Physical Dimensions of Aging

Waneen W. Spirduso, EdD
The University of Texas

Human Kinetics

Library of Congress Cataloging-in-Publication Data

Spirduso, Waneen Wyrick.
    Physical dimensions of aging / Waneen W. Spirduso.
      p.   cm.
    Includes bibliographical references and index.
    ISBN 0-87322-323-3
    1. Aging--Physiological aspects.   I. Title.
   QP86.S65   1995
   612.6'7--dc20   94-43969
                                     CIP

ISBN: 0-87322-323-3

95-1091

Copyright © 1995 by Waneen W. Spirduso

Cover photo of runner Carl Llewellyn courtesy Ric Dugan/Herald-Mail Company.
Chapter 9 photo courtesy Mary Langenfeld Photo.
Chapter 14 photo of rower Sam Daniels, courtesy Craig Daniels.
Part I center, chapter 2, chapter 3, chapter 6, Part IV upper right, and chapter 10 photos © 1995 Connie Springer.
Part I lower right, chapter 1, Part II center, Part II upper left, chapter 4, chapter 5, Part III center, Part III lower right, chapter 7, chapter 8, Part IV center, chapter 11, chapter 12, chapter 13, Part V center, and Part V upper left photos © Terry Wild Studio.

Developmental Editor: Larret Galasyn-Wright; **Assistant Editors:** Julie Marx Ohnemus and Dawn Roselund; **Copyeditor:** Dianna Matlosz; **Proofreader:** Nedra Lambert; **Indexer:** Theresa J. Schaefer; **Typesetters:** Julie Overholt and Angie Snyder; **Layout:** Denise Lowry; **Text Designer:** Judy Henderson; **Cover Designer:** Jack Davis; **Illustrator:** M.R. Greenberg; **Printer:** Braun-Brumfield

Printed in the United States of America

10 9 8 7 6 5 4 3 2 1

Human Kinetics
P.O. Box 5076, Champaign, IL 61825-5076
1-800-747-4457

Canada: Human Kinetics, Box 24040,
Windsor, ON N8Y 4Y9
1-800-465-7301 (in Canada only)

Europe: Human Kinetics, P.O. Box IW14,
Leeds LS16 6TR, England
(44) 532 781708

Australia: Human Kinetics, 2 Ingrid Street,
Clapham 5062, South Australia
(08) 371 3755

New Zealand: Human Kinetics, P.O. Box 105-231
Auckland 1
(09) 309 2259

To my mother, who has spent a lifetime being my biggest fan, but who sometimes wondered whether she would ever see this book in her lifetime; to Comel, who takes such good care of my biggest fan; and to Craig, for his love, support, and forbearance.

Contents

Foreword

Here is a book many of us have been waiting for. While the field of aging is notable for its rich collections of data, it has also suffered from a general lack of integration. But with the publication of *Physical Dimensions of Aging* by Waneen Spirduso, that is no longer the case. Not only does Dr. Spirduso thoroughly review the *facts* about physical aging, but more important, she *synthesizes* those facts into a coherent story that reveals how our bodies age.

Dr. Spirduso's years of productive research give her a unique perspective that enables her to "shake the theoretical trees" of our field. What is significant about this book is the way she pulls together so many diverse concepts, data sets, theories, and interpretations of physical aging.

Taking an organismic point of view that should be encouraged in students and researchers, Dr. Spirduso examines biological and environmental factors that influence aging and physical performance. (One of her recurring themes deals with the source of individual differences and how these differences are reflected in individual aging patterns.) She cites a range of material culled from respected journals in physiology, psychology, medicine, sports medicine, and gerontology to address basic concepts of energy, work, and efficiency and how they relate to the physical performance of fit and unfit adults of different ages.

There are few scholarly attempts to rival Dr. Spirduso's; it obviously took years for her to review and integrate the body of literature that forms the foundation of this book. I, for one, am glad she was willing to take on such a task. *Physical Dimensions of Aging* is the benchmark against which other such books will be judged. I will use it frequently, and I advise you to do the same.

James E. Birren, Director
Borun Center for Gerontological Research
UCLA School of Medicine

Preface

One of the certainties of life, perhaps the only one, is that every day everyone grows older. A time comes in each of our lives when this fact becomes personally relevant. The time is different for everyone, and the awareness may be sudden or subtle, but at some age each of us *really* understands for the first time that we are not immortal. For many people this revelation is precipitated by a physical experience—a father's unexpected loss to his son in a short race, sore muscles following softball at the company picnic, the first time you wonder if you can climb all the steps to the top of the monument on vacation. Of all human dimensions, the physical is usually the first to convince us that no one is an exception to the rule—we all are aging. Not only does the physical dimension provide us with clues to this effect, but it becomes a constraining factor in what we can do; and if we live long enough, physical aging begins to define our quality of life. Because physical function is central to most of our activities, our physical efficiency permeates all aspects of our life. Physical aging affects us cognitively, psychologically, socially, and spiritually.

This book discusses how people age physically and how this aging affects other dimensions of life. It will be of interest to anyone who is personally experiencing signs of aging, which includes almost everyone over the age of 40. Primarily, however, *Physical Dimensions of Aging* is written for undergraduate and graduate students planning to be professionals or researchers who work with adults and the elderly, in such areas as counseling psychology, gerontology, health promotion, medicine, psychiatry, nursing, pharmacy, physical fitness, physical therapy, and social work. Because the book is research based, researchers who study physical aging in these professions and in disciplines such as biomechanics, exercise physiology, and psychology will find this book to be a resource. I have integrated findings on physical aging from over a hundred different journals in myriad fields, creating interdisciplinary coverage of the topic.

Interest in gerontology has accelerated remarkably since the early 1980s, leading to growing numbers of research centers, undergraduate and graduate courses, and graduate programs on gerontological topics. I believe that every health professional who works with older adults needs to understand the nature of physical aging and the profound impact it can have. This belief is apparently shared by the developers of many gerontology programs, because a triad of core courses—covering the biology of aging, the psychology of aging, and the sociology of aging—is usually required as an introduction to the subject. Peterson (1985)*, reporting on required courses in graduate gerontology programs, found that courses addressing the biology of aging were ranked third in number, and courses that covered health and aging were ranked seventh. Since Peterson's report, the numbers of gerontology programs and students in them have increased, as has interest in the health and physical capabilities of the elderly.

Although it is important for professionals to understand basic concepts of the biology of aging (survival curves, interspecies aging patterns, theories of aging, evolutionary aspects of aging, etc.) equally important are the age-related changes in the body's major physical systems and how these changes impact physical capacity, mobility, and performance. Professionals must also understand not only the full range of physical function but also how function can be manipulated by health habits and, perhaps more importantly, how these physical changes influence other aspects of human mental and social functioning.

The term *physical dimensions* is deliberate in the title of this book, emphasizing the multidimensional effect of physical aging on individuals from late-middle to old age. From beginning to end, I emphasize the importance of our physical being in the process of all aspects of aging and the contribution that maintenance of physical capacity and performance makes to successful aging. It is because I believe that the various physical dimensions of aging should be studied in an integrated and cohesive manner that I decided to write this book alone rather than to edit a collection of chapters from the most celebrated experts on each topic. Several fine books of that type already exist, but they provide primarily resource information on specific topics, rather than an informational base of understanding of the physical dimensions of aging and their impact on the aging individual. In this book I introduce students and professionals to the basic concepts of age-related changes in energy, work, efficiency, motor control, coordination, and skill; to the concept of functional age; and to the role that health habits and physical exercise play in modifying functional age. Because physical health and competency play an increasingly important role in determining the quality of life of aging adults, I address the interdependence of physical health, mental function, emotional control, and self-esteem at every level, from the frail elderly to exceptionally capable Senior Olympians and masters competitors.

From the moment I conceived of this book, I decided that, although based on research information, it should be primarily an introductory survey of the various dimensions of physical aging. Thus, the professionals and researchers who focus on specific areas may view the background information on their specialties to be simplistic, but they should find its applications to the aging process informative. My students, undergraduates and graduates from many different professions and disciplines, found this to be true. They discovered, to their surprise, that the information in chapters outside their areas of specialization added important information to their knowledge. For example, exercise physiologists who specialize in older adult physical performance found little new information in the chapter on aerobic work capacity. However, they did find the chapters on physical development, physical function of the frail elderly, and comparisons of elite athletes' performances to be useful in their work. Similarly, gerontological physical therapists with substantial knowledge about strength, posture, and locomotion found they also needed information on elderly work capacity, functional testing of the frail elderly, and the role of mobility in emotional function and well-being. Without exception, my students found that this integrated approach to the understanding of the physical dimensions of aging widened their perspectives of their work, gave them a greater appreciation of the impact of physical aging, and made them more effective in their professions.

The book begins with an introductory chapter on the concept of aging in terms of longevity and quality and quantity of life. Because one of the most characteristic aspects of aging is how different it is for each person, the second chapter emphasizes individual differences. The rest of the book presents information related to four major areas of human movement: energy, work, and efficiency; motor control, coordination, and learning; involvement, interdependence, and skill; and physical performance. The physical aspects of growth and form, that is changes in body composition, bone, flexibility, and skin are discussed in chapter 3. Chapters on work capacity, muscular strength, and endurance discuss the capacities of individuals in terms of energy, work, and efficiency. Effects of aging on motor control, coordination, and physical skill are organized as posture, locomotion, and simple movements (chapter 6), behavioral speed (chapter 7), and coordination and skill in complex movements (chapter 8). How the physical dimension influences our involvement in life, our dependence on others, and our achievements involves the relationship of health and physical fitness to cognition (chapter 9), emotional function (chapter 10), and our general feeling of well-being (chapter 11).

Finally, I conclude the book with a section on how aging affects older adults' physical performance in society. Physical function in the frail elderly, with all of its limitations and psychological implications, is discussed in chapter 12, and the role of physical capabilities in societal job discrimination, from airplane pilots at age 45 to white-collar workers in their 70s, is presented in chapter 13. I have saved the performance of the elite athletes for the last, chapter 14. With so much negative news about one's aging physical ability, an analysis of the great athletic performances of some of our septuagenarians and octogenarians is inspiring and uplifting. I believe that almost all professionals underestimate the physical abilities and potentials of the elderly. At a time in their lives when so many people are telling the elderly that they can't, we professionals at least should be telling them that they can.

Gerontology is a relatively new field, incredibly complex and multidisciplinary. In the study of human gerontology, physical, psychological, social, and environmental systems interact so that it is extremely difficult to identify causal relationships. Thus, each chapter has several controversial issues. I have presented these as fairly as I can, but no one person can be an expert in every field. I am, therefore, indebted to a number of people who have helped me find information, critiqued my writing, and helped me think through the ideas and concepts that I present. For their time, energy, creativeness, and encouragement, I also am grateful to many colleagues: Larry Abraham, Ann Scarborough, Ed Coyle, Russell Ewan, Roger Farrar, Jan Hutchinson, Sid Liebes, Priscilla MacRae, Bob Malina, David Reuben, and Joe Starnes. Several graduate students also read the manuscript and provided excellent suggestions: Gary Etgen, Tina Geithner, and Steve Seiler. Susan Jay improved the form and substance of the manuscript with meticulous editing and extensive research. A special note of gratitude goes to Wojtek Chodzko-Zajko and Max Vercruyssen, both of whom read the manuscript from cover to cover, made many suggestions, found many mistakes, and supplied additional information, articles, and references. Their comments have had a significant impact on the book and have improved its quality immeasurably. I also am indebted to the creativeness and ingenuity of Rosalind Lee and Kelly McQueary, who provided me with special technical assistance and skills throughout the writing of the book.

Finally, I view this book as a beginning. I hope that it will evolve over the years, through my own growth and understanding and through my interaction with others, and become a book that will be truly useful to a great many people. I therefore encourage readers to send me their comments, suggestions, and critiques.

Department of Kinesiology
The University of Texas
Austin, TX 78712
Fax: 512/471-0946
spirduso@mail.utexas.edu

---

*Peterson, D.A. (1985). Employment experience of gerontology master's degree graduates. *The Gerontologist*, **25**, 514-519.

PHYSICAL
DIMENSIONS
OF AGING

PART I

An Introduction to Aging

The first truth about aging is that everybody does it. The second truth is that everybody does it differently.

It is impossible to talk about the effects of physical aging without considering first the human life span, the notion of time, and how differently each individual moves through his or her life. Why do some people live longer than others? Why do some seem to age quickly, whereas others seem to resist aging? If living longer means living in sickness and morbidity, is it ethical for scientists to continue to search for ways to extend the human life span? What is normal aging? Is it different from sickness and disease? This section introduces the basic concepts of the biology of aging, the theories of aging, and the compression of morbidity. This section also introduces one of the most important concepts of aging: Individuals differ in the way they age and the way they react to aging. Indeed, one of the factors that makes the study of aging so difficult is that a "typical" older adult does not exist. Finally, the last chapter in this section discusses the major developmental changes that occur with aging: changes in body size and form, in muscle, fat, and bone composition, in joint flexibility, and in the skin.

CHAPTER 1

Issues of Quantity and Quality of Life

Aging is one of the great enigmas of life. Apart from birth and death, it is perhaps the only experience that every human being shares. As ubiquitous as aging is, no one fully understands it. Many throughout human history have pondered the same questions about aging: What is aging? What is its nature? Why do living organisms age? Can aging be stopped or slowed down?

Although all people age, they do so in different ways and at different rates. Some people live longer and have a higher quality of life than others. The basis of gerontology is the study of these differences, their causes, and the factors that amplify or attenuate them. The length of time, or quantity of life, that people live is easily measured. Statistical survival curves have been developed to describe the life spans of many species, and from these, predictions can be made about the quantity of life and the rate of aging. But scholars and scientists want more. They want to understand the fundamental processes and causes of aging so that the quantity of life for humans can be maximized. The results of their studies of basic mechanisms have provided the basis for several theories of aging.

Understanding the fundamental processes of aging is not only essential to determining what causes aging, but it is also necessary if interventions are to be developed to interfere with, postpone, or stop the aging process. The goal of applied health and social scientists is to change the shape of the human survival curve so that most individuals can live long lives, and several controllable factors, such as food restriction and nutrition, general activity level, and physical activity have some promise in fulfilling that goal. Most people would agree that long life without health and physical mobility is undesirable, yet many people live their terminal years in a state of morbidity, or complete physical dependence and poor health. A substantial thrust in recent research has thus been to determine whether the occurrence and duration of morbidity in the population can be compressed. Discussions of extending the life span are always entangled with issues of the quality of life.

This chapter introduces some of the fundamental questions and basic terminology of gerontology. What is aging? How is it described? What causes it? Can the aging process be slowed? And how is the quantity of life related to the quality of life?

What Is Aging?

On the simplest level, physical age seems easy to define. It is the chronological time something has existed, or the number of elapsed standard time units between birth and a date of observation. On this level, age and time are synonymous. On another level, however, the physical dimension and meaning of time depend totally on the biological, psychological, and social significance attached to it; for that reason the concept of time has been the subject of philosophical debate for centuries. Because time and chronological aging can be

viewed as synonymous, it is impossible to divorce aging from the passage of time. Yet biological processes that occur in youth are thought of as developmental, whereas time-related changes that lead to disability and dysfunction are thought of as adult aging, or senescence. When does this change in definition occur? Does aging begin in all body cells simultaneously or in different systems at different times? When does aging start? As complex as these issues are, rational discussion requires some agreement on definitions among professionals.

I use the term *aging* to refer to a process or group of processes occurring in living organisms that with the passage of time lead to a loss of adaptability, functional impairment, and eventually death. These processes are distinct from daily or seasonal biological rhythms and any other temporary change. It is particularly important to distinguish aging effects from *secular effects*, which are environmental effects that influence all people who live within an identified period. For example, during the late 1970s and early 1980s serum cholesterol levels dropped over 7-year intervals in all age groups studied in the Baltimore Longitudinal Study of Aging (BLSA). The dietary cholesterol and fiber of these subjects also changed. Attributing the drop in cholesterol to aging would be an inaccurate conclusion. Much more probable is that many of the BLSA subjects, as well as countless numbers of nonsubjects, changed their diets as a result of heavy media advertising regarding the benefits of low-fat and high-fiber diets.

Aging is a logical extension of the physiological processes of growth and development, beginning with birth and ending with death. The emphasis of this text is on the later portion of this continuum of life span growth and development.

Aging occurs with the relentless march of time, but relatively few people actually die of old age. Most die because the body loses the capacity to withstand physical or environmental stressors. Through youth, bodies have reserve physiological capacities and system redundancies that enable them to adapt to physical challenges or insults, such as exposure to viruses or to extreme heat and cold. Accompanying aging, however, is a loss in reserve capacity and redundancy, which reduces the ability to adapt quickly and effectively. For example, a young adult might be able to dodge an oncoming automobile on a hot summer day and avoid being struck. An older person, however, who has suffered cumulative losses in peripheral vision, hearing, muscular strength, reaction time, and heat adaptation, might marshal his or her resources just a step too late and be hit by the car.

Although physical age differences are apparent, the physiological effects of aging are hardly visible between a 20-year-old and a 70-year-old when the two are sitting quietly in chairs. But these differences are more noticeable when they rise and walk across the room, and they are striking if an alarm sounds and the two must leave the room as quickly as possible. The age differences will be even more dramatic if the older person has had frequent sicknesses and accidents, has one or more chronic diseases, and has chronically insulted her or his body (e.g., by smoking or using drugs). Losses in (for example) vision, hearing, and strength are primary aging, and the accelerated aging that occurs as a result of disease or environmental factors is secondary aging.

Primary and Secondary Aging

Aging processes are different from *the process of aging.* Aging processes represent universal changes with age within a species or population that are independent of disease or environmental influence (Hershey, 1984). The onset of puberty in children and menopause in women, for example, are age-related changes that are not disease-dependent. The process of aging refers to clinical symptoms (the syndrome of aging) and includes the effects of environment and disease. Busse (1969) describes aging processes as primary aging and the process of aging (which includes the interaction of aging processes with disease and environmental influences) as secondary aging. Although the causes of primary and secondary aging are distinct, they do not act independently. Rather, they strongly interact with each other. Disease and environmental stress can accelerate basic aging processes, and aging processes increase one's vulnerability to disease and environmental stress.

The Rate of Aging

The *rate of aging* is the change in function of organs and systems per unit of time. In normal aging these deleterious changes roughly follow a linear senescence over the life span. It had been thought that the rate of aging was roughly exponential after age 40, that is, mortality intensity would double following equal periods of time after a person reached 40 years of age. But the aging rate is different in men and women (Ekonomov, Rudd, & Lomakin, 1989). The rate at which males age slows monotonically with time, whereas females age at a slower rate between 45 to 60 years of age than they do between 70 to 80 years of age. Disease and accident can change the rate of deterioration, and thus of aging, in a system, but although many researchers have tried, only two interventions, caloric restriction and genetic manipulation, have been shown to change the rate of aging positively by increasing the life span. These changes thus far have been accomplished only in rodents and *C. elgans*, a species of nematode (Johnson, 1990).

How Is Aging Described?

The simplest way to describe aging is to categorize it. *Age categories* are divisions of chronological age, such as those shown in Table 1.1, that are used for purposes of discussion and clarification in gerontology. These divisions seem straightforward, but a major problem in gerontological research has been that age categories have not been standardized across the field of gerontology. Some professionals describe a 55-year-old as old, whereas others call the same-aged person middle-aged. Within the gerontology literature, 20 different terms have been used to describe middle-aged or old adults (Crandall, 1991). Reviewing several research studies will show that subjects ranging in age from 35 to 100 years have been labeled "old." This is an unfortunate state of affairs, for in order to interpret the results of research studies in which old are compared to young, it is important to know what "old" means. (For purposes of discussion, the age categories shown in Table 1.1 will be used in this text; the term *older* or *old* refers to persons older than those in the *middle-age adult* category, i.e., ≥65 years of age. The *young-old* category, comprised of those between 65 and 74, is a relatively new division by which gerontologists acknowledge the growing number of older Americans who, by virtue of their active lifestyles, have continued behaving as young and middle-aged people well into the ages that were once described as old. Ronald Reagan, who was able to keep up the demanding pace of a president of the United States from age 70 to 77, is an excellent example of members of the young-old age

**Table 1.1
Age Categories**

Description	Age (years)	Decade
Infant	0-2	1st
Child	3-12	1st-2nd
Adolescent	13-17	2nd
Young adult	18-24	2nd-3rd
Adult	25-44	3rd-5th
Middle-age adult	45-64	5th-7th
Young-old	65-74	7th-8th
Old	75-84	8th-9th
Old-old	85-99	9th-10th
Oldest-old	100+	11th

category. Most young-old can maintain their jobs and productivity if they choose to do so.

Another important point shown in Table 1.1 is that the first decade of life includes children from birth to age 9, the second decade includes individuals from 10 to 19 and so on. Thus, if someone describes individuals as being in their sixth decade, they are chronologically between 50 and 59. Yet another way to describe older adults is as sexagenarians (60-69), septuagenarians (70-79), octogenarians (80-89), nonagenarians (90-99), and centenarians (100+).

All individuals in an age category may be loosely described as *cohorts*, that is, people who are more likely to experience common environmental conditions and events, such as wars, environmental disasters, or economic booms or downturns. *Birth cohorts* include all people who have the same year of birth and who are compared from the same fixed time origin. Although all individuals have very different personalities and experiences, persons who were beginning their career during World War II and who also lived through the Great Depression, for example, collectively share some attitudes and behaviors that are different than those of young adults who began their careers in the post-Vietnam era. The radically different life events that shaped different cohorts play a substantial role in shaping their behaviors, so that what might be interpreted as an aging effect in one cohort could be in reality an effect of a specific environmental event experienced by one cohort but not by the other. Physical and social environments that differ in health risks and medical care impact upon the life expectancy of a cohort.

The most highly publicized cohort in American society includes individuals born between 1946 and 1960, the *baby boomers*. This cohort is the largest in the United States. After World War II, babies were born at a faster rate in this country than in any other period of time. Consequently, one out of three people in our society is a baby boomer. The sheer size of this cohort has influenced every aspect of our society—schools, housing, marketing, job availability—and continues to do so as this cohort ages. Indeed, one reason that gerontology and issues of aging are attracting so much attention today is that the baby boomers are now at midlife and are requiring more and more health care. Many are predicting that when the baby boomers reach retirement age, if health insurance, medical disability, and retirement policies are not radically changed, the health care system will completely collapse under the weight of the needs of this large cohort of society.

The Human Survival Curve

Another way to describe aging is to develop a human survival curve, depicting the percentage of a population that survives at each age throughout the life span of the entire population. Survival curves for any species are important in order to describe changes and shifts in populations, as well as to understand the factors that influence these changes. Life spans determined from the survival curves of several species are shown in Table 1.2. In the human species, each person has a specific life span, ranging from perhaps only a few minutes to over 100 years. In fact, Gompertz, who lived from 1779 to 1865, worked out several mathematical equations in 1825 to describe and predict the rate of aging at each age and showed that after 40 years of age the actuarial aging rate stayed roughly the same. His formulas, called the Gompertz equations, are still used today, although their generalization across genders and geographical locations has been challenged recently (Ekonomov et al., 1989). Several aspects of the human survival curve are shown in Figure 1.1 (page 10). The percent of persons surviving out of 100,000 is shown on the vertical axis for each age group.

Since the mid-19th century, the life expectancy of the United States population at birth has nearly doubled from 40 to almost 80 years. Figure 1.1 shows that many more people born in 1980 can expect to live to be 80 years of age than the number

Table 1.2
**Maximum Recorded Life Spans for Selected Mammals,
Birds, Reptiles, Amphibians, and Fish**

	Scientific name	Common name	Maximum life span (years)
Primates	*Papio papio*	Baboon	27
	Macaca mulatta	Rhesus monkey	29
	Pan troglodytes	Chimpanzee	44
	Gorilla gorilla	Gorilla	39
	Homo sapiens	Human	115
Carnivores	*Felis catus*	Domestic cat	28
	Canis familiaris	Domestic dog	20
	Ursus arctos	Brown bear	36
Ungulates	*Ovis areis*	Sheep	20
	Sus scrofa	Swine	27
	Equus caballus	Horse	46
	Elephas maximus	Indian elephant	70
Rodents	*Mus musculus*	House mouse	3
	Rattus rattus	Black rat	5
	Sciurus carolinensis	Gray squirrel	15
	Hystrix brachyura	Porcupine	27
Bats	*Desmodus rotundus*	Vampire bat	13
	Pteropus giganteus	Indian fruit bat	17
Birds	*Streptopelia risoria*	Domestic dove	30
	Larus argentatus	Herring gull	41
	Aquila chrysaëtos	Golden eagle	46
	Bubo bubo	Eagle owl	68
Reptiles	*Eunectes murinus*	Anaconda	29
	Macroclemys temmincki	Snapping turtle	58+
	Alligator sinensis	Chinese alligator	52
	Testudo elephantopus	Galapagos tortoise	100+
Amphibians	*Xenopus-laevis*	African clawed toad	15
	Bufo bufo	Common toad	36
	Cynops pyrrhogaster	Japanese newt	25
	Rana catesbiana	Bullfrog	16
Fish	*Gadus morrhua*	Atlantic cod	20+
	Aphya pellucide	Gobie	1
	Esox lucius	Pike	40+
	Hippoglossus hippoglossus	Halibut	60+
	Lebistes reticulatus	Guppy	6
	Acipenser sp.	Sturgeon	82+

Note. From Robert Arking, *Biology of Aging: Observations and Principles*, © 1991, p. 109. Reprinted by permission of Prentice Hall, Englewood Cliffs, NJ.

of people born in 1900 who exceeded 80 years. The longer the life expectancy of each new cohort, the greater the percentage of the total population represented by the older cohort and the older the population as a whole (Figure 1.2). Whereas only 3% of the United States population was older than 80 in 1890, 12.3% was older than 80 in 1988. At the beginning of this century, the median age of the U.S. population was 24 years and the average life expectancy for those born was 47. This is far different from the life expectancy today, where the median age is 31.5 and the life expectancy for babies born is over 75 for females. In 2010 it is projected that the median age will be 39. That is,

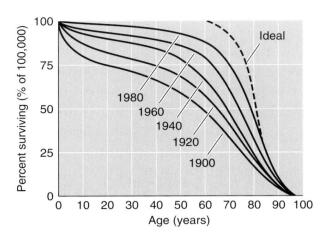

Figure 1.1   Cumulative survival curves for both sexes. The increasing life expectancy for each cohort (1920, 1940, 1960, and 1980) reveals that the survival curves are becoming more rectangular. One goal of medical science is to find ways to reduce accidents and eliminate disease, thus rectangularizing the human survival curve so that most individuals can expect to live the average biological life span for humans.

From *Vitality and Aging* (p. 7) by J.F. Fries and L.M. Crapo, 1981, New York: Freeman. Copyright 1981 by J.F. Fries and L.M. Crapo. Adapted by permission.

half of all the people living in the U.S. will be older than 39 years.

The most dramatic increases in the number of people over 80 are projected to occur between 1990 and 2000. Predictions of growth for this age group range from 30.3% to 45.3% in 80+ men and 23.7% to 36.4% for women. The period of greatest overall growth for people of both genders 65 and older will be from 2010 to 2020, when the baby boomers reach retirement age. Predictions for this group range from 29.7% to 36.4% growth. The fastest growing age category are the centenarians, those over 100 years old. It is estimated that 25,000 Americans are over 100 years old, and projections are that 100,000 centenarians will be living in this country by the year 2000. Those now living are predominantly female and white, approximately half live in homes rather than institutions, most have very low incomes, and more than 75% are native-born Americans.

Most of the increases in life expectancy in the early part of this century were due to declining rates in neonatal, infant, and maternal mortality. In recent years, gains in life expectancy have been achieved by reducing mortality due to cardiovascular disease. Thus deaths from infectious diseases have been replaced by deaths from chronic degenerative diseases. It is estimated that the life expectancy of males at age 30 could be increased by more than 15 years if major known risk factors, such as smoking, high cholesterol, high blood pressure, and obesity, were eliminated. Dramatic changes in the life expectancy of women have accompanied the technological advances in the monitoring of childbearing. Figure 1.3 shows the distribution of deaths at all ages per 100,000 females for the cohort born in 1900

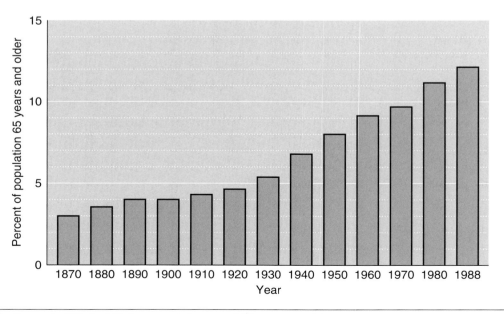

Figure 1.2   Percent of United States population aged 65 years or older.
Data from Crandall (1991, p. 41).

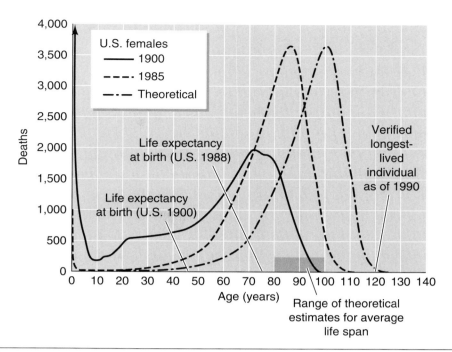

Figure 1.3 Observed and theoretical distribution of deaths of females in the United States, 1900 and 1985. From "In Search of Methuselah: Estimating the Upper Limits to Human Longevity" by S.J. Olshansky, B.A. Carnes, and C. Cassel, 1990, *Science*, **250**, p. 635. Copyright 1990 by the American Association for the Advancement of Science. Reprinted by permission.

and the hypothetical distribution for the cohort born in 1985, represented by a dashed line (Olshansky, Carnes, & Cassel, 1990). Note that the life expectancy of the 1988 cohort (75 years) is 28 years longer than that of the 1900 cohort (47 years). In the 1900 cohort, a sharp increase in deaths occurred in women at childbearing age, approximately ages 16 to 25, and the majority died between the ages of 50 and 70. A large percentage of the causes of death for these women was infectious disease. The 1985 cohort, conversely, is almost free of these causes of death and will die of chronic diseases between the ages of 70 and 100. The curve shown by dotted lines represents a hypothetical life span as the average approaches 100 years, perhaps because of medical breakthroughs and dramatic changes in lifestyle health habits. In this figure the theoretical estimates for average life span are 80 to 100 years.

Whether life expectancy at birth will increase from present levels to the average biological limit of life (age 85), or even higher, is a topic of hot debate in gerontology. The attention of researchers interested in extending life expectancy has turned to finding ways to eradicate cancer (which causes about one fifth of all deaths in the U.S.) and heart disease. Some researchers believe that

the ceiling of human life expectancy has almost been reached, because eliminating all forms of cancer would increase life expectancy at birth by only 3.17 years for females and 3.2 years for males (Olshansky et al., 1990). For that to occur, mortality rates from all causes of death would have to decline at all ages by 55% and at ages 50 and over by 60%. This seems highly unlikely (Olshansky et al., 1990).

Maximum Life Span Potential

The maximum life span potential is the survival potential of members of a population. If life is thought of as a race, one could describe it by either how long it is or how far most of the runners actually go. In Figure 1.4, imagine an aerial view of all the runners at the starting line (i.e., birth). Those shown at the bottom of the figure are all born in the same year and, in this example, are baby boomers. The distance of the race is the maximum life span potential, the upper bound on life expectancy determined by the biological limits of the species. (The members of a species who live the longest provide an operational definition of the maximum life span for that population.) As of 1990, the oldest verified age for

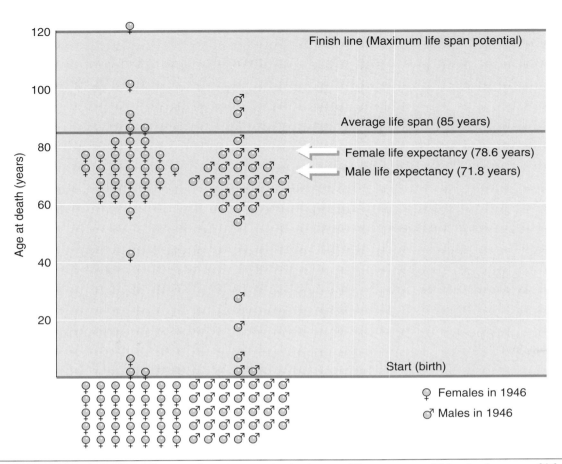

Figure 1.4   A hypothetical aerial view of participants in the human life span race. All begin the race of life at birth. A few die from accidents or disease early in life, but the majority of deaths occur at the average life expectancy for that cohort. Almost all of the participants are deceased by the average biological life span; a few will exceed the average life span and live past 100 years. The length of the race, the finish line, is defined by the participant who lives the longest and is termed the *maximum life span potential.* Symbols do not represent exact numbers or proportions.

a human was 120 years (Olshansky et al., 1990). Some demographers believe that, in the absence of some genetic or medical technological breakthrough, 115 to 120 years will prove to be the maximum human life span potential (Rothenberg, Lentzner, & Parker 1991).

The Average Life Span

The average life span is the average age by which all but a very small percentage of the members of a population are deceased. Note that in Figure 1.4, the majority of race participants have died by the age of 85. Most gerontologists agree that the average biological limit to human life is approximately 85 years, although a few individuals live to be more than 100 years old. Figure 1.5 shows the distribution of age at death in the hypothetical

situation where no premature death occurs from accident or disease (Fries, 1980). This suggests a genetically endowed limit to life even for a member of a population free of all exogenous risk factors. Indeed, the life span of humans has not changed much since the beginning of recorded history. The 90th Psalm in the Bible declares man's natural life span to be three-score years and ten, or 70 years, which is not radically different from present values.

Life Expectancy

Life expectancy is the average number of years of life remaining for a population of individuals, all of the same age, usually expressed from birth as the average number of years of life that newborns might expect to live. In the analogy of a race, life expectancy answers the question, How far do

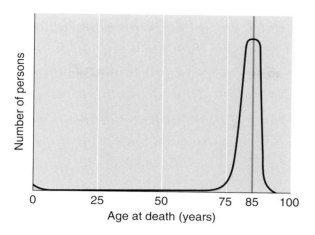

Figure 1.5 Mortality according to age in the absence of premature death. If the survival curve were completely rectangularized, that is, everyone died of old age and no one died prematurely (due to accidents, war, disaster, etc.), almost all natural deaths would occur at about 85 ± 10 years of age, which is the average human life span.

Adapted, by permission of *The New England Journal of Medicine*, from "Aging, Natural Death, and the Compression of Morbidity" by J.F. Fries, 1980, *New England Journal of Medicine*, **303**, p. 134.

most of the runners actually go? The answer is different for males and females (see Figure 1.4). For those born in 1946 in the United States, the life expectancy is 71.8 for males and 78.6 for females. That is, the largest number of deaths in this group occurs at these ages. Although life expectancy is usually thought of as length of life from birth, it can also be expressed as the life expectancy of 50-year-olds. In this case, life expectancy is defined as the average number of years of life remaining. In contrast to the average life span, life expectancy for both genders increased significantly throughout most of the 20th century in most countries. Life expectancy is different for people of different ages, cohorts, genders, and ethnic backgrounds. It is also greatly influenced by geographic locations. However, of all the biological, social, and cultural differences in life expectancies, one of the most striking is that of gender.

Gender Differences

One of the interesting questions of longevity is why women throughout the world outlive men by 4 to 10 years. Although more males are conceived than females, the female survival advantage begins at conception and increases throughout

life. More spontaneous abortions, miscarriages, and stillbirths are male, and as shown in Figure 1.6, the ratio of males to females decreases throughout life. James V. Neel of the University of Washington was quoted as saying, "We really are the weaker sex, biologically less fit than females at every step of the way" (Holden, 1987).

The gender gap was significant at the beginning of the 20th century and widened considerably until approximately 1970, at which time it leveled off. It has not increased within recent years, at least partly because the life expectancy for females is leveling off. In Figure 1.7, the number of years that females live longer than males is shown on the vertical axis. The higher the regression line of the graph, the greater the gender gap. The increase in the gender gap from 1900 to 1960 is conspicuously larger than that from 1960 to 1980.

In 1987 the gender gap was intriguing enough to be the subject of a conference sponsored by the National Institute on Aging. At this international conference, a great many scholars discussed biologically and behaviorally known facts that could explain the gender gap, but they could not draw any satisfactory conclusions. Many of the conferees expressed the belief that it would be a long time before the gender gap is fully understood. Why *do* women live longer than men? Several explanations, which may be categorized as genetic, hormonal, or social, have been proposed.

Genetics Theory

One argument for why women live longer is that because women have two sets of the female determining X-linked genes, cells can operate on instructions from genes on either X chromosome. If a male has an X-linked gene for a recessive gene disease such as muscular dystrophy, he will develop the disease because the gene is on the only X chromosome he has. But if a woman has an X-linked recessive gene, theoretically she could function on the other X chromosome, which may be free of the X-linked disease-producing gene. For this reason males have more sex-linked recessive gene diseases. As long ago as 1953, Montague, in his popular book, *The Natural Superiority of Women*, made this argument. Some suggest that this same type of argument might be made if an X-linked gene or gene system related to longevity is someday identified, or if some aspect of the replication and repair mechanism of cells is X chromosome–linked.

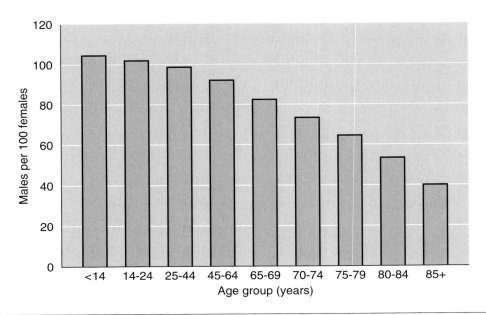

Figure 1.6   The ratio of males to females in the United States.
Data from Crandall (1991, p. 49).

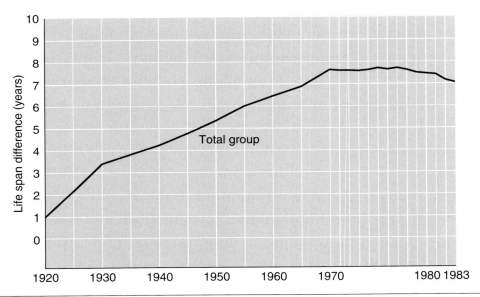

Figure 1.7   The gender gap over six decades (1920 to 1983).
Adapted from Miller (1986, p. 59).

Although the X-linked gene argument continues to be intuitively compelling, it is probably too simplistic in its present form. As has been emphasized by many, one of the X chromosomes in most women is inactivated, so women really are operating on a single X chromosome, just as are men. However, another hypothesis has been that longevity is influenced by differences in the male Y chromosome. The familial genetics of an Amish culture were followed for four generations, and the investigators found that Amish men who lacked an arm of the Y chromosome lived significantly longer than men who were not of their culture and longer than women who were (Holden, 1987). The average age of Amish men with the Y chromosome difference was 82.3, whereas the average age of Amish women was 77.4. Compare this to non-Amish women who lived to their mid-70s and to non-Amish men who lived only to their late 60s. Note that in this genetic line the males on the average lived 5 years longer than the females who experienced the same environmental influences. Therefore, even though the relationship is obviously very complex, the evidence seems to lean toward some genetic contribution to gender differences in longevity.

Hormonal Differences

Another explanation for the greater longevity of women is based on the observation that women do not die in their 50s and 60s from heart disease in the percentages that men do. Estrogen, the hormone responsible for female characteristics, is also well known to protect against heart disease by lowering levels of low-density lipoproteins (LDLs) and increasing levels of high-density lipoproteins (HDLs), which protect against the development of atherosclerosis. Conversely, androgens, the male hormones, lower the protective HDLs and raise the atherosclerotic-inducing LDLs. The high levels of premenopausal estrogen in women are conducive to greater longevity. After menopause, this advantage evaporates.

Hormonal differences also affect the immune system. Females have greater and faster immune responses to foreign objects in the blood, a beneficial effect in youth in terms of warding off antigen-produced diseases. For example, the results of research on mice have suggested that the greater immune activity may provide greater resistance to the development of tumors. In general, women are more frequently sick than men as they age, but their illnesses tend to be chronic and debilitating rather than fatal. The faster response of the female immune system is detrimental in terms of autoimmune diseases. Thus, diseases in which the immune system of an individual attacks him or herself, such as arthritis, lupus, and myasthenia gravis, are much more prevalent in women. As the immune system ages, it becomes less and less accurate in identifying foreign versus self-produced antigens, and thus the autoimmune system is more likely to attack its own host.

Social Explanations

The different social roles and behaviors of males and females in society are also used to explain the gender gap. These explanations center on the disparate work roles and responsibilities of men and women and sex-related differential health habits such as smoking and the use of health resources.

During the first three quarters of the 20th century, females generally have been in less dangerous and stressful environments. Boys are more likely to have serious or fatal accidents than girls, and, although the work-related responsibilities of women are increasing, men continue to hold a high percentage of working positions in which job-related stress is high. Historically, women in the first half of their lives have always been less subject to violent death due to war, homicide, suicide, or accident. Even in the 1991-92 war in Kuwait, in which women made up a larger proportion of the U.S. military than ever before, they were for the most part limited to supportive stations in combat zones. Insurance rates attest to the fact that generally women do not drive automobiles as fast nor are they as accident prone as men are. These social role disparities are slowly changing, but they exist at present.

Until relatively recently, women have always participated less than men in the high risk habit of smoking. There is much controversy over whether the difference in smoking habits of men and women can account for a substantial portion or all of the gender gap. One argument used to support this hypothesis is that the gender gap is larger in the working class, and smoking is more prevalent among blue-collar males than any other group. Miller and Gerstein (1983) have gone so far as to say that the different smoking habits of the two genders may account for *all* of the gender gap. They challenged many of the studies that found a large gender gap because they claimed that smoking was not a well-controlled factor; that is, former smokers were not identified and distinguished from nonsmokers. Miller and Gerstein (1983) suggest that if these analyses are done, when the number of women smokers catches up with that of men, the gender gap almost disappears. Miller (1986) insists that if the male–female longevity difference is plotted over six decades, this difference follows smoking trends (see Figure 1.7). Before World War I, few men smoked and the gender gap was small. During and after World War II, smoking became popular, many men smoked, and the gender gap began to climb. African-Americans also began to smoke in larger numbers and their gender gap increased. Women, perhaps attracted to the advertisement, "You've come a long way, baby!" began to smoke in much greater numbers in the late 1970s and 1980s, after which time the gender gap began to attenuate. By 1980, African-Americans were smoking as much as Caucasian Americans, which was reflected by the gender gap. The 1964 Surgeon General's Report on the dangers of smoking motivated more Caucasians than African-Americans to stop smoking, and this too is reflected in a racial gap.

Another way that scientists have tried to explain the gender gap is by studying nonsmoking populations of men and women so that smoking is not a factor. Among the nonsmoking populations of the Irish in Sleive Loughner, Ireland, and the Amish in Lancaster County, Pennsylvania, men tend to live as long as or longer than women (Casey & Casey, 1971). However, in several studies in which smoking was well controlled and in studies of other nonsmoking populations, these claims were refuted (Friedman, Dalles, & Ury, 1979). Although many agree that "women who smoke like men will die like men" and the gender gap trend seems to be decreasing, others in the research community believe that smoking may account for only 50% to 75% of the gender gap (Enstrom, 1984), with genetics and hormonal differences also contributing.

Another social explanation of why women live longer than men is that women tend to have more contact with the health system. They are more consistent in having annual medical examinations and quicker to go to the doctor if a symptom appears. They also are more social and are more likely to have friends who can assist them in their health needs.

An irony of the gender gap is that although females live longer and use the health care system more, they have more acute illnesses and nonfatal chronic conditions (Figure 1.8). Older females have a higher incidence of arthritis, sinusitis, colitis, soft tissue disorders, and chronic constipation. Conversely, older males experience more emphysema, heart disease, and cerebrovascular disease. Older women as a group presumably experience more emotional stress, exercise less than men (Holden, 1987), have high incidences of disability, and are more dependent.

It is clear that descriptive analyses have produced a wealth of information about aging. From studies of the human survival curve and comparisons of it with the survival curve of other species have come the concepts of primary and secondary aging, the rate of aging, maximum life span potential, average life span, and life expectancy. The curious gender difference in life expectancy also has been revealed. But these descriptions only inform researchers about what appears to exist; they do not answer the questions of why aging takes place.

What Causes Aging?

Throughout recorded history humans have been trying to understand why people age, partly out of curiosity, but more urgently because most humans would like to discover a process by which aging

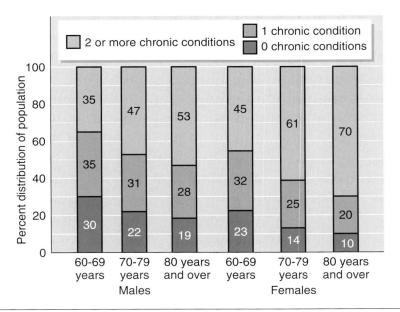

Figure 1.8   Percent distribution of population 60 years and older by number of chronic conditions, according to age group and sex, in the United States, 1984.
Adapted from Guralnik, LaCroix, Everett, and Kovar (1989, p. 4).

might be stopped, slowed, postponed, or reversed. One of the motivations for searching for immortality is that many, if not most, humans suffer from *thanatophobia*—a fear of death—and therefore one of the great quests of science has been to extend the maximum life span. Hippocrates (460-377 B.C.) is credited with being the first to propose a theory of aging—that aging is an irreversible and natural event caused by the gradual loss of body heat. Galen (A.D. 130-201) expanded this theory by suggesting that age-related changes in the body humors began early in life and that these changes gradually caused a slow increase in dryness and coldness of the body. Roger Bacon (1210-1292), in his monograph "Cure of Old Age and Preservation of Youth," subscribed to the Greek belief that aging was caused by a loss of body heat, but Bacon was the first to suggest that this process might be slowed by good hygiene. He also was the first to articulate the "wear and tear" theory of aging, that continual abuses and insults to body systems eventually ages them.

Darwin (1731-1762) thought aging was due to a loss of irritability in nervous and muscular tissue. By this time many scholars were attributing aging to a loss of some type of vital force or physical essence that was necessary for intrinsic energy. A popular theory in the late 19th century was that aging was caused by intestinal putrefaction, which led Charles Brown-Sequard (1817-1894) to inject animal testicular extracts into his own body when he was 72 years old in an effort to postpone aging. Because he died 5 years later, it is safe to say that his efforts were unsuccessful.

By the mid-19th century, the anatomic and physiological changes in the major organ systems were being systematically documented, and it was agreed that with time cells eventually die and are not replaced. But serious and prolific scientific interest in the causes of aging and the aging process is a relatively recent phenomenon. The term *geriatrics*, described for the first time by Ignatz Nascher (1914/1979) as a medical specialization on aging processes, was not coined until 1914 in the title of his book *Geriatrics: The Diseases of Old Age and Their Treatment.* The first geriatric medical journal began publication in 1945, and the first gerontologic conference on aging did not occur until 1950. In the United States, serious interest in a phenomenon is usually expressed by the creation within the National Institutes of Health of an institute dedicated to the topic, yet the National Institute on Aging was not created until 1974. The

realization that the baby boomers of this country will begin to reach retirement age in 2010 has greatly stimulated the interest in the effects of aging on all aspects of life. Research on aging is increasing as each year passes. The questions researchers hope to answer are: What determines the average life span of a population? What determines the life span of an individual? To what maximum could the life span of humans be extended?

Theories of Aging

Because even the definition of aging is controversial, it may seem premature to develop theories of aging before a consensual definition is articulated. Nevertheless, theories abound. Modern theories of aging, a consequence of dramatic advancements in science and technology, are sophisticated and complex and beyond the scope of this book, but a brief summary is appropriate. These theories fall into three major categories—genetic theories, damage theories, and gradual imbalance theories.

Genetic Theories

Supporters of genetic theories propose that the entire process of aging, from birth to death, is programmed by our genes. Age-related events such as puberty and menopause are markers of the biological clock programmed into each cell. In these theories, life span, as well other age-related events, may be controlled by one or more specific, positively acting genes (either major or minor) operating independently or with others for longevity. As yet, no longevity genes have been identified. Nevertheless, these theories suggest that one or more genes dictate cellular aging within the nucleus of the cell or that certain genes are expressed or repressed during the normal developmental process of living.

An early genetic theory proposed that cells began aging if errors occurred during somatic mutations, chromosomal rearrangements, or transcription of genetic material. This theory was called the error-catastrophe theory. Research discounting this theory has accumulated to the extent that Lints (1983) stated, "It may now be said with a reasonable certainty that the error-catastrophe and related theories have been experimentally disproven" (p. 54). However, another expression of this theory has been proposed recently: that DNA mutations of the mitochondria (the energy producers of the cells) build up during an individual's lifetime thus causing aging (Miguel, 1991).

One of the most well-known expressions of a genetically based theory was formulated by Leonard Hayflick in 1977. What is now called the *Hayflick limit* states that cells will divide and reproduce themselves only a limited number of times and that this number is genetically programmed. Thus, the physiological age of the cell (the number of divisions left before it stops reproducing) is determined by the genetic material in the nucleus of the cell, and just as the process of puberty is "turned on" during the growth period, the process of senescence is turned on sometime in middle age. The argument against this theory holds that the long, gradual process of aging is not at all similar to the growth spurts observed in youth. Although it seems intuitive that growth spurts are turned on by genes, it seems less so that the same mechanism accounts for the quite different pattern of slow, gradual aging.

Damage Theories

These theories are based on the concept that chemical reactions that occur naturally in the body begin to produce a number of irreversible defects in molecules. In addition, small but daily chemical damage may occur from the air breathed, the food or other substances eaten, tobacco smoke, or from products of the body's own metabolism. The suggestion by proponents of these damage theories is that if chemical damage could be minimized, the aging process could be slowed and people would live longer. A prominent example of this type of theory is shown in Figure 1.9. Johnson (1985) suggests that, beginning at birth, micro-injuries are unavoidable, universal, and ubiquitous. In the first box of the figure are examples of small insults (viruses, trauma, free radicals) that are a result of metabolic products, background environmental radiation, and a high body temperature, which encourages molecular instability. Repeated small insults eventually lead to injury, which is either repaired or results in a loss of function. The body's natural repair processes can either be overwhelmed or become less effective with aging. If the repair processes cannot keep up with the injuries, a system failure occurs. Loss of function therefore occurs throughout life, but because of the great redundancy in physiological systems, a system failure does not occur until a

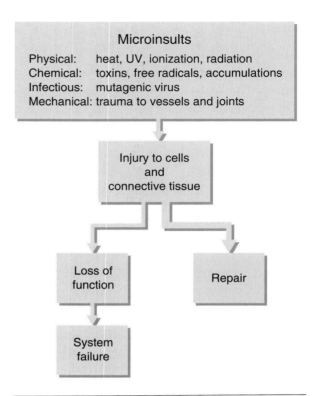

Figure 1.9   The damage-inflicted model of aging. From "Is Aging Physiological or Pathological?" by H.A. Johnson. In *Relations Between Normal Aging and Disease* (p. 241) by H.A. Johnson (Ed.), 1985, New York: Raven Press. Copyright 1985 by Raven Press, Ltd. Reprinted by permission.

considerable amount of function has been lost. Johnson also argues that if a disease is defined as "a gradual accumulation of incompletely repaired injuries due to countless microinsults," then aging per se may be viewed as a disease.

A prominent example of damage theories is the cross-linkage theory. Some highly reactive cellular components made up of atoms or molecules have chemically active sites that can link to the DNA helix within the cell. When one of these cross-linking agents attaches to a strand of DNA, the body's defense mechanism cuts out the piece of corrupted DNA (where the agent is connected) and then repairs the strand using the other strand of the helix as a template. But if the repair process is too slow, or if the cross-linked agent also connects to the corresponding site on the other DNA strand, then this site is cut out of both DNA strands. Thus, no template is available and the damage cannot be repaired. As cross-linking occurs between these molecules, large tangles form, thus impeding intracellular transport of nutrients and information. Because cross-linking occurs on the strands of the DNA helix itself, a very small input can result in a very large change.

Many cross-linking agents are molecules called *free radicals*, which are products of oxygen metabolism. These chemical compounds contain an unpaired electron in an outer orbital and thus are able to link to tissue and cause damage. This damage theory is called the *free-radical theory*. Free radicals oxidize and attack other cellular components, causing alterations and malfunctions that accumulate throughout life. Eventually, so much cellular damage has occurred that the cell dies, a scenario that occurs in more and more cells as one's age increases.

A suggested strategy for reducing free radicals and thus slowing the rate of aging is the consumption of supplementary doses of vitamin C and E and beta-carotenes. Vitamin E and beta-carotenes are antioxidants and are proposed as attackers and destroyers of the damaging free radicals continually created in the body. A number of scientists are presently studying this strategy, but at the present no clear evidence exists in humans to support the use of these vitamin supplements as anti-aging agents. Another cross-linking agent is aluminum, a metal that is plentiful in the environment and used in many common products (e.g., cans, cookware, etc.). Several scientists have proposed that the intake of aluminum is highly damaging and contributes to aging (Bjorksten, 1989; Ganrot, 1986).

Detrimental cross-linking of proteins may also occur in the presence of excessive levels of the blood sugar, glucose. One of the most stressful internal changes that occurs with aging is an increase in blood glucose. The increase occurs because receptors in the pancreas, which supplies insulin to remove glucose, become less sensitive to circulating levels of glucose. Researchers have shown that glucose can randomly attach itself chemically to places on proteins and nucleic acid where it is not normally found. When this happens, it triggers a series of chemical reactions that cross-link proteins in undesirable ways. Regardless of how cross-links are made, the random attachment of proteins and the development of large tangles of malfunctioning molecules lead to many of the problems and systems that are associated with aging: stiffening of tissue, rigidity of blood vessels, tight ligaments and muscle tendons, cataracts, atherosclerosis, and many more.

Gradual Imbalance Theories

Gradual imbalance theories state that the brain, the endocrine glands, or the immune system gradually begin to fail to function. Not only do they begin to fail, they may age at different rates, producing an imbalance among the systems as well as reduced effectiveness within each system. Both the central nervous system and the neuroendocrine system serve as regulators and integrators of cellular functions and organ systems. Failures of the immune system challenge these control mechanisms and leave older individuals vulnerable to diseases of many types. Because aging is more apparent when complex coordination and integration of systems is required for proper function, many researchers have proposed that a general aging theory can be developed through a better understanding of these control mechanisms. An early theory of aging stated that death occurred when one or more of these regulatory processes failed (Frolkis, 1968). Evidence continues to accumulate that regulatory processes seem particularly vulnerable to aging.

The *neuroendocrine regulatory systems* integrate cellular, tissue, and organ activities and enable the body to adapt to real or perceived environmental challenges, such as increases or decreases in temperature, increases in physical work, or psychological threats. The neuroendocrine system requires the proper functioning of both the central nervous system and the endocrine system. Hypothalamic releasing and inhibiting hormones secreted by the hypothalamus of the brain regulate the pituitary gland. The pituitary gland in turn regulates the thyroid, the adrenal gland, and the release of the sex hormones, estrogen and testosterone.

The hypothalamus-pituitary axis has been a prime target of aging theories, and it has even been postulated that within the hypothalamus resides some type of "biological clock" that controls the rate of aging. The pituitary is a master gland because of its wide influence on other hormonal functions. It controls the release of human growth hormones, thyroid hormones, and glucocorticoids, which in turn control metabolic rate. The thyroid hormone is not really a regulatory hormone, but it interacts with other hormones to enhance their functions; for example, it enhances the actions of growth hormone, cortisone, and estrogen. When thyroid hormone is insufficient, as in hypothyroidism, aging symptoms are accelerated. Thyroid hormone replacement therapy, however, reduces or eliminates these symptoms of increased aging.

Adequate levels of estrogen in females seem to protect against some symptoms of aging, for example, a deterioration of cardiovascular function. After menopause, when estrogen levels fall sharply, biological aging accelerates. Estrogen hormone replacement seems to reverse this process. If the control processes of these regulatory hormones break down, an imbalance occurs, further stressing the control mechanisms. A regulatory system out of balance causes malfunctions in each of its components, and each malfunction places an even greater stress on the other components of the system. Thus, age-related changes in certain aspects of the neuroendocrine control mechanisms result in initial endocrine imbalances, producing other physiological and metabolic imbalances that further alter control mechanisms. Eventually the balance of many hormonal and physiological systems is disrupted, a result that Finch (1976) called a cascade of metabolic disturbances described as aging symptoms.

Another type of gradual imbalance theory is the *autoimmunity theory.* Proponents of this theory propose that during aging the immune system, which normally attacks foreign substances such as viruses or cancerous cells in the body, loses the capacity to distinguish foreign antigens from normal body materials. Antibodies are formed that react with normal cells and destroy them or that fail to recognize and destroy the small detrimental mutations that occur in cells. This is called autoimmunity, doubly lethal because the immune system not only becomes less protective against foreign objects, but it actively begins to destroy its host. According to this theory, autoimmunity may be the underlying mechanism of aging.

Although genetic, damage, gradual imbalance, neuroendocrine regulatory, and autoimmunity theories of aging have been discussed independently, the more they are studied, the more it appears that they may not be totally independent of each other. Some aspects of these theories are complementary rather than exclusive of each other: A gene, perhaps related to immune function, becomes defective, rendering it more vulnerable to free radical attack, which in turn disturbs the neuroendocrine immunity balance. Thus, aging may occur because of an interaction among genetic, damage, and system theories. Complicated though the process of aging is, the search for and understanding of its basic mechanism has intensified over the past several years. The "holy grail" for researchers in gerontology is to find a way to retard or stop the aging process. The search continues unabated, and some success has already been achieved.

Can the Aging Process Be Slowed?

If the aging process could be stopped, people could live indefinitely. On the basis of present knowledge, this is impossible. It does not even appear possible to extend the maximum life span potential by any significant amount in the near future. It may be possible, by some behavioral interventions, to slow the rate of secondary aging; that is, fewer people would die at ages younger than the average human life span. If almost everyone lived to the full human life span, an ideal situation from a survival perspective, the shape of the human survival curve would be more like a rectangle. This was shown in Figure 1.1 (page 10), where the size of each older cohort became greater and greater.

Rectangularizing the human survival curve means maximizing the number of persons who approach the average life span of humans (85 years) by eliminating chronic diseases and accidents. This was expressed not as survival data but as mortality data in Figure 1.5 (page 13). In this scenario, almost everyone would live until he or she was very close to the average human life span, somewhere between the ages of 75 and 90. Many would exceed the average life span age. Factors that influence the shape of the human survival curve are medical progress, reductions of levels of environmental pollutants, a decline in the rates of smoking, drinking, and drug abuse, decreases in the rate of violent crime, and increases in the number of people willing to make lifestyle changes that promote longevity. Mortality has also been associated with health, general activity level, quality of life, independence, cognitive function, demographic indicators, and happiness. Three factors—improving nutrition and decreasing the total amount of food consumed, maintaining adequate general activity, and moderate amounts of physical exercise—have been of particular interest to those who wish to decrease secondary aging and thus increase life expectancy.

Food Restriction (Undernutrition)

Food restriction is the only strategy that appears to alter the *rate* of aging. In this strategy, the major nutrients, minerals, and vitamins that are necessary for health are maintained in the diet, but the total amount of food is reduced to about two thirds of normal consumption. This strategy, tested almost exclusively in rats, has been successful. It has been shown with little doubt that rats fed only two thirds of the food that they would normally eat live longer than rats that eat as much as they want. The proposed mechanisms by which this strategy works are that energy that would have been used for reproduction or for unstimulated levels of cellular proliferation and other processes is redirected into essential maintenance and repair processes of the organism. In addition, undernutrition may cause global changes in gene expression that result in greater longevity (Walford & Crew, 1989).

The results of food restriction studies with rats have been so striking that a few scientists have advocated food restriction for humans. The strongest proponent of this life extension technique is Dr. Roy Walford, a biochemist at the University of California at Los Angeles, who at one time personally followed a food restriction diet by eating only every other day (Walford, 1983). However, the application of this strategy to humans has evoked some highly negative reactions among the scientific community, with criticisms centering on the great differences between rats and humans. The food that the rats in these studies had been eating, detractors say, was extremely high in protein and was developed to encourage rapid and artificial growth. It was, they claim, developed to produce large numbers of rats that grew fast but didn't necessarily live a long time. The calorie-restricted diet purported to extend their life span (the rats were fed only every other day) was beneficial only because it enabled the rats to live to their normal average life expectancy. It did not, they claimed, increase the maximum life span of the species. Nevertheless, the effect on extending the life span is so well documented in rats that it is used as a biomarker of aging, and any theory of aging must pass the test of accounting for undernutrition before it can be considered viable.

General Activity Level

The general activity hypothesis has been prevalent in the gerontological community for almost 30 years. Succinctly, the theory states that persons who are more generally active live longer than their sedentary counterparts. Unlike the food restriction hypothesis, which has been experimentally verified many times, the general activity hypothesis is based mainly on anecdotal and associative information. No one has ever shown that general activity actually alters the rate of aging, but it does seem to enable more people to achieve their maximum life span potential. This theory is understood by almost all lay people, and in fact individuals who are exceptionally old often attribute their longevity to staying active. Subjects over the age of 85 listed activity ("hard work," exercise, and keeping active, physically and mentally) as first on their list of secrets to long life (Hogstel & Kashka, 1989). Their other "secrets" were heredity, lifelong good health, strong religious beliefs, a positive attitude toward self and others, abstinence from alcohol, smoking, and drugs, good nutrition, a good support system (parents, spouse, or children), helping others, adequate rest and sleep, and use of health care resources.

Activity inventories have been developed to assess the activities of individuals in three categories: interpersonal activities (family and friend involvement, community or voluntary organization activity), physical or manipulative activities (household activities, exercise habits), and intellectual or solitary activities (Arbuckle, Sissons, & Harsany, 1986-1987; Stones & Kozma, 1986). Many researchers have found that in both community and institutional settings, activity level is a potent predictor of survival. Indeed, in an institutional setting, a young age and a high level of activity were the strongest predictors of survival (Stones, Dornan, & Kozma, 1989). General activity was an even higher predictor than health status in these institutionalized subjects, and the authors concluded that "mortality was found to relate more to lifestyle than to ill health" (p. P78). Conversely, other investigators have failed to find a relationship between general activity level and mortality (Lee & Markides, 1990). An obstacle that makes it difficult to clarify the relationship between general activity level and mortality is that investigators of the various studies use different activity inventories, so they may not be assessing similar activity constructs. The subjects in their samples are also different. For example, 70% of the sample in the Lee and Markides study (1990) was composed of Mexican Americans. Taking these factors into account, the consensus of researchers provides cautious support for the notion that general activity level is a factor in longevity.

Physical Activity

It is now generally accepted that chronic and systematic exercise throughout life, when accompanied by reasonable health habits, increases life expectancy. Increased longevity in exercised animals compared to sedentary animals has been shown many times (Drori & Folman, 1976; Edington, Cosmas, & McCafferty, 1972; Goodrick, 1980; Retzlaff, Fontaine, & Futura, 1966; Sperling, Loosli, Lupien, & McCay, 1978), and Holloszy (1988) concluded from a mini-review of the role of exercise in longevity of rats that exercise does indeed counteract the deleterious effects of a sedentary life combined with overeating. Exercise made it possible for more rats to live to an old age. One dissenting group of researchers found no significant effect in rats, but in this study the exercise activity was voluntary and started from mid- to late-life (Goodrick, Ingram, Reynolds, Freeman, & Cider, 1983).

The results of human studies also support the exercise-longevity relationship. Some evidence is available that track athletes live longer than nonathletes (Shephard, 1978). A 32-year longitudinal study of highly fit male amateur ice skaters in the Netherlands, who are capable of ice skating for 8.5 hours or more, supported the conclusion that these men have a longer life expectancy than the average population, although curiously this did not extend to the professional ice skating racers in the study (van Saase, Noteboom, & Vandenbroucke, 1990). However, the level of physical activity associated with longer survival does not have to approximate the levels of these ice skaters. Much more moderate levels of exercise have been shown to extend the life span of individuals.

One of the most definitive studies to support the idea that physically active individuals live longer was a study of 16,936 Harvard graduates aged 35 to 74 (Paffenbarger, Hyde, Wing, & Hsieh, 1986). In the mid-1960s these investigators used a detailed questionnaire to determine the general health and living habits of these graduates and followed them through 1978. In this study, physical exercise level was expressed in calories expended per week, and those men who expended at least 2,000 calories a week had mortality rates that were 25% to 30% lower than those men who exercised less. This amount of activity is roughly equivalent to about 5 hours of brisk walking or 4 hours of jogging a week. Figure 1.10 shows the relative risk of death according to the amount of physical activity. Relative mortality risk for the sedentary graduates was much higher in the two oldest age groups than in the two youngest age groups. But exercise increased longevity only up to a point. Those who exercised beyond 3,500

calories a week seemed to have exercise-induced detrimental effects that countered the benefits seen at lower levels.

Being a varsity Harvard athlete did not provide additional longevity for these graduates. The mortality rates of former athletes were similar to those of nonathletes. If they remained active after graduation, their mortality rate was decreased, and if they became sedentary, their mortality rate increased. The inescapable conclusion is that the benefits of exercise and physical activity cannot be stored for a later date. The number of additional years of life projected on the basis of physical activity are probable only so long as the individual remains active.

A surprising result of this study was that exercise also seemed to have the beneficial effect of countering some diseases. Hypertensive men who exercised had half the mortality rate of hypertensive men who did not exercise. The mortality rate of smokers who exercised was 30% less than that of smokers who did not exercise.

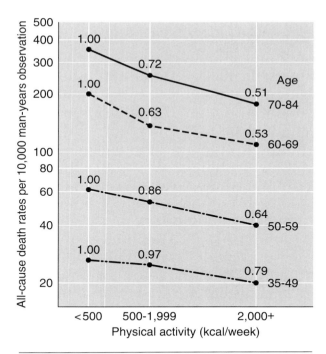

Figure 1.10 Age-specific mortality from all causes among 16,936 Harvard alumni from 1962 to 1978, according to physical activity levels. Relative risks are noted above plot points.
Reprinted, by permission of *The New England Journal of Medicine*, from "Physical Activity, All-Cause Mortality, and Longevity of College Alumni" by R.S. Paffenbarger, Jr., R.T. Hyde, A.L. Wing, and C.C. Hsieh, 1986, *New England Journal of Medicine*, **314**, p. 608.

A group of researchers at the Institute for Aerobics Research in Dallas, Texas, documented the survival or mortality of the 13,344 healthy men and women who had participated in their evaluation and fitness programs over an 8-year period (Blair et al., 1989). This study was unique in that it used an objective measure of aerobic fitness, $\dot{V}O_2$max (described in detail in chapter 4), along with many other demographic and health attributes, for all of the subjects. The subjects were grouped into five categories, ranging from those who were sedentary to those who ran 30 to 40 miles a week (Figure 1.11, a-b). Men who were in the lowest fitness category died at 3.5 times the rate of the most fit men. For women, the difference was even greater; those in the least fit category died at a rate 4.5 times greater than women in the highest fit category. Both men and women in the least fit category had higher incidences of cancer as well as cardiovascular disease.

A new finding that emerged from this study that may have particular relevance to the elderly is that the most important predictor of longevity was *not being in the lowest fit category*. Additional levels of fitness, although increasing longevity somewhat, did not increase it in substantially greater increments. That is, the researchers concluded that

systematic exercise at relatively low levels will increase longevity almost as much as more intensive exercise. In fact, Dr. Blair now lectures that even a little exercise is better than none in terms of the maintenance of health and survival.

To this point, discussions of aging have centered on the quantity, or length, of life. It is important to remember, however, that these results are specific to survival and do not necessarily speak to *quality* of life. Higher levels of systematic exercise provide many benefits, other than just staying alive. Higher levels of cardiorespiratory and neuromuscular strength and flexibility enable any individual to be more generally active and expand the range of activities in which one can participate. These contributions of exercise-induced health and physical fitness and their role in psychological and social dimensions of life are discussed in more detail in chapters 9 through 11.

How Does Physical Aging Affect the Quality of Life?

Modern medicine, science, and technology have been triumphant in this country in bringing the majority of infectious and endemic diseases and nutritional deficiencies under control. The positive

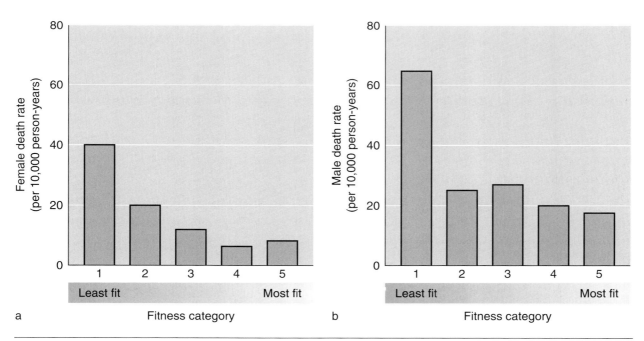

Figure 1.11   The role of physical fitness in preventing premature death among (a) females and (b) males. Even relatively light exercise programs increased the life span of a substantial percentage of the subjects. Increasing the intensity of the exercise program did not provide substantial additional gains in life expectancy.
Data from Blair et al. (1989).

impact of this major accomplishment is that a very high proportion of people born in this country can expect to live a very long time. The consequence of this increased longevity is that degenerative diseases have become and will increasingly be our largest health care problem. The negative impact of a longer life span for mentally competent individuals is the potential for suffering blindness, deafness, arthritis, osteoporosis, diabetes, hypertension, heart disease, incontinence, and physical frailty, and it many times becomes questionable whether life can be enjoyed fully under these morbid conditions that constrain activities so much.

Morbidity

Morbidity is the absence of health, and all too frequently it is a condition in which many frail elderly live for a long time before they die. Sometimes it is caused by terminal or chronic illness. The term *morbidity* is used to describe the condition in which an individual is so physically or mentally disabled by chronic disease that he or she becomes immobile and dependent on the care of others. The "four Ds" of morbidity are discomfort, disability, doctor problems, and drug-interactions (among multiple medications). The major chronic diseases that eventually lead people into a condition of morbidity are atherosclerosis, cancer, osteoarthritis, diabetes, emphysema, and cirrhosis of the liver. These diseases generally start early in life and progress throughout the life span.

Even during youth, some degenerative changes begin to take place, but the body is able to compensate for the slight loss of function, particularly in the neuromuscular system. The great redundancy in this system suppresses overt symptoms for some time. Eventually, however, the pathologic changes become sufficiently extensive and the disease becomes symptomatic, leading inexorably to a morbid condition in which survival is dependent upon extensive use of medical support systems. Table 1.3 shows the average age at which symptoms of these chronic diseases begin to appear. The chronic diseases go through six stages: the start, noticeable, subclinical, problematic, severe, and terminal stage. Many times individuals have one or more of these diseases, with each disease exacerbating the effects of the other. Living with multiple chronic diseases predisposes an individual to a very poor quality of life, and it may be this poor quality of life in conjunction with the financial problems some elderly have that lead to the significantly higher suicide rate among these cohorts. The national suicide rate in the late 1980s was 12.8 per 100,000 individuals. For those 65 and older the rate was 21.5 (Crandall, 1991). Suicide and emotional control are discussed in chapter 10.

The social consequences of an unhealthy aged population are great. Not only does the society have a large number of miserable and unproductive citizens and their extended families, but the financial burden on society as a whole is staggering. The financial burden is determined by the total number of elderly in the society and the percent of these elderly who are incapacitated or ill.

Table 1.3
Accumulative Increases in Chronic Disease

Age (years) Stage	20 Start	30 Noticeable	40 Subclinical	50 Problematic	60 Severe	70 Terminal
Emphysema	Smoking	Mild airway obstruction	X-ray hyper-inflation	Shortness of breath	Recurrent hospitalization	Chronic irreversible oxygen debt
Diabetes	Obesity	Glucose intolerance	Elevated blood glucose	Sugar in urine	Medication required	Blindness Neuropathy
Osteoarthritis	Abnormal cartilage staining	Joint space narrowing	Bone spurs	Mild joint pain	Moderate pain Stiffness	Disability
Atherosclerosis	Elevated cholesterol	Appearance of small plaques	Larger plaques	Leg pain with exercise	Angina pectoris	Heart attack

If the least conservative estimates are used, by the year 2040 the average life expectancy of older people could increase 20 years. Some projections are that by the middle of the 21st century there will be 16 million Americans over 85 years of age. Prognosticators also say that the average 65-year-old will spend 7.5 years of the remaining 17 years living with some functional disability (Wilkins & Adams, 1983). If the present rate at which people are being added to the category of those experiencing morbidity is projected to the future, a 600% increase in health costs will occur. By 2040, Medicare costs, in constant 1987 dollars, will rise sixfold, dementia will ultimately afflict 28% or more of the elderly, and 800,000 hip fractures can be expected annually (Schneider & Guralnik, 1990). Social and medical programs are directly linked to the size and health status of the elderly population of a society. Thus, it is not only the number of years that seniors live but the way they live their remaining years that will determine the quality of life not only for them but for all Americans.

The Compression of Morbidity

Given the projections for the number of individuals experiencing morbidity and the fact that raising the life expectancy ceiling is producing relatively fewer gains, the emphasis in gerontological research has shifted from lengthening life to increasing years of health. The goal is to compress the period of time in which individuals live in a state of morbidity. If the results of scientific advances and medical technology serve only to increase the life span 15 or 20 years and in so doing merely increase the number of years of pain and suffering, then few individuals would accept that as a desirable goal. Figure 1.12 illustrates the concept of the compression of morbidity. First, the hypothesized present morbidity is shown for an average life span of 75 years, with an increasing number of the population experiencing morbidity, beginning at about age 55. Scenario 1 shows a hypothetical situation in which life span is extended to age 85 through technological advances and medical breakthroughs, but the onset of morbidity begins at about the same average age. In this situation, which is clearly undesirable, more people experience morbidity for a longer time, because more people live longer but the incidence and increase in morbidity remains the same. Extension of years of life without changes in health habits would only expand the period of morbidity. But extension of years of life accompanied by changes in health habits can compress the period of morbidity, as shown in Scenario 2. Because chronic diseases begin early in life and develop gradually, a healthy lifestyle can prevent or greatly postpone the start of some of these chronic diseases, such as adult onset diabetes, emphysema, cirrhosis of the liver, and heart disease. Thus, the start or appearance of noticeable symptoms of those diseases would be postponed to a later age.

As shown in Figure 1.13, the longer diseases are prevented, the less time an individual would

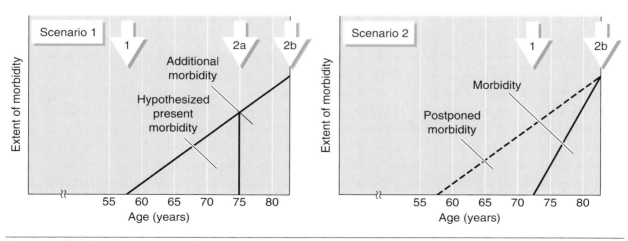

Figure 1.12   The compression of morbidity. The future of population health depends on relative movement of the two arrows: Arrow 1 represents the average age at initial onset of disease or infirmity and Arrows 2a and 2b represent average age at death.

From "Health Promotion and the Compression of Morbidity" by J.F. Fries, L.W. Green, and S. Levine, 1989, *The Lancet*, **8636**, p. 481. Copyright 1989 by *The Lancet*, Ltd. Adapted by permission.

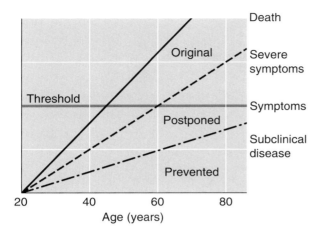

Figure 1.13 Schematic of the hypothetical development of chronic illness. The universal, chronic diseases begin early in life, progress through a clinical threshold, and eventuate in disability or death. Altering the rate (slope) at which symptoms develop postpones the clinical appearance of the illness, "preventing" it.
From *Vitality and Aging* (p. 82) by J.F. Fries and L.M. Crapo, 1981, New York: Freeman. Copyright 1981 by J.F. Fries and L.M. Crapo. Adapted by permission.

experience morbidity in the terminal years. Individuals who practice sound health habits and prevent the onset of chronic disease for many years may *never* experience morbidity. For example, one of the positive outcomes for a group of healthy older adults who participated in a 2-year program of aerobic exercise was that as a group they evidenced a delay in the onset of cardiovascular disease symptoms (Topp et al., 1989). It is highly probable that a healthy lifestyle may also prevent or delay the threshold stage of other diseases such as osteoarthritis and some types of cancer.

Some gerontology scholars argue that a compression of morbidity cannot occur, and others argue vigorously that it can. The doubters see no evidence that individuals who change their lifestyle may experience a lower incidence of morbidity; they argue that even if there were evidence the majority of individuals will not or cannot change their lifestyles. Fries (1980), however, summarized several large studies in which substantial reductions in morbidity were accomplished by education and the initiation of health promotion programs. The evidence from these studies showed that for each hour of exercise a week, there was a 10% improvement in reported health status. There were health risk reductions (19%) and a significant reduction in work-time lost after

6 months of these health promotion programs. Doctor visits and hospitalization time also decreased. An important point that Fries made in his review of these studies was that the average rate of death did not decrease as a result of these health promotion studies, but the morbidity markers did significantly decrease, and thus the quality of life was increased for many of the program participants.

The doubters are also concerned that fixing the responsibility of a contemporary illness on the behavior of individuals is "blaming the victim," which is not consistent with the caring goals of service professions. However, the preventive contributions of good health habits and their effects on the quality of life outweigh their effects on the quantity of life, and individuals must take responsibility for the quality of their own lives. It is important for the health professions to develop and enhance life-extending strategies, but only if professionals also provide strategies that enable people to live as well as they can while continuing to be the best they can be. Of course, for individuals to optimize their abilities, they must actually use these strategies.

Quality of Life Components

In 1990, the Anna and Harry Borun Center for Gerontological Research of the University of California, Los Angeles, sponsored a symposium entitled "Measuring the Quality of Life in the Frail Elderly." At that pioneering conference it was generally agreed that 11 factors constitute quality of life for the frail elderly. The factors of cognitive and emotional function reflect everyone's desire to maintain productivity, independence, and an active interaction with the environment. Life satisfaction and a feeling of well-being represent emotional control and mental heath. Economic independence, though not essential, has the potential of enhancing quality of life. Social function, recreation, and sexual function enable people to enrich their lives. These factors, which are also highly relevant to healthy older persons, are shown in Figure 1.14. But it is also clear that the physical dimension of life, which includes health, physical function, and energy and vitality, contributes in a very significant way to quality of life for the elderly. It is noteworthy that of the 11 factors thought to be essential for a high quality of life in the last years, three of these relate to the physical dimension.

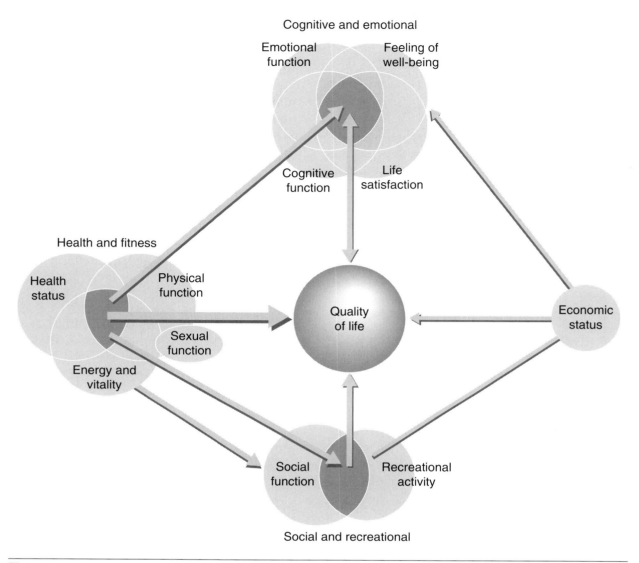

Figure 1.14   Factors affecting the quality of life. These factors are shown as three major constellations: cognitive and emotional, health and fitness, and social and recreational. Economic status also contributes in many direct and indirect ways but is deemed less important by older adults.

Health status, energy and vitality, and physical function, which support the execution of physical tasks, are generally taken for granted by the average young person; but age-related deficits in performance, which begin to concern middle-aged adults, become of greater concern to the young-old and grow to be a primary concern to some old and many of the oldest-old. Physical ability is the basis for performing the activities of daily living, such as walking, eating, bathing, and dressing; job-related tasks, such as typing, writing, lifting, and reaching; and participation in sport and recreational pursuits. This strong contribution of health, energy and vitality, and physical function to the quality of life is shown in Figure 1.14 by

the broad line connecting the health and fitness cluster to the quality of life sphere. The integrity of this threesome will have a profound influence on one's active life expectancy.

Active life expectancy is a term coined by Katz and his colleagues (1983) that combines mortality and disability data. Active life expectancy refers to the number of remaining years of life that an individual may expect to be able to conduct the basic activities of daily living (BADLs). The BADLs are activities such as walking, dressing, bathing, eating, and getting up from a bed or chair. Individuals who cannot carry out these activities are in a state of morbidity, are dependent upon others, and do not have a high quality of life by most people's standards.

Physiological changes accompany aging and these changes eventually constrain motor performance. However, it is difficult to distinguish physiological changes due to aging per se from those due to declining physical activity, decreases in motivation, lower societal expectations, and the occurrence of disease. Many exercise physiologists suggest that most symptoms that people (especially those 50-75 years of age) attribute to aging are really the result of the "rotting, corrosion, and rust" that develops in a stagnant system. The dimensions of the physical components also extend directly to other facets of the quality of life. These are shown in Figure 1.14 by thinner lines that depict the relationship to mental functions (cognitive and emotional function, life satisfaction, and feelings of well-being) and social function. The interrelationships of the physical dimension with mental and social dimensions are explored in chapters 12 and 13.

One of the ways that quality of life has been addressed is by considering whether individuals have an active life or are just alive.

Health and Fitness Contributions in Different Age Categories

Because the physical dimension is so inextricably interwoven with other human life dimensions, and because health and physical activities have a high probability of contributing to the compression of morbidity in the population, good health habits and consistent exercise are beneficial for everyone. Individuals of all ages gain better health, higher levels of physical function, and emotional and mental benefits from habitual physical activity and good health habits. But the primary contribution of consistent physical activity for quality of life varies with age. These differences are summarized in Table 1.4. In children, adolescents, and young adults, physical activity contributes to growth, development, refinement, and self-knowledge of abilities and skills. In middle-aged adults and the young-old, good health habits and exercise can maintain near peak performance and postpone premature aging. For the old, consistent physical activity can substantially enhance the quality of life, enabling the elderly to continue to participate in many of the most enriching experiences of life. The effects of preventive health measures on quality of life may outweigh their effects on quantity of life. Health and fitness in 70-year-olds provide them with the vitality to hike, ski, swim, take walking tours, and deal with the physical demands of shopping, traveling, or socializing. Physical capacity in the oldest-old is the difference between mobility and helplessness, maintaining independence and being dependent upon others, and eventually between life and death.

It is customary to think of physical capacity and performance as improving through the early years, peaking in the third decade, and then declining linearly until death. However, each person is a unique individual, and the interaction of aging and life experiences decreases the consistency of performance within individuals and increases the differences among individuals on many variables across the life span (Sprott, 1988). The differences in physical function of old adults is striking. Capacities range from the frail older adult living in a

Table 1.4
The Role of Physical Activity in Life Stages

Description	Age (years)	Role of physical activity
Infant	0-2	Mobility
Child	3-12	Mobility, development identity, self-esteem, recreation, social interaction
Adolescent	13-17	Development identity
Young adult	18-24	Self-esteem, recreation, social interaction
Adult	25-44	Recreation, self-esteem, social interation
Middle-age adult	45-64	Self-esteem, maintenance (function, job)
Young-old	65-74	Maintenance (mobility, job), recreation, social interaction
Old	75-84	Mobility, IADL, ADL, eating, bathing, dressing, walking, social interaction
Old-old	85-99	Mobility, ADL, independent living
Oldest-old	100+	Mobility, ADL, independent living

long-term care facility, who experiences severe difficulty walking, bathing, and dressing, to an 80-year-old living independently, who can run a 26.2-mile marathon race in a masters' track meet. The concept of "average" ability for a specific age group becomes less and less appropriate for individual performance with increasing age.

In Summary

Life can be described in terms of quantity (how long it is) and quality (how satisfying it is). Quantity is described by several different terms: the maximum life span potential, operationally defined by the longest living survivor of the species; the average life span, which is the average age by which almost all of the members of a population are deceased; life expectancy, which is the average number of years of life remaining for an individual; and the rate of aging, which is the change in organ and system function over time. Another important definition is that of birth cohorts, which include all people born within a similar time frame. The most visible cohort is that of the baby boomers, who are an example of a birth cohort born between the years of 1946 and 1960.

The life expectancy of humans has almost doubled since the beginning of the 20th century, but the average life span has remained relatively stable. The number of individuals over the age of 80 will increase dramatically between now and the year 2000, but the fastest growing age group will be the centenarians, those over 100 years old.

Several theories, which can be categorized as genetic, damage, or gradual imbalance theories, have been developed to describe and understand aging. These age theories have been developed in hopes of attaining the major goal of the life sciences and professions: to rectangularize the human survival curve. Three factors that contribute to increased life expectancy are food restriction (undernutrition), general activity level, and physical exercise. Activity level and exercise result in more adults living longer, not an increase in the maximum human life span. An interesting aspect of the human survival curve is the gender gap. Women throughout the world outlive men by 4 to 10 years. Theories proposed to account for the gender gap include genetics, hormonal differences, and social behavioral differences (primarily smoking habits).

Quantity of life is only of value, however, if the quality of life is endurable, and the goal of extending the life span is only viable if a reasonable quality of life can be maintained throughout the terminal years. Maintaining health and postponing the onset of debilitating disease as long as possible is called compression of morbidity.

The quality of life in the elderly, particularly the frail elderly, is affected by 11 major factors: health status, physical function, energy and vitality, cognitive and emotional function, life satisfaction and a feeling of well-being, sexual function, social function, recreation, and economic status. Most of these factors highly interact with each other. Of particular interest in this book is the substantial contribution that health and fitness, physical function, and energy and vitality can make to the quality of life.

References

Arbuckle, T.Y., Sissons, M.E., & Harsany, M. (1986/1987). Development of a measure of intellectual, social, and physical activity for use with young and older adults. *Research Bulletins of the Centre for Research in Human Development, Concordia University,* **5**(4).

Arking, R. (1991). *Biology of aging: Observations and principles.* Englewood Cliffs, NJ: Prentice Hall.

Bjorksten, J. (1989). The role of aluminum and age-dependent decline. *Environmental Health Perspectives,* **81**, 241-242.

Blair, S., Kohl, H.W., Paffenbarger, R.S., Clark, D.G., Cooper, K.H., & Gibbons, L.W. (1989). Physical fitness and all-cause mortality: A prospective study of healthy men and women. *Journal of the American Medical Association,* **262**, 2395-2401.

Busse, E.W. (1969). Theories of aging. In E.W. Busse & E. Pfeiffer (Eds.), *Behavior and adaptation in later life* (pp. 11-32). Boston: Little Brown.

Casey, A.E., & Casey, J.G. (1971). Long-lived male population with high cholesterol intake in Slieve Loughner, Ireland. *Alabama Journal of Medical Science,* **7**, 21.

Crandall, R.C. (1991). *Gerontology: A behavioral science approach* (2nd ed.). New York: McGraw-Hill.

Drori, D., & Folman, Y. (1976). Environmental effects on longevity in the male rat: Exercise, mating, castration, and restricted feeding. *Experimental Gerontology,* **11**, 25-32.

Edington, D., Cosmas, A.C., & McCafferty, W.B. (1972). Exercise and longevity: Evidence for a threshold age. *Journal of Gerontology*, **27**, 341-343.

Ekonomov, A.L., Rudd, C.L., & Lomakin, A.J. (1989). Actuarial aging rate is not constant within the human life span. *Gerontology*, **35**, 113-120.

Enstrom, J.E. (1984). Smoking and longevity studies. *Science*, **225**, 878.

Finch, C.E. (1976). The regulation of physiological changes during mammalian aging. *Quarterly Review of Biology*, **51**, 49-83.

Friedman, G.D., Dalles, L.G., & Ury, N. (1979). Mortality in middle-aged smokers and nonsmokers. *New England Journal of Medicine*, **300**, 213-217.

Fries, J.F. (1980). Aging, natural death, and the compression of morbidity. *New England Journal of Medicine*, **303**, 130-135.

Fries, J.F., & Crapo, L.M. (1981). *Vitality and aging*. New York: Freeman.

Fries, J.F., Green, L.W., & Levine, S. (1989). Health promotion and the compression of morbidity. *The Lancet*, **8636**, 481-483.

Frolkis, V.V. (1968). Regulatory process in the mechanisms of aging. *Experimental Gerontology*, **3**, 113-123.

Ganrot, P.O. (1986). Metabolism and possible health effects of aluminum. *Environmental Health Perspectives*, **56**, 363-441.

Goodrick, C.L. (1980). Effects of long-term voluntary wheel exercise on male and female Wistar rats. *Gerontology*, **26**, 22-33.

Goodrick, C.L., Ingram, D.K., Reynolds, M.A., Freeman, J.R., & Cider, N.L. (1983). Differential effects of intermittent feeding and voluntary exercise on body weight and life span in adult rats. *Journal of Gerontology*, **38**, 36-45.

Guralnik, J.M., LaCroix, A.Z., Everett, D.F., & Kovar, M.G. (1989). Aging in the eighties: The prevalence of comorbidity and its association with disability. *Advance Data, National Center for Health Statistics*, **170**, 1-8.

Hayflick, L. (1977). The cellular basis for biological aging. In C.E. Firch and L. Hayflick (Eds.), *Handbook of the biology of aging* (pp. 159-186). New York: Van Nostrand Reinhold.

Hershey, D. (1984). *Must we grow old?* Cincinnati: Basal Books.

Hogstel, M.O., & Kashka, M. (1989, Jan/Feb). Staying healthy after 85. *Geriatric Nursing*, pp. 16-18.

Holden, C. (1987). Why do women live longer than men? *Science*, **238**, 158-160.

Holloszy, J. (1988). Exercise and longevity: Studies on rats. *Journal of Gerontology: Biological Sciences*, **43**, B149-B151.

Johnson, H.A. (1985). Is aging physiological or pathological? In H.A. Johnson (Ed.), *Relations between normal aging and disease* (pp. 239-247). New York: Raven Press.

Johnson, T.E. (1990). Increased life span of age-1 mutants in *Caenorhabditis elegans* and lower Gompertz rate of aging. *Science*, **249**, 908-912.

Katz, S., Branch, L.G., Branson, M.H., Papsidero, J.A., Beck, J.C., & Greek, D.S. (1983). Active life expectancy. *New England Journal of Medicine*, **309**, 1218-1224.

Lee, D.J., & Markides, K.S. (1990). Activity and mortality among aged persons over an eight-year period. *Journal of Gerontology: Social Sciences*, **45**, S39-S42.

Lints, F.A. (1983). Genetic influences on life span in *Drosophila* and related species. *Review of Biological Research in Aging*, **1**, 51-72.

Miguel, J. (1991). An integrated theory of aging as the result of mitochondrial-DNA mutation in differentiated cells. *Archives of Gerontology and Geriatrics*, **12**, 99-117.

Miller, G.H. (1986). Is the longevity gender gap decreasing? *New York State Journal of Medicine*, **86**, 59-60.

Miller, G.H., & Gerstein, D.R. (1983). The life expectancy of nonsmoking men and women. *Public Health Report*, **98**, 343-349.

Montague, A. (1953). *The natural superiority of women*. New York: Macmillan.

Nascher, J.L. (1979). *Geriatrics: The diseases of old age and their treatment*. New York: Arno Press. (Original work published 1914)

Olshansky, S.J., Carnes, B.A., & Cassel, C. (1990). In search of Methuselah: Estimating the upper limits to human longevity. *Science*, **250**, 634-640.

Paffenbarger, R.S., Jr., Hyde, R.T., Wing, A.L., & Hsieh, C.C. (1986). Physical activity, all-cause mortality, and longevity of college alumni. *New England Journal of Medicine*, **314**, 605-613.

Retzlaff, E., Fontaine, J., & Futura, W. (1966). Effect of daily exercise on life span of albino rats. *Geriatrics*, **21**, 171-177.

Rothenberg, R., Lentzner, H.R., & Parker, R.A. (1991). Population aging patterns: The expansion of mortality. *Journal of Gerontology: Social Sciences*, **46**, S66-S70.

Schneider, E.L., & Guralnik, J. (1990). The aging of America: Impact on health care costs. *Journal of the American Medical Association*, **263**, 2335-2340.

Shephard, R.J. (1978). *Physical activity and aging*. Chicago: Yearbook Medical Publishers.

Sperling, G.A., Loosli, J.K., Lupien, P., & McCay, C.M. (1978). Effect of sulfamerazine and exercise on life span of rats and hamsters. *Gerontology*, **24**, 220-224.

Sprott, R.L. (1988). Age-related variability. In J.A. Joseph (Ed.), *Central determinants of age-related declines in motor function. Annals of the New York Academy of Sciences*, **515**, 121-123.

Stones, M.J., & Kozma, A. (1986). "Happy are they who are happy . . ." A test between two causal models of relationships between happiness and its correlates. *Experimental Aging Research*, **12**, 23-29.

Stones, M.J., Dornan, B., & Kozma, A. (1989). The prediction of mortality in elderly institution residents. *Journal of Gerontology: Psychological Sciences*, **44**, P72-P79.

Topp, B., Windsor, L.A., Sans, L.P., Gorman, K.M., Bleiman, M., Cherkas, L., & Posner, J.D. (1989). The effect of exercise on morbidity patterns of healthy older adults. *The Gerontologist*, **29**, 192A.

van Saase, J.L.C.M., Noteboom, W.M.P., & Vandenbroucke, J.P. (1990). Longevity of men capable of prolonged vigorous physical exercise: A 32-year follow-up of 2,259 participants in the Dutch Eleven Cities Ice Skating Tour. *British Medical Journal*, **301**, 1409-1411.

Walford, R. (1983). *Maximum life span.* New York: Norton.

Walford, R.L., & Crew, M. (1989). How dietary restriction retards aging: An integrative hypothesis. *Growth, Development, and Aging*, Winter, 139-140.

Wilkins, R., & Adams, O. (1983). Health expectancy in Canada, late 1970s: Demographic, regional, and social dimensions. *American Journal of Public Health*, **73**, 1073-1080.

CHAPTER 2

Individual Differences

Aging is an individual experience, for people differ not only in their attributes and behaviors but in the way these change over time. The results of hundreds of experiments and research projects using both human and animal subjects have shown that chronological age is not a good predictor of function or performance for an individual on most variables. Aging is a highly personal process, with individuals not only being different from each other but also having physiological systems that age at different rates. The average blood pressure, for example, gradually increases in an age cohort with the passing of time. But when individuals are measured longitudinally, blood pressure does not increase at all in some people. In those whose blood pressure is unchanged, however, other systems may be deteriorating more rapidly. Also, random variations in many physiological variables are frequently seen in individuals throughout their life span, so the differences seen among individuals over time do not remain entirely stable.

Several other factors contribute to individual differences. The assessment of aging rate may be influenced by the measurements taken or the tasks used for testing. Each individual begins life with different attributes and behaviors, with aging rates that differ for different systems, and the interactions among these attributes and their aging rates also interact with the measurements made. The result is a unique aging pattern for each person. *Individual differences*, the term used to describe the great variability among people, describes a phenomenon that is just as much a hallmark of aging as the concept of age-related functional decline. Considering that individual differences exist among the elderly, it is no wonder that chronological age is such a poor predictor of function for an individual.

Measuring Individual Differences

The differences that exist among people are measured by determining the spread of scores on a particular variable from the mean (average) score for that age group. Figure 2.1a shows the range of performance on a hypothetical strength test for individuals of different ages. The filled circles indicate the average score for each age group, but the unfilled circles show the strength of each person in each age group. Notice that in this particular example no single person has exactly the mean score. The mean adequately represents the amount of force that most of the members of each age group can produce, but it cannot accurately predict each individual's score. In some individuals, such as subjects S83 and S62, the mean is a very poor estimate of their strength. Subject 83 may have strength-trained all his life and consequently has superior scores not only for his age group but for persons in the other age groups as well. Subject 62, an extremely sedentary individual, has a very low level of strength. This individual's strength is extraordinarily different from that of others in his age group.

The amount of individual difference (*inter*individual variability) among people in an experimental group is measured by the standard deviation of the scores about the mean. The standard deviation roughly represents an average of the distances of the subjects' strength scores from the mean score of the age group. It is calculated by taking the square root of the squared difference of each score from the group mean divided by the total number of subjects in the group ($\sqrt{\Sigma x^2/N}$). The distance of each score from the mean is shown by the brackets in the 40-year-old group (Figure 2.1a). The greater the spread of scores from the mean, the more different the members of the group are and the less accurate the mean is in estimating individuals' strength. Figure 2.1b shows a hypothetical distribution of resting heart rates. Resting heart rates do not change significantly with age, and the standard deviations are small. In this figure two points are important: First, the magnitude of individual differences varies with the attribute or function being measured. Physiological variables tend to have smaller individual differences than do psychological variables. Second, particularly in variables with large individual differences, the means do not accurately predict the individual scores.

Because they arise from different sources, between-subject differences increase with age in many variables. For example, human gestation requires 280 ± 5 days, onset of menarche occurs at 151.8 ± 14.1 months, and age at menopause is 50 ± 8 years (Baker & Sprott, 1988). Psychomotor test scores (Figure 2.2, a-b, page 36) are examples of variables on which the individual differences increase with age. The average coefficient of variation [(*SD*/*M*) · 100] across six psychomotor tasks for 20-, 50-, 60-, and 70-year-olds is shown in Figure 2.2a. The standard deviations are larger in the older age groups. Reaction time, measured in cross-sectional studies, also increases in individual differences as age increases (Botwinick, 1973; Fozard, Thomas, & Waugh, 1976; Hertzog, 1985). In Figure 2.2b, the individual differences in choice reaction time (CRT) are shown across five age groups (Spirduso, Light, & Reilly, 1990). The coefficient of variation reveals that large individual differences exist among a group of 8-year-olds, that the individuals in the 12- and 20-year-old groups are the most alike, but that individual differences increase substantially in the oldest two age groups. The larger between-subject variability in older people seen in reaction time data could be due either to a larger range of reaction

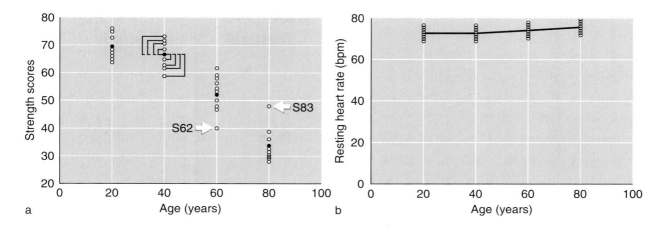

Figure 2.1 Hypothetical distributions of (a) strength scores and (b) resting heart rate.

times or to a more highly skewed distribution, that is, one in which just a few individuals are either much faster or much slower than the group as a whole. But the greater differences that exist among older adults are not a statistical artifact. When reaction times are measured longitudinally, individuals appear to become more different from each other. Individuals stay at about the same place in the distribution from one longitudinal measure to the next, but the distance among them increases. For example, individual differences in 8 out of 15 variables measured six times over a 13-year period were maintained throughout the period studied (Maddox & Douglass, 1974). In 5 out of the 15 variables analyzed in those longitudinal studies, the between-subject variance increased with increasing age. It should be remembered, however, that individual differences do not increase on all variables with aging. Body weight, perhaps due to selective mortality, is an example of a variable on which individual differences are stabilized throughout the life span.

Another way to observe individual differences is to study the cumulative frequency distributions of scores from individuals of different ages (Figure 2.3). In cumulative frequency distributions, the scores of each person in each age group are plotted, beginning with the lowest score in the distribution on the X axis of the graph, adding each score in ascending order, and plotting them against the percentage of scores on the dependent variable of interest that are below each score. Several observations about individual differences can be made from this cumulative frequency graph of choice reaction times. First, the cumulative frequency curve of the oldest group (60-year-olds) is displaced to the right, that is, their reaction times

are slower. Second, the cumulative frequency regression line of the 20-year-olds is much more vertical, meaning that all of the scores of the 20-year-olds fall between a narrow range of reaction times. In this example, the 20-year-olds' CRTs fall between 250 and 360 ms, a range of 110 ms. The cumulative frequency curve of the 60-year-olds is flatter and more spread out, meaning that the older subjects' reaction times range from 280 to 490 ms, a difference of 210 ms.

Sources of Individual Differences

Individual differences arise from many sources. Individuals inherit different attributes, behaviors, and predispositions, and a lifetime of interacting with the environment and developing unique compensatory behaviors magnifies these differences. People differ in age, weight, height, gender, skin color, eye color, strength, intelligence, and a host of other variables, each of which alone and in combination contributes to individual differences. Additionally, physiological systems age at a different rate for each person. Also, as people grow older they perform less consistently on many types of tests. Gender, cultural differences, education, and socioeconomic status are additional sources of individual differences. Finally, the research designs used in gerontology research also contribute to the observations of individual differences.

Genetic Differences

People are born with unique genotypes (genetic make-ups), which vary on several dimensions and

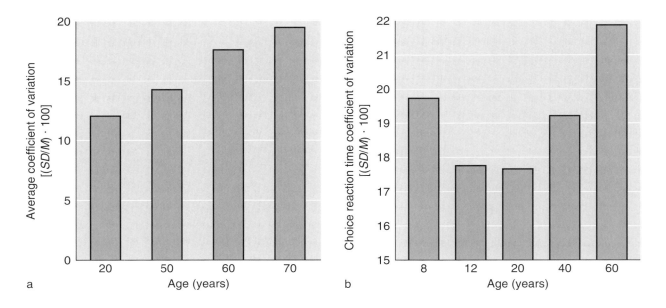

Figure 2.2 Average coefficients of variation (*CV*) for (a) six psychomotor tasks and (b) a choice reaction time test. The *CV* [(*SD*/*M*) · 100] is a way to assess the relative variability that exists within several distributions of scores, each of which have different units of measure. By discussing the standard deviation of each distribution as a function of its mean, the sizes and discrepancies of means are neutralized. In this figure the average *CV* from six psychomotor tasks increases with increases in age. The tasks were stationary tapping, between-target tapping, simple reaction time (foot), discrimination reaction time (foot), trailmaking, and digit-symbol substitution. The *CV*s for choice reaction times from five age groups also increased with adult aging, but 8-year-old children were equally different within their group.
Data from Spirduso, Light, and Reilly (1990).

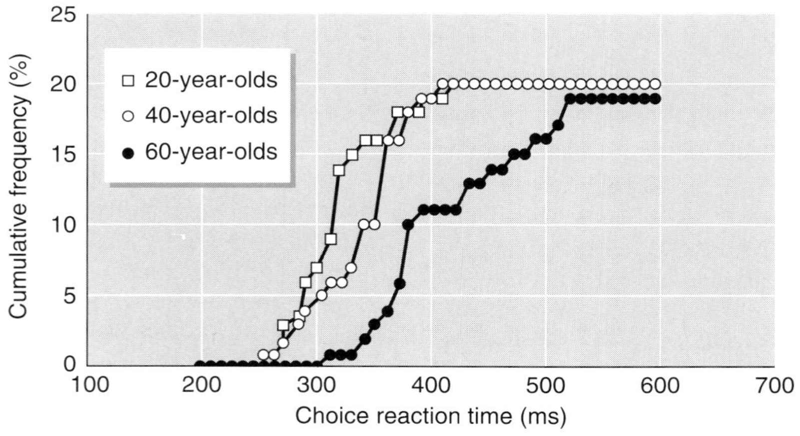

Figure 2.3 Cumulative frequency distribution for 20-, 40-, and 60-year-olds on choice reaction time. The fastest reaction time score produced by the group of 20-year-old subjects was 250 ms. Because it was the fastest score in that group, the percentage of scores below it is 0%. The next score plotted was 265 ms, and because only one person in the distribution was below that score, its cumulative frequency is 5%, meaning that only 5% of the scores were lower. The slowest score in the distribution for 20-year-olds was approximately 400 ms, and because it was the slowest, 100% of the scores are below this value. In this cumulative frequency graph, the line representing 60-year-olds is the most spread out, indicating that individual differences are greater in this group than in the other two groups. The 20-year-olds' line is almost vertical, indicating small individual differences.

in hundreds of attributes. Not only are many individual differences in attributes and function genetically expressed, but behavioral genetics studies of children have shown that social and physical activity habits are also strongly determined by heredity (Buss & Plomin, 1984). Studies of adult twins have indicated that the genetic influence on physical activity persists into the second half of the life span (Plomin, Pedersen, McClearn, Nesselroade, & Bergeman, 1988). In other words, some patterns of behavior with which individuals interact with their environment are relatively stable throughout the life span, and many lines of evidence suggest that these patterns may reflect an individual difference propensity for certain behaviors that originates in genetic inheritance and early experiences (Stones, Dornan, & Kozma, 1989). Research on aging animals strongly supports the role of genetics in aging (Collier & Coleman, 1991). Same-aged mice and rats of different strains age differently in different tasks. Aging mice of some strains lose the capacity to balance on a moving rod but retain the ability to find an underwater target better than mice of other strains. Individual differences in behavior are therefore partially a function of inherited traits but are also partially shaped by a genotype that predisposes individuals to interact with their environment in certain ways. The abilities that they have and their predispositions to maximize their talents and compensate for their inadequacies allow wide disparities of function to occur among individuals. For example, the aging of a system, such as the cardiovascular system, is modified by the use of medications and alcohol, by smoking, by diet and exercise habits, by the incidence of disease, and by social factors. The different interactions, partly genetic, that people exhibit also increase individual differences. Genetic interactions with environmental experiences have also been demonstrated in animal research. Mice that were handled daily by technicians during the first 3 weeks of their lives managed stress better as they aged than did nonhandled mice (Levine, 1962).

Disease and Aging

People differ in the extent to which they experience disease, because each unique genotype supports different types and frequencies of inherited pathologies, different vulnerabilities to certain environmental challenges, and different levels of immune system effectiveness. Clearly, disease accelerates aging in some systems, and stress on these affected systems eventually stresses other systems. Events such as a heart attack, an environmental toxic stress, or the onset of depression following the death of a spouse can radically affect behavior and thus the aging process. In Johnson's (1985) model of aging (see Figure 1.9, page 18), diseases such as diabetes or cardiovascular disease would exacerbate injuries to cells and connective tissue and accelerate the loss of function of a system. Although it has not been possible to measure the different time courses, reaction to, frequency of, and intensity of disease among people and predict life span, it is likely that these pathologies are related to biological aging and account for some of the individual differences that are seen in physical function of the elderly.

Differential Aging of Body Systems

Another contributor to individual differences is the different rate at which physiological and behavioral systems age within the individual. The deterioration of systems is progressive but not at the same rate across all sensory modalities and physiological systems. Nowhere has this been shown more clearly than in the classic graph published by Shock in 1962 (Figure 2.4). For example, nerve conduction velocity declines relatively little throughout the life span, but maximal breathing capacity deteriorates greatly. Vital capacity decreases substantially, but the cardiac index declines much less. Even in a single system, for example the cardiovascular system, maximum heart rate slowly but gradually declines in the active older adult while other cardiovascular components such as stroke volume and cardiac output do not. Fast-twitch muscle fibers become harder to recruit, but slow-twitch fibers age very slowly. Some aspects of psychomotor function, such as long-term memory, are maintained, while others, such as rapid decision making, deteriorate. In a longitudinal study, Schaie (1990) observed that no subjects universally declined on all abilities monitored (verbal meaning, spatial orientation, inductive reasoning, and number and word fluency). In addition, age-related change in different systems can follow different patterns of decline, shown in Table 2.1.

Within-Subject Variability in Aging

Another source of individual differences is within-subject variability, or subject consistency. When

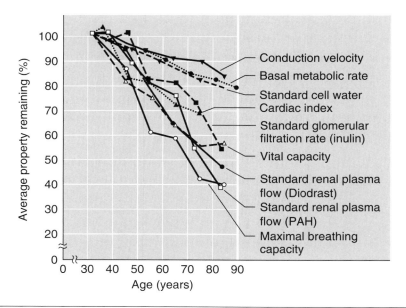

Figure 2.4   Age changes in physiologic functions from age 30. Data are derived from cross-sectional studies. Reprinted from "Physical Activity and the Rate of Aging" by N.W. Shock, 1967, *Canadian Medical Association Journal,* **96,** p. 836. Copyright 1967 by the Canadian Medical Association. Reprinted by permission of the publisher.

Table 2.1
Patterns of Change With Age[a]

Change pattern	Example
1. Stability, absence of change	Resting heart rate, some personality factors
2. Disease-related changes	Careful health screening showed that plasma testosterone does not decline in healthy men, contradicting earlier research. Thus, apparent age-related declines in testosterone are likely to be disease-related.
3. Steady decline in function in healthy persons	Creatinine clearance
4. Disease-accelerated aging of a system that declines in healthy persons[b]	The decline in forced expiratory ventilation, which is inevitable even in healthy individuals, is exacerbated by the development of ischemic heart disease.
5. Changes that occur precipitously in old age	Dementia (These changes are often expressions of disease.)
6. Compensatory changes	Frank-Starling mechanism to maintain cardiac output during exercise; represents the body's attempts to maintain function with advancing age
7. Cultural changes	Reduction of dietary cholesterol has nothing to do with aging but represents a change in behavior that influences other patterns.

Note. [a]Data from Shock et al. (1984, p. 208).
[b]From Fozard, Metter, and Brant (1990, p. P119).

researchers measure functions or behaviors of subjects, they hope that their measurement represents the true value of that function or behavior. But true scores of a function or behavior can only

be estimated by obtaining two or more measurements from the same subject and using the average of these several observations. The amount of variation that occurs in several measures of a variable from the same subject is called the *within-subject variability*. This variation is described by the standard deviation of all the subject's trials about the *subject's* mean. The principle is the same as that used to determine individual differences within a group: To determine individual differences, the average distance of each person's score from the mean of the group is calculated. To determine within-subject variability, the average distance of each score of a subject from the subject's own mean is calculated. A comparison of the calculations for between-subject variation (individual differences) and within-subject variability (consistency) is shown in Figure 2.5. The subjects are placed in the figure according to their within-subject variance (standard deviation), that is, from the most consistent (S1) to the least consistent (S10).

In some variables, within-subject variation is very small. Multiple measures of nerve conduction velocity, for example, provide almost identical values unless the measurements are taken at different times of the day. If resting heart rate is measured 10 times for 1 minute, the result will not be identical on all 10 trials, but the measures will be very close. Within-subject variability may occur due to the nature of biological oscillating systems, or it may be caused by errors of measurement. In other variables, such as reaction time, the responses of subjects are so variable that a large number of trials have to be taken so that the average or median of these trials can be used to estimate the subject's true response speed. Subject motivation, fatigue, learning, and the experimental use of different strategies on different trials explain some of the within-subject variability in these behaviors.

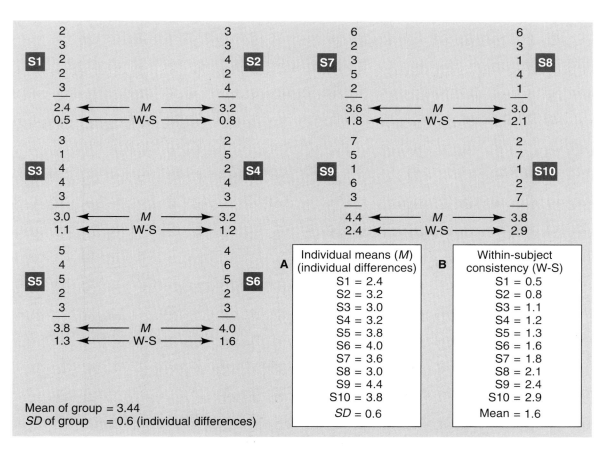

Figure 2.5   The calculation of individual differences and within-subject consistency. The average score (estimated true score) for each individual is the mean derived from each subject's set of scores, and the average score for the group is the mean of all the subjects' means, or *M* = 3.44 (see bottom of figure). The measure of individual differences for the group is the standard deviation of the means of all the subjects, or *SD* = 0.6 (also, bottom of figure). A subject's consistency of performance is determined by calculating the standard deviation of the subject's set of scores about his or her mean. The average consistency of individuals within this group is shown in Box B by the mean of all subjects' standard deviations, or 1.6.

The extent to which within-subject variability is stable throughout the life span probably differs with the function measured. Conflicting results have been obtained for reaction time. Within-subject variability stayed the same over a 13-year period with six measures of reaction time according to Maddox and Douglass (1974) but increased with age according to Fozard, et al. (1976).

Variations in Lifestyle

Variations in lifestyle also contribute to individual differences. Some people optimize specific capacities by selectively maintaining them through training or practice. For example, playing contract bridge weekly maintains memory and reasoning but not reaction time (Clarkson-Smith & Hartley, 1990). Playing racquetball may maintain reaction time but perhaps not the ability to reason. The social and personal lifestyles that people adopt also influence their aging (Stones & Kozma, 1986).

The patterns of exercise, physical activity, and health habits that people adopt also contribute to individual differences within specific age cohorts. Even though more and more people are participating in systematic exercise, individuals vary considerably in the extent to which they adhere to an exercise schedule. A typical 65-year-old cohort might be characterized as follows: A large portion of the group were sedentary all of their lives, preferring to watch others be physically active rather than be active themselves. As these individuals approached 65 years of age, they grew more and more sedentary with increasing age and are now at risk for developing a hypokinetic disease, becoming debilitated and prematurely dependent, and being classified among the frail elderly. Another portion of this 65-year-old cohort were physically active in their first two decades but participated in less and less physical activity with each ensuing decade until at 65 years they participate in little or no physical activity. Only 14% of men and 13% of women in their 70s and 80s report that they participate in some type of systematic exercise program four or more times a week (Cullen & Weeks, 1978). They too are at risk for joining the ranks of the frail elderly. (It remains to be seen whether the larger numbers of physically active individuals who are now in their 30s and 40s will remain active through their 70s and 80s.)

Another portion of the 65-year-old group were sedentary individuals who became motivated in their 40s and 50s to change their lifestyles and to become physically active. Now they are very active and the majority are healthy. A much smaller percent of the 65-year-old group have engaged in vigorous physical activity all of their lives, and it is accurate to describe them as the "physically elite" elderly. Their capacities and activities are elaborated in chapter 14. Clearly this 65-year-old cohort exemplifies the vast individual differences that exist in the physiological function and physical performance of this age group. The wide differences in their levels of physical activity also contribute to increasing individual differences in psychological functioning and social interactions, which is discussed in more detail in Part IV, "Physical-Psychosocial Relationships."

Compensatory Behaviors of Older Adults

One of the necessities of life is to learn to compensate for inadequacies and to develop strategies that maximize personal goal acquisition. Young people develop compensatory strategies to achieve their objectives if they are lacking in relevant talents or skills. Adults develop compensatory strategies when they begin to lose skills or talent. For example, the elderly learn how to handle heavy objects using the larger muscle groups. As typists grow older, they learn to anticipate what is to be typed in order to compensate for their slower eye-hand coordination. They begin cognitively processing the typing of a letter or character earlier than young subjects so that their performance is not hampered by their slower central nervous system function (Salthouse, 1988). The magnificent human cognitive intellect provides behavioral flexibility, that is, the ability to choose different strategies, which adds to the plasticity of the system. But in so doing, it also adds to the individual differences that are observed in groups of people.

Gender, Cultural Differences, Education, and Socioeconomic Status

Gender differences in physiological function and psychosocial role expectations contribute substantially to individual differences in aging on some physical dimensions. The observations that women live longer than men, have less atherosclerosis than men, and use health care resources more than men, whereas men have fewer debilitating diseases in the very-old age categories, all are examples of gender as a source of individual differences.

Cultural and subcultural differences exist in all aspects of life. Cultural membership affects personality, patterns of familial and friendship interaction, the ways people cope with and adapt to perturbations of their environment, and also the way people age (Jackson, Antonucci, & Gibson, 1990). More specifically, cultures have specific views of the role of physical activity in the lives of members, and strong expectations exist among the members of the culture concerning which physical activities are appropriate for different age groups. Individual differences in youth and middle age may also be accentuated with increasing age, because in many cultures social constraints on older people are relaxed. Older people in most cultures have more freedom to behave in the ways they want to behave.

Yet another source of individual differences is education. The vastly different educational background of 70- and 80-year-olds compared to 20-year-olds makes it exceptionally difficult to understand age-related cognitive changes that are independent of educational background. If researchers simply compare 20- and 80-year-olds' cognitive performance, they also compare groups that have vastly different educational experiences. Conversely, if they match for educational level, so that they only study subjects who have the same amount of education, they are studying a group of 80-year-olds who represent a population more educationally elite than that of the 20-year-olds. This is particularly true when studying females. So few women went to college in the 1930s that any 80-year-old women who did may represent a population with a very different intellectual and personality profile. The influence of educational level is not isolated to cognitive tests. It is also related to many types of physical performance as well.

Socioeconomic status provides an entirely different environment for individuals and is thus yet another source of individual differences. Another way that socioeconomic status can influence a researcher's analysis of individual differences is that low-income older adults who are financially stressed may volunteer for a study just for monetary incentive, whereas young adults may volunteer to participate in the study for reasons other than financial incentive.

Research Design Effects on Individual Differences

The study of individual differences in aging, and particularly the rate of aging for individuals and groups, is not as straightforward as it might seem. The appropriate design for such study appears intuitively to be a longitudinal design, in which the same people are measured on a particular variable over a number of years. But people live too long for this to be feasible in most instances. It would be extremely costly, and many of the subjects might outlive the researcher. The design used by most researchers is the cross-sectional research design shown in Figure 2.6, in which people of different ages are compared. A longitudinal study (e.g., Row 2 of the figure) involves measurement of the same people, the 1940 cohort, in the years 1970, 1980, and 1990. A cross-sectional study (e.g., Column 3) involves the measurement during 1 year, 1990, of people born in 1950 (40-year-olds), 1940 (50-year-olds), 1930 (60-year-olds), and 1920 (70-year-olds). Some combinations of cross-sectional and longitudinal designs over limited time periods have also been used,

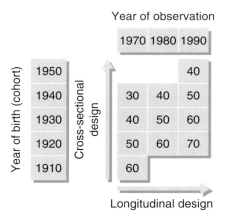

Figure 2.6 Comparison of cross-sectional and longitudinal research designs. In cross-sectional research designs, measurements are down a column (i.e., in 1970, 30-, 40-, 50-, and 60-year-olds would be measured). A longitudinal analysis involves measuring one or more birth cohorts over several years (i.e., the 1930 cohort would be measured in 1970 at age 40, again in 1980 at age 50, and yet again in 1990 at age 60).

Adapted from "Research Methods" by J. Botwinick. In *Aging and Behavior* (p. 389) by J. Botwinick (Ed.), 1984, New York: Springer. Copyright 1984 by Springer Publishing Co., Inc., New York, 10012. Used by permission.

but these combinations comprise a very small percentage of research.

The cross-sectional design, however, is not a good design for determining individual differences on many variables for several reasons. First, cross-sectional analyses can only assess age *differences*, not age *changes*. Second, old and young people do not volunteer and remain in studies in the same percentages. Third, the pattern of mortality, disability, and health status in aging adults affects the results. Fourth, the number of subjects in the various age groups is usually unequal, with far more younger than older subjects. Last, the sampling techniques to acquire older subjects for study may be different than those techniques used to obtain young subjects.

Age Differences Versus Age Changes

Individuals age at different rates, but it is not possible to measure the rate of aging of selected functions unless the same individuals are measured over an extended period of time. Most of the information about capacities and abilities at various ages comes from cross-sectional studies in which variables are measured in individuals of different ages. Thus, oxygen consumption is said to decline with increased age, because the average oxygen consumption values are lower in the older groups. However, these are age differences *not* age changes. The results of longitudinal studies, such as the Baltimore Longitudinal Study of Aging and the Duke Longitudinal Studies I and II (Palmore, 1970, 1981), produced similar descriptions of age changes that occur in healthy adults. When individuals are measured longitudinally for a period of time, relatively few of them actually follow the means that are plotted for a variable from cross-sectional studies (i.e., studies of different people at different ages). Even fewer would follow the average sample means derived cross-sectionally for several different parameters. Graphs of average aging patterns provide only a rough approximation of the actual pattern of aging followed by an individual. Thus, the researchers involved in the Baltimore and the Duke studies concluded from their analyses that cross-sectional studies are not very accurate in predicting individual aging patterns. It is all too easy to fall into the trap of interpreting differences between age groups as age-related changes, but as noted in the discussion of selective mortality,

such interpretations can lead to completely inaccurate conclusions.

Differential Attrition of Subjects

Subjects drop out of studies for a variety of reasons. They may become sick, disabled, or disinterested; but whatever their reasons, they represent a very different sample of their age group than those who continue in a study. Those who remain in studies typically have higher self-reported measures of physical health, psychological well-being, life satisfaction, self-esteem, and social support—all factors that describe successful aging. The dropouts generally participate less in personal, recreational, and social-interpersonal activities (Powell et al., 1990) and exhibit more incidence of depression than the remaining research participants. Clearly, studying individual differences among age groups can be affected if the older groups include people who are successfully aging, whereas the younger groups contain a mixture of those who will successfully age and those who will not. Many older people who are unhealthy or who feel that they cannot perform as well as their peers may refuse to participate in a study or may refuse to return as a subject for the second or third testing in a longitudinal study. If these older people are accurate in their self-evaluation, then the scores from those who return for testing will *overestimate* the abilities or functions of people of that age group and may artificially reduce the individual differences observed.

Selective Mortality

Another problem that occurs when averages are taken cross-sectionally from different age groups is that the results can be distorted by *selective mortality*. Selective mortality describes the phenomenon that only a "select few" live to be 80 or 90 years old. More than half of a birth cohort die before their 70th birthday. Some of those who are measured in their 30s and 40s in present experiments will not live to be 70, whereas the 70- or 80-year-olds in the study obviously already have lived that long. Consequently, the comparisons that are drawn between 20-year-olds and 70-year-olds are comparing a mixture of select and nonselect 20-year-olds with only select 70-year-olds. The 70-year-old sample may have smaller individual differences because of the selective process.

Figure 2.7, a through c, shows how selective mortality in cross-sectional studies can mislead researchers in hypothetical situations in which a) no change occurs with aging, b) there is a floor effect, and c) there is a lethal limit that varies with age.

Unequal Numbers of Subjects in Age Groups

It is difficult to find older adults who are willing to be tested. The more difficult the test and the more energy it requires, the less easy it is to convince older adults to participate. Also, as discussed

previously, more older adults than younger adults may drop out of an experiment. Consequently, in most research projects the number of subjects dwindles for each older age group. For example, a study of young, middle-aged, and old adults may have 50 young adults, 32 middle-aged adults, and 18 old adults. But compounding this inequality of sampling is the fact that the age ranges are also usually unequal. The young group may have an age range of 9 years (20-29), the middle-aged group an age range of 13 years (40-53), and the old group, often referred to as the "60+" group, a range of 23 years (60-83). Thus the individual differences within each age group increase with

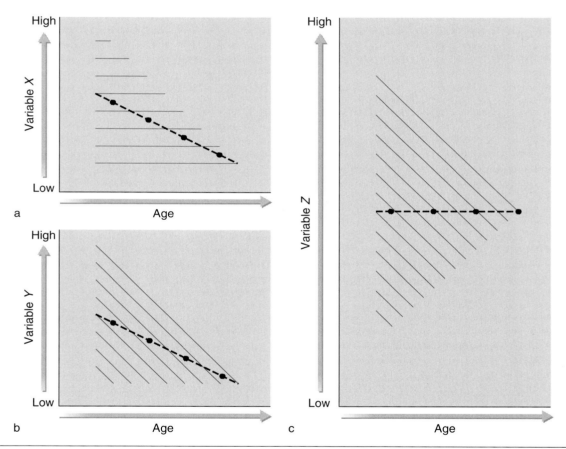

Figure 2.7 (a) Confounding effect of selective mortality on inferences about age changes. Each solid line segment represents the pattern of change in an individual (in this case there is no change with aging, and death occurs at the end of the line). High values for *X* are assumed to be deleterious. The closed circles represent mean values obtained in a cross-sectional study; the dashed line connecting these dots then correctly represents age *differences* among age groups, but the inference that age *changes* were occurring in individuals would be erroneous. (b) Confounding effect of selective mortality on the magnitude of age changes. A floor effect or lethal limit is assumed for the variable. In this case, the dashed line representing age differences underestimates true aging. (c) Confounding effect of selective mortality as a result of which age changes are not revealed in cross-sectional studies. A lethal limit that varies with age is assumed. In this case, the dashed line shows no age *differences*, although there were large age changes in individuals.
Adapted from Shock et al. (1984, pp. 6-8).

increasing age, contaminating the results of the age group comparisons.

The smaller number of subjects in the oldest age group not only contaminates the age group comparisons by compromising the statistical analyses, but also represents a situation in which the population of one age group—the oldest age—is less represented than the other two age populations. Take the measurement of muscular strength: A researcher wishing to know how aging affects the maximum amount of weight a man can lift analyzes the records of weight-lifting contests. But the number of 20-year-old men who weight-train and compete in weight lifting is many times larger than the number of 70-year-old men who compete. The 20-year-olds' weight-lifting records, because they are obtained from a much larger number of contestants, probably estimate the population mean for that age group more reliably than the 70-year-olds' records do for their age group. So few old individuals participate in strength and power athletic events that the records surely must underestimate the upper limits of human strength and power in the seventh, eighth, and ninth decades. This problem is discussed in more detail in chapter 14, which compares the numbers of competitors in each age and weight class of powerlifting competitions.

Selective Sampling

Researchers generally are reluctant to force elderly adults to do anything that is against their desires, so most investigators use only those old adults who volunteer to serve as subjects. Volunteers of any age, by their nature, are different from randomly selected subjects on a wide variety of variables. Young volunteers have been shown from various studies to be more sociable, to have a greater need for social approval, to be more easily influenced by the presence and opinions of others, and to be more intelligent. Females tend to volunteer in greater numbers for research projects that are relatively standard or unthreatening, whereas males volunteer more frequently for experiments that are more unpredictable.

Studies of aging tend to be studies of volunteers, and this is another source of individual differences that is independent of aging effects. Furthermore, when recruiting old adults as subjects for research for studies, many investigators are tempted, for ease of testing, to use intact groups of people.

such as college faculty members, residents of nursing homes, retirement communities, or long-term care facilities, Veterans Administration hospital outpatients, members of garden clubs, or participants of social service groups, such as Meals on Wheels. Although such groups are more convenient to measure, the very factors that caused them to be in those groups also contribute another source of individual differences that can contaminate the comparisons made to younger groups.

Research Process Effects on Individual Differences

To understand the effects of aging on various behaviors, the process of measuring older adults, comparing them with younger adults, and interpreting the results must distinguish between competence and performance. This distinction is not a serious problem in the measurement of many physiological variables, such as blood proteins, muscle tissue composition, or bone calcium analysis, although some variables, such as oxygen consumption and blood pressure, thought by some researchers to be totally free of psychosocial influences, are not. The difference between competence and performance is most apparent in behavioral variables when the subject must produce his or her best effort. Examples of this type of variable are tests of memory, reaction time, balance, and strength. Larger individual differences in older groups compared to younger groups on these types of measurements arise from several sources, thus making the comparison of age differences more difficult to understand.

Two prime behavioral characteristics long thought to inflate individual differences in performance are intrinsic motivation (need achievement and anxiety) and self-efficacy. Several researchers have reported in the psychological literature that older adults are not as motivated as young adults to do their best in performance tests; the need achievement of adults declines with age (e.g., Verhoff, Reuman, & Feld, 1984) while the anxiety related to testing increases. Another frequently posed relationship is that how need achievement and anxiety interact depends on the type of test. For example, women in their 70s may have little interest in producing the highest strength score within their capability, but they may be very interested in providing a good short-term memory performance. The women want to prove to themselves and to others that their memory is still excellent. A 20-year-old man, on the other hand, may be relatively disinterested in a short-term memory test, which he may consider irrelevant to anything he cares about, but be very anxious to produce the highest muscular strength performance he can. In this example, age and gender account for large individual differences, but the different motivations these subjects have with regard to the test variables also contribute to the individual differences seen in their performances. Kausler (1990), however, points out that although differential age-related motivation effects on performance are almost dogma in the gerontological field, few investigators have addressed the issue. Results from these studies were contradictory and inconsistent, and he concluded that the results were so ambiguous that neither need achievement nor anxiety appeared to account for the age differences in performance. Nevertheless, because it has been well established that motivation influences performance at *any* age, and because inadequately or unequally motivated subjects contribute artificially to the individual differences seen, the conscientious researcher must plan the research design and measurement procedures so that any differences seen are related to age and gender, not to motivation.

Self-efficacy is an individual's perception of his or her capability to successfully execute a certain behavior. It may be considered a "situation-specific" measure of self-confidence. Self-efficacy is not related to the skills an individual possesses but rather to that individual's perceived confidence about his or her skills. It is affected by performance accomplishments, vicarious experiences, verbal persuasion (social expectations), and physiological arousal (Bandura, 1977). The strongest source of efficacy information is performance accomplishments. In the previous example, a 70-year-old woman who is to be tested on strength and short-term memory has probably not been tested in more than 50 years on any type of test. When she was young, it was not "proper" for young ladies to exhibit high strength; thus, she may never have been tested on strength and have no feeling for a maximum strength effort. Conversely, the 20-year-old man's memory has been tested in every school class he has taken for the past 12 or more years. He has found many ways to test his strength against his peers and may even

have taken weight-training classes in school. Thus the confidence that he brings to the testing situation is likely to be very different from the confidence that an older woman feels when entering the laboratory.

If tests are short and completed in 1 day for a shot-gun-type of experiment, it is unlikely that the older subjects will be able to approach the tests with the same confidence in their ability that younger adults have. Older people are also more likely than younger people to attribute poor performance to their own ability, which further detrimentally affects self-efficacy and interacts with task performance (Lachman & McArthur, 1986). Yet individual differences in the variable of interest may be more related to the scores of the older subjects being contaminated by intimidation rather than to true age differences.

Biological Age

Individual differences are nowhere better represented than in the concepts of biological or functional age. Casual observations of people provide ample evidence that individuals differ dramatically in the way they age. Some individuals seem very young for their chronological age, whereas others appear to be much older than their age-group peers. This is implied when a woman is described as "aging gracefully" or a man is told that he "doesn't look his age." The observation seems straightforward enough, but how can it be defined and measured?

Determining biological age would require measurement of the gradual breakdown and decline of physiological and cognitive systems *irrespective* of chronological age, so that an assessment could be made of how far an individual is along the life course. Obviously individuals differ greatly in their chronological age at death, but they may not differ substantially if age were represented by the biological status of physical systems. The issue is a very complex one, however, further complicated by the fact that the gerontological scientific community has been unable to develop a consensual definition of aging. The time-related decline of physical systems clearly interacts with environmentally-induced, as well as hereditary, disease processes (Ludwig & Smoke, 1980). Yet theorists disagree as to whether the results of disease processes should be included in a definition of aging.

The concept of biological age is not new. Historically scientists have assessed biological age in children by measuring skeletal and dental characteristics. Sexual maturation has been measured by anthropometrics, and physiological and physical changes have been associated with puberty and menopause. The accuracy of these measures is clearer in children, however, and the measurements themselves tend to be more useful for determining landmark stages of development than for quantifying the slow, progressive changes in the physical dimension associated with adult aging.

Definition of Biological Age

Biological aging is the process or group of processes that causes the eventual breakdown of mammalian homeostasis with the passage of time. It is expressed as a progressive decrease in viability and an increase in vulnerability of the body with the passage of time, both of which lead eventually to death. In this sense, biological aging refers to the organism as a whole. Biological aging can only be inferred from measurements of variables that represent physical and mental functions, and because it is correlated with chronological aging in the general population, people tend to think of biological age and chronological age as being synonymous. Everyday observations, however, which quickly reveal that some individuals do not appear to be as "old" in some behaviors as others of the same age, have led researchers to seek a measure of biological age that is independent of chronological age. Such a measure could be used as a biomarker of aging. The essential criteria for biomarkers are that they be able to determine the rate of change in a function or performance that is related only to the passage of time and not to disease processes, and that they be measured without altering the basic biological processes and behavior of the individual. Biomarkers also should reveal directional change—decreased viability and increased vulnerability to death with increasing chronological age. These general criteria are expressed more specifically in Table 2.2 (Mooradian, 1990).

Several biomarkers, none of which meet all of these criteria, have been proposed on the basis of research on lower life forms. For example, if a nematode (a type of worm) has a life span of 60 days and is observed to wiggle 60 times a minute when touched with a pencil on its first day of life,

59 times a minute on its second day and so on, with the wiggles decreasing by 1 wiggle a minute each day of its life, one would only have to touch any nematode and count the wiggles per minute to know how many days of life remained. It would not be necessary to know the date of birth. In this case, the wiggles-per-minute behavior would be a perfect biomarker, for it would predict the age and the time of death for members of that species. This type of biomarker seems unattainable in humans at the present time.

Researchers had hoped for a biomarker or combination of biomarkers that represent a point on the life-course of an individual that would be relatively independent of chronological age. Unfortunately the aging process in humans is more complicated and complex, and a biomarker of aging that can meet all the criteria mentioned above has been elusive.

Measurement of Biological Age

Without the ability to measure humans on one or more variables throughout the life span, most researchers resort to chronological age as the criterion. The method used to derive most biological age scores is that when the average score on a variable is calculated, those individuals whose score is higher than the average for their age group are said to be "older" than those whose scores fall below the average. Figure 2.8 shows average choice reaction times (CRTs), which become slower with age, for individuals aged 20 through 80 on a hypothetical test. The average CRT (shown by open circles on the graph) is 310 ms for 20-year-olds, 340 ms for 50-year-olds, and 368 ms for 80-year-olds. The CRT of a 50-year-old female is represented by a filled circle and that of a 60-year-old male by a filled square. The 50-year-old's CRT is faster (lower time) than the average for her age group; indeed, her CRT is identical to the average CRT of women who are 30 years old. Thus, according to her CRT, she is biologically younger than her age cohort. Conversely, the 60-year-old male's CRT is slower (higher time) than the average for his cohort. His CRT is equivalent to the average for 80-year-olds; thus, on this CRT variable, he is biologically older than his age group.

Biological age scores can be calculated for any variable by correlating the scores of the subjects with their ages. This procedure produces an equation that describes the linear relationship between

Table 2.2
Suggested Criteria for Identifying Biomarkers of Aging

A. Primary criteria
   1. Quantitative correlation between the biologic parameter and age of subjects, or a qualitative change observed only in those achieving at least 90% of the life span potential of that species.
   2. The biologic parameter is not altered by any known disease process, or the alteration with disease is not in the same direction as that of aging.
   3. The age-related alteration is not secondary to metabolic or nutritional changes of aging.
   4. Factors that modulate the aging rate should appropriately alter the putative biomarker.
   5. Absence of the biomarker in immortal cell lines.

B. Secondary criteria
   1. Applicability of the biomarker of aging to different tissues with similar replicative capacity.
   2. Generalizability of the biomarker of aging across the species.
   3. Applicability of the biomarker to different syndromes of premature aging.

C. Other desirable features
   1. Testing should not cause the death of the animal.
   2. Reliable changes within relatively short interval of time compared to life span.

Note. From "Biomarkers of Aging: Do We Know What to Look For?" by A.D. Mooradian, 1990, *Journal of Gerontology: Biological Sciences,* **45**, p. B184. Copyright 1990 by The Gerontological Society of America. Reprinted by permission.

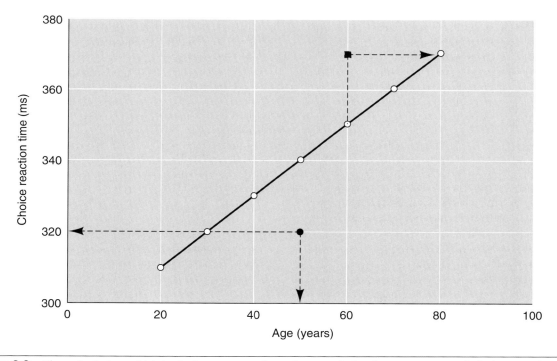

Figure 2.8 The calculation of biological age scores from the correlation between age and choice reaction time. The diagonal line represents the correlation between age and choice reaction time. Individuals whose scores are above the line, that is higher than the average for their age group, have a higher (older) biological age. Individuals whose scores are lower than the average for their age group have lower (younger) biological ages.

age and the variable for all subjects in the group as a whole:

$$Y = a + bX,$$

where Y = the predicted scores, a = a constant representing the magnitude of the scores, b = the change in variable scores with the change in age, and X = the age of an individual subject.

Using the correlation between performance and age, an individual's biological age on a particular variable can be determined by substituting the individual's age for X in the equation and predicting Y. Then the individual's actual score on the variable is subtracted from the predicted score, yielding the biological age score. Thus, biological age can be determined for many variables.

Scores on tests are converted to standard scores for comparative purposes so that distributions of scores from several tests will have the same standardized means and standard deviations. (Statistically, this also eliminates the need for the constant in the equation.) The scores are transformed further so that scores above the mean represent being biologically older, (i.e., exhibiting poorer function) and scores below the mean represent better or younger function or performance. If an individual's score on a variable is exactly the same as the average for his or her age group, the predicted score also would be the same and that individual's biological age would be 0, or the same as his or her age group. It is important to note that individuals of vastly different ages—even 20-year-olds and 60-year-olds—can have the same biological age on a variable, because the biological score is a measure only of their performance relative to the mean of their own age groups. That is, biological age calculated in this way is a measure of an individual's aging status relative to his or her cohort age group. *It is not a measure of the rate of aging* of a person on that variable.

Animal research, however, has also provided "overwhelming support [for] the concept of divergent chronological and biological aging" (Collier & Coleman, 1991, p. 690). In addition to the studies showing that same-aged animals lose abilities differentially, many investigators have shown that biological age can be manipulated by underfeeding, by regulating glucocorticoid function, and by administering certain molecular compounds (Collier & Coleman, 1991). These three types of manipulation have resulted in rats achieving substantially longer life spans. Such manipulation, which actually changes the rate of aging, clearly supports the concept of differentiation between chronological and biological age.

Criticisms of the Biological Age Concept

The notion of biological and functional age, especially when used to describe humans, is not without its critics. When individuals appear as healthy as people half their age, or when their performance scores on physical fitness, strength, or reaction time tests are better than those of much younger people, it is tempting to say, "He has the body of a man half his age," or "That 60-year-old woman can run as fast as most women half her age. She has the legs of a 30-year-old!" But several objections have been raised against both this type of metaphoric explanation and the underlying assumptions of the concept of measuring biological age.

First, theories of biological age, especially those that suggest the existence of a single biological age score, assume the existence of a general aging factor, that is, a uniform rate of aging across different systems. Thus, extending the metaphor used previously, the tacit assumption would be that a woman who has the legs of a person half her age would also have the kidneys and brain of a person half her age. Yet, the research evidence discussed at the beginning of this chapter does not support the existence of a single aging process. Shock's (1962) work (Figure 2.4, page 38) exemplified this, and the fact that aging occurs at different rates in different systems has been confirmed several times. Costa and McCrae (1980) analyzed changes in several anthropometric and laboratory variables over 5- and 10-year periods and found no evidence for a single aging factor. Also, if there were a unitary biological rate of aging, the correlation among physiological function and test performances should be higher with each other than they are with chronological age. Yet, this pattern of correlation among functions does not occur. In most test batteries for humans, age correlates more highly with each item than the items do with each other.

Second, the metaphor of a 60-year-old man with the heart of a 30-year-old carries with it the inference that such a man could live as many more years as a 30-year-old. That is, with the average biological limit for life span (discussed in chapter 1) at 85 years, this 60-year-old could expect to live

55 more years. This would make him (and all others at his biological age) 115 years old at his death, almost surpassing the world record of human longevity. This prospect is highly unlikely.

Third, most critics of multiple regression research on biological age find it ironic that researchers have turned to test batteries of attributes and performances because they are dissatisfied with chronological age as a marker of biological age. Yet, these researchers base the validity of their biomarkers on the correlation of these markers to chronological age!

Finally, people who are biologically younger than their peers should age at a slower rate on tests of functional capacities measured over time; but Costa and McCrae (1980) failed to find any evidence that this was the case. In a position paper, they suggested that the individual differences seen in an age group are more likely due to differences in initial levels, the presence or absence of illness, or measurement error than to a hypothetical rate-of-aging factor (Costa & McCrae, 1985). They suggested that, rather than postulating a single, unicausal process of aging, researchers should emphasize the interacting influences of biological processes, social forces, and health behaviors of individuals.

One way that researchers have addressed these criticisms is by foregoing attempts to determine a unitary measure of biological age and, instead, designing biological age test batteries to determine the biological age of a system by testing several organs and systems. The biological age scores of individuals at different ages are compared and analyzed collectively, because the scores are all calculated as scores relative to the mean of their age groups. Similarly, the biological age scores of all variables can be analyzed simultaneously, because the biological age scores are derived from standard scores.

Those who design biological age test batteries establish criteria for selection in order to determine which variables should be included in the test batteries. For example, the criteria used by Borkan and Norris (1980) were:

1. The variables should show a clear directional trend (either positive or negative in slope) during adulthood which is evident in both cross-sectional and longitudinal data.
2. A cross-sectional score on a particular parameter should primarily be the result of change over time rather than genetic endowment, measurement error, or daily or short-term fluctuation.
3. The variables selected should cover a wide range of physical functions and not be restricted only to known deleterious aspects of aging. (p. 178)

In some of the biological age profile approaches, statistical techniques have been used to determine how highly each variable in the test battery is correlated with age. Stones and Kozma (1988) proposed a technique for computing biological age in which the relative contribution of each variable to biological age is estimated statistically. Similarly, Chodzko-Zajko and Ringle (1989) used a statistical technique to weigh the variables in their Index of Physiological Status (IPS).

Several examples of biological age test batteries are shown in Table 2.3. The biological age batteries of Webster and Logie (1976) were directed toward physiological aging, whereas the test battery of Botwinick, West, and Storandt (1978) was designed for cognitive function. The test batteries of Furukawa et al. (1975) and Borkan and Norris (1980) were more ambitious, attempting to develop a battery so comprehensive that it would assess overall biological age. Because systems age at different rates, a test of global biological age would have to include test scores that represent cardiovascular, cognitive, psychomotor, neuromuscular, hormonal, and other systems.

Borkan and Norris (1980) extended the notion of a biological age by developing a biological age profile for individuals. A biological age score for each variable in their battery was determined for each subject, and a biological age profile was established. An example of the biological age profile for one of their male subjects is shown in Figure 2.9 (page 51). The standard biological age score of 0.0 represents a score for this individual that is exactly the same as his age group. (Recall that biological age is derived by subtracting an individual's measured score from the score predicted for him from the group equation.) His biological age on six variables (MBC, systolic and diastolic blood pressure, hemoglobin count, globulin, auditory threshold, and visual acuity) is almost exactly 0.0 on the Y axis, meaning that his function on these variables is at the average for his age group. All variables for which his biological age is older than that of his age cohort appear as points above the line, and variables on which he has a younger biological age score appear below the line. In this

Table 2.3
Examples of Biological Age Test Batteries

Webster & Logie, 1976	Furukawa et al., 1975
Forced expiratory volume Systolic blood pressure Plasma urea nitrogen Plasma cholesterol	Height Weight Systolic and diastolic blood pressure Vital capacity Renal function Visual accommodation Vibration sense

Botwinick, West, & Storandt, 1978	Borkan & Norris, 1980

Wechsler Memory Scale:
  paired associates
  visual reproduction
  following instructions
Perception:
  Bender-Gestalt
  Hooper visual organization
Psychomotor:
  WAIS digit-symbol
  Crossing-off
  Trailmaking A
Personality:
  Neuroticism scale
  Zung depression scale
  Life satisfaction
  Control rating
Self-health rating
	Forced expiratory ventilation
	Vital capacity
	Systolic blood pressure
	Blood proteins (albumin, globulin)
	Central nervous system function:
	  tapping, medium distance
	  tapping, close distance
	  simple reaction time
	  choice reaction time

Note. From "Predicting Death From Behavioral Test Performance" by J. Botwinick, R. West, and M. Storandt, 1978, *Journal of Gerontology*, **33**, p. 757. Copyright 1978 by The Gerontological Society of America. Reprinted by permission.

example, his status relative to his peers is considerably younger for two variables, creatinine clearance and plasma glucose, but he seems to be considerably older on eleven other variables, particularly those that represent neuromuscular and central nervous system function. Borkan and Norris (1980) hoped to account for the discrepancy in system aging rates by using this profile strategy.

One way to validate the use of biological age scores as biomarkers would be to obtain scores on the variables of the biological age test battery, wait several years, and then compare the biological age scores of those subjects who were deceased with those who survived. If the concept of biological age is valid and if the biological age test battery scores reliably measure biological age, then those who had younger biological age profiles could be expected to live longer than subjects whose biological age profiles were older than that

of their age group. This was the strategy first used by Botwinick, West, and Storandt (1978). They began their study by developing a potential biological age battery composed of psychological variables (see Table 2.3), such as demographic factors; cognitive, perceptual, and psychomotor abilities; personality and morale factors; and health and social activities. One of their analyses revealed that, taken together, eight of the performance measures correctly classified 71% of the living subjects and 64% of the deceased. None of the variables had any predictive value when used as a single predictor.

The Borkan and Norris (1980) biological age test battery included only tests of physiological and neuromotor function and excluded assessments of personality factors. They also used deceased-survivor status as a criterion, and their efforts to predict whether subjects were in the

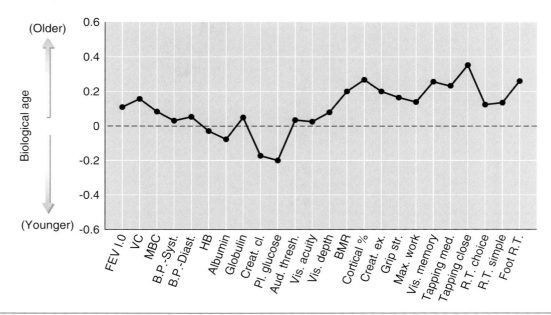

Figure 2.9   Biological age profile of a single individual. This profile demonstrates that an individual may be biologically older on some parameters than others.

From "Assessment of Biological Age Using a Profile of Physical Parameters" by G.A. Borkan and A.H. Norris, 1980, *Journal of Gerontology*, **35**, p. 180. Copyright 1980 by The Gerontological Society of America. Reprinted by permission.

deceased or survivor group appear in Figure 2.10. The deceased group's biological age scores were significantly older on nine of the test battery variables (shown by an asterisk on the graph). Their biological age scores were especially higher on systolic blood pressure and ventilation, measures of blood proteins (serum albumin and globulin), and four behavioral measures of central nervous system function (two speed-tapping and two reaction-time tasks). The five variables on which the group was biologically younger did not statistically differ from the average. Thus, the ability of 9 of the 24 variables to differentiate significantly survivors from decedents supports the concept of biological age and suggests that these nine variables operating together may have some clinical usefulness for determining aging. These nine variables also seem intuitively useful as biological age scores, because other researchers have found them to be interdependent (see chapter 9).

Several other researchers have used the biological age concept to study individual differences. A Japanese research group (Furukawa et al., 1975) found that the ages they predicted from anthropometric and physiological measures of individuals in several different samples differed significantly from the subject's chronological ages. Using measures of each subject's height (H), weight (W),

systolic blood pressure (SBP), diastolic blood pressure (DBP), vital capacity (VC), renal function (PSP), visual accommodation, right eye (VAr), visual accommodation, left eye (VAl), vibration sense, right (Vr), and vibration sense, left (Vl), they predicted age based on the formula

$$Age = 95.232 - 0.138(H) - 0.180(W) \\ + 0.142(SBP) - 0.072(DBP) - 0.003(VC) \\ - 0.252(PSP) - 1.433(VAr) - 0.816(VAl) \\ + 0.262(Vr) + 0.315(Vl).$$

To see if their estimated biological age scores could discriminate between a group with a chronic disease and a group in good health, these researchers independently predicted the ages of a group of clinically hypertense subjects who, they hypothesized, should have a higher biological age than nonhypertense subjects. They did indeed find that the ages they predicted using these anthropometric and physiological data were higher than those of the nonhypertense subjects. In Figure 2.11 the middle line represents the ages of healthy subjects as estimated by their equation; ages that fall between the two lines on either side of the midline are also considered normal for healthy subjects. Almost half of the ages estimated for the hypertensive subjects are above the top line, indicating that their estimated ages are considerably

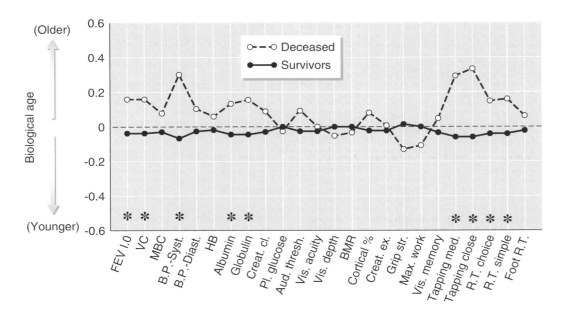

Figure 2.10   Biological age profile comparison of deceased and surviving study participants. Dotted line represents mean biological age scores of 166 men who died since being measured in the Baltimore Longitudinal Study on Aging. Solid line represents mean scores for all other participants (*n* = 922) who were alive in 1977. Parameters marked with an asterisk represent significantly different mean scores.

From "Assessment of Biological Age Using a Profile of Physical Parameters" by G.A. Borkan and A.H. Norris, 1980, *Journal of Gerontology*, **35**, p. 181. Copyright 1980 by The Gerontological Society of America. Reprinted by permission.

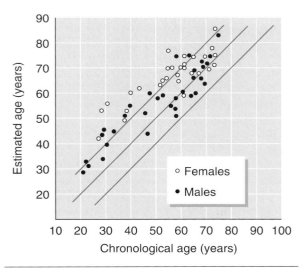

Figure 2.11   Estimated age of hypertensives by the regression formula of healthy subjects. The upper and the lower solid lines represent the tolerance limit (± 1.0 *SD*) of healthy subjects.

From "Assessment of Biological Age by Multiple Regression Analysis" by T.M. Furukawa et al., 1975, *Journal of Gerontology*, **30**, p. 428. Copyright 1975 by The Gerontological Society of America. Reprinted by permission.

older than their chronological ages. Thus, hypertension represents a factor that substantially widens the individual differences seen in biological age at *any* age.

Webster and Logie (1976) took the opposite approach and found that a group of exceptionally healthy women had lower predicted biological ages than a group of women rated merely average in health. Their biological age test battery included chronological age and several physiological variables.

The biological age batteries developed for humans to date have not improved much upon chronological age as a descriptor of the aging process, nor can they successfully predict aging rate. No unitary biomarker has been identified that can predict aging of individuals across several physiological and psychological systems. Nevertheless, biological age test scores have been successful in distinguishing groups that seem to age at different rates. Genetic research also is following lines of inquiry that may lead to the discovery of some causal factors for aging. Because there has been some limited success, and progeria (a disease characterized by acutely accelerated aging) and genetic research seem promising, it is likely that researchers will continue to search for one or more human biomarkers that will describe aging and predict the rate of aging.

The Importance of Individual Differences in Understanding Aging Research

Aging is a very personal, individualized process, and averages of function and behavior for different chronological age groups are just that—averages. As pointed out in Figure 2.1 (page 35), averages do not very accurately estimate the capacities of many individuals. Nevertheless, comparisons of the function and performance of individuals serve many important purposes in biological, psychological, and social sciences. Professionals such as nurses, psychologists, physical therapists, social workers, and health promotion specialists need estimates of abilities of various age groups in order to maximize their services. Consequently, a great many average values of function and performance for different chronological ages are available in the literature, and these will be discussed throughout this book. Average values provide an idea of the capacities of a large number of people at a given age, but the student of aging and the professional should interpret all of these from within the framework of individual differences.

In Summary

Aging is a highly individual process, with individuals aging at rates that may be very different than those of others at the same chronological age. Indeed, individual differences are just as much a hallmark of aging as age-related decline in function. They are measured by calculating the standard deviation of the individuals within the group of people measured. Individual differences also can be displayed graphically and analyzed as a cumulative frequency distribution.

The many sources of individual differences include genetic differences, disease, and different rates of aging of physiological and biological systems within individuals. Variations in lifestyle and compensatory behaviors of older adults also create differences. Other sources are gender, culture, education, and socioeconomic status.

Time-related changes in function and performance follow different patterns: no change (stability), disease-related change, steady decline in function, precipitous expression of disease, compensatory change, and cultural changes. This diversity of ways that change can occur (or not occur) within and among individuals increases individual differences.

The research designs used to study aging and the research process itself sometimes magnify individual differences. Then, too, older people are less consistent in their performance than younger people, which means more differences in older groups than in younger groups.

Biological age has been used as a descriptor to explain the individual differences seen on variables within chronological age groups. Biological age is defined statistically as the distance of an individual from the mean of the chronological age cohort. It has been calculated as a value derived from the linear relationship between the scores on a variable and the age of the subjects. Individuals whose scores on a variable are higher than the average of their age group are described as older for their age than those whose scores fall below the average. Biological age test batteries have been used to develop profiles of aging on variables known to be related to chronological age. These test batteries and profiles have been used successfully in a few studies to predict longevity and the presence of health risk factors.

Although the evidence from animal research supporting the concept of biological age is compelling, it is not without its critics when used in the context of human age. The notion of biological age assumes an underlying general age factor, which has not been supported by research on humans. The fact that different systems age at different rates in different people leads many scientists to believe that the notion of a unicausal mechanism controlling the rate of aging is too simplistic and that it will be many years before the mechanisms of aging are discovered.

References

Baker, G.T., III, & Sprott, R.L. (1988). Biomarkers of aging. *Experimental Gerontology,* **23**, 223-239.

Bandura, A. (1977). Self-efficacy: Toward a unifying theory of behavior change. *Psychological Review*, **84**, 191-215.

Borkan, G.A., & Norris, A.H. (1980). Assessment of biological age using a profile of physical parameters. *Journal of Gerontology*, **35**, 177-184.

Botwinick, J. (1973). *Aging and behavior*. New York: Springer.

Botwinick, J. (1984). Research Methods. In J. Botwinick (Ed.), *Aging and behavior* (pp. 381-403). New York: Springer.

Botwinick, J., West, R., & Storandt, M. (1978). Predicting death from behavioral test performance. *Journal of Gerontology*, **33**, 755-762.

Buss, A.H., & Plomin, R. (1984). *A temperament theory of personality development*. Hillsdale, NJ: Erlbaum.

Chodzko-Zajko, W., & Ringle, R.L. (1989). Evaluating the influence of physiological health on sensory and motor performance changes in the elderly. In A.C. Ostrow (Ed.), *Aging and work behavior* (pp. 307-323). Indianapolis: Benchmark Press.

Clarkson-Smith, L., & Hartley, A.A. (1990). The game of bridge as an exercise in working memory and reasoning. *Psychology and Aging: Psychological Sciences*, **45**, P233-P238.

Collier, T.J., & Coleman, P.D. (1991). Divergence of biological and chronological aging: Evidence from rodent studies. *Neurobiology of Aging*, **12**, 685-693.

Costa, P.T., Jr., & McCrae, R.R. (1980). Functional age: A conceptual and empirical critique. In S.G. Haynes & M. Feinleib (Eds.), *Proceedings of the second conference on the epidemiology of aging* (p. 23) (NIH Publication No. 80-969). Washington, DC: U.S. Government Printing Office.

Costa, P.T., Jr., & McCrae, R.R. (1985). Concepts of functional or biological age: A critical view. In R. Andres, E.L. Bierman, & W.R. Hazzard (Eds.), *Principles of geriatric medicine* (pp. 30-37). New York: McGraw-Hill.

Cullen, K.J., & Weeks, P.J. (1978). Sporting activities and exercise habits of the 1975 Busselton population. *Medical Journal of Australia*, **1**, 69-71.

Fozard, J.L., Metter, E.J., & Brant, L.J. (1990). Next steps in describing aging and disease in longitudinal studies. *Journal of Gerontology: Psychological Sciences*, **45**, P119.

Fozard, J.L., Thomas, J.C., & Waugh, N.C. (1976). Effects of age and frequency of stimulus repetitions on two-choice reaction time. *Journal of Gerontology*, **31**, 556-563.

Furukawa, T.M., Inoue, M., Kajiya, F., Inada, H., Takasugi, S., Fukui, S., Takeda, H., & Abe, H. (1975). Assessment of biological age by multiple regression analysis. *Journal of Gerontology*, **30**, 422-434.

Hertzog, C. (1985). An individual differences perspective: Implications for cognitive research in gerontology. *Research on Aging*, **7**, 7-45.

Jackson, J.S., Antonucci, T.C., & Gibson, R.C. (1990). Cultural, racial, and ethnic minority influences on aging. In J.E. Birren & K.W. Schaie (Eds.), *Handbook of the psychology of aging*, (3rd ed., pp. 103-123). New York: Academic Press.

Johnson, H.A. (1985). Is aging physiological or pathological? In H.A. Johnson (Ed.), *Relations between normal aging and disease*. New York: Raven Press.

Kausler, D.H. (1990). Motivation, human aging, and cognitive performance. In J.E. Birren & K.W. Schaie (Eds.), *Handbook of the psychology of aging* (3rd ed., pp. 172-182). New York: Academic Press.

Lachman, M.E., & McArthur, L.Z. (1986). Adult age differences in causal attributions for cognitive, physical, and social performance. *Psychology and Aging*, **1**, 127-132.

Levine, S. (1962). Plasma-free corticosteroid response to electric shock in rats stimulated in infancy. *Science*, **135**, 795-796.

Ludwig, F.C., & Smoke, M.E. (1980). The measurement of biological age. *Experimental Aging Research*, **6**, 497-522.

Maddox, G.L., & Douglass, E.B. (1974). Aging and individual differences: A longitudinal analysis of social, psychological, and physiological indicators. *Journal of Gerontology*, **29**, 555-563.

McArdle, W.D., Katch, F.I., & Katch, V.L. (1981). *Exercise Physiology*. Philadelphia: Lea & Febiger.

Mooradian, A.D. (1990). Biomarkers of aging: Do we know what to look for? *Journal of Gerontology: Biological Sciences*, **45**, B183-B186.

Palmore, E. (1970). *Normal aging*. Durham, NC: Duke University Press.

Palmore, E. (1981). *Social patterns in normal aging*. Durham, NC: Duke University Press.

Plomin, R., Pedersen, N.L., McClearn, G.E., Nesselroade, J.R., & Bergeman, C.S. (1988). EAS temperaments during the last half of the life span: Twins reared apart and twins reared together. *Psychology of Aging*, **4**, 43-49.

Powell, D.A., Furchtgott, E., Henderson, M., Prescott, L., Mitchell, A., Hartis, P., Valentine, J.D., & Milligan, W.L. (1990). Some determinants of attrition in prospective studies on aging. *Experimental Aging Research*, **16**, 17-24.

Salthouse, T.A. (1988). Cognitive aspects of motor functioning. In J.A. Joseph (Ed.), *Central determinants of age-related declines in motor function. Annals of New York Academy of Sciences* (pp. 33-41). New York: New York Academy of Sciences.

Schaie, K.W. (1990). Intellectual development in adulthood. In J.E. Birren & K.W. Schaie (Eds.), *Handbook of the psychology of aging* (3rd ed., pp. 291-309). New York: Academic Press.

Shock, N.W. (1962). The science of gerontology. In E.C. Jeffers (Ed.), *Proceedings of seminars, 1959-61* (pp. 123-140). Durham, NC: Council on Gerontology & Duke University Press.

Shock, N.W. (1967). Physical activity and the rate of aging. *Canadian Medical Association Journal,* **96**, 836-840.

Shock, N.W., Greulich, R.C., Andres, R., Arenberg, D., Costa, P.T., Jr., Lakatta, E.G., & Tobin, J.D. (1984). *Normal human aging: The Baltimore Longitudinal Study of Aging* (NIH Publication No. 84-2450). Washington, DC: U.S. Department of Health and Human Services.

Spirduso, W.W., Light, K., & Reilly, M. (1990). Effects of practice on within- and between-subject variability. Unpublished manuscript.

Stones, M.J., Dornan, B., & Kozma, A. (1989). The prediction of mortality in elderly institution residents. *Journal of Gerontology: Psychological Sciences,* **44**, P72-P79.

Stones, M.J., & Kozma, A. (1986). Happiness and activities as propensities. *Journal of Gerontology,* **41**, 85-90.

Stones, M.J., & Kozma, A. (1988). Physical activity, age, and cognitive/motor performance. In M.L. Howe & C.J. Brainerd (Eds.), *Cognitive development in adulthood: Progress in cognitive development research* (pp. 273-321). New York: Springer-Verlag.

Verhoff, J., Reuman, D., & Feld, S. (1984). Motives in American men and women across the adult life span. *Developmental Psychology,* **20**, 1142-1158.

Webster, I.W., & Logie, A.R. (1976). A relationship between functional age and health status in female subjects. *Journal of Gerontology,* **31**, 546-550.

Physical Development and Decline

When a baby is born, one of the first things that people ask is "How much does he weigh?" or "How long is she?" As the child grows, family and friends mark the progression with measurements of height and weight. One of Norman Rockwell's wonderful covers for the *Saturday Evening Post* showed a father's annual ritual of recording his son's growth by adding a pencil mark on the wall. Throughout the growth and development phase of life, the various changes of size are important and are often recorded. At maturity, except for some concerns about increases in body weight, social interest in changes in physical dimensions becomes less important. But although physical dimensions may not be measured and publicly recorded or announced, the age-related changes in body dimensions and composition do not stop. Height and weight continue to change with increasing age for most people. Body composition, primarily the composition of bone, fat, and muscle, also change both absolutely and relatively. The range of motion of the joints is also affected by time and disuse. The skin undergoes profound age-related changes. This chapter describes the age-related changes that occur in these basic physical components of the body, discusses some of the pathologies that interact with aging, and illustrates the role that physical activity plays in aging.

Body Dimensions

The dimensions of the body are obtained by anthropometry, which literally means measures of the body. They are usually made in millimeters (10 mm = 2.54 in.) and in kilograms (1 kg = 2.2 lb). In addition to measures of height and weight, anthropometric dimensions include many breadths (e.g., the breadth of the hips) and circumferences (e.g., the circumference of the upper thigh), segment lengths, and skinfolds. These are often used to estimate the general shape and composition of the body.

Height

Height, or more specifically standing height, is the distance from the floor to the top of the head without shoes. It is distributed approximately normally (on a bell-shaped curve) at each age, except that the population has a few more tall than short people (positively skewed distribution). Average heights and weights for American males and females are shown in Figure 3.1, a and b. In males, height increases until about age 25 to 29 years and then begins to decrease slowly. Females reach their peak height somewhat sooner, between ages 16 to 29 years, and then their height gradually declines (Frisancho, 1990). Height and weight patterns across age are not the same for all countries. Small variations in height and in the age at peak height for both males and females have been reported not only for different countries but for different geographical areas within a country (e.g., Rosenbaum, Skinner, Knight, & Garrow, 1985; Chandler & Bock, 1991).

Females lose height faster than males. A major reason why women lose stature at a faster rate than men is that so many develop osteoporosis, a degenerative bone disease. Osteoporosis occurs in all bones, especially a few years before and after menopause when significant bone loss occurs. In the vertebral column, the vertebrae are depressed (Riggs et al., 1986). The cartilaginous disks between vertebrae, which in youth are resilient, make up 20% to 30% of the total length of the spine. Each day the incessant pull of gravity compresses the disks very slightly, but by morning they have returned to their full size. As adults age these disks become less resilient so that they remain compressed, and the vertebral bone is eroded by osteoporosis. Thus, height is gradually lost (Galloway, Stini, Fox, & Stein, 1990). Osteoporosis is discussed in more detail later in this chapter. Other factors that probably contribute to a loss of stature are diet, heredity, weight, and physical activity patterns. Height is related to social class. Figure 3.2, a and b, shows the heights of males and females in England who were categorized as being in one of six social classes (1 & 2 [highest], 3-nonmanual, 3-manual, and 4 & 5). With but a few exceptions, the heights of males and females decline in relationship to their class membership. Those in the first two classes are substantially taller than those in the lower two classes. These differences reflect the important roles that nutrition and health status play during the years of growth.

Weight

The average body weight of American females continues to increase until somewhere between the ages of 45 and 50, and then stabilizes before beginning a decline in the 70s. Males follow a similar increasing weight pattern to age 40, but then begin a slow, gradual decline in weight (Frisancho, 1990; see Figure 3.1b). Almost all body weight data are cross-sectional, but a few longitudinal studies exist. Figure 3.3, a and b (page 60), shows the body weights of 9 males and 7 females after age 70. The males in this figure lost about 5% of their weight at age 70, and the females lost about 7%. It is thought that, although stature is more influenced by a high genetic component, body weight also has a moderate to high genetic component (Korkeila, Kaprio, Rissanen, & Koskenvuo, 1991). The extent to which heredity influences body weight, especially in women, declines with increasing age in both sexes (Fabsitz, Feinleib, & Hrubec, 1980; Korkeila et al., 1991; Stunkard, Harris, Pedersen, & McClearn, 1990).

Just as body weight is used as a gross marker of growth and health in children, the unusual or

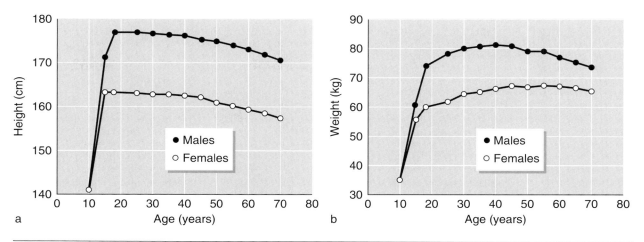

Figure 3.1 (a) Body height and (b) weight of males and females. Standard errors are so small that they are not visible in this figure.
Adapted from Frisancho (1990, p. 27).

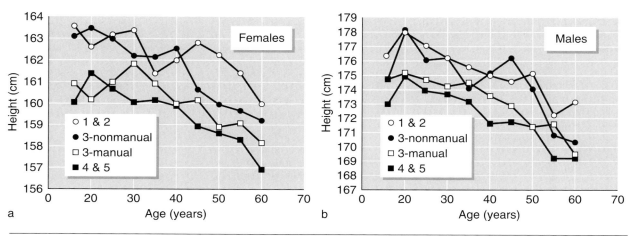

Figure 3.2 Heights by social class based on data from (a) 1,785 females and (b) 1,544 males randomly sampled from electoral registers in England. Standard errors are so small that they are not visible on this figure.
Data from Rosenbaum, Skinner, Knight, and Garrow (1985, p. 117).

sudden loss of body weight in the elderly is considered a cause for concern. The rate of body-weight loss accelerates rapidly between the ages of 70 and 80 (Steen, Lundgren, & Isaksson, 1985), but the acceleration should be merely an increase in rate of loss, not a precipitous drop in weight. When a precipitous loss occurs, the loss is unexplainable in about 24% of cases, but other sudden losses have heralded the onset of cancer (16%), depression (18%), gastrointestinal ailments such as ulcers (11%), an overactive thyroid gland (9%), neurological problems (7%), and the effects of or responses to medications (9%) (Thompson & Morris, 1991).

Body Mass Index

The body mass index (BMI) is one way of expressing weight in relation to stature. It also relates well

to relative fatness (Roche, Siervogel, Chumlea, Reed, & Valadian, 1982). BMI is calculated by dividing body weight (kg) by height^2 (m). BMI was recommended by the National Institutes of Health Consensus Development Conference Panel (NIH, 1985) as a clinical way to measure obesity in adults. The higher the BMI, the more likely an adult is to have a high proportion of fat, although in young weight-trained individuals, greater muscle mass would also create a high BMI. BMI is not a direct measure of relative fatness, and it is not very sensitive to redistributions of fat mass relative to fat-free mass, but it relates well to and is often used as a proxy for relative fatness. Table 3.1 shows BMI classifications. Another gross measure of obesity recommended by the National Institutes of Health is the Metropolitan Relative Weight (MRW), which

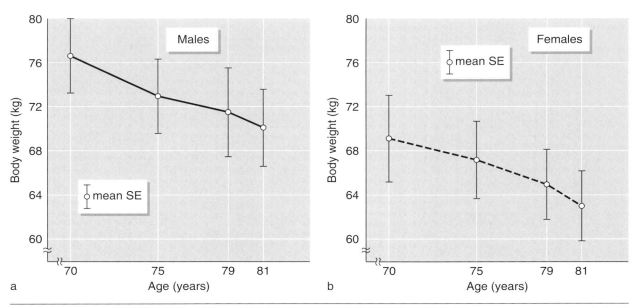

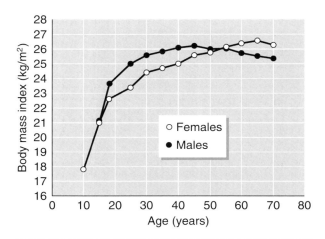

Figure 3.3   Body weight in (a) males and (b) females at ages 70, 75, 79, and 81. Values shown are means ± *SEM.* Adapted from *Nutrition, Immunity, and Illness in the Elderly* (pp. 49-52) by R.K. Chandra (Ed.), 1985, New York: Pergamon Books.

is body weight divided by the midpoint of the desirable weight range for medium frame in the 1959 Metropolitan Life Table. The MRW is based, however, only on insured individuals whose heights were measured while wearing shoes. In many cases, heights and weights for these tables were obtained by interviews, not by direct measurement.

BMIs of males and females in the United States are shown in Figure 3.4. Men reach their highest BMI between the ages of 45 and 49 and then begin a slow decline in BMI. Women, on the other hand, do not reach their peak BMI until between 60 and 70 years of age. This means that women continue to become heavier relative to their height for 25 years after mens' BMIs have stabilized and begun

to decline! This is probable because men experience a substantial loss of muscle mass while women are experiencing both a loss of muscle mass and an accumulation of fat.

The BMI is related in complex ways to mortality. In Figure 3.5 the relationship between mortality, ratio, and BMI in the population is U- or J-shaped (Andres, 1988). The point at which the curve reaches its lowest level, its nadir, is the BMI group that has the fewest number of deaths; this BMI is shown in the box on the lower right aspect of the figure. For example, among the 20- to 29-year-old

Table 3.1
Body Mass Index (BMI)

Weight class	BMI
Underweight	<20
Normal weight	21-24
Overweight	25-29
Obese	>30

Note. BMI = weight (kg)/height^2(m). If the weight of an individual divided by the height^2 is between 21-24, the individual is classified as having normal weight.
Data from National Institutes of Health (1985).

Figure 3.4   Body mass index (BMI) of American males and females. Standard errors are so small they are not visible on this figure.
Data from Frisancho (1990).

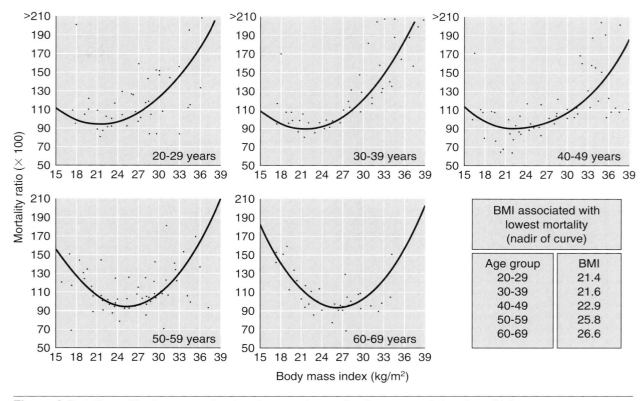

Figure 3.5   Effect of body mass index (BMI) on total mortality for men in 5 decades of life. Curves were constructed from the following regression equation: mortality ratio = a + b Age = c · Age².
From "Discussion: Assessment of Health Status" by R. Andres. In *Exercise, Fitness, and Health* (p. 135) by C. Bouchard et al. (Eds.), 1990, Champaign, IL: Human Kinetics. Copyright 1990 by Human Kinetics Publishers, Inc. Reprinted by permission.

subjects of this study, those with BMIs close to 21.4 contributed the least to the number of deaths. In the 60- to 69-year-old group, those with BMIs around 26.6 had the lowest risk for death. Different BMIs are associated with different causes of death, however. For example, the lowest mortality rates among those with coronary heart disease or diabetes occur among those with the lowest BMIs. In pneumonia, influenza, and suicide, however, the lowest mortality ratios are associated with higher BMIs than those for heart disease. Different mortality rates for extreme BMIs probably occur for different reasons. The critical risk factor for very low BMIs may be a deficiency in muscle mass, whereas at very high BMIs, excessive fat is the critical risk factor.

Body Composition

Understanding age-related developmental changes in body size (i.e., height and weight) or weight relative to height is inadequate for understanding the actual changes that occur, because the body is composed of many different tissues. Adults may have the same weight and height but have very different body compositions. One person may be very muscular and lean with a substantial percentage of the weight coming from metabolically active muscle tissue, whereas another may be very sedentary and pudgy with a large percentage of the weight accounted for by inert fat tissue. Even within individuals, changes in body composition occur over time with changes in nutrition, physical activity, and aging. A 40-year-old former athlete may actually weigh less than she did when she competed as a youth but, due to inactivity and 20 years of aging, may wear a skirt size larger than the one she wore in earlier years. She has traded muscle, which weighs more, for fat, which weighs less.

Clinically, body composition is viewed in terms of two compartments: fat and fat-free mass (Blanchard, Conrad, & Harrison, 1990). Fat mass (FM) plus fat-free mass (FFM), which is made up of protein, water, and mineral (most of which is in bone), equals total body mass. Biochemical components of FFM are generally total body water (TBW), muscle, bone, and viscera. Many techniques are available to estimate FM and FFM, but they all involve indirectly measuring either FM or FFM and deriving the other by subtraction. More specific descriptions of body fat, such as isolating internal abdominal fat from subcutaneous peripheral fat, can be made by more sophisticated and expensive laboratory instrumentation.

Although body composition, as well as the age-related changes in it, has a strong genetic component, it is also influenced by environmental factors. The primary influences are nutrition, disease, and physical activity. For example, failure to consume sufficient protein and calories in the diet can limit the development of muscle tissue or negatively influence the maintenance of muscle tissue, and failure to have adequate calcium in the diet has a major negative impact on bone formation and remodeling. Diseases such as osteoporosis drastically impact bone, and it has been well established that consistent, daily physical activity of a moderate intensity plays an important role in developing bone density at healthy levels and maintaining an appropriate body:muscle-to-fat ratio.

Age-related changes in body composition have important implications for successful aging. Such changes alter the pharmacokinetic and pharmacodynamic properties of drugs, so that dosages and schedules that are appropriate for young individuals are not appropriate for older adults. Because changes in body composition are related to disease and function, it is useful to monitor changes. For a variety of reasons, older adults eat less as they age, and it is easy for them to become undernourished. Careful monitoring of BMI and body composition can prevent malnutrition and simultaneously provide information about the effectiveness of maintenance, reduction, and weight gain programs.

Total Body Water

Depending on body fatness, 60% to 65% of the body is water, which is absolutely essential for life. Most nutrients ingested are comprised of water. Waste materials exit the body via a water medium, as in urine, sweat, and feces. Water softens tissues, so that gases can diffuse across cellular membranes. The chemical exchanges that occur in the body, such as the movement of calcium and sodium through the cells, depend upon appropriate amounts of water in the cells. Water also serves as the body's buffer against over-heating, because it can absorb high amounts of heat without increasing its own temperature at the same rate. Muscle has more water (~70%) than fat does (<25%). Thus, individual differences in body water greatly influence body composition. Those who have higher percentages of body fat also have a lower percentage of their total weight made up by body water.

Body water, which can be measured by isotope dilution methods, linearly decreases with age, as is shown in Figure 3.6 (Steen, 1988). Humans begin as embryos, which are about 90% water, but gradually water is replaced by solids during growth. During the adult years water is steadily lost until it is less than 50% of total body weight in very old bodies (Steen, 1988). The loss of body water may be the most important cause of loss of body weight beyond the age of 70. Older adults do not drink as much water following thirst-producing situations as do younger adults. Consequently, they run the risk of dehydration, which results in the concentration of electrolytes, lipids, and proteins in plasma and urine (Steen, 1988). Decreased body water, in combination with a decreased sweating rate and a less efficient cardiovascular system, makes the elderly more vulnerable to heat stress. Elderly people who live in temperate or tropical climates and who cannot afford air conditioning are at an increased risk for heat stroke. Each year, when

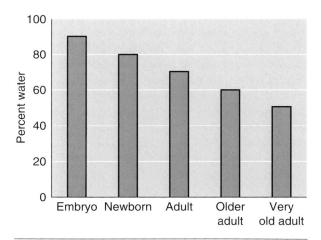

Figure 3.6   Changes in percent body water with increasing age.
Data from Steen (1988, p. 17).

temperatures soar above 100 °F in southern climates, reports of heat-related deaths occur primarily among the elderly. Also, because many elderly take diuretics to reduce edema due to congestive heart failure or to improve their ability to concentrate urine, they are even more at risk for dehydration. Diuretics cause the body to draw water from the plasma, which lowers plasma volume, thus decreasing the body's ability to withstand heat. Because older adults have a relatively lower volume of body water, a given dose of medication will be more concentrated in the elderly than in the young and will take longer to clear from the bloodstream.

Body Fat

Body fat generally has negative implications in this country because so many people have more of it than they wish, and they are constantly bombarded by media messages that emphasize these negative aspects. Diets and other schemes to lose fat are a way of life for millions of people. But a certain level of fat is necessary for normal function. Fat is a source of energy, a storage site for some vitamins, and necessary for cell membrane integrity. Fat makes up a large percentage of brain tissue and also protects the internal organs against physical damage. Another commonly known function of fat is that of insulation for the body against extreme cold. Of course, the insulating property of fat, which slows the release of heat from the body, is a negative factor when the environment is hot and the dissipation of body heat is desirable.

Body fat is of two types, *essential fat*, which is necessary for normal function of the central nervous system and other organs of the body, and *storage fat*, which is fat stored in adipose tissue. As shown in Table 3.2, the reference woman has considerably more total fat than the reference man. It is assumed by most researchers that the larger amounts of fat in women of normal weight have sex-specific functions that are related to reproductive function.

Estimations of Body Fat

Estimates of body fat can be roughly grouped into three types: clinical or field estimations, estimates from densitometry, and more direct measures through radiography and computed tomography.

Table 3.2
Body Composition for a Young Reference Man and Woman

	Man	Woman
Age (years)	20-24	20-24
Stature (cm)	170.0	163.8
Mass (kg)	70	56.7
Total % fat	15.0%	27.0%
% storage fat	12.0%	15.0%
% essential fat	3.0%	12.0%
Muscle	44.8%	36.0%
Bone	14.9%	12.0%
Remainder	25.3%	25.0%
LBM[a] (kg)	61.7	48.5
essential fat	3.0%	14.0%
muscle	50.0%	42.0%
bone	17%	14%

[a]LBM = lean body mass.

Note. From *Evaluation and Regulation of Body Build and Composition* (p. 123) by A.R. Behnke and J.H. Wilmore, 1974, Englewood Cliffs, NJ: Prentice Hall. Copyright 1974 by Allyn & Bacon. Reprinted by permission.

Clinically, body fat is estimated primarily by obtaining the anthropometrics of skinfold thickness, in addition to measures of stature and weight. Skinfold calipers that have a constant tension are used to measure the thickness of a double fold of skin along with the adipose tissue that lies immediately beneath it at critical sites, such as above the front of the hip, the abdomen, upper thigh, below the shoulder blade, and the back of the upper arm. In laboratories where more precise estimates are desired, circumferences, body segment lengths, body weight, and stature are also measured. Metric tapes are used to measure the girths at the waist, chest, hips, thigh, calf, and upper arm. A combination of skinfold, trunk and extremity diameters, and girth measurements, such as the ratio of waist circumference to hip circumference, usually provide an acceptable estimation of fat distribution (Schwartz et al., 1990), but they are not as reliable at distinguishing between subcutaneous and internal fat deposits as are more sophisticated methods of measurement, such as computed tomography.

Another way to estimate body fat is to measure the density of the body. Muscle and bone are more dense than fat; that is, a particular volume of muscle or bone is heavier than the same volume of fat. Therefore, fat floats better than muscle and bone, so weighing people underwater (also called hydrostatic weighing or densitometry) is a way to distinguish those who have relatively more body fat than others. From these measures statistical equations have been developed to predict total body fat. Densitometry is considered the "gold standard" for estimating body composition and is used to determine the validity of clinical measures. For example, Pollock, Laughridge, Coleman, Linnerud, and Jackson, (1975) correlated the skinfold, girth, and diameter measures of young and middle-aged women with body density estimated by hydrostatic weighing (Table 3.3) and found that these correlations were generally higher in middle-aged than in young women.

Radiography, computed tomography, and magnetic resonance imaging provide a more direct measure of the fat that is within the particular site of measurement. From these scans, total body fat can be determined by using equations designed to estimate the fat surface area of the body. Although these technologies provide more reliable assessments of fat, they are very expensive and are usually available only on an experimental clinical basis.

Body Fat Distribution

On average, males and females differ in the way they store fat, and these differences begin early in life (Baumgartner et al., 1986). At about 9 years of age, boys begin to deposit more fat in the abdomen (centripetal fat pattern), whereas girls begin to deposit more fat in the hips and legs (Durnin & Womersley, 1974; Malina & Bouchard, 1991). These two gender-differentiated patterns, which become more pronounced with puberty and maturation, are called the *android* (male) and the *gynoid* (female) fat patterns. Men depicting the typical android pattern are sometimes described as apple-shaped, because their fat is primarily stored on the trunk, chest, back, and abdomen, whereas women depicting the gynoid pattern are described as pear-shaped and are characterized by greater fat deposition on the hips and legs (Bray, 1985; Kissebah, Freedman, & Prinis, 1989; Gillum, 1987). Significant gender differences also exist in the size of fat cells and in an enzyme (lipoprotein lipase) that synthesizes fat and is involved in fat/lipid storage (Hirsch, Fried, Edens, & Leibel, 1989).

Age Effects on Body Fat

Although the increase in body weight throughout life begins to level off at about age 50 and even begins to decline in the seventh decade (see Figure 3.1b, page 59), body fat continues to increase. A small percent of the elderly over 70, for various reasons, greatly reduce food intake and experience undernutrition. In these elderly, body fat is decreased. But in most older adults body fat, as a proportion of body weight, continues to increase with age. For example, among 70-year-olds some average values of body fat are about 21% for men and about 39% for women (Fülöp et al., 1985).

As men and women age, they increase body fat and maintain the basic android and gynoid characteristics (Figure 3.7, page 66). Body fat is redistributed somewhat with aging, however, with the redistribution differing for the two genders. In men, subcutaneous fat decreases on the body's periphery, but the deposition of fat increases both centrally (subcutaneous torso fat) (Schwartz et al., 1990) and internally (fatty organs, e.g., heart, kidneys, and liver) (Borkan, Hults, Gerzof, Robbins, & Silbert, 1983; Borkan & Norris, 1977; Schwartz et al., 1990; Skerlj, Brozek, & Hunt, 1953). The redistribution begins in the late 20s and continues through the 60s, but about 40% of the increase in intraabdominal fat occurs by the fifth decade. In computed tomography (CT) scans of the abdomens of men between the ages of 60 and 82 years, compared with young men ages 24 to 31 years, Schwartz et al. (1990) found that intraabdominal fat in the older men was four times greater than the amount of fat on their thighs. Older men also had more subcutaneous abdominal fat, but the ratio of intraabdominal fat to subcutaneous fat was more than 2-1/2 times greater in the older men compared with the younger men. The greater intraabdominal fat levels in the older men were even more pronounced when corrected for body size or total body fat. The proportion of total body fat situated internally increases with aging (Durnin & Womersley, 1974).

In women, total body fat increases with aging, but the subcutaneous fat may remain stable after about 45 years of age. Thus, the increasing amount of total body fat in women is primarily due to an increase in internal body fat (Durnin & Womersley, 1974). Most of the studies of fat distribution have employed anthropometric techniques, which cannot measure internal and intramuscular fat. Schwartz et al. (1990), however, used CT scans to assess intraabdominal fat in men and were able to confirm earlier findings of an age-related shift in the percentage of fat from subcutaneous to internal fat. Thus, both in men and women, it is

Table 3.3
Skinfold, Girth, and Diameter Measures of Young and Middle-Aged Women and Their Correlation With Body Density

Variable	Young women[a]	Middle-aged women[a]	t-Ratio[b]	Correlation with density Young	Correlation with density Middle-aged
Skinfolds (mm)					
Chest	14.0 ± 4.2	14.0 ± 5.6	0.12	−0.54	−0.70
Axilla	13.3 ± 5.6	16.9 ± 7.5	3.19	−0.60	−0.78
Triceps	18.8 ± 5.0	22.2 ± 6.5	3.52	−0.65	−0.75
Subscapular	15.3 ± 6.5	17.3 ± 7.4	1.64	−0.60	−0.70
Abdominal	22.8 ± 7.2	29.6 ± 11.6	4.23	−0.59	−0.79
Suprailiac	15.3 ± 6.2	17.3 ± 9.1	1.61	−0.68	−0.82
Thigh	28.8 ± 6.8	33.1 ± 7.9	3.46	−0.73	−0.67
Knee	17.4 ± 6.2	17.3 ± 5.6	0.49	−0.50	−0.49
Girths (cm)					
Shoulder	99.7 ± 5.5	100.9 ± 5.1	1.37	−0.39	−0.57
Chest, high	84.6 ± 4.8	87.1 ± 4.9	2.98	−0.38	−0.66
Chest, middle	87.7 ± 5.6	90.8 ± 6.8	2.99	−0.44	−0.77
Chest, low	75.5 ± 4.4	78.1 ± 4.5	3.39	−0.38	−0.65
Abdominal	67.1 ± 4.7	71.8 ± 6.1	5.21	−0.47	−0.80
Waist	75.0 ± 6.5	82.7 ± 9.2	5.86	−0.56	−0.83
Gluteal	93.1 ± 5.3	97.5 ± 7.0	4.20	−0.58	−0.75
Thigh	56.5 ± 4.2	57.6 ± 4.7	1.48	−0.56	−0.69
Calf	33.9 ± 2.2	34.4 ± 2.3	1.25	−0.43	−0.42
Ankle	20.8 ± 1.2	20.8 ± 1.3	0.19	−0.30	−0.48
Arm	27.0 ± 2.2	28.6 ± 2.6	3.98	−0.50	−0.71
Forearm	23.8 ± 1.3	24.4 ± 1.3	2.73	−0.37	−0.46
Wrist	14.8 ± 0.6	15.1 ± 0.7	2.56	−0.19	−0.40
Diameters (cm)					
Shoulder	41.4 ± 2.4	41.8 ± 2.0	1.12	−0.36	−0.49
Biacromial	36.8 ± 1.8	36.7 ± 1.5	0.56	−0.05	−0.18
Chest	27.8 ± 1.7	28.6 ± 1.9	2.63	−0.31	−0.64
Bi-iliac	29.9 ± 1.9	31.2 ± 1.9	3.97	−0.44	−0.71
Bitrochanteric	34.0 ± 1.9	35.3 ± 2.6	3.40	−0.49	−0.64
Knee	9.3 ± 0.7	9.6 ± 0.9	2.31	−0.65	−0.65
Wrist	5.1 ± 0.3	5.2 ± 0.3	2.16	−0.03	−0.19
Bra size (cm)	86.9 ± 4.1	88.1 ± 4.1	1.43	−0.23	−0.53
Cup size	1.96 ± 0.8	2.28 ± 0.1	3.11	−0.30	−0.68

[a]Values are means ± *SD*
[b]t-Ratio 1.98 = $p < 0.05$; t-Ratio 2.62 = $p < 0.01$.
Note. From "Prediction of Body Density in Young and Middle-Aged Women" by M.L. Pollock et al., 1975, *Journal of Applied Physiology*, **38**, p. 746. Copyright 1975 by the American Physiological Society. Reprinted by permission.

likely that fat distribution shifts in a gender-specific pattern from subcutaneous to more internal and intramuscular fat. Muscles appear to be partially replaced by fat tissue—fat and connective tissue infiltrate fibers within the muscle during aging (Allen, Anderson, & Langham, 1960).

Chapter 4 will point out that the measure of fitness, $\dot{V}O_2max$, is higher in young people than in older adults and higher in men than in women. Because the actively metabolizing tissue that contributes to the measurement of $\dot{V}O_2max$ is almost exclusively muscle, age and gender differences in the muscle-to-fat ratio exaggerate differences in $\dot{V}O_2max$ between young and old and males and females. Body fat as a percentage of total body weight is about twice as high in women as in men,

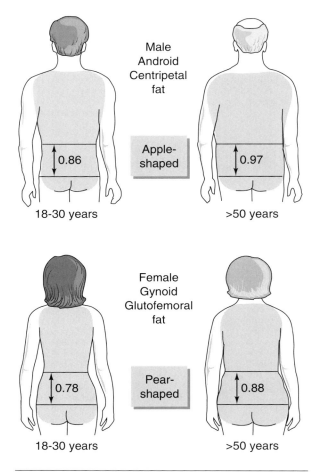

Figure 3.7 A pictorial diagram of age-related changes in body shape and fat distribution. The indexes ranging from .78 to .97 are the waist-to-hip ratios; a smaller number indicates a greater fat deposition on the hips relative to the waist, whereas a higher number indicates that the waist is closer to the size of the hips.

whereas lean body mass is the actively metabolizing tissue. When resting oxygen consumption is expressed per unit of fat-free mass (ml $O_2 \cdot$ kg FFM $\cdot$ min^{-1}), gender differences in resting oxygen consumption tend to disappear (McLaren, 1988): Thus, measures of $\dot{V}O_2$max and even resting oxygen consumption probably should include a calculation in terms of lean body mass.

Factors Influencing Body Fat

That adults almost universally gain weight and fat as they age from decade to decade has been known for many years. The puzzle has been whether this weight gain and fat accumulation results from a genetically programmed pattern, age-related changes in diet and physical activity, or an interaction between these factors. Even though the basic metabolic rate of individuals slows about 10% each decade, metabolic changes alone are unlikely to account for the general fatness of the average American adult. Considering that even obese individuals do not overeat more than normal-weight adults (Braitman, Adlin, & Stanton, 1985) and that they may even have basal metabolic rates that are higher than their normal-weight counterparts (Jequier, 1987), probably a decline in the amount, duration, and intensity of physical activity throughout the life span contributes highly to age-related weight accumulation.

Most evidence points to a relation between excessive body weight and physical inactivity. Although a few investigators have not found this relationship (Tryon, 1987), many others have (e.g., Chirico & Stunkard, 1960; Klesges, Eck, Isbell, Fulliton, & Hanson, 1991; Sallis, Patterson, Buouno, & Nader, 1988). A major problem in understanding this relationship is that defining and measuring daily physical activity have been difficult and unreliable. To determine whether physical activity is related to body fat, the activity must be defined in terms of energy expenditure, intensity, duration, frequency and mode of movement, and whether it is occupational or recreational. Almost none of the existing physical activity assessment inventories has considered each of these factors. However, Klesges et al. (1991) combined scores from several of the best measuring instruments of physical activity into composite scores: They found a significant, but low, correlation ($r = -0.26$) between excessive body fat and physical inactivity. They found that aerobic recreational physical activity, rather than work activity, was the best predictor of body fat.

Little doubt exists that systematic and long-term endurance-type exercise programs invariably result in a reduction of body fat. The fat loss for men and women occurs preferentially in the central regions of the body, but the effects of exercise on body fat distribution may be different in men and women (Kohrt, Obert, & Holloszy, 1992). These researchers found that the waist-to-hip ratios decreased in the men, but stayed the same in the women.

Another way to determine the relationship between body fat and physical activity is to study the percentage of body fat of masters athletes who train and compete in different sports. The body build of 756 masters competitors is shown in Table

3.4. These older individuals, who participate in extremely vigorous activities (distance running, cycling, canoeing) occurring over a relatively long time period, tend to have lower relative fat mass than people who participate in sports requiring relatively less energy expenditure over a shorter time period (racket sports, team sports). All competitors are on the lower end of body fat percentages compared with physically inactive adults of the same age, but they have higher body fat percentages than young athletes. In a review of six studies, Pollock, Foster, Knapp, Rod, and Schmidt (1987) found that the body fat of masters runners ranged from 5% to 10% higher than that of elite young runners.

Obesity, which is an excess of body fat compared to body weight, is often described as a BMI greater than 30 (kg/m^2), or more than 30% body fat in females and 25% body fat in males (Bray, 1985). Obesity is associated with coronary heart disease, cerebral vascular disease, abnormal glucose tolerance, a high-risk lipid profile, hypertension, osteoarthritis, and premature death. Adults who have high waist-to-hip ratios (abdominal fat profiles) are likely to have high triglycerides (Sönnichsen, Richter, & Schwandt, 1991). Animal studies also show that body weight is related to the development of several different kinds of malignant tumors and that premature death increases with increasing body weight (Roe et al., 1991). In humans, obesity is often associated with poor nutritional habits and low physical activity patterns, both thought to contribute to earlier mortality.

Fat-Free Mass

Fat-free mass (FFM) includes nonfat components of the body: muscle, skin, bone, and viscera. FFM of the body is estimated by subtracting fat mass (FM) from the total body mass, but FFM of specific components of the body can also be estimated. The FFM of organs can be measured by radiography or imaging techniques, such as magnetic resonance imaging (MRI). MRI uses extremely high magnetic fields and radio waves to translate the differential energy released from tissues into colorful images. It is particularly useful for differentiating between soft tissues of the body, such as muscle and fat. Muscle mass can also be estimated by analyzing amounts of specific chemicals that are excreted in urine, and total bone mass can be assessed by several techniques discussed later. Lean body mass (LBM) is a term sometimes used interchangeably with FFM, although LBM includes

Table 3.4
Body Build of 756 Masters Competitors

	Men			Women		
		Lean body			Lean body	
Event	Height (cm)	mass (kg)	Body fat (%)	Height (cm)	mass (kg)	Body fat (%)
Short-distance track	173.4[a]	58.6	19.7	165.7	43.1	28.8
Long-distance track	175.7	60.5	18.3	163.2	41.7	23.5
Short-distance swim	176.4	62.6	20.4	164.6	45.0	27.2
Long-distance swim	177.9	63.9	19.2	166.7	45.1	28.6
Cycling	175.0	61.4	17.2	166.9	48.2	25.9
Racket sports	174.8	61.0	21.6	161.0	43.6	29.5
Rowing	179.9	64.8	20.4	—	—	—
Canoeing	177.2	64.8	17.9	165.5	44.6	26.9
Sailing	174.8	59.3	19.3	168.1	47.0	32.9
Synchronized swimming	—	—	—	161.9	41.7	30.4
Team sports	176.3	64.0	22.2	—	—	—
Fencing	—	—	—	157.7	42.6	30.5

[a]The highest and lowest values in each column are underlined.

Note. From "Can Regular Sports Participation Slow the Aging Process?" by T. Kavanaugh and R.J. Shephard, 1990, *The Physician and Sportsmedicine*, **18**, p. 96. Copyright 1990, reprinted by permission of McGraw-Hill, Inc.

essential fat. However, in this text, only the term FFM will be used.

Loss of Fat-Free Mass

Beginning in middle adulthood, FFM begins to decline gradually both in men and women, primarily due to the wasting of muscle tissue. Obviously, because FFM is calculated by subtracting FM from total body weight, and because older adults gain FM throughout their lives, FFM declines with increasing age. FFM is significantly lower in elderly women than in younger women (Blanchard et al., 1990), and it is estimated that FFM decreases 3 kg per decade, on average, in middle-aged to elderly sedentary healthy adults (Forbes & Reina, 1970). This loss is almost 1-1/2 times as great in men as in women, because men were found to lose FFM at the rate of 0.34 kg/year whereas women lost FFM at the rate of 0.22 kg/year (Forbes, 1976). Creatinine loss, which is used as an estimate of total body protein, is shown for men in Figure 3.8. Between 40 and 80 years of age, men lose FFM at the rate of 5% each decade, whereas women lose about 2.5% FFM each decade (Rudman et al., 1991). At these rates, men and women lose approximately 20% and 10% of total FFM, respectively, between ages 40 and 80 years. Thus, while

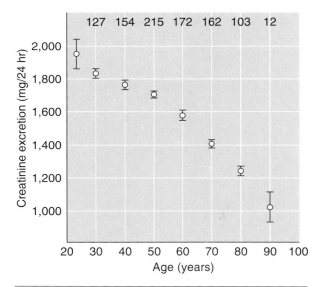

Figure 3.8   Creatinine excretion over 24 hr (means ± *SEM*) for men grouped by age.
From "Effect of Muscle Mass Decrease on Age-Related Basal Metabolic Rate Changes" by S.P. Tzankoff and A.H. Norris, 1977, *Journal of Applied Physiology: Respiratory, Environmental, and Exercise Physiology,* **43**, p. 1002. Copyright 1977 by the American Physiological Society. Reprinted by permission.

FM is increasing with age, FFM is decreasing (Figure 3.9).

Factors Influencing Fat-Free Mass

A major cause of FFM loss is the steady decrease in growth hormone (GH) levels that accompanies aging. In an elegant experiment, Rudman and his colleagues (1991) discovered that men who took GH supplements for 18 months increased their FFM 6% and the sum of 10 muscle areas 11%, while decreasing their fat mass 15%. These changes, however, were accompanied in some subjects by the incidence of the unpleasant side effects of carpel tunnel syndrome and sometimes painful enlargement of the breasts. Both the positive changes and negative side effects disappeared 3 months after discontinuing the GH supplement.

Another major factor influencing the loss of FFM is the type and frequency of physical activity that an individual experiences. Tennis players, for example, have been shown to have a greater FFM than their non–physically active peers (Laforest, St-Pierre, Cyr, & Gayton, 1990). Pollock et al. (1987) found that among masters competitors the FFM decreased as much in those who continued to compete as it did in those who stopped competing but continued to train at a reduced intensity. However, on closer analysis, most of the subjects in both groups had greatly curtailed training frequency and intensity. Of the 24 subjects, the only three who maintained their FFM over the 10-year study period were also the only three who participated in weight training, and one of them was a vigorous cross-country skier. It has been estimated that continued exercise training at moderate-to-high levels can prevent about 25% of the loss of FFM that occurs during the aging process (Buskirk & Hodgson, 1987).

Bone

The skeleton not only provides mechanical support for the body, it also serves as a reservoir for minerals, systemic regulatory hormones, and inflammation-mediated factors. Major quantitative and qualitative changes occur in bone tissue during growth and maturation. Recently, it has also become apparent that the combination of good nutrition and exercise produce a healthy bone density in youth. In fact, it appears that the development of bone mass can be continued until age 30, and that a large development of bone mass

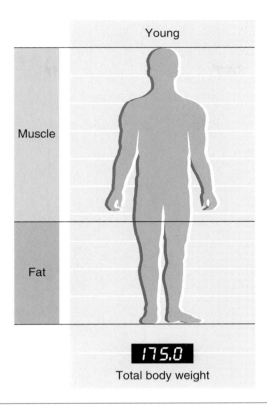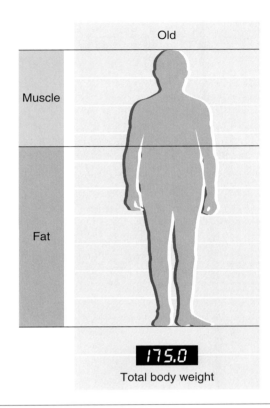

Figure 3.9   Age-related redistribution of fat-free mass and total body fat.

serves as a reservoir of bone and calcium, which can alleviate later inevitable bone loss during aging (Recker et al., 1992). A large reservoir of bone at menopause lessens the risk for developing osteoporosis. Not so well known are the transformations that occur in bone development between adulthood and old age. This section discusses how age-related bone changes are measured, the changes in bone, the factors that influence bone changes, the relationship of bone integrity to muscle strength, and some of the age-related pathologies of bone.

Measurement

The integrity of bone is assessed by *bone mass* (the amount of bone), *bone mineral content* (calcium, phosphorous, magnesium, boron, and manganese), *density* (the amount of calcium or minerals per unit volume of bone), *bone geometry* (internal structure of bone), and *rate of bone loss*. From these measures taken over time, an assessment of *bone gain, bone maintenance, bone loss, rate of bone gain,* and *rate of bone loss* can be made.

Methods used to measure bone parameters include X-ray, single photon absorptiometry, and more recently, dual photon absorptiometry and

computerized tomography (CT), also called computerized axial tomography (CAT). In each of these, a narrow beam of radiation passes through the bone. In the case of photon absorptiometry, low-energy photons measure bone mineral content directly through layers of soft tissue. This measurement provides information on bone mineral content (BMC, in g/cm), which is the total BMC per unit length of the bone being scanned; bone width (BW, in cm); and BMC/BW (in g/cm^2), which is the BMC per unit area of bone. CAT is used to determine bone geometry. In this case the trabecular structure of the bone is assessed, and the cross-sectional bone area and diameter are measured.

Bone gain or loss is calculated as the net increase or decrease in bone mass that occurs from one measurement point in time to the next. Bone maintenance is defined as no change in bone mass from one measuring point to the next, or it may be inferred if less bone loss is seen than might be expected according to the age of the subject. Assessments are made more frequently in forearm (radius) and spinal (lumbar) bones, but measurements are also reported for many other bones. Measurements of bone parameters in one bone do not always correlate well with measurements in other bones, therefore it is important to remember that measurements are specific to the bones that were measured. This is because different bones are exposed to different weight-bearing stresses, and age-related changes in bone are not equally distributed across bones.

Bone Development and Aging

Adult bones are composed of two types of bone tissue: compact (dense) bone and cancellous (spongy or honeycomb-like) bone. Some bones, such as those in the spine, hips, and wrist, have a higher proportion of cancellous bone than compact bone. Bone loss begins earlier and is greater in cancellous bone (Poss, 1992; see Figure 3.10, a-b). The growth of bone occurs in youth and is driven primarily by blood hormone levels.

Throughout life, bone continually undergoes a process of *remodeling*, in which old bone is replaced by new bone. In youth, old bone is resorbed, but because new bone is formed at a faster rate, total bone increases. In young adulthood, resorption and formation occur at about the same rate, so there is no net loss of bone. During growth remodeling, bones are reshaped through specific, local stresses, for example, the widening and increase in robustness of the bones of a tennis player's playing arm (Huddleston, Rockewell, Kulund, & Harrison, 1980; Jones, Priest, Hayes, Tichenor, & Nagel, 1977) or a baseball player's throwing arm (Watson, 1973). Such differences are related to the level of resistance encountered by the bone on a daily basis during weight bearing, chronic use, or training. Thus, the bones of weight

lifters are stronger and thicker than the bones of joggers, whose bones are stronger than those of swimmers (Nillsson & Westlin, 1971). Some investigators believe that the modeling process provides a larger bone "bank" or reserve above the needs of normal daily activity (Frost, 1989). This reserve might postpone the inevitable onset of microfractures at an older age (Schultheis, 1991).

Beginning about the middle of the third decade, the rate of formation begins to fail to keep pace with resorption, and bone loss occurs (approximately 1% a year). In fully developed osteoporosis, the annual loss of bone ranges from 2% to 3% (Parfitt & Kleerkoper, 1984). The change in the ratio of formation to resorption is said to become *uncoupled*. Although this uncoupling process is not well understood, some possible explanations, all age-related, include changes in calcium-regulating hormones, decreased perfusion of bone tissue as a result of changes in bone bloodflow, changes in the properties of bone mineral material, and a decrease in the number and metabolic activity of the cells that produce bone (Kiebzak, 1991). It is important to remember that the balance between resorption and formation of bone differs substantially not only in different bones (e.g., weight-bearing vs. non–weight-bearing), but also in different areas within a single bone.

During aging, resorption occurs at a faster rate than formation, thus major architectural and other compensatory changes occur within the bone. Men may be able to make better compensations to preserve bone strength than women (e.g., Martin & Burr, 1989), although this is a controversial proposal. A remodeling cycle occurs over 3 to 6

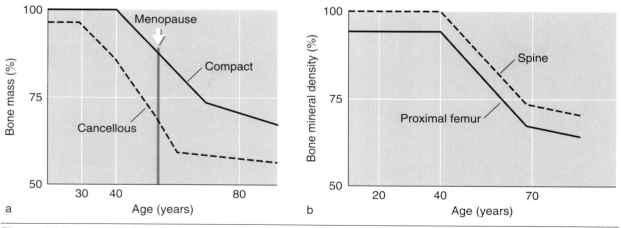

Figure 3.10 (a) Cancellous and compact bone loss and (b) loss of bone mineral density.
From "Natural Factors that Affect the Shape and Strength of the Aging Human Femur" by R. Poss, 1992, *Clinical Orthopaedics*, **274**, pp. 195-196. Copyright 1992 by J.B. Lippincott Co. Reprinted by permission.

months, but because remodeling is slower with increased age, microfractures begin to accumulate. Eventually, the accumulation of microfractures compromises the integrity of the bone and a major bone fracture occurs. Aged bone actually becomes more highly mineralized, causing it to be more brittle and vulnerable to fatigue and microfractures. However, because bone also becomes more porous and there is actually less of it in older people, measurements of bone mineral content are always lower in aged samples than in younger ones. Bone mineral content is related to bone strength, but the architecture of the bone is also very important.

The changes in bone that occur over the life span are diagrammed in Figure 3.11. Men and women begin losing bone as early as their mid-20s. By age 90, some women may have lost 90% of their cancellous bone mass, whereas men may have lost 10% to 25% (Kiebzak, 1991). An example of age-related loss of cancellous bone is shown in Figure 3.12, a and b, with the comparison of normal and osteoporotic bone. The amount of bone loss is specific to the individual and varies widely in different types of bone and across gender, race, and geographic area. Generally, the rate of bone loss is steady, except that it may decrease with age (Davis, Ross, Wasnich, MacLean, & Vogel, 1989). Although some women immediately after menopause lose a substantial amount of bone very quickly, they usually do not continue to lose bone at the same fast rate throughout their remaining life span (Hui, Slemenda, & Johnston, 1989). Rather, the bone loss stabilizes.

Factors Influencing Bone Changes

Three major factors influence bone changes in the elderly: changes in bone-related hormones, dietary deficiencies, and decreased physical activity. Hormonal factors include changes in estrogen, testosterone, and growth hormone; dietary deficiencies are primarily related to low intake of calcium- or vitamin-D–rich foods; and decreased physical activity has an impact on the development and maintenance of bone.

Hormonal Changes. In normal healthy women, menopause is probably the best predictor of bone mineral loss (Hagino, Yamamoto, Teshima, Kishimoto, & Kagawa, 1992). Menopausal-related hormonal changes, especially the withdrawal of estrogen, result in a rapid increase in the processes that deteriorate bone, and simultaneously, the cells

that manufacture bone are impaired. These changes also may contribute indirectly to bone loss, because estrogen depletion reduces absorption of calcium in the intestine (Schultheis, 1991). Also, calcitonin and some vitamin-D metabolites, hormones that regulate calcium homeostasis in bone, decrease with age. The decrease in these hormones and the age-related increase in parathyroid hormone favor bone resorption over bone formation (Kiebzak, 1991). Increased calcium intake of 170 mg a day nearly doubles bone density over approximately 1 year (Albanese, Edelson, Lorenze, Wein, & Carroll, 1985), and injections of vitamin D and estrogen replacement therapy show promise for bone restoration (LeBlanc & Schneider, 1991). The combination of these treatments with exercise is especially effective in reducing age-related bone mineral loss in women. In men, osteopenia, which can lead to osteoporosis in men, is related to the onset of puberty. Men who attain puberty late, that is, experience neuroendocrine changes later than average, do not begin increasing their bone mineral content as soon as, and therefore not as long as, men who are average in sexual maturity status. Because peak bone-mineral density obtained during youth predicts bone mineral density in later life, men with delayed puberty are at greater risk for osteoporotic bone fractures in their older years (Finklestein, Neer, Biller, Crawford, & Klibanski, 1992). Osteoporosis may also be caused by endocrine disease, but other equally likely causes are drugs and toxins, genetic and other disorders, chronic illness, and malnutrition (Jackson & Kleerkoper, 1990).

Diet. Many adults, particularly women, tend to have inadequate calcium, vitamins, and minerals in their diets. Part of the explanation is that many elderly people simply lose interest in food and consume so little that they cannot get as much of these essential nutrients as they need. Another reason is that the dietary patterns of the elderly often do not include milk and other calcium-rich foods. Also, older adults lose some ability to produce, through sun exposure to their skin, the vitamin-D metabolites so important to calcium utilization in bone. Consequently, it has been natural to question whether supplemental dietary calcium could eliminate, postpone, or slow the losses of bone mass in postmenopausal women. The evidence from a meta-analysis of many studies is consistent and clear. Women who took no supplemental calcium lost about 2% of their bone mass a year in early menopause, whereas women who took supplemental calcium lost only about 0.8%

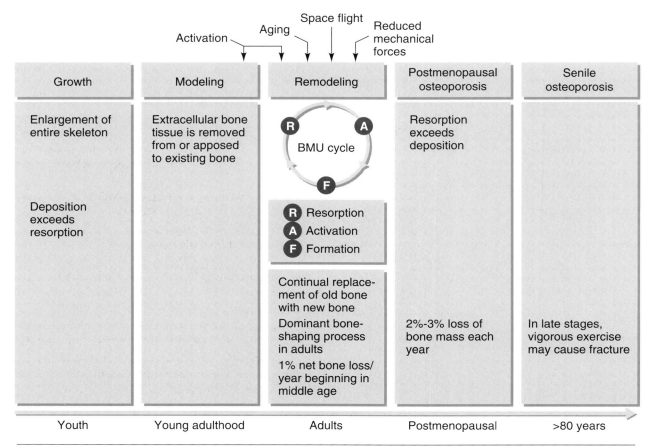

Growth	Modeling	Remodeling	Postmenopausal osteoporosis	Senile osteoporosis
Enlargement of entire skeleton	Extracellular bone tissue is removed from or apposed to existing bone	BMU cycle R Resorption A Activation F Formation	Resorption exceeds deposition	
Deposition exceeds resorption		Continual replacement of old bone with new bone Dominant bone-shaping process in adults 1% net bone loss/year beginning in middle age	2%-3% loss of bone mass each year	In late stages, vigorous exercise may cause fracture
Youth	Young adulthood	Adults	Postmenopausal	>80 years

Figure 3.11 Changes in bone over the life span. BMU = basic multicellular units, which are groups of cells that work together. Within a BMU, osteoclasts (cells that resorb bone) and osteoblasts (cells that form bone) interact in a cycle of activation, resorption, and formation.

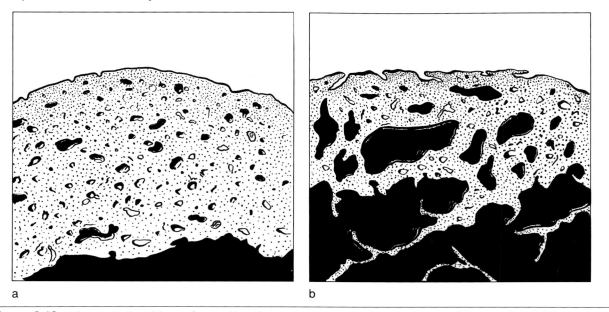

a   b

Figure 3.12 The age-related loss of cancellous bone can be seen when comparing (a) normal and (b) osteoporotic bone.

Previously appeared in *Exercise Programming for Older Adults* (p. 19) by K. Van Norman, 1994, Champaign, IL: Human Kinetics. Illustrated by Beth Young.

a year (Cumming, 1990). This suggests that a calcium supplement of at least 1,000 mg a day in early postmenopausal women might prevent nearly half the bone loss that occurs in untreated women. Saving approximately 1% of bone mass each year over a 10-year period could have a striking impact on the risk of bone fracture. Heaney (1986) suggested that the effects of supplemental calcium may have a threshold effect, because they seem to be more effective in older women who had low baseline levels of calcium than in those who had developed clinical symptoms of osteoporosis. Recker et al. (1992), mentioned previously, found that physical activity and supplemental calcium increased the rate of still-growing bone tissue in young women in their 30s, which contradicts Heaney. Also, the National Institute of Health panel on osteoporosis has recommended that premenopausal women should ingest a minimum of 1,000 mg of calcium a day, and postmenopausal women who are not undergoing estrogen therapy should ingest 1,500 mg of calcium a day.

Exercise. Exercise might be expected to have a beneficial influence on the maintenance of bone, because bed rest, immobilization, and disuse of muscles are disastrous for bone mineralization (Schneider & McDonald, 1984; Weinreb, Rodan, & Thompson, 1989). Subjects of one study lost 1% of bone a week following 1 month of bed rest and only regained it at a rate of 1% a month (Krølner & Toft, 1983). The evidence from spaceflights, both for experimental animals and human astronauts, was that an unabated loss of bone, due to a lack of mechanical stress (i.e., gravity) on the bone, occurred during all flights. NASA-sponsored studies of bed rest have shown that calcium and bone mineral are lost steadily throughout the period of immobility. Yet when mobility is reinitiated, the recovery of bone components is much slower than was the rate of bone loss (LeBlanc & Schneider, 1991). Indeed, exercise may be critically important in increasing bone formation, because the effect of weight-bearing loading is essential for bone formation, whereas calcium supplements and estrogen treatment work only to slow down bone resorption (Franck, Beuker, & Gurk, 1991; Heaney, 1986). Both muscular contraction and gravity apply force to bones that influences the structure and integrity of the bone. When bone is stressed, it converts mechanical energy to electrical energy, a process that activates the bone-forming cells in the area of the stress and increases calcium levels (Smith, 1982).

Most investigators using a cross-sectional research methodology have shown that bone mineral content is higher in exercising than in sedentary older groups (Dalsky et al., 1988; Dilson, Berker, Ordl, & Varan, 1989; Jacobson et al., 1984). However, exercise groups in cross-sectional studies differ from nonexercise groups in many ways other than just bone quality. Intervention studies, such as those in which the bone mineral content of adults who adopted a daily 30-min walk was higher than in those control subjects who did not walk, are more convincing than cross-sectional studies or measures of higher BMC in exercising than in sedentary groups (Rundgren, Aniansson, Ljungberg, & Wetterqvist, 1984; Smith & Raab, 1986). Several investigators who have used exercise intervention techniques have reported positive relationships between exercise and bone maintenance or gain (Chow, Harrison, & Notarius, 1987; Gleeson, Protas, LeBlanc, Schneider, & Evans, 1990; Michel, Lane, Bloch, Jones, & Fries, 1991). Even in very old women (average age 84 years), an exercise program of 30 min a day, 3 days a week for 3 years resulted in an increase in bone mineral content of 2.29% (Smith, 1982). Meanwhile, the nonexercising control group lost 3.28% of bone mineral. Many readers of this study have noted that if the 3.28% of bone loss that did not occur in the exercise group is added to their 2.29% gain, the overall benefit for the exercisers would be 5.57%. Some have found bone mass increases as high as 5% to 10% above baseline following an exercise training program (Dalsky, 1989).

Animal research confirms these findings. A vigorous 4-month running program significantly increased the bone calcium in mature female rats, a finding which is particularly compelling because the investigators were able to remove the bones and directly measure total bone calcium in both spinal and limb bones (Darby, Pohlman, & Lechner, 1985). The results of this study and those mentioned earlier support the premise that vigorous and extensive weight-bearing exercise can slow the loss of bone in postmenopausal women. The exercise must place a load on the bones, as researchers who have used mild exercises failed to find a postponement of bone loss. Also, that chronic swimmers did not exhibit increased bone mineralization, whereas weight lifters, throwers, runners and soccer players did, supports the proposal that the exercise must be weight bearing. A minimum level may be 30 to 60 min a day, 2 or

3 days a week (Schoutens, Laurent, & Poortmans, 1989). The *type* of weight-bearing exercise seems unimportant; aerobic dancing was as effective as conventional types of conditioning exercise such as walking, jogging, stair climbing, and upright rowing. Nor are changes in bone mass and mineralization correlated with $\dot{V}O_2$max. Some researchers have tried to relate $\dot{V}O_2$max to bone mineral density in hopes of finding a way to predict bone density increase for a known measure of physical fitness, but their results have not been very successful (Bevier et al., 1989) The key factors for bone benefit are the intensity, duration, and mechanical stress that are put on the bone during exercise.

Even though research seems to support the hypothesis that vigorous systematic exercise can slow bone loss in postmenopausal women, Gerber and Rey (1991) pointed out in their review of 10 controlled longitudinal studies (Table 3.5) that the available evidence is not conclusive enough to be considered proof. They found several research design problems. Most of the studies lacked randomization procedures and had small sample sizes. Nor were the exercise compliance rates, estrogen status, muscle mass, and strength measures controlled in all the studies. Furthermore, all were studies of elderly women, whereas it is possible that exercise effects might be even more potent in younger women. In all of the studies, only measures of bone mineral content or density were analyzed, whereas other parameters, such as bone geometry and bone quality, might be more predictive of the effects of exercise on bone strength. Finally, various investigators analyzed different bones, and it is possible that compact and cancellous bone may respond to different degrees of mechanical stress (Notelovitz et al., 1991) and that cancellous bone, because it is more metabolically active, may respond faster to mechanical stress (Pruitt, Jackson, Bartels, & Lehnhard, 1992).

Although the relationship between exercise and bone loss seems compelling, it is far from straightforward and probably depends heavily on estrogen status and age. One study that did not support an exercise-bone maintenance relationship was that of Heikkinen et al. (1991), who found that 1 hour a day of resistive exercise at least twice a week failed to confer additional beneficial bone-mineral effects above those associated with the supplementary estrogen that the treatment groups received. Cavanaugh and Cann (1988) also reported that brisk walking failed to alleviate bone

loss in postmenopausal women, and Ballard, McKeown, Graham, and Zinkgraf (1990) reported that neither exercise nor estrogen therapy maintained bone in older women. Drinkwater (1986) found that although women athletes who were menstrually cycling monthly had vertebral densities well above those of inactive women, the bone densities of amenorrheic athletes were actually lower than those of the controls. Presumably these amenorrheic athletes trained as intensely and as often as the eumenorrheic athletes, but the exercise per se did not protect them from bone loss. Similarly, fitness and vertebral bone mineral density were moderately and positively correlated in young eumenorrheic women but not in amenorrheic women (average age 59 years) who completed an exercise program (Kirk et al., 1989).

Notelovitz et al. (1991) found that the spinal bone mineral density of women who exercised in a variable-resistance strength program for 1 year *in addition to* estrogen therapy increased 8.6%, whereas that of the estrogen-alone group did not improve significantly (Figure 3.13). In a compelling 2-year study, Prince et al. (1991) found that an exercise program plus estrogen replacement is an effective way to maintain bone mineral density, much more effective than exercise alone, or exercise in addition to calcium supplements. This was a particularly encouraging finding, because osteoporosis of the

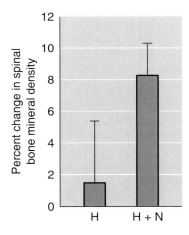

Figure 3.13   Percent change in the bone mineral density of surgically menopausal women after 1 year of hormone therapy alone (nonsignificant) or hormone therapy plus resistive strength exercise (*p* = <0.002).

From "Estrogen Therapy and Variable-Resistance Weight Training Increase Bone Mineral in Surgically Menopausal Women" by M. Notelovitz et al., 1991, *Journal of Bone and Mineral Research,* **6**, p. 587. Copyright 1991 by Mary Ann Liebert, Inc. Reprinted by permission.

Table 3.5
Effect of Exercise on Postmenopausal Bone, Controlled Longitudinal Trials

Author, year	Health status	Age (years)	Randomization	Group size (E = exercisers, C = controls)	Exercise intensity, sessions/ week × min	Duration (months)	Results	Comment
Aloia et al., 1978	Healthy	53	–	E = 9 C = 9	Vigorous 3 × 60	12	Exercisers > controls	Compliance not recorded.
Smith et al., 1981	Healthy	81	–	E = 19 + 18 C = 26 + 17	Mild 3 × 30	36	Exercisers > controls	Compliance not recorded.
Krølner et al., 1983	Healthy or posttraumatic	69	–	E = 116 C = 15	Moderate 2 × 60	8	Exercisers >>[a] controls	Previous radius fracture in half of patients. 3 controls still pre- or perimenopausal. Estrogen supplied to 21 + 1 C.
White et al., 1984	Healthy	56	±	E = 27 + 25 C = 21	Walking or aerobic dancing 4 ×	6	Dancers > walkers > controls	Compliance recorded. Compliance recorded. Some received estrogens.
Kriska et al., 1986 and Sandler et al., 1987	Healthy	57	+	E = 114 C = 115	Walking (7 miles/week)	36	Walkers ≥ controls	Compliance recorded. Positive results in walkers only with good grip strength.
Dalsky et al., 1988	Healthy	62	–	E = 17 (11) C = 18 (6)	Vigorous walking, jogging, rowing 3 × 50–60	9 (22)	Exercisers >> controls	Bone mass returned to baseline following cessation of exercises.

(continued)

Table 3.5
(continued)

Author, year	Health status	Age (years)	Randomization	Group size (E = exercisers, C = controls)	Exercise intensity, sessions/week × min	Duration (months)	Results	Comment
Cavanaugh & Cann, 1989	Healthy	56	–	E = 8 C = 9	Brisk walking 3 × 15–40	12	Walkers = controls	Compliance recorded.
Sinaki et al., 1989	Healthy	56	+	E = 34 C = 31	Prone lying extension, 5 ×	24	Exercisers = controls	Compliance not recorded.
Smith et al., 1989	Healthy	50	–	E = 80 C = 62	Vigorous dancing, pushing, lifting 3 × 45	48	Exercisers > controls	Pre-, peri- and postmenopausal. Compliance not recorded. Nonspinal bone only.
Simkin et al., 1987	Osteoporosities	63	–	E = 14 C = 26	Moderate arm + whole body 3 × 45–50	5	BMC[b]: exercisers = controls BMD[c]: exercisers > controls	Compliance not recorded.

[a]>> = much greater than
[b]BMC = bone mineral content
[c]BMD = bone mineral density

Note. From "Can Exercise Prevent Osteoporosis or Reverse Bone Loss?" by N.J. Gerber and B. Rey. In *Physiotherapy: Controlled Trials and Facts. Rheumatology* (Vol. 14, p. 50) by P. Schlapbach and N.J. Gerber (Eds.), 1991, Basel, Switzerland: Karger. Copyright 1991 by S. Karger AG, Basel. Reprinted by permission.

spine is so common in older women, and there is some evidence that benefits derived from estrogen therapy alone may dissipate a few years after therapy is ceased (Lindsay et al., 1976). Exercise and estrogen status apparently interact to protect against bone loss, but the exact mechanisms by which this protection occurs remain to be identified. Nevertheless, Notelovitz et al. (1991) concluded that resistive strength exercises for all muscle groups in which the emphasis is more on heavy resistance than on repetition will increase bone mineral, and they support an osteopenia prevention program based on calcium supplements, estrogen replacement, and exercise (Notelovitz, 1986). The estrogen modulates the activity of the bone cells that break down bone (osteoclasts), the calcium facilitates mineralization, and the weight-bearing exercises stimulate new bone formation. Even moderate jogging once a week appeared to increase bone mineral content in women between the ages of 38 and 64 (Jónsson, Ringsberg, Josefsson, Johnell, & Birch-Jensen, 1992).

Most research on the effects of exercise training on bone deals with bone mass, bone density, bone formation, and bone mineralization. These studies assume that these variables are related to bone strength and that increases in these variables will produce bones that are more resistant to stress. Raab, Smith, Crenshaw, and Thomas (1990) directly measured the breaking strength of bones by studying this phenomenon in young and old rats that were either exercised for 10 weeks or were sedentary. After the animals were exercised, they were sacrificed and the force necessary to break the bones was measured. It took a much greater force to break the bones of the exercised rats, both young and old, than those of the sedentary rats.

Bone tissue of young organisms may respond differently to exercise than the bone tissue of the aged. Young bone is still growing, whereas the length and volume of mature bones have stabilized. Young bones may respond to exercise by increasing in volume, whereas old bone may increase in bone calcium (Darby et al., 1985). Because bone serves as a reservoir for the body's calcium needs, an exercise-induced increase in bone calcium in the aged should enable the body to provide calcium to other parts of the body when needed.

Relationship to Strength

Bone mass and muscle mass develop together during youth and decline together during aging.

In men and women ages 61 to 84 years, several measures of strength are correlated to spinal bone density (Bevier et al., 1989; Halle, Smidt, O'Dwyer, & Lin, 1990). Grip strength is correlated to forearm and spine density, but back strength is the best predictor of bone density in elderly men. Body mass also significantly predicts bone density in elderly women, perhaps because the greater the body mass, the greater the gravitational and stress forces on the bones. Although muscular strength correlates positively with bone density, increases in bone density cannot necessarily be inferred from increases in muscular strength (Pocock et al., 1988).

Bone Fractures

The many factors that contribute to bone fracture are shown in Figure 3.14. One of the most important of these factors is the age-related decrease in bone mass that makes adults vulnerable to bone fractures, particularly those of the hip, wrist, and vertebrae (Ross, Davis, Vogel, & Wasnich, 1990). As individuals age, some bone loss is inevitable. Bone mass, the rate of bone loss, body mass index, and chronological age all significantly predict fractures. Chronological age is a somewhat better predictor of bone fracture than direct measures of forearm bone mass (Hui, Slemenda, & Johnston, 1988), and bone mass predicts fractures better than the rate of bone loss (Gärdsell et al., 1991). Body mass index is inversely related to risk of bone fracture. Women with very low BMIs, that is, with very low levels of body fat, have almost twice the risk of fracturing a hip than do women with higher BMIs. The excess weight of fatter women places a greater-than-average mechanical stress on some bones, perhaps slowing the rate of bone loss (Harris, Dallal, & Dawson-Hughes, 1992). Then, too, women with fatter hips have more protection against damage when they fall. Bone fractures are a serious threat to the elderly, because they are a major contributor to morbidity and to the high cost of medical care (Cummings, Kelsey, Nevitt, & O'Dowd, 1985). The incidence of hip fractures in women is twice that of men. Furthermore, a substantial percentage of women who experience a hip fracture will never regain their mobility, and as many as two out of five may die from complications of the fracture.

Osteoporosis

Osteoporosis is a crippling, irreversible disease that increases the risk of fracturing bone due to

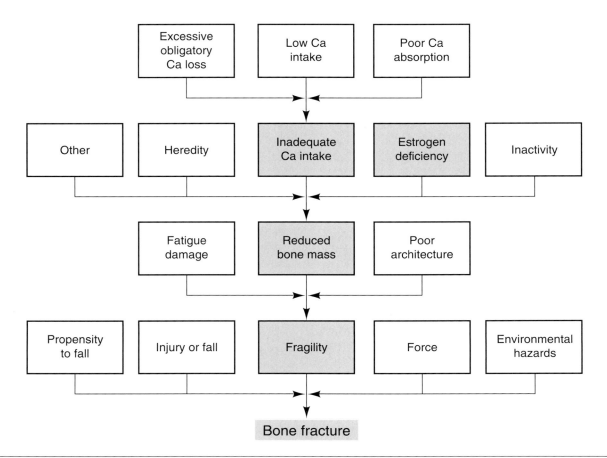

Figure 3.14   Factors that contribute to bone fracture. The shaded boxes are factors particularly problematic for the elderly.
Adapted from "Calcium in the Prevention and Treatment of Osteoporosis" by R.P. Heaney, 1992, *Journal of Internal Medicine*, **231**, p. 170.

lack of bone mass. It affects many more women than men. Osteoporosis may or may not be preceded by *osteopenia*, the routine loss of mineralized bone that occurs in all individuals (Gerber & Rey, 1991). In osteoporosis, so much bone mineral is lost that the bones become fragile and brittle. The spine can become so deformed that height is lost, and this may be accompanied by bone pain. Although there are many causes of osteoporosis, such as hyperparathyroidism, hypercortisolism, hypogonadism, and abuse or misuse of drugs, Kiebzak (1991) differentiates two independent types of osteoporosis, *postmenopausal osteoporosis* and *senile osteoporosis*.

Postmenopausal osteoporosis is described as "estrogen-dependent osteopenia with resultant fractures superimposed on age-related osteopenia," whereas senile osteoporosis is "excessive age-related bone loss with fractures in the elderly of both sexes" (Kiebzak, 1991, p. 179). The same factors lead to bone loss in both senile and postmenopausal osteoporosis: low levels of estrogen,

which follow menopause, low dietary intake of calcium, and the lack of mechanical load (muscular stress) on the bone that accompanies a sedentary lifestyle.

Women are more affected by osteoporosis than are men for several reasons. Women generally consume less calcium in their diets because they are more likely to avoid milk products, which they perceive as fattening. Many women are chronic dieters; thus, they do not consume enough food to ensure an adequate calcium intake. Women have less bone mass, but they live longer. They may also deplete some body calcium during pregnancy and lactation. Bone loss continues to occur with increasing age. Thus, many factors converge to predispose women to lose more bone tissue than men do.

Although substantial work has been completed on the effects of supplements and weight-bearing exercise on the maintenance of some parameters of bone, such as bone mineral content, the effect of supplements and exercise on adults who already have full-blown osteoporosis is not known.

More specifically, whether increased weight-bearing exercise can increase or recover lost bone mass in an adult skeleton remains unknown (LeBlanc & Schneider, 1991).

Exercise-Induced Losses in Bone

Heavy running and very intense exercise have been shown to decrease bone mass and bone mineral content in young amenorrheic women and in young men (Bilanin, Blanchard, & Russek-Cohen, 1989; Drinkwater et al., 1984). Similarly, in beagle dogs who ran very long distances (up to 40 km, or 24 miles) every day for 55 weeks, the bone mineral content was lower than in non-running controls (Puustjärvi et al., 1991). Also, bone mineral density was less in over-exercised (>5 hrs a week) women than in normal exercisers (Michel et al., 1991). The latter group concluded that excessive exercise, especially in women over age 55, may be detrimental to bone maintenance. Malina (1991) reviewed several studies in which testosterone levels in men who were chronic runners were lower than in nonrunners, although they were within normal physiological ranges. He concluded, however, that the evidence suggests that intensive endurance training may alter the function of the hypothalamic-pituitary-gonadal axis in a way that is similar to the changes that occur in the menstrual function of intensively endurance-trained women. Alterations such as these could explain losses in bone mineral density in excessively trained men and women.

Joints

Bones are linked together at articulations (joints) by ligaments, tendons, connective tissue, and in some cases direct attachment of muscles to bones. The attachment is also supported by the muscles that cross the joint. A smooth, rubbery covering of hyaline cartilage covers the ends of bones so that they can move with relatively little friction. This cartilage also absorbs shock when the two bones are pressed together by muscular action or by external forces. Within the joint space is a synovial membrane containing synovial fluid, which bathes the cartilage on the bone endings, keeping it soft and pliable. The synovial membrane also contains the nerve endings that signal pain when insults to the joint occur. Lastly, the

joint capsule surrounding the articulating bones of the joint helps to hold them together.

The purpose of most joints, except for those in the skull and spine, is to provide an opportunity for a wide range of movements. Joint flexibility is described by the extent to which the linked bones can move before being stopped by bony structures or tight ligaments, tendons, or muscles. For example, the ability to touch the floor with the fingers while keeping the knees locked depends on the flexibility of the hip joint. Flexibility, in turn, is dependent on the state and condition of the soft tissues of the joint, the tendons, ligaments, and muscles. When these tissues are soft and pliant, the joint is allowed its full range of motion.

Flexibility

Flexibility is maintained in a joint by using the joint and by participating in physical activities that stretch the muscles across the joint. When a joint is relatively unused, the muscles that cross it shorten, thus reducing its range of motion. Joint flexibility is crucial for effective movement. It would serve little purpose to have strong bones and muscles if the bones cannot be moved through their range of motion enough to manipulate objects or to locomote. Therefore, flexibility (like cardiovascular and muscular endurance and muscular strength) is considered an essential component of physical fitness. The loss of flexibility not only reduces the amount and nature of movement that can be made at a joint, it also increases the possibility of injury to the joint or to the muscles crossing the joint. Inflexibility can lead to muscle strains or to muscle, tendon, or ligament damage or detachments.

Flexibility is extremely difficult to measure, in part because it is difficult to locate landmarks on the body to use as starting and ending points of the measurement, and in part because the measures depend to some extent on the amount of pain that the subject is willing to tolerate. That is, if the instructions to the subject are to stretch as far as possible before experiencing pain, some subjects' threshold of pain is lower than that of others, so they will not push themselves as far. Nevertheless, flexibility is generally measured with a goniometer, which is essentially a movable protractor with two long arms. If the two arms are stretched out to make a straight line, they measure 180°. If they are positioned to make a right angle, they measure 90°. Using the goniometer, flexibility at the fingers, elbow, shoulder, ankle, knee, and hip can be determined. The measures of flexibility in the fingers, elbow, and knee are primarily in one anatomical plane. Shoulder- and hip-joint movements, however, are three-dimensional. Shoulders and hips are attached to limbs that can flex and extend, but they can also abduct (move away from the body) and adduct (move toward the body) in another plane. A typical way to measure flexibility of the hip joint is to have individuals sit on the floor with their legs fully extended, so that the heels are in line with a tape measure placed on the floor. The distance that they can lean forward relative to their heels is a clinical assessment of hip flexibility, and indirectly, of the tightness of the hip, lower back, and knee flexor/extensor muscle groups.

Adults lose a significant amount of flexibility as they age, and these losses can be measured whether individuals themselves actively move the limb through the range of motion or whether the limb is passively moved by the clinician (Chapman, deVries, & Swezey, 1972). The loss in flexibility occurs surprisingly early. Figure 3.15, a through d, shows the spinal flexibilities of women ages 20 through 84 (Einkauf, Gohdes, Jensen, & Jewell, 1987). The greatest losses in flexibility were seen in back extension, and they sharply increased between the 30- to 39-year-old and 40- to 49-year-old age groups. The losses were least severe in anterior flexion (bending forward). The authors interpreted these results as an indication of the types of daily activities in which most people participate. Few occasions arise in the course of daily life to lean backward, whereas many activities of daily living involve leaning forward. Also, as people age, their balance is compromised, and they are much less likely to lean backward—and probably less likely to "stretch themselves" to lean backward in a laboratory test of flexibility.

The ankle joint also loses flexibility with aging. Women have been shown to lose 50% of their range of motion in the ankle joint, and men lose about 35% from the age of 55 to 85 (Vandervoort et al., 1992). Age-related weakness in the muscles that flex the ankle upward and an increase in muscle resistance due to increases in the connective tissue of old muscles mean that the ankle is not flexed as much during walking. Decreased use eventually leads to a loss of range of motion at or about the ankle joint, which when added to the

age-related strength losses increases the risk for falling.

Exercise and Flexibility

Exercise contributes significantly to joint stability and flexibility. Resistive exercises enhance the tensile strength of tendons and ligaments, and flexibility exercises maintain the suppleness of tendons, ligaments, and muscles, thus allowing a full range of joint motion. Stretching exercises of specific types are essential to maintain range of motion in young people and are even more important in middle-aged and elderly individuals. Stretching exercises are a major component of physical therapy and rehabilitation procedures following injury, accident, or disease that has curtailed the range of motion of joints. Stretching and a progressive-resistance exercise program produced the same percentage of improvement in range of motion of elderly subjects (aged 63-88 years) as in young subjects (15-19 years), although their joints remained stiffer than the joints of the younger men (Chapman, deVries, & Swezey, 1972). Raab, Agre, McAdam, and Smith (1988) reported that a 25-week exercise program improved joint flexibility in ankle plantar flexion, shoulder flexion, shoulder abduction, and left neck rotation, but no improvements were seen in hip flexion, right neck rotation, wrist flexion or extension, or ankle dorsiflexion. It is likely that the exercise program emphasized movement of those joints in which flexibility was improved while excluding those in which no changes in flexibility were seen. Brown and Holloszy (1991) also found improvements in joint ranges of motion in those who followed a 5-day a week exercise program for 3 months. This program included stretching exercises, and the largest improvement they found (35%) was in hip flexion.

Osteoarthritis

Osteoarthritis is one of several chronic diseases that cause significant physical disability in the elderly; others are cardiovascular disease (including hypertension), diabetes mellitus, and chronic lung disease. Osteoarthritis is a degenerative disease of the joints that affects approximately 80% of adults over age 65 (roughly 16 million people). More women are affected than men.

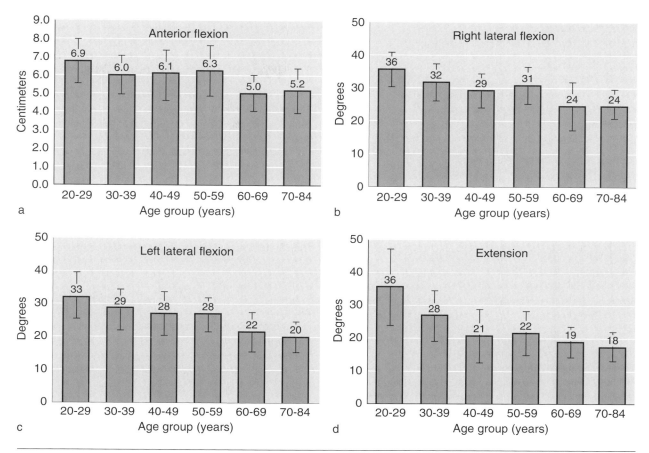

Figure 3.15 Changes in spinal flexibility with age for females: (a) anterior flexion, (b) right lateral flexion, (c) left lateral flexion, (d) extension. Bar graphs represent means and standard deviations by age group.
From "Changes in Spinal Mobility With Increasing Age in Women" by D.K. Einkauf, M.L. Gohdes, G.M. Jensen, and M.J. Jewell, 1987, *Physical Therapy*, **67**, p. 374. Copyright 1987 by the American Physical Therapy Association. Reprinted from *Physical Therapy* with the permission of the American Physical Therapy Association.

As osteoarthritis develops, the cartilage that normally covers bone, reducing friction and absorbing shock, begins to change in consistency, crack, and wear away, eventually exposing the bone to the surface of other bones at the joint. Changes in texture and suppleness also occur in the soft tissues of the joint: the muscles, tendons, ligaments, and joint capsule. In fact, it is estimated that a very high percentage of joint stiffness can be attributed to soft tissue changes that occur with age (Johns & Wright, 1962). Over time, the joint may develop bone spurs, abnormal thicknesses, and fluid-filled pockets. All of this can result in periodic or chronic inflammation, usually but not always accompanied by pain of varying degrees.

The causes of osteoarthritis have not been completely identified, but it seems clear that both heredity and multiple environmental factors contribute. At least some aspects of osteoarthritis may be genetically determined, because osteoarthritis appears in several generations of some families. But adults have also thrown their joints out of alignment or damaged the cartilage through accidents, or have abused their joints by placing excessive force on them or overusing them in sports or work activities during their youth. When joints are misaligned or the supportive cartilaginous structures are damaged, osteoarthritis can occur. Osteoarthritis that seems to develop from a known cause, such as old injuries or abuse to the joints, is called *secondary osteoarthritis*. When osteoarthritis develops without an obvious cause, it is called *primary osteoarthritis*.

Osteoarthritis can occur in any joint but is a very common occurrence in the joints of the fingers. When osteoarthritis occurs in the hip or knee joints, the resultant pain and discomfort seriously impair mobility. A related negative consequence of impaired mobility is the cost of adaptive mobility. The compensatory physical movements that persons with arthritis make often result in movements that are metabolically cost-inefficient. In other words, inefficient movement places a greater load on the cardiorespiratory system (Waters, Conaty, Lunsford, & O'Meara, 1987). These compensatory changes also can lead to biomechanical misalignment, which adds additional metabolic costs to movement. Thus, it becomes increasingly difficult for such individuals to rise from a chair, walk long distances, or climb up and down stairs. The associated pain often motivates the person to be less mobile, which predisposes the joint to stiffen and become even less flexible, which in turn causes the person to be even less mobile. Low mobility can reduce muscular strength to approximately 45% to 75% of normal function (Ekdahl & Broman, 1992).

Several strategies are used to reduce pain and enhance the function of those with osteoarthritis, One strategy used by many physicians is drug therapy, which employs salicylates, nonsteroidal anti-inflammatory drugs, and intra-articular steroids (Wigley, 1984). Other nondrug techniques include reduction of the joint work load, use of technology to assist joint action, exercise, surgical procedures, and joint replacement. If the older adult is overweight (and many are), one of the best ways to reduce the work load at all joints of the lower limbs is to lose weight. The impact of each step taken while walking, which can be several times greater than one's total body weight, can be reduced 9 to 15 lb for every 3 lb of weight lost (Liang, 1992).

Exercise and Osteoarthritis

Whether moderate exercise can prevent, postpone, rehabilitate, or provide relief for symptoms of osteoarthritis is not well established. However, preliminary evidence suggests that individuals with rheumatoid arthritis and osteoarthritis can benefit from regular systematic exercise (Panush et al., 1986). Passive nonstressful stretching of muscles across joints will keep the range of motion at those joints from decreasing. The preliminary evidence is sufficiently promising, and the Arthritis Foundation has recommended several exercises for the lower limbs. Fuller and Winters (1991) biomechanically analyzed these exercises in terms of the joint loads produced and recommended revisions that would decrease the muscular forces produced at the joint during back and side kicks. Puhl, Maier, and Günther (1992) suggested that

some sports are appropriate for those with osteoarthritis, some can be participated in if modified, and others are inappropriate (Table 3.6). Of particular benefit are sports that require stretching of muscles so that the range of motion of joints is maintained.

Exercise can assist the person with arthritis in several ways. The increased strength and flexibility derived from exercise can reduce pain. If the exercise is aerobic and is continued long enough, weight loss can occur, which will reduce the forces produced at the joints. Exercise also increases mobility; but because heavy forces on joints exacerbate arthritic conditions, low-impact exercises, such as those suggested by the Arthritis Foundation, or swimming and bicycling are recommended.

Exercise also can increase one's sense of well-being (see chapter 11). Joisten and Albrecht (1992) suggested that appropriate sports activities can provide this very important benefit for arthritic patients, too. They point out that arthritis often diminishes the self-assurance and self-image of those with the condition, and suggest that professionals who work with patients with arthritis point out improvements in physical appearance, mood, or feeling that accrue from participation in physical activity. Sports activities are also excellent activities to counter the tendency of individuals with arthritis disabilities to withdraw from social interactions.

Many people have questioned whether a lifetime of heavy running may aggravate and stress joints to such an extent that the runners develop osteoarthritis. There is little information regarding the relationship between training and osteoarthritis, but it does not support a negative effect of chronic running (Lane et al., 1986; Panush et al., 1986; Puhl et al., 1992). Running did not accelerate the development of osteoarthritis in runners between the ages of 50 and 72 years (Lane et al., 1993). These researchers compared the incidence of bone spurs, sclerosis, and joint space narrowing in the same subjects between 1984 and 1989. They found that although the incidence of osteoarthritis increased in both groups, the runners had not developed more arthritis than the nonrunners.

Skin

The skin is one of the most remarkable organs of the body. It is the interface between the internal

Table 3.6
Appropriateness of Various Sports for Adults With Osteoarthritis

Appropriate

Swimming	Crawl stroke or altered stroke may be necessary.
Walking on level ground	
Table tennis	
Cross-country skiing	Not for patients with compromised hip motility
Rowing	Contraindicated for gonarthrosis
Cycling	Level ground only for patients with gonarthrosis
Gymnastics	
Hydrogymnastics (water exercise)	
Isokinetic exercise	Permits muscle training without joint movement

Conditionally appropriate

Tennis	Doubles tennis rather than singles; proper shoes must be worn to prevent high-friction ground forces; proper techniques must be used.
Badminton	Suitable footwear must be worn.
Bowling	Only for patients with uncompromised hip and knee joint motility
Horse riding	Limited suitability for patients with compromised abduction and rotation of the hip joint
Downhill skiing	Only for excellent skiers
Jogging	For patients with lower leg arthrosis; only with suitable footwear; only if joint positions are normal

Unsuitable

Mountain hiking
Squash
Throwing (discus, shot put, etc.)
Soccer
Ice skating

Not appropriate

Walking on mountainous terrain

Note. From "Effects of Physical Activity on Degenerative Joint Disease" by W. Puhl, P. Maier, and K.P. Günther. In *Rheumatic Diseases and Sport. Rheumatology* (Vol. 16, pp. 132-134) by H.-W. Baenkler (Ed.), 1992, Basel, Switzerland: Karger. Copyright 1992 by S. Karger AG, Basel. Reprinted by permission.

body and the external world, providing protection against bacteria, chemicals, sun irradiation, blows to the body, and temperature extremes. The sense of touch, which comes from receptors in the skin, contributes important information that enables people to manipulate objects and maintain their balance. Touch also provides important, unique information about the environment. Babies want to touch and hold every object they see, because they learn more about it through touch than they do by just visualizing it. This need to touch does not change over one's life span, as evidenced by the signs in stores, museums, and gift shops that say "Please do not touch." Finally, the skin is important in communication. Touching, whether it is soft and gentle, direct, or harsh, conveys emotional expressions, and because emotional changes cause rapid circulatory adaptations, observing people's skin conveys information about their emotional state. Persons who are highly agitated or stressed may exhibit large red blotches across their necks and faces. Everyday speech conveys these observations: He was so mad he was red-faced. She was as white as a sheet. You can talk until you are blue in the face and you won't convince him!

Skin Composition

The skin is composed of two major layers, the *epidermis* and *dermis*. The epidermis, or outermost layer, also has several layers of skin cells. The innermost layers of the epidermis are living cells, which proliferate and reproduce. The cells in each successive layer of the epidermis are less and less able to reproduce themselves, so that those in the external layer are dead cells, sloughed off on a daily basis.

The dermis, which lies immediately underneath the epidermis, contains fine, fibrillar collagen and elastin fibers, oil glands, the skin's circulatory system, sweat glands, nerve endings, and hair follicles. Collagen and elastin provide the padding and elasticity of skin, giving it its shape and quality and allowing it to return to its original shape when displaced. Oil (sebaceous) glands lubricate the skin and help to keep it pliable. Nutrients are provided to the skin by the microcirculatory system of the dermis. This system also removes heat from the deep structures of the body to the surface and then transports the heat from the skin to the outside via sweat produced by the sweat glands. Approximately 2 to 4 million sweat glands are distributed throughout the surface of the body. As sweat evaporates on the surface of the skin, it cools the blood in the circulatory system of the dermis, thus cooling the body. Heat is also lost from the body through respiration, but sweating is the body's major mechanism for cooling.

Because the control of blood flow through the skin is responsive to both internal and external temperature changes and emotional states, the rate of bloodflow is extremely variable. Capillaries can become constricted, cutting off almost all blood to an area within seconds, or can perfuse an area rapidly. Metabolic work and external temperature changes have the most effect on the rate of bloodflow to the skin. During metabolic work (i.e., exercise), substantial body heat is produced, the capillaries of the skin become greatly dilated and perfused, and the skin of the exercising person turns red. In high heat environments, the skin also appears to be red. But, emotional states also make major changes in the circulatory system of the skin. These capillary changes are what affect the color of skin: Perfused capillaries make skin look red; deoxygenated blood in skin capillaries creates a blue appearance; and if blood is cut off from an area, the skin becomes white. Not only does the skin become white, but the lowered bloodflow also cools the skin, which is perceived as wet and clammy.

Underneath the dermis lies a layer of *subcutaneous tissue*, which contains fat cells, capillaries, nerve endings, and hair follicles. The fat cells in subcutaneous tissue provide padding for contact with the environment and protect against blows to the body.

Age-Related Changes to Skin

Skin is the tattletale of aging. Because the skin is constantly exposed to environmental stresses, such as temperature and humidity changes as well as chemicals, toxins, and mechanical pressure, it reveals its age. Also, the innermost tissues of the epidermis are not nourished as effectively, because blood profusion of these tissues decreases; consequently, the aging epidermal cells do not reproduce as rapidly. The organization of the epidermal cells throughout cell turnover is not maintained well, consequently skin cells become haphazardly grouped together, dryer, and rough. Because of a preponderance of dead, scaly cells on the surface of the skin, the skin may become chalky in appearance.

Aging is also accompanied by a breakdown of collagen and elastin fibers, so that the dermis becomes thinner and less pliable. The collagen fibers coarsen and appear in bundles. The elastin fibers become more cross-linked and more calcified (Partridge, 1970). These changes in the resiliency and compliance of the skin can be observed by pinching a fold of skin on the back of the hand. Hold the skin in the pinch for a few seconds, and then let go. The skin will return to its original shape, and the location of the pinch can no longer be seen. If 20 people representing ages 20 to 80 were to do this "pinch test" simultaneously, the 20-year-old's skin would return to normal almost instantaneously after releasing the skin, but the location of the pinched skin of the 80-year-old might be visible 10 or 15 s after release.

Contributing to these age-related changes in the quality of skin is that the circulation to the dermis decreases and becomes less efficient. The result of these inevitable age-related changes in the characteristics of skin is that it becomes paler, wounds do not heal as quickly, and it becomes more vulnerable to sun damage, less able to produce sweat, less efficient at thermoregulation, more permeable, and less able to make an inflammatory response. Increased dryness of skin is caused by a loss of some oil glands.

As skin becomes less and less resilient and compliant, losing tone and elasticity, the constant displacement of skin that occurs at joints and other places where the skin is pushed together or folded (e.g., when people smile, laugh, frown, and express other emotions) evolves into wrinkles. Each time a young person quits laughing, the skin that has been displaced returns to its original position. After thousands of laughs and many years, however, a stiffer, dryer, less elastic skin does not return as easily and begins to form folds. Consequently, wrinkles of skin, which begin forming early in life, become more and more visible. Wrinkles reflect the predominant positions of skin. Thus, people who frown most of the time have frown wrinkles on their foreheads, and people who smile most of the time have smile wrinkles around their mouths. Because it damages skin and makes it dryer, exposure to the sun accelerates the development of wrinkles. The constant squinting of the eyes and furrowing of the brow by people who are in the sun for long periods of time create large, multiple wrinkles in their skin.

Chronic exposure to sunlight causes sagging skin (Daly & Odland, 1979; Matsuoka & Uitto, 1989), changes in the elasticity of the skin (elastosis), and a reduction in the microcirculation to the skin (Montagna & Carlisle, 1979). Although it has been commonly believed for hundreds of years that constant exposure to sunlight is very damaging and accelerates the aging process in skin, this belief has not been scientifically confirmed until recently. Warren et al. (1991) used high-resolution facial photography, image analysis, instrumentation to measure elasticity, and histologic examinations to compare the faces of young (aged 25-31 years) and older (aged 45-51 years) women who had either been exposed to <2 hr of sun a week or >12 hr of sun a week for the previous year. They did not find a significant effect of chronic sun exposure on the elasticity, skin color, or wrinkles of the young women, but the results for the older women were very different. In the older high-sun-exposed group, significantly more wrinkles and less elasticity were present. Also, the older high-sun-exposure group was perceived by a panel of 24 untrained women judges, 20 to 60 years old, to be significantly older than the older women who were exposed to the sun very little. Figure 3.16 shows the correlation between perceived age and facial wrinkles, supporting the well-known observation that those with a high prevalence of facial wrinkles are perceived to be older than their chronological age. That sun

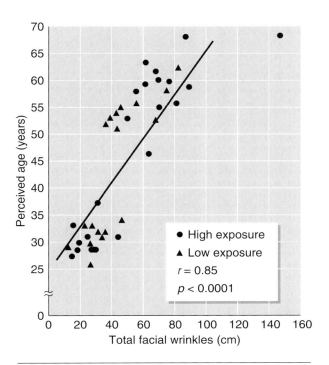

Figure 3.16 Correlation plot between perceived age and total facial wrinkles.
From "Age, Sunlight, and Facial Skin: A Histologic and Quantitative Study" by R. Warren et al., 1991, *Journal of the American Academy of Dermatology*, **25**, p. 759. Copyright 1991 by Mosby-Year Book, Inc. Reprinted by permission.

exposure is detrimental to skin can be further supported by comparisons of the skin of any individual to that person's skin in areas never exposed to the sun. Fortunately, sun damage can be prevented by using sunscreen, by wearing protective clothing, or by avoiding or limiting outdoor activities. Some improvements can be made if formerly exposed skin is removed from high-sun exposure for a prolonged period of time. Gerstein and Freeman (1963) showed that sun-damaged skin improves when it is transplanted to a solar-protected area.

In Summary

Aging is associated with visible and sometimes dramatic changes in the physical body. Indeed, the relentless decline of the physical body is perhaps the most routinely used marker of chronological age. Both men and women lose height, but women lose more, faster. Losses of bone and the compression of cartilage between the vertebrae cause women especially to lose height and to develop the dowager's hump characteristic of osteoporosis.

Both men and women gain weight until late-middle age, at which time womens' weights stabilize and mens' weights decline. Although body weight stabilizes or declines in the later years, body composition continues to change. Younger men and women have about 15% to 25% body fat and about 36% to 45% muscle. Beginning in the late 20s and 30s, the ratio of body fat to muscle steadily changes. Muscle mass is lost, especially in men, and body fat increases, until average men and women in their 70s have between 25% to 40% body fat. This redistribution of body fat and muscle and loss of height result in a body mass index that continues to climb with age, even though body weight may stay relatively the same during the last one third of life. The percent body fat can be profoundly affected by the amount of physical exercise that a person experiences.

Total body water decreases with aging. The combination of decreased total body water and increased body fat presents problems of stabilizing body temperature in extremes of environmental temperature. It also creates problems for the prescription of drugs, because both age and body composition influence the time that it takes a drug to clear the system.

Bone loss begins to occur in the mid- to late-20s in everyone, regardless of gender, race, or geographic location. Losses occur in bone mass, bone density, and bone geometry, largely due to hormonal changes, dietary deficiencies, and physical inactivity. Women lose more bone faster than men, because they begin with less bone mass and they experience a more drastic hormonal change with age. Bone losses can be somewhat attenuated by hormonal therapy, diet, dietary supplements, and exercise. Estrogen replacement has been the most effective way to prevent excessive bone loss in postmenopausal women, but increasing evidence for exercise as a way to retard bone loss has been accumulating in the last few years. Estrogen replacement (in women) combined with an exercise program and a diet that includes all of the required nutrients, especially calcium, appears to be the best preventive measure against premature and needless bone loss.

Bones that maintain mass and mineral density are stronger and less vulnerable to bone fracture. Osteoporosis, a crippling and painful degenerative disease of bone, has a genetic component and is also caused by the same factors that cause bone loss. Although the evidence is mounting that exercise may play a role in the prevention of osteoporosis, it is not yet known what contribution exercise can make to the amelioration of osteoporosis. Although exercise training that involves weight-bearing work, such as running, appears to be beneficial to bone, excessive and unduly intensive exercise may be detrimental to bone.

Another physical loss with age is that of flexibility. The range of motion at most joints is severely curtailed if stretching exercises are not implemented on a regular basis. Another factor that reduces flexibility is the development of osteoarthritis, a degenerative disease of the joints in which the cartilaginous and ligamentous components of the joint become damaged, causing substantial pain and impaired mobility. Techniques used to reduce pain and enhance function in osteoarthritic elderly include the reduction of joint work load, employment of movement-assisting technology, exercise, surgical procedures, and joint replacement. Systematic exercise assists in maintaining muscle and controlling body weight and optimizes the range of motion of joints, thus reducing work load at the joint. The Arthritis Foundation has recommended a program of low-impact and flexibility exercises for those with osteoarthritis.

In addition to the visible changes in physical appearance that occur, age-related changes in body composition also have implications for physical function and health. The redistribution of and increase in fat and the loss of muscle mass result in a substantial decrease in aerobic capacity. These changes in body composition in combination with the loss of bone mass and the development of osteoporosis and osteoarthritis can result in decreased function of muscles (e.g., decreased strength) and organs (e.g., kidney and liver malfunction). Finally, increased body fat, particularly upper-body or abdominal fat (expressed by higher BMIs), is associated with increased risk for cardiovascular disease and diabetes, and earlier mortality.

The last physical changes discussed in this chapter were those that occur to the skin. Skin is the tattletale of aging—of all the physical changes that occur, those to the skin are the most obvious. Much of the damage that occurs to the skin over a lifetime is due to sun exposure; consequently a substantial amount of age-related skin degradation can be prevented by protecting the skin from the sun.

References

Albanese, A.A., Edelson, H., Lorenze, E.J., Wein, E.H., & Carroll, L. (1985). Effect of age and fractures on bone loss and calcium needs of women

45 to 85+ years of age. *Nutrition Reports International*, **31**, 1093-1115.

Allen, T.H., Anderson, E.C., & Langham, W.H. (1960). Total body potassium and gross body composition in relation to age. *Journal of Gerontology*, **15**, 348-357.

Andres, R. (1990). Discussion: Assessment of health status. In C. Bouchard, R.J. Shephard, T. Stephens, J.R. Sutton, & B.D. McPherson (Eds.), *Exercise, fitness, and health* (pp. 133-136). Champaign, IL: Human Kinetics.

Ballard, J.E., McKeown, B.C., Graham, H.M., & Zinkgraf, S.A. (1990). The effect of high level physical activity (8.5 METs or greater) and estrogen replacement therapy upon bone mass in postmenopausal females, aged 50-68 years. *International Journal of Sports Medicine*, **11**, 208-214.

Baumgartner, R.N., Roche, A.F., Gleo, S., Lohman, T., Baileall, R.A., & Slaughter, M.H. (1986). Adipose tissue distribution: The stability of principal components by sex, ethnicity, and maturation stage. *Human Biology*, **58**, 719-735.

Behnke, A.R., & Wilmore, J.H. (1974). *Evaluation and regulation of body build and composition*. Englewood Cliffs, NJ: Prentice Hall.

Bevier, W.C., Wiswell, R.A., Pyka, C., Kozak, K.C., Newhall, K.M., & Marcus, R. (1989). Relationship of body composition, muscle strength, and aerobic capacity to bone mineral density in older men and women. *Journal of Bone and Mineral Research*, **4**, 421-432.

Bilanin, J.E., Blanchard, M.S., & Russek-Cohen, E. (1989). Lower vertebral bone density in male long-distance runners. *Medicine and Science in Sports and Exercise*, **21**, 66-70.

Blanchard, J., Conrad, K.A., & Harrison, G.G. (1990). Comparison of methods for estimating body composition in young and elderly women. *Journal of Gerontology: Biological Sciences*, **45**, B119-B124.

Borkan, G.A., & Norris, A.H. (1977). Fat redistribution and the changing body dimensions of the adult male. *Human Biology*, **49**, 495-514.

Borkan, G.A., Hults, D.E., Gerzof, S.G., Robbins, A.H., & Silbert, C.K. (1983). Age changes in body composition revealed by computed tomography. *Journal of Gerontology*, **38**, 673-677.

Braitman, L.E., Adlin, E.V., & Stanton, J.L., Jr. (1985). Obesity and caloric intake: The National Health and Nutrition Examination Survey of 1971-1975 (NHANES I). *Journal of Chronic Diseases*, **38**, 727-732.

Bray, G.A. (1985). Obesity: Definition, diagnosis, and disadvantages. *Medical Journal of Australia*, **142**, 52-58.

Brown, M., & Holloszy, J.O. (1991). Effects of a low-intensity exercise program on selected physical performance characteristics of 60- to 71-year-olds. *Aging*, **3**, 11, 129-139.

Buskirk, E.R., & Hodgson, J.L. (1987). Age and aerobic power: The rate of change in men and women. *Federation Proceedings*, **46**, 1824-1829.

Cavanaugh, D.J., & Cann, C.E. (1988). Brisk walking does not stop bone loss in postmenopausal women. *Bone*, **9**, 201-204.

Chandler, P.J., & Bock, R.D. (1991). Age changes in adult stature: Trend estimation from mixed longitudinal data. *Annals of Human Biology*, **18**, 433-440.

Chandra, R.K. (Ed.) (1985). *Nutrition, immunity, and illness in the elderly*. New York: Pergamon Books.

Chapman, E.A., deVries, H.A., & Swezey, R. (1972). Joint stiffness: Effects of exercise on young and old men. *Journal of Gerontology*, **27**, 218-221.

Chirico, A.M., & Stunkard, A.J. (1960). Physical activity and human obesity. *New England Journal of Medicine*, **263**, 935-940.

Chow, R., Harrison, J.E., & Notarius, L. (1987). Effect of two randomized exercise programmes on bone mass of healthy postmenopausal women. *British Medical Journal*, **295**, 1441-1444.

Cumming, R.G. (1990). Calcium intake and bone mass: A quantitative review of the evidence. *Calcified Tissue International*, **47**, 194-201.

Cummings, S.R., Kelsey, J.L., Nevitt, M.C., & O'Dowd, K.J. (1985). Epidemiology of osteoporosis and osteoporotic fractures. *Epidemiologic Reviews*, **7**, 178-208.

Dalsky, G.P. (1989). The role of exercise in the prevention of osteoporosis. *Comprehensive Therapy*, **15**, 30-37.

Dalsky, G.P., Stocke, K., Ehsani, A.A., Slatopolsky, E., Waldon, C.L., & Stanlexy, J.B. (1988). Weight-bearing exercise training and lumbar bone mineral content in postmenopausal women. *Annals of Internal Medicine*, **108**, 824-828.

Daly, C.H., & Odland, G.F. (1979). Age-related changes in the mechanical properties of skin. *Journal of Investigative Dermatology*, **73**, 84-87.

Darby, L.A., Pohlman, R.L., & Lechner, A.J. (1985). Increased bone calcium following endurance exercise in the mature female rat. *Laboratory Animal Science*, **35**, 382-386.

Davis, J.W., Ross, P.K., Wasnich, R.D., MacLean, C.J., & Vogel, J.M. (1989). Comparison of cross-sectional and longitudinal measurements of age-related changes in bone mineral content. *Journal of Bone and Mineral Research*, **4**, 351-357.

Dilson, G., Berker, C., Ordl, A., & Varan, G. (1989). The role of physical exercise in prevention and management of osteoporosis. *Clinical Rheumatology*, **8**, 70-75.

Drinkwater, B. (1986). Osteoporosis and the female masters athlete. In J.R. Sutton & R.M. Brock (Eds.), *Sports medicine for the mature athlete* (pp. 353-359). Indianapolis: Benchmark Press.

Drinkwater, B.L., Nilson, K., Chestnut, C.H. III, Bremner, W.J., Shainholtz, S., & Southworth, M.B. (1984). Bone mineral content of amenorrheic and eumenorrheic athletes. *New England Journal of Medicine*, **311**, 277-281.

Durnin, J.V.G.A., & Womersley, J. (1974). Body fat assessed from total body density and its estimation from skinfold thickness: Measurements of 481 men and women aged from 16 to 72 years. *British Journal of Nutrition*, **32**, 77-97.

Einkauf, D.K., Gohdes, M.L., Jensen, G.M., & Jewell, M.J. (1987). Changes in spinal mobility with increasing age in women. *Physical Therapy*, **67**, 370-375.

Ekdahl, C., & Broman, G. (1992). Muscle strength, endurance, and aerobic capacity in rheumatoid arthritis: A comparative study with healthy subjects. *Annals of Rheumatic Diseases*, **51**, 35-40.

Fabsitz, R., Feinleib, M., & Hrubec, Z. (1980). Weight changes in adult twins. *Acta Genetics Medicine Gemello*, **29**, 273-279.

Finklestein, J.S., Neer, R.M., Biller, B.M.K., Crawford, J.D., & Klibanski, A. (1992). Osteopenia in men with a history of delayed puberty. *New England Journal of Medicine*, **326**, 600-604.

Forbes, G.B. (1976). The adult decline in lean body mass. *Human Biology*, **48**, 161-173.

Forbes, G.B., & Reina, J.C. (1970). Adult lean body mass declines with age: Some longitudinal observations. *Metabolism*, **19**, 653-663.

Franck, H., Beuker, F., & Gurk, S. (1991). The effect of physical activity on bone turnover in young adults. *Experimental and Clinical Endocrinology*, **98**, 42-46.

Frisancho, A.R. (1990). *Anthropometric standards for the assessment of growth and nutritional status*. Ann Arbor: University of Michigan Press.

Frost, H.M. (1989). Mechanical usage, bone mass, bone fragility: A brief overview. In M. Kleerekoper & S.M. Krane (Eds.), *Clinical disorders of bone and mineral metabolism: Proceedings of the Laurence and Dorothy Fallis International Symposium* (pp. 15-40). New York: Mary Ann Liebert.

Fuller, J.S., & Winters, J.M. (1991). Joint loading during stretching exercises recommended for osteoarthritis: A biomechanical analysis. *Topics in Geriatric Rehabilitation*, **6**, 25-33.

Fülöp, T., Jr., Wórum, I., Csongor, J., Fóris, G., Varga, P., & Leövey, A. (1985). Body composition in elderly people. *Gerontology*, **31**, 150-157.

Galloway, A., Stini, W. A., Fox, S.C., & Stein, P. (1990). Stature loss among an older United States population and its relation to bone mineral status. *American Journal of Physical Anthropology*, **83**, 467-476.

Gärdsell, P., Johnell, O., & Nilsson, B.E. (1991). The predictive value of bone loss for fragility fractures in women: A longitudinal study over 15 years. *Calcified Tissue International*, **49**, 90-94.

Gerber, N.J., & Rey, B. (1991). Can exercises prevent osteoporosis or reverse bone loss? In P. Schlapbach & N.J. Gerber (Eds.), *Physiotherapy: Controlled trials and facts. Rheumatology* (Vol. 14, pp. 47-60). Basel, Switzerland: Karger.

Gerstein, W., Freeman, R.G. (1963). Transplantation of actinically damaged skin. *Journal of Investigative Dermatology*, **41**, 445-450.

Gillum, R.F. (1987). The association of body fat distribution with hypertension, hypertensive heart disease, coronary heart disease, diabetes, and cardiovascular risk factors in men and women aged 18-79 years. *Journal of Chronic Diseases*, **40**, 421-428.

Gleeson, P., Protas, E.J., LeBlanc, A.D., Schneider, V., & Evans, H.J. (1990). Effects of weight lifting on bone mineral density in premenopausal women. *Journal of Bone and Mineral Research*, **5**, 153-158.

Hagino, H., Yamamoto, K., Teshima, R., Kishimoto, H., & Kagawa, T. (1992). Radial bone mineral changes in pre- and postmenopausal healthy Japanese women: Cross-sectional and longitudinal studies. *Journal of Bone and Mineral Research*, **7**, 147-152.

Halle, J.S., Smidt, G.L., O'Dwyer, K., & Lin, S. (1990). Relationship between trunk muscle torque and bone mineral content of the lumber spine and hip in healthy postmenopausal women. *Physical Therapy*, **70**, 690-699.

Harris, S., Dallal, G.E., & Dawson-Hughes, B. (1992). Influence of body weight on rates of change in bone density of the spine, hip, and radius in postmenopausal women. *Calcified Tissue International*, **50**, 19-23.

Heaney, R.P. (1986). Calcium, bone health, and osteoporosis. *Journal of Bone and Mineral Research*, **4**, 255-301.

Heaney, R.P. (1992). Calcium in the prevention and treatment of osteoporosis. *Journal of Internal Medicine*, **231**, 169-180.

Heaney, R.P. (1982). Paradox of irreversibility of age-related bone loss. In J. Menczel, G.C. Robin, M. Makin, & R. Steinberg (Eds.), *Osteoporosis: The proceedings of an international symposium held at the Jerusalem Osteoporosis Center in June 1981.* (pp. 15-20). New York: Wiley.

Heikkinen, J., Kurttila-Matero, E., Kyllönen, E., Vuori, J., Takala, T., & Vuäänänen, H.K. (1991). Moderate exercise does not enhance the positive effect of estrogen on bone mineral density in postmenopausal women. *Calcified Tissue International*, **49**, (Suppl.), 583-584.

Hirsch, J., Fried, S.K., Edens, N.K. & Leibel, R.L. (1989). The fat cell. *Medical Clinics of North America*, **73**, 83-110.

Huddleston, A.L, Rockewell, D., Kulund, D.N., & Harrison, R.B. (1980). Bone mass in lifetime tennis athletes. *Journal of the American Medical Association*, **244**, 1107-1109.

Hui, S.L., Slemenda, C.W., & Johnston, C.C. (1988). Age and bone mass as predictors of fracture in a prospective study. *Journal of Clinical Investigation, 81*, 1804-1809.

Hui, S.L., Slemenda, C.W., & Johnston, C.C. (1989). Rapid bone losers: Permanent or temporary classification? *Journal of Bone and Mineral Research, 4* (Suppl. 1), 414.

Jackson, J.A., & Kleerkoper, M. (1990). Osteoporosis in men: Diagnosis, pathophysiology, and prevention. *Medicine, 69*, 137-152.

Jacobson, P., Beaver, W., Janeway, D., Grubb, S., Taft, T., & Talmage, R. (1984). Bone density in women: College athletes and older athletic women. *Journal of Orthopaedic Research, 2*, 328-332.

Jequier, E. (1987). Energy utilization in human obesity. In R.J. Wurtman & J.J. Wurtman (Eds.), *Human obesity* (pp. 73-83). New York: New York Academy of Sciences.

Johns, R.J., & Wright, V. (1962). Relative importance of various tissues in joint stiffness. *Journal of Applied Physiology, 17*, 824-828.

Joisten, U., & Albrecht, H.J. (1992). Physical activity and spondylarthritis. In H.W. Baenkler, *Rheumatic diseases and sport. Rheumatology* (Vol. 16, pp. 153-159). Basel: Karger.

Jones, H.H., Priest, J.D., Hayes, W.C., Tichenor, C.C., & Nagel, D.A. (1977). Humeral hypertrophy in response to exercise. *Journal of Bone and Joint Surgery, 59A*, 204-208.

Jónnson, B., Ringsberg, K., Josefsson, P.O., Johnell, O., & Birch-Jensen, M. (1992). Effects of physical activity on bone mineral content and muscle strength in women: A cross-sectional study. *Bone, 13*, 191-195.

Kavanaugh, T., & Shephard, R.J. (1990). Can regular sports participation slow the aging process? Data on masters athletes. *Physician and Sportsmedicine, 18*, 94-104.

Kiebzak, G.M. (1991). Age-related bone changes. *Experimental Gerontology, 26*, 171-187.

Kiebzak, G.M., Smith, R., Howe, J.C., & Sacktor, B. (1988). Bone mineral content in the senescent rat femur: An assessment using single photon absorptiometry. *Journal of Bone and Mineral Research, 3*, 311-317.

Kirk, S., Sharp, C.F., Elbaum, N., Endres, K., Simons, S.M., Mohler, J.G., & Rude, R.K. (1989). Effect of long-distance running on bone mass in women. *Journal of Bone and Mineral Research, 4*, 515-522.

Kissebah, A.H., Freedman, D.S., & Prinis, A.N. (1989). Health risks of obesity. *Medical Clinics of North America, 73*, 111-138.

Klesges, R.C., Eck, L.H., Isbell, T.R., Fulliton, W., & Hanson, C.L. (1991). Physical activity, body composition, and blood pressure: A multimethod approach. *Medicine and Science in Sports and Exercise, 23*, 759-765.

Kohrt, W.M., Obert, K.A., & Holloszy, J.O. (1992). Exercise improves fat distribution patterns in 60- to 70-year-old men and women. *Journal of Gerontology: Medical Sciences, 47*, M99-M105.

Korkeila, M., Kaprio, J., Rissanen, A., & Koskenvuo. M. (1991). Effects of gender and age on the heritability of body mass index. *International Journal of Obesity, 15*, 647-654.

Krølner, B., & Toft, B. (1983). Vertebral bone loss: An unheeded side effect of therapeutic bed rest. *Clinical Science, 64*, 537-540.

Laforest, S., St-Pierre, D.M.M., Cyr, J., & Gayton, D. (1990). Effects of age and regular exercise on muscle strength and endurance. *European Journal of Applied Physiology, 60*, 104-111.

Lane, N., Bloch, D.A., Jones, H.H., Marshall, W.H., Jr., Wood, D.D., & Fries, J.F. (1986). Long-distance running, bone density, and osteoarthritis. *Journal of the American Medical Association, 255*, 1147-1151.

Lane, N., Michel, B., Bjorkengren, A., Oehlert, J., Shi, H., Bloch, D.A., & Fries, J. F. (1993). The risk of osteoarthritis with running and aging: A 5-year longitudinal study. *Journal of Rheumatology, 20*, 461-469.

LeBlanc, A., & Schneider, V. (1991). Can the adult skeleton recover lost bone? *Experimental Gerontology, 26*, 189-201.

Liang, M.H. (1992). A joint endeavor. *Harvard Health Letter, 17* (6), 1-3.

Lindsay, R., Hart, D.M., Aitkin, J.M., MacDonald, E.B., Anderson, J.B., & Clarke, A.C. (1976). Long-term prevention of postmenopausal osteoporosis by oestrogen: Evidence for an increased bone mass after delayed onset of oestrogen treatment. *The Lancet, 1*, 1038-1040.

Malina, R.M. (1991). Darwinian fitness, physical fitness, and physical activity. In C.G.N. Mascie-Taylor & G.W. Lasker (Eds.), *Applications of biological anthropology to human affairs*. Cambridge: Cambridge University Press.

Malina, R.M., & Bouchard, C. (1991). *Growth, maturation, and physical activity*. Champaign, IL: Human Kinetics.

Martin, R.B., & Burr, D.B. (1989). *Structure, function, and adaptation of compact bone*. New York: Raven Press.

Matsuoka, L.Y., Uitto, J. (1989). Alterations in the elastic fibers in cutaneous aging and solar elastosis. In A.K. Balin & A.M. Kligman (Eds.), *Aging and the skin* (pp. 141-151). New York: Raven Press.

McLaren, D.S. (1988). Letter to the editor. *Science, 241*, 399-400.

Michel, B.A., Lane, N.E., Bloch, D.A., Jones, H.H., & Fries, J.F. (1991). Effect of changes in weight-bearing exercise on lumbar bone mass after age fifty. *Annals of Medicine, 23*, 397-401.

Montagna, W., & Carlisle, K. (1979). Structural changes in aged human skin. *Journal of Investigative Dermatology*, **73**, 47-53.

National Institutes of Health. (1985). Health implications of obesity. *NIH Consensus Development Conference Statement* (Doc. No. 21111). Bethesda, MD: U.S. Government Printing Office.

Nillsson, B.E., & Westlin, N.E. (1971). Bone density in athletes. *Clinical Orthopaedics*, **77**, 179-182.

Notelovitz, M. (1986). Postmenopausal osteoporosis: A practical approach to its prevention. *Acta Obstetricia et Gynecologica Scandinavica*, **65**, 67-80.

Notelovitz, M., Martin, D., Tesar, R., Khan, F.Y., Probart, C., Fields, C., & McKenzie, L. (1991). Estrogen therapy and variable-resistance weight training increase bone mineral in surgically menopausal women. *Journal of Bone and Mineral Research*, **6**, 583-590.

Panush, R.S., Schmidt, C., Caldwell, J.R., Edwards, N.L., Longley, S., Yonker, R., Webster, E., Stork, J., & Pettersson, H. (1986). Is running associated with degenerative joint disease? *Journal of the American Medical Association*, **255**, 1152-1154.

Parfitt, A.M., & Kleerkoper, M. (1984). Diagnostic value of bone histomorphometry and comparison of histologic measurements and biochemical indices of bone remodeling. In C. Christiansen, C.D. Arnaud, & B.E.C. Nordin (Eds.), *Osteoporosis* (pp. 111-120). Copenhagen International Symposium on Osteoporosis. Copenhagen: Glostrupt Hospital.

Partridge, S.M. (1970). Biological role of cutaneous elastin. In W. Montagna, J.P. Bentley, & R.L. Dobson (Eds.), *Advances in biology of skin* (Vol. 10, pp. 69-87). New York: Meredith Corporation.

Pocock, N.A., Eisman, J.A., Gwinn, T.H., Sambrook, P.N., Yeates, M.G., & Freund, J. (1988). Regional muscle strength, physical fitness, and weight but not age predict femur bone mass. *Journal of Bone and Mineral Research*, **3**, 584.

Pollock, M.L., Foster, C., Knapp, D., Rod, J.L., & Schmidt, D.H. (1987). Effect of age and training on aerobic capacity and body composition of master athletes. *Journal of Applied Physiology*, **62**, 725-731.

Pollock, M.L, Laughridge, E.E., Coleman, B., Linnerud, A.C., & Jackson, A. (1975). Prediction of body density in young and middle-aged women. *Journal of Applied Physiology*, **38**, 745-749.

Poss, R. (1992). Natural factors that affect the shape and strength of the aging human femur. *Clinical Orthopaedics*, **274**, 194-201.

Prince, R.L., Smith, M., Dick, I.M., Price, R.I., Webb, P.G., Henderson, N.K., & Harris, M.M. (1991). Prevention of postmenopausal osteoporosis. *New England Journal of Medicine*, **325**, 1189-1195.

Pruitt, L.A., Jackson, R.D., Bartels, R.L., & Lehnhard, H.J. (1992). Weight-training effects on bone mineral density in early postmenopausal women. *Journal of Bone and Mineral Research*, **7**, 179-185.

Puhl, W., Maier, P., & Günther, K.P. (1992). Effects of physical activity on degenerative joint disease. In H.-W. Baenkler (Ed.), *Rheumatic diseases and sport. Rheumatology* (Vol. 16, pp. 129-141). Basel, Switzerland: Karger.

Puustjärvi, K., Karjalainen, P., Nieminen, J., Helminen, H.J., Soimakallio, S., Kivimäki, T., & Arokoski, J. (1991). Effects of long-term running on spinal mineral content in dogs. *Calcified Tissue International*, **49**, S81-S82.

Raab, D.M., Agre, J.C., McAdam, M., & Smith, E.L. (1988). Light resistance and stretching exercise in elderly women: Effect upon flexibility. *Archives of Physical Medicine and Rehabilitation*, **69**, 268-278.

Raab, D.M., Smith, E.L., Crenshaw, T.D., & Thomas, D.P. (1990). Bone mechanical properties after exercise training in young and old rats. *Journal of Applied Physiology*, **68**, 130-134.

Recker, R.R., Davies, K.M., Hinders, S.M., Heaney, R.P., Stegman, M.R., & Kimmel, D.B. (1992). Bone gain in young adult women. *Journal of the American Medical Association*, **268**, 2403-2408.

Riggs, B.L., Wahner, H.W., Melton, L.J., III, Richelson, L.S., Judd, H.W., & Offord, K.P. (1986). Rates of bone loss in the appendicular and axial skeletons of women: Evidence of substantial vertebral bone loss before menopause. *Journal of Clinical Investigation*, **77**, 1487-1491.

Roche, A.F., Siervogel, R.M., Chumlea, W.C., Reed, R.B., & Valadian, I. (1982). Serial changes in subcutaneous fat thickness of children and adults. *Monogram of Pediatrics*, **17**, 29-99.

Roe, F.J.C., Lee, P.N., Conybeare, G., Tobin, G., Kelly, D., Prentice, D., & Matter, B. (1991). Risks of premature death and cancer predicted by body weight in early adult life. *Human and Experimental Toxicology*, **10**, 285-288.

Rosenbaum, S., Skinner, R.K., Knight, I.B., & Garrow, J.S. (1985). A survey of heights and weights of adults in Great Britain, 1980. *Annals of Human Biology*, **12**, 115-127.

Ross, P.D., Davis, J.W., Vogel, J.M., & Wasnich, R.D. (1990). A critical review of bone mass and the risk of fractures in osteoporosis. *Calcified Tissue International*, **46**, 149-161.

Rudman, D., Feller, A.G., Cohn, L., Shetty, K.R., Rudman, I.W., & Draper, M.W. (1991). Effects of human growth hormone on body composition in elderly men. *Hormone Research*, **36** (Suppl. 1), 73-81.

Rundgren, A., Aniansson, A., Ljungberg, P., & Wetterqvist, H. (1984). Effects of a training programme for elderly people on mineral content of the heel bone. *Archives of Gerontology and Geriatrics*, **3**, 243-248.

Sallis, J.F., Patterson, T.L., Buouno, M.J., & Nader, P.R. (1988). Relation of cardiovascular fitness and physical activity to cardiovascular disease risk factors in children and adults. *American Journal of Epidemiology*, **127**, 933-941.

Schneider, V.S., & McDonald, J. (1984). Skeletal calcium homeostasis and countermeasures to prevent disuse osteoporosis. *Calcified Tissue International*, **36**, S151-S154.

Schoutens, A., Laurent, E., & Poortmans, J.R. (1989). Effects of inactivity and exercise on bone. *Sports Medicine*, **7**, 71-81.

Schultheis, L. (1991). The mechanical control system of bone in weightless spaceflight and in aging. *Experimental Gerontology*, **26**, 203-214.

Schwartz, R., Shuman, W.P., Bradbury, V.L., Cain, K.C., Fellingham, G.W., Beard, J.C., Kahn, S.E., Stratton, J.R., Cerqueira, M.D., & Abrass, I.B. (1990). Body fat distribution in healthy young and older men. *Journal of Gerontology: Medical Sciences*, **45**, M181-M185.

Skerlj, B., Brozek, J., & Hunt, E.E., Jr. (1953). Subcutaneous fat and age changes in body build and body form in women. *American Journal of Physical Anthropology*, **11**, 577-600.

Smith, E.L. (1982). Exercise for the prevention of osteoporosis: A review. *Physician and Sports Medicine*, **3**, 72-80.

Smith, E.L., & Raab, D.M. (1986). Osteoporosis and physical activity. *Acta Medica Scandinavica*, (Suppl. 711), 149-156.

Sönnichsen, A.C., Richter, W.O., & Schwandt, P. (1991). Body fat distribution and serum lipoproteins in relation to age and body weight. *Clinica Chimica Acta*, **202**, 133-140.

Steen, B. (1988). Body composition and aging. In *Nutrition and Aging*. Suppl. 24 of Näringsforskning, årgång, **32**, 13-19.

Steen, B., Lundgren, B.K., & Isaksson, B. (1985). Body composition at age 70, 75, 79, and 81 years: A longitudinal population study. In R.K. Chandra (Ed.), *Nutrition, immunity, and illness in the elderly* (pp. 49-52). New York: Pergamon Press.

Stunkard, A.J., Harris, J., Pedersen, N.L., & McClearn, G.E. (1990). The body mass index of twins who have been reared apart. *New England Journal of Medicine*, **322**, 1483-1487.

Thompson, M.P., & Morris, L.K. (1991). Unexplained weight loss in the ambulatory elderly. *Journal of the American Geriatrics Society*, **39**, 497-500.

Tryon, W.W. (1987). Activity as a function of body weight. *American Journal of Clincal Nutrition*, **46**, 451-455.

Tzankoff, S.P., & Norris, A.H. (1977). Effect of muscle mass decrease on age-related basal metabolic rate changes. *Journal of Applied Physiology: Respiratory, Environmental, and Exercise Physiology*, **43**, 1001-1006.

Vandervoort, A.A., Chesworth, B.M., Cunningham, D.A., Paterson, D.H., Rechnitzer, P.A., & Koval, J.J. (1992). Age and sex effects on mobility of the human ankle. *Journal of Gerontology: Medical Sciences*, **47**, M17-M21.

Warren, R., Gartstein, V., Kligman, A.M., Montagna, W., Allendorg, R.A., & Ridder, G.M. (1991). Age, sunlight, and facial skin: A histologic and quantitative study. *Journal of the American Academy of Dermatology*, **25**, 751-760.

Waters, R.L., Conaty, P.J., Lunsford, B., & O'Meara, P. (1987). The energy cost of walking with arthritis of the hip and knee. *Clinical Orthopaedics and Related Research*, **214**, 278-284.

Watson, R.C. (1973). Bone growth and physical activity in young males. In R.B. Mazess (Ed.), *International Conference on Bone Mineral Measurement* (NIH #75-683; pp. 380-386). Chicago, IL: Department of Health, Education, & Welfare.

Weinreb, M., Rodan, G.A., & Thompson, D.D. (1989). Osteopenia in the immobilized rat hind limb is associated with increased bone resorption and decreased bone formation. *Bone*, **10**, 187-194.

Wigley, F.M. (1984). Osteoarthritis: Practical management in older patients. *Rheumatology*, **39**, 101-120.

PART II

Energy, Work, and Efficiency

They are tiny but ominous harbingers of aging—the first time an ordinary trip up the stairs causes an unusually fast heartbeat, the first time the legs tremble after lifting a child up to a water fountain. Fortunately, exercise and determination can postpone these warnings for a very long time.

*I*t is a common observation that cardiorespiratory function and endurance decrease with aging in the average person. Maximum heart rate, cardiac output, and oxygen consumption decline as individuals grow older. How much aerobic capacity and how much strength and endurance are lost? More importantly, how much of the difference between the aerobic endurance and strength of a 20-year-old and a 60-year-old is due to aging, and how much is due to disuse? This section discusses the effects of aging on various components of the cardiovascular and respiratory system. Although much is known about the age-related deteriorations of these systems, a number of controversies, such as whether cardiac output actually declines in highly trained individuals or whether the nature of the muscle tissue actually changes with aging, still exist.

CHAPTER 4

Cardiovascular and Pulmonary Function

The capacity to perform physical work draws on the function of several interrelated and interdependent systems. The structure and function of the heart, lungs, arteries, and veins, the ability of the system to convert oxygen to energy over an extended period, and the ability of the system to perform short-term work in the absence of oxygen are all crucial to independent physical functioning. In youth, routine activities of daily living place minimal physical demands on these systems; therefore physical capacity differences between physically fit and non–physically fit young persons are not obvious. These differences only become observable when dynamic physical exertion is demanded, such as dashing up a long flight of stairs, loading heavy boxes onto a vehicle, or running a mile. With increasing age, however, less physically demanding tasks require increasingly more of the work capacity reserves. Early in life, increased age provides developmental processes necessary to reach the peak potential of physical performance. After the early 20s, however, aging begins to erode many functions. Conversely, exercise training enhances physiological systems. Aging and chronic exercise, therefore, drive several key body functions in opposite directions. Aging degrades the systems that support work capacity, whereas systematic exercise generally enhances these systems. Older individuals who maintain as high a level of physical function as possible increase their distance from fatigue. Therefore, the amount of physical activity in one's lifestyle is a highly significant determiner of individual differences in the physical capacity of the elderly.

This chapter describes the major age-related changes that occur in heart and lung structure, cardiovascular and pulmonary function, and hemodynamics and discusses the benefits of physical training of each of these systems. This discussion emphasizes the debilitating effects of disuse and their relationship to human frailty and briefly summarizes how chronic exercise programs affect normal, healthy, aging adults and people with cardiovascular disease, hypertension, and diabetes. The chapter concludes with a discussion of the ultimate postponement of age-related loss of aerobic capacity exemplified by athletes.

Cardiovascular Function

Cardiovascular function is dependent on the structure and function of the heart, the aorta and arterial tree, and the components and volume of blood. In reality, resting cardiovascular parameters in a healthy adult change so little with aging, except for systolic blood pressure, that they are adequate to meet the body's need for blood pressure and bloodflow (Gerstenblith, Renlund, & Lakatta, 1987; Lakatta, 1990). The cardiovascular response to exercise, however, is greatly reduced in the average person. The contrast in aging effects on resting and exercise cardiorespiratory performance can be seen in Figure 4.1, where resting parameters change only moderately but some of the exercise responses decline substantially.

Structural Changes to the Heart

Not many gross or microscopic changes occur in the heart due to aging alone. There is some evidence of degeneration in the heart cells and the loss of some cells, but these changes are not thought to lead to functional abnormalities. Some age-related mechanical changes that have been identified are a lengthened contraction duration and an increase in the time during which the heart cannot be stimulated (the refractory period). Aging heart muscle also takes longer to reach its peak force. These mechanical changes in the heart result in incomplete relaxation during early diastolic filling. The rate of left ventricular filling decreases roughly 50% between the ages of 20 and 70. Alterations may occur in the relaxation phase and in the viscoelastic properties of the cardiac muscle (Klausner & Schwartz, 1985). The valves of the heart, particularly the aortic and pulmonary valves, increase in circumference. But by far the greatest changes in the heart are pathological changes, brought about by disease processes and lifestyle changes.

The left ventricle of the heart, which pumps blood to all portions of the body except the lungs, increases in wall thickness approximately 30% between the ages of 25 and 80, probably in compensation for the age-related increase in systolic blood pressure (Fleg, 1986; Lakatta, 1990). As blood pressure increases, the heart muscle has to work harder. The heart muscle, like an arm or leg muscle, hypertrophies with additional work, thus the ventricle walls grow thicker. Left ventricular hypertrophy is also a normal adaptation to regular exercise. However, the ventricular cavity dimensions and systolic ventricular function during rest are unaffected by these structural changes. Additional exercise training seems to have little effect on resting left ventricular function (Ehsani, 1987), except to lower the resting heart rate.

End diastolic volume is the amount of blood that fills the chambers of the heart when it is relaxed. End diastolic volume depends on the rate of venous blood return to the heart and on the amount of time the blood has to return to the heart between beats. The aortic and pulmonary valves, which are closed during diastolic filling, increase in circumference. Early diastolic filling rate is reduced, but an increased atrial contribution compensates for the decreased ventricular filling in elderly individuals so that filling volume is maintained at a normal level. In fact, in one group of healthy, physically active subjects over 65 years of age, the atrial contribution to ventricular filling was almost twice (37%) that of 25-year-old men (19%) (Pearson, Gudipati, & Labovitz, 1991). The heart ventricle of older adults does not relax as

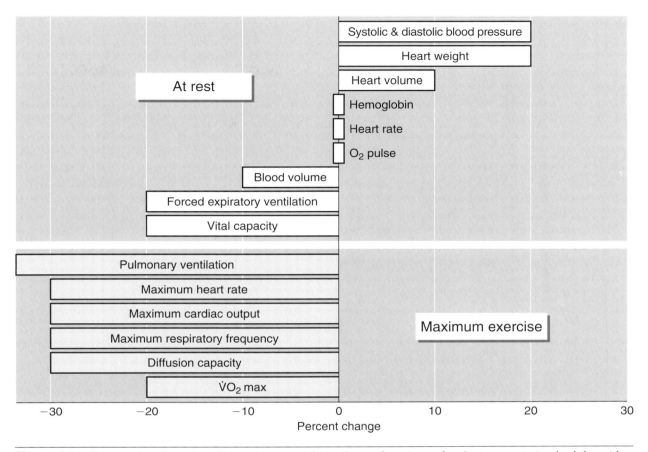

Figure 4.1 Changes in selected cardiorespiratory and circulatory functions of sedentary, untrained adults with aging.

completely (thus allowing complete filling) as it does in young adults, so older adults compensate with a hypertrophied atrium that actively ejects more blood into the ventricle. Systolic pressure at rest increases with age, but the increase in the left ventricular wall thickness compensates partially so that the resting end-systolic volume and ejection fraction are not changed (Lakatta, 1990). Also, an intensive exercise program improves left ventricular systolic performance in older men (Ehsani, Takeshi, Miller, Spina, & Jilka, 1991).

The aorta and the arterial tree become thicker and less compliant with aging, contributing to increased systolic blood pressure and imposing a greater load on the heart (Fleg, 1986). Very small arteries, the arterioles, also become less responsive during physical activity to neurohumoral cues for dilation, thus remaining inappropriately constricted. These changes, plus increased peripheral resistance, are the major contributors to the development of hypertension (Safar, 1990). In spite of these age-related changes, heart function in the nondiseased aged individual is adequate for resting and light physical work. The development of

atherosclerotic coronary artery disease, however, significantly alters cardiovascular structure and function in most aged people and, in combination with hypertension, forces the cardiovascular system to work under a substantial stress even during relatively light physical work. Vigorous physical activity overwhelms the diseased heart, rendering it incapable of supplying the periphery with the blood required for the task.

Neural Control Mechanisms of the Heart, Arteries, and Capillaries

Neural control of the heart occurs through the parasympathetic and sympathetic nervous systems. Parasympathetic nerve fibers innervate the pacemaker of the heart, releasing acetylcholine, which slows the heart rate. Sympathetic nerve fibers innervate the heart muscle itself and release norepinephrine, increasing the rate and force of contractions. Sympathetic activation also stimulates the adrenal medulla to release epinephrine and norepinephrine (catecholamines). Resting levels of norepinephrine are not higher in older persons, but when measured during submaximal and maximal exercise, norepinephrine levels are elevated. Conversely, epinephrine levels are higher in older persons under all conditions: resting, submaximal exercise, and maximal exercise (Fleg, Tzankoff, & Lakatta, 1985). Two groups of receptors are sensitive to these catecholamines, alpha (α) receptors and beta (β) receptors. The β-receptors predominate in the heart and are also found in the smooth muscle walls of the arterial tree. The catecholamines, via β-adrenergic stimulation, increase the heart rate. They also increase the contractility of the heart muscle, which contributes to amplifying stroke volume. These effects allow the heart to adjust to moderate and vigorous exercise.

With aging, the heart and vasculature become less sensitive to β-adrenergic stimulation; thus, the aging heart cannot achieve the maximum heart rate levels that were possible during youth. Cardiovascular adaptation to the onset and offset of exercise also slows. The age-related impairment of β-adrenergic function is an important limiting factor of cardiovascular performance during physical stress. In fact, this loss is thought to be one of the primary changes in cardiovascular function that occurs with aging in normal individuals who are free of cardiovascular disease (Lakatta, 1986).

The α-receptors are found on all smooth muscle cells in the walls of the arterial tree, whereas there are very few in the heart itself. Thus, α-adrenergic activity primarily assists in causing the blood vessels to constrict through smooth muscle contraction, whereas β-adrenergic stimulation causes smooth muscles to relax and blood vessels to dilate. With aging, the arterial wall smooth muscle becomes less sensitive, largely due to a decreased number of β-receptors, to the β-adrenergic dilator effects of catecholamines. Alpha-adrenergic responsiveness of the vasculature appears to remain intact (Lakatta, 1986), but the decrease in β-adrenoreceptors changes the balance between alpha and beta adrenoceptor function, so that peripheral vasculature leans toward vasoconstriction, thus increasing peripheral resistance. The smaller radius of the constricted arterioles provides a smaller tube through which blood must be pumped and consequently increases resistance to the pumping heart. Vanhoutte (1988) suggests that these changes are the hallmark of aging in precapillary vessels.

Total peripheral resistance represents the ease with which blood can flow from the smallest arteries (arterioles) into the capillaries. It is decreased by enlarging the radius of the arterioles. Total peripheral resistance increases about 1% a year with aging, even in the absence of coronary artery disease, due partly to increased rigidity of arterial vessels and partly to decreased biochemical mechanisms of vasodilation. Chronic exercise can dramatically decrease the total peripheral resistance in elderly individuals. Figure 4.2, a and b, shows the bloodflow to the calf muscle before and after several months of training. In this case the training

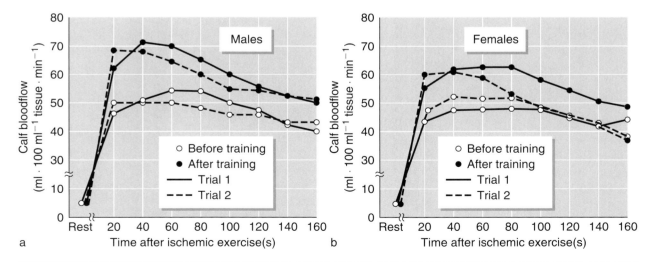

Figure 4.2 Changes in vasodilatory capacity of 60- to 72-year-old (a) males and (b) females.
From "Exercise Training Enhances Leg Vasodilatory Capacity of 65-Year-Old Men and Women" by W.H. Martin et al., 1990, *Journal of Applied Physiology*, **69**, p. 1807. Copyright 1990 by the American Physiological Society. Reprinted by permission.

effect appears to be greater for men than for women.

Age-related changes in neural control mechanisms of the arterial tree are also seen in *postural hypotension,* which is a loss in responsiveness of homeostatic reflexes. When young individuals rise quickly, their heart rate and diastolic blood pressure also rise to ensure an adequate blood supply to the brain. Baroreceptors in the aortic arch and the carotid sinus are sensitive to changes in blood pressure and initiate cardiovascular responses such as an increased heart rate to restore systemic blood pressure. These reflexes assist in maintaining bloodflow to vital organs when systemic blood pressure suddenly drops. When many elderly people move suddenly from a lying to a standing position, however, the baroreflexes fail and a substantial drop of systemic blood pressure occurs. This condition, postural hypotension, results in dizziness, confusion, weakness, or fainting. Age-related declines in baroreceptor reflex function occur even if the lack of response is not severe enough to be expressed as postural hypotension. Postural hypotension is fairly common in the elderly, ranging from 22% to 30% in the young elderly and 30% to 50% in those over 75 years of age (Docherty, 1990).

Although these changes in cardiovascular physiology are accepted by most researchers in the aging field, not all agree. Bennett and Gardiner (1988) suggest that if the most rigorous standards are applied to the available literature on the subject, the substantive evidence is weak for "well-known" age-related changes such as baroreflexes, sympathetic hyperactivation, adrenoreceptor dysfunction, and neurohumoral abnormalities. Nevertheless, until more valid information to the contrary is produced, it appears that substantive age-related changes do occur in the neural control of the cardiovascular system.

Heart Rate

The average resting heart rates of older adults are not significantly different from those of young adults, although the younger heart rates are more variable (Lipsitz, 1989). The maximum rate at which the heart can beat during heavy exercise, however, decreases about 5 to 10 beats a decade (Shephard, 1987), and no amount of training seems to be able to halt the inevitable decline. The average maximum heart rates of young (ages 24-28) and older (ages 50-68) men, taken from 15

research studies, are shown in Figure 4.3. The inevitability of an age-related decrease in maximum heart rate is clear. In all of these studies, the maximum heart rate was higher for young men than old, and training status had no effect.

Some older persons in good cardiovascular health develop greater end-diastolic volume, which increases stroke volume enough to compensate for the decrease in exercise heart rate. But when these individuals exercise, end-systolic volume is greater and the ejection fraction increase is less than that of younger individuals (Lakatta, 1990). The major contributor to the decline in the body's maximum ability to use oxygen is the slowing of the maximal heart rate, not a decreased stroke volume or a decrease in oxygen use in the peripheral musculature (Stamford, 1988).

The heart rates of older people also remain higher and recover more slowly after maximal exercise. Active older people who exercise consistently can walk longer during a treadmill test (Steinhaus et al., 1988), and the age effect on heart rate recovery after they complete the test is either greatly attenuated (Darr, Bassett, & Morgan, 1988) or nonexistent (Chick, Cagle, Vegas, Poliner, & Murata, 1991).

During submaximal work at a moderate intensity, the heart rate drifts slowly upward in both young and old people. That is, the heart beats faster for the same work load during the latter part of the work. In older individuals the upward drift is less than in young individuals, probably because the attenuation of sympathetic β-adrenergic stimulation that occurs with increasing age

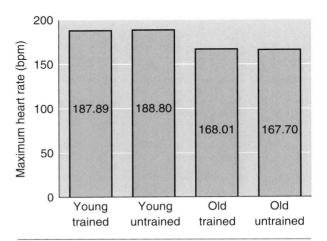

Figure 4.3 Maximum heart rate for young and old, trained and untrained subjects. Ages and standard deviations of subjects were: young trained = 27.09 ± 2.36; young untrained = 26.4 ± 1.98; old trained = 61.6 ± 4.9; old untrained = 59.1 ± 8.9.

depresses the heart rate's upward drift in older people. Van Loan et al. (1989) reported the heart rate response to a maximal voluntary isometric contraction, such as lifting a heavy weight, to be approximately 7 beats per minute (bpm) lower in older people, but Goldstraw and Warren (1985) failed to find any age differences. The first cardiac adaptation to isometric work is the withdrawal of parasympathetic stimulation of the heart; the second response is direct cardiac sympathetic stimulation.

Stroke Volume

Stroke volume is the amount of blood (in ml) that is pumped from the heart with each beat. The heart has the ability to regulate the strength of its own contractions. If a greater amount of blood is returned to the heart from the periphery, it increases the amount of blood in the heart ventricle and stretches the heart wall. The heart responds by contracting more vigorously. In this way the heart can respond to increased work demands by increasing the stroke volume. Stroke volume in the aging heart has been reported to decrease moderately, perhaps due to a decrease in preloading (i.e., the pumping action of exercising muscles, forced respiratory movements, and passive constriction of the veins). The decrease in stroke volume may also be caused by an increase of afterloading (increased peripheral resistance), a decrease of ventricular power, and the slower time that it takes the heart to reach peak force.

Total blood volume in older individuals is less, the tone of the peripheral veins is not as substantive, and the walls of their heart ventricles are stiffer than those of young people. Also, many older individuals have some degree of varicosity in their veins. All of these conditions decrease the blood volume that enters the heart ventricle during the preloading phase, thus reducing the amount of stretching of the heart muscle. The consequence is that less blood is available to eject. Safar (1990), however, contends that if subjects are screened for cardiovascular disease, little or no age-related change is seen in any of these variables.

Generally, individuals who remain physically active retain youthful function in many cardiovascular parameters. Regular exercise is estimated to retard the physiologic decline associated with old

age by as much as 50%. Systematic exercise produces several changes that enhance stroke volume and consequently retard age-related changes. One of the responses to exercise is the slowing of heart rate (bradycardia), which has the effect of increasing the diastolic phase of the cardiac cycle, improving the oxygen supply to the myocardium, and enabling stroke volume to be better maintained at high work levels. Physical training also increases total blood volume and the tone of peripheral veins, reducing vascular resistance, which in turn increases the preloading of the heart and amplifies stroke volume (Hagberg et al., 1985; Weisfeldt, Gerstenblith, & Lakatta, 1985). These effects are exactly opposite to those of bed rest, where blood volume decreases and stroke volume is reduced. Thus, stroke volume is greatly increased in exercisers and cardiac output is maintained even though their maximum heart rate decreases as they age (Landin, Linnemeier, Rothbaum, Chappelear, & Noble, 1985; Mahler, Cunningham, & Curfman, 1986; Zauner, 1985). In highly trained older persons, stroke volume may exceed that of much younger persons (Weisfeldt et al., 1985).

Cardiac Output

Cardiac output is the total amount of blood ejected from each ventricle of the heart in 1 min, expressed as $\dot{Q}$ (L/min). In exercise, it represents the ability of the system to deliver oxygen to the muscles. $\dot{Q}$ can also be expressed relative to body size, by dividing it by an estimate of body surface area. This ratio is called the *cardiac index*. Maximum cardiac output is calculated by multiplying the total amount of blood that can be ejected in one heart contraction (the maximum stroke volume) by the total number of times the heart can beat in one time period (the maximum heart rate). The higher the volume of blood pumped to the periphery, the greater the oxygen uptake and transport.

Researchers do not completely agree on the effects of aging on cardiac output; in fact, the literature on age-related changes in $\dot{Q}$ is somewhat confused. One reason for this confusion is that researchers have not carefully specified two factors that are critically important in understanding cardiac output: whether $\dot{Q}$ was measured under submaximal or maximal exercise conditions, and whether the subjects measured were trained or untrained. Some early researchers, such as Brandfonbrener, Landowne, and Shock (1955), found significant age-related declines in resting $\dot{Q}$, but their measures were of unhealthy subjects. Conversely, Rodeheffer et al. (1984), from data of the Baltimore Longitudinal Study, found no relation between $\dot{Q}$ and age at rest but significant increases in cardiac output with age at submaximal and maximal exercise. In healthy aging individuals free of cardiac disease, the major age-related cardiovascular change is a decrease in *maximum* heart rate. Therefore, resting and submaximal $\dot{Q}$ are relatively unchanged with age.

However, even in the face of an inevitable decline in maximum heart rate, $\dot{Q}$ in vigorous exercise may be maintained in aging individuals through a greater reliance on the Frank-Starling mechanism. (The Frank-Starling mechanism is a property of muscle tissue: When a muscle is stretched, it contracts with more force. This characteristic may be seen in Figure 5.4 (page 126), where changes in force are plotted against different lengths [degree of stretch] of muscle.) In other words, the age-related decline in maximum heart rate can be compensated for by increasing ventricular filling during the heart's relaxation phase (end-diastolic volume), leading to the ejection of a larger blood volume during systole. Young adults, therefore, increase cardiac output by increasing heart rate, whereas older adults increase cardiac output by a smaller increase in heart rate but a greater reliance on the Frank-Starling mechanism (Mann, Denenberg, Gash, Makler, and Bove, 1986). Because the Frank-Starling reflex can be enhanced and used as a compensatory mechanism, the cardiac output of healthy older individuals, both at rest and during exercise, can be maintained (Fleg, 1986; Geokas, Lakatta, Makinodan, & Timiras, 1990; Lund-Johansen, 1988). Persons with hypertension do, however, experience an age-related decline in cardiac output (Lund-Johansen, 1989).

Aerobic exercise training increases diastolic heart volume, stroke volume, and hence, cardiac output. At rest, and at submaximal workloads, cardiac output is similar for trained and untrained people. But as the exercise intensity increases, particularly during maximum exercise, trained people have a higher cardiac output than untrained people of the same age.

Arteriovenous Oxygen Difference

At the tissue level, some of the oxygen carried by arterial blood diffuses from the capillary, where it is highly concentrated, across the capillary membrane to the active tissue. There, oxygen is consumed and CO_2 is generated when food (glucose and fats) is metabolized to provide usable energy. Therefore, blood that has traversed the tissue capillary bed and entered the veins has less oxygen. At a given bloodflow rate through this tissue, the more oxygen used by the tissue, the greater the difference in the amount of oxygen contained in the arterioles and venules. This difference, which represents the efficiency of oxygen transfer to the tissues, is called the arteriovenous difference and is described as a-vO_2 difference (ml · L^{-1}). Hemoglobin concentration (g · L^{-1}) and bloodflow determine the quantity of available oxygen. Arteriovenous oxygen difference (ml · L^{-1}), at the whole body level, represents the efficiency with which tissue extracts the available oxygen.

The aging system is less able to redirect blood from inactive muscles, viscera, and skin to working muscles (Shephard, 1987). Thus, both the a-vO_2 difference measured directly in muscle and the difference in oxygen level between the arterial and venous blood that returns to the heart are lower during moderate to heavy exercise (Niinimaa & Shephard, 1978). Because chronic exercise increases the ability to redirect blood to working muscles and the muscle's ability to extract oxygen (aerobic metabolism) from the blood, it increases the a-vO_2 difference (Larson & Bruce, 1987).

Systolic and Diastolic Blood Pressure

Each time the heart contracts, it ejects a rush of blood that enters the arteries faster than that amount can be taken up by the arterial system and organs. Consequently, the pressure that is built up in the system with each heart beat is called the systolic pressure, and the pressure that remains in the arterial system while the heart is at rest is called the diastolic pressure. Systolic pressure reflects the amount of work that the heart is performing and also the strain of the arterial walls against ventricular contraction. Diastolic pressure indicates the amount of peripheral resistance encountered, or the ease with which blood is circulated to organs or muscles. A high diastolic pressure indicates that the pressure within the arteries remains high throughout much of the cardiac cycle. One way to express this is by *mean arterial pressure*, which is the average force exerted by the blood against the walls of the arteries throughout the full cardiac cycle. Arterial pressure increases with age, systolic

more than diastolic (Lakatta, 1990). Both pulse pressure (the difference between systolic and diastolic pressure) and systolic pressure increase.

With aging, the major blood vessels increase in rigidity, causing these arteries to accept the cardiac stroke volume less rapidly. The outcome is an age-related increase in resting pulse pressure and systolic blood pressure. A systolic pressure greater than 160 mmHg or a diastolic pressure greater than 95 mmHg is viewed as pathological, or hypertensive. At least 40% of people over age 65 have hypertension (Vokonas, Kannel, & Cupples, 1988). This percentage has ominous forebodings, because 65% to 70% of fatal and nonfatal cardiovascular events occur in hypertense persons (Klag, Whelton, & Appel, 1990). A high resting systolic pressure is also related to postural-related changes in blood pressure. Discussed more fully in chapter 6, one of the causes of falling for individuals over the age of 70 is that when they change position suddenly (e.g., stand up from being seated for a while), if blood pressure cannot be maintained adequately in the brain, they become dizzy or faint. The inability to maintain cerebral blood pressure upon standing (postural hypotension) is associated with high levels of systolic blood pressure (Harris, Lipsitz, Kleinman, & Cornoni-Huntley, 1991).

Many researchers and physicians regard regular exercise, which lowers systemic blood pressure slightly in many hypertensive and normotensive people, in combination with nutrition and behavior modification to be one of several nondrug treatments for hypertension. In one study, 641 Caucasian women between the ages of 50 and 89 were divided into physical activity categories of light (58%), moderate (24%), heavy (6%), or no activity (12%). As the activity intensity increased, systolic blood pressure decreased. The systolic blood pressure was approximately 20 mmHg lower in the heavy-activity group than in the no-activity group. Lower rates of hypertension were also associated with higher physical activity (Reaven, Barrett-Connor, & Edelstein, 1991).

The mechanisms by which exercise may reduce resting blood pressure (shown in Table 4.1) have been deduced largely from research on young to middle-aged subjects and perhaps should not be inferred to apply to all older populations. For example, the cardiovascular response of hypertensive elderly people during exercise is somewhat different. Maximum cardiac output and stroke volume decrease, systolic and diastolic blood pressures increase, and total peripheral resistance is

higher. These alterations need not preclude exercise programs for the hypertensive, however, because the myocardial demands of rehabilitation exercise programs are not excessive in older hypertensive persons (Montain, Jilka, Ehsani, & Hagberg, 1988). Physical exercise for the hypertensive elder is beneficial if the hypertension is controlled by medication and if the guidelines for exertion follow the principle of perceived exertion rather than external standards. Systolic pressure was lowered in postcoronary patients who exercised vigorously over a 3-year period. However, even though the drop in systolic pressure with exercise was statistically significant, it was also so small that its therapeutic significance was questionable (Shephard, 1987).

Peripheral Circulation

Bloodflow in the peripheral vasculature has only been *directly* measured in senescent beagles

**Table 4.1
Mechanisms by Which Exercise May
Reduce Resting Blood Pressure**

Cardiovascular
  Reduces resting heart rate
  Decreases resting cardiac output
  Reduces peripheral vascular resistance
  Increases capillary density, vascularization
  Reduces plasma volume

Endocrinal, metabolic
  Decreases body fat
  Reduces sympathetic nervous system responsiveness
  Reduces plasma insulin levels
  Increases insulin sensitivity
  Improves glucose tolerance

Nutritional, body composition
  Reduces body salt (diuretic effect)
  Decreases body fat
  Increases muscle mass and strength

Behavior
  Reduces stress
  Decreases anxiety

Note. From "Physical Exercise in the Elderly" by A.P. Goldberg and J.M. Hagberg. In *Handbook of the Biology of Aging* (3rd ed.) (p. 415) by E.L. Schneider and J.W. Rowe (Eds.), 1990, New York: Academic Press. Copyright 1990 by Academic Press, Inc. Reprinted by permission.

(Haidet & Parsons, 1991), not in elderly humans. In these senescent dogs, peripheral circulation was maintained during exercise. That is, even though the dogs' cardiac output and functional capacity were reduced, bloodflow per unit of muscle was maintained in both submaximal and maximal exercise. One mechanism by which Haidet and Parsons (1991) explained the maintenance of peripheral bloodflow in aging muscle is that blood is shunted from splanchnic areas, such as kidneys, intestine, pancreas, spleen, and stomach, to active muscle tissue. Although their explanation was based on canine physiology (dogs have a larger spleen blood volume reserve relative to humans and can release higher levels of red blood cells into the circulation during exercise), it is known that an absolute work load elicits a greater sympathetic nervous system response from older adults than young ones. One of the characteristics of a sympathetic response to exercise is that splanchnic bloodflow decreases. Indeed, the perfusion of the active muscle may be relatively greater in old than in young muscles, because maximal exercise occurs at lower absolute aerobic capacity levels in old animals. This relatively larger peripheral perfusion in older muscles may compensate partially for age-related reductions of maximal cardiac output, decrements in peripheral metabolic potential, and lower arterial O_2 content.

Aerobic exercise greatly improves peripheral bloodflow, regardless of age or gender. Hagberg et al. (1985) reported that the peripheral resistance of older male masters athletes who had engaged in strenuous physical training for many years was nearly 30% lower during exercise than that of their sedentary age-matched peers. This response of the peripheral vasculature to training also occurs rather quickly in both young and old adults. After only a few months of training, previously sedentary older subjects can achieve the same peripheral bloodflow responses to exercise exhibited by highly trained older road racers (Martin et al., 1990). The physical conditioning of the peripheral vasculature is related more to the occurrence of physical activity per se than to a high exercise capacity (Martin et al., 1991). Of course in elderly individuals who have pathological peripheral circulation conditions, such as phlebitis or intermittent claudication, peripheral bloodflow is impaired and exercise capacity is limited.

Blood Volume and Blood Constituents

The major constituents of blood are plasma, white blood cells, and red blood cells. Of these, the number and hemoglobin content of red blood cells determine the oxygen-carrying capacity of the blood. The proportion of red blood cells to total blood volume, the *hematocrit*, provides an approximation of the hemoglobin content of the blood. Hemoglobin, an iron-containing protein in the blood that has the ability to carry oxygen, is a main component of red blood cells. About 98% of the oxygen transported in the blood is carried by hemoglobin, which is expressed as grams per liter $(g \cdot L^{-1})$. Normal variations in hemoglobin concentration (140-180 and 115-160 $g \cdot L^{-1}$ of blood, for men and women respectively) have an effect on the oxygen-carrying capacity of blood, but this effect is not functionally important at rest or during submaximal exercise. If the iron content of the red blood cell is significantly decreased, such as occurs in iron deficiency anemia, it decreases the blood's oxygen-carrying capacity. Individuals who have certain types of anemia, or low hemoglobin levels, have a lessened capacity for even mild aerobic exercise.

If hematocrit and hemoglobin decline with aging, the change is very small and gradual. Bowdler and Foster (1987) propose that aging is associated with a slight but significant, gradual decline in hematocrit, beginning in the relatively early decades. However, Timiras and Brownstein (1987) found that mean hemoglobin levels were maintained in healthy aging individuals until about 85 years of age, at which time the levels decreased slightly. The results of animal research have suggested that the ability to replace red blood cells is maintained in aged mice, but the ability to increase red blood cells after hemorrhage or trauma may be reduced. Boggs and Patrene (1985) found that although the survival of red blood cells was not different in old mice, the recovery of hematocrit began more slowly after experimentally-induced extensive bleeding. They also reported that the ability to use iron in order to develop new red blood cells following extensive bleeding was twice as fast in young mice.

Anemia is prevalent among older individuals, especially those over age 70, but it is difficult to tell whether the decline in hematocrit and hemoglobin values are a function of aging or of other, more indirect factors. In a review of 1,024 geriatric screening charts, 17.7% of males and 8.4% of females were classified as anemic (Timiras & Brownstein, 1987). A major cause of anemia in older individuals is change in diet, which may entail not only a decrease in total calories per day but changes in types of food consumed. Many older people, especially those living alone, are challenged by loss of appetite, impaired mobility to obtain groceries, reduced income to purchase food, and lowered capacity to cook. Other age-related contributors to anemia may be unrecognized internal bleeding or deterioration of gastrointestinal absorption of iron or vitamin B_{12}. Some evidence suggests, however, that mean hemoglobin levels are not different in the elderly, except in males over 85, and should not be expected to change with advancing age.

Daily exercise is thought to stimulate a more rapid rate of red blood cell development. The number of red blood cells may be higher in highly conditioned older athletes, a condition which should provide optimum oxygen delivery to the tissues, but there is also more destruction of red blood cells during exercise. Hemoglobin levels fell significantly in elderly men aged 62 to 72 while running a 2,100-km relay over a 17-day period. The loss of hemoglobin was 20% more than that experienced during their training period for this race (Nye, Sutherland, Jefferson, & Robertson, 1985). This amount of physical work is highly unusual for either young or old people, and though these hemoglobin losses indicate that strenuous exercise can reduce hemoglobin, the information is not likely to be applicable to elderly who are participating in normal daily exercise programs.

Lipids are fats that circulate in the blood. The two most well known, because they are identified as risk factors leading to heart disease, are cholesterol and triglycerides. Serum cholesterol, which is comprised of several types of fat, increases with age. The cholesterol that is identified as a high-density lipoprotein (HDL) represents less risk and may even have some protective benefits. High levels of low-density lipoproteins (LDL), however, are considered to present a risk for cardiovascular disease. Saltin and Grimby (1968) found that even in elderly orienteers (extremely active overland hikers) serum cholesterol levels were higher than in younger people but still lower than levels in their age group peers. Generally, chronic aerobic exercise increases the protective HDL-cholesterol commensurate with the intensity of the exercise, but the effect is lost when the exercise program is terminated. Some researchers suggest that even brisk walking from 2-1/2 to 4 hours a week increases HDLs, though others maintain that there is no documented effect of low-intensity exercise on cholesterol (Foster, Hume, Byrnes, Dickinson, & Chatfield, 1989). Goldberg and Hagberg (1990)

concluded after reviewing several studies that aerobic exercise increases HDLs. The effect of exercise on HDLs in the elderly is less clear. Seals, Allen, et al. (1984) and Seals, Hagberg, et al. (1984) suggested that physical conditioning improves lipoprotein lipids in older people, but only when weight is lost in conjunction with the exercise program. In another intervention study, the level of HDLs in men and women over age 60 was significantly increased 7% after a 3-day-a-week, 14-month exercise training program (Blumenthal et al., 1991). Although HDL seems to be augmented, there were no increases in some of the HDL components (Allen, Willcox, Teague-Baker, & Lei, 1985). Exercise may also reduce LDLs (Schwartz, 1988).

Moderate levels of physical activity may attenuate age-related elevation of some blood lipids. A decrease in serum triglycerides was observed in two groups of women, one relatively younger (27-40 years) than the other (43-59 years), who participated in an 8-month physical fitness program (Van der Eems & Ismail, 1985). Goode, Firstbrook, and Shephard (1966) also reported decreases in triglycerides in subjects who followed a vigorous exercise program.

Pulmonary Function

All living cells in the body use oxygen for metabolism and produce carbon dioxide as a by-product. The pulmonary system acts as an exchange mechanism through which oxygen can enter the bloodstream and carbon dioxide can be expelled. Therefore, in conjunction with the circulatory system, the pulmonary system provides a means by which oxygen is delivered to cells and carbon dioxide is removed. The pulmonary system includes the lungs, into which ambient air is drawn by breathing, and airways that bring air into contact with the delicate lung tissues in which oxygen and carbon dioxide are exchanged.

The aging effects on the pulmonary system are primarily limited to its function during maximal strenuous exercise, which challenges lung volumes and the ventilatory capacity of the lungs. Aging reduces the elasticity of the lung tissue and chest walls, which in turn increases the work involved in breathing. For a given external effort, older people have a higher respiratory work rate. Aerobic training improves some pulmonary functions, but as will be discussed later, age-related decreases in pulmonary function are not the major limiting factor in work capacity. Age-related pulmonary deficits, however, do reduce respiratory support for speech, which in turn negatively affects the quality of life (Ringel & Chodzko-Zajko, 1987).

Lung Volumes

The volume of air that is cycled through the lungs is customarily categorized into four major volumes: tidal volume, inspiratory reserve, expiratory reserve, and residual volume. These volumes, as described in average young individuals, are shown graphically in Figure 4.4. The effects of aging are shown as dotted lines in the figure.

Most pulmonary volumes change very little with aging. During resting conditions, *tidal volume* (TV), the volume of air inspired or expired during each respiratory cycle, and respiratory rate change imperceptibly with increasing age. In fact, tidal volume is relatively unaffected by either aging or physical training. *Functional residual capacity* (FRC), the amount of air remaining in the lungs after a normal expiration, is also relatively unchanged, as are the *inspiratory reserve volume* (IRV), the amount of air that can be inhaled above the peak inhalation point of tidal volume, and the *expiratory reserve volume* (ERV), the amount of air that can be expired after a normal expiration.

Residual volume (RV), the amount of air remaining in the lungs after a complete expiratory effort (normal expiration + expiratory reserve), changes relatively little in elderly, healthy, nonsmokers. In extremely sedentary individuals and smokers, however, residual volume increases slightly with age, although in the absence of pathology, this increase probably has little significance for the resting level oxygen-carbon dioxide exchanges necessary for daily activities.

The total volume of air in the lungs at the end of a maximal inspiration, *total lung capacity* (TLC, tidal volume + inspiratory reserve + expiratory reserve + residual volume), also remains unchanged with age. Although total lung capacity does not change much with age, the fact that residual volume increases means that the *ratio* of residual volume to total lung capacity (RV/TLC) increases with age in sedentary persons. In young individuals, the residual volume is about 20% of the total lung capacity. In persons over age 60, it increases to about 40%.

One of the lung volumes that is affected by age is *forced vital capacity* (FVC), the maximum amount of air that can be exhaled after a maximum inhalation. In other words, it is the total volume of air that can be voluntarily moved from maximum inspiration to maximum expiration. Forced vital capacity decreases linearly approximately 4% to 5% each decade in the average population. Unusual decreases may be indicative of pulmonary pathology.

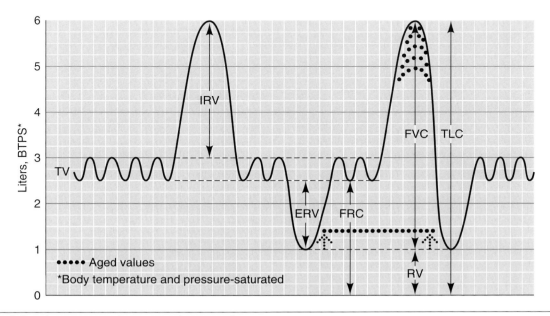

Figure 4.4 Changes in pulmonary volumes with aging.
From *Exercise Physiology* (p. 240) by W.D. McArdle, F.I. Katch, and V.L. Katch, 1991, Philadelphia: Lea & Febiger. Adapted by permission.

Figure 4.5 shows that the forced vital capacity of 65-year-old men and women differs considerably from that of 25-year-olds. In a longitudinal study of well-trained individuals, however, the forced vital capacity of these persons at ages 40 to 45 was the same as when they were in their 20s (Åstrand, Åstrand, Hallback, & Kilbom, 1973; Shephard, 1987).

Another method of assessing pulmonary function is to determine dynamic volumes, that is, the ventilatory capacity for a given period. The amount of air that can be forced out of the lungs in 1 min (forced expiratory volume, $FEV_{1.0}$) decreases progressively with age. Extraordinary losses in $FEV_{1.0}$ indicate obstructive pulmonary disease. Shephard (1987) showed that $FEV_{1.0}$ decreased more with age than vital capacity, even in healthy individuals. However, as long as $FEV_{1.0}$ is 70% or more of the maximum, daily function and even exercise should not be affected. Other measures of pulmonary dynamic function, such as the maximum voluntary ventilation, peak expiratory air flow, and the amount of air that can be forcefully expired in 1 s decrease with age.

Alveolar-to-Arterial Gas Exchange

Oxygen and carbon dioxide, driven by differential pressures, pass back and forth between the alveoli of the lungs and the blood through the alveolar membrane. It is through this alveolar-to-arterial gas exchange that the body is able to move oxygen from the air in the lungs to the bloodstream, which transports the oxygen to all body tissues. This exchange decreases in efficiency over the years

(Mahler, Cunningham, & Curfman, 1986), and pulmonary pressure and pulmonary vascular resistance also increase even in the absence of coronary artery disease (Davidson & Fee, 1990). These changes, although not fully understood, may be attributed to age-related changes in systemic circulation, such as an increased systemic afterload resistance. Pulmonary diffusing capacity for oxygen is lower among the elderly. Unfortunately, chronic exercise has very little influence on the gas exchange system. Although the total amount of blood flowing in the lungs (pulmonary bloodflow) rises linearly with exercise-enhanced work capacity (Dempsey, Johnson, & Saupe, 1990), lung diffusion capacity and pulmonary capillary blood volume remain unchanged, even in highly trained individuals. The capacity of the lungs to diffuse oxygen to the blood, as well as the total volume of blood in lung capillaries, is also uninfluenced by training. Nor does training appear to change the capability of the airways to produce higher flow rates (Dempsey et al., 1990).

Ventilation

Ventilation ($\dot{V}_E$) is the volume of air breathed per minute. Not only does pulmonary ventilation during maximal exercise in men and women decrease with aging, it also recovers more slowly in older untrained people (Figure 4.6). At the end of recovery, younger people have higher $\dot{V}_E$ than older people, perhaps because the young develop higher lactic acid levels at maximum work. During a submaximal work bout, pulmonary ventilation increases slowly for both young and old, but the ventilation in younger people increases more than in older persons. After submaximal work ends, the recovery of ventilation is slower in older individuals. Postsubmaximal exercise recovery also is slower in older people, regardless of their fitness level (Chick et al., 1991). The age-related differences in recovery time occur, however, in the kinetics of recovery, not in the extent of recovery. At 10 min postexercise, the recovery rates of older persons have caught up to those of the younger exercisers (Chick et al., 1991).

The percentage of maximal voluntary pulmonary ventilation that a person can breathe during maximal work is lower in the average older person, but this is more a function of health status than chronological age. Older individuals who have been sedentary, through participation in an

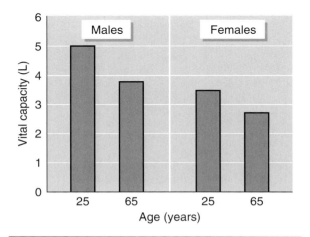

Figure 4.5 Changes in pulmonary gas volumes with aging.
Data from Shephard (1987, p. 57).

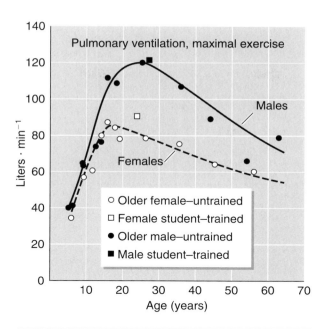

Figure 4.6 Pulmonary ventilation measured after maximal exercise.
From *Textbook of Work Physiology* (p. 232) by P.O. Åstrand and K. Rodahl, 1986, New York: McGraw-Hill. Copyright 1986 by P.O. Åstrand and K. Rodahl. Reprinted by permission.

aerobic exercise program, can increase their percentage of maximal voluntary pulmonary ventilation during maximal exercise to that of highly trained athletes of similar age (Yerg, Seals, Hagberg, & Holloszy, 1985). The pulmonary ventilatory equivalent, another measure of lung function (i.e., the number of liters of pulmonary ventilation needed to transport a liter of oxygen), does not change much with age.

To a large extent, respiration is controlled by the contraction and relaxation of the diaphragm as well as other muscles located in the thoracic cavity. Thus, respiration can be termed an energy consuming activity. The cost of respiration for a given exercise task is higher for older people, increasing about 3% to 5% each year (Brischetto, Millman, Peterson, Silage, & Pack, 1984; Takishima, Shindoh, Kikuchi, Hida, & Inoue, 1990). Also, the lower the overall aerobic capacity of the individual, the higher the cost of respiration when compared to the total aerobic capacity. In very old people, the cost of respiration in combination with a very low total oxygen capacity leaves considerably less oxygen available for physical work.

What factors contribute to an increased cost of respiration? The rib cage becomes stiffer with age, and the compliance of the chest wall decreases.

This increased stiffness may lead to a restriction of chest wall movement and an increase in elastic load on the respiratory muscles. Also, airway resistance increases and the amount of air that can be forcefully expired in 1 min decreases, leading to an increase in the resistive load of the respiratory system. Respiratory muscle strength decreases with age, which for a given level of pulmonary ventilation may require recruitment of accessory muscles, which in turn increases the oxygen cost of breathing. Finally, some of the physical changes that take place with aging, such as arthritis and a loss of coordination, may create a greater challenge to the respiratory process and contribute to an increased cost of breathing. Chronic physical exercise can decrease the cost of respiration during submaximal exercise.

Generally, in healthy individuals the aged pulmonary system functions very well under resting and moderate exercise conditions. Because maximal oxygen consumption (discussed in the following section) is related to the amount of oxygen absorbed by the lungs, one might assume that pulmonary function is an important limiting factor in maximal work capacity. However, the pulmonary system is usually not the limiting factor in exercise performance, although in some cases it can be. People quit a physical work bout because of the limitation on cardiac output caused by a decreased maximum heart rate, not severe breathlessness. The lungs offer no major barrier to gas exchange, at least in individuals younger than age 70.

Aerobic Capacity

Aerobic capacity is the ability of the cardiopulmonary system to deliver blood and oxygen to active muscles and of these muscles to use oxygen and energy substrates to perform work during maximum physical stress (Åstrand & Rodahl, 1986). Aerobic capacity is determined by measuring the maximal oxygen uptake ($\dot{V}O_2max$) that can be achieved during physical work. Usually it is measured while subjects walk or jog on a treadmill or ride a bicycle ergometer. However, $\dot{V}O_2max$ can be measured in any type of physical work condition in which inspired and expired air can be monitored. Although assessing an individual's physical fitness status is so complex that there really is no one measurement that perfectly summarizes an individual's physical fitness, medical personnel, sports medicine specialists, and exercise physiologists consider $\dot{V}O_2$max to be the best single index of fitness available. The amount of oxygen that an individual can consume is a good measure of how much energy that person can expend.

$\dot{V}O_2$max, which is measured either in absolute terms (liters of oxygen per minute [L · min^{-1}]), or in terms relative to body mass (milliliters of oxygen per minute per kilogram body weight [ml · kg^{-1} · min^{-1}]), is, in cross-sectionally derived averages from sedentary adults, 1% lower in each additional year of life. Figure 4.7 shows $\dot{V}O_2$max values, gleaned from many studies in the literature, for four categories of physical activity: athletes, physically active adults, short-term trained adults, and sedentary adults. It is very clear from this graph that $\dot{V}O_2$max declines somewhat with aging, irrespective of the amount of training that an individual undergoes. All of the regression lines in Figure 4.7 have a downward slope.

The decline appears to be greater when $\dot{V}O_2$max is measured in longitudinal research designs than when it is measured in cross-sectional designs, probably because subjects at older ages who volunteer to be measured in cross-sectional fitness studies tend to be more physically fit than those who do not volunteer. The few studies in which subjects have been followed over an extended period suggest that the loss in $\dot{V}O_2$max each year may be greater than has been estimated.

A major reason why $\dot{V}O_2$max decreases with age is that maximum heart rate decreases with age, but at least part of the $\dot{V}O_2$max decline is probably due to an age-related decrease in muscle

mass, the ability to redirect bloodflow from organs to working muscles, and the ability of muscles to use oxygen. Because $\dot{V}O_2$max is calculated from both the amount of oxygen that can be delivered to muscles and the amount used by the muscles, the magnitude of muscle mass has a large bearing on the $\dot{V}O_2$max value. For example, work capacity is higher for males than females at any age, largely because males have more muscle mass than females do. When work capacity is compared in older subjects, the total work that can be done on a bicycle ergometer in 30 s is also higher in males than in females (Makrides, Heigenhauser, McCartney, & Jones, 1985). Age-related loss of performance is also greater in women than in men (Shephard, 1987), perhaps because although a substantial loss of muscle occurs in both genders, women lose a higher percentage of their muscle mass than do men. Also, body fat is 2 to 2-1/2 times higher in women than in men, so even if women had the same muscle mass men have, their $\dot{V}O_2$max would be lower in terms relative to total body mass.

If $\dot{V}O_2$max is related to muscle mass rather than body weight, the loss of $\dot{V}O_2$max each decade and the gender differences are not so great. In one study, when $\dot{V}O_2$max was normalized for an estimate of the amount of muscle, the decline attributable to age went from 60% to 14% in men and from 50% to 8% in women. With age, however, the ability to shunt blood from nonworking to working muscles decreases. Muscles also become less effective in extracting oxygen from blood to support work (Shephard, 1987).

A minimum $\dot{V}O_2$ of 13 ml · kg^{-1} · min^{-1} is considered necessary for independent living. The decreased $\dot{V}O_2$ that accompanies aging may accelerate from age 65 to 75 and again from 75 to 85. Thus, if the downward slope of $\dot{V}O_2$max in Figure 4.7 is followed to these older ages, it is apparent that the oxygen delivery and utilization system of many of the least fit older individuals falls below the minimum necessary to maintain an independent lifestyle (Shephard, 1987), and many 65-year-old sedentary people are poised perilously near the edge of disability.

Exercise training, although it cannot prevent an age-related loss in $\dot{V}O_2$max, can substantially change the overall levels of $\dot{V}O_2$max. Cumulative findings from research on training effects in the elderly support the notion that a substantial amount of physical deterioration previously attributed to aging can be prevented, delayed, or in

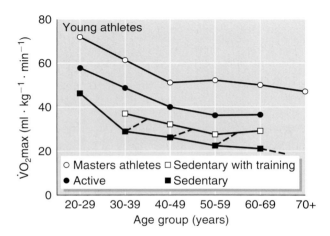

Figure 4.7   Average maximal oxygen uptake values.

many cases even reversed (Rowe & Kahn, 1987). In fact, the existing evidence seems to support the notion that a lifestyle of habitual intensive exercise makes a striking difference in the aging of physiological markers such as $\dot{V}O_2$max (Kasch, Boyer, Van Camp, Verity, & Wallace, 1990). Clearly, when sedentary elderly people begin exercise programs, aerobic capacity can be restored to acceptable levels (Posner, Gorman, Klein, & Woldow, 1986), and training effects are similar for both males and females (Hopkins, Murrah, Hoeger, & Rhodes, 1990). These beneficial exercise effects can be seen in both oxygen pulse (the oxygen uptake per beat of the heart) and $\dot{V}O_2$max. Figure 4.8 shows the cross-sectional oxygen pulse values obtained from 13 studies. Although older trained men (average age ~61) did not have higher oxygen pulse values than younger trained men (average age ~26), their values were higher than those of untrained younger men (average age ~26). Also, in 10 of the intervention studies, the average oxygen pulse values increased 15% from pre- to post-exercise tests.

The effects of training on $\dot{V}O_2$max can be seen in Figure 4.7. Training in older persons raises the overall level of oxygen use, in some cases higher than the values for much younger individuals. Thus, trained adults at any age are on a higher parallel-aging curve than untrained individuals. The highest levels of $\dot{V}O_2$max at any age are those exhibited by competitive runners who maintain an intense, daily training schedule and who compete on a regular basis. These high levels, which are not approached even by the physically active group, undoubtedly are due largely to genetic

talent for running in addition to intense, prolonged training. In one longitudinal study, Kasch and his colleagues (1990) reported a decline in $\dot{V}O_2$max of only 13% in a group of older men (ages 45-68) who maintained their exercise training over an 18-year period. This decline was much less than the 41% decline in maximal oxygen consumption of the older men (ages 52-70) who had not exercised over a similar period. The "Sedentary with training" line in Figure 4.7 shows that when middle-aged or older individuals begin a training program, they can achieve significant improvements, ranging from 10% to 25%, in cardiovascular function and aerobic capacity (Blumenthal et al., 1991; Shephard, 1987), even in individuals 70 to 79 years old who have never exercised before (Hagberg et al., 1989). The "Sedentary with training" group line represents the average of the improvements made by sedentary older groups in several different studies. The small dotted lines that go from the "Sedentary" to the "Sedentary with training" group line represent the improvements that might be predicted for sedentary groups at each age who undergo exercise-training programs.

Older individuals do not achieve the same absolute gains in maximal oxygen consumption that younger people achieve, but their relative gains are very similar. Even the oldest age groups respond favorably to physical conditioning *if* the exercise programs are individually prescribed, cautiously increased, and carefully supervised by professionals. In nursing-home patients or frail-but-independent elderly who have been sedentary all their lives, even low-intensity programs provide an adequate training stimulus (Foster et al., 1989; Naso, Carner, Blankfort-Doyle, & Coughey, 1990).

It is clear that the elderly can derive great benefits from a consistent exercise program. The American College of Sports Medicine has summarized this in a position statement: "Age in itself does not appear to be a deterrent to endurance training" (1978, p. 8). Shephard (1987) suggests that an increase in $\dot{V}O_2$max of 20%, even though it may be small in absolute amount, is not trivial. He maintains that a gain of this size "offers the equivalent of 20 years of rejuvenation—a benefit that can be matched by no other treatment or lifestyle change" (1987, p. 5). But to maintain aerobic capacity, exercise must be continued on a systematic basis throughout life. Marti and Howald (1990) showed that even former highly-trained runners

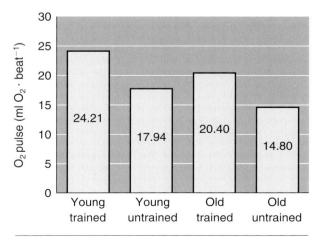

Figure 4.8   Oxygen pulse (ml $O_2 \cdot$ beat^{-1}) for young and old, trained and untrained men.

decreased in aerobic capacity and increased body fat if they did not continue training. These statements refer primarily to aerobic exercise programs, which have been shown to be much better than isometric strength-training programs at improving physical capacity in the elderly (Sagiv, Fisher, Yaniv, & Rudoy, 1989).

Anaerobic Capacity

In the absence of oxygen, anaerobic processes can provide energy. Anaerobic glycolysis is the primary energy mechanism used to produce energy during strenuous exercise that cannot be maintained for longer than about 120 to 150 s. It allows such activities as dashing up a flight of stairs or running for a bus without having to wait for the cardiorespiratory system to "catch up" and supply oxygen to the muscles. The anaerobic energy system is a short-term system in which stored energy in the form of glycogen is used; but it incurs oxygen debt. Also, lactic acid, produced in muscle as a by-product of the anaerobic processes, eventually must be removed. The appearance of significant lactic acid levels in the blood indicates that the energy demands of the muscle cell are no longer being met solely by oxidative metabolism; therefore blood lactate concentration may be used as an index of anaerobic metabolism and circulatory characteristics of the contracting muscle (Karlsson, 1985). As exercise becomes more intense, the lactic acid increase accelerates. When lactic acid reaches certain levels, nonoxidative energy production and the lactate removal process cannot keep blood lactate low, therefore exercise must be discontinued (Karlsson, 1985).

Anaerobic work capacity is difficult to measure clinically. One performance test of anaerobic capacity is the Katch test (1973) in which subjects must pedal a bicycle ergometer as fast as possible for 40 s against a high resistance. Anaerobic capacity is determined by the total amount of work done. Another test involves 30 s of all-out supermaximal exercise on an arm-cranking device. The assumption made in these tests is that the average power produced represents the individual's glycolytic capacity. These tests are rarely appropriate for or applied to the average elderly person; older individuals are much more adapted to aerobic than to power work. In the unusual

circumstances where anaerobic capacity is assessed, researchers generally use tests of blood lactate.

Both lactic acid production and removal decline as people age. The aged anaerobic system does not work as quickly to produce energy (thus increasing lactic acid levels), and when lactic acid is produced, it is not cleared as quickly. The probable reasons for the decline in the anaerobic system are loss of large-muscle mass and a decrease in the size and number of glycolytic fast-twitch muscle fibers, which are known to rely more on glycolysis. Intramuscular bloodflow is also lower in older people, which contributes to a slower recovery from high-lactate conditions.

Lactic acid is not produced only during short, intensive power activities but also during moderate, submaximal aerobic work. Lactic acid remains at low levels in an untrained individual until the work load reaches about 50% to 55% of the person's maximal aerobic capacity. At that time, the individual's oxidative systems are unable to keep up with the energy demands required for that level of work. The measurement of lactic acid produced during a longer bout of endurance work is obtained by using maximal endurance-testing protocols, such as treadmill running to exhaustion. In such tests, the point at which the rate of lactic acid accumulation dramatically increases above resting level is called the blood lactate threshold. After a run to exhaustion, the blood lactates of young men, though higher than those of older men, are cleared from the blood quicker. This is shown in Figure 4.9; blood lactate levels of younger individuals at 7 min after the treadmill test had already stabilized, indicating that their tissues were clearing lactate rapidly. However, the blood lactates of older men (ages 35-65) continued to rise 3 to 7 min *after* exercise (Tzankoff & Norris, 1979). The observation that the oldest group was also stable in lactate levels was an unexpected finding in this study. Tzankoff and Norris speculated that, because it is unusual for 75-year-olds to train intensively, this particular group of older subjects might have been demonstrating the "survivor effect" of superior performance often seen in exceptional older performers. This group also had the smallest number of subjects of any age group in the study ($n = 10$) and might have been a biased sample of the 75-year-old age category. Slower clearing of blood lactate in older adults may partially explain age-related decrements in endurance.

The blood lactate threshold occurs earlier for older adults than for young adults at a similar work

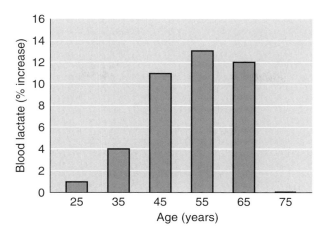

Figure 4.9 Blood lactate concentrations after maximal treadmill exercise.

From "Endurance Training for Elderly Women: Moderate vs. Low Intensity" by V.L. Foster et al., 1989, *Journal of Gerontology: Medical Sciences*, **44**, p. M186. Copyright 1989 by The Gerontological Society of America. Reprinted by permission.

load. For example, if both age groups jog at the same speed and cover the same distance, older adults will accumulate lactic acid sooner, because they will reach a work load of 50% to 55% of their maximum oxygen consumption sooner. If both groups exercise to exhaustion, however, the young adults will eventually accumulate higher levels of lactic acid, because young men have more muscle mass to produce lactate. During these tests, at the same submaximal work level, oxygen uptake increases slowly in proportion to the rise in plasma lactic acids, but the $\dot{V}O_2$ drift is less in older individuals than in younger individuals (Chick et al., 1991).

Anaerobic power is the ability of the individual to mobilize energy stored in the muscles during an ultrashort exercise, such as a vertical jump. The jump for height can be used as an indirect measure of anaerobic power. Even in power-trained or endurance-trained masters athletes, anaerobic power declined 50% by age 75 (Grassi, Cerretelli, Narici, & Marconi, 1991).

Like aerobic exercise, life-long training of the anaerobic system appears to maintain the system. Reaburn and Mackinnon (1990), measuring lactic acid accumulation in masters competitors after a sprint swimming race, found no age-related deterioration trends in the anaerobic energy system. Swimmers aged 46 to 56+, who were elite competitors training for the 1988 World Masters Swimming Championships, did not differ from 25- to 35-year-old swimmers in producing and removing lactic

acid. The researchers concluded, on the basis of these results, that the ability of older male swimmers to produce, translocate, and remove lactic acid over short periods is maintained by rigorous, systematic training in swimming.

What mechanisms could explain this finding? Training may eliminate the age-associated declines in myocardial contractility, muscle mass, and the number and size of fast-twitch muscle fibers. Suominen et al. (1980) found that the fast-twitch fiber areas in aged endurance runners were greater than those of their sedentary counterparts. The number of motor units may also be maintained with endurance training. A more complete discussion of the effects of training on muscular strength and endurance is presented in chapter 5. For the present, it is important to note that high-intensity exercise training is necessary to produce the changes that affect lactate production and removal (Foster et al., 1989).

The Debilitating Effects of Disuse

Throughout this chapter the positive effects of physical activity on the decline of cardiovascular functions have been noted. However, the long-term negative effects of physical inactivity are so debilitating, not only cardiovascularly but also on the whole body, that further discussion is merited. Experiments on bed rest have shown that only a short period of physical inactivity, even in relatively young subjects, can have negative effects on cardiovascular function, blood pressure, and hormonal responses to exercise. A lifetime of physical disuse can have catastrophic effects, eroding strength and mobility and eventually transforming an individual into an exceedingly frail, immobile, and totally dependent human being. To compound the problems of disuse, the low levels of daily caloric expenditure that accompany physical inactivity contribute to an increase in body fat, especially upper body fat, and an increased ratio of body fat to muscle mass. An increase in body fat, particularly in the upper body, increases the prevalence of risk factors for atherosclerosis and Type II diabetes.

Human frailty has three dimensions (Bortz, 1983), shown in Figure 4.10. The first dimension, time, relentlessly drains energy and vitality. No one has yet found a way to halt the passage of time. Inevitably—for everyone—when enough

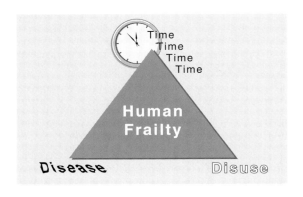

Figure 4.10   The three dimensions of human frailty: time, disease, and disuse.

time passes, death occurs. The second dimension, disease, is due to internal errors or external agents that damage body systems and lead to weakness, system fatigue, frailty, and eventually death. Science and technology have developed miraculous preventives and cures for many diseases; thus, limited control over the second dimension is available. The third dimension, disuse, although far less publicized, is also significant in the transformation from robustness to frailty. In contrast to the previous two dimensions, the majority of individuals have, within some constraints, almost total control over the extent to which they choose to use their mental, physical, and social capacities.

Bortz (1983) was led to articulate the deleterious effects that disuse has on the physical system from his personal experience with a leg broken in a skiing accident.

> When the cast was removed, I found my leg giving all the appearance of the limb of a person forty or fifty years older. It was withered, discolored, stiff, painful. I could not believe this leg belonged to me.
>
> The similarity of changes due to enforced inactivity to those commonly attributed to aging was striking. And, in fact, if one were to go to all the standard textbooks of geriatrics and write down all the changes which seem to accompany aging, set the list aside, and then go to the textbooks of work physiology and write down all the changes subsequent to inactivity—and then compare the two lists, one would see that they are virtually identical.
>
> The coincidence is not random. It is intense. It forces the conclusion that at least part of what passes as change due to age

is not caused by age at all but by disuse. (p. 2)

Information on the debilitating effects of disuse, which has largely surfaced from research on bed rest, water immersion, and more recently, from research on weightlessness in space, is compelling. All of these conditions drastically alter three classes of stimuli that humans experience: hydrostatic pressure, compression force on long bones, and level of physical exercise (Greenleaf, 1984). Prolonged periods of sitting in recliners or on couches simulates bed rest, and transient bed-rest effects are easily seen. For example, when many older people stand up from prolonged sitting or lying, the relatively sudden change in fluid compartment volumes lowers blood pressure so that they experience a light-headed sensation. If the fall in blood pressure is significant, they will faint (Convertino, Montgomery, & Greenleaf, 1984). Exercising the lower limbs assists in the venous return process, improving the bloodflow and pressure needed to maintain adequate perfusion of the brain. Exercise also maintains important reflexes that compensate for changes in posture.

Especially in the elderly, there are three major problems that can develop from bed rest in healthy people as well as those confined for medical reasons: lung edema, venous and arterial thrombi, and hydrostatic pneumonia (Booth, 1982; Greenleaf, 1984). Other symptoms associated with bed rest include bed sores, foot drop, general muscular weakness and atrophy, muscle shortening, knee-joint stiffness, restriction of joint motion, loss of appetite, minor dyspepsia and heartburn, constipation and occasional intestinal obstruction, increased tendency for urinary calculi, and accentuation of symptoms during the course of multiple sclerosis and tabes dorsalis (Greenleaf, 1984).

The extent of the effects of disuse depends on the degree of disuse, but the results are clear. Disuse is devastating to the physical system, and even mild physical activity goes a long way in the prevention of some of the more serious disuse-precipitated diseases.

Exercise as Remediation in Older Populations

At first thought it might seem that physical exertion would be contraindicated for chronically ill adults.

To the contrary, exercise plays an important role in the rehabilitation of those with chronic cardiovascular disease, hypertension, and diabetes.

Cardiovascular Disease

Because individuals differ in genetic backgrounds and health behaviors, some experience an early, intense onset of cardiovascular heart disease whereas others remain almost free of symptoms to a very old age. The differential extent and rate of development of cardiovascular heart disease account largely for the increase in individual differences in work capacity that is seen in each older decade. Atherosclerotic coronary heart disease and hypertension accelerate aging of the cardiovascular system. It is becoming increasingly clear that systematic physical exercise retards the development of cardiovascular heart disease. Thus, individuals in their 60s and 70s range from those who are severely impaired and barely mobile to those who have little evidence of cardiovascular disease and who can run marathons. In a review of seven epidemiological studies involving a total of 55,859 people from the United States, England, and Norway, Paffenbarger (1990) concluded that even moderate levels of exercise substantially reduce the risk of coronary heart disease. The average relative risk of death due to cardiovascular disease is approximately 50% less in those individuals considered highly physically active (Table 4.2).

Habitual exercise has both preventive and remedial benefits for aging persons. Most physicians prescribe low-intensity exercise for the treatment of cardiovascular disease, even in individuals who have never exercised. In most people daily exercise decreases the resting and exercise heart rate at any given submaximal work load, which leads to an increase in the preload and thus a decrease in work load and energy demand on the heart. Exercise programs that include stationary cycling,

Table 4.2
Relative Risks of Coronary Heart Disease (CHD)
by Levels of Physical Activity in Selected Populations

British civil servants[a]	Sessions of vigorous sports in past 4 weeks	% of men	CHD rate per 100 men[b]	Relative risk of CHD
9-year follow-up, 1976-1985	0	83	6.3	1.00
	1-3	8	5.1	0.81
	4-7	5	3.6	0.57
	8+	4	2.0	0.32
Multiple risk factor interventional trial[c]	Tertiles of physical activity in kcal/day		CHD rate per 100 men[d]	Relative risk of CHD
8-year follow-up, 1973-1981	Low		7.2	1.00
	Moderate		6.4	0.88
	High		5.8	0.81
Harvard alumni[e]	Physical activity index in kcal/week	% of man-years	CHD rate per 1,000 man-years[f]	Relative risk of CHD
10-year follow-up, 1962-1972	<2,000	62	5.8	1.00
	2,000+	38	3.5	0.61

[a]7,820 men, ages 45 to 59 years at entry.
[b]Adjusted for age-differences; $p = 0.03$.
[c]12,138 men, ages 35-57 at entry.
[d]Adjusted for age-differences; $p = 0.01$.
[e]16,936 men, ages 35 to 74 years at entry.
[f]Adjusted for differences in age, cigarette habit, and blood-pressure status; $p < 0.01$.
Note. From "Physical Activity, Physical Fitness, and Coronary Heart Disease" by R.S. Paffenbarger, 1990, *Atherosclerosis Reviews*, **21**, p. 36. Copyright 1990 by Raven Press, Ltd. Reprinted by permission.

stretching, weight training, and walking can produce significant improvements in submaximal aerobic work capacity, heart rate, resting heart rate, hamstring flexibility, and abdominal strength in chronically ill individuals (Morey et al., 1989). Testimonials of dramatic improvements in the function and quality of life of diseased patients who begin a cautious yet habitual exercise program abound. A particularly striking example was described by Biegel (1984):

> Only five feet three inches tall and weighing 100 pounds for the past 40 years, Eula Weaver had developed cardiovascular disease and was treated for angina at age 67. At age 75 she was hospitalized with a severe heart attack; by age 81, she had developed an arthritic limp and had congestive heart failure, hypertension, and angina. When she began a regimen of dieting and walking at age 81, her limp limited her walking to 100 feet; the circulation in her hands was so impaired that she wore gloves in the summer to keep her hands warm. Gradually increasing her walking, she was able, by age 82, to be free of drugs and her previous symptoms. After four years of increased activity, she participated in the Senior Olympics in Irvine, California, where she won gold medals in the half mile and mile running events. The following year, age 86-1/2, she repeated those runs for another two gold medals. Each morning she runs a mile and rides her stationary bicycle 10-15 miles; three times weekly she works out in a gymnasium; and she follows her diet strictly. (p. 31)

In a preventive mode, exercise acts as a countermeasure to the development of cardiovascular heart disease; in a remedial mode, it serves to reverse symptoms and improve quality of life for those individuals who have developed disease. It has been said that aging impairs cardiopulmonary and metabolic function, but physical inactivity, obesity, and the pattern of fat distribution also control significant physiological functions such as aerobic capacity (Meyers et al., 1991).

Blood Pressure and Hypertension

Although the immediate effect of acute exercise is to raise the blood pressure (more so in older adults than in younger ones), the long-term effect of chronic exercise is to lower resting systolic and diastolic blood pressure about 10 mmHg in nonhypertensive individuals (Lund-Johansen, 1988; Montoye, Metzner, Keller, Johnson, & Epstein, 1973). Moderate-to-vigorous chronic exercise presumably enhances cardiovascular function, tones endocrine and metabolic function, balances nutritional and body composition, and relieves tension and anxiety.

Systematic exercise also lowers blood pressure in hypertensive persons, although the hemodynamics of young hypertensive persons are substantially different from those of elderly hypertensive people. Older hypertensives have less efficient responses to exercise than young hypertensive individuals. A high resting cardiac output is seen in young hypertensives, whereas in the elderly, cardiac output is very low and total peripheral resistance is very high (Montain et al., 1988). These differences are not so great, however, that these researchers advise against exercise. They suggest that older persons with essential hypertension can handle adequately the myocardial demands of exercise of the intensity usually prescribed in rehabilitation programs. The cardiovascular response to exercise in elderly hypertensives is also different from that of older individuals with normal blood pressure. Hypertensive elderly individuals have a lower cardiac output and stroke volume, higher systolic, diastolic, and mean blood pressure, and a higher total peripheral resistance during exercise.

Adult Onset Diabetes

The combination of a less and less physically active lifestyle and a decrease of the basal metabolic rate of 10% each decade means that it is extremely difficult for most aging adults to maintain their youthful body weight. Discussed in more detail in chapter 3, body composition changes with aging so that older adults have almost twice as much fat as younger adults. Adult onset diabetes, or Type II, non–insulin-dependent diabetes mellitus, is highly associated with obesity. Chronic exercise can play an extremely important role in the prevention and control of this type of diabetes (Kart, Metress, & Metress, 1992).

Glucose tolerance measures the efficiency with which glucose is metabolized for energy, an efficiency that declines with increased age. Insulin resistance indicates a tissue-, or whole body-, dampened response to insulin, and therefore, a decreased ability of insulin to stimulate glucose uptake into cells. Insulin resistance becomes more pronounced with aging. Type II diabetes is characterized by a decreased glucose tolerance and increased insulin resistance, which result in circulating levels of glucose (in a nonfasting state) far above normal (hyperglycemia) in spite of elevated insulin levels (hyperinsulinemia). In the average person, blood glucose levels increase about 5 to 6 mg per 100 ml of plasma each decade. The disease occurs 10 times more often in people over age 45 and affects 20% of people over age 60.

Type II diabetes, which in older adults is precipitated primarily by overeating and underexercising, is a dangerous disease, because the high circulating levels of glucose are detrimental to the pancreas, kidneys, liver, heart and blood vessels, eyes, and central and peripheral nervous systems. The formation of lipid plaques in arterial vessels accelerates, which decreases bloodflow to major organs, including the brain, and reduces cardiovascular performance. Thus, a downward cascade of negative events begins. Compromised circulation encourages less physical activity (and perhaps higher levels of food consumption), which results in a further impairment of glucose tolerance. An individual in this downward spiral may have to rely heavily on insulin medication.

Muscular contraction enhances the transport of glucose into the muscle cells regardless of the presence of insulin, thereby compensating for insulin resistance. It is commonly accepted that chronic exercise can play an important role in the prevention of diabetes and should be incorporated in medical prescriptions to control diabetes. In mild cases of Type II diabetes, weight loss to normal levels and increased physical activity may be all that is necessary to control the disease (e.g., Berger & Berchtold, 1982).

The Work Capacity of Masters Athletes

A masters athlete is an individual who competes in events categorized by age. In most sports the age categories for masters athletes begin at 50 years. Most masters athletes have been competing in sport all their lives, with a few beginning to compete relatively late. Although these athletes constitute a tiny percentage of the elderly population, it is not uncommon to find 70- and 80-year-old men and women who have sustained a daily physical training schedule for many years. Consequently, these athletes who train in aerobic sports, such as running, cycling, and swimming, provide a "gold standard" against which age-related physical decline not accelerated by physical disuse and disease can be compared. Generally, athletes who aerobically train also adhere to other beneficial health habits, such as good nutrition, good sleep habits, and freedom from drug abuse. Thus, these masters athletes not only provide information about the heights of performance and physiological adaptation that are possible at advanced ages, they also provide a source of inspiration to all aging individuals who realize that their physical abilities are weakening.

Although declines in maximum heart rate, maximal pulmonary ventilation, and maximal oxygen consumption are inevitable, and although these older athletes rarely continue to train as hard in their senior years as they did when they were competing 20-year-olds, they nevertheless come closer than any other group to being the models of how the human body can withstand the passage of time if it is well cared for and if exercise consistency and intensity are maintained. Discussions of training effects in this highly fit group, therefore, focus not on how much improvement can be made with exercise but rather on how intensive, systematic exercise can maintain cardiovascular function and aerobic capacity within the framework of an aging system.

There is one caveat: It cannot be assumed that the work capacity of all individuals, if they followed a similar lifestyle, would be similar to that of masters athletes, because a moderately high percentage of an individual's maximal force, power, or capacity is attributed to genetic factors. In addition, the extent to which individuals respond to physical training also has a high genetic component (Bouchard & Malina, 1983). In other words, if some miracle occurred and every baby born today trained aerobically every day, the average $\dot{V}O_2$max of 70-year-olds (assuming each baby lived to this age) in the year 2060 would probably be significantly lower than that of the average 70-year-old masters runner today, simply because today's masters runners probably are an elite and genetically talented group. Nevertheless, they do provide evidence of the long-term benefits of aerobic training and good health habits.

Results from cross-sectional studies show that masters athletes, having achieved dramatically higher aerobic capacities in their youth, also experience less decline in maximal aerobic capacity with aging. Shown previously in Figure 4.7 (page 108), the $\dot{V}O_2$max of masters athletes is considerably higher than that of former athletes and sedentary people. Recent cross-sectional research has found that the decrease in $\dot{V}O_2$max known to occur in masters athletes may be somewhat less than has been previously thought (Fuchi, Iwaoka, Higuchi, & Kobayashi, 1989). Longitudinal studies have provided additional evidence that the decline in aerobic capacity of masters athletes may be even less than was proposed on the basis of cross-sectional studies. In masters athletes who were screened for the absence of cardiovascular disease, losses of only 2% to 5% $\dot{V}O_2$max per decade were found (Dehn & Bruce, 1972; Pollock, Foster, Knapp, Rod, & Schmidt, 1987). In the Pollock et al. (1987) study, 24 male track athletes between the ages of 50 and 82 were evaluated to determine the effect of age and training on $\dot{V}O_2$max over a 10-year period. During the test period about half of the athletes remained highly competitive and continued to train at the same intensity, whereas the other half quit competition and reduced their training intensity. The $\dot{V}O_2$max of those who continued competing hardly changed over the test period (54.2-53.3 ml · kg^{-1} · min^{-1}), whereas the $\dot{V}O_2$max of those who quit competing declined significantly (52.5-45.9 ml · kg^{-1} · min^{-1}). Even in genetically gifted competitors, therefore, $\dot{V}O_2$max declines more in those who decrease the frequency and intensity of their exercise program than in those who continue competing.

How do these masters athletes maintain their $\dot{V}O_2$max throughout the years? Maximum heart rate is unaffected by training, declining about seven beats per minute per decade both in sedentary people and masters competitors. But highly trained individuals develop increased left ventricular and diastolic dimensions and wall thickness. They are able to maintain stroke volume and the arteriovenous oxygen difference, and they retain a greater peripheral vasodilatory response (Hagberg et al., 1985). Peripheral resistance is much lower in trained older athletes and contributes to their greater stroke volume, cardiac output, and $\dot{V}O_2$max. The small decline of $\dot{V}O_2$max seen in aging athletes is attributable more to central circulatory factors, such as maximum heart rate and cardiac output, than to peripheral factors, such as

arteriovenous difference. These athletes also have greater maximal voluntary ventilation (MVV) and a greater ratio of $\dot{V}_E$max to MVV than sedentary adults. When compared at the same relative submaximal work load, masters athlete and young athlete runners have similar stroke volumes and arteriovenous O_2 differences, as well as a lower ventilatory-to-submaximal exercise ratio at the same O_2 uptake value ($\dot{V}_E/\dot{V}O_2$).

The encouraging aspect of these studies of highly trained aged competitors is that a decade of aging may have little effect on a highly exercised cardiovascular system. The maximum heart rate and $\dot{V}O_2$max of a masters athlete, shown in Figure 4.11, a and b, reveal strikingly youthful cardiovascular function. But for individuals who would like a quick and easy solution to aging, the results are discouraging in that they emphasize that the cardiovascular maintenance benefits of exercise are only effective as long as the exercise intensity is maintained. In fact, some measures of fitness decline by 50% within 3 weeks, and all exercise benefits may be lost to previously light or moderate exercisers within a few months. Thus, in order to be beneficial on a long-term basis, exercise must become an integral, weekly part of an individual's lifestyle.

In Summary

The most observable physiological changes associated with aging are a decline in maximal exercise capacity and maximum heart rate, an increase in systolic blood pressure and left ventricle wall thickness, and a deterioration in glucose and lipid metabolism. Heart function in most elderly is adequate at rest. Normal aging changes in heart size, end-systolic volume, and the volume of blood ejected at rest are minimal. More structural and functional deterioration is due to pathological processes, such as coronary atherosclerosis rather than the actual aging process.

Systolic and diastolic blood pressure increase with age, due primarily to a thickening and hardening of the aorta and arterial tree but also to an increase in peripheral resistance. The heart and vasculature also become less sensitive to β-adrenergic stimulation, and thus the aging heart cannot achieve maximum heart rate levels that were possible during youth. The heart rate of

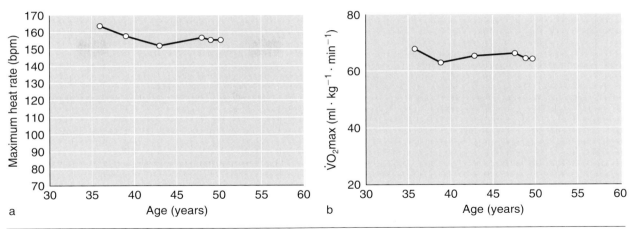

Figure 4.11 Cardiovascular parameters of a masters runner from age 35 to 50: (a) Maximum heart rate and (b) V̇O₂max.
Data from Costill (1986).

older people also remains higher and recovers more slowly after maximal exercise.

Postural hypotension, a loss in responsiveness of homeostatic reflexes, is present in almost one third of the young elderly and almost one half of those over age 75. Postural hypotension, which predisposes an individual to dizziness, confusion, weakness, or fainting, is related more to high levels of systolic blood pressure than to aging processes.

Generally, in healthy individuals the aged pulmonary system functions very well under resting and moderate exercise conditions. Even under heavy exercise conditions, pulmonary function is not usually a limiting factor in maximal work capacity. The limiting factor is more attributable to the limit that a decreased maximum heart rate places on cardiac output.

The maximum amount of oxygen that a sedentary individual can consume during work decreases about 10% each decade. In chronic exercisers, however, maximal oxygen consumption can be maintained at much higher levels. Most elderly chronic exercisers, even those over age 60, have a higher oxygen uptake and can out perform many sedentary 20-year-olds in work capacity. The benefits that these exercisers receive include:

- enhanced stroke volume, which assists in maintaining cardiac output;
- increased maximal oxygen consumption;
- increased total blood volume and tone of peripheral veins, which reduces vascular resistance;
- reduced vascular resistance, which increases preloading of the heart and amplifies stroke volume;

- decreased resting heart rate, which lengthens diastolic filling of the ventricle; and
- increased HDL lipids and possibly reduced LDL lipids.

However, the cardiovascular maintenance effects of habitual exercise are only effective as long as exercise intensity is maintained.

Anaerobic performance in maximal exercise tests decreases with age, but when the anaerobic processes during short time periods (<1.0 min) are measured in elderly athletes, age differences are negligible.

Habitual exercise serves as both a preventive and an effective nondrug supplement in the remediation of cardiovascular disease, hypertension, and diabetes. In this sense it postpones many symptoms of aging. Conversely, disuse, such as occurs in long periods of sitting in recliners or chairs or during bed rest, dramatically accelerates aging of most physiological processes.

Masters athletes provide a gold standard of exercise habits and performance against which age-related decline that is not accelerated by physical disuse and disease can be compared. Age-related decreases in work capacity occur at lower rates in these individuals, who sometimes show almost negligible losses in work capacity over a full decade.

Generally, as people age, their capacity to perform work declines. But the work capacity of individuals is very different, and these individual differences in work capacity grow greater with each decade. The influence of genetics, widely different behavioral patterns, and the development of cardiovascular disease cause people to become more different than alike in work capacity as they age.

References

Allen, D., Willcox, K.K., Teague-Baker, T.S., & Lei, K.Y. (1985). Alterations in HDL lipoprotein and apolipoprotein profiles consequent to 20 weeks of aerobic training in older men. *Medicine and Science in Sports and Exercise*, **17**, 275 (abstract).

American College of Sports Medicine. (1978). Position statement on the recommended quantity and quality of exercise for developing and maintaining fitness in healthy adults. *Medicine and Science in Sports*, **10**, 7-10.

Åstrand, I., Åstrand, P.O., Hallback, I., & Kilbom, A. (1973). Reduction in maximal oxygen uptake with age. *Journal of Applied Physiology*, **35**, 649-654.

Åstrand, P.O., & Rodahl, K. (1986). *Textbook of work physiology*. New York: McGraw-Hill.

Bennett, T., & Gardiner, S.M. (1988). Physiological aspects of the aging cardiovascular system. *Journal of Cardiovascular Pharmacology*, **12** (Suppl. 8), 51-57.

Berger, M., & Berchtold, P. (1982). Physical training as part of the therapy for adult onset diabetes. *Annals of Clinical Research*, **14** (Supp. 34), 69-73.

Biegel, L. (1984). *Physical fitness and the older person*. Rockville, MD: Aspen Systems.

Blumenthal, J.A., Emery, C.F., Madden, D.J., Coleman, R.E., Riddle, M.W., Schniebolk, S., Cobb, F.R., Sullivan, M.J., & Higginbotham, M.B. (1991). Effects of exercise training on cardiorespiratory function in men and women >60 years of age. *American Journal of Cardiology*, **67**, 633-639.

Boggs, D.R., & Patrene, K.D. (1985). Hematopoiesis and aging III: Anemia and a blunted erythropoietic response to hemorrhage in aged mice. *American Journal of Hematology*, **19**, 327-328.

Booth, F.W. (1982). Effect of limb immobilization on skeletal muscle. *Journal of Applied Physiology: Respiration, Environment, and Exercise Physiology*, **52**, 1113-1118.

Bortz, W.M., II. (1983). On disease . . . aging . . . and disuse. *Executive Health*, **20**(3), 1-6.

Bouchard, C., & Malina, R.M. (1983). Genetics of physical fitness and motor performance. *Exercise and Sport Sciences Reviews*, **11**, 306-339.

Bowdler, A.J., & Foster, A.M. (1987). The effect of donor age on the flow properties of blood. Part I: Plasma and whole blood viscosity in adult males. *Experimental Gerontology*, **22**, 155-164.

Brandfonbrener, M., Landowne, M., & Shock, N.W. (1955). Changes in cardiac output with age. *Circulation*, **12**, 557-566.

Brischetto, M.J., Millman, R.P., Peterson, D.D., Silage, D.A., & Pack, A.I. (1984). Effect of aging on ventilatory response to exercise and CO_2. *Journal of Applied Physiology*, **56**, 1143-1150.

Cantwell, J.D., & Watt, E.W. (1974). Extreme cardiopulmonary fitness in old age. *Chest*, **65**, 357-359.

Chick, T.W., Cagle, T.G., Vegas, F.A., Poliner, J.K., & Murata, G.H. (1991). *Journal of Gerontology: Biological Sciences*, **46**, B34-B38.

Convertino, V.A., Montgomery, L.D., & Greenleaf, J.E. (1984). Cardiovascular responses during orthostasis: Effect of an increase in $\dot{V}O_2$max. *Aviation Space and Environmental Medicine*, **55**, 702-708.

Costill, D.L. (1986). *Inside running: Basics of sports physiology*. Indianapolis: Benchmark Press.

Darr, K.C., Bassett, D.R., & Morgan, B.J. (1988). Effects of age and training status on heart rate recovery after peak exercise. *American Journal of Physiology*, **254**, H340-H343.

Davidson, W.R., Jr., & Fee, E.C. (1990). Influence of aging on pulmonary hemodynamics in a population free of coronary artery disease. *American Journal of Cardiology*, **65**, 1454-1458.

Dehn, M.M., & Bruce, R.A. (1972). Longitudinal variations in maximal oxygen intake with age and activity. *Journal of Applied Physiology*, **33**, 805-807.

Dempsey, J.A., Johnson, B.D., & Saupe, K.W. (1990). Adaptations and limitations in the pulmonary system during exercise. *Chest*, **97**(3)(Suppl.), 81S-87S.

Docherty, J.R. (1990). Cardiovascular responses in aging: A review. *Pharmacological Review*, **42**, 103-125.

Ehsani, A.A. (1987). Cardiovascular adaptations to exercise training in the elderly. *Federation Proceedings*, **46**, 1840-1843.

Ehsani, A.A., Takeshi, O., Miller, T.R., Spina, R.J., & Jilka, S.M. (1991). Exercise training improves left ventricular systolic function in older men. *Circulation*, **83**, 96-103.

Fleg, J.L. (1986). Alterations in cardiovascular structure and function with advancing age. *American Journal of Cardiology*, **57**, 33C-44C.

Fleg, J.L., Tzankoff, S.P., & Lakatta, E.G. (1985). Age-related augmentation of plasma catecholamines during dynamic exercise in healthy males. *Journal of Applied Physiology*, **59**, 1033-1039.

Foster, V.L., Hume, G.J., Byrnes, W.C., Dickinson, A.L., & Chatfield, S.J. (1989). Endurance training for elderly women: Moderate vs. low intensity. *Journal of Gerontology: Medical Sciences*, **44**, M184-M188.

Fuchi, T., Iwaoka, K., Higuchi, M., & Kobayashi, S. (1989). Cardiovascular changes associated with decreased aerobic capacity and aging in long-distance runners. *European Journal of Applied Physiology*, **58**, 884-889.

Geokas, M.C., Lakatta, E.G., Makinodan, T., & Timiras, P.S. (1990). The aging process. *Annals of Internal Medicine*, **113**, 455-466.

Gerstenblith, G., Renlund, D.G., & Lakatta, E.G. (1987). Cardiovascular response to exercise in younger and older men. *Federation Proceedings*, **46**, 1834-1839.

Goldberg, A.P., & Hagberg, J.M. (1990). Physical exercise in the elderly. In E.L. Schneider & J.W. Rowe (Eds.), *Handbook of the biology of aging* (3rd ed., pp. 407-428). New York: Academic Press.

Goldstraw, P.W., & Warren, D.J. (1985). The effect of age on the cardiovascular responses to isometric exercise: A test of autonomic function. *Gerontology*, **31**, 54-58.

Goode, R.C., Firstbrook, J.B., & Shephard, R.J. (1966). Effects of exercise and a cholesterol-free diet on human serum lipids. *Canadian Journal of Physiology and Pharmacology*, **44**, 575-580.

Grassi, B., Cerretelli, P., Narici, M.V., & Marconi, C. (1991). Peak anaerobic power in master athletes. *European Journal of Physiology*, **62**, 394-399.

Greenleaf, J.E. (1984). Physiological responses to prolonged bed rest and fluid immersion in humans. *Journal of Applied Physiology: Respiration, Environment, and Exercise Physiology*, **57**, 619-633.

Hagberg, J.M., Allen, W.K., Seals, D.R., Hurley, B.F., Ehsani, A.A., & Holloszy, J.O. (1985). A hemodynamic comparison of young and older endurance athletes during exercise. *Journal of Applied Physiology*, **58**, 2041-2046.

Hagberg, J.M., Graves, J.E., Limacher, M., Woods, D.R., Leggett, S.H., Cononie, C., Gruber, J.J., & Pollock, M.L. (1989). Cardiovascular responses of 70- to 79-year-old men and women to exercise training. *Journal of Applied Physiology*, **66**, 2589-2594.

Haidet, G.C., & Parsons, D. (1991). Reduced exercise capacity in senescent beagles: An evaluation of the periphery. *American Journal of Physiology*, **260**, (Heart Circulation Physiology, 29), H173-H182.

Harris, T., Lipsitz, L.A., Kleinman, J.C., & Cornoni-Huntley, J. (1991). Postural change in blood pressure associated with age and systolic blood pressure. *Journal of Gerontology: Medical Sciences*, **46**, M159-M163.

Hopkins, D.R., Murrah, B., Hoeger, W.W., & Rhodes, R.C. (1990). Effect of low-impact aerobic dance on the functional fitness of elderly women. *Gerontologist*, **30**, 189-192.

Karlsson, J. (1985). Metabolic adaptations to exercise: A review of potential beta-adrenoceptor antagonist effects. *American Journal of Cardiology*, **55**, 48D-58D.

Kart, C.S., Metress, E.K., & Metress, S.P. (1992). *Human aging and chronic disease*. Boston: Jones & Bartlett.

Kasch, F.W., Boyer, J.L, Van Camp, S.P., Verity, L.S., & Wallace, J.P. (1990). The effects of physical activity and inactivity on aerobic power in older men (a longitudinal study). *Physician and Sportsmedicine*, **18**, 73-83.

Katch, V.L. (1973). Kinetics of oxygen uptake and recovery for supramaximal work of short duration. *Internationale Zeitschrift fur Angewandte Physiologie*, **31**, 197-207.

Klag, M.J., Whelton, P.K., & Appel, L.J. (1990). Effect of age on the efficacy of blood pressure treatment strategies. *Hypertension*, **26**, 700-705.

Klausner, S.C., & Schwartz, A.B. (1985). The aging heart. *Clinical Geriatric Medicine*, **1**, 119-141.

Lakatta, E.G. (1986). Diminished beta-adrenergic modulation of cardiovascular function in advanced age. *Cardiac Clinics*, **4**, 185-200.

Lakatta, E.G. (1990). Changes in cardiovascular function with aging. *European Heart Journal*, **11** (Suppl. C), 22-29.

Landin, R.J., Linnemeier, T.J., Rothbaum, D.A., Chappelear, J., & Noble, R.J. (1985). Exercise testing and training of the elderly patient. *Cardiovascular Clinics*, **15**, 201-218.

Larson, E.B., & Bruce, R.A. (1987). Health benefits of exercise in an aging society. *Archives of Internal Medicine*, **147**, 353-356.

Lipsitz, L.A. (1989). Altered blood pressure homeostasis in advanced age: Clinical and research implications. *Journal of Gerontology: Medical Sciences*, **44**, M179-M183.

Lund-Johansen, P. (1988). The hemodynamics of the aging cardiovascular system. *Journal of Cardiovascular Pharmacology*, **12** (Suppl. 8), S20-S32.

Lund-Johansen, P. (1989). Age hemodynamics and exercise in essential hypertension: Difference between β-blockers and dihydropyridine antagonists. *Journal of Cardiovascular Pharmacology*, **14** (Suppl. 10), S7-S13.

Mahler, D.A., Cunningham, D.P.E., & Curfman, G.D. (1986). Aging and exercise performance. *Clinical Geriatric Medicine*, **2**, 433-452.

Makrides, L., Heigenhauser, G.J., McCartney, N., & Jones, N.L. (1985). Maximal short-term exercise capacity in healthy subjects aged 15-70 years. *Clinical Science*, **69**, 197-205.

Mann, D.L., Denenberg, B.S., Gash, A.K., Makler, P.T., & Bove, A.A. (1986). Effects of age on ventricular performance during graded supine exercise. *American Heart Journal*, **111**, 108-115.

Marti, B., & Howald, H. (1990). Long-term effects of physical training on aerobic capacity: Controlled study of former elite athletes. *Journal of Applied Physiology*, **69**, 1451-1459.

Martin, W.H., Kohrt, W.M., Malley, M.T., Korte, E., & Stoltz, S. (1990). Exercise training enhances leg vasodilatory capacity of 65-year-old men and women. *Journal of Applied Physiology*, **69**, 1804-1809.

Martin, W.H., III., Ogawa, T., Kohrt, M., Malley, M.T., Korte, E., Kieffer, P.S., & Schechtman, K.B. (1991). Effects of aging, gender, and physical training on peripheral vascular function. *Circulation*, **84**, 654-664.

McArdle, W.D., Katch, F.I., & Katch, V.L. (1991). *Exercise physiology*. Philadelphia: Lea & Febiger.

Meyers, D.A., Goldberg, A.P., Bleecker, M.L., Coon, P.J., Drinkwater, D.T., & Bleecker, E.R. (1991). Relationship of obesity and physical fitness to cardiopulmonary and metabolic function in healthy older men. *Journal of Gerontology: Medical Sciences*, **46**, M57-M65.

Montain, S.J., Jilka, S.M., Ehsani, A.A., & Hagberg, J.M. (1988). Altered hemodynamics during exercise in older essential hypertensive subjects. *Hypertension*, **12**, 479-484.

Montoye, H.J., Metzner, H.L, Keller, J.B., Johnson, B.C., & Epstein, F.H. (1973). Habitual physical activity and blood pressure. *Medicine and Science in Sports*, **4**, 175-181.

Morey, M.C., Cowper, P.A., Feussner, J.R., DiPasquale, R.C., Crowley, G.M., Kitzman, D.W., & Sullivan, R.J. (1989). Evaluation of a supervised exercise program in a geriatric population. *Journal of the American Geriatrics Society*, **37**, 348-354.

Naso, F., Carner, E., Blankfort-Doyle, W., & Coughey, K. (1990). Endurance training in the elderly nursing home patient. *Archives of Physical Medicine and Rehabilitation*, **71**, 241-243.

Niinimaa, V., & Shephard, R.J. (1978). Training and oxygen conductance in the elderly. II. The cardiovascular system. *Journal of Gerontology*, **33**, 362-367.

Nye, E.R., Sutherland, W.H., Jefferson, N.R., & Robertson, M.C. (1985). Serum lipoprotein lipids and hematological variables in veteran runners, before and after a 2100-km relay run. *Clinical Physiology*, **5**, 521-529.

Paffenbarger, R.S. (1990). Physical activity, physical fitness, and coronary heart disease. *Atherosclerosis Reviews*, **21**, 35-41.

Pearson, A.C., Gudipati, C.V., & Labovitz, A.J. (1991). Effects of aging on left ventricular structure and function. *American Heart Journal*, **121**, 871-875.

Pollock, M.L, Foster, C., Knapp, D., Rod, J.L., & Schmidt, D.H. (1987). Effect of age and training on aerobic capacity and body composition of master athletes. *Journal of Applied Physiology*, **62**, 725-731.

Posner, J.D., Gorman, K.M., Klein, H.S., & Woldow, A. (1986). Exercise capacity in the elderly. *American Journal of Cardiology*, **57**, 52C-58C.

Reaburn, P.R.J., & Mackinnon, L.T. (1990). Blood lactate responses in older swimmers during active and passive recovery following maximal sprint swimming. *European Journal of Applied Physiology*, **61**, 246-250.

Reaven, P.D., Barrett-Connor, E., & Edelstein, S. (1991). Relation between leisure-time physical activity and blood pressure in older women. *Circulation*, **83**, 559-565.

Ringel, R.L., & Chodzko-Zajko, W.J. (1987). Vocal indices of biological age. *Journal of Voice*, **1**, 31-37.

Rodeheffer, R.J., Gerstenblith, G., Becker, L.C., Fleg, J.L., Weisfeldt, M.L. & Lakatta, E.G. (1984). Exercise cardiac output is maintained with advancing age in healthy human subjects: Cardiac dilation and increased stroke volume compensates for adminished heart rate. *Circulation*, **69**, 203-213.

Rowe, J.W., & Kahn, R.L. (1987). Human aging: Usual and successful. *Science*, **237**, 143-149.

Safar, M. (1990). Aging and its effects on the cardiovascular system. *Drugs*, **39** (Suppl. 1), 1-18.

Sagiv, M., Fisher, N., Yaniv, A., & Rudoy, J. (1989). Effect of running versus isometric training programs on healthy elderly at rest. *Gerontology*, **35**, 72-77.

Saltin, B., & Grimby, G. (1968). Physiological analysis of middle-aged and old former athletes. Comparison of still-active athletes of the same age. *Circulation*, **38**, 1104-1115.

Schwartz, R.S. (1988). Effects of exercise training on high density lipoproteins and apolipoprotein A-I in old and young men. *Metabolism*, **37**, 1128-1133.

Seals, D.R., Allen, W.K., Hurley, B.F., Dalsky, G.P., Ehsani, A.A., & Hagberg, J.M. (1984). Elevated high-density lipoprotein cholesterol levels in older endurance athletes. *American Journal of Cardiology*, **54**, 390-393.

Seals, D.R., Hagberg, J.M., Hurley, B.F., Dalsky, G.P. Ehsani, A.A., & Holloszy, J.O. (1984). Glucose tolerance in young and older athletes and sedentary men. *Journal of Applied Physiology*, **56**, 1521-1525.

Shephard, R.J. (1987). *Physical activity and aging*. Rockville, MD: Aspen Publishers.

Stamford, B.A. (1988). Exercise and the elderly. *Exercise and Sport Sciences Review*, **16**, 341-379.

Steinhaus, L.A., Dustman, R.E., Ruhling, R.O, Emmerson, R.Y., Johnson, S.C., Shearer, D.E., Shigeoka, J.W., & Bonekat, W.H. (1988). Cardiorespiratory fitness of young and older active and sedentary men. *British Journal of Sports Medicine*, **22**, 163-166.

Suominen, H., Heikkinen, E., Parkatti, T., Forsburg, S., & Kiiskinen, A. (1980). Effects of "lifelong" physical training on functional aging in men. *Scandinavian Journal of Social Medicine*, Suppl. 14, 225-240.

Takishima, T., Shindoh, C., Kikuchi, Y., Hida, W., & Inoue, H. (1990). Aging effect on oxygen consumption of respiratory muscles in humans. *Journal of Applied Physiology*, **69**, 14-20.

Timiras, M.L., & Brownstein, H. (1987). Prevalence of anemia and correlation of hemoglobin with age in a geriatric screening clinic population. *Journal of the American Geriatrics Society*, **35**, 639-643.

Tzankoff, S.P., & Norris, A.H. (1979). Age-related differences in lactate distribution kinetics following maximal exercises. *European Journal of Applied Physiology and Occupational Physiology*, **42**, 35-40.

Van der Eems, K., & Ismail, A.H. (1985). Serum lipids: Interactions between age and moderate intensity exercise. *British Journal of Sports Medicine*, **19**, 112-114.

Vanhoutte, P.M. (1988). Aging and vascular responsiveness. *Journal of Cardiovascular Pharmacology*, **12**, S11-S18.

Van Loan, M.D., Massey, B.H., Boileau, R.A., Lohman, T.G., Misner, J.E., & Best, P.L. (1989). *Journal of Sports Medicine and Physical Fitness*, **29**, 262-268.

Vokonas, P.S., Kannel, W.B., & Cupples, L.A. (1988). Epidemiology and risk of hypertension in the elderly: The Framingham study. *Journal of Hypertension*, **6** (Suppl. 1), S3-S9.

Weisfeldt, M.L., Gerstenblith, G., & Lakatta, E.G. (1985). Alterations in circulatory function. In E.L. Bierman & W.R. Hazzard (Eds.), *Principles of geriatric medicine* (pp. 248-279). New York: McGraw-Hill.

Yerg, J.E., Seals, D.R., Hagberg, J.M., & Holloszy, J.O. (1985). Effect of endurance exercise training on ventilatory function in older individuals. *Journal of Applied Physiology*, **58**, 791-794.

Zauner, C.W. (1985). Physical fitness in aging men. *Maturitas*, **7**, 267-271.

CHAPTER 5

Muscular Strength and Endurance

Moderate levels of strength are necessary for a surprising number of activities of daily living: carrying groceries and packages from shopping malls, lifting potted plants, climbing stairs, and getting up from chairs or out of automobiles. Low to moderate levels of strength are necessary to retain certain types of jobs for those who wish to extend their work life beyond traditional retirement ages. Also, in elderly adults strength plays a significant role in preserving the ability to participate in social activities, such as dancing and traveling on vacations, and to continue some lifelong hobbies, such as cabinet making or gardening.

Muscular strength and endurance are important resources for all individuals, but they become even more important as individuals age. A substantial loss of leg and back strength in the elderly not only impairs locomotion but is also associated with an increased risk of falling (Tinetti & Speechley, 1989; Tobis, Friis, & Reinsch, 1989). Adequate leg strength may prevent a fall by enabling an individual to correct momentary losses of balance in time to prevent catastrophic falling events, and strength of the upper-body musculature may reduce the amount of injury that results from a fall by breaking the force of the fall or by stabilizing the joints during the fall.

The first part of this chapter discusses the age-related changes that occur in muscular strength, the potential causes of these changes, and the role that resistive and repetitive exercise plays in the maintenance of strength. The second part of the chapter discusses the impact of these same factors on muscular endurance.

Muscular Strength

Maximal muscular strength is achieved during young adulthood, the 20s or 30s, and then declines with age (e.g., Cunningham, Morrison, Rice, & Cooke, 1987; Laforest, St-Pierre, Cyr, & Gayton, 1990; Vandervoort, Kramer, & Wharram, 1990). A good cross-sectional example of the lower-arm and shoulder strength of older men was provided by Shock and Norris (1970; Figure 5.1). The maintenance of strength through approximately age 60 followed by a precipitous decline in the later years is a relatively common pattern. Another cross-sectional example of age-related loss of strength is provided in Figure 5.2. Longitudinal data from Kallman, Plato, and Tobin (1990) show that even though grip strength in the general population is related to aging, people differ greatly in the amount of strength lost. Many of the older subjects in this population lost *less* strength over a 10-year period than did middle-aged and young subjects, and about 29% of the middle-aged subjects and 15% of older subjects *lost no strength at all* over the 10 years. These findings do not necessarily mean that the strength losses that occur before or after the 10-year measurement period can be predicted by this single 10-year period, but the results are an excellent example of individual differences, which were discussed in chapter 2.

Force Production

The strength function of a muscle is determined by the amount of force it can produce, either isometrically or dynamically. *Isometric muscular strength* is the force that can be generated against a resistance that does not yield to the muscular contraction, and thus the muscle length is held constant throughout the contraction. Isometric

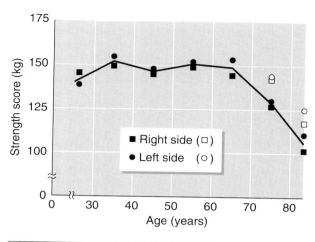

Figure 5.1 Composite strength score for the arm and shoulder muscles.
From "Neuromuscular Coordination as a Factor in Age Changes in Muscular Exercise" by N.W. Shock, and A.H. Norris, 1970, *Medicine and Sport,* **4**, p. 96. Copyright 1970 by S. Karger AG, Basel. Reprinted by permission.

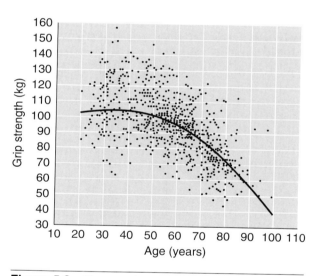

Figure 5.2 Changes in grip strength for 847 males from 20 to 100 years of age.
From "The Role of Muscle Loss in the Age-Related Decline of Grip Strength: Cross-Sectional and Longitudinal Perspectives" by D.A. Kallman, C.C. Plato, and J.D. Tobin, 1990, *Journal of Gerontology: Medical Sciences,* **45**, p. M83. Copyright 1990 by The Gerontological Society of America. Reprinted by permission.

strength is defined as the maximum force or tension generated by a muscle, and it is measured during a single maximal contraction. Isometric or static strength can be measured with a dynamometer, such as a hand grip dynamometer, which measures the maximum amount of strength that an individual can produce in gripping. *Dynamic strength* is the greatest amount of strength that can be produced in a one-repetition maximum contraction (1-RM; McArdle, Katch, & Katch, 1986). An example of dynamic strength measurement is the back-leg lift dynamometer test, in which the maximal amount of weight an individual can lift at one time is recorded. The individual attempts to lift a specific weight, and if successful, an additional weight is added. Weights are added until the person can no longer lift the weight in a single lift. Computer-assisted isokinetic strength-measuring devices provide measures of peak torque (rotary force), or the amount of force that is generated throughout the range of motion of the muscle. *Isokinetic strength* is a measure of work and power output at constant movement velocity. Thus the average amount of force and work that the muscle can generate at any given point throughout the muscle's contraction can be determined.

The age-related deficits in absolute strength that are seen in humans are analyzed in more detail in controlled studies of single, whole muscles excised from animals. In these studies, the muscle is stimulated electrically, and precise measurements are made of its contractile properties and morphology. The contractile properties of whole muscle, shown in Figure 5.3a, are the total amount of force that it can generate (maximum isometric force), the total amount of time that it takes to generate that force (contraction time), the speed with which it contracts (maximum contraction velocity), its ability to relax (one-half relaxation time), and its ability to keep contracting (fatigability). With aging, the maximal isometric force that can be produced decreases and the fatigability of the muscle increases (Figure 5.3b). The age-related loss of force in an isolated muscle is graphically depicted in Figure 5.4. In this figure the peak twitch tension of the fast-twitch plantaris rat muscle is much lower in old rats than in young rats (Arabadjis, Heffner, & Pendergast, 1990). Generally, the force produced by isolated muscles from old animals is about one third that produced by young animals. For example, Brooks and Faulkner (1988) reported that the maximum absolute power of an isolated mouse muscle was 30% lower than the power of a young mouse muscle, and power normalized according to the amount of muscle mass was 20% lower in older mice. These findings from animal studies are relevant for humans. For example, the force per cross-sectional area is also reduced in aged men (Young, Stokes, & Crowe, 1985).

The rate of tension development is also slower in aged muscle (Arabadjis et al., 1990; Newton & Yemm, 1986). Shown in Figure 5.5, the greater the peak force the greater the difference in rate of tension development between old and young muscle. Old muscles do not reach half relaxation as quickly as young muscles (Arabadjis et al., 1990; Fitts, Troup, Witzmann, & Holloszy, 1984). Walters, Sweeney, and Farrar (1990), however, argue that none of the characteristics of the fast-twitch muscle of the rat strain that they studied deteriorated in young, middle-aged, and old rats. They found no age changes in maximum isometric tetanic force, contraction time, half-relaxation time, maximum contraction velocity, or fatigability. Brooks and Faulkner (1988) agree that age-related changes in time-dependent or force-velocity relationships do not occur, but they maintain that a 10% to 20% decrease occurs in maximum isometric tetanic force and in maximum specific force. The differences in the results of these investigators may be due to differences in the subject species (mouse, rat, or human), the strain of rat (F344, Wistar, etc.), or alterations that are muscle specific, such as fiber type or location of the muscle. The location and function of the muscle may also expose the muscle to a much different history of tension than a similar muscle that has an antagonistic function about the same joint. Researchers might observe different age effects on muscle structure and function because they analyze muscles that undergo different types of activity or experience different degrees of muscle involvement in that activity.

Strength is not lost uniformly across all muscles and in all types of movement in either humans or animals. Table 5.1 (page 127) shows some generalizations about the loss of muscle strength. Results from laboratory testing and clinical observations indicate that muscle strength of the lower body declines faster with age than muscle strength of the upper body (Asmussen & Heebøl-Neilsen, 1961; Larsson, 1978; Larsson, Grimby, & Karlsson, 1979; Murray, Duthie, Gambert, Sepic, & Mollinger, 1985; Murray, Gardner, Mollinger, & Sepic, 1980). Also, in assessments of physical function of the frail elderly, losses of lower-body strength are a bigger problem than losses of upper-body strength (Jette, Branch, & Berlin, 1990). However, for laboratory tests of strength to reflect the maximum strength that a subject can produce, the subject must be highly motivated and must be well practiced at performing the task. Rarely are these two conditions met in a research study.

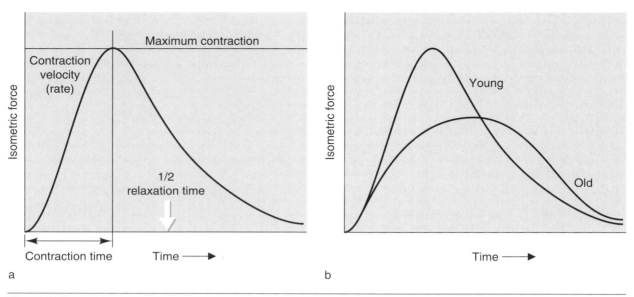

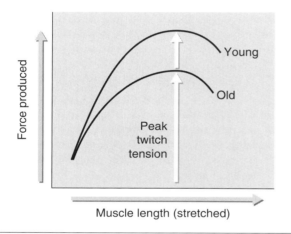

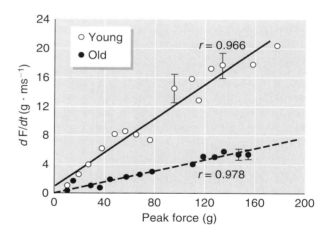

Figure 5.3   (a) Schematic diagram of contractile properties of whole muscle. (b) Effects of aging on muscle force-time curves.

Figure 5.4   Maximal isometric twitch force as a function of increases in muscle length.

Figure 5.5   Rate of force development as a function of peak force. The rate of force development was calculated for each contraction at different muscle lengths and peak tensions and plotted as a function of peak tension, with average ± *SD* where multiple points accrued at the same peak tension.
From "Morphologic and Functional Alterations in Aging Rat Muscle" by P.G. Arabadjis, R.R. Heffner, and D.R. Pendergast, 1990, *Journal of Neuropathology and Experimental Neurology*, **49**, p. 603. Reproduced with permission from the *Journal of Neuropathology and Experimental Neurology*.

A better way to compare losses of maximum strength in upper- and lower-body muscles is to make those comparisons in the various age groups who compete in powerlifting. The dead lift, although requiring some arm and grip strength to hold the weight, primarily requires brute strength of the legs and back. In the bench press, the competitor, while lying on the back, lifts a barbell with arm strength only. In Figure 5.6 the losses in arm strength (bench press) and leg strength (dead lift) are shown as a percentage of the American record performance for each event. A lower percentage of the record in one type of lift means that greater strength losses occur in that lift compared to others. In the comparison shown in Figure 5.6,

little or no differences between upper- or lower-body strength are seen until ages 70 to 75. In these two age groups, the greatest losses (~ 6-9%) were in upper-body, not lower-body, strength. These results provide evidence of relative strength losses when all health, physical, psychological, and

Table 5.1
Summary of Strength Changes With Aging

Better maintenance	Greater decline
Muscles used in daily activities	Muscles used infrequently in specialized activities
Isometric strength	Dynamic strength
Eccentric contractions	Concentric contractions
Slow velocity contractions	Rapid velocity contractions
Repeated low-level contractions	Power production
Strength using small joint angles	Strength using large joint angles
Males' strength	Females' strength

social conditions are maximized and support the notion that a substantial percentage of the loss of muscular strength in both upper and lower body is due to disuse, not aging. Age effects on strength, in regard to powerlifting and weight lifting, are discussed in more detail in chapter 14.

The strength of frequently used muscles, such as those used in a grip-strength test or in a test of plantar and dorsiflexion of the feet (Kauffman,

1985; Petrofsky, Burse, & Lind, 1975), is maintained much better than that of infrequently used muscles (Bosco & Komi, 1980; Wilmore, 1991). Isometric strength is maintained better than dynamic strength (Laforest et al., 1990), and strength during eccentric, lengthening contractions seems to be maintained better than strength during concentric, shortening contractions of the muscle (Vandervoort et al., 1990). Thus, an aged woman may experience less difficulty in lowering herself into a chair, which requires a lengthening contraction of the quadriceps muscles, than in rising from the chair, which requires a shortening contraction of these same muscles.

When speed of contraction is entered into the equation, the aging muscle is at a greater disadvantage in developing absolute tension. Figure 5.7 shows that the higher the velocity at which the force must be produced, the lower the relative tension that the aged muscle can generate (Laforest et al., 1990). This is demonstrated in Figure 5.8a, where the absolute amount of force produced by older men is less than that produced by young men at specific time intervals throughout the contraction. However, the aged muscle can arrive at its maximal force output as quickly as a young muscle (dF/dt) if the task is to produce a maximum contraction as fast as possible (Clarkson, Kroll, & Melchionda, 1981). Figure 5.8b shows that the relative amount of time necessary to produce a particular percentage

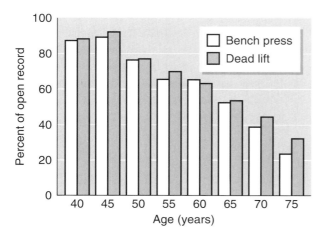

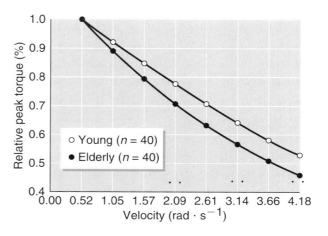

Figure 5.6 Comparison of losses in upper- and lower-body strength by comparing powerlifting performance in the upper arms (bench press) and lower limbs (dead lift). Percent loss was calculated by dividing the age-group record by the 1991 Open Record for the 181-lb weight class.
Unpublished data from the United States Powerlifting Federation, P.O. Box 389, Roy, VT 84064.

Figure 5.7 Relative peak torques produced at various velocities. Double points indicate significant differences between groups at $p < 0.01$.
From "Effects of Age and Regular Exercise on Muscle Strength and Endurance" by S. Laforest, D.M.M. St-Pierre, J. Cyr, and D. Gayton, 1990, *European Journal of Applied Physiology*, **60**, p. 106. Copyright 1990 by Springer-Verlag. Reprinted by permission.

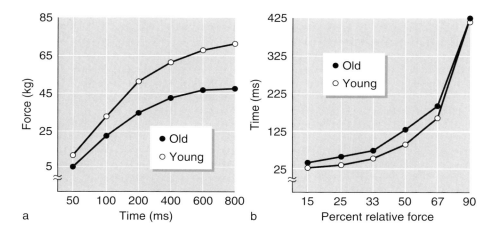

Figure 5.8 Force-time characteristics of a fast maximal voluntary contraction: (a) absolute force developed at specified contraction time; (b) time required to develop specified percentages of maximal isometric strength. Abscissa intervals are unequal.
From "Age, Isometric Strength, Rate of Tension Development, and Fiber Type Composition" by P. Clarkson, W. Kroll, and A.M. Melchionda, 1981, *Journal of Gerontology*, **36**, p. 650. Copyright 1981 by The Gerontological Society of America. Reprinted by permission.

of maximum strength is almost the same for both young and old men.

Muscle Mass

The amount of force that an individual can produce depends substantially on the amount of working muscle that is brought to the task. Individual muscle cells of the same size and training condition produce about the same amount of force in all contexts, whether in males or females, old or young. Differences in strength occur when individuals have a much larger muscle mass than other individuals. Males, for example, who on the average are stronger than females, also have greater muscle mass.

Muscle mass, which can be measured by computer tomography (CT) scanning, substantially declines with aging, and it is well established that this loss accounts for a large amount of the age-related decline in muscle strength (Green, 1986; Kallman et al., 1990). It has been reported that the maximal cross-sectional area of the quadriceps may be 25% lower in 70-year-olds compared to 20-year-olds (Young et al., 1985). The decline in muscle mass has been attributed to changes in the components of the muscle, such as decreases in number and size of muscle fibers and the loss of entire motor units (the motor neuron, axon, and all of the muscle fibers that it innervates). In older

adults, a substantial amount of muscle tissue is replaced by connective tissue (Lexell, 1992).

Although muscle mass declines with aging, it declines significantly less in individuals who maintain a lifelong practice of good nutrition accompanied by resistive training. Many elderly adults lose their interest in food, and as a result their nutritional status deteriorates. The combination of poor nutrition and physical inactivity can initiate a downward cycle of muscular wasting. As mentioned in chapter 4, the loss of muscle mass not only decreases the amount of strength and functional capacity of the individual, it also accounts for some of the decreased aerobic fitness capability that occurs with aging. The primary measure of fitness, $\dot{V}O_2$max, is highly dependent on the amount of muscle working during the measurement. Thus, significant losses in muscle mass can result in a loss of physical function, fitness reserves, and in time, the mobility that is essential for independent living.

Skeletal Muscle Characteristics

Studying the age-related changes in microstructural characteristics of human muscle is difficult, because the available techniques are invasive and not completely free of discomfort. To obtain skeletal muscle tissue, a biopsy needle is used to remove a small amount of muscle. However, because this process is invasive, the needle must be small and the number of samples from each muscle must be kept to a minimum. Consequently, studies of human muscle characteristics are plagued with sampling problems. The amount of tissue available is usually only a few milligrams and contains only a few hundred muscle fibers. Therefore, biopsies taken from different locations and depths within the muscle have produced different results, and according to Elder, Bradbury, and Roberts (1982), the variability of fiber-type composition between biopsy sites is larger than the variability within a single biopsy site.

Because of these substantial problems associated with human analyses (e.g., nutritional and physical activity differences) and because animal muscle tissue is very similar to human muscle tissue, much of the available information regarding the effects of aging on skeletal muscle characteristics has been derived from animal studies. The entire muscle of an animal, usually the rat, can be excised and studied cross-sectionally or longitudinally in intricate detail, fiber by fiber. Though the number of animal studies of muscle far exceeds the number of human studies, both provide important information regarding aging effects on muscle.

A muscle is organized into several subunits, shown in Figure 5.9, a and b. The first subunit is the fasciculus, which is a packet of muscle fibers. Each muscle fiber (i.e., muscle cell) is a subunit composed of myofibrils, which are made up of myofilaments. Each myofilament is primarily made up of the proteins actin and myosin. Muscles increase in size (hypertrophy) by increasing, through use, the amount of myofibrillar protein, thus resulting in an increase in the cross-sectional area of the muscle. The prevailing view has always been that most of the strength gained occurs by hypertrophy of the existing muscle fibers, not by increasing the number of fibers. One exception, discussed in the training section of this chapter, was the study done by Gonyea and co-workers (1986), who used a unique animal-training model to induce substantial hypertrophy in the muscles and then applied a technique that allowed them to count the actual number of muscle fibers. They reported an increase of 10% in the number of fibers after heavy resistance training.

Muscle fibers are characterized by physiologists as slow- or fast-twitch fibers, with fast-twitch fibers being further subdivided into two groups. Slow-twitch fibers contract very slowly, using the aerobic energy system to drive the contractions. These fibers metabolize glycogen for energy, and, as long

as the work load is at a relatively low-to-moderate intensity, energy can be supplied at the same rate at which it is being consumed by the fibers. Because slow-twitch fibers can maintain a balance between energy production and consumption at moderate work loads for a relatively long time, they are fatigue resistant and are called slow oxidative (SO) fibers. Morphologists (those who study cell structure, not function) call such fibers Type I fibers. The body depends primarily on SO, or Type I, muscle fibers when muscular contractions must be maintained for long periods, such as in long-distance running, cycling, or swimming. Although muscles generally have a mix of both major types of muscle fibers, some muscles like the soleus, which is used almost exclusively in slow postural movements, are composed primarily of slow-twitch fibers.

Fast-twitch muscle fibers contract very rapidly, using energy derived from immediate stores of adenosine triphosphate (ATP) and from anaerobic energy processes to develop tension quickly. They convert, via a short-term anaerobic process called glycogenolysis, some of the glycogen stored in the muscle to energy. Because of this capability, fast-twitch fibers are also called fast-glycolytic (FG) fibers, or Type IIb fibers. FG, or Type IIB, fibers contract two to three times faster than SO, or Type I, fibers. Type IIb muscle fibers produce the rapid, powerful contractions needed for running sprint races and throwing a discus or shot put. The muscles that are used in these types of activities, especially the muscles of athletes who train in power events, have a high percentage of fast-twitch fibers.

Some Type II fast-twitch fibers are intermediate in contraction speed and combine both aerobic and anaerobic properties. They are called fast oxidative-glycolytic, or Type IIa, fibers. A third but much less frequently seen type of fast-twitch fiber in humans has characteristics between those of Type IIa and IIb fibers. These are Type IIx muscle fibers and appear when these fibers are undergoing transition from Type IIb to Type IIa.

Muscle Fiber Quantity

More scientists agree that there is a loss in the number of muscle fibers with increased aging than can agree on almost any other issue regarding the aging muscular system (Green, 1986; Lexell, Henriksson-Larsen, Wimblad, & Sjöström, 1983). In fact, the age-related decline in muscle mass,

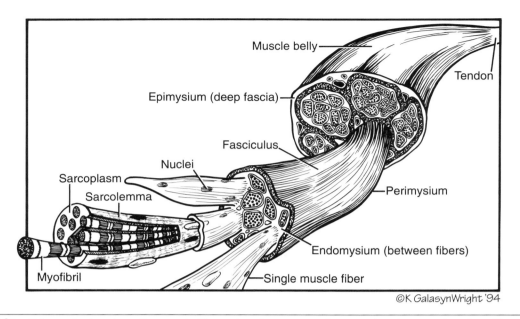

©K GalasynWright '94

Figure 5.9a Schematic drawing of a muscle illustrating three types of connective tissue: epimysium (the outer layer), perimysium (surrounding each fasciculus, or group of fibers), and endomysium (surrounding individual fibers).
Copyright 1994 K. Galasyn-Wright, Champaign, IL, 1994.

particularly after age 70, is thought to be due in large part to a decrement in the size and number of muscle fibers (Green, 1986) and to disuse. However, the age-related loss of muscle fibers is relatively small, on the order of 5% (Arabadjis et al., 1990).

Muscle Fiber Type and Composition

Although the loss of muscle fibers with age is relatively well accepted, agreement on which fiber types are lost is not at all easy to obtain. If one type of muscle fiber were lost in greater quantities than another, it would change the fiber type composition of the muscle. For example, if more fast-twitch fibers were lost than slow-twitch, then the muscle would have a higher proportion of slow-twitch fibers. Three hypotheses explain the effect of age on muscle fiber-type composition, but none of the three enjoys consensus of agreement at this time. One hypothesis is that the proportion of muscle fiber types remains relatively constant throughout life, with a loss of all fiber types. A second hypothesis is that more fast- than slow-twitch fibers are lost with aging. This is thought to result from the progressive and selective death of the large motoneurons that activate fast-twitch motor units. The third hypothesis is that fast-twitch motor units transform, primarily through disuse, into slow-twitch units, changing the fast-to-slow-twitch ratio and making it appear that fast-twitch fibers have been lost.

Green (1986), in reviewing the most recent evidence, was convinced that the age-related loss of muscle fibers is not fiber-type specific, but the selective loss of fast-twitch muscle fibers continues to be a controversial topic. Several investigators have reported that fast-twitch fibers are more affected by aging than slow-twitch fibers and that Type II fibers are selectively lost (Engel, 1970; Larsson, 1978). Others, however, have found no difference in the slow-twitch-to-fast-twitch ratio, either in young and older humans (Essen-Gustavsson & Borges, 1986; Lexell et al., 1983) or in rats (Eddinger, Moss, & Cassens, 1985; Kovanen & Suominen, 1987). The resolution of the fiber-type ratio controversy may hinge on the specific ages studied and a technology better able to differentiate aging, disuse, and pathological changes. Several investigators have shown that, indeed, no differences exist in fiber-type ratio in men and women ranging in age from 20 to 60 years. In subjects older than 60, however, unlike the young subjects, fewer Type IIa and IIb fibers were found. When only the number of Type II fibers was compared for the different ages, there seemed to be slightly more IIa (oxidative-glycolytic) than IIb (glycolytic) fibers (Aniansson, Hedberg, Henning, & Grimby, 1986; Grimby, Danneskiold-Samsoe, Hvid, & Saltin, 1982; Grimby & Saltin, 1983). Some Type II fibers that lose their innervation may be reinnervated by Type I motor neurons (Grimby & Saltin,

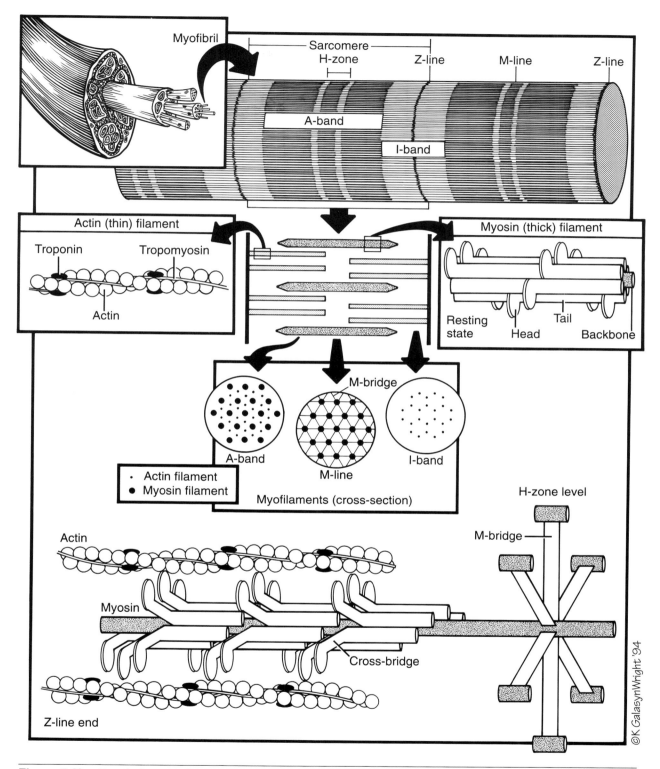

Figure 5.9b Detailed view of the myosin and actin protein filaments in muscle. The arrangement of myosin (thick) and actin (thin) filaments gives skeletal muscle its striated appearance.

Copyright 1994 K. Galasyn-Wright, Champaign, IL, 1994.

1983). This would result in an apparent maintenance of slow-twitch fibers and a loss of fast-twitch fibers, although in fact some slow-twitch fibers may have been lost.

Much of the controversy about whether fast- or slow-twitch fibers are lost selectively is probably because different investigators study different muscles and different species, use different methodologies, and sample different areas of muscle. The selective loss of specific fiber types has been shown to depend on whether the muscle fiber being examined was taken from the belly or the ends of the muscle (Arabadjis et al., 1990). It may be that when fiber types are relatively unused in a particular muscle, or a particular area of the muscle, they decline with age in that muscle. For example, fast-twitch muscle fibers may deteriorate selectively in the soleus muscle, which is predominantly a slow-twitch-fiber muscle. Because the demands on the soleus are almost exclusively slow contractions or aerobic work, fast-twitch motor units in this muscle are rarely activated. A small percentage may, through disuse, eventually die. Arabadjis, Heffner, and Pendergast (1990) suggest that this might be a good explanation for rat muscle, but it may be too simplistic to explain the selective losses in humans, because human muscles have a more mixed fiber-type composition than rat muscles. It is also possible that as individuals age the histochemical and functional differences between fast-twitch and slow-twitch muscle fibers decrease. That is, the contraction speed of fast fibers slows down some and slow fibers contract somewhat more quickly. The slow fibers demonstrate these changes sooner than fast fibers (McCarter, 1978). However, in a study designed to overcome many methodological problems, autopsied human vastus lateralis (thigh) muscle tissue was analyzed for muscle area, fiber density, total number of fibers, and proportion of fiber types (Lexell, Taylor, & Sjöström, 1988). They found that the major cause of muscle atrophy was a loss of fibers. Losses were approximately the same in fast- and slow-twitch fibers.

Another age-related change is that the fiber-type arrangement shifts somewhat with aging. In young muscles, fiber types—slow- and fast-twitch—are interspersed. In old muscles, more incidences of fiber type grouping are seen (Lexell, 1992).

Consensus is growing among biogerontologists that many age-related changes in muscle are more specific to muscle function than to age. Although many investigators support the observation that the number of muscle fibers significantly declines

with aging, almost all indicate that the relatively small percentage of fibers lost does not account for the much larger percentage of lost muscular force. Some mechanism other than muscle fiber loss and atrophy must be involved in the loss of muscular strength and power.

Muscle Fiber Size

Several researchers of human muscle (Denis et al., 1986; Lexell et al., 1988) and of rat muscle (Brown, 1987; Kovanen & Suominen, 1987) have found the size of the muscle fiber to be smaller in aged muscle, but most investigators of both human and animal muscle have found no difference in the mean fiber size (Arabadjis et al., 1990; Lexell et al., 1983; Walters et al., 1990).

Contractile Properties of Muscle Fiber

The integrity of individual muscle fibers, regardless of number and ratio, for both slow- and fast-twitch types seems to be maintained with aging. That is, if muscle fibers are isolated in an animal preparation and electrically stimulated to contract, old muscle fibers contract with as much tension as young muscle fibers (McCarter, 1978; McCarter & McGee, 1987). Thus, the decreased force produced by the entire aged muscle is not due to declines in the maximum amount of tension that can be produced by individual fibers but to a smaller number of functional motor units (Campbell, McComas, & Petito, 1973). Nor is the decreased force due to the inability of the neurons to activate the muscle. Older individuals can fully activate their muscles, so the loss of muscular force must be due to other factors (Phillips, Bruce, Newton, & Woledge, 1992).

Capillary Density

The smallest arteries (arterioles) branch into even smaller, almost microscopic blood vessels called capillaries. Some capillaries are so small that they are microscopic, having a capillary wall only one cell thick and allowing only one blood cell to squeeze through them at a time. The larger the number of capillaries per square millimeter of tissue, the greater the capillary density. An estimate of the capillary density of human skeletal muscle (vastus lateralis) is 585 ± 40 capillaries per square millimeter (Åstrand & Rodahl, 1986). The capillarization of muscle, however, is one vascular function that appears not to change with aging

(Aniansson et al., 1981; Brown, 1987; Grimby et al., 1982; Walters, Sweeney, & Farrar, 1990). Capillary density seems to be maintained throughout aging.

Metabolism

Within the muscle cells (as in other types of cells throughout the body) are organelles called mitochondria, in which enzymatic processes take place to convert the energy from food into a type of energy that the body can use. The maximum ability of the muscle cells to use oxygen in the production of energy is called the muscle respiratory capacity. The capacity of this system is lower in some muscles in aged humans (Trounce, Byrne, & Marzuki, 1989) and animals (Farrar, Martin, & Ardies, 1981; Hansford & Castro, 1982), but the magnitude of age-related decline is not uniform for all skeletal muscles or all respiratory enzymes (Hansford & Castro, 1982). Farrar and his group have found that although the oxidative capacity of slow oxidative and fast oxidative-glycolytic fibers is lower in old animals, it is not different in fast-glycolytic fibers (Walters et al., 1990). They proposed that the primary reason that differences are seen in the oxidative enzymatic activity in young and old rats is that, just as is true of people, old rats are less and less physically active as they age. That is why, they suggest, age differences are seen in muscles that are highly oxidative, such as the gastrocnemius (calf muscle), but not in muscles that are primarily fast-glycolytic muscles, such as the flexor digitorum longus (toe flexors). The muscles that have a greater number of fast oxidative-glycolytic fibers would be more affected by an age-related decrease in physical activity. When physical activity is not decreased with aging, the age differences in respiratory capacity disappear, as discussed later in the section on training effects on respiratory capacity.

Neurological Function

Muscle fibers are innervated by a motor neuron, and the motor neuron, its axon, and all of the muscle fibers that it innervates are called a motor unit. The muscle fiber types are the same in specific motor units, so that motor units also can be categorized as slow oxidative, fast-glycolytic, and fast oxidative-glycolytic.

Some motor units are lost with aging (Green, 1986; Grimby, 1988), a loss that is thought to be due to the death of the motor neurons in the spinal cord. Surviving motor units, which are likely to be slow-twitch units, increase in fiber number by reinnervating some of the fibers that were innervated by a motor neuron that has died (Campbell et al., 1973). Thus, the number of muscle fibers per motor neuron (the motor neuron innervation ratio) may grow larger in the aged adult (Fitts, 1981). If the innervation ratio is substantially changed, fine control of muscle contraction (muscular coordination) may be impaired. Although some motor units are lost, there appears to be no age-related alteration in the neuromuscular function of those remaining; that is, the motor neuron stimulation, the myoneural junction, and the muscular characteristics are unchanged (Walters et al., 1990).

Effects of Physical Activity and Training on Strength

The effects of regular, systematic physical activity on the muscular system of the aging adult are impressive, and the result of a well-planned, scientifically based, resistive strength-training program can be spectacular. Of all the bodily systems, the neuromuscular system can demonstrate the most visibly dramatic difference between a completely sedentary, inactive person and a person who conscientiously trains. In Figure 5.10, a through d, a series of photographs taken of Clarence Bass over a 40-year period clearly demonstrates the capacity of an individual to maintain muscle mass with training for many years. Over this period of time, he has maintained a lifestyle that includes resistive strength-training, aerobic training, and an excellent diet. What is remarkable about his accomplishments is that his training program is so well organized that it requires only 4 hours a week ("Clarence Bass's Testing," 1993).

Differences in neuromuscular function can range from the 80-year-old who cannot lift a 10-lb weight to a person of the same age who can lift 200 lb, from an octogenarian who cannot get up out of a chair to one who can run a 26.2-mile marathon in a masters track meet. The muscular system is maintained to a great extent by the amount of daily physical activity an individual experiences, either in work or in leisure pursuits such as sports. Older adults who stay physically active have greater strength levels than do sedentary persons (Viljanen, Viitasalo, & Kujala, 1991).

Figure 5.10   Clarence Bass at age (a) 15, (b) 31, (c) 43, and (d) 55.
Photos courtesy of Clarence Bass, *Lean for Life*, Ripped Enterprises, 528 Chama NE, Albuquerque, NM 87108.

The types of movements people make during their daily activities throughout their lives will determine the amount of functional capacity that they can maintain in their musculoskeletal system. Muscles that are never used will deteriorate with the passage of time. Individuals who are physically very active and who make it a point to resistance-train all of their muscle groups throughout the muscles' ranges of motion will maintain an adequate amount of strength well into their senior years.

The muscular system responds profoundly to strength training. The training effects are highly specific not only to the type of training, whether aerobic or anaerobic, but to the muscle that is being used and the way it is being used. Improvements in the amount of force that can be produced are relatively rapid, occurring within 2 months. Also, during this short period, visible changes occur in the shape and tone of body muscles. For these reasons, strength-training programs provide a psychological feeling of accomplishment for many of the elderly who participate in them (see chapter 10).

Habitual Physical Activity

Individuals who remain physically active by participating in sports, or who work in a strength-demanding job, are stronger in measures of both isometric and isokinetic strength than inactive adults, suggesting that the age-related decrements in muscle strength are a function of the type and amount of activity in which adults participate (Aniansson, Sperling, Rundgren, & Lehnberg, 1983; Dummer et al., 1985; Frontera, Meredith, O'Reilly, Knuttgen, & Evans, 1988; Petrofsky & Lind, 1975). For example, amateur tennis players of both genders in their mid-60s had stronger knee extensors and flexors, when measured by an isokinetic dynamometer, than their sedentary counterparts (Laforest et al., 1990). Women who maintained a physically active lifestyle had higher levels of grip strength than sedentary women (Rikli & Busch, 1986). Two research groups failed to find a relationship between habitual activity and increased strength of the lower limbs, but both of these groups studied very small samples and used a questionnaire to define an "active" lifestyle (Cunningham et al., 1987; Fugl-Meyer, Gustafsson, & Burstedt, 1980). In both cases, the investigators admitted that the questionnaire was not a suitable way to establish

the level of physical activity in which the subjects participated.

Adults who continue working at jobs that require strength above the levels required for a sedentary lifestyle generally maintain much higher levels of strength. Figure 5.11 shows the grip-strength data from machine shop workers of various ages. These workers' hand-grip strength did not change at all over a period of 40 years.

Strength-Training Programs

Resistive exercise can increase strength substantially in adults at any age (Frontera et al., 1988; Moritani & deVries, 1980; Tomanek & Wood, 1970) and in aged animals (Goldspink & Howells, 1974). Table 5.2 shows the results of several studies on the effects of strength training on muscular strength of older adults. For example, the percentage of strength gained was related to the intensity and length of the strength-training program. The results of the Frontera et al. (1988) study show that when dynamic strength training at high levels of resistance was continued for 12 weeks, strength gains were as high as 227%. Note also that older people have the same absolute rate of strength gain that young people have, but because they usually start an exercise program in a weaker condition, their relative gains are greater.

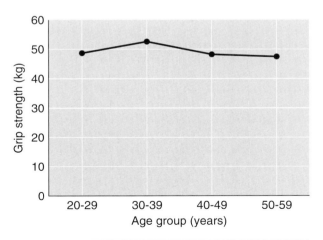

Figure 5.11 Grip strength of machine shop workers of various ages.
From "Aging, Isometric Strength and Endurance, and Cardiovascular Responses to Static Effort" by J.S. Petrofsky and A.R. Lind, 1975, *Journal of Applied Physiology,* **38**, p. 92. Copyright 1975 by the American Physiological Society. Reprinted by permission.

Table 5.2
Strength-Training Trials in the Elderly

Source	Number of subjects and sex (F,M)	Mean age, years	Type of training[a]	Resistance	Duration, week[b]	Muscle group	Mean strength increase, %
Perkins & Kaiser	15 F	73.6	Static	High	6	Knee extensors	57
	5 M		Dynamic	Moderate	6	Knee extensors	64
Liemohn	6 M	61-70	Static	High	6	Knee extensors and flexors	17 and 24, respectively
Aniansson & Gustafsson	12 M	71	Static and dynamic	Low	12	Knee extensors	9-22
	12 M (controls)	71	Static and dynamic	Low	12	None	0
Moritani & deVries	5 M	70	Dynamic	High	8	Elbow flexors	23
	5 M	22	Dynamic	High	8	Elbow flexors	30
Larsson	18 M	22-65	Dynamic	Low	15	Knee extensors	2.9-7.5[c]
Kauffman	10 F	69	Static	High	6	Abductor digiti minimi	72
	10 F	23	Static	High	6	Abductor digiti minimi	95

Study	N/sex	Age	Type	Intensity	Weeks	Muscle groups	Result
Frontera et al.	12 M	60-72	Dynamic	High	12	Knee extensors and flexors	107 and 227, respectively
Hagberg et al.	23 M,F	70-79	Dynamic	Low-moderate	26	Upper and lower body	18 and 9, respectively
Current study (Fiatarone et al., 1990)	10 M,F	90	Dynamic	High	8	Knee extensors	174

[a]Static indicates isometric; dynamic indicates isotonic.
[b]All training sessions were conducted 3 days a week except for those by Larsson, which were 2 days a week.
[c]Not significant.

Note. From "High-Intensity Strength Training in Nonagenarians" by M.A. Fiatarone et al., 1990, *Journal of the American Medical Association*, **263**, p. 3033. Copyright 1990, American Medical Association. Reprinted by permission.

The results of a study by Kauffman (1985), however, questioned the dogma that older adults always start an exercise program with lower strength levels than young subjects. Kauffman obtained premeasures of and then trained the abductor digiti minimi (the abductor of the little finger) of young and older women. This muscle is rarely used, and so the effects of a strength-training regimen uncontaminated by exercise history could be determined. Surprisingly, all the women started out at similar strength levels and made about the same gains throughout the three sessions a week, 6-week training program (see Figure 5.12). Even though it appears that the young women gained more strength in the fifth and sixth weeks, those gains were not significant. These data emphasize that strength losses are not the same for all muscles, and all muscles do not necessarily lose mass.

Physicians, researchers, and exercise physiologists traditionally have been very cautious in prescribing strength training or approving weight lifting for older adults. When researchers first began testing the effects of strength training on older adults, their "old" subjects tended to be in their late 40s and 50s. They found that these older subjects increased their maximal arm strength the same percentage (20%) as young subjects after 8 weeks of progressive strength training (Moritani & deVries, 1980). Subjects of

older and older ages were eventually tested, and at all ages the *relative* strength gains from training were not different. Men between the ages of 60 and 72 improved the strength of their knee flexors (227%) and extensors (107%) during a 12-week strength-training program and increased the isokinetic peak torque that they could produce with their knee extensors and flexors by 10% to 18.5% (Frontera et al., 1988). These strength gains were also accompanied by significant muscular hypertrophy as measured by computerized tomographic scans and girth measurements.

Pavel Dobrev is a relative pioneer in resistive strength-training programs for older adults; he has encouraged them to participate in resistive exercise for many years. He claims to have made longitudinal research observations since 1960 in his weight-training school in Bulgaria that document the preventive, rehabilitative, and remedial effects of resistive exercise in persons over 70 years old. He has even reported beneficial effects of resistive exercise training for persons suffering from high blood pressure and atherosclerosis and those who have experienced myocardial infarctions (see Dobrev, 1980). But although his weight-training school has been an object of considerable interest to many biologists, doctors, weight lifters, and rehabilitation experts who visited the school, his work has not been fully embraced by the scholarly and medical community, because it has not been documented via the traditional research channels in this country.

Physicians in the United States have been dubious about weight lifting and resistive exercise for older adults who have hypertension or a history of cardiovascular problems, and these physicians' concerns have extended also to their prescriptions for normal, healthy older adults. Many physicians and exercise physiologists actively discourage participation in high-intensity resistance exercise. Their attitude is exemplified in the following statement from the American College of Sports Medicine *Guidelines for Exercise Testing and Prescription:* "High intensity exercise should be discouraged. Isometric exercise is not strictly contraindicated in hypertensive patients, however, high intensity exercise and activities with a significant isometric component should be minimized in those with established hypertension. Weight training should be prescribed using low resistances and high repetitions" (ACSM, 1991, p. 166).

The concern has been that the high pressures that can develop within the chest cavity during contractions against heavy resistance could result

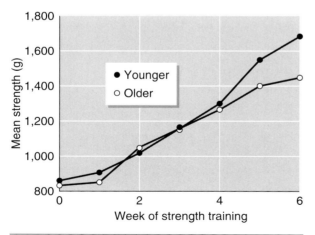

Figure 5.12 Cumulative strength scores of the abductor digiti minimi (little finger adduction) of women ages 20 to 26 and 65 to 73 over a 6-week strength-training program.

From "Strength-Training Effect in Young and Aged Women" by T.L. Kauffman, 1985, *Archives of Physical Medicine and Rehabilitation,* **65**, p. 224. Copyright 1985 by the American Congress of Rehabilitation Medicine. Reprinted by permission of W.B. Saunders Company.

in a great resistance to bloodflow through the vessels in the thoracic cavity and precipitate cardiovascular or cerebrovascular accidents. However, Lewis et al. (1983) have shown that not much difference exists in the blood pressure responses between isometric and dynamic exercises if similar activities are compared. Under the careful supervision of a physician, exercise physiologist, or rehabilitation specialist, older adults who have a relatively low risk for cardiac problems and who have normal ventricular function could safely participate in strength and resistance training (Pollock & Wilmore, 1990). Heavy lifting and heavy resistance training are not recommended for adults who are at a high risk for a cardiac crisis.

Some of the oldest adults to be resistance-trained were studied by Fiatarone et al. (1990), who found large gains in the muscular strength, endurance, and mobility of 86- to 96-year-old subjects. In this study, 10 very frail individuals who lived in a long-term care facility and who also had one or more combinations of osteoarthritis, coronary artery disease, osteoporotic fractures, and hypertension, participated in an 8-week progressive resistance strength-training program under careful medical supervision. The subjects exercised only one muscle group, the knee extensors, by executing three sets of eight knee extensions at 80% of their maximum strength. The results of this study were remarkable. The average increase in strength was 174% on the right leg and 180% on the left leg. The strength gain continued throughout the 8 weeks and had not reached a plateau by the end of the program. More important, however, were the changes in mobility that occurred following the strength-training program. The nonagenarians improved 48% in a measure of gait speed that required more balance than their habitual gait speed required. Whereas in healthy adults who are highly mobile, correlations between leg strength and gait speed are near zero (Buckner & deLateur, 1991), there is a substantial inverse relationship between strength and walking time of institutionalized patients who have extremely low levels of strength (see Figure 5.13).

After participating in the Fiatarone group's (1990) training program, two subjects were able to eliminate the use of their canes to walk, and one of three subjects who, prior to training, were unable to rise from a chair without using their arms was able to do so. Considering the fact that these individuals were at a very advanced age,

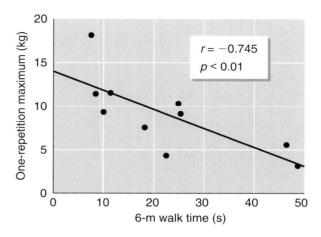

Figure 5.13 Comparison of initial muscle strength and functional mobility of the knee extensors of subjects 86 to 96 years old before strength training. From "High-Intensity Strength Training in Nonagenarians" by M.A. Fiatarone et al., 1990, *Journal of the American Medical Association*, **263**, p. 3031. Copyright 1990, American Medical Association. Reprinted by permission.

had lived an extremely sedentary life, had multiple chronic diseases and functional disabilities, had nutritional inadequacies, and exercised only one muscle group during this experiment, these results are a remarkable testimony to the benefits that can be gained from a properly conducted strength-training program. Because of these results and those from other studies of slightly younger old adults, many gerontological fitness specialists now suggest that progressive resistance exercise should supplement aerobic work in the weekly exercise program of individuals at any age.

For those very old persons who cannot participate in a progressive high-resistance strength program like that described previously, substantial gains in strength, flexibility, and mobility can still be made even with very-low-impact and light exercise programs (Brown & Holloszy, 1991; Gillett, 1989; Sager, 1984). A relatively low-intensity exercise program 5 days a week for 3 months resulted in significantly better standing balance for women ages 60 to 71 (Brown & Holloszy, 1991).

Average healthy 80-year-olds may be at or very near the threshold value of quadriceps strength necessary to rise from a chair. Therefore, in the frail elderly, exercise programs may have to begin with very small movements while the participants are seated in chairs (Reynolds & Garrett, 1989). Because the frail elderly have such limited physical capacity, these low-impact programs provide small increases in strength and endurance. However, for frail elderly adults, gains in relative strength are more important than gains in absolute strength. The strength necessary to climb stairs, for example, depends on how much body weight must be lifted. Relative strength, therefore, is:

$$\text{strength (in newton-meters of torque)}/\text{height [m]} \cdot \text{weight [kg]}.$$

Commonly, relative strength declines because body fat increases and lean body mass decreases with age; thus, the amount of body weight to be lifted increases whereas the amount of muscle tissue available to do the work decreases. If relative strength gains in adults unable to climb stairs can be made through a training program so that stair climbing can be resumed, then the stair climbing itself will maintain enough relative strength to continue stair climbing (Fisher, Pendergast, & Calkins, 1991).

Long-term research data are not available to provide answers as to whether these small increases can really prevent or postpone immobility or falling, but because strength, mobility, and flexibility are associated with a decreased risk of falling (Tobis et al., 1989), the chances are good that these programs may reduce the incidence of falling in the frail population. At least 40% of those over age 80 who live in the community experience a fall (Prudham & Grimley-Evans, 1981), but the percentage of persons who fall is much higher (61%) among those in institutions (Tinetti, 1987). Strength plays an important role in the prevention of falling by enabling individuals to correct momentary losses of balance in time to prevent catastrophic falling events. It is probable that much more research will be conducted in the near future on strength training in older populations, because the National Institute of Aging has placed the causes of disability and the prevention of falling as one of their highest funding priorities for the 1990s (Gibbons, 1991).

Exercise and Muscle Mass

Whether muscle mass increases in older adults as a result of training has been a topic of interest to many researchers. A certain amount of strength development is attributable to improved neural activation of muscles, which occurs before any increase in muscle size. The responses of muscles to strength or resistance training occur in three

stages (Jones, 1989). In the first stage, a rapid, dramatic improvement in strength and power occurs without any change in the size, characteristics, or biochemical aspects of the muscle tissue. These initial increases in strength are due to improved neurological coordination of the motor units used to carry out the task, to an improved understanding of the task (i.e., learning), and perhaps to increased expectations and motivation. The second stage is characterized by increased strength of an individual muscle without a change in the area of the muscle. Only in the third stage does a slow but steady increase in size and strength of exercised muscle occur. Many have questioned, therefore, whether older adults who participate in strength-training programs ever achieve the final stage of increased muscle mass.

An increase in muscle mass requires a progressive resistance strength-training program in which individuals repeat 8 to 12 times the production of a force that is greater than 40% of their maximum force output. At first it was thought that most of the strength gained by older individuals who participated in strength training was due to improved nervous system activation and not to muscular hypertrophy (Moritani & deVries, 1980). However, the more recent use of CT scans to determine cross-sectional area of muscle has shown clearly that muscle mass does increase in the elderly. Figure 5.14a is a diagram of a digitized CT scan of the relative proportions of leg muscle, bone, and fat. From this type of diagram the cross-sectional area of muscle can be calculated. Figure 5.14, b and c, shows the increases in muscle mass after 6 and 12 weeks of training on a thigh-knee dynamic machine (Frontera et al., 1988). Twelve 60- to 72-year-old sedentary subjects performed 3 sets of 8 repetitions of knee extension and flexion three times a week for 12 weeks. Complementing the findings of Frontera et al. (1988) that leg muscle mass increased with training, Brown, McCartney, and Sale (1990) showed that muscle mass also increased in arm muscles after 12 weeks of strength training.

The exercise-induced increases (11%) in muscle mass of the Fiatarone et al. (1990) subjects, frail 86- to 96-year-olds, were within the range of increases seen in younger subjects (3%-22%). Before these frail old subjects began their strength program, the muscle mass of their legs accounted for only 31% of the total cross-sectional area of their thighs. Several investigators have found that muscle mass in elderly people increases in response to progressive resistance exercise training basically the same

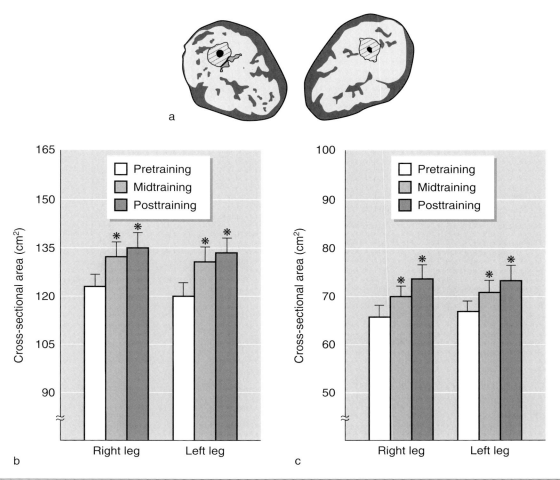

Figure 5.14 (a) Cross-sectional digitized CT scan of thigh muscle, showing muscle mass (light gray), bone (cross-hatched), and fat (dark gray); changes in thigh muscle mass as a result of training: (b) image analysis and (c) planimetric analysis. An asterisk indicates a difference from pretraining measurements ($p < 0.05$).
From "Strength Conditioning in Older Men: Skeletal Muscle Hypertrophy and Improved Function" by W.R. Frontera et al.,1988, *Journal of Applied Physiology*, **64**, p. 1042. Copyright 1988 by the American Physiological Society. Reprinted by permission.

way it does in young people (Brown, McCartney, & Sale, 1990; Frontera et al., 1988; Kauffman, 1985). However, the increases in muscle mass are not as large as the increases in strength.

Strength training by older adults results in substantial improvements in strength, and a lifestyle that incorporates strength training will surely maintain muscle mass to some degree. No lifetime longitudinal studies of the effects of resistance training on the maintenance of muscle mass have been conducted, however, so the extent to which strength training is effective is not known. Observations of aged weight lifters provide some evidence, but only force output, not muscle mass, is quantified in these competitive events. What has become clear is that endurance training cannot prevent the deterioration in muscle mass. Daily

exercise training will attenuate age-related loss of muscle mass, but it will not prevent it (Zacour & Gardiner, 1986). Even when rats of two different strains exercised at levels far beyond those to which most humans would willingly comply, they nonetheless suffered some loss of muscle mass (Cartee & Farrar, 1987; Farrar et al., 1981).

Skeletal Muscle Fiber Response to Exercise

Muscle fibers have an amazing ability to adapt to the demands placed on them. Both the contractile apparatus and the energy metabolism systems become more efficient with exercise training. With endurance exercise, both Type I oxidative muscle and Type IIa fibers hypertrophy and increase their ability to produce energy on a long-term basis (Kovanen & Suominen, 1987; McCarter, 1978). Type IIb fibers also hypertrophy with training (MacDougall & Davies, 1984; MacDougall, Elder, Sale, Moroz, & Sutton, 1980).

Muscle Fiber Quantity

The consensus has always been that individuals are born with a certain number of muscle fibers and that this number is not changed by exercise. Certainly aerobic training does not increase the quantity of fibers (Daw, Starnes, & White, 1988; Mitchell, Byrnes, & Mazzeo, 1991). However, in the mid-80s, Gonyea and his group (1986) conducted a series of fascinating studies of the changes in muscle composition of cats as they progressed through a resistance exercise program. The cats were taught to lift a weight with one paw in order to get their food. Each week the weight was increased, so that the cats were eventually lifting very heavy weights for their size. After the training program, the fiber characteristics for the muscle from the strength-trained paw were compared to those fibers from the untrained paw. By counting instead of estimating their numbers, Gonyea and his colleagues reported that the strength-trained paw had 9% more fibers than the untrained paw. We may conclude that with endurance-type training and even moderate-intensity strength training, the quantity of muscle fibers is not likely to increase. But if muscle undergoes progressive high-resistance training for several months, the number of fibers in the muscle may be increased by a very small percentage.

Muscle Fiber Type and the Fast-Twitch/Slow-Twitch Ratio

Methodological problems that make it difficult to determine the effects of aging on muscle fiber-type composition also present barriers to understanding the role of exercise training in maintaining or changing the muscle fiber-type ratio in aging individuals. Some researchers suggest that endurance exercise training changes the fast-twitch–slow-twitch (FT/ST) ratio in muscles. Evidence supporting these changes comes from three sources: cross-sectional studies of individuals who have trained for long periods of time, studies of animals that have been trained throughout their

lives and that have proportionately more slow-twitch fibers than their nontrained counterparts, and resistance-training studies.

Muscle Fiber-Type Composition

One of the first ways that researchers attempted to discover whether participation in physical work would change fiber types was to study the fiber-type composition of athletes in endurance sports. Older individuals in general have a higher percentage of slow-twitch muscle fibers than young people have, but endurance athletes, both young and old, have even higher percentages of slow-twitch fibers (e.g., Clarkson et al., 1981; Gollnick, Armstrong, Saubert, Piehl, & Saltin, 1972; Melichna et al., 1990). Animals that ran on a treadmill throughout their lifetimes had higher percentages of slow-twitch fiber types than did animals that never exercised (Kovanen & Suominen, 1987). Support for the conclusion that endurance training changes fiber-type composition also comes from comparing the fiber types of older athletes who quit training with those of senior athletes who continue their training. When older oarsmen terminated their competitive careers, the number of Type I fibers (determined histochemically) and the percentage of total area contributed by Type I fibers decreased compared to those oarsmen who continued training and competing (Larsson & Ansved, 1985).

Other evidence that exercise affects fiber-type ratios is that although average older persons have a smaller number of glycolytic fibers (Type IIb) than younger people, this is not the case when older athletes are compared to younger athletes. Thus, the training of older athletes, in addition to maintaining Type I fibers, may also enable the athletes to be more physically active and to recruit Type II fibers. If Type IIb fibers are recruited and used, they may be better maintained. Also, because daily endurance training in older individuals prevents the attrition of both slow- and fast-twitch fibers (Faulkner, Maxwell, Brook, & Lieberman, 1971), individuals who exercise vigorously on a daily basis may more successfully maintain the capacity to recruit Type IIb fast-twitch fibers.

Bear in mind that most of these studies are cross-sectional studies of trained versus untrained individuals. This type of research design does not tell whether the differences in fiber types that are seen between young and old, trained and untrained are due to genetic factors, training, or aging. However, evidence that strength training can change fiber-type composition in older subjects is persuasive. Individuals who have participated in resistive strength training have increased the relative area of their fast-twitch fibers by 9% to 22% (Aniansson & Gustafsson, 1981; Klitgaard et al., 1989; Larsson, 1982).

One reason that endurance-trained individuals may have a higher percentage of slow-twitch fibers is that their fast-twitch glycolytic fibers (IIb) may be converted to fast-twitch oxidative-glycolytic fibers (Type IIa). Or, Type IIa fibers may be transformed to Type I fibers (Faulkner, Maxwell, Brook, & Lieberman, 1971; Melichna et al., 1990). Transformations of this kind cannot be validated in cross-sectional studies nor even in studies of humans where muscle tissue has been compared before and after an exercise program, because the researcher can never be sure that the samples have been taken from the same location in the muscle. But laboratory studies of animal muscles in which long-term endurance contractions have been simulated by electrically stimulating the muscles for long periods of time have shown that under intense and extended endurance training, Type II fibers may transform into Type I, and Type IIb fibers into Type IIa (Pette, 1984). This transformation, or plasticity, was not as great in old rats as it was in young rats (Walters, Sweeney, & Farrar, 1991) in that the time course of adaptation was slowed. However, at the end of 90 days the magnitude of change was similar.

Muscle Fiber-Type Proportions

Even though many researchers support the hypothesis that endurance training prevents the often observed age-related change in the fiber-type composition of muscles, others believe that endurance training does not change fiber-type composition (Andersen, 1975; Denis et al., 1986; Gollnick, Timson, Moore, & Riedy, 1981; Suominen, Heikkinen, & Parkatti, 1977). Mitchell et al. (1990) suggested that it may be difficult to see a change in fiber-type ratio of some muscles if the percentage of Type I fibers in the muscle is very high. An example of this is the soleus muscle, which is composed of 96% to 99% Type I fibers.

Muscle Fiber Size

The number of muscle fibers in a muscle does not increase with training, except under the unusual

circumstances discussed in the study by Gonyea et al. (1986). Therefore, the major mechanism by which muscle girth increases in size with resistive training is through a change in the diameter and size of muscle fibers. Specifically, the myofibrillar diameter increases (Goldspink, 1983). When athletes were compared to nonathletes, the muscle fiber diameters of athletes were reported to be larger for all fiber types (Melichna et al., 1990). In addition, the diameters of Type I fibers were larger in older than young athletes. Again, because this information came from a cross-sectional study, the cause of larger muscle fibers is ambiguous. It could be due to heredity just as well as to long-term training, or to an interaction between genotype and environmental training. However, Frontera et al. (1988) reported that sizes of both Type I and II fibers increased 30% in men aged 60 to 72 after 12 weeks of training.

The evidence that training increases muscle fiber size is not conclusive. Larsson and Ansved (1985) failed to find any change in muscle fiber diameter after 42 months of training or after detraining. They suggested that muscle fiber size is genetically determined and that large muscle fibers are a prerequisite for athletic success; hence the muscle fiber diameters of athletes are always observed to be larger compared to those of nonathletes. Even more damaging to the hypothesis that training enlarges muscle fibers was the finding by Kovanen and Suominen (1987) that endurance training in rats did not prevent either Type I or Type II muscle fibers from decreasing in size with aging.

Contractile Properties

No change occurs in the time to peak twitch tension with strength training, but there is an increase in half-relaxation time of the muscle (Brown et al., 1990). The half-relaxation time of older muscles increases with training, just as it does in younger muscles. Increasing half-relaxation time means that the muscle can maintain tension longer at the same frequency of motor unit firing. Illustrated in Figure 5.15, strength training shifts the force-frequency relationship to the left. Considering that the contraction time of older untrained muscles is slower, this training adaptation should enable older trained individuals to reach their maximal muscular force at lower motor unit firing rates, which in turn may increase their resistance to fatigue.

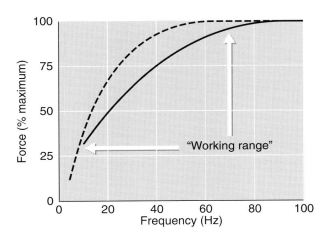

Figure 5.15   Relationship between motor unit firing rate and force output of the muscle fibers. The relationship between frequency of stimulation and force output takes the form of a force-frequency curve (solid-line curve), which has a relatively steep portion of the lower frequencies; thus, small changes in frequency cause large changes in force output. The dotted curve shows the force-frequency curve expected for a motor unit with a longer twitch contraction time. A lower frequency is sufficient to achieve a given percentage of maximum force output in a more slowly contracting muscle. The "working range" of a motor unit (about 6-50 Hz) corresponds to the commonly observed range of motor unit firing rates in sustained (vs. ramp or ballistic) contractions. From "Influence of Exercise and Training on Motor Unit Activation" by D.G. Sale, 1987, *Exercise and Sport Sciences Reviews*, **15**, p. 116. Copyright 1987 by Williams & Wilkins. Reprinted by permission.

The technique of electrically stimulating muscle during a maximal contraction provides evidence of whether the individual can neurologically recruit all of the motor units in the muscle in order to make a maximal voluntary contraction. Using this technique, Vandervoort and McComas (1986) found that older subjects were able to activate all of their motor units just as well as young subjects.

Exercise Effects on Muscular Bloodflow

Exercise increases the number of capillaries per muscle fiber area in humans (Andersen, 1975; Ingjer, 1978) and in animals (Carrow, Brown & Van Huss, 1967). Denis et al. (1986) found that the number of capillaries in contact with muscle fibers increased after training in both old and young adults. The young adults' increases were 11% (Type I) and 15% (Type IIa), but these increases were not significant. The old adults' increases were 15% (Type I) and 20% (Type IIa) and

were significant. The authors cautioned, however, that the apparent increased capillarization might be due to decreased fiber area and not capillary proliferation (Denis et al., 1986). Increased capillarity was seen in exercised animals, but the amount of increase in capillarity was not as great in old animals as in young animals (Mitchell, Byrnes, & Mazzeo, 1990). Some have found a preferential increase in the number of capillaries per muscle fiber area of Type I fibers with treadmill running, but others have reported a selective increase in the capillaries-fiber ratio of Type II fibers (Carrow, Brown, & Van Huss, 1967). The effect of exercise and aging on capillarization per muscle fiber area is not completely resolved at this time.

Exercise has effects other than increased capillarity that are beneficial to muscle contractility (Table 5.3). By stimulating bloodflow, exercise may enhance contractility and permeability of blood vessels, thus preventing local ischemia (Samorajski, 1976). A healthy circulation also stabilizes temperature in the extremities, which in turn maintains functions such as normal nerve conduction velocity and spinal reflex loops.

Exercise Effects on Neuronal Innervation of Muscle

Frequent firing of action potentials may postpone nerve cell aging (Vogt & Vogt, 1946). Retzlaff and

---

Table 5.3
Peripheral Adaptations to Exercise Training in Older People

- Increased skeletal muscle capillarization
- Increased skeletal muscle oxidative enzyme levels
- Maintained or increased muscle mass
- Increased muscle strength
- Improved peripheral bloodflow distribution
- Reduced peripheral vascular resistance
- Increased insulin sensitivity and glycogen stores
- Increased blood vessel diameter

Note. From "Physical Exercise in the Elderly" by A.P. Goldberg and J.M. Hagberg. In *Handbook of the Biology of Aging* (3rd ed.) (p. 411) by E.L. Schneider and J.W. Rowe (Eds.), 1990, New York: Academic Press. Copyright 1990 by Academic Press, Inc. Reprinted by permission.

Fontaine (1965) determined from an examination of stained motoneurons from exercising and non-exercising rats that controlled exercise delays the onset of physiological aging in motoneurons. They also found that the nerve conduction velocity of their exercised old rats was considerably faster than that of their control rats. Eccles (1973) proposed that muscular contraction has a trophic effect on its innervating neuron and immediate central connections in the spinal cord. Although it has not been documented, it is plausible that the neural activity produced before, during, and after muscular activity might confer some benefit on the entire multilevel neuronal network contributing to the movement. It has already been shown that when neurons are chronically inactive, the quantity of neuronal firing is reduced and the frequency of discharge in those neurons that remain active decreases (Smith & Dugall, 1965). Fibers in the nerve will atrophy when muscle function is reduced, but some evidence suggests that this atrophy may be reduced with lifelong exercise. The diameters of the posterior tibial nerve fibers were larger in mice that had exercised on a running wheel from age 3 months to age 24 months (Samorajski & Rolsten, 1975). Thus the diameter of the nerve fiber may reflect the changes in functional status of the nerve cell body that are associated with changes in the active muscle fiber.

Muscular Endurance

Muscular endurance is the capacity of the muscle to contract continuously at submaximal levels, whereas muscular strength is the amount of force that a muscle produces in one contraction. Muscular endurance is measured by determining the length of time an individual can maintain a certain percentage of maximal force until fatigued or by recording the number of times an individual can contract a muscle repeatedly at a specified percentage of that individual's maximum contraction. Thus, if the maximum amount of force that an individual can produce is 150 kg, the individual's maximum voluntary contraction, then the muscular endurance is measured by determining how many times the person can produce a force that is 40% (or some other submaximal percentage) of that maximal voluntary contraction. In animals, muscular endurance is determined in excised

whole muscles by electrically stimulating the muscle directly, or through its nerve, and then observing the fall in peak tension that occurs with each subsequent contraction.

The gradual, subtle loss of muscular endurance that occurs throughout aging was shown by Nakao, Inoue, and Murakami (1989), who measured 7,412 Japanese subjects from the ages of 13 to 79. Nevertheless, muscular endurance is maintained better throughout aging than is muscular strength (Aniansson, Sperling, Rundgren, & Lehnberg, 1983; Burke, Tuttle, Thompson, Janney, & Weber, 1953; Dummer et al., 1985). For example, the knee extensors of both women and men in their mid-60s were not as strong as those of younger men and women, but their knee extensor endurance was statistically the same (Laforest et al., 1990).

In another example, older women who trained the same number of hours in swimming as younger women were not as strong as the younger swimmers, but their endurance was not different (Dummer et al., 1985). The older swimmers, however, had both more strength and more endurance than women their age who did not exercise. One explanation for why these older swimmers were not as strong as the younger swimmers might be that swimming is basically an endurance activity, so the older women were training for endurance rather than strength. Another explanation is that even though the older women in that study trained for about the same length of time an equivalent number of times each week, they actually swam only half the distance of the youngest group each day. Therefore, the younger swimmers were using more muscular power to travel twice as far in the same amount of time.

Muscular endurance specific to the involved muscle groups is also maintained in various occupations that require physical exertion. For example, older men who continued to be employed in a machine shop had just as high a task-specific endurance as the younger men (Petrofsky & Lind, 1975). Human muscular endurance withstands the onslaughts of time very well.

Effects of Aerobic Training on Muscular Endurance

Muscular endurance is maintained and enhanced by improving the oxidative capacity of the slow-twitch Type I and fast oxidative-glycolytic Type IIa fibers. If the fatigability of oxidative fibers of old sedentary individuals is compared to that of young individuals, little difference is found between them (McCarter & McGee, 1987). But the oxidative capacity can be greatly enhanced in both old and young by endurance training (Orlander & Aniansson, 1980). This results in the ability of older athletes of both sexes, such as tennis players (Laforest et al., 1990), competitive swimmers (Dummer et al., 1985), and runners (Fugl-Meyer, Gerdle, & Langstrom, 1985), to maintain much better muscular endurance than sedentary individuals of similar age.

The oxidative capacity of primarily slow-twitch muscles depends on the function of the mitochondria in the muscle cells, and the efficiency and energy production of these mitochondria are increased greatly with systematic physical training (Beyer et al., 1984; Farrar et al., 1981; Holloszy & Coyle, 1984; Orlander & Aniansson, 1980). Exercise stimulates an increase in some of the enzymes that metabolize aerobic energy. The training effect occurs at all ages (Cartee & Farrar, 1987). In humans, for example, the mitochondrial oxidative capacity of five 70- to 75-year-old men increased greatly after a 12-week program of walking, jogging, and exercises (Orlander & Aniansson, 1980). Results from animal studies provide convincing support that muscle respiratory capacity improves with exercise (Holloszy & Booth, 1976; Young, Chen, & Holloszy, 1983). In fact, both old and young rats attained identical muscle respiratory capacity after the same exercise program (Cartee & Farrar, 1987; Farrar, Martin, & Ardies, 1981). Therefore, a decline in the muscle respiratory capacity of primarily slow oxidative muscles is not inevitable. It may be postponed by maintaining physical activity throughout life. Humans who sit on their couches all day and rats that sit in small cages every day lose their ability to generate muscular energy as they age, but both can prevent this loss by daily exercise.

It should be clear that disuse accelerates aging. When muscles are not used, the number of muscle fibers remains the same but the fibers atrophy. The most dramatic demonstration of this effect is when the muscles of one arm or leg that have been in a cast for 6 weeks are compared to the muscles of the other arm or leg. Bortz (1983) described the impact of this effect in chapter 4. Not only has the previously casted limb not been used, the other has been used more in compensation for the cast. The casted leg is withered and

shrunken and may be only two thirds the size of the noncasted leg. The muscles of the atrophied leg also do not contract as quickly.

Because people tend to be less and less active as they age, it is difficult to determine which changes and to what degree these changes in muscle structure and function can be attributed to aging and which occur because of disuse. The examples of elderly athletes and the profound improvements in strength and endurance that result from training programs clearly support the conclusion that a considerable proportion of strength and endurance loss in older adults can be attributed to the fact that as they age, they simply stop using their neuromuscular system except for very basic daily activities. The levels of muscular performance that can be maintained through participation in sports skills, such as weight lifting, running, or cycling, are the subject of chapter 14.

In Summary

The changes in strength throughout aging are basically quantitative changes rather than qualitative changes. Small but gradual decreases in strength occur until about age 60, after which a more marked decline occurs. Losses in submaximal strength are hardly noticeable in muscles that remain active throughout life, either from work experiences or from daily living activities. Losses are greater in women than in men (probably because women are more inactive than men), greater in the lower than the upper extremities of the frail elderly, and greater in fast rather than slow velocity movements.

Strength losses are attributed largely to a loss of muscle mass, which is due to losses of muscle fiber. The losses may be greater in fast-twitch than in slow-twitch fibers, although this hypothesis is still controversial and a topic of considerable research interest. Intuitively, a selective loss of fast-twitch fibers should account for the greater decreases in rapid movements and power production and the lower rate of tension development that is seen in the aged. However, most investigators agree that although an overall loss of muscle mass accounts for the largest portion of the loss of strength, it does not account for all of the loss. When older individuals undergo strength training, their increases in strength are greater than their increases in muscle mass, thus other impaired mechanisms have not yet been identified. Very few age-related changes occur in capillary density and neuromusuclar function.

The oxidative capacity of slow oxidative and fast oxidative-glycolytic fibers is lower in old animals, but the metabolism of fast-glycolytic fibers is unchanged. The lower respiratory capacity of old fibers is more likely due to an age-related decrease in physical activity than to aging.

Some motor units, most likely fast-twitch motor units, are lost with aging, and when their abandoned muscle fibers are reinnervated by surviving motor neurons, it increases the fiber-to-neuron ratio. An increase in this ratio with aging may contribute to impairments in coordination.

Chronic resistance strength training enables individuals to maintain high levels of strength for many years and also provides individuals who have not been involved in strength training an opportunity to reverse many of the age-related deterioration processes that are observed in the muscles of sedentary people. Adults who continue participating in endurance sports maintain their muscular strength much better than sedentary adults do, and adults of any age, even a very old age, can experience remarkable and dramatic gains in strength following a resistance strength-training program. Strength-training programs increase muscle mass in old adults as well as in young adults, with individual muscle cells increasing in size and protein level. Even daily strength training, however, cannot postpone indefinitely the inevitable deterioration in muscle mass.

Strength and aerobic exercise training can prevent the age-related decline of both slow- and fast-twitch fibers. The number of muscle fibers does not increase with normal strength-training programs, but the size of the active muscle fibers does increase. Other effects of strength training on muscle fiber are increases in the half-relaxation time of the muscle (which means that the muscle can maintain tension longer at the same motor unit-firing frequency), the number of capillaries per muscle fiber area in both young and older adults, and the efficiency and energy production of mitochondria in both young and old.

Frequent muscular training may also have beneficial effects on the neurons that innervate the active muscles. Neural fibers atrophy when their target muscle is not used. There is some evidence that the number of nerve fibers innervating a muscle, the diameters of the nerve fibers, and the

health of the neuron are maintained through systematic activation of the muscle.

Adults who participate regularly in endurance sports or aerobic exercise can maintain superior muscular endurance for many years, an accomplishment that enables them to continue working if they wish and to maintain their independence. One of the clearest findings in the literature on strength and aging is that disuse accelerates aging. In fact, most of the decline seen in strength and muscular endurance, at least until age 70, is due more to disuse of the neuromuscular system than to aging.

References

American College of Sports Medicine. (1991). *Guidelines for exercise testing and prescription.* Philadelphia: Lea & Febiger.

Andersen, P. (1975). Capillary density in skeletal muscle of man. *Acta Physiologica Scandinavica,* **95**, 203-205.

Aniansson, A., Grimby, G., Hedberg, M., & Krotkiewski, M. (1981). Muscle morphology, enzyme activity, and muscle strength in elderly men and women. *Clinical Physiology,* **1**, 73-86.

Aniansson, A., & Gustafsson, E. (1981). Physical training in elderly men with special reference to quadriceps muscle strength and morphology. *Clinical Physiology,* **1**, 87-98.

Aniansson, A., Hedberg, M., Henning, G.B., & Grimby, G. (1986). Muscle morphology, enzymatic activity, and muscle strength in elderly men: A follow-up study. *Muscle Nerve,* **9**, 585-591.

Aniansson, A., Sperling, L., Rundgren, A., & Lehnberg, E. (1983). Muscle function in 75-year-old men and women: A longitudinal study. *Scandinavian Journal of Rehabilitation Medicine* (Suppl.), **193**, 92-102.

Arabadjis, P.G., Heffner, R.R., & Pendergast, D.R. (1990). Morphologic and functional alterations in aging rat muscle. *Journal of Neuropathology and Experimental Neurology,* **49**, 600-609.

Asmussen, E., & Heebøll-Neilsen, K. (1961). Isometric muscle strength of adult men and women. *Danish National Association of Infantile Paralysis,* **11**, 1-43.

Åstrand, P.O., & Rodahl, K. (1986). *Textbook of work physiology.* New York: McGraw-Hill.

Beyer, R.E., Starnes, J.W., Edington, D.W., Lipton, R.J., Compton, R.T., & Kwasman, M. (1984).

Exercise-induced reversal of age-related declines of oxidative reactions, mitochondrial yield, and flavins in skeletal muscle of the rat. *Mechanisms of Ageing and Development*, **24**, 309-323.

Bortz, W.M., II. (1983). On disease . . . aging . . . and disuse. *Executive Health*, **20**(3), 1-6.

Bosco, C., & Komi, P.V. (1980). Influence of aging on the mechanical behavior of leg extensor muscles. *European Journal of Applied Physiology*, **45**, 209-219.

Brooks, S.V., & Faulkner, J.A. (1988). Contractile properties of skeletal muscles from young, adult and aged mice. *Journal of Physiology*, **404**, 71-82.

Brown, M. (1987). Change in fibre size, not number, in ageing skeletal muscle. *Age and Ageing*, **16**, 244-248.

Brown, A.B., McCartney, N., & Sale, D.G. (1990). Positive adaptations to weight-lifting training in the elderly. *Journal of Applied Physiology*, **69**, 1725-1733.

Brown, M., & Holloszy, J.O. (1991). Effects of a low-intensity exercise program on selected physical performance characteristics of 60- to 71-year-olds. *Aging*, 129-139.

Buckner, D.M., & deLateur, B.J. (1991). The importance of skeletal muscle strength to physical function in older adults. *Annals of Behavioral Medicine*, **13**, 91-98.

Burke, W.E., Tuttle, W.W., Thompson, C.W., Janney, C.D., & Weber, R.J. (1953). Relation of grip strength and grip-strength endurance to age. *Journal of Applied Physiology*, **5**, 628-630.

Campbell, M.J., McComas, A.J., & Petito, F. (1973). Physiological changes in aging muscles. *Journal of Neurology, Neurosurgery, and Psychiatry*, **36**, 174-182.

Carrow, R., Brown, R., & Van Huss, W. (1967). Fiber sizes and capillary to fiber ratios in skeletal muscle of exercised rats. *Anatomical Record*, **159**, 33-40.

Cartee, G.D., & Farrar, R.P. (1987). Muscle respiratory capacity and $\dot{V}O_2$max in identically trained young and old rats. *Journal of Applied Physiology*, **63**, 257-261.

Clarence Bass's testing at the Cooper Clinic: Personification of lifetime body building and balanced training. (1993, February). *Master Trainer*, **3**(1), 1-4.

Clarkson, P., Kroll, W., & Melchionda, A.M. (1981). Age, isometric strength, rate of tension development, and fiber type composition. *Journal of Gerontology*, **36**, 648-653.

Cunningham, D.A., Morrison, D., Rice, C.L., & Cooke, C. (1987). Ageing and isokinetic plantar flexion.

European Journal of Applied Physiology, **56**, 24-29.

Daw, C.K., Starnes, J.W., & White, T.P. (1988). Muscle atrophy and hypoplasia with aging: Impact of training and food restriction. *Journal of Applied Physiology*, **64**, 2428-2432.

Denis, D., Chatard, J., Dormois, D., Linossier, M., Geyssant, A., & Lacour, J. (1986). Effects of endurance training on capillary supply of human skeletal muscle on two age groups (20 and 60 years). *Journal of Physiology (Paris)*, **81**, 379-383.

Dobrev, P.A. (1980). Complex experimental investigations of the influence of weight training on persons in middle, advanced, and old age. *Scientific Methodical Bulletin*, **3**, 27-28.

Dummer, G.M., Clark, D.H., Vaccaro, P., Vander Velden, L., Goldfare, A.H., & Sockler, J.M. (1985). Age-related differences in muscular strength and muscular endurance among female masters swimmers. *Research Quarterly for Exercise and Sport*, **56**, 97-110.

Eccles, J.C. (1973). Trophic influences in the mammalian central nervous system. In M. Rockstein (Ed.), *Development and aging in the nervous system* (pp. 89-104). New York: Academic Press.

Eddinger, T., Moss, R., & Cassens, R. (1985). Fiber number and type composition in extensor digitorum longus, soleus, and diaphragm muscles with aging in Fischer 344 rats. *Journal of Histochemistry and Cytochemistry*, **33**, 1033-1041.

Elder, G.C., Bradbury, K., & Roberts, R. (1982). Variability of fiber type distributions within human muscle. *Journal of Applied Physiology*, **53**, 1473-1480.

Engel, W.K. (1970). Selective and nonselective susceptibility of muscle fiber types: A new approach to human neuromuscular diseases. *Archives of Neurology*, **22**, 97-117.

Essen-Gustavsson, B., & Borges, O. (1986). Histochemical and metabolic characteristics of human skeletal muscle in relation to age. *Acta Physiologica Scandinavica*, **126**, 107-114.

Farrar, R.P., Martin, T.P., & Ardies, C.M. (1981). The interaction of aging and endurance exercise upon the mitochondrial function of skeletal muscle. *Journal of Gerontology*, **36**, 642-647.

Faulkner, J.A., Maxwell, L.C., Brook, D.A., & Lieberman, D.A. (1971). Adaptation of guinea pig plantaris muscle fibers to endurance training. *American Journal of Physiology*, **221**, 291-297.

Fiatarone, M.A., Marks, E.C., Ryan, N.D., Meredith, C., Lipsitz, L.A., & Evans, W.J. (1990). High-intensity strength training in nonagenarians. *Journal of the American Medical Association*, **263**, 3029-3034.

Fisher, N.M., Pendergast, D.R., & Calkins, E. (1991). Muscle rehabilitation in impaired elderly nursing home residents. *Archives of Physical Medicine and Rehabilitation*, **72**, 181-185.

Fitts, R.H. (1981). Aging and skeletal muscle. In E.L. Smith & R.C. Serfass (Eds.), *Exercise and aging: The scientific basis* (pp. 31-44). Hillside, NJ: Enslow.

Fitts, R.H., Troup, J.P., Witzmann, F.A., & Holloszy, J.O. (1984). The effect of ageing and exercise on skeletal muscle function. *Mechanisms of Ageing and Development*, **27**, 161-172.

Frontera, W.R., Meredith, C.N., O'Reilly, K.P., Knuttgen, H.G., & Evans, W.J. (1988). Strength conditioning in older men: Skeletal muscle hypertrophy and improved function. *Journal of Applied Physiology*, **64**, 1038-1044.

Fugl-Meyer, A.R., Gerdle, B., & Langstrom, M. (1985). Characteristics of repeated isokinetic plantar flexion in middle-aged and elderly subjects with special regard to muscular work. *Acta Physiologica Scandinavica*, **124**, 213-222.

Fugl-Meyer, A.R., Gustafsson, L., & Burstedt, Y. (1980). Isokinetic and statis plantar flexion characteristics. *European Journal of Applied Physiology*, **45**, 221-234.

Gibbons, A. (1991). Aging research: A growth industry. *Science*, **252**, 1483.

Gillett, P. (1989). Aerobic and muscle fitness in high-risk and overweight senior women. *The Gerontologist*, **29**, 258A.

Goldberg, A.P., & Hagberg, J.M. (1990). Physical exercise in the elderly. In E.L. Schneider & J.W. Rowe (Eds.). *Handbook of the biology of aging* (3rd ed., pp. 407-428). New York: Academic Press.

Goldspink, G. (1983). Alterations in myofibril size and structure during growth, exercise, and changes in environmental temperature. In L.D. Peachey, R.H. Adrian, & S.R. Geiger (Eds.), *Handbook of physiology* (pp. 539-554). Bethesda, MD: American Physiological Society.

Goldspink, G., & Howells, K.F. (1974). Work-induced hypertrophy in exercised normal muscles of different ages and the reversibility of hypertrophy after cessation of exercise. *Journal of Physiology*, **239**, 179-193.

Gollnick, P.D., Armstrong, R.B., Saubert, C.W., IV, Piehl, K., & Saltin, B. (1972). Enzyme activity and fiber composition in skeletal muscle of untrained and trained men. *Journal of Applied Physiology*, **33**, 312-319.

Gollnick, P., Timson, B., Moore, R., & Riedy, M. (1981). Muscle enlargement and number of fibers in skeletal muscles of rats. *Journal of Applied Physiology*, **50**, 936-943.

Gonyea, W.J., Sale, D.G., Gonyea, F.B., & Mikesky, A. (1986). Exercise-induced increases in muscle fiber number. *European Journal of Applied Physiology*, **55**, 137-141.

Green, H.J. (1986). Characteristics of aging human skeletal muscles. In J.R. Sutton & R.M. Brock (Eds.), *Sports medicine for the mature athlete* (pp. 17-26). Indianapolis: Benchmark Press.

Grimby, G. (1988). Physical activity and effects of muscle training in the elderly. *Annals of Clinical Research*, **20**, 62-66.

Grimby, G., Danneskiold-Samsoe, B., Hvid, K., & Saltin, B. (1982). Morphology and enzymatic capacity in arm and leg muscles in 78- to 81-year-old men and women. *Acta Physiologica Scandinavica*, **115**, 125-134.

Grimby, G., & Saltin, B. (1983). The ageing muscle. *Clinical Physiology*, **3**, 209-218.

Hansford, R.G., & Castro, F. (1982). Age-linked changes in the activity of enzymes of the tricarboxylate cycle and lipid oxidation, and of carnitine content, in muscles of the rat. *Mechanisms of Ageing and Development*, **19**, 191-201.

Holloszy, J.O., & Booth, F. (1976). Biochemical adaptations to endurance exercise in muscle. *Annual Review of Physiology*, **37**, 273-291.

Holloszy, J.O., & Coyle, E.F. (1984). Adaptations of skeletal muscle to endurance exercise and their metabolic consequences. *Journal of Applied Physiology*, **56**, 831-838.

Ingjer, F. (1978). Maximal aerobic power related to the capillary supply of the quadriceps femoris muscle in man. *Acta Physiologica Scandinavica*, **104**, 238-240.

Jette, A.M., Branch, L.G., & Berlin, J. (1990). Musculoskeletal impairments and physical disablement among the aged. *Journal of Gerontology: Medical Sciences*, **45**, M203-M208.

Jones, D.A. (1989). Physiological changes in skeletal muscle as a result of strength training. *Quarterly Journal of Experimental Physiology*, **74**, 233-256.

Kallman, D.A., Plato, C.C., & Tobin, J.D. (1990). The role of muscle loss in the age-related decline of grip strength: Cross-sectional and longitudinal perspectives. *Journal of Gerontology: Medical Sciences*, **45**, M82-M88.

Kauffman, T.L. (1985). Strength-training effect in young and aged women. *Archives of Physical Medicine and Rehabilitation*, **65**, 223-226.

Klitgaard, H., Brunet, A., Maton, B., Lamaziere, C., Lesty, C., & Monod, H. (1989). Morphological and biochemical changes in old rat muscles: Effect of increased use. *Journal of Applied Physiology*, **67**, 1409-1417.

Kovanen, V., & Suominen, H. (1987). Effects of age and life-time physical training on fibre composition of slow and fast skeletal muscle in rats. *Pflugers Archives*, **408**, 543-551.

Laforest, S., St-Pierre, D.M.M., Cyr, J., & Gayton, D. (1990). Effects of age and regular exercise on muscle strength and endurance. *European Journal of Applied Physiology*, **60**, 104-111.

Larsson, L. (1978). Morphological and functional characteristics of the ageing skeletal muscle in man. *Acta Physiologica Scandinavica*, **103**, (Suppl. 457), 1-29.

Larsson, L. (1982). Physical training effects on muscle morphology in sedentary males at different ages. *Medicine and Science in Sports and Exercise*, **14**, 203-206.

Larsson, L., & Ansved, T. (1985). Effects of long-term physical training and detraining on enzyme histochemical and functional skeletal muscle characteristics in man. *Muscle and Nerve*, **8**, 714-722.

Larsson, L., Grimby, G., & Karlsson, J. (1979). Muscle strength and speed of movement in relation to age and muscle morphology. *Journal of Applied Physiology*, **46**, 451-456.

Lewis, S.F., Taylor, W.F., Bastian, B.C., Graham, R.M., Pettinger, W.A., & Blomqvist, C.G. (1983). Haemodynamic responses to static and dynamic handgrip before and after autonomic blockage. *Clinical Science*, **64**, 593-599.

Lexell, J. (1992). The structure and function of the ageing human muscle. In G.E. Stelmach & V. Hömberg (Eds.), *Sensorimotor impairments in the elderly: Are they reversible?* Boston: Kluwer Academic.

Lexell, J., Henriksson-Larsen, K., Wimblad, B., & Sjöström, M. (1983). Distribution of different fiber types in human skeletal muscles: Effects of aging studies in whole muscle cross-sections. *Muscle and Nerve*, **6**, 588-595.

Lexell, J., Taylor, C., & Sjöström, M. (1988). What is the cause of ageing atrophy? Total number, size, and proportion of different fiber types studied in whole vastus lateralis muscle from 15- to 83-year-old men. *Journal of Neurological Sciences*, **84**, 275-294.

MacDougall, J.D., Elder, G.C.B., Sale, D.G., Moroz, J.R., & Sutton, J.R. (1980). Effects of strength training and immobilization on human muscle fibers. *European Journal of Applied Physiology*, **43**, 25-34.

MacDougall, M.J.N., & Davies, C.T.M. (1984). Adaptive response of mammalian skeletal muscle to exercise with high loads. *European Journal of Physiology*, **52**, 139-155.

McArdle, W.D., Katch, F.I., & Katch, V.L. (1986). *Exercise physiology*. Philadelphia: Lea & Febiger.

McCarter, R. (1978). Effects of age on contraction of mammalian skeletal muscle. *Aging*, **6**, 1-21.

McCarter, R., & McGee, J. (1987). Influence of nutrition and aging on the composition and function of rat skeletal muscle. *Journal of Gerontology*, **42**, 432-441.

Melichna, J., Zauner, C., Havlíčková, L., Novák, J., Hill, D.W., & Colman, R.J. (1990). Morphologic differences in skeletal muscle with age in normally active human males and their well-trained counterparts. *Human Biology*, **62**, 205-220.

Mitchell, M.L., Byrnes, W.C., & Mazzeo, R.S. (1990). A comparison of skeletal muscle morphology with training between young and old Fischer 344 rats. *Mechanisms of Ageing and Development*, **58**, 21-35.

Moritani, T., & deVries, H.A. (1980). Potential for gross muscle hypertrophy in older men. *Journal of Gerontology*, **35**, 672-682.

Murray, M.P., Duthie, E.H., Gambert, S.R., Sepic, S.B., & Mollinger, L.A. (1985). Age-related differences in knee muscle strength in normal women. *Journal of Gerontology*, **40**, 275-280.

Murray, M.P., Gardner, G.M., Mollinger, L.A., & Sepic, S.B. (1980). Strength of isometric and isokinetic contractions. *Physical Therapy*, **60**, 412-419.

Nakao, M., Inoue, Y., & Murakami, H. (1989). Aging process of leg muscle endurance in males and females. *European Journal of Applied Physiology*, **59**, 209-214.

Newton, J.P., & Yemm, R. (1986). Changes in the contractile properties of the human first dorsal interosseous muscle with age. *Gerontology*, **32**, 98-104.

Orlander, J., & Aniansson, A. (1980). Effects of physical training on skeletal muscle metabolism and ultrastructure in 70- to 75-year-old men. *Acta Physiologica Scandinavica*, **109**, 149-154.

Pette, D. (1984). Activity-induced fast to slow transitions in mammalian muscle. *Medicine and Science in Sports and Exercise*, **16**, 517-528.

Petrofsky, J.S., Burse, R.L., & Lind, A.R. (1975). Comparison of physiological responses of women and men to isometric exercise. *Journal of Applied Physiology*, **38**, 863-868.

Petrofsky, J.S., & Lind, A.R. (1975). Aging, isometric strength and endurance, and cardiovascular responses to static effort. *Journal of Applied Physiology*, **38**, 91-95.

Phillips, S.K., Bruce, S.H., Newton, D., & Woledge, R.C. (1992). The weakness of old age is not due to failure of muscle activation. *Journal of Gerontology: Medical Sciences*, **47**, M45-M49.

Pollock, M.L., & Wilmore, J.H. (1990). *Exercise in health and disease*. Philadelphia: Saunders.

Prudham, D., & Grimley-Evans, J. (1981). Factors associated with falls in the elderly: A community study. *Age and Ageing, 10*, 141-146.

Reynolds, B., & Garrett, C. (1989). Effects of exercise on elderly ambulatory functions. *The Gerontologist, 29*, 258A.

Retzlaff, E., & Fontaine, J. (1965). Functional and structural changes in motor neurons with age. In A.T. Welford & J.E. Birren (Eds.), *Behavior, aging, and the nervous system* (pp. 340-352). Springfield, IL: Charles C Thomas.

Rikli, R., & Busch, S. (1986). Motor performance of women as a function of age and physical activity level. *Journal of Gerontology, 41*, 645-649.

Sager, K. (1984). Exercises to activate seniors. *Physician and Sportsmedicine, 5*, 144-151.

Sale, D.G. (1987). Influence of exercise and training on motor unit activation. *Exercise and Sport Sciences Reviews, 15*, 95-151.

Samorajski, T. (1976). How the human brain responds to aging. *Journal of American Geriatrics Society, 24*, 4-11.

Samorajski, T., & Rolsten, C. (1975). Nerve fiber hypertrophy in posterior tibial nerves of mice in response to voluntary running activity during aging. *Journal of Comparative Neurology, 159*, 553-558.

Shock, N.W., & Norris, A.H. (1970). Neuromuscular coordination as a factor in age changes in muscular exercise. *Medicine and Sport, 4*, 92-99.

Smith, L.P., & Dugall, L.D. (1965). Age and spontaneous running activity of old male rats. *Canadian Journal of Applied Physiology and Pharmacology, 43*, 852-856.

Suominen, H., Heikkinen, E., & Parkatti, T. (1977). Effect of 8 weeks' physical training on muscle and connective tissue of the M. vastus lateralis in 69-year-old men and women. *Journal of Gerontology, 32*, 33-37.

Tinetti, M.E. (1987). Factors associated with serious injury during falls by ambulatory nursing home residents. *Journal of the American Geriatrics Society, 35*, 644-648.

Tinetti, M.E., & Speechley, M. (1989). Prevention of falls among the elderly. *New England Journal of Medicine, 320*, 1055-1059.

Tobis, J.S., Friis, R., & Reinsch, S. (1989). Impaired strength leads to falls in the community. *The Gerontologist, 29*, 256A-257A.

Tomanek, R.J., & Wood, Y.K. (1970). Compensatory hypertrophy of the plantaris muscle in relation to age. *Journal of Gerontology, 25*, 23-29.

Trounce, I., Byrne, E., & Marzuki, S. (1989). Decline in skeletal muscle mitochondrial respiratory chain function: A possible factor in ageing. *The Lancet, 1*(8639), 637-639.

Vandervoort, A.A., Kramer, J.F., & Wharram, E.R. (1990). Eccentric knee strength of elderly females. *Journal of Gerontology: Biological Sciences, 45*, B125-B128.

Vandervoort, A.A., & McComas, A.J. (1986). Contractile changes in opposing muscles of the human ankle joint with aging. *Journal of Applied Physiology, 61*, 361-367.

Viljanen, T., Viitasalo, J.T., & Kujala, U.M. (1991). Strength characteristics of a healthy urban adult population. *European Journal of Applied Physiology, 63*, 43-47.

Vogt, C., & Vogt, O. (1946). Aging of nerve cells. *Nature, 58*, 304.

Walters, T.J., Sweeney, H.L., & Farrar, R.P. (1990). Aging does not affect contractile properties of Type IIb FDL muscle in Fischer 344 rats. *American Journal of Physiology, 258* (Cell Physiology 27), C1031-C1035.

Walters, T.J., Sweeney, H.L., & Farrar, R.P. (1991). Influence of electrical stimulation on a fast-twitch muscle in aging rats. *Journal of Applied Physiology, 71*, 1921-1928.

Wilmore, J.H. (1991). The aging of bones and muscle. In R.K. Kerlan (Ed.), *Sports medicine in the older adult* (pp. 231-244). Philadelphia: Saunders.

Young, A., Stokes, M., & Crowe, M. (1985). The size and strength of the quadriceps muscles of old and young men. *Clinical Physiology, 5*, 145-154.

Young, J.C., Chen, M., & Holloszy, J.O. (1983). Maintenance of the adaptation of skeletal muscle mitochondria to exercise in old rats. *Medicine and Science in Sports and Exercise, 15*, 243-246.

Zacour, M.E., & Gardiner, P.F. (1986). Long-term mild endurance exercise effects on the age-associated evolution of hindlimb muscle characteristics in hamsters. *Mechanisms of Ageing and Development, 37*, 13-26.

PART III

Motor Control, Coordination, and Skill

Older people sometimes lose their balance, and they cannot react as quickly to a stoplight turning green. But then there is Artur Rubinstein, who in his late 80s performed piano concerts that melted the hearts of his audience.

he steady, inexorable pull of gravity against the upright human posture begins to take its toll as maturity turns into aging. Balance becomes more difficult, falling is more probable, and jogging and running are replaced by walking. Reactions to environmental events are slower, and motor coordination of complex and novel skills is less efficient. This section discusses what is known about age-related changes in motor skill. Several questions about topics in this section remain to be answered. What are the factors that can prevent the premature loss of balance: increased leg strength, increased endurance, locomotor training? Can the speed with which individuals react to an environmental stimulus be increased through long-term practice? How can hand function be maintained throughout old age? What types of education or technological assistance could prolong the length of time that the oldest-old might continue to drive their automobiles? How important is physical skill to maintaining an acceptable quality of life?

Balance, Posture, and Locomotion

Changes in balance, posture, and locomotion are so commonly observed in the elderly that they are thought to be synonymous with aging. Advanced age is associated with a slumped, flexed posture and tenuous balance. Many elderly people have a gait characterized by short, slow steps and a wide base of support. These balance, postural, and gait characteristics are so typical of aging that younger actors adopt them to portray older individuals; people who exhibit these characteristics simply *look* older.

155

Balance

Balance is the ability to maintain the body's position over its base of support, whether that base is stationary or moving. Controlling postural sway during quiet standing is called *static balance*. Using pertinent internal and external information to react to perturbations of stability and activating muscles to work in coordination to anticipate changes in balance are called *dynamic balance*. Many different tests have been developed to test both static and dynamic balance. These tests, categorized by Duncan, Studenski, Chandler, and Prescott (1992) as laboratory or clinical tests, are shown in Table 6.1.

Static Balance

It is impossible to stand absolutely motionless. Even when people stand quietly on both feet, the body sways over its base of support. Postural sway is determined by measuring the location and amount of change that occurs in the position of the total vertical force vector projected onto a horizontal plane. This measurement determines where the average center of pressure or center of force is located and how much variability of this location occurs during the measurement. When older people stand quietly, the amplitude and frequency of postural sway is greater than in younger individuals (e.g., Brocklehurst, Robertson, & James-Groom, 1982) and more so in women than in men (Overstall, Exton-Smith, Imms, & Johnson, 1977). In the anteroposterior direction, sway was 52% greater in subjects 70 to 80 years of age than in subjects of 30 to 39 years (Lucy & Hayes, 1985). Postural swaying is exaggerated in all ages, but especially so in the elderly, if the eyes are closed or if the situation involves unusual balance requirements (Hasselkus & Shambes, 1975).

Even though the range of postural sway in old, compared with young, people during quiet standing is significantly larger, the absolute amount of age difference is relatively small. The age differences increase considerably, however, when postural stability is slightly perturbed: It takes the aged longer to recover postural stability. Stelmach, Zelaznik, and Lowe (1990) measured how long it took old people to recover from the perturbation of swinging their arms several times to a preset rhythm. They also analyzed the amount of sway

that occurred during the recovery when the subjects performed attention-demanding tasks: a mathematical problem or a maximum grip strength task. The results are shown in Figure 6.1 (page 158). During the baseline postural conditions, little difference was seen between the two age groups. Swinging the arms exaggerated the differences in stability between the two age groups, and working mathematical problems delayed the return of the older group to stable conditions. Thus, postural stability, normally considered to be under automatic control processes, requires more conscious attention in the elderly than it does in younger individuals. As locomotion and basic mechanisms of balance deteriorate, older people have to focus more attention on formerly automatic processes to compensate for the loss of feedback and neuromuscular integration.

Postural sway is functionally significant because it is related to the risk of falling (e.g., Brocklehurst et al., 1982; Lichtenstein, Shields, Shiavi, & Burger, 1988; Overstall et al., 1977; Overstall, Johnson, & Exton-Smith, 1978). This relationship is only relevant for those elderly who fall without warning and without a loss of consciousness, as opposed to those who trip and fall (Overstall et al., 1978). Postural sway is of interest because it may identify older people at risk for falling, for whom behavioral strategies can be developed to help prevent falls.

Maintaining static balance on one foot is much harder than maintaining stability over two feet because the base of support is so much smaller when standing on one foot and the available neuromuscular-skeletal apparatus is so much more restricted. Not surprisingly, age differences in postural sway are much more pronounced when balance is maintained on only one foot (Era & Heikkinen, 1985). In fact, among 128 tests of behavioral neurologic function, standing on one leg with the eyes closed was one of the most sensitive measures of aging (Potvin, Syndulko, Tourtellottee, Lemmon, & Potvin, 1980). Stones and Kozma (1987), however, found that one-foot balance performance with the eyes open was both more age-sensitive and more reliable.

Many older people cannot maintain balance on one foot long enough for researchers to obtain reliable measures. Postural sway is increased and in addition, other compensatory mechanisms are incorporated to counteract the increased frequency with which the body's center of gravity moves outside the smaller base of support. The

Table 6.1
Established Test Characteristics of Measures of Balance

Tests	Reliability		Validity		Sensitivity to change
	Interobserver	Test-Retest	Criterion	Construct	
Laboratory measures					
Postural sway	Not applicable	No	Yes	Concurrent—Not well established	No
Center of pressure excursion	Not applicable	Yes (but marginal)	No	Concurrent—Yes; Predictive—No	No
EMG analysis of platform perturbation	Not applicable	EMG latency—Yes EMG latency—No patterns	No	Concurrent—Not well established Predictive—No	No
Maki-Pseude random perturbations	Not applicable	No	No	Concurrent—No; Predictive—Yes	No
Anticipatory postural adjustments	Not applicable	No	No	Concurrent—Not well established Predictive—No	No
Sensory-organization test	Not applicable	No	No	Concurrent—Not well established Predictive—No	No
Clinical measures					
Romberg	Not tested	No (in the elderly)	No	Concurrent—No; Predictive—No	No
One-leg stance	No	No	No	Concurrent—No; Predictive—No	No
Postural stress test	Yes	Yes	Yes	Concurrent—Yes; Predictive—No	No
Sternal push	No	No	No	Concurrent—No; Predictive—No	No
Lee maximal load test	No	No	No	Concurrent—Poor association with other measures of balance, but discriminated individuals with pathology Predictive—No	No
Tinetti performance-oriented mobility assessment	Yes	No	No	Concurrent—No; Predictive—Yes	No
Mathias Get-Up-and-Go test	Yes	No	No	Concurrent—Yes; Predictive—No	No
Functional reach	Yes	Yes	Yes	Concurrent—Yes; Predictive—Yes	Yes

Note. From "Functional Reach: Predictive Validity in a Sample of Elderly Male Veterans" by P.W. Duncan, S. Studenski, J. Chandler, and B. Prescott, 1992, *Journal of Gerontology: Medical Sciences*, **47**, p. M94. Copyright 1992 by The Gerontological Society of America. Reprinted by permission.

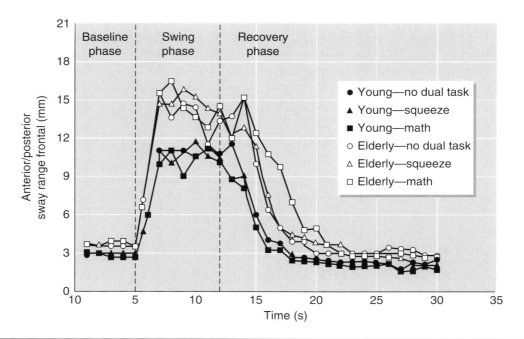

Figure 6.1   Mean range of frontal sway over 1-s intervals for elderly and young subjects under the three experimental swing conditions.
From "The Influence of Aging and Attentional Demands on Recovery From Postural Instability" by G.E. Stelmach, H.N. Zelaznik, and D. Lowe, 1990, *Aging*, **2**, p. 158. Copyright 1990 by Editrice Kurtis S.R.L. Reprinted by permission.

standard tests for one-foot balance are the one-legged stance test (OLST—see Bohannon, Larkin, Cook, Gear, & Singer, 1984) and the Romberg test (SR—see Graybiel & Fregly, 1966; Figure 6.2).

Dynamic Balance

Reaching for objects, pressing elevator buttons, or opening doors all require subjects to lean forward, sideways, or backward, thus challenging their balance. During movement activities people must

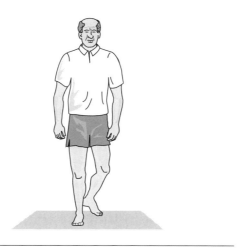

Figure 6.2   One-legged balance test, eyes open.

maintain control of the body's center of gravity while moving it over the base of support, a situation that occurs when upper-body movements shift the center of gravity or when the position of the body changes from one location to another, as in locomotion. Tests that have been used to study age-related differences in dynamic balance include Wolfson's postural stress test (Wolfson, Whipple, Amerman, & Kleinberg, 1986), the center of pressure excursion test (COPE—see Murray, Seireg, & Sepic, 1975), and Nashner's (1976) platform perturbation test. These tests are all basically static balance tests, but they have a very potent dynamic early component which challenges dynamic balance. Wolfson's test is an ordinal ranking of subjects' postural responses to a gravity-induced posterior displacement of their body and balance. In the COPE test, subjects stand on a force platform and the center of pressure is measured as the subject leans forward, backward, or sideways. Elderly subjects' centers of pressure do not approach the edges of their base of support as closely as do those of young subjects. In other words, the area of stability over the base of support is smaller in older subjects. A clinical version of this test, called the Functional Reach test, was developed to analyze the ability of older individuals to maintain equilibrium while reaching for an object (Duncan, Weiner, Chandler, & Studenski, 1990). In this test, functional reach (FR) is defined as the maximal distance a subject can reach forward beyond his or her own arm's length, while maintaining a fixed base of support in the standing position. In Figure 6.3, a and b, a subject is shown taking the FR test, and Figure 6.4 shows the effect of aging on FR.

Another test of dynamic balance is to determine how well individuals can regain their balance when the support surface on which they are standing moves unexpectedly. Nashner (1976) developed such a platform perturbation test. A diagram of Nashner's test apparatus is shown in Figure 6.5, where the muscular response patterns also are described in more detail. The perturbation of the platform in this test is analogous to an unexpected lurch one might experience while standing in a moving bus. In the laboratory, the platform is unexpectedly shifted slightly forward or backward, and the adaptations that people make to the shift are monitored by electromyographic recordings of muscle activity, film analysis, and ataxiameters. These measures may be obtained individually or in combination. The support immediately under the ball of the foot and the heel also may be unexpectedly raised or lowered, so that the ankle position and muscle length can be altered independently of horizontal shifts of the platform. This perturbation provides information about the in-

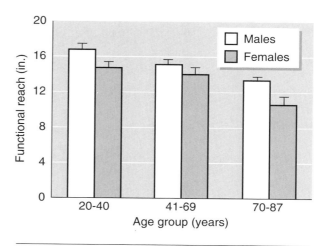

Figure 6.4 Age and gender differences in functional reach measured by the Functional Reach test. From "Functional Reach: A New Clinical Measure of Balance" by P.W. Duncan, D.K. Weiner, J. Chandler, and S. Studenski, 1990, *Journal of Gerontology: Medical Sciences*, **45**, p. M194. Copyright 1990 by The Gerontological Society of America. Reprinted by permission.

tegrity of the feedback produced by ankle joint rotation, independent of forward and backward displacements of the body. Furthermore, information from the visual, vestibular, and somatosensory systems can also be suppressed or distorted so that their roles in maintaining balance can be studied.

When the support surface of the subjects in these experiments unexpectedly moves forward,

a   b

Figure 6.3 The Functional Reach test. (a) The clinical version in which the normal reach of the subject is measured by a leveled 48-in. measuring device on the wall; (b) the laboratory version in which the subject extends one arm as far as possible while maintaining balance on a force platform.

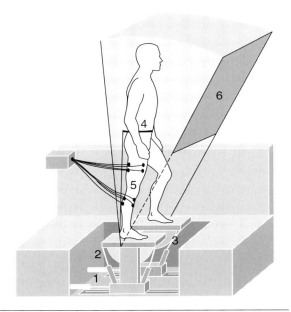

Figure 6.5 Diagram of a perturbation platform used to measure muscular postural adjustments to changes in the base of support. Displacements of the platform are made horizontally by moving the platform support base (1) forward or backward. Vertical displacements are made by moving the base of support up and down (2 & 3 together). The response to ankle rotation is obtained by moving the platforms under the heels (2) or toes (3) only. A belt attached to the hips (4) moves a device that measures body sway. Surface electromyographic electrodes (5) measure electrical activity of active muscles. A visual barrier (6) is used when visual cues are to be manipulated or eliminated (see Woolacott, Shumway-Cook, and Nashner (1982, p. 104).

the counterbalance response of young people is to contract, in sequence, the tibialis anterior (shin muscle), the quadriceps (anterior thigh), and abdominal muscles. Conversely, an unexpected movement of the support surface backward results in contractions of the gastrocnemius (calf muscle), biceps femoris (posterior thigh), and paraspinal muscles (back muscles). Older people begin contracting the first muscles in the sequence later than young people do, and sometimes the optimal sequence of muscle contractions is reversed in the aged (Woollacott, Inglin, & Manchester, 1988). Furthermore, when a source of information about the balance process is lost, such as occurs when the experimenter distorts the sensations of ankle movements or when vision is impaired, the balance of older people is more affected than is the balance of young persons (Teasdale, Stelmach, & Breunig, 1991). Conflicting feedback (e.g., when the experimenter artificially manipulates visual, sensory, or kinesthetic

feedback) also results in greater losses of balance in the elderly (Woollacott, Shumway-Cook, & Nashner, 1986).

Still, there are wide variations of static and dynamic balance among older adults (Alexander, Shepard, Gu, & Schultz, 1992). Not only do they vary more in their responses to balance perturbations, but they also differ greatly in the degrees of pathology present in the balance systems. Because it is difficult to find people over age 60 who are completely free of pathology, it is probable that even in subject groups described as healthy old adults, different degrees of pathology, some of which are very subtle, may affect balance measures. Few investigators have rigorously screened and excluded from their studies older subjects with slight neuromuscular pathologies.

Sensory Systems That Maintain Balance

The major sensory systems that enable people to balance are the visual system, vestibular system (the inner ear), and the somatosensory system. The visual system plays an important role in providing information about where the body is in space, how fast it is moving, and what obstacles are likely to be encountered. It also can compensate to some extent for inadequacies or losses in the other two major balance systems. The vestibular system provides reference information necessary to control postural sway and dynamic balance. Because the eyes can move while the head is stationary and the head can move while the eyes remain fixed on a target, the role of the vestibular system is crucial because it provides information that is independent of visual cues. The somatosensory system is crucial to balance, for it includes information from the skin (cutaneous input), from the joints, and from vibratory sensors, all of which provide information about body position. Several types of reflexes are triggered by somatosensory input. *Spinal reflexes*, such as the patellar tendon reflex (knee jerk), are activated when information from muscle activity is sent to motor neurons in the spinal cord, which then respond by contracting the appropriate muscles to counteract small deviations from balance. These reflexes are extremely rapid and may initiate postural adjustments without commands from the brain. Another class of reflexes that are recruited without voluntary control are *righting reflexes*, which are activated when the head is suddenly displaced from its normal upright position.

Ankle rotation provides stimuli that activate compensatory postural responses, including complex reflexes known as *long-latency reflexes*. Long-latency reflexes are thought to initiate the first useful phase of muscular activity in the total body pattern of muscular contraction that counteracts losses of balance. The long-latency reflexes, in cooperation with other reflexes, make up motor response synergies that operate to maintain static and dynamic balance. Clearly, the visual, vestibular, and somatosensory systems provide a vast array of information to assist the maintenance of posture and stability.

Vision

The visual system is a major contributor to balance, providing information about the environment and the location, direction, and speed of movement of the individual. Because many postural reflexes triggered by the vestibular system can also be triggered by visual stimulation, vision can compensate for some loss of vestibular function. However, in most very old individuals, vision also is degraded and provides decreased or distorted information. Consequently, poor visual acuity is correlated with the number of falls older people experience (Tobis, Nayak, & Hochler, 1981; Tobis, Reinsch, Swanson, Byrd, & Scharf, 1985). With aging, people often lose the ability to detect spatial information that would assist in balance. On average, they need three times more contrast to see some stimuli at slow frequencies (Sekuler, Hutman, & Owsley, 1980), and their depth perception is poorer. They also progressively lose their peripheral vision (Manchester, Woollacott, Zederbauer-Hylton, & Marin, 1989; Sekuler & Hutman, 1980). Peripheral vision makes a very important contribution to the control of anterior-posterior sway of the body. Woollacott et al. (1988), after comparing older adults to younger adults in dynamic balance under conditions of central vision only, peripheral vision only, and visual feedback unrelated to body sway, concluded that "older adults rely more on peripheral vision than young adults and that absence of peripheral vision leads to a greater number of falls" (p. 46).

Almost all elderly people use bifocal eyeglasses, which requires the processing of dual information systems, especially for those with extreme corrective lenses. Trying to operate within a dual mode of information processing (i.e., with and without

glasses) has the potential to create conflicting peripheral versus central vision information, which could be confusing and maladaptive.

The Vestibular System

The vestibular system, located in the inner ear, is a system of receptors that provides information about movements of the head. One type of receptors, the *otoliths* in the saccule and utricle, provide a static vertical reference during postural standing and signal the head's position with respect to gravity (i.e., whether the head is upside down, sideways, or tilted). If the head is tilted, these receptors indicate the direction and extent of tilt. Another type of sensor in the inner ear is the *semicircular canals*, which are composed of three half-circle canals aligned with the three planes of the body: frontal, saggital, and horizontal (Figure 6.6). The semicircular canals are filled with a fluid that moves in response to head movements. The receptors that are triggered by this fluid movement then provide information about the turning of the head. The neurons of both of these vestibular structures have powerful direct influences over the motor neurons in the spinal cord that activate muscles (especially extensor muscles) and thus contribute substantially to balance.

Vestibular neurons decrease both in numbers and in size of nerve fiber with aging, beginning at about age 40 (Bergstrom, 1973a, 1973b; Rosenhall & Rubin, 1975). Persons over age 70 may have lost 40% of the sensory cells within the vestibular system. Nonetheless, the results of many studies in which the vestibular function of older adults has been compared to that of younger people are inconclusive. Some researchers have found older people to be even more sensitive to vestibular stimuli than young people, whereas others have found the sensitivity of the elderly to be relatively unchanged. For example, only 6% of elderly people revealed vestibular impairment in the tilt test, in which the subject's chair is tilted and the vestibular responses are measured (Brocklehurst et al., 1982). One explanation for these widely divergent findings is that aging first affects an area of the brain that increases the excitability of brain tissue (reticular activating system). With more advanced aging, the sensitivity of the peripheral receptors of the vestibular system is reduced. Thus, individuals would be hypersensitive, normal, or hyposensitive to vestibular stimulation depending on where they were in the aging process (Bruner & Norris, 1971).

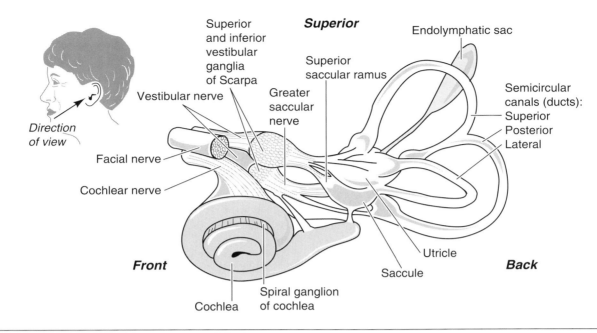

Direction of view

Superior and inferior vestibular ganglia of Scarpa

Vestibular nerve

Superior

Superior saccular ramus

Greater saccular nerve

Endolymphatic sac

Semicircular canals (ducts):
Superior
Posterior
Lateral

Facial nerve

Cochlear nerve

Front

Cochlea

Spiral ganglion of cochlea

Saccule

Utricle

Back

Figure 6.6 The vestibular apparatus of the inner ear.

Still, persons known to have vestibular losses may sway excessively or fall, especially when the other major systems that support balance (e.g., vision and the somatosensory system) are also impaired. These individuals may resort to using patterns of muscular contraction that are different from those seen in young individuals.

The Somatosensory System

The somatosensory system, which is critical to balance and motor control, provides information related to body contact and position. It includes cutaneous receptors that provide information about touch and vibration and muscle receptors that provide information about the position of the limbs and body. Muscle receptors also signal changes in limb and body positions. The control of movement is dependent upon constant and accurate information from the somatosensory system.

Cutaneous Contributions. Cutaneous receptors in the skin signal when any mechanical stimulus is applied to the body surface. Thus, when the skin is contacted and changes in pressure on the skin occur, neural impulses are directed centrally. The importance of this information is fully appreciated when one experiences the difficulty of balancing or walking when this information is absent. Normal individuals often experience the loss of these receptors when they sit in one position for a long time, restricting the blood supply to the lower limbs. This

causes a temporary loss of the function of cutaneous receptors; the feet and lower legs feel numb, and we say, "my foot has gone to sleep." Clearly, the contact of the skin with the shoes and the changes in pressure that result as the body weight shifts from heel to toe are important sources of information in the maintenance of balance.

Cutaneous sensation grows less sensitive with aging. This has been measured by determining how accurately individuals can detect vibration of the skin, because vibration sense in the legs is used to control postural sway (Brocklehurst et al., 1982). In this technique, a vibrator is placed on the skin surface, displacing the skin slightly with each vibration. Persons who have a keen sense of vibration can detect very low levels of vibration, but persons with less sensory acuity may be able to detect only very fast vibrations. Although the ability to detect cutaneous and vibratory stimuli is greatly influenced by disease and nutrition, it also declines significantly with aging (Skinner, Barrack, & Cook, 1988; Whanger & Wang, 1974). The speed with which vibration information reaches central control centers and the amplitude of this information also decreases. Another test of cutaneous sensitivity that clearly indicates this decline with age is the two-point discrimination test. In this test, the skin is touched lightly with an instrument that has two prongs. The subject's task is to determine whether the prongs are separated or together. If the prongs are far apart, as much as a half an inch, it is very easy to detect the two points of touch. However, as the prongs are brought closer together, it becomes much more difficult to determine whether the touch is by one or two prongs. The smaller the distance between the two prongs that the subject can still detect as two touches, the more sensitive the sense of touch. Older individuals lose some sensitivity of touch (Bolton, Winkelman, & Dyck, 1966).

Muscle Receptors and Joint Information. Muscle proprioceptors provide information about mechanical displacements of muscles and joints. When muscles are stretched (e.g., the calf muscles when the body leans forward), stretch receptors in the muscle signal the change in muscle length to central mechanisms. Reflexively, the muscle is contracted so that the desired muscle length and tension is obtained. Similarly, when a joint angle is changed, information is provided from joint receptors. Joint-position sense at the knee and ankle is measured either by moving the subject's knee and asking what the new angle of the joint is or by moving the subject's limb to a new position and asking the subject to duplicate that position in the next trial.

The ability of older people to detect motion of their limbs is significantly impaired when these manipulations are done at a slow speed, but when fast rates of joint extension are used, the age differences are minimal (Skinner, Barrack, & Cook, 1988). Because fast rates of joint extension are required for many dynamic balance needs, these investigators concluded that age-related differences in position sense are not functionally important. Whatever age differences exist in the ability to perceive motion of the joints appear only when the extremes of age groups are compared to each other. Thus, joint-position sense in the joints of the arms and legs does not markedly decline with aging (Kokmen, Bossemeyer, & Williams, 1978). A gradual loss of cervical articular mechanoreceptor functions has been shown by Wyke (1979), indicating that perceptions about the position of the neck and head may grow less accurate with aging.

Posture

Posture can be described as the alignment of the various parts of the body in relation to each other at any given point in time. Degenerative changes in the spinal column deleteriously affect posture. With aging the intervertebral discs become progressively flatter and less resilient, and osteoporosis causes the bones to become more porous. The result is a gradual wedging of the lower thoracic vertebrae, which results in a compensatory misalignment of the lower cervical and upper thoracic vertebrae known as "dowager's hump" (often seen in elderly women). Walking, rising from a chair, climbing stairs, and bending place added mechanical stresses on these precariously positioned vertebrae. Pain from these stresses makes older individuals reluctant to move more than necessary. Long periods of sitting, however, exacerbate the increased spinal curvature in the neck, shoulders, and lower back, resulting in even more destructive posture with increased pain and decreased mobility. In addition, a lifetime of wear, contracture, injury, and poor posture can produce differences in leg lengths, which may cause postural compensations while standing and walking that are conducive to falling.

Posture during standing or locomotion is maintained by several reflex systems, exquisitely integrated by central nervous system programs. Reflex systems that contribute to posture are monosynaptic reflexes (such as knee and ankle jerk reflexes), righting reflexes, and motor response synergies.

Spinal or Monosynaptic Reflexes

Spinal reflexes are activated when a muscle is stretched, sending neural impulses to the spinal cord. These impulses, which travel directly to the motor neurons in the spinal cord that control the stretched muscle, stimulate motor neurons to contract the muscle in an attempt to return it to its initial or appropriate length. The classic example of this type of reflex is seen when a person nods off to sleep in a boring meeting. The head begins to nod forward, and when the nodding reaches a certain velocity and the head drops to a certain level, the neck extensor muscles are stretched, and the head is suddenly jerked upright. Other monosynaptic reflexes are the well-known knee jerk (patellar tendon reflex) and the Achilles tendon reflex, which is evoked by tapping the tendon with a small hammer just below the knee or at the back of the ankle. Reflex mechanisms are also activated as people sway forward and backward or sideways over their base of support. Monosynaptic reflexes are thought by some to be active in counteracting postural sway, minimizing the movement and maintaining a substantial amount of balance without engaging the central command systems in the brain. These reflexes, which are active in standing and in locomotion, may not involve enough musculature to counter the sway, but they may "tune" other higher level response synergies that are capable of maintaining body sway within the tolerance limits for maintaining balance.

The degree to which aging slows monosynaptic reflexes and the functional significance that these changes, if they exist, have for postural stability remain somewhat controversial. Many researchers have reported very little, if any, changes in these reflexes. Conversely, several investigators have found significant age differences. In the largest study, which involved 9,774 subjects, Carel, Korczyn, and Hochberg (1979) correlated a measure of the Achilles tendon reflex to age. Similarly, Laufer and Schweitz (1968) found that Achilles tendon reflexes were significantly slower in individuals older than 50, whereas Vandervoort and Hayes (1989) found a higher incidence of absent ankle reflexes in old people.

These findings of age decrements in monosynaptic reflexes seem reasonable, because the speed with which neural impulses travel along peripheral nerves is slowed with age. But even though these slowed reflexes in aged individuals may be statistically significant, their functional significance has not been resolved. If fast-acting monosynaptic reflexes assist in the prevention of ankle sprains, then persons who have slower reflex reactions to perturbations of stability around the ankle joint also may have a higher risk for ankle sprains and other injuries. If this is the case, then age-related slowing of monosynaptic reflexes may compromise balance in old adults and predispose them to injury.

Exercise and chronic physical activity may assist in maintaining these reflexes (Hart, 1986), although Clarkson (1978) found no differences between reflex components of physically active and healthy sedentary older adults. Both of these investigators found that individuals who led an active lifestyle, which included exercise on a daily basis, had faster patellar tendon reflexes.

Righting Reflexes

Most people are familiar with the extraordinary righting reflexes of animals. When a cat is held upside down (even very close to the ground) and then suddenly dropped, it will land on its feet by recruiting its amazingly fast righting reflexes. In humans, these quick, fast-acting reflexes may be seen in the efforts to recover from the sudden and unexpected loss of balance that occurs when people trip on a stairway. These reflexes are triggered by visual and vestibular system activation, indicating that the body is accelerating and rotating about one or more of its axes. Dynamic sensors in the semicircular canals and in the utricle and saccule detect changes in the head position and initiate vestibular reflexes that mobilize antigravity muscles in the lower limbs and link them to compensatory counterbalancing movements of the upper body and arms.

Aging effects on righting reflexes have not been studied very much in humans, but animal studies suggest that righting reflexes may change very little with age (Wallace, Krauter, & Campbell, 1980). The ability to initiate a righting response may not be slowed much with aging, but the ability to respond with a muscular response that is substantive enough to implement the righting response and prevent a fall may be impaired. For example, the size of the response to a startling stimulus was greatly reduced in old rats when compared to that of younger rats (Krauter, Wallace, & Campbell, 1981).

Synergistic Motor Responses

Visual, vestibular, and somatosensory information must be integrated and coordinated in such a way that neural commands to the posture-stabilizing muscles of the legs and trunk can correct almost instantaneously for deviations in balance. Because these corrections occur so rapidly, in less than a quarter of a second, there must be central nervous system programs, much like computer programs, that organize balance information subconsciously from the different systems and then automatically activate the appropriate correction mechanisms. Sensory input from the visual, vestibular, and somatosensory systems triggers a response selection center; then a central mechanism selects, organizes, and initiates the corrective postural response (Stelmach & Worringham, 1985). An example of a corrective synergistic program in the legs and trunk is the mechanism that counteracts horizontal movements of the body's center of gravity caused by respiration movements (Gurfinkel, Kots, Paltsev, & Feldman, 1971). Two other motor response synergies are a *sway synergy* and a *suspensory synergy*, each of which has muscular patterns of activation that are characteristic and specific to their functions (Nashner & Woollacott, 1979).

A central command center integrates spinal reflex circuits by opening and closing them in a coordinated fashion. The command center is activated by *long-latency reflexes* that are triggered by the rotation of the ankles during movement. Thus, long-latency reflexes are part of an elegant postural reflex system that is active continuously when individuals are standing or moving about and that is integrated with voluntary movement. Response synergies are active when sudden perturbations to balance occur, and they are also an integral part of the preparation, planning, and execution of willful movement.

Synergistic Motor Response to a Loss of Balance

When the base of support during standing is suddenly perturbed forward, as in Nashner's paradigm (Figure 6.5, page 160; see Nashner, 1976), a young person's counterbalance response is to contract in sequence the tibialis anterior (shin muscle), the quadriceps (anterior thigh), and abdominal muscles. Conversely, an unexpected movement of the support surface backward results in contractions of the gastrocnemius (calf muscle), biceps femoris (posterior thigh), and paraspinal muscles (back muscles). Woollacott (1990) observed that some older people differ from young subjects in these response synergies in four ways.

First, the muscles in the front of the leg, which counteract a postural sway backward, contract slightly slower than those of young subjects, though the muscles in the calf, which counteract a backward platform perturbation, are not significantly slower. Thus, the postural response of the foot flexors may be more slowed by aging than the foot extensors (Inglin & Woollacott, 1988). Perhaps because the force applied by the foot extensors in walking is greater than the force required to flex the foot in the swing phase of the gait, the muscles responsible for foot extension are better maintained. Also, foot extensors are involved in tonic extension activity during standing. Thus, if chronic muscular usage has any beneficial effect on the maintenance of reflexes, the reflexes that depend on foot extension should be maintained, whereas those that depend on foot flexion would deteriorate.

Second, the activation sequence of the older subjects' muscles was occasionally disrupted. The older subjects used the joint information from the ankle to initiate response synergies to compensate for the changing balance over the base of support. Perhaps because they could not generate adequate muscular force during foot flexion and extension or because neurological deficits reduced the amount of information provided by ankle joint rotation, on some trials, old subjects employed a hip strategy in which the hip muscles were activated first, and then the thigh muscles (Woollacott et al., 1988). Third, the relative amplitudes of muscle activation in the synergistic response of older people were more variable than those of young subjects.

Fourth, a greater amount of co-contraction of antagonists was observed in older people during postural sway. By simultaneously contracting muscles that work against each other, older people stiffened the joints, which reduced the amount of movement they had to control to maintain balance. Lack of confidence about their balance probably partially accounts for this co-contraction pattern. When people of any age are not confident about their balance, they tend to produce a more global muscular contraction, that is, they contract muscles that do not contribute to maintaining balance. In fact, this phenomenon, the contraction of muscles nonspecific to the task, also occurs when people are learning a new skill and when they begin to fatigue in a well-learned skill. Loss of confidence, which also contributes to falling, will be discussed later in the chapter.

Synergistic Motor Preparation for Changes in Balance

Motor response synergies also are activated before and after voluntary movements in order to prepare for the change in dynamic state, including a new base of support, new external forces applied to the body, and a new changing position. For example, if a person plans to open a door, postural adjustments are activated *before* the extension of the hand toward the door to counter the change in dynamic state that will occur when force is applied to the door handle by the arm and hand. This type of postural muscle activation is described as a feedforward *anticipatory postural adjustment* and is specific to the movement to be made. A central command system yokes the anticipatory postural adjustment to the muscle activation command. Synergistic motor responses of this type have been studied by measuring the onset of contraction of the postural muscles (via electromyography) in a standing reaction time paradigm (Figure 6.7). When subjects raise one lower leg to a position horizontal to the floor, either as quickly as possible in response to a stimulus light or at their own pace, electrodes on the lower limb muscles indicate that the muscles in the leg not to be lifted contract *before* the moving leg begins to rise. This pattern is specific to the type of movement that is required.

The anticipatory postural response pattern of older adults is primarily the same as that of young people in slow movements, but it may be delayed in fast movements. Man'kovskii, Mints, and Lysenyuk (1980) suggested that because the voluntary response is not initiated until the postural stabilization has occurred, the slower anticipatory postural responses of older individuals delay the onset of the voluntary response. They also proposed that

when a fast movement is called for, the postural preparation that is supposed to precede the action overlaps the voluntary response. The synergy is disrupted, and the quality of the movement response is degraded. This is seen in young adults, too, but it may occur more frequently in older adults (Lee, Buchanan, & Rogers, 1987). Rogers, Kukulka, and Soderberg (1992), however, failed to find any age differences in the frequency and temporal ordering of anticipatory postural adjustments. They concluded that it is not likely that age-related deficits in postural or balance control can be accounted for by an absence of anticipatory postural adjustments.

Another reaction time experiment examined the standing postural activity linked to pushing or pulling a handle (Inglin & Woollacott, 1988). In this study, the postural anticipatory adjustment patterns were primarily similar in young and old subjects, but some changes in the muscular patterns occurred in some of the trials of the older subjects. Similar to the analysis of postural sway, the foot

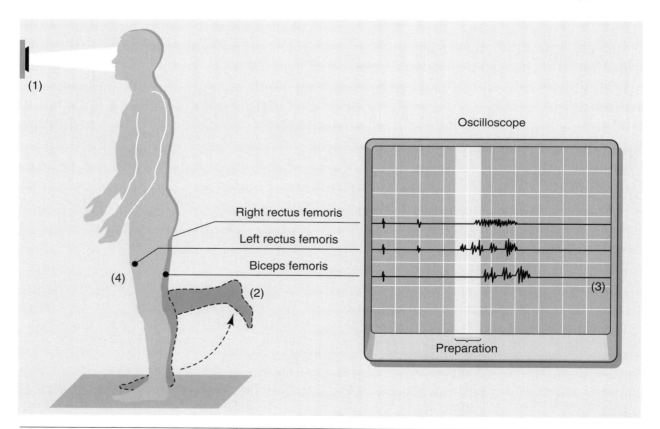

Figure 6.7   Measuring preparatory postural adjustments to anticipated movement. When the stimulus light (1) is activated, the subject lifts the lower right leg (2) to a position horizontal to the floor. EMG electrodes on the right leg record electrical activity from the moving limb (3). Electrodes on the left leg (4) record the preparatory postural activity that occurs before the left leg becomes the sole base of support. This diagram describes an experiment by Man'kovskii, Mints, and Lysenyuk (1980).

flexor responses were slower than the foot extensor responses. Anticipatory postural adjustments depend on the initial posture of individuals and may also depend on the strategy used to accomplish the task as well as the integrity of the neuromuscular system. The observation that older people's simple reaction time is actually faster when they are sitting down compared to their reaction time in a standing position suggests that the integration of postural stabilizing mechanisms with voluntary response initiation contributes significantly to the slowing of reaction time of the elderly (Stelmach, Populin, & Müller, 1990).

The age-related breakdown of stabilizing muscular responses and voluntary movement also occurs in situations where subjects initiate a voluntary body sway from their ankles. In older subjects, the timing and sequencing of muscle activity broke down, so that the functional coordination of their postural reflexes with voluntary sway was impaired (Stelmach, Phillips, DiFabio, & Teasdale, 1989). Future researchers in this area undoubtedly will question whether the age-related differences seen in anticipatory postural patterns are due to different initial postures of the elderly and their use of different strategies to solve the laboratory tasks. Also, it is well known that the voluntary reaction response of older persons is significantly slower (see chapter 7), but the contribution that postural slowing makes to the overall response delay has not been completely determined. Anticipatory postural adjustment, and its relationship to the voluntary movement, changes according to the nature of the conditions under which the movement is to be made. Determining how aging interacts with the nature of premovement conditions will be an important challenge for future researchers.

System Redundancy

The global input from the visual, vestibular, and somatosensory systems provides redundant information; that is, normal individuals can compensate for the partial loss of one of these systems by relying more heavily on the remaining two. In experimental situations where information from vision and the somatosensory system is unavailable or distorted, aging subjects have a more difficult time adapting and maintaining balance. Thus, when vision is lost or when somatosensory information is dulled through aging, the greater reliance on a vestibular system that is also aging results in a more fragile balance.

Other Factors That Affect Balance

In addition to the major systems that provide information and corrective actions relative to the body's posture and stability, muscular strength and self-confidence also contribute to the maintenance of balance.

Leg Strength

Loss of lower leg strength may not contribute to the increased postural sway seen in older people, because the amount of lower limb muscular activity that occurs during quiet standing is very limited. But lower leg strength is a factor in static balance testing, and it certainly is important in maintaining dynamic balance, walking, and in preventing falls (DiPasquale, et al., 1989; MacRae, Reinsch, & Tobis, 1989). The muscles that exert force against the ground during walking and provide stabilization around the ankle joint are considerably weakened with aging (Vandervoort & Hayes, 1989). In fact, in fallers the strength of the dorsiflexors of the ankle was found to be 7.5 times less than the strength of a control group of nonfallers (Whipple, Wolfson, & Amerman, 1987). Also, weak leg musculature may prevent older individuals from using the minimal number of lower leg muscles required to maintain balance when the support surface is moved. When balance is unexpectedly threatened, older people often resort to a strategy that incorporates more and larger body muscles (McCollum, Horak, & Nashner, 1984). To maintain balance, they may bring more muscles into play by bending at the hip or waist. Even younger individuals resort to this strategy when their balance is greatly challenged in activities such as walking on a narrow beam. Older individuals would probably display these compensatory strategies when trying to maintain balance while standing on a moving support, such as a moving walkway in an airport or on an escalator. Decreased strength of the muscles that support the knees has been associated with a greater incidence of falling (Tinetti, Williams, & Mayewski, 1986). In walking, age-related decreases in strength result in failure to lift the foot high enough during the swing phase of the gait, thus tripping becomes more problematic.

Decreased leg strength also is a major contributor to the loss of walking speed, which causes problems when older people must cross the street within the time period of a traffic light or when they must avoid an oncoming automobile by increasing their gait speed. Calf muscle strength, when combined with height and the presence of health problems, accounts for almost half of the variance associated with walking speed (Bendall, Bassey, & Pearson, 1989). It is highly probable, therefore, that walking exercises, strength training, and encouragement to walk faster could greatly improve the walking speed and thus the mobility of older adults.

Confidence

Many older adults lack confidence in their mobility and fear falling. In one study, 41% of the subjects said that they avoided certain activities in order to prevent the possibility of falling, and 34% feared that they might experience a fall within the year (Walker & Howland, 1991). In that study, subjects who feared falling rated their fear as greater than their fear of robbery, forgetting important appointments, or financial difficulties. In the elderly, lack of self-confidence and fear of falling may actually increase the risk of falling. When older adults were divided into groups of fallers/nonfallers and fear-of-falling/non–fear-of-falling, the group that feared falling performed significantly less well in blindfolded, spontaneous-sway tests and in eyes-open, one-leg balance tests (Maki, Holliday, & Topper, 1991). It was not possible in this study to determine whether those individuals who had the poorest balance were also the most afraid of falling or whether the fear of falling actually created a situation in which falling would be more likely to occur.

Many professionals strongly believe that a fear of falling contributes to a "stiffening" of the body, the unnecessary contraction of muscles, and a flexed posture, which produces a pattern of adjustment to losses of balance different from the adjustments made by young people. All people protect against falling backward, but older adults have exaggerated fears of falling backward and hitting their heads or breaking their backs or hips. Because the consequences of falls are much more serious for the elderly, they bias their posture so that if a fall occurs, it is a fall forward so they can use their arms to break the fall. In other words, they develop a flexed posture to lessen the chances of falling backward. Flexing the ankles does put the body in a more stable position, but because it requires more muscular output to maintain this position, the increased stability comes at the expense of an increased reliance on muscular strength and endurance. The flexed posture places the muscular load at the hips and knees and shifts the base of support to the front of the feet over the toes. Falls from this position may result in broken wrists or arms.

The fear of falling often causes individuals to avoid walking whenever possible, thereby weakening their muscles and minimizing the use of physiological balance systems. Impaired mobility engenders a fear of falling, which leads the elderly to lose their confidence in ambulation, to refuse to walk, and consequently, to become more immobile. Under these conditions, family and friends only exacerbate the problem when they discourage walking after a fall, because they reinforce the individual's fear of falling. It is ironic that a perceived sense of insecurity of balance may actually amplify the possible occurrence of the feared event. The ways in which these physiological, psychosocial, and environmental hazards interact and accumulate to increase the risk of falling are shown in Figure 6.8.

Locomotion

Although adult locomotion, primarily walking, appears to be a relatively simple process that for the majority of one's life span requires little conscious attention, it is in reality a complicated process that involves many physiological systems. It requires control at three levels: basic reflexive stride and support patterns, postural and equilibrium control, and mechanisms that allow the body to adapt to unexpected changes in the environment. Vision is used to monitor the direction and speed of movement, the vestibular system maintains equilibrium and provides information about acceleration, and proprioceptive information from the muscles, joints, and skin is used to determine muscular forces produced and the angles of the joints. Walking is basically the process of transferring the center of gravity from one foot to the other in a series of successive losses of balance. Thus in the act of walking the mechanical equilibrium of the body is disturbed continuously as it forms new bases of support by moving the legs forward alternately.

Gait Changes

Perhaps the most prominent feature of the movement of old people is that they move much slower

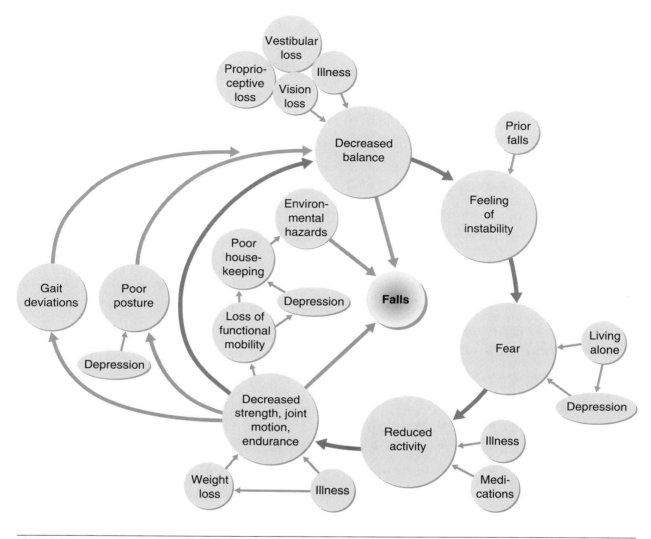

Figure 6.8 A "vicious circle" that eventually leads to falling.
Figure developed by Stephen Allison, PhD, PT, while a graduate student at The University of Texas, 1993. Reprinted by permission.

than younger people. Just as older people respond more slowly to environmental stimuli (chapter 7), plan and execute coordinated movements more slowly (chapter 8), and are slower when executing job skills (chapter 13), they also have a slower gait. Their slowness is not wholly because they cannot walk faster but rather because they prefer to walk at a slower pace. In Figure 6.9 the average walking speed of men and women age 20 is compared to the walking speed of individuals 60 to 80 years old. These comparisons were made of different people of different ages, because gait speed has not been measured longitudinally. It is likely, however, that walking speed slows gradually throughout the life span, decreasing at a faster rate between 65 and 85 years of age. Shown in

Figure 6.9, speed of walking declines more for older women than for older men. Older women walk with slower velocity, higher cadence, and shorter step length (Molen, 1973). The flexed posture that they sometimes assume to prevent falling leads to earlier fatigue, decreased joint excursion, and a decreased stride and gait speed.

Age-related changes in gait pattern can be seen in measures as simple as foot contact patterns. Because these patterns are the final outcome of stride length and cadence, relatively unsophisticated but clinically useful measures can be obtained by having subjects walk across a long piece of paper with ink-saturated material attached to the toe and heel of their shoes (Figure 6.10). To understand more clearly what is happening in the

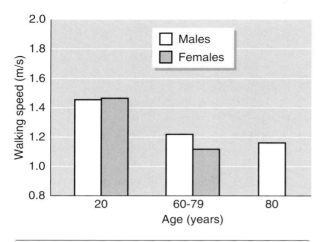

Figure 6.9 Average walking speed of males and females in three age groups. Figure composed from means of several studies in the literature (20-year-olds, *n* = 6 studies; 60-79-year-olds, *n* = 6 studies; 80-year-olds, *n* = 14 studies).
Data from Vandervoort and Hill (1990, p. 81).

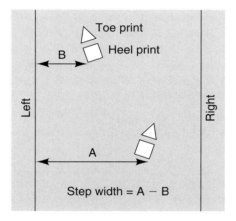

Figure 6.10 Step width measured from linked footprints.
From "Balance Performance and Step Width in Non-Institutionalized, Elderly, Female Fallers and Nonfallers" by D.K. Heitmann, M.R. Gossmann, S.A. Shaddeau, and J.R. Jackson, 1989, *Physical Therapy*, **69**, p. 926. Copyright 1989 by the American Physical Therapy Association. Reprinted from *Physical Therapy* with permission of the American Physical Therapy Association.

gait of older people, however, the gait patterns are measured in the laboratory by electromyography, film analysis, and force platforms.

Laboratory analyses reveal that the gait pattern of people older than 65 years has shorter and broader stride dimensions, more limited ankle movement, and lower swing-to-stance time ratios so that the period of double support is increased (Ferrandez, Pailhous, & Serratrice, 1988; Hageman & Blanke, 1986; Murray, Kory, Ross, &

Clarkson, 1969). Old adults, therefore, take more steps to cover the same distance, and the time when both feet are on the ground is longer. These differences are shown graphically in Figure 6.11. Age differences in gait characteristics, however, can be attributed almost solely to the slower gait of older people. When the gait patterns of young and old subjects who were free of neurological or neuromuscular pathologies were compared under similar walking speeds, the differences were minimal (Ferrandez, Pailhous, & Durup, 1990). Also, differences in gait are minimized when stride length is equalized across ages (Elble, Thomas, Higgins, & Colliver, 1991). Both young and old subjects manipulate stride length, swing phase, and stride frequency to slow or speed up their walking voluntarily. However, older subjects tend to favor increasing their stride frequency whereas younger adults tend to increase their stride length (Larish, Martin, & Mungiole, 1988). Older adults may not use the strategy of increasing their stride length either because they are less flexible or their balance is somewhat compromised. Increasing stride length also decreases the amount of double-support time, a pattern which requires greater balance. At an enforced very slow walking speed, old subjects tend to prolong the double-support phase of the gait cycle in order to enhance their balance (Gillis, Gilroy, Lawley, Mott, & Wall, 1986).

Another factor that is important to the age differences seen in gait is the factor of economy of motion. Locomotion requires the expenditure of energy, which is determined by the measurement of oxygen consumption, or $\dot{V}O_2$. A major theory of locomotion is that both humans and animals prefer the gait speed that is the most economical in terms of energy consumption. Horses, for example, will break into a trot when increases in fast walking become less economical than trotting. Similarly, they will change to a gallop when fast trotting reaches a speed that is less economical than galloping. Individual humans, presumably, prefer certain speeds of walking because those speeds are the most economical for them based on their body structure, weight, muscular strength, flexibility, and a host of other variables. Walking speeds ranging from 0.81 to 1.88 m/s are less economical for older adults than young adults, and therefore older walkers may use the strategy of increasing stride frequency rather than length because it also maximizes their economy of motion (Larish et al., 1988).

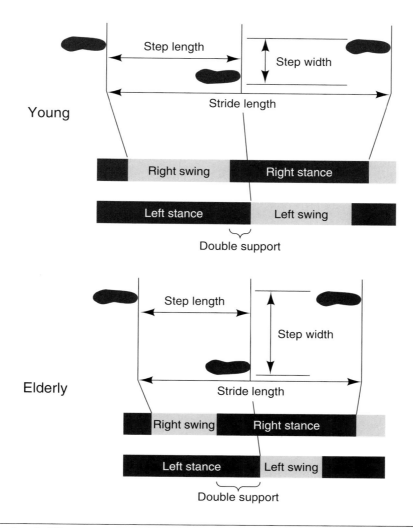

Figure 6.11   Age-related differences in step length, step width, period of double support, stance, and swing phases during walking.

From "Biomechanics of the Human Gait" by E.Y.S. Chao. In *Frontiers in Biomechanics* (p. 226) by G.W. Schmid-Schonbein, S.L.-Y. Woo, and B.W. Zweifach (Eds.), New York: Springer-Verlag. Copyright 1986 by Springer-Verlag. Adapted by permission.

Overall, locomotion of even the very old healthy individual is normal during slow walking and differs by shorter, more frequent strides during fast walking. There are several explanations for the preferred slow gait of older people. Endurance of weaker muscles in the lower limbs is maximized with the use of shorter strides, and the energy cost of walking is minimized. Less flexible ankle and knee joints constrain the stride length. Having a more precarious balance on one foot encourages individuals to spend less time in the single-support phase of the gait. Except for unexpected perturbations of balance, a slower gait also allows an older person more time to monitor the progress and result of walking and to react to changes in the environment. Just as the elderly drive automobiles more slowly so they can have more time to read street signs, stop the car, and react to emergencies (see chapter 8 for automobile driving skills), so also might they slow their walking to gain better control over their environment. A slower gait optimizes the adaptability of older people at all three locomotor control levels: basic reflexive stride and support patterns, postural and equilibrium control, and mechanisms that allow the body to adapt to unexpected changes in the environment. However, slow walking also has its disadvantages in society. Swedish investigators (Lundgren-Lindquist, Aniansson, & Rundgren, 1983) found that none of their 70-year-old subjects could cross a street intersection at their preferred walking speed within the time that was allowed by the street light, which required a walking speed of 1.4 m/s. At their maximum speed, only 32% of the women and 72% of the men could successfully cross the intersection before the light changed.

Gait pattern changes in normal walking with aging are minimal in healthy individuals who do not have physical impairments, such changes being predicted more by health status (Engle, 1986), physical inactivity (Larish et al., 1988), or pathological conditions (Imms & Edholm, 1981) than by chronological age. Several conditions are required for normal mobility. Besides having a negotiable environment, a person must have skeletal, muscular, and neural control systems that are intact (Table 6.2). Many older people, however, have articular (joint) problems of the toes, ankles, knees, hips, or spine that result from osteoporosis or osteoarthritis. The pain associated with these diseases causes the elderly to attempt to relieve the mechanical stress that occurs during walking by making gait changes (Wigley, 1984). Some of these skeletal disorders and the effect they have on mobility are shown in Table 6.3. In fact, because many diseases and disorders influence gait patterns, the gait changes that occur can be used as predictors of pathology. Table 6.4 (page 174) shows a list of different causes of changes in gait pattern. A comprehensive understanding of pathological effects on gait can be combined with skillful analyses of gait to be used as a screening device for many pathologies. For example, a slow, rigid

gait with small, mincing steps and a tendency for retropulsion can indicate parkinsonism, whereas a staggering, unsteady, irregular, wide-based gait may be a clue to cerebellar ataxia (Cunha, 1988).

Postural stability and gait efficiency are related to mobility, the ability to get around the home and community. Because walking reflects the health and function of the neuromuscular system, it is frequently part of a test of the activities of daily living (ADLs). Tinetti (1986) developed a more comprehensive assessment of mobility, shown in Table 6.5 (page 174), called the Mobility Index. This test includes objective ratings of balance, gait, and flexibility. The Mobility Index includes two scales, one composed basically of balance items and one of gait items. Subjects are awarded points (0, 1, or 2, as shown in Table 6.5) for an item if they successfully complete it. The higher the score, the better the subject's balance and gait. Lichtenstein, Burger, Shields, and Shiavi (1990) found that the more stable the postural sway, when measured on a force platform, and the more efficient the gait, measured by videotape analysis, the higher the scores on the Tinetti Mobility Index. That is, subjects who had a greater range of motion in the ankle and knee joints, longer strides, and faster gaits scored higher on the Mobility Index. Correlations of the total score of the Mobility Index with postural sway were moderate: for knee range of motion, $r = 0.52$; for stride length, $r = 0.68$; and for stride speed, $r = 0.75$. The relationship between measures of postural sway and mobility was

Table 6.2
Requirements for Safe, Normal, Confident Mobility

Category	Considerations
Skeletal system	Symmetry of the lower-limb segments Bone strength for stress absorption Base of support Pain-free, functional joint motion
Muscular system	Muscle size and fiber composition Strength of key muscles for gait Power of rapid-reflex contractions Muscular endurance
Neural control	Peripheral neuromuscular function Lower level central nervous system control of balance Motor planning for skilled movement
Environment	Elimination of hazards in the home and community to prevent falls

Note. From "Mobility Impairment and Falling in the Elderly" by A. Vandervoort, K. Hill, M. Sandrin, and V.M. Vyse, 1990, *Physiotherapy Canada*, **42**, p. 100. Copyright 1990 by the Canadian Physiotherapy Association. Reprinted by permission.

Table 6.3
Skeletal Disorders and Resultant Effects on Mobility

Disorder	Site	Pathology	Types of Effect
Osteoporosis	Vertebrae	Cancellous bone loss	Hypokinesis Avoidance of jarring movement
	Intervertebral disk	Flatter and less resilient	Flexed posture Slowed walking
	Hip	Compact bone loss	Immobilization Femoral fracture
Osteoarthritis	Cervical spine	Impaired movement and mechanoreceptor function	Limitations to gaze direction Imbalance
	Knee	Reduced range Loss of knee locking mechanism	Abnormal gait Knee "gives way"
	Hip	Degenerative changes	One-sided weight-bearing
	Feet	Deformities (hallux valgus)	Pain, tentative stepping

Note. From "Mobility Impairment and Falling in the Elderly" by A. Vandervoort, K. Hill, M. Sandrin, and V.M. Vyse, 1990, *Physiotherapy Canada,* **42,** p. 101. Copyright 1990 by the Canadian Physiotherapy Association. Reprinted by permission.

highest for the one-leg, eyes-open balance. Lichtenstein et al. (1990) suggest that this measurement should be predictive of mobility and risk of falling, because one-leg balance is required both in walking and when climbing stairs. In fact, the Mobility Index has been correlated to the incidence of falls in a long-term care facility (Tinetti, 1986).

Walking velocity is a higher predictor of mobility than is age. Imms and Edholm (1981) found that, in the older aged, they could predict the time necessary to traverse an obstacle course better by knowing how fast an individual normally walked than by knowing the individual's age. It helped to know how great the postural sway was, but this was not as important as knowing the walking velocity. Postural sway is moderately related to walking velocity ($r = -0.599$), and consequently, it also is related to mobility.

Negotiating Obstacles

Older adults approach obstacles and negotiate them in somewhat different ways than young people do. According to a comprehensive analysis conducted by Chen, Ashton-Miller, Alexander, and Schultz (1991), the minimum swing foot clearance over an obstacle is not different in older adults. But older adults do use a more cautious strategy when they cross over obstacles. They use a slower crossing speed, a shorter step length, and the distance from the rear edge of the obstacle to the heel of their swing foot at heel strike is shorter. They also cross the obstacle so that it is 10% further forward in their crossing step. More mistakes are made by older adults as they negotiate obstacles. Although none of Chen et al.'s (1991) older adults actually tripped while crossing over an obstacle, 17% of them stepped on an obstacle while attempting to cross over it. Thus, because older adults make more obstacle contact, their risk of tripping or falling while negotiating an obstacle is higher.

Falling—When Balance Fails

Losing balance and falling during standing or locomotion becomes an ever increasing threat to the safety and health of the elderly, especially those at advanced ages. One third to one half of the population over 65 years old, or one out of every three older persons, will fall at least once a year (Nickens, 1985; Perry, 1982).

Hospitalization for hip fracture, which is extremely expensive, is increasing approximately

---

Table 6.4
**Causes of Gait Disorders
in Old Age**

Neurological
    État lacunaire
    Dementia
    Chronic subdural hematoma
    Normal-pressure hydrocephalus
    Cerebellar ataxia
    Stroke
    Parkinson's disease
    Progressive supranuclear palsy
    Peripheral neuropathy
    Spinal cord lesions
        Cervical spondylotic myelopathy
        Cervical tumors
        Vitamin B_{12} deficiency
        Posterior column degeneration

Psychological
    Depressive states
    Fear of falling

Orthopedic
    Osteoarthrosis
    Osteomalacia
    Foot problems
    Unsuspected fractures

Endocrinological
    Hypothyroidism

General
    General muscle weakness

Drugs

Senile gait

Associated conditions

Note. From "Differential Diagnosis of Gait Disorders in the Elderly" by U.V. Cunha, 1988, *Geriatrics*, **43**, p. 34. Copyright 1988 by Edgell Communications. Reprinted by permission.

9% each year. Approximately 50% of fallers who break their hips are never functional walkers again. Women fall more frequently (Nickens, 1985; Perry, 1982), but men who fall have a higher mortality rate. Risk factors that predispose the elderly to falling are shown in Table 6.6.

Craik (1989) suggests that the cause of falls can be divided into two categories: the stimulus that results in the loss of balance, and the inability of the older person to correct for the unexpected loss of balance. Examples of stimuli that can cause falling are dizziness, fainting, or uneven surfaces. Inability to correct for an unexpected loss of stability results

---

Table 6.5
**Gait and Balance Evaluations
With Mobility Index**

Balance measures (range 0-24)	Scoring
Sitting balance	0, 1
Rising from a chair	0, 1, 2
Attempts to rise	0, 1
Immediate standing balance (first 5 s)	0, 1, 2
Prolonged standing balance	0, 1, 2
Withstanding nudge on chest	0, 1, 2
Neck range of motion	0, 1, 2
Stance with eyes closed	0, 1
Turning balance (through 360°)	
Step continuity	0, 1
Steadiness	0, 1
One-leg balance (5 s)	
Right leg	0, 1
Left leg	0, 1
Back extension	0, 1, 2
Reaching up	0, 1
Bending over	0, 1
Sitting down	0, 1, 2

Highest possible total = 24

**Gait measures
(range 0-16)**

Initiation of gait	0, 1
Step symmetry	0, 1
Step continuity	0, 1
Step length	
Right leg	0, 1
Left leg	0, 1
Step height	
Right leg	0, 1
Left leg	0, 1
Path	0, 1, 2
Walk stance	0, 1
Trunk	0, 1, 2
Turning	0, 1, 2
Able to accelerate walking speed	0, 1, 2

Highest possible total = 16

Note. From "Comparison of Biomechanics Platform Measures of Balance and Videotaped Measures of Gait With a Clinical Mobility Scale in Elderly Women" by M.J. Lichtenstein, M.C. Burger, L.L. Shields, and R.G. Shiavi, 1990, *Journal of Gerontology: Medical Sciences*, **45**, p. M50. Copyright 1990 by The Gerontological Society of America. Adapted by permission.

Table 6.6
Risk Factors for Falling

- Balance abnormalities
- Muscular weakness
- Visual disorders
- Gait abnormalities
- Cardiovascular disease
- Cognitive impairment
- Medication

from decreased reaction time, diminished central nervous system integration, decreased strength, and loss of joint mobility.

Several factors operate on either the stimulus causing the fall or the reactive ability of the aged person to prevent the fall. These factors include the status of the skeletoneuromusuclar system, visual system, cardiovascular system, cognition, use of medication, and the status of the environment. Neuromuscular pathologies that produce abnormal gait patterns are a major cause. Neuromuscular pathologies also are frequently combined with arthritis, resulting in restricted neck movements and limited hip movement, all of which increase the risk for falling. Even when neuromuscular pathology is not apparent, the muscles responsible for coordinated postural reactions weaken and slow (by remaining in stretched positions for years). Another major cause of falling in the elderly is tripping, which occurs when the step height is reduced during the swing phase of the gait (Overstall et al., 1977).

In addition to disorders of the neuromuscular, vision, vestibular, and somesthetic systems, other factors associated with falling are impaired cardiovascular function, Parkinson's disease, and medication (Brocklehurst, 1973). Reduced cardiac output disorders, cardiac arrhythmias and conduction defects, anemia, and orthostatic hypotension can reduce the amount of blood that is necessary for consciousness and for the postural control centers of the brain to operate. Cerebral bloodflow declines with aging, and in many elderly people, blood pressure increases. This shifts the threshold for cerebral mechanisms that maintain bloodflow to higher levels of blood pressure. Thus, a relatively small change in cerebral blood pressure produces a relatively large ischemia that can in turn cause dizziness or fainting. Older people are more affected by drugs designed to regulate blood pressure, and they react

less quickly to challenges of homeostasis (Jonsson & Lipsitz, 1990). Kauffman (1990) diagrammed the multiple interactive forces that govern static and dynamic balance and showed how these factors affect posture and falling (see Figure 6.12).

Medication and Falling

The use of one or more medications is very common in the elderly, and many drugs can affect balance and increase the risk of falling (Wells, Middleton, Lawrence, Lillard, & Safarik, 1985). In a study of 1,042 elderly members of a community, researchers correlated the prevalence of falls with the frequency of falling. Only 25% of individuals who were taking no medication had experienced a fall, whereas 48% of individuals taking five medications had fallen (Blake et al., 1988). Medications such as diuretics (prescribed for congestive heart failure) have been associated with falling, but several researchers have failed to find an increased risk due to the use of diuretics or antihypertensives.

Psychotropic drugs (hypnotics, tricyclic antidepressants, antipsychotics) increase the risk of falling in the elderly. The effects of these drugs also increase with age and dose. For example, 39% of hospitalized patients over age 70 had reactive symptoms of drowsiness, confusion, and ataxia to the psychotropic drug flurazepam (Greenblatt, Allen, & Shader, 1977). Ray and Griffin (1990) analyzed many epidemiological studies of the association between age, psychotropic drug symptoms, and falling and found that older people in both community and hospital environments have increased rates of dizziness, postural hypotension, psychomotor impairment, and falls associated with medication. In fact, the relative risk of falling among elderly psychotropic drug users is twice that of nonusers. Hypnotic drugs, such as barbiturates, are an important cause of falls at night and in the morning withdrawal periods (MacDonald & MacDonald, 1977). Sobel and McCart (1983) reported that in one group of elderly described as fallers, diuretics were prescribed three times more than for the nonfallers, and 60% more fallers used sedatives or hypnotics than did nonfallers. Medication can contribute to falling by inducing dizziness, reversible dementia, confusion, withdrawal insomnia, and ataxia. Tricyclic antidepressants, antipsychotics, sedatives and hypnotics, insulin, levodopa, and monoamine oxidase inhibitors may

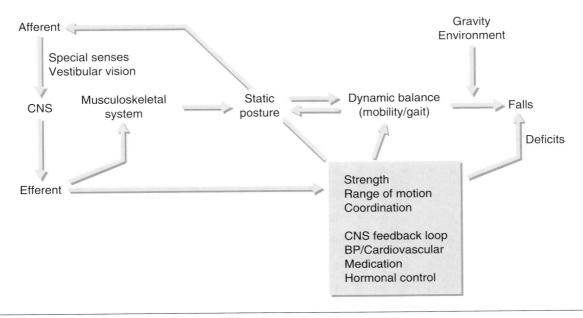

Figure 6.12 Factors affecting posture and falls.
Reprinted from Kauffman, T., Impact of Aging-Related Musculoskeletal and Postural Changes on Falls, *Topics in Geriatric Rehabilitation*, Vol. 5:2, p. 36, with permission of Aspen Publishers, Inc., © 1990.

lower blood pressure directly or interact with antihypertensive agents to cause postural hypotension, which is a risk factor for falling. Postural hypotension, discussed more fully in chapter 4, can occur when elderly people move suddenly from a lying to a standing position. The resultant rapid drop in systemic blood pressure (>20 mmHg) sometimes results in fainting, which in turn causes falling. But other studies of this risk factor have failed to find an association. The long-acting benzodiazepines impair psychomotor function, which in turn degrades balance, increases the risk of falling, and decreases the capability of executing a positive reaction and preventing the fall.

Increased incidence of falling, which has the serious consequences of injury or even death, is just one outcome of what some individuals deem an abuse of medication for patient-control purposes in institutions and long-term care facilities.

Environmental Hazards

Many falls that community-living elderly experience in the home are caused by environmental hazards. Indoor causes of falls are slippery bathtub floors, absence of grab bars, low toilet seats, torn or loose rugs, inaccessible light switches, wet or waxed floors, shelves that are too high, and wobbly tables and chairs (DeVito et al., 1988; Tinetti

et al., 1986). Ten percent of falls occur on stairs, with more falls occurring during the descent than the ascent. Some outdoor hazards include unsafe stairways, broken or uneven pavement, poorly marked curbs, and high bus steps. Finally, Gabell, Simons, and Nayak (1985) reported that 40% of the falls analyzed in their study could have been prevented by proper footwear. Many falls could also be prevented by habitual wearing of prescription glasses.

Environmental hazards may be less predictive of falls and accidents in institutionalized elderly than in those older adults living at home. In one study, 60% of the falls reported by elders living independently in the community were associated with inattention and hazardous activities (Reinsch, MacRae, Lachenbruch, & Tobis, 1992). But although environmental hazards play a slight role in falls of institutionalized elders, other factors are much more predictive of future accidents (Svensson et al., 1991). Table 6.7 compares the contribution of various intrinsic causes to environmental causes for accidents that occurred among 4,862 patients in a geriatric hospital and its associated nursing homes in Sweden during 1 year. Although the information in this table pertains to all accidents, many were related to falling. In these institutionalized patients, accidents were more likely to occur in patients with a history of previous accidents, moderate confusion, episodes of dizziness, moderate imbalance, moderate impairment on the

Table 6.7
Probable Causes of All Accidents

	Major accidents (n = 308) (%)	Minor accidents (n = 519) (%)
Intrinsic		
Dizziness	33	29
Anxiety and confusion	21	9
Impaired balance	16	31
Exhaustion and pain	6	6
Acute disorders (TIA, insult, infarct)	4	4
Poor vision	4	6
Environmental		
Slipperiness	9	7
Nursing staff or fellow patients	3	3
Furniture	2	3
Lighting	1	2
Clothing	1	0

Note. From "Accidents in the Institutionalized Elderly: A Risk Analysis" by M.L. Svensson et al., 1991, *Aging*, **3**, p. 189. Copyright 1991 by Editrice Kurtis S.R.L. Reprinted by permission.

ADL scale, and high drug use. Major risk factors did *not* include environmental hazards such as slippery floors, poor lighting, or ill-fitting clothing.

Characteristics of Fallers

Those individuals who have a history of falling and are therefore at a high risk for falling share particular characteristics. They are most likely to be adults who take more steps to turn 360°, cannot stand up from a chair without pushing off, have a high prevalence of antidepressant use, and have impaired position sensation; they are also more likely to be women (Lipsitz, Jonsson, Kelley, & Koestner, 1991). They also have unusually weak hip adductors, knee extensors, knee flexors, and ankle dorsiflexors (MacRae, Lacourse, & Moldavon, 1992). Besides a history of previous accidents, they may be moderately demented, experience episodes of dizziness, are moderately impaired on the ADL scale, and have impaired gait (Morse, Tylko, & Dixon, 1987). They also routinely take several medications. Individuals who have one or more of these characteristics have a higher risk of falling.

Consequences of Falling

Falls can result in major or minor physical injuries, psychological anxieties about falling, and decreases in physical activity. Major injuries are joint dislocation, lacerations, and bone fractures, whereas minor injuries are small cuts, bruises, abrasions, and sprains. Major injuries occur in only 6% of elders living in the community, and although hip fractures occur in only about 1% of the falls, the consequences of this major injury are most often catastrophic (Nevitt, Cummings, & Hudes, 1991). Few individuals who have serious hip fractures ever regain their previous functional levels. Indeed, more than half of all those hospitalized from a fall do not live more than a year (Rubenstein, Miller, Pastel, & Evans, 1983). In addition, falls account for 87% of all fractures in the elderly. More than two thirds of accidental deaths in people over age 75 are caused by falling (Azar & Lawton, 1964). Hip fractures, which occur at higher percentages in nursing homes than among the oldest-old living in the community, have serious health, economic, and social consequences even when death does not occur. The national health cost of fall-related injuries is in the multibillion dollars range.

Minor injuries are more likely to occur when protective responses are impaired. For example, individuals with slow reflexive or reactive responses may initiate protective movements too late to avoid injury, weakened upper-body strength may reduce the individual's chances of diverting some of the force of the fall with hands and arms, and a decoupling of reflexive and voluntary response mechanisms (loss of coordination) may result in the individual being unable to dissipate the force across a wider surface area of the body. In addition to strength and reaction time, psychomotor efficiency, mental status, and visual acuity also contribute to the likelihood of minor injuries resulting from falls (Nevitt et al., 1991).

Exercise Programs as a Strategy to Prevent Falling

Because muscular weakness, inflexibility, degraded synergy and programming mechanisms, and motor control difficulties all contribute to falling, a high level of physical fitness is an effective strategy to prevent falling: It increases muscular strength, flexibility, and motor control. The changes in body composition that accompany a successful exercise program (i.e., decreased total body weight and body mass) also contribute to the maintenance of balance by making the task easier for the neuromuscular system (Era & Heikkinen, 1985). Older masters athletes were better at controlling their balance in clinical and functional (walking) tests than their nonactive peers (Brown & Mishica, 1989). Older subjects of a balance perturbation experiment who were physically fit usually showed the muscle pattern activation that was seen in young subjects (Manchester et al., 1989). Also, because performance on the one-leg balance test improves with practice (Fansler, Poff, & Shepard, 1985; Heitman, Gossmann, Shaddeau, & Jackson, 1989), chronic physical activity might reasonably be expected to enhance balance by providing daily challenges and practice opportunities for balance mechanisms. Stones and Kozma (1987) related postural control to fitness training by showing that performance on the one-leg balance test was correlated significantly with vital capacity ($r = 0.384$) and forced expiratory volume ($r = 0.382$; see chapter 4 for more information about vital capacity and forced expiratory ventilation). Presumably, increased lower-limb strength and endurance accompany the increased fitness necessary to increase vital capacity and forced expiratory volume. The continued practice and use of the balance mechanisms that occur in chronic physical activity also increased the self-confidence of older people in their abilities, in turn enhancing mobility (Overstall, 1980; Roberts & Fitzpatrick, 1983).

Although Era and Heikkinen (1985) observed a relationship between aerobic fitness, grip strength,

and postural sway, others believe that increases in postural sway may represent a deterioration of the nervous system that cannot be improved by exercise training. These investigators found that a 12-week exercise program aimed at increasing postural stability produced no apparent changes in the postural sway of women ages 72 to 92 (Crilly, Willoms, Trenholm, Hayes, & Delaquerriere-Richardson, 1989) even though their fitness improved. Reinsch et al. (1992) also found no decrease in the number of falls occurring in 230 elders from senior centers after 1 year of either an exercise program, a lecture discussion, or a combination of both that were designed to decrease falls. They suggested that either their exercise program was not intense enough (they also found no increases in strength or balance), or the exercise and discussion programs might have given the elders more confidence, which led them to become more venturesome and thus have more accidents.

Nonetheless, the findings of all studies on the subject of exercise and falling, when taken together, suggest that an exercise program that significantly increases strength, maintains a body weight and composition that are efficient for locomotion, and improves balance should decrease the number of falls seen in older people. Daily physical activity and exercise are also likely to contribute to the prevention of falling in other ways. Reflex and motor synergy integration may be enhanced, postural hypotension that can lead to falls is less likely, and the physically active elder may need less medication and be able to sleep better (see Table 6.8). All of these conditions contribute to an enhanced self-confidence in physical ability. Such activity-related physical enhancements may reduce the severity and consequences of a fall when it does occur (Nevitt et al., 1991).

In Summary

Maintaining balance, although usually accomplished without conscious control, is nonetheless an extraordinary neuromuscular achievement. Because it requires the integration of multiple body systems, and because each of these systems ages at a different rate for different individuals, the effects of aging on static and dynamic balance, locomotion, and falling are extremely varied for different individuals. Individual differences in balance, posture, and locomotion are striking in the elderly. Nonetheless,

Table 6.8
How Physical Exercise Contributes to the Prevention of Falling in the Elderly

- Strengthens leg and back muscles
- Enhances reflex and motor synergy postural reactions
- Improves gait
- Increases flexibility
- Maintains body weight so balance is less challenging
- Improves mobility to avoid unexpected threats
- Decreases cardiovascular disease risk
- Reduces the risk of postural hypotension
- Lowers the probability of needing medication
- Enhances sleep and reduces insomnia
- Raises self-confidence in physical abilities

aging does eventually exact a toll on everyone, and some generalizations may be made.

The amount of postural sway over a standing base of support increases with aging, more so in women than in men, and more in one-legged balance than in quiet standing. People who are classified as fallers, that is, who fall not because of tripping or encountering an overwhelming obstacle, but because of giddiness, loss of balance, turning the head, or rising from a chair, exhibit greater postural sway than nonfallers. Both static and dynamic tests are relatively sensitive behavioral measures of neurologic dysfunction in older adults. The one-leg balance test measures static balance, and functional reaching, postural stress tests, and sudden perturbations of the support surface measure dynamic balance. Performance on all of these tests decreases with aging.

Impairments in the visual, vestibular, and somatosensory systems that are natural outcomes of the aging process also contribute to decreases in balance. Monosynaptic reflexes, which contribute to standing balance, become less sensitive with aging, but aging effects are not as great in these reflexes as they are in more complex reflexes and muscle synergies.

Older people are slower to make postural adaptations to an unexpected loss of balance. Also, when making postural responses to a perturbation of balance, older individuals sometimes demonstrate a different order of muscle activation than

that executed by young persons. They sometimes activate hip flexors "out of order" in the pattern, perhaps to recruit stronger muscles to make the compensatory response earlier. Preparatory postural adjustments are similar in young and old people when the movement to be made is a slow one. When the movement must be made quickly, older people sometimes demonstrate postural preparation that is so slow that it is overlapped by the voluntary response, thus disrupting the motor synergy and degrading the quality of the movement.

Lower-leg strength is important in maintaining dynamic balance, walking, and preventing falls. Physical exercise, because it strengthens muscles, increases flexibility, maintains body weight, decreases cardiovascular disease risk, and lowers the probability of needing medication, can contribute substantially to the prevention of falling.

Locomotor gait is slower in older individuals, and it is the slowness of speed that causes the elderly gait pattern to have shorter, broader step dimensions, a higher cadence, and a lower swing-to-stance time ratio. When older people are asked to accelerate their walking, they do so by increasing the cadence of their gait. Young adults, in contrast, increase their stride length. Aging per se changes gait pattern and mobility much less than pathology does. Even very old people who are free of disease have relatively normal gaits and mobility. Individuals who have osteoarthritis, osteoporosis, and peripheral neurological pathology, however, modify their gait to relieve mechanical stress and pain.

Increased falling is due both to a physiological decline in postural control with advancing age and to a decline due to disease of the central nervous system. Factors that contribute to falling include disorders of the neuromuscular, visual, vestibular, and somatosensory systems and cardiovascular disease. Medication is also a frequent cause of falling. Drug-related symptoms of drowsiness, confusion, dizziness, postural hypotension, and psychomotor impairment contribute to falling. The relative risk of falling among elderly psychotropic drug users is twice that of nonusers. A substantial number of falls among the elderly could be prevented by eliminating environmental hazards, improving footwear, and wearing prescription glasses.

References

Alexander, N.B., Shepard, N., Gu, M.J., & Schultz, A. (1992). Postural control in young and elderly adults when stance is perturbed: Kinematics. *Journal of Gerontology: Medical Sciences*, **47**, M79-M87.

Azar, G., & Lawton, A. (1964). Gait and stepping as factors in the frequent falls of elderly women. *The Gerontologist*, **4**, 83-84, 103.

Bendall, M.J., Bassey, E.J., & Pearson, M.B. (1989). Factors affecting walking speed of elderly people. *Age and Ageing*, **18**, 327-332.

Bergstrom, B. (1973a). Morphology of the vestibular nerve. II. The number of myelinated vestibular nerve fibers in man at various ages. *Acta Otolaryngologica*, **76**, 173-179.

Bergstrom, B. (1973b). Morphology of the vestibular nerve. III. Analysis of the caliber of the myelinated vestibular nerve fibers in man at various ages. *Acta Otolaryngologica*, **76**, 331-338.

Blake, A.J., Morgan, K., Bendall, M.J., Dallosso, H., Ebrahim, S.B.J., Arie, T.H.D., Fentem, P.H., & Bassey, E.J. (1988). Falls by elderly people at home: Prevalence and associated factors. *Age and Ageing*, **17**, 365-372.

Bohannon, R.W., Larkin, P.A., Cook, A.C., Gear, J., & Singer, J. (1984). Decrease in timed balance test scores with aging. *Physical Therapy*, **64**, 1067-1070.

Bolton, C.F., Winkelman, M.D., & Dyck, P.J. (1966). A quantitative study of Meissner's corpuscles in man. *Neurology*, **16**, 1-9.

Brocklehurst, J.C. (1973). *Textbook of geriatric medicine and gerontology*. Edinburgh: Churchill Livingstone.

Brocklehurst, J.C., Robertson, D., & James-Groom, P. (1982). Clinical correlates of sway in old age: Sensory modalities. *Age and Ageing*, **11**, 1-10.

Brown, M., & Mishica, G. (1989). Effect of habitual activity of age-related decline in muscular performance: A study of master athletes. *The Gerontologist*, **29**, 257A.

Bruner, A., & Norris, T.W. (1971). Age-related changes in caloric nystagmus. *Acta Otolaryngologica*, Suppl. 282, 5-24.

Carel, R.S., Korczyn, A.D., & Hochberg, Y. (1979). Age and sex dependency of the Achilles tendon reflex. *American Journal of the Medical Sciences*, **278**, 57-63.

Chao, E.Y.S. (1986). Biomechanics of the human gait. In G.W. Schmid-Schonbein, S.L.-Y. Woo, & B.W. Zweifach (Eds.), *Frontiers in biomechanics* (p. 226). New York: Springer-Verlag.

Chen, H., Ashton-Miller, J.A., Alexander, N.B., & Schultz, A.B. (1991). Stepping over obstacles: Gait patterns of healthy young and old adults. *Journal of Gerontology: Medical Sciences*, **46**, M196-M203.

Clarkson, P.M. (1978). The relationship of age and level of physical activity with the fractionated components of patellar reflex time. *Journal of Gerontology*, **33**, 650-656.

Craik, R. (1989). Changes in locomotion in the aging adult. In M.H. Woollacott & A. Shumway-Cook (Eds.), *Development of posture and gait across the life span* (pp. 176-201). Columbia: University of South Carolina Press.

Crilly, R.G., Willoms, D.A., Trenholm, K.J., Hayes, K.C., & Delaquerriere-Richardson, L.F. (1989). Effect of exercise on postural sway in the elderly. *Gerontology*, **35**, 137-143.

Cunha, U.V. (1988). Differential diagnosis of gait disorders in the elderly. *Geriatrics*, **43**, 33-42.

DeVito, C.A., Lambert, D.A., Sattin, R.W., Bacchelli, S., Ros, A., & Rodriguez, J.G. (1988). *Journal of the American Geriatrics Society*, **36**, 1029-1035.

DiPasquale, R., Morey, M., Sullivan, R., Crowley, G., Cowper, P., & Feussner, J. (1989). Strength improvements in geriatric exercise: Falls history and deficits. *The Gerontologist*, **29**, 39A.

Duncan, P.W., Studenski, S., Chandler, J., & Prescott, B. (1992). Functional reach: Predictive validity in a sample of elderly male veterans. *Journal of Gerontology: Medical Sciences*, **47**, M93-M98.

Duncan, P.W., Weiner, D.K., Chandler, J., & Studenski, S. (1990). Functional reach: A new clinical measure of balance. *Journal of Gerontology: Medical Sciences*, **45**, M192-M197.

Elble, R.J., Thomas, S.S., Higgins, C., & Colliver, J. (1991). Stride-dependent changes in gait of older people. *Journal of Neurology*, **238**, 1-5.

Engle, V.F. (1986). The relationship of movement and time to older adults' functional health. *Research in Nursing and Health*, **9**, 123-129.

Era, P., & Heikkinen, E. (1985). Postural sway during standing and unexpected disturbance of balance in random samples of men of different ages. *Journal of Gerontology*, **40**, 287-295.

Fansler, C.L., Poff, C.L., & Shepard, K.F. (1985). Effects of mental practice on balance in elderly women. *Physical Therapy*, **65**, 1332-1338.

Ferrandez, A.M., Pailhous, J., & Durup, M. (1990). Slowness in elderly gait. *Experimental Aging Research*, **16**, 79-89.

Ferrandez, A.M., Pailhous, J., & Serratrice, G. (1988). Locomotion in the elderly. In B. Amblard, A. Berthoz, & F. Clarac (Eds.), *Development adaptation and modulation of posture and locomotion* (pp. 115-124). Amsterdam: Elsevier.

Gabell, A., Simons, M.A., & Nayak, U.S.L. (1985). Falls in the healthy elderly: Predisposing causes. *Ergonomics*, **28**, 965-975.

Gillis, B., Gilroy, K., Lawley, H., Mott, L., & Wall, J.C. (1986). Slow walking speeds in healthy young and elderly females. *Physiotherapy Canada,* **38,** 350-352.

Graybiel, A., & Fregly, A.R. (1966). A new quantitative ataxia test battery. *Acta Otolaryngologica (Stockholm),* **61,** 292-312.

Greenblatt, D.J., Allen, M.D., & Shader, R.I. (1977). Toxicity of high-dose flurazepam in the elderly. *Clinical Pharmacology and Therapeutics,* **21,** 355-361.

Gurfinkel, V.S., Kots, Y.M., Paltsev, E.I., & Feldman, A.G. (1971). The compensation of respiratory disturbances of the erect posture of man as an example of the organization of interarticular interaction. In I.M. Gelfand, V.S. Gurfinkel, S.V. Fomin, & M.L. Tsetlin (Eds.), *Models of the structural-functional organization of certain biological systems.* Cambridge, MA: The MIT Press.

Hageman, P.A., & Blanke, D.J. (1986). Comparison of gait of young women and elderly women. *Physical Therapy,* **66,** 1382-1387.

Hart, B.A. (1986). Fractionated myotatic reflex times in women by activity level and age. *Journal of Gerontology,* **41,** 361-367.

Hasselkus, B.R., & Shambes, G. (1975). Aging and postural sway in women. *Journal of Gerontology,* **30,** 661-667.

Heitman, D.K., Gossmann, M.R., Shaddeau, S.A., & Jackson, J.R. (1989). Balance performance and step width in non-institutionalized, elderly, female fallers and nonfallers. *Physical Therapy,* **69,** 923-931.

Imms, F.J., & Edholm, O.G. (1981). Studies of gait and mobility in the elderly. *Age and Ageing,* **10,** 147-156.

Inglin, B., & Woollacott, M.H. (1988). Anticipatory postural adjustments associated with reaction time arm movements: A comparison between young and old. *Journal of Gerontology: Medical Sciences,* **43,** M105-M113.

Jonsson, P.V., & Lipsitz, L.A. (1990). Cardiovascular factors contributing to falls in the older adult. *Topics in Geriatric Rehabilitation,* **5,** 21-33.

Kandel, E.R., Schwartz, J.H., & Jessell, T.M. (1991). *Principles of neuroscience.* New York: Elsevier.

Kauffman, T. (1990). Impact of aging-related musculoskeletal and postural changes on falls. *Topics of Geriatric Rehabilitation,* **5,** 34-43.

Kokmen, E., Bossemeyer, R.W., Jr., & Williams, W.J. (1978). Quantitative evaluation of joint motion sensation in an aging population. *Journal of Gerontology,* **33,** 62-67.

Krauter, E.E., Wallace, J.E., & Campbell, B.A. (1981). Sensory-motor function in the aging rat. *Behavioral and Neural Biology,* **31,** 367-392.

Larish, D.D., Martin, P.E., & Mungiole, M. (1988). Characteristic patterns of gait in the healthy old.

In J.A. Joseph (Ed.), *Central determinants of age-related declines in motor function: Annals of the New York Academy of Sciences,* **515,** 18-31.

Laufer, A.C., & Schweitz, M.D. (1968). Neuromuscular response tests as predictors of sensory-motor performance in aging individuals. *American Journal of Physical Medicine,* **47,** 250-263.

Lee, W.A., Buchanan, T.S., & Rogers, M.W. (1987). Effects of arm acceleration and behavioral conditions on the organization of postural adjustments during arm flexion. *Experimental Brain Research,* **66,** 257-270.

Lichtenstein, M.J., Burger, M.C., Shields, L.L., & Shiavi, R.G. (1990). Comparison of biomechanics platform measures of balance and videotaped measures of gait with a clinical mobility scale in elderly women. *Journal of Gerontology: Medical Sciences,* **45,** M50.

Lichtenstein, M.J., Shields, S.L., Shiavi, R.G., & Burger, M.C. (1988). Clinical determinants of biomechanics platform measures of balance in aged women. *Journal of the American Geriatrics Society,* **36,** 996-1002.

Lipsitz, L.A., Jonsson, P.V., Kelley, M.M., & Koestner, J.S. (1991). Causes and correlates of recurrent falls in ambulatory frail elderly. *Journal of Gerontology: Medical Sciences,* **46,** M114-M122.

Lucy, S.D., & Hayes, K.C. (1985). Postural sway profiles: Normal subjects and subjects with cerebellar ataxia. *Physiotherapy Canada,* **37,** 140-148.

Lundgren-Lindquist, B., Aniansson, A., & Rundgren, A. (1983). Functional studies in 79-year-olds. III. Walking performance and climbing ability. *Scandinavian Journal of Rehabilitation Medicine,* **15,** 125-131.

MacDonald, J.B., & MacDonald, E.T. (1977). Nocturnal fracture and continuing widespread use of barbiturate hypnotics. *British Medical Journal,* **2,** 483-485.

MacRae, P.G., Lacourse, M., & Moldavon, R. (1992). Physical performance measures that predict faller status in community-dwelling older adults. *Journal of Occupational and Sports Physical Therapy,* **16,** 123-128.

MacRae, P.G., Reinsch, S., & Tobis, J. (1989). Strength, muscular endurance, balance, and reaction time as predictors of faller status in the older adult. *The Gerontologist,* **29,** 159A.

Maki, B.E., Holliday, P.J., & Topper, A.K. (1991). Fear of falling and postural performance in the elderly. *Journal of Gerontology: Medical Sciences,* **46,** M123-M131.

Manchester, D., Woollacott, M., Zederbauer-Hylton, N., & Marin, O. (1989). Visual, vestibular, and somatosensory contributions to balance control in the older adult. *Journal of Gerontology: Medical Sciences*, **44**, M118-M127.

Man'kovskii, N.B., Mints, A.Y., & Lysenyuk, V.P. (1980). Regulation of the preparatory period for complex voluntary movement in old and extreme old age. *Human Physiology*, **6**, 46-50.

McCollum, G., Horak, F.B., & Nashner, L.M. (1984). Parsimony in neural calculations for postural movements. In J. Bloedel, J. Dichgans, & W. Precht (Eds.), *Cerebellar functions* (pp. 52-65). Berlin: Springer-Verlag.

Molen, H.H. (1973). *Problems on the evaluation of gait.* Unpublished doctoral dissertation, Institute of Biomechanics and experimental Rehabilitation, Free University, Amsterdam.

Morse, J.M., Tylko, S.J., & Dixon, H.A. (1987). Characteristics of the fall-prone patient. *The Gerontologist*, **27**, 516-522.

Murray, M., Kory, P., Ross, C., & Clarkson, B.H. (1969). Walking patterns in healthy old men. *Journal of Gerontology*, **24**, 169-178.

Murray, M.P., Seireg, A.A., Sepic, S.B. (1975). Normal postural stability and steadiness: Quantitative assessment. *Journal of Bone and Joint Surgery*, **57-A**, 510-516.

Nashner, L.M. (1976). Adapting reflexes controlling the human posture. *Experimental Brain Research*, **26**, 59-72.

Nashner, L.M., & Woollacott, M. (1979). The organization of rapid postural adjustments of standing humans: An experimental-conceptual model. In R.E. Talbott & D.R. Humphrey (Eds.), *Posture and movement* (pp. 243-257). New York: Raven Press.

Nevitt, M.C., Cummings, S.R., & Hudes, E.S. (1991). Risk factors for injurious falls: A prospective study. *Journal of Gerontology: Medical Sciences*, **46**, M164-M170.

Nickens, H. (1985). Intrinsic factors in falling among the elderly. *Archives of Internal Medicine*, **145**, 1089-1093.

Overstall, P.W. (1980). Prevention of falls in the elderly. *Journal of the American Geriatrics Society*, **28**, 481-484.

Overstall, P.W., Exton-Smith, A.N., Imms, F.J., & Johnson, A.L. (1977). Falls in the elderly related to postural imbalance. *British Medical Journal*, **1**, 261-264.

Overstall, P.W., Johnson, A.L., & Exton-Smith, A.N. (1978). Instability and falls in the elderly. *Age and Ageing*, **7**, 92-96.

Perry, B.C. (1982). Falls among the elderly: A review of the methods and conclusions of epidemiologic studies. *Journal of the American Geriatrics Society*, **30**, 367-371.

Potvin, A.R., Syndulko, K., Tourellottee, W.W., Lemmon, J.A., & Potvin, J.H. (1980). Human neurologic function and the aging process. *Journal of the American Geriatrics Society*, **28**, 1-9.

Ray, W.A., & Griffin, M.R. (1990). Prescribed medications and the risk of falling. *Topics in Geriatric Rehabilitation*, **5**, 12-20.

Reinsch, S., MacRae, P., Lachenbruch, P.A., & Tobis, J.S. (1992). Attempts to prevent falls and injury: A prospective community study. *The Gerontologist*, **32**, 450-456.

Roberts, B.L., & Fitzpatrick, J.J. (1983). Improving balance: Therapy of movement. *Journal of Gerontological Nursing*, **9**, 151-156.

Rogers, M.W., Kukulka, C.G., & Soderberg, G.L. (1992). Age-related changes in postural responses preceding rapid self-paced and reaction time arm movements. *Journal of Gerontology: Medical Sciences*, **47**, M159-M165.

Rosenhall, U., & Rubin, W. (1975). Degenerative changes in the human vestibular sensory epithelia. *Acta Otolaryngologica*, **79**, 67-81.

Rubenstein, H.S., Miller, F.H., Pastel, S., & Evans, H.B. (1983). Standards of medical care based on consensus rather than evidence: The case of routine bedrail use for the elderly. *Law and Medical Health Care*, **11**, 271-276.

Sekuler, R., & Hutman, L.P. (1980). Spatial vision and aging. I: Contrast sensitivity. *Journal of Gerontology*, **35**, 692-699.

Sekuler, R., Hutman, L., & Owsley, C. (1980). Human aging and spatial vision. *Science*, **209**, 1255-1256.

Skinner, H.B., Barrack, R.L., & Cook, S.D. (1988). Age-related declines in proprioception. *Clinical Orthopaedics*, **184**, 208-211.

Sobel, K.G., & McCart, G.M. (1983). Drug use and accidental falling in an intermediate care facility. *Drug Intelligence and Clinical Pharmacy*, **17**, 539-542.

Stelmach, G.E., Phillips, J., DiFabio, R.P., & Teasdale, N. (1989). Age, functional postural reflexes, and voluntary sway. *Journal of Gerontology: Biological Sciences*, **44**, B100-B106.

Stelmach, G.E., Populin, L., & Müller, F. (1990). Postural muscle onset and voluntary movement in the elderly. *Neuroscience Letters*, **117**, 188-193.

Stelmach, G.E., & Worringham, C.J. (1985). Sensorimotor deficits related to postural stability. *Clinics in Geriatric Medicine*, **1**, 679-694.

Stelmach, G.E., Zelaznik, H.N., & Lowe, D. (1990). The influence of aging and attentional demands on recovery from postural instability. *Aging*, **2**, 155-161.

Stones, M.J., & Kozma, A. (1987). Balance and age in the sighted and blind. *Archives of Physical Medicine and Rehabilitation*, **66**, 85-89.

Svensson, M.L., Rundgren, A., Larsson, M., Odén, A., Sund, V., & Landahl, S. (1991). Accidents in the institutionalized elderly: A risk analysis. *Aging,* **3**, 181-192.

Teasdale, N., Stelmach, G.E., & Breunig, A. (1991). Postural sway characteristics of the elderly under normal and altered visual and support surface conditions. *Journal of Gerontology: Biological Sciences,* **46**, B238-B244.

Tinetti, M.E. (1986). Performance-oriented assessment of mobility problems in elderly patients. *Journal of the American Geriatrics Society,* **34**, 119-126.

Tinetti, M.E., Williams, T.F., & Mayewski, R. (1986). Fall risk index for elderly patients based on number of chronic disabilities. *American Journal of Medicine,* **80**, 429-434.

Tobis, J.S., Nayak, L., & Hochler, F.K. (1981). Visual perception of verticality and horizontality among fallers. *Archives of Physical Medicine and Rehabilitation,* **62**, 619-622.

Tobis, J.S., Reinsch, S., Swanson, J.M., Byrd, M., & Scharf, T. (1985). Visual perception dominance of fallers among community-residing older adults. *Journal of the American Geriatrics Society,* **33**, 330-333.

Vandervoort, A.A., & Hayes, K.C. (1989). Plantarflexor muscle function in young and elderly women. *European Journal of Applied Physiology,* **58**, 389-394.

Vandervoort, A., & Hill, K. (1990). Neuromuscular performance of the aged. In M.L. Howe, M.J. Stones, & C.J. Brainerd (Eds.), *Cognitive and behavioral performance factors in atypical aging* (pp. 69-101). New York: Springer-Verlag.

Vandervoort, A., Hill, K., Sandrin, M., & Vyse, V.M. (1990). Mobility impairment and falling in the elderly. *Physiotherapy Canada,* **42**, 99-107.

Walker, J.E., & Howland, J. (1991). Falls and fear of falling among elderly persons living in the community: Occupational therapy interventions. *American Journal of Occupational Therapy,* **45**, 119-122.

Wallace, J.E., Krauter, E.E., & Campbell, B.A. (1980). Motor and reflexive behavior in the aging rat. *Journal of Gerontology,* **3**, 364-370.

Wells, B.G., Middleton, B. L., Lawrence, G., Lillard, D., & Safarik, J. (1985). Factors associated with the elderly falling in intermediate care facilities. *Drug Intelligence and Clinical Pharmacy,* **19**, 142-145.

Whanger, A.D., & Wang, H.S. (1974). Clinical correlates of the vibratory sense in elderly psychiatric patients. *Journal of Gerontology,* **29**, 39-45.

Whipple, R.H., Wolfson, L.I., & Amerman, P.M. (1987). The relationship of knee and ankle weakness to falls in nursing home residents: An isokinetic study. *Journal of the American Geriatrics Society,* **35**, 13-20.

Wigley, F.M. (1984). Osteoarthritis: Practical management in older patients. *Geriatrics,* **39**, 101-120.

Wolfson, L., Whipple, R., Amerman, P., & Kleinberg, A. (1986). Stressing the postural response: A quantitative method for teaching balance. *Journal of the American Geriatrics Society,* **34**, 845-850.

Woollacott, M.H. (1990). Changes in posture and voluntary control in the elderly: Research findings and rehabilitation. *Topics in Geriatric Rehabilitation,* **5**, 1-11.

Woollacott, M.H., Inglin, B., & Manchester, D. (1988). Response preparation and posture control in the older adult. In J. Joseph (Ed.), *Central determinants of age-related declines in motor function* (pp. 42-51). New York: New York Academy of Sciences.

Woollacott, M.H., Shumway-Cook, A., & Nashner, L. (1982). Postural reflexes and aging. In J.A. Mortimer, F.H. Pirozzolo, & G.J. Maletta (Eds.), *The aging motor system* (pp. 98-119). New York: Praeger.

Woollacott, M.H., Shumway-Cook, A., & Nashner, L. (1986). Aging and posture control: Changes in sensory organization and muscular coordination. *International Journal of Aging and Human Development,* **23**, 97-114.

Wyke, B. (1979). Conference on the ageing brain. Cervical articular contributions to posture and gait: Their relation to senile dysequilibrium. *Age and Ageing,* **8**, 251-257.

CHAPTER 7

Behavioral Speed

One of the most visible landmarks of aging is the slowing of behavior, especially physical movements. Although it does so in a very individualistic manner, the speed with which individuals initiate, execute, and complete physical movements gradually and inexorably decreases with advancing years. This age-related change in physical movement speed is so profound that actors portraying older characters capitalize on this common phenomenon by exaggerating the slowness of individual movements.

Response Speed

A reduction in the speed with which older people can react and move has substantial significance for all aspects of their life. It takes longer to complete physical tasks, which means that fewer tasks can be accomplished in a day. It takes a longer time for dressing, grooming, and completing daily home management chores. Employers are less likely to be satisfied if older workers produce fewer units within a specified period of time or cannot keep up with externally paced industrial tasks. If "time is money," then older individuals may make less of it. In one very early study, for example, older dentists were observed to take longer to fill cavities (Klein, Dollar, & Bagdonas, 1947).

Slower reaction and movement speeds also modify the behaviors of older automobile drivers and contribute to an increased accident rate at home, in the yard, at work, and in other aspects of life. The pressure to respond and move quickly—to write out a check in the grocery line, to enter the freeway from the access road, to provide a credit card as quickly as possible to the salesperson—is rampant in our society. This societal pressure to hurry can be socially intimidating to older people, discouraging them from active involvement in community activities outside the home.

More important to the researcher in gerontology, however, is that some types of age-related changes in central nervous system (CNS) processes can be measured by the speed with which individuals physically respond. Slower physical response capacity also appears to affect performance on some intellectual and cognitive tasks. The importance of speed of behavior with regard to study of the brain was underscored by Birren, Woods, and Williams (1979) several years ago in the title of their article, "Speed of Behavior as an Indicator of Age Changes and the Integrity of the Nervous System."

This chapter divides behavioral speed into two components: the speed with which individuals can react to environmental stimuli and the speed with which they can move their limbs. The focus is on the reactivity and speed of limb movements that occur in psychomotor laboratory tasks and some types of functional movements, such as typing and coordinating small movements. Age-related changes in large body movements such as sports, dance, and work activities are discussed in Part V, "Physical Performance and Achievement." Health and physical fitness are thought to influence the maintenance of response speed, but because this influence is widely debated and of great importance, it is discussed separately in chapter 9.

Reaction Time

Reaction time is the time interval from the onset of a stimulus to the initiation of a volitional response. When an obstacle suddenly appears in the road and the driver must stop as quickly as possible, the time that passes from the driver's first sight of the obstacle to the lifting of the foot from the accelerator is called simple reaction time. When the situation involves only one stimulus (the obstacle) and one response (to stop), the response is called a *simple reaction time* (SRT). The fastest possible reactions occur when the driver is told that an obstacle *will* appear, but he or she does not know when. If a driver is told that an obstacle *may* appear, just the uncertainty as to whether it will increases his or her reaction time. This is called a *discrimination reaction time*. If the driver has to choose between stepping on the brake pedal or further depressing the accelerator, then the interval between the perception and the reaction is called a *choice reaction time* (CRT).

In the laboratory, reaction time is a type of psychomotor task that is frequently used to determine the effects of aging on response speed. Almost any factor that enhances or disrupts CNS function is reflected by a change in reaction time. Drugs, sleep deprivation, arousal level, disease, and maturation are factors that affect CNS function and also cause changes in reaction time. For this reason, reaction time may be thought of as a behavioral window through which scientists can study CNS function. Gerontologists have used reaction time for many years as an index of the effects of aging on the integrity of the CNS.

The reaction time stimulus may be visual, auditory, or tactile and may be simple or complex. The response, which also may be simple or complex, may be made with the musculoskeletal system or the vocal apparatus. In both SRT and CRT, the time between the stimulus onset and the first response of the muscle is assumed to represent CNS processing that is necessary to complete the task. When the response is initiated and the movement begins, other central mechanisms are responsible for controlling and monitoring the movement.

Throughout the following discussions of reaction time and aging, many references will be made to observations that reaction times are slower in older people. An important point to remember, however, is that most of the data reported are *average* or *median* reaction times from many individuals at different ages (i.e., cross-sectional sampling) rather than reflections of change within individuals over a series of years (i.e., longitudinal analysis). Very wide individual variation exists in reation time at all ages, and some people in their 50s who are almost as fast as the fastest 20-year-olds are considerably faster than many of their cohorts. Aging rates also vary, so that some individuals may lose very little behavioral speed over a long period, whereas others may slow significantly each decade or precipitously before death. Thus, when discussions mention "reaction times of 20-year-olds or 40-year-olds," bear in mind the discussion of individual differences in chapter 2: These are averages of many individuals within each age category.

Simple Reaction Time

SRT is so named because it requires a very simple behavior, usually lifting one finger from a switch or button, in response to the activation of a stimulus. SRT requires relatively low-level CNS processing: perception of the stimulus (such as seeing a light or hearing a buzzer), remembering its significance and the behavior to be associated with it, and programming and executing a movement response. SRT represents speed of response, that is, the speed with which a person can move a finger or limb when almost no calculation, integration, or decision making is required. It is thought to represent the general responsiveness of the central nervous system and has been described as "a general primary response mechanism of the CNS" (Gottsdanker, 1982, p. 342).

The slowing of SRT with aging has been observed so many times that it is considered one of the most measurable and recognizable behavioral changes that occurs with aging. The simplest auditory reaction time slows approximately 0.6 ms a year between ages 20 and 96 (Fozard, Vercruyssen, Reynolds, & Hancock, 1990). Adding one decision to be made about the stimulus, as occurs in a discrimination reaction time, increases the slowing to 1.5 ms a year. Requiring additional decisions further increases the slowing effect. Francis Galton, an English scientist who between 1884 and 1890 measured the SRTs of thousands of people of all ages, was the first to report that 60-year-olds were approximately 13% slower than

20-year-olds (Galton, 1899). Later his data were reanalyzed and confirmed using more advanced statistical techniques (Koga & Morant, 1923; Johnson et al., 1985). Since then, almost every researcher who has measured reaction time has found it to be significantly slower in older people. Age-related slowing is apparent even as soon as the late 30s and early 40s (Myerson, Hale, Hirschman, Hansen, & Christiansen, 1989). Figure 7.1 shows a replication by Wilkinson and Allison (1989) of Galton's work. Their measurement of 5,325 visitors to the Science Museum in London showed, like Galton's results, that whether one considers the average, fastest, or most consistent SRTs, they are significantly slower and somewhat more variable in older people. Note, however, that although significant age differences cannot be eliminated entirely, the magnitude of the age differences seen in most SRT studies is due partially to the fact that many investigators use a single test session in which only a few trials are provided. If experimental factors such as novelty, practice, stimulus quality, and performance expectations are held constant, age differences in simple reaction time can be minimized. If only the fastest reactions are analyzed, age differences can be reduced to almost zero (Gottsdanker, 1982).

In almost all studies of SRT and CRT, males are reported to be faster than females at all ages except among the youngest (< 15 years old) and the oldest (70+ years old) (Fozard et al., 1990). Hodgkins (1963) measured the SRTs of 930 men, women, and children ranging from age 5 to 84 years and found that males were faster than females except for the youngest group (first graders) and the two oldest groups (ages 55-84). Figure 7.2 presents similar results, except that the age range in which gender differences were significant was 20 to 70 years (Noble, Baker, & Jones, 1964). Gender differences are probably more a product of our society, however, than a difference in neurophysiological function. Yandell and Spirduso (1981) tested the SRT of college-age males and females, the ages in which gender differences were greatest, over a 5-day period. After the first day, a different motivational technique (extrinsic, intrinsic, social, or monetary reward) was used each day on all subjects to maximize their response speed. All subjects were strongly encouraged to produce a faster reaction than they had on the previous day. On the first day of testing the researchers found classic male superiority in speed. But on each successive day, the females gained until on the fifth day the

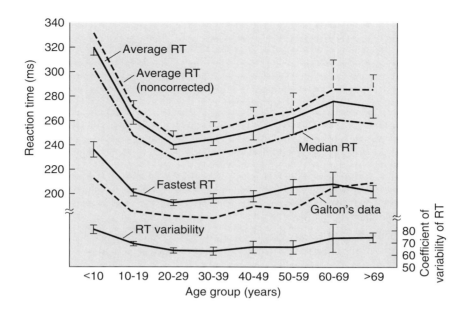

Figure 7.1   Population SRTs: average RT, median RT, fastest RT, and RT variability as a function of age. Confidence limits (95%) are shown for three of the scores. The variable breadth of these limits is a function of the number in each age group as well as the intrinsic variability of subjects within each group. The dashed curve gives average RT data derived as for the full curve for that score but without removing unduly long RTs more than twice the duration of the average for the test concerned. For comparison, Galton's data are plotted on the same scale and for approximately the same age groups.

From "Age and Simple Reaction Time: Decade Differences for 5,325 Subjects" by R.T. Wilkinson and S. Allison, 1989, *Journal of Gerontology: Psychological Sciences*, **44**, p. P31. Copyright 1989 by The Gerontological Society of America. Reprinted by permission.

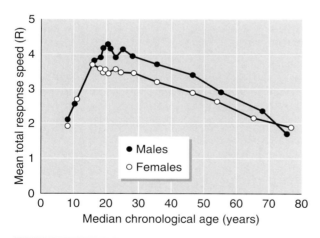

Figure 7.2   Typical gender differences in mean total response speed between the ages of 8 and 75. Each point is based on the data for 20 subjects, averaged over the entire practice period.

Reproduced with permission of authors and publisher from: Noble, C.E., Baker, B.L., and Jones, T.A. "Age and sex parameters in psychomotor learning." *Perceptual and Motor Skills*, 1964, **19**, 935-945. © *Perceptual and Motor Skills*, 1964.

significant differences between males and females disappeared. Thus, the purported male superiority in response latency, rather than reflecting gender-related differences in neurophysiological processing, probably represents the different expectations that society has for the physical performance of men and women.

Although SRT is less complicated than many other behaviors, it contains several components that enable researchers to study CNS function. For example, it has been used as a measure of basic central control mechanisms. Increases in latency of response that are associated with an increase in the complexity of the movement to be made (e.g., a smaller target or a longer distance to be moved) are taken to indicate that a more complex motor program is necessary to activate the movement. Older individuals react more slowly when greater accuracy is required (Griew, 1959). The SRTs of preferred versus nonpreferred hands are thought to reflect the extent of CNS laterality, although laterality seems to be unaffected by age (Stern, Oster, & Newport, 1980). Basic coordination of the two brain hemispheres has also been studied by comparing simple unilateral response latencies with bilateral response latencies. It takes longer to react simultaneously with both hands to a single stimulus than it does to react with only one hand, presumably because information yoking the two hands together must be integrated between the motor areas of the two sides of the brain before the two hands can be coordinated to react. With increased age, bilateral SRT increases more than unilateral SRT, purportedly because the transfer of information across the brain provides an opportunity for greater information loss and perhaps distortion due to neural noise (Stern et al., 1980).

Understanding the phenomenon of attention has also been enhanced by SRT paradigms. Even when one stimulus and one response are used, the length of the interval of time between the warning signal and the stimulus onset (preparatory interval) greatly affects the SRT. Long preparatory intervals produce the greatest age deficits (Wilkinson & Allison, 1989), perhaps because long preparatory intervals require an individual to attend to the task for a longer period of time and attention deteriorates with increased age in many older people. Some researchers have suggested that young adults can better sustain attention and make use of a longer period in which to prepare to respond.

SRT is a useful behavior to measure in aging because it is significantly related to other psychomotor tasks. For example, Laufer and Schweitz (1968) found that the SRTs of older adults were the only one of a battery of neurophysiological phenomena, such as reflex latency, nerve conduction velocity, and information transfer time, significantly correlated to the behavioral task of placing pegs in a board as quickly as possible.

Choice Reaction Time

In a CRT paradigm, more than one stimulus is presented and a specific movement must be paired with each stimulus. The subject must choose the movement that is associated with the stimulus presented. For instance, if a red light is activated the subject releases a right hand key, whereas if the green light is activated the subject releases the left hand key. CRT paradigms can become very complicated, for example, when several possible stimuli are paired with specific responses of varying degrees of complexity.

CRT has at least three components: the perceptual process of identifying the stimulus; the decision process, in which the stimulus-response code is retrieved and the response is selected; and the motor process required to initiate the response. The perceptual process and the motor process are relatively stable and represent the base level of response in an SRT paradigm. It is the middle component, the processing of the stimulus-response code and the selection of the motor response, that varies with the complexity of the choices to be made in the CRT paradigm. The choices relate to the number and type of stimuli to be selected, although the nature and difficulty of the response movement to be made also affect the response latency. Both the difficulty of the decisions to be made and the difficulty of the movement response contribute to the response complexity.

Stimulus and Decision Complexity

As early as 1959, researchers understood that the higher the nervous system function required to complete a task, the greater the age differences. Welford (1959), focusing on behavioral responses, championed the concept that CRT can be expressed by the equation

$$CRT = a + bX,$$

where a represents the relatively constant neurological base level of response speed, b represents a slope function that indicates the proportionally increasing time required to centrally process the stimulus and response decisions, and X represents the number of stimulus alternatives. Other researchers (Fozard, Thomas, & Waugh, 1976; Waugh, Fozard, Talland, & Ervin, 1973) divided total CRT into sensory-motor (a factor) components and decision (b factor) components and argued that the age effects were greater for the decision components than for the sensory-motor components; but they made no direct comparison of the magnitude of age trends in the two components.

Nevertheless, Welford (1977a) provided convincing evidence that the more complex the stimulus display and the decisions to be made, the greater the differences in reaction speed of young and old subjects. A graph of his results is shown in Figure 7.3. The age differences are significant for all tasks (A-D). Changing the stimulus display by degrading the clarity and increasing the quantity of stimuli increased the latency of response for most individuals and disproportionately increased the latencies of older persons. More recently, from

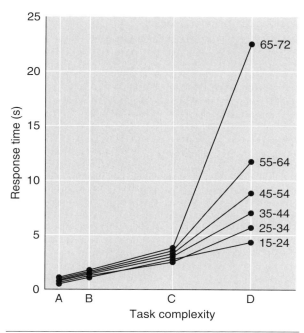

Figure 7.3 Increase in latency of response with increase in complexity of central processing. Each of the A, B, C, and D tasks is progressively more difficult in terms of the combination of spatial transposition with symbolic translation required in order to relate the signal to the response. As task difficulty increases, the difference between the age groups increases.
From "Causes of Slowing of Performance With Age" by A.T. Welford, 1977, *Interdisciplinary Topics in Gerontology,* **11**, p. 46. Copyright 1977 by S. Karger AG, Basel. Reprinted by permission.

their analysis of nine studies, Hale, Myerson, and Wagstaff (1987) confirmed Welford's supposition that as the task difficulty increases, the reaction latencies of old subjects are disproportionately slower than those of the young. In other words, advancing age has a greater impact on the central processing components than on the perceptual and motor output components of the CRT response.

As stimulus discriminations and choices to be made increase (Simon & Pouraghabagher, 1978), so do age differences. However, practice minimizes age differences caused by complexity. In fact, Jordan and Rabbitt (1977) found that in increasingly complex tasks, practice eliminated all age differences except the basic age lag in SRT.

Complicating the issue, however, is the increase with age in the variability within individuals and between subjects in both the perceptual motor and the decision-making components. Because there is a neurophysiological limit on the shortest amount of time in which a response can be made, and because theoretically there is no maximum time limit, the longer the latencies, the greater the within-subject variability. Older persons' responses are longer, and the extent to which increased variability contributes to the age differences has not been resolved. Fozard et al. (1976) argued that what appear to be systematic age-related differences in decision making may be greatly affected by the age-related increase in the variability of information-processing strategies. They pointed out, as have many researchers, that a tremendous overlap exists in behavioral speed at all ages and that chronological age is a poor basis for describing individual differences in reactivity.

Response Complexity

Besides the reactive latency delay induced by a complicated stimulus display, can the delay also be attributed to the difficulty of the response? Response complexity is another factor that contributes to the complexity of the task, delays response speed, and makes age differences more pronounced. Regardless of how simple the stimulus is, a response that is more complex in terms of its duration, timing, rhythm, number of component parts, compatibility, and accuracy requirements increases both the SRT and the CRT necessary to program and initiate the movement. Griew (1959) measured the SRT of subjects in a paradigm in which they were to touch a stylus to a target as quickly as possible when a stimulus light was illuminated. He found that the more manipulations the older subjects had to make with the stylus preceding target contact, the slower their reactions compared to the young subjects. There is ample evidence that the more complex the movement to be made, the greater the age disparity in response latency (e.g., Cerella, Poon, & Williams, 1980).

Another example of the slower responses of older individuals on movements of greater complexity is when subjects must select between movements that are customarily made (i.e., the motor components of the movement are compatible) and motor components that are not usually done together. Light and Spirduso (1990) required subjects to respond either with one index finger, the index finger and thumb in a pinching movement, both index fingers, or both pinching movements (see Figure 7.4). Pinching movements are frequently used in daily activities, but

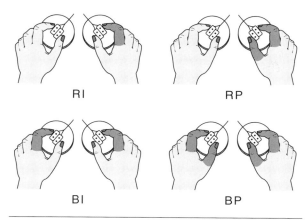

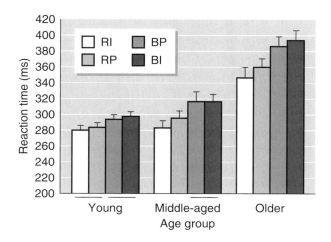

Figure 7.4 Movements used to initiate a reaction. CRT responses were made to a light stimulus by closing a RT switch with either the right index finger (RI), the right index finger and the thumb in a pinching motion (RP), both index fingers simultaneously in a bilateral response (BI), or a bilateral pinch (BP).

Figure 7.5 Age differences in initiating movements of varying complexity. Reaction time means and standard errors for young (M = 22), middle-aged (M = 43), and older (M = 63) subjects for right index (RI), right pinch (RP), bilateral pinch (BP), and bilateral index (BI) movements. Age effect and movement-type effect were both significant ($p < 0.001$). The interaction between age and movement was also highly significant ($p < 0.001$). Nonsignificant differences among the movements for each age group are depicted by connecting lines under the abscissa.

From "Effects of Adult Aging on the Movement Complexity Factor of Response Programming" by K. Light and W. Spirduso, 1990, *Journal of Gerontology: Psychological Sciences*, **45**, p. P108. Copyright 1990 by The Gerontological Society of America. Reprinted by permission.

the bilateral index response is rarely made. In each of the testing conditions, two of the four movements were paired and subjects reacted to whichever movement was signaled. Each time the stimulus was activated, the subjects had to choose one of those two movements. Throughout the testing session, every movement was paired in the stimulus display with every other movement, and the CRT for each movement was an average of the response latencies for that movement when paired with every other movement. Because the subjects had to make a binary choice of movements in every response, the major difference between the reaction latencies for different movements was attributed to the complexity of the movement. Older subjects were significantly slower than young adults on the two more complex movements, the bilateral pinch and the bilateral index response (see Figure 7.5). However, only in the oldest group (70-80 years) were the differences in the speed with which they could initiate the two bilateral movements significant. Light and Spirduso (1990) concluded that the response programming capability of older women was more sensitive to small changes in movement complexity and less consistent than that of younger women.

The data of Stern et al. (1980) provide a comparison of the effects of increasing the stimulus and decision-making complexity to increasing the complexity of the movement response (see Figure 7.6). SRT, with a simple stimulus and simple compatible response, was the fastest for all

ages. Bilateral reaction time, which required a more complex movement (the coordination of two limbs to a simple stimulus), was somewhat slower. CRT, which required a decision about which of two limbs to move, consumed more time than either of the previous two simple stimulus conditions. Reverse choice reaction time (RCRT), in which the subjects determined which stimulus was activated but had to respond with the opposite limb, was the slowest response. In this study, the reaction times were lengthened because the CRT task added increased alternatives from which to choose and the RCRT task required an incompatible stimulus-response association (right-hand response to left light) and an unusual movement, which made the reactions even longer. Age differences occurred on each of the four tasks, but it was only in the two tasks, CRT and RCRT, that required substantial decision making (i.e., took longer to process) with regard to matching the response to the stimulus display that *disproportionate* age differences occurred.

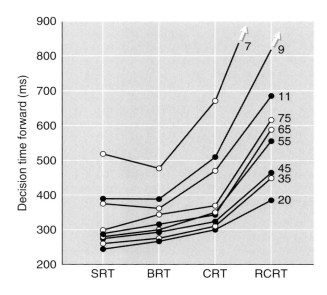

Figure 7.6 Comparison of effects of complexity of stimulus display with response complexity. Decision time forward is a function of age. Numbers next to the lines are the average age of each group. SRT = simple reaction time; BRT = bilateral reaction time; CRT = choice reaction time; RCRT = reverse choice reaction time.

From "Reaction Time Measures, Hemispheric Specialization, and Age" by J.A. Stern, P.J. Oster, and K. Newport. In *Aging in the 1980s: Psychological Issues* (p. 316) by L.W. Poon (Ed.), 1980, Washington, DC: American Psychological Association. Copyright 1980 by the American Psychological Association. Reprinted by permission.

Central and Peripheral Reaction Time Events

To understand more fully the effects of age on central versus peripheral response speed, reaction time has been broken into several components by using electroencephalographic (EEG) and electromyographical (EMG) analyses to determine when specific mechanisms of the response become active. If EEG electrodes are placed on the scalp overlying the cerebral visual cortex (for a visual stimulus) and motor cortex of the brain (for a motor potential response) and an EMG electrode is placed over the belly of the muscle to be used, the combination of records from the electrodes and the chronoscope microswitches (or computer keys) provides a more detailed analysis of the response (see Figure 7.7).

Visual evoked potentials (VEPs, from the EEG records), which indicate when the visual stimulus has reached the area of the brain that receives visual information, have provided evidence that

older individuals receive the stimulus more slowly than younger individuals. The time between the VEP and the motor potential (MP), which is taken to be a measure of central processing time (CPT) uncontaminated by peripheral nerve conduction velocity (NCV) and muscle contraction time (CT), is the major source of slowing, especially in a CRT paradigm. Also, certain features of the VEP, such as a specific slow wave called the P300, are sensitive to age-related changes in perceptual and cognitive processing but not to response-related processes (Coles, Gratton, Bashore, Eriksen, & Donchin, 1985). The P300 is known as the decision wave of the VEP, because it is highly associated with the decision that the subject has to make about the stimulus display. Premotor time (PMT), the time that lapses between the onset of the stimulus and the beginning of muscle activity, is substantially slower in older individuals. Contractile time (CT) represents the time necessary for the muscle to contract sufficiently to initiate limb movement. Used as an estimate of the time taken by muscle mechanics to generate enough force to start movement of the limb, it is considered a peripheral rather than a central processing event. Unless the movement is resisted, CT is less affected by aging than measures of central processing. The activation of the reaction key (either SRT or CRT) records the time from stimulus onset to the beginning of the reaction (RT), and because this includes CPT, PMT, and CT, SRT and CRT reveal the cumulative age-related slowing that occurs in both central and peripheral processing. Finally, the movement of the limb from the reaction key to the target key, which provides a measure of limb movement speed called movement time (MT), is also slower in older individuals. (MT is discussed in more detail later in this chapter.) When these components are added together, the result is the total response time (TRT). TRT differs from SRT and CRT in that it includes both reaction time (SRT or CRT) and movement time (MT).

Shown in Figure 7.8 (page 194), in descending order from left to right, are the relative effects of aging that were seen in two fractionated RT studies (Clarkson, 1978; Hart, 1980). Because the same equipment and paradigm were used in these two studies and the parameter values were very similar, the age factors derived from each study could be averaged. Clarkson (1978) studied males whereas Hart (1980) studied female subjects. The only parameter values of the two genders to differ were PMT, in which the males typically were

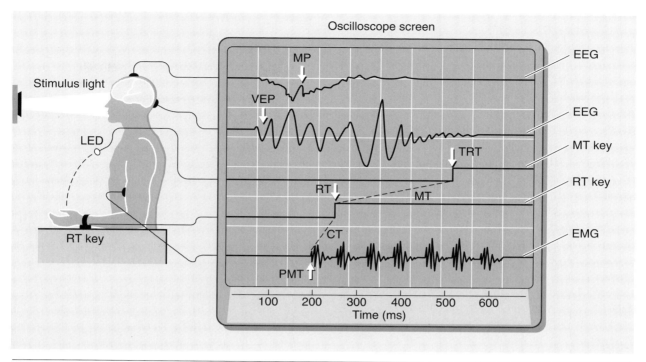

Figure 7.7 Fractionation of reaction time. As soon as the stimulus light is activated, the subject lifts the forearm to the shoulder as quickly as possible. The stimulus light initiates five traces across the oscilloscope. Lifting the forearm releases the switch attached to the subject's arm and causes an offset on the trace labeled RT key, an indication of reaction time. Passing the wrist through the beam emitted by the light-emitting diode (LED) activates the MT switch causing an offset of the total response time (TRT) trace. The *motor potential* (MP), which is the time when the activity of the motor cortex controlling the movement is coupled with the stimulus, is recorded on an electroencephalographic trace (EEG). The *visual evoked potential* (VEP) is an EEG record of activity in the cortical occipital lobe that is coupled to the stimulus. It reflects the receipt of the visual stimulus in the brain. The beginning of electrical activity in the muscle (before the arm moves) signals the arrival of the movement command to the muscle. The time between the stimulus and this arrival is called the *premotor time* (PMT). From these observed values, it is possible to calculate the other variables:

IP = MP − VEP (information-processing time)
NCV = PMT − MP (nerve conduction velocity)
CT = RT − PMT (time required to contract the muscle sufficiently to move the wrist off the RT key)
MT = TRT − RT (movement speed independent of reaction)

faster, and MT, which should not be compared across studies unless the movement distance is carefully equated. The age factor, however, was very similar across the two studies. The greatest aging effects were on the component considered the purest measure of central processing, the PMT, whereas the smallest effects were on the most peripheral component, the CT.

Age differences are generally greater when processing times are longer. If the reaction occurs in a CRT paradigm in which the central processing time is long, age differences are greater than if the central processing time is short. Even when the processing time required is short, as in SRT, if the movement to be initiated is made more difficult, such as requiring a response of the entire body mass or applying a resistance to the movement,

the CT component of the reaction becomes much longer and age differences are more pronounced. In an SRT experiment in which younger and older subjects flexed or extended their forearms as quickly as possible after a stimulus, Rich (1987) found that the age differences in RT were relatively small, but when she attached a magnet on the table apparatus to a wrist cuff and provided resistance equal to 15% of a subject's maximum strength to the flexion, substantial age differences appeared. It took the older subjects longer to generate enough muscle tension to make the movement against resistance. Age-related slowing in this case was primarily due to the peripheral component of CT and not to central processing mechanisms required for this particular SRT paradigm. The significantly longer CTs of the older subjects were

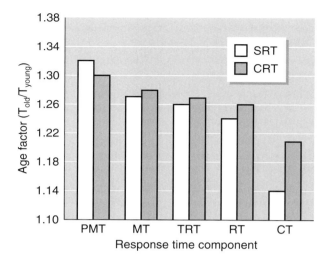

Figure 7.8 Aging factors derived from data from Clarkson (1978) and Hart (1980). In this task, the subject chose between two stimulus lights and kicked the appropriate stimulus-matched target by rapidly extending the lower limb. The absolute MT in this task depends substantially on the distance the leg must be moved, but the movement distance in these studies was the same for all age groups. T = time; PMT = premotor time; MT = movement time; TRT = total response time; RT = reaction time; CT = contractile time.

enough to create a significant TRT effect under the resisted conditions in SRT. Clarkson (1978), on the other hand, found significantly longer CTs in older people even when the movement was not resisted. One explanation for the difference in these two results may be that Clarkson analyzed lower-leg muscle extension, whereas Rich analyzed forearm flexion and extension. Lower-limb strength may deteriorate faster than upper-body strength (Larsson & Karlsson, 1978). Also, common observations tell us that flexion of the forearm is a much more frequent occurrence in the daily living activities of the elderly than rapid, forward leg kicking at a target.

Any condition that lengthens either PMT or CT also amplifies age differences. Increases in stimulus complexity lengthen PMT because more neural networks must be enlisted to process the stimulus and some of the neural connections of the networks may be faulty. Increases in the length of time required for motor unit fibers to contract and in the number of motor units needed to make the movement also slow the total response. However, although both a lengthened processing time and a lengthened CT amplify age differences, because they increase the total amount of reaction time, the age

effects on central processing time account for more of the age-related slowing than does CT, because processing time generally constitutes more of the TRT than does CT.

Vocal Reaction Time—An Exception?

One possible exception to age-related slowing of reaction time is vocal reaction time. In some studies, when researchers asked subjects to respond as quickly as possible by saying "yes" or "no," or "right" or "left," older subjects were not substantially slower than younger subjects. In other words, when decisions regarding nonverbal stimuli were mapped onto the vocal apparatus, older subjects were no slower than younger ones (Nebes, 1978; Salthouse & Somberg, 1982b). Several investigators have suggested that the CNS structure, function, and mechanisms that control skeletal muscle may age at a different rate than those controlling the vocal apparatus, but many factors dispute this hypothesis. First, the vocal apparatus is activated much more frequently than are the movements used in a reaction time task. Most individuals talk and respond to others many hours of each day. In fact, it is not uncommon for people to react very quickly with a vocal response to prevent an event from happening, such as when a grandmother shouts "No!" to a child who is about to touch a hot stove. Second, it is much more problematic to measure the onset of a vocal utterance than to measure a hand or finger response, consequently many methodological questions have been raised about vocal reaction time research. Third, it is difficult to match the compatibility of a stimulus and response in two different modalities. Whether a finger response to a visual stimulus is equitable to a vocal response to a sound stimulus is questionable. It is, therefore, very difficult to tell if the absence of age difference in vocal reaction time paradigms is a real phenomenon or an artifact of measurement.

Baron and Journey (1989) attempted to control for compatibility and differences in measurement by comparing the slopes of vocal RT over increasing alternatives in a CRT paradigm. They found age differences in vocal responses, but the age differences did not increase with increasing alternatives (i.e., complexity). Usually older adults are disproportionately slower with increasingly complex stimulus or response demands, but in this study, the slopes of vocal RT of the old subjects were the same as those of the young despite increasing alternatives. The implication of similar slopes across increasingly complicated decision making is that when responses are made vocally, information processing, that is, the central component thought to be a major source of slowing (compared to perception and CT), was no slower in older than in younger subjects.

Osborne (1987) found that when task complexity in the two response modes was more equal, and when ample practice was provided in the manual mode, old and young men did not differ in vocal reaction time. Of the two levels of complexity provided in both the vocal and manual response modes, the older subjects were disproportionately slower only when reacting with the complex manual response. There are many well-controlled studies in which investigators failed to find an age difference in vocal reaction time, yet other investigators *have* reported age differences in vocal responses. Salthouse (1985) reviewed 18 research reports in which vocal reaction time was used as a response. Of these, 6 found no age deficits in vocal reaction time, whereas 12 found vocal differences. These age differences were reported in studies where vocal reaction time signaled perceptual judgments, memory scanning, or higher order cognitive functions, and the reaction times were long. The investigators who reported that vocal reactions appeared to be resistant to age effects utilized experimental procedures that produced reactions of less than 400 ms (Nebes, 1978; Osborne, 1987; Salthouse & Somberg, 1982b).

The general slowing hypothesis (Birren, 1965) provides no apparent basis on which to propose that the diffuse age-related neurochemical and structural changes in the brain might be spared in the vocal motor system. The nature of the observed physiological changes argues against the notion of a vocal system that is spared from aging. Age-related biochemical changes in the brain tend to keep it in a lower state of subliminal excitation. From EEG studies, it is apparent that evoked sensory potentials shift in the direction of slower wave forms, long latencies, and lower amplitudes. Thus many of these age-related changes appear to be global in nature, rather than system specific. Nevertheless, the issue should be studied further. Vocal responses may be the most highly practiced motor responses that individuals ever make, and the motor control system of vocal responses is most certainly functionally different from that of the skeletal muscle system (Inhoff & Bisiacchi, 1990). The possibility that the vocal motor system is less affected by age will probably continue to intrigue investigators.

Theories of Response Slowing

Age-related behavioral slowing has been observed so long and so consistently that many theories have been developed to explain the phenomenon. They can be categorized into three broad groups that explain behavioral slowing as some type of information-processing model, an aging attributes model, or a biological degradation model. Salthouse (1985), using computer terminology, has suggested that information-processing models explain aging effects as "bugs" in the software of the system, that is, impairments within the programs that are constructed and used to interact with the environment. Aging attributes models ascribe age-related slowing to changes in other behaviors and characteristics of aging individuals. The biological degradation model, which suggests that physical deterioration of the CNS accounts for behavioral slowing, locates impairments in the hardware of the computer.

Information-Processing Models

Mechanisms that explain the mental processes that intervene between the onset of a signal and the rapid initiation of a single or coordinated movement are called information-processing models (Schmidt, 1988). Such models describe the initiation and execution of movements as being controlled by sequential or parallel stages of mental function, such as stimulus perception, encoding, storage retrieval, attention, decision making, motor programming, and initiation and execution of movement. When using reaction time as a psychomotor behavior to study information processing, researchers vary the amount of verbal manipulation required (Hale et al., 1987), the nature and types of decision making required, and the relative proportion of decision making and motor programming to sensorimotor function that occurs.

An example of reactive slowing explained by an information-processing model is seen in the data from Salthouse and Somberg (1982a), shown in Figure 7.9. These researchers assumed that the information processing necessary to initiate the response included stimulus encoding, comparison, and the selection of the response. The task was designed so that if these stages existed and if people of different ages processed information differently, age differences would be seen on some aspects of the task but not on others. The visual stimuli were presented throughout the reaction-time trials in two ways, either intact (easily seen

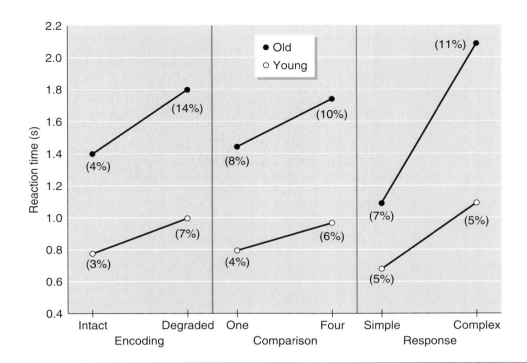

Figure 7.9 Example of a study in which age is proposed to interact with different stages of information processing: encoding, comparison, and response programming. The numbers in the parentheses represent the percentage of incorrect responses in the condition. *Encoding* is the process of perceiving stimulus characteristics, *comparison* is a theoretical processing stage in which several stimuli are compared, and *response* (i.e., selection) is a theoretical stage in which the correct movement response is selected.

From "Isolating the Age Deficit in Speeded Performance" by T.A. Salthouse and B.L. Somberg, 1982, *Journal of Gerontology*, **37**, p. 61. Copyright 1982 by The Gerontological Society of America. Reprinted by permission.

and discernible) or degraded (difficult to discern). Better performance on the trials with intact rather than degraded stimuli would substantiate the premise that stimulus encoding must take place in order to complete the task. Better performance by the young than the old subjects on the trials with degraded stimuli would indicate that age has a negative effect on the information-processing stage of stimulus encoding. The task also required one or four comparisons of stimuli and either a simple or a complex response. Although it appears in Figure 7.9 that aging affects the response selection stage more than the other two stages, this difference was not supported statistically. Older subjects were significantly slower than the younger subjects under all task conditions; therefore this study did not validate use of the information-processing model to explain aging effects. Rather, aging seemed to have a global slowing effect on all stages studied.

Perhaps because the effect of aging *is* global, age effects have been reported in most of the postulated information-processing stages: memory visual search (Fisk, Rogers, & Giambra, 1990),

selective attention, especially in complex tasks (McDowd & Birren, 1990), sensory memory (Craik, 1977), and visual iconic sensory memory (Walsh, 1976; Walsh & Thompson, 1978). Salthouse (1985) reviewed several studies in which age differences were reported in comparison operations, response selection, and central decision making. A diagram of a hypothetical information-processing model appears in Figure 7.10. This model is not intended to imply that information processing is a serial process, for ample evidence exists that many processes occur in parallel. Rather, it portrays the concept of *stages* of central motor control and the slowing of any response that is processed through several stages rather than a few. Overall, at least one study can be found to support an age effect for every stage of processing.

An example of the hypothesis that aging degrades some stages of processing but not others is the proposal that aging differentially affects the capacity of working memory; that is, as people age, they have a smaller working memory space within which to conduct information-processing functions. The inability to process information and

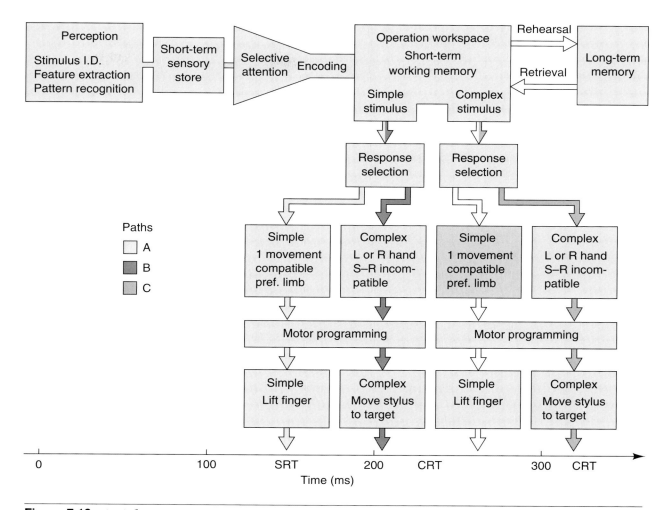

Figure 7.10 An information-processing model. In this hypothetical model, the stimulus enters the system and progresses through stages, either serially or in parallel. Each step through the stages is assumed to take a finite amount of time, so that a task with complex stimulus processing followed by a complex response requires more steps to process and hence a longer processing time. Task requirements such as an SRT that require almost no memory, comparisons, or transformations and require only simple response programming can follow Path A and be completed in less time than tasks that must be processed via Paths B or C.

quickly complete mental operations such as coding, retrieval, comparing, and selecting means that the information necessary to conduct these operations in the short-term memory "workspace" begins to decay before the operations can be completed. This in turn may affect more complex intellectual functions, because transferring information necessary to complete the task between the smaller working space and a larger capacity secondary storage system is time consuming (Salthouse, 1985). If adults lose working memory capacity with aging it would explain, at least in part, the age-related slowing in response time that is seen in the elderly. This hypothesis has not been supported by research, however; Craik (1977)

concluded that working memory is unaffected by increased age. Furthermore, although the evidence that age difference in CRTs of older persons increases with increasing task complexity is supportive of the concept of a smaller working memory space, the observation that age differences also exist in SRT is not compatible with the hypothesis.

More accepted today is the *information loss model*, which was elegantly explained and supported by Myerson and his colleagues (Myerson, Hale, Wagstaff, Poon, & Smith, 1990). According to this model, both young and older adults process stimuli and formulate responses in discrete steps, with each step taking a finite amount of time. The duration of each step is inversely related to the amount of information available. That is, if a substantial amount of information is available, the step takes little time; if not much information is available, the step takes longer. Aging increases the amount of information lost in each step. Therefore, aging has the effect of increasing the amount of time that each step takes, so that although older adults go through the same number of steps in similar ways, because each step takes longer, older people need more time to execute the entire task. According to this hypothesis, the magnitude of age-related slowing is not dependent on the type of task or the specific stage of processing, but on the length of time required to complete the task.

Myerson et al. (1990) showed that any factor, such as task complexity or practice, can be explained by this model. Task complexity increases the number of steps necessary to process a task, thus making the processing duration longer for young adults but even longer for older adults. Conversely, practice has the effect of shortening the amount of processing time required (by decreasing the number of steps), but both young and old adults perform the task in a shorter amount of time. The older adults; however, because they take longer for each step, continue to be proportionately slower at the task than the young adults. At present, the arguments for the information loss model are compelling; however, one challenge to the model has been offered.

Stelmach and his colleagues (Stelmach, Goggin, & Amrhein, 1988; Stelmach, Goggin, & Garcia-Colera, 1986) found age differences in a specific stage of motor programming that was shorter than other stages in which age differences did not exist. They found, as has everyone else, that the elderly take more time than young people to specify movement dimensions, such as the selection of the limb, the direction, and the extent to which the limb should be moved. But more importantly, they found that the elderly took differentially longer to specify (i.e., program) the *extent* of the movement than to specify which limb to move or the direction in which to move it. This occurred even though specifying the extent of the movement took both young and old less time than did specifying the movement dimensions (direction, side of body). This finding contradicts the information loss model and will no doubt receive more attention in future research.

Age-Related Differential Processing. Another premise of the information-processing model explaining the slower responses of older people is that changes occur in the way information is processed rather than in specific stages of processing.

Four ways that processing might change include the extent to which concurrent processing can occur, the accessibility of procedural operations, the preparation that individuals make to produce a behavior, and the extent to which they use stimulus information.

Concurrent Processing. One possible change in information processing is the extent to which information is concurrently, or parallel, processed. Because of low motivation or distractions, older persons may allocate only part of their CNS resources to a task and may process serially what could, with increased effort, be processed concurrently. Proponents of this explanation suggest that older persons are frequently underaroused or undermotivated. Scientists who tested this hypothesis, including those who used instructional or monetary incentives, concluded that the evidence is so mixed that it is inconclusive. (For a review, see Marsh & Watson, 1980; Strayer, Wickens, & Braune, 1987).

Inaccessibility of Procedural Operations. A second possibility is that some procedural operations (programs) may become less available with increased age, particularly if they are unused for long periods. If some operations are in a low state of availability, it would take more time to perform a task that depends on those operations. If this hypothesis is true, practice should reduce or eliminate age differences, because it would make these operations more accessible. The results of only two studies support this hypothesis (Murrell, 1970; Rabbitt & Birren, 1967).

Poor Preparation. A third process-change explanation for the slower responses of the elderly is poor preparation. Years ago Talland (1965) asked an important question and then provided an interesting proposition. He wondered why many famous but very old musicians were able to maintain their skills and abilities, revealing incredible motor coordination and speed, when almost all athletes have to retire from their sport in their early 40s. Aside from the obvious differences—muscular power, energy expenditure, and muscle groups required—that exist between piano and violin playing and swinging a baseball bat or dribbling a basketball, Talland suggested,

> More relevant seems to be the fact that music follows a detailed program; each bar, each note can be anticipated, and if all goes well the event confirms the expectancy. In tennis, the goal is to confound the

opponent's prediction, to face him suddenly with the unexpected. As we grow older, we may indeed need more time to respond to the unforeseen with finger or wrist, arm or leg, but it is the response to the isolated event, coping with uncertainty, rather than acting unprepared that becomes harder with age. (p. 527)

In the laboratory, older individuals appear not to develop optimal readiness for a specific signal. To determine whether older people have a decreased ability to maintain a highly prepared state, researchers manipulate the duration or regularity of the preparatory interval preceding the stimulus in a reaction time paradigm or record psychophysiological measures of arousal or attention during their subjects' preparation for the stimulus.

Laboratory test results have supported this observation. When investigators provided a condition of uncertainty in testing situations, the difference between young and old subjects increased. Some have suggested that the uncertainty that exists in a choice reaction time paradigm contributes to the greater age difference seen in CRTs than in SRTs. Plude, Hoyer, and Lazar (1982) reported that uncertainty contributed more to differential age-related slowing of responses than did the complexity of the movement to be made. Their older subjects who were tested for 2 days under a predictable target set condition were not significantly slower, after practice, than the young subjects in initiating either a simple or a complex movement. But the age differences in movement complexity were significant when the target sets were unpredictable, and additional practice did not eliminate these age differences. However, in a paradigm where the complexity issue affected the decision and not the response, the results were different. When subjects were allowed to predict the location of the stimulus and their latencies to the stimulus were analyzed according to whether their prediction was correct or not, both young and old subjects were faster on the trials that they correctly predicted. However, old subjects did not gain proportionately more speed on those trials that they correctly predicted (Waugh & Vyas, 1980). Salthouse (1985), after an extensive review of studies in which preparation was experimentally manipulated, concluded that "the data presently available provide little evidence that age differences in expectancy or preparation contribute to the slower performance of older adults in most behavioral activities" (p. 412).

Inefficient Use of Stimulus Information. A fourth way in which information processing might change is that older individuals may use stimulus information inefficiently. It has been suggested that older persons cannot ignore irrelevant foresignals in a reaction time paradigm (Botwinick, 1970; Rabbitt, 1965). Older subjects who were unable to ignore irrelevant information became distracted by presignals and attended to redundant signal sources. On the basis of this information, Gottsdanker (1980) generalized that at least some older adults cannot use advance information to help them prepare for a response. Salthouse (1985) insisted that this hypothesis had not been directly tested, either by Rabbitt or anyone else, and that no one had shown that age differences are eliminated under conditions that maximize ease of information use.

Aging Attributes Models

An alternative category of explanations to information-processing models for age-related slowness in response speed might be termed the aging attributes model. This category includes explanations that rely not on proposed CNS deterioration and processing, but on an evolution of the tendencies, preferences, and characteristics of older individuals. The first of these explanations is that as individuals age, they develop a decreased tolerance for making errors, which causes them to trade speed for accuracy. Another explanation is that older individuals, being more inactive than young, simply do not activate some of their capacities as frequently, and so these capacities suffer from disuse. A third explanation is that older people may not use the same strategies to solve problems and control movements that young individuals use.

The Speed-Accuracy Trade-Off Hypothesis. Because advanced age is often blamed for errors, older adults may view making errors as an indication of aging. In an effort not to be seen as old or incompetent, they try very hard to be accurate. In order to be accurate, they perform a task more slowly. Thus, the explanation for the slower responses of older people in motor performance testing is that, rather than a progressive biological deterioration in CNS processing, the old are just operating at a different point on the speed-accuracy trade-off continuum than the young. Thus, the purported difference in their information-processing capacity is more accurately attributed to a difference in the speed-accuracy setpoint (Figure 7.11). There is ample evidence supporting the speed-accuracy trade-off model. In fact, Rabbitt's (1980) work suggests that it is essential to know the speed-accuracy trade-off factor of subjects and provide a generous amount of practice before CRT can be fully understood.

Several sources of evidence suggest that the speed-accuracy phenomenon, although confirmed many times, is inadequate to explain completely the age differences in response slowing. First, if it were true, then all of the studies in which the speed and accuracy of young and old individuals are observed together would result in old individuals being slower but also more accurate. Plude, Cerella, and Raskind (1984) found otherwise. They assembled data from 201 information-processing conditions and found that the slower latencies of the old were not always accompanied by higher accuracy. Second, in at least two very well-controlled studies, age differences, although attenuated, continued to be present when the speed-accuracy trade-off was equated in two age groups (Salthouse & Somberg, 1982c; Strayer et al., 1987). Third, in investigations of response speed in which animals were used as subjects, old animals were significantly slower than young animals. It is unlikely that animals are concerned about accuracy in experiments that were analogous to those in which human subjects were tested (Birren, Wood, & Williams, 1980; MacRae, Spirduso, & Wilcox, 1988).

Disuse Hypothesis. Slower responses of the aged could be due to decreased use of the systems used to make the response. As people age, many tend to withdraw from mental and social interactions, and disuse of any ability (at all ages) generally leads to less efficient use of that ability. This hypothesis suggests that age-related slowing of response speed is due more to the inequitable use of psychomotor function between the old and young than to deterioration of information processing or to neurophysiological decrements. If this hypothesis is true, sufficient practice should compensate for the age deficits seen in initial response speeds.

Little doubt remains that older persons improve and maintain their performance on motor tasks with frequent use, as do younger persons. Clark, Lanphear, and Riddick (1987), for example, found that playing video games improved the psychomotor performance of older subjects. Both age groups also performed better when information was available that enabled them to predict what movements were necessary to complete the task at hand, and practice improved their ability to predict what to do. Practice provides older people with an opportunity to acquire optimal strategies, and the frequent performance of a task should enhance the optimum state of availability for all operations relevant to completing the task. Extreme practice also should make tasks "automatic" so that aging, a factor that limits processing, would have less impact. Practice also reduces novelty, a factor well known to have a more negative impact on the performance of older rather than younger subjects. Whether older individuals' performances are enhanced more by practice than those of younger individuals, however, is not a simple question to answer.

The question is really twofold. Does practice improve the response speed of older persons more than that of younger, and can practice completely eliminate age differences? With regard to the latter question, Murrell (1970) analyzed 20,000 reaction time trials of three secretaries, two 17- to 18-year-olds and one 57-year-old. Although it took the 57-year-old secretary 300 trials of practice, she eventually eliminated the differences between her reaction time and those of the two younger females. Salthouse (1984) also found that skilled 60-year-old typists' interkey interval speeds were not significantly different from those of 20-year-old typists, whereas these

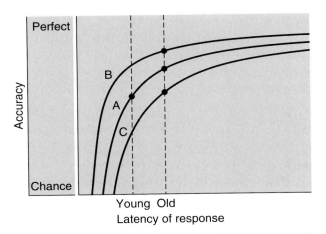

Figure 7.11 Speed-accuracy trade-off. Latency alone is inadequate to explain age differences. The greater latency of the old may occur because the older subjects have a lower capacity (Curve C), or because, though they have the same capacity as the young (Curve A) or better (Curve B), they require more accuracy.
From "Aging and Information-Processing Rate" by J. Cerella. In *Handbook of the Psychology of Aging* (3rd ed.) (p. 213) by J.E. Birren and K.W. Schaie (Eds.), 1990, New York: Academic Press. Copyright 1990 by Academic Press, Inc. Reprinted by permission.

same older typists were significantly slower at standard laboratory psychomotor tests (CRT, stationary tapping, and the Digit-Symbol Substitution test). He proposed that the older typists maintained their typing speed not by actually retaining processing speed, but by a compensatory strategy in which they used their experience to anticipate forthcoming word combinations more efficiently (Salthouse, 1984).

Indeed, most investigators have found that age differences in psychomotor speed cannot be completely eliminated with practice. Hertzog, Williams, and Walsh (1976) reported that age differences remained stable throughout practice over a 5-day period. Salthouse (1985) reviewed six studies, all of which failed to find that extensive practice eliminated significant age differences. In fact, Salthouse indicated that age differences could not be eliminated through at least 50 hours of experience with the task. So little systematic research has been conducted on age differences in truly highly skilled, highly practiced tasks that it is difficult to know by how much an age deficit can be reduced through practice. Clearly, laboratory tests of psychomotor performance provide inadequate levels of practice to answer this question. Rarely are investigators, who assess response speed on a 1-day basis, really measuring baseline capacities of older people.

Cerella (1990) presented the results of a comprehensive review of age-related practice effects on information-processing latencies. He analyzed 10 different studies in which at least four levels of practice were provided. The latency differences, which he plotted, of the young and old before and after practice are shown in Figure 7.12. If practice (i.e., a reduction of disuse) could eliminate age differences, then the final difference scores on the ordinate would all be zero, distributed across the abscissa depending on where the initial scores fell. A range of initial deficits would be expected, but the final deficits should all be near zero. If, however, the age deficits after extensive practice were the same as they were before practice, the points that represent the relationship between the initial and final difference scores would be distributed across the diagonal line. This configuration would indicate that practice did not reduce the age deficits and, thus, would support a biological decrement or strategy change hypothesis. In Cerella's chart, the data fell between these two extremes; although practice seemed to reduce the age differences about 11%, 89% of the initial age deficit was irreversible. Therefore, although

disuse impairs performance somewhat, it is not the best explanation of age-related differences in response speed.

Strategy Shift Hypothesis. Another explanation for increased latencies is that older people do not solve a problem in the same way that younger people do. In other words, their latencies are slower not because their hardware (CNS integrity) or their software (information-processing systems and programs) is defective, but because they choose to use different software to solve the problem. No good explanation has been suggested regarding why individuals shift information processing strategies with age. Because age differences increase as task complexity increases, it has been proposed that increased complexity provides greater opportunity to use different strategies. The fact that age differences are smaller in SRT than in CRT is given as an example. But again, increased practice should provide older subjects ample time to learn optimum strategies, thus decreasing or eliminating age differences, and it has

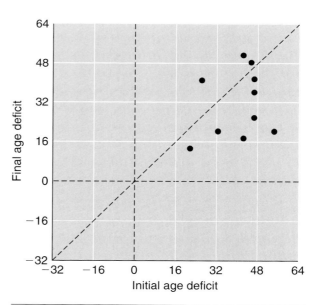

Figure 7.12 Age deficit after practice. A survey of 10 studies that tracked the performance of young and old subject groups over multiple sessions shows that the final age deficit matched the initial age deficit fairly closely; if the age differences had been eliminated by practice, all points would fall on the horizontal axis.

From "Aging and Information-Processing Rate" by J. Cerella. In *Handbook of the Psychology of Aging* (3rd ed.) (p. 214) by J.E. Birren and K.W. Schaie (Eds.), 1990, New York: Academic Press. Copyright 1990 by Academic Press, Inc. Reprinted by permission.

already been shown that practice does *not* completely eliminate age differences in overall speed. Also, that the rank order of task difficulty for many different tasks is the same for old as for young people (Salthouse, 1985) does not support this hypothesis.

Biological Degradation Models— Hardware Differences

The third category of theories relating to age-related differences in speed of response explains response slowing in terms of biological changes that occur with aging. Many age-related CNS changes, such as declines in neurotransmitters, enzymes, and neural receptors; the loss of neural cells, dendrites, and synaptic contacts; a deterioration of the myelin covering of nerve axons; and an accumulation of lipofuscin have been confirmed. Based on these observed structural and functional changes in both the central and peripheral nervous system, several explanations have been developed that could be called biological degradation models. The earliest theory was the neural noise theory, followed by the general slowing hypothesis, which was extended into a neural network hypothesis. Each model built on the ideas of its predecessor; consequently, the models share some basic concepts.

Neural Noise Theory. The forerunner of biological explanations of response speed slowing was the neural noise hypothesis, coined by Crossman and Szafran (1956) and later adopted by Welford (1977b). According to this theory, the biological deterioration that occurs in the nervous system creates noise in the system. Noise increases due to changes in magnitude or control of inhibitory processes or the persistence of previously activated neural networks. A diffuse loss of neurons or the inability to activate neurons relevant to the task accounts for a reduction in stimulus signal strength. The weakened stimulus signal, therefore, has to be discriminated from a greater background of noise. The reduction in signal-to-noise ratio means that the older individual requires more samples of the stimulus and takes additional time to integrate these samples before coming to a decision (Crossman & Szafran, 1956; Welford, 1958, 1959, 1965, 1977b, 1981).

General Slowing Hypothesis. Birren (1965) extended the concept of biological deterioration resulting in neural noise to the more general conclusion that this deterioration caused most, if not

all, fundamental neural events to become slower with increasing age. The same neurological processes are carried out in old and young persons but at a slower rate in the old. This concept was imaginatively described by Salthouse (1985) as a kind of electrical brown-out of the nervous system. By viewing the structure and function of the nervous system in computer terms, he described this hypothesis as a cycle-time hypothesis. That is, aging produces a difference in the hardware that makes cycle time per operation slower than it is in the younger system. If the same operations are performed in the same sequence, the system with a faster cycle time (i.e., the younger subject) will provide a faster response. According to this hypothesis, differences progressively increase as the complexity of CNS function required to complete the task increases. One way to examine this hypothesis is to express the response speed of older persons on tasks of varying complexity as a function of the response speed of younger subjects. In Figure 7.13, Salthouse and Somberg (1982) has done just that: This graph shows that age differences increase in magnitude as the task increases in complexity and requires more central processing time.

Cerella et al. (1980) tested this hypothesis by analyzing numerous studies and found that as the difficulty of a task increases (measured by the length of time it takes to do the task), the detrimental effect of aging increases, regardless of the nature of the task. Because the type of task contributed almost nothing to the prediction of age effects, they concluded that their analysis supported a general slowing factor hypothesis.

The hypothesis of general slowing is also compatible with the work of Surwillo (1964), who found a high relationship between reaction time and the alpha wave of the electroencephalogram. He suggested that the alpha rhythm of the electroencephalogram serves as a central timing mechanism for neural operations and that internal processing operations are performed at specific periods in a timing cycle. Older individuals have slower alpha rhythm cycles; consequently, their slower cycles result in slower timing, and slower timing results in slower processing and responses.

How does the neural noise hypothesis compare to the general slowing hypothesis? In the context of a generalized slowing concept, neural noise can be viewed as one of several results of the slowing of the entire CNS. Inhibitory networks, normally called on to inhibit neuronal activity not appropriate for the task, are slow to respond. Also, because the stimulus sampling time for older persons

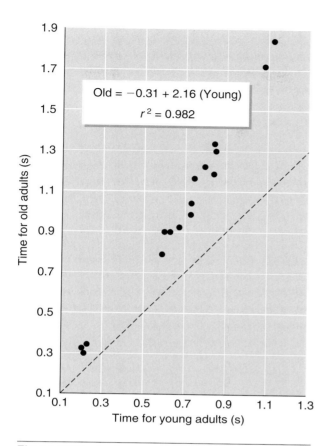

Old = −0.31 + 2.16 (Young)
$r^2 = 0.982$

Figure 7.13 Performance time of old adults as a function of performance time of young adults on different versions of a digit-symbol substitution task. Each point represents the time of young and old adults in a given experimental condition.
From "Isolating the Age Deficit in Speeded Performance" by T.A. Salthouse and B.L. Somberg, 1982, *Journal of Gerontology*, **37**, p. 62. Copyright 1982 by The Gerontological Society of America. Reprinted by permission.

is slower, the combination of increased noise and slow sampling times would require many more samples before the older subject could detect a stimulus.

Aging in a Neural Network. In a more recent refinement of the biological decay model, the brain is viewed as a neural network composed of links and nodes. Forming the response to a stimulus begins with the propagation of a signal from the input end to the output end of the network. Each step through the network takes a fixed amount of time, but with aging, links in the network are broken at random with a constant probability over time. Because, as shown in Figure 7.14, a neural signal must detour broken links in its path, whenever the neural signal encounters a break, the path length is increased by one step,

which adds time to the final latency. The breakages in links accumulate over time, create more detours, and increase the latency exponentially over a lifetime. Thus, the longer a task takes to be processed, the greater the age differences that occur, because more breakages would be encountered during longer processing in the neural network. This accounts for the greater age differences that accompany greater task complexity.

The exponential increase in latency with age that was shown previously in Figure 7.11 (page 200) suggests that the aging process is cumulative and that the exponential increase in latency may reflect an exponential decline in neuronal connectivity (Greene, 1983). It could be argued that these breakages in links are a source of the neural noise that Crossman and Szafran (1956) envisioned.

Based on an extensive analysis of several studies, Cerella (1990) has pointed out that age effects on response speed in these studies vary with the *amount* but not the *kind* of information. His results led him to conclude that "the singular regularity of the age outcome [in all the studies he analyzed] is independent of every aspect of task content except for task duration" (Cerella, 1990, p. 207). Furthermore, the increase in response latency with aging can best be described by a curvilinear, not a linear, function. Thus he proposed three plausible curvilinear models, based on the concept of neural network theory, that build on the original idea of a generalized, linear slowing that accompanies increasing age. Although more research must be completed before the accuracy of these models can be determined, any one of them could explain the disproportionate slowing of older persons with increased task duration. The three models Cerella proposed are the organizational overhead model, the information loss model, and the multilayered slowing model.

In the *organizational overhead model*, each microprocess has a unit duration, and age adds an "overhead" penalty (a kind of attenuation of the microprocess) to the duration of each unit step in the network processing. The overhead penalty grows with each additional step. Thus, simple tasks that require only elementary processing with few steps are relatively unimpaired; but when many steps must be organized into sequences, the longer the sequence, the more time a given step takes. In the *information loss model*, Myerson (1987) argued that because latencies of young subjects increased with greater task duration (i.e.,

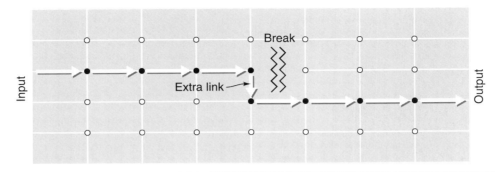

Figure 7.14   Schematic neural network; nodes represent neurons and horizontal and vertical white lines represent axon connections between neurons. The illustrated network performs no computation, merely transmits signals from left to right.
From "Aging and Information-Processing Rate" by J. Cerella. In *Handbook of the Psychology of Aging* (3rd ed.) (p. 203) by J.E. Birren and K.W. Schaie (Eds.), 1990, New York: Academic Press. Copyright 1990 by Academic Press, Inc. Reprinted by permission.

complexity), the microprocess duration of the young also increases with the step. This also occurs in old subjects, but they also lose a constant fraction of information, which he termed the *slowing factor*, at each step of a computation. Thus, the more steps that must be taken to process a task, the more information is lost and the greater the age difference.

The *multilayered slowing model* was proposed by Cerella (1987) to account for the fact that a two-factor model described some data sets better than a single linear function (Cerella, 1985; Hale et al., 1987). In earlier work, Cerella et al. (1980) observed that the sensorimotor component of a task slowed only slightly by a factor of 1.14, but the mental component slowed by a factor of 1.6 or 1.7. Cerella's multilayered model latency is comprised of two processing stages, a perceptual-motor stage and a computational stage. The perceptual-motor stage is assumed to be constant when the same response is made to signal the completion of different mental tasks; therefore, increases in latency with increased complexity must be caused primarily by the computational factor. Age may impair each stage by a different factor, but the perceptual-motor stage is impaired less than the computational stage. The two-factor model, which could account for both perceptual-motor and computational components, fits the data better. Therefore, Cerella suggested that a speeded response is composed of a layer of processing that is marginally affected (perceptual-motor) and a layer that is substantially affected (computational). This view is compatible with that of Hale et al. (1987), who suggested that because verbal abilities generally decline with aging much

more slowly than motor capacities, performance changes on nonverbal tasks may be qualitatively different from performance changes on verbal tasks.

Summary of Theories of Response Slowing

Salthouse's (1985) comprehensive review of theories of age-related response speed slowing did not find substantial support for the aging attributes model, and both his and Cerella's (1990) analysis and synthesis of many studies have seriously challenged the notion that stage-specific information processing is the most useful way to explain age-related changes. Little doubt exists that factors such as stimulus quality, stimulus and response compatibility and complexity, and preparatory interval duration differentially influence specific stages of information processing. The key is whether the differences due to these factors that increase processing time in stages are really greater for aged subjects than for young subjects. Cerella's (1990) review clearly shows that skill acquisition, speed-accuracy trade-off, attentional capacity, strategy differences, and other phenomena operate in the same way for young and old subjects. If this is true, they are not good explanations for an age deficit. In fact, the evidence that all information-processing stages show age-related differences is more supportive of a biological degradation hypothesis. Cerella concludes, "Information-processing latencies taken from elderly subjects match exactly, qualitatively and quantitatively, those that would be expected from a brain whose interconnections were systematically disrupted or attenuated" (1990, p. 219). He predicts that model parameters, such as the connectivity constant or signal loss rate, may emerge as powerful predictors of individual differences.

Movement Speed

The speed with which an individual can move digits (fingers or toes), a limb (arm or leg), or limb components (forearm or lower leg) independent of the time necessary to start the movement is called *movement speed*. Movement speed is important, because fast movement time could, for example, enable an individual to copy an address or phone number from a television screen before the screen changes to something else. It is also important in tasks such as moving the foot from the accelerator of an automobile to the brake in an emergency. The response to stop the car as quickly as possible requires a simple reaction time to begin to move the foot. Once the foot leaves the accelerator, however, the time that it takes to move from the accelerator to the brake is independent of the initial reaction. Quick reactions are important in many situations in life, but the ability to move quickly after the initial reaction can be equally important.

A straightforward way to determine movement speed is to measure how fast an individual can move a limb from one location to another when the individual self-initiates the movement. Most researchers, however, measure movement speed in an RT paradigm, because they can obtain both RT and movement speed on the same trial. Thus, they acquire two measurements instead of one. In the RT context, the amount of time consumed by the movement, independent of time taken to react to the stimulus, is usually called *movement time* (MT). The independence of RT and MT is shown very clearly in Figure 7.7 (page 193).

Movement Time—Movement Speed in an RT Paradigm

Movement time is the time after the release of the reaction-time key to the contact of a target at some specified distance. In Figure 7.7 movement time was diagrammed as a part of a reaction time paradigm. Even though MT is frequently measured in a reaction time paradigm and may in some cases be slightly correlated with RT, it is clearly independent of reaction time (Henry, 1961). As shown in Figure 7.8 (page 194), the MT of older subjects in a fractionated response is significantly longer than that of younger subjects, and Stern et al. (1980) suggested that movement time is faster in the preferred limb for young and middle-aged, but not older, adults. A question often asked in these paradigms is whether MT or RT is more affected by aging. Pierson and Montoye (1958) found that MT was more affected than SRT, but whether aging slows movement time more than reaction time probably depends on the task parameters. Highly complex movements that can be initiated by simple decisions reveal greater age differences in movement time. Conversely, when simple movements are initiated by a complex stimulus array, more age differences are seen in the reaction time. The greatest age effects occur in the cumulative condition, where the decision process is complicated and the movement to be made is complex.

Movement Speed in Psychomotor and Neuropsychological Tests

Another way to assess movement speed is to determine the amount of time necessary to complete a task when almost all decisions about which movement to make are removed, such as when copying numbers or dealing playing cards without regard to their suit. In all cases, investigators try to reduce the amount of CNS monitoring and maximize the speed that can be controlled and produced. In copying tests, the tasks are designed so that it is unnecessary to remember or interpret the symbols to be copied. When timing movements in card dealing, no requirement is made to deal the cards by suit or number. This type of speed is generally called *copying time, motor speed,* or *movement speed* and is a component in many psychomotor or neuropsychological test batteries. These terms are distinct from the term movement time, which is reserved for the time lapsed between movements of limbs from one target to another, described previously.

In almost all tests measuring movement speed, older individuals are slower than younger ones in their movements. Welford, Norris, and Shock (1969) showed many years ago that in an aiming speed test (reciprocal tapping), if target width and distance are held constant, slowed position sense and motor control decline more for the aged than do the decisional processes responsible for accuracy in hitting a target. Figure 7.15 shows that movement time (called *transit time* by Stern et al., 1980) decreases with increased decision complexity. That is, having to make a decision about which movement to make slows that movement once the response is initiated. But this decrease in movement speed with an increase in premovement stimulus complexity occurs in young subjects as well as the old. Thus, although the older subjects were clearly slower in their movement speed than the young subjects, the age differences did not increase with increasing decision complexity. Also, it is clear in this figure that age differences in movement time are not as discrete and neatly ordered by decades as are the age differences in decision-making time shown in Figure 7.6 (page 192).

Movement Speed: Repetitive Movements

Making repetitive movements as quickly as possible exaggerates age differences in movement speed. Almost all investigators who have studied repetitive measures have found large age differences. A common laboratory measurement of repetitive movements is tapping speed, in which the subject taps a finger or a stylus in one place as many times as possible within a specified time, usually 10 or 15 s. In a stationary tapping test, shown in Figure 7.16, the "home" button is tapped repeatedly. The stationary tapping task (sometimes called *finger oscillation* or *repetitive tapping*) involves only the activation and control of the appropriate muscles with minimal monitoring required. Because the task requires only that the individual repeat the process of starting and terminating a movement as rapidly as possible, repetitive tapping is thought to measure motor outflow integrity, similar to the way flicker fusion frequency is thought to measure visual perceptual integrity. (*Flicker fusion frequency* is the frequency at which a blinking light begins to appear to be an uninterrupted beam of light. When the perceptual apparatus cannot complete the processing of one flash of light before the next one arrives, the light begins to appear as a steady beam.)

Stationary tapping is limited by how fast movements can be started and stopped and is a good behavioral test of the processing speed. This assumption is based on the premise that tapping the finger or a pencil-type stylus for such a short period requires almost no muscle strength, endurance, flexibility, or accuracy, so the delimiting factor has to be the speed with which the CNS can issue a repeated motor command. Stationary tapping is so sensitive to age differences that it has been used frequently in neuropsychological test batteries (e.g., Halstead-Reitan Neuropsychological Test Battery). Often it represents a so-called "pure" motor component in psychomotor or perceptual motor test batteries.

Another measure of movement speed is reciprocal (target) tapping; the subject moves the finger or stylus from one target to another as rapidly as possible within a specified period, generally 10 to 15 s (Figure 7.16; see also Figure 8.3, page 219). This task requires not only initiating and terminating movements, but depending on the accuracy requirements of the targets, the monitoring of the movements. The speed with which reciprocal target tapping is accomplished is a function of the relationship between speed and accuracy, expressed by Fitts' law,

$$MT = a + b [\log_2(2A/W)],$$

where MT = movement time, a = the movement

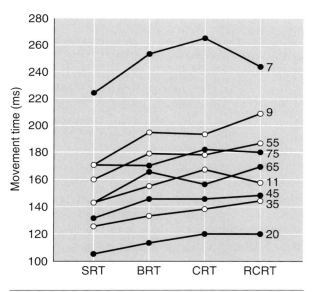

Figure 7.15 Movement time as a function of age. Numbers next to lines are average age of each group. SRT = simple reaction time; BRT = bilateral reaction time; CRT = choice reaction time; RCRT = reverse choice reaction time.

From "Reaction Time Measures, Hemispheric Specialization, and Age" by J.A. Stern, P.J. Oster, and K. Newport. In *Aging in the 1980s: Psychological Issues* (p. 317) by L.W. Poon (Ed.), 1980, Washington, DC: American Psychological Association. Copyright 1980 by the American Psychological Association. Reprinted by permission.

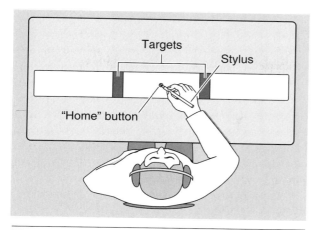

Figure 7.16 Stationary or target tapping. The subject taps the stylus on one plate as many times as possible in 10 s. In target tapping, the subject taps the stylus on the left and right plates alternately as rapidly as possible.
From "Perceptual-Motor Skills Learning" by P.M. Fitts. In *Categories of Human Learning* (p. 258) by A.W. Melton (Ed.), 1964, New York: Academic Press. Copyright 1964 by Academic Press, Inc. Reprinted by permission.

speed that would occur in a movement of zero accuracy difficulty, as in repetitive (intercept) tapping, and b = the added time to move caused by increasing the index of difficulty of the movement slope. The index of difficulty is defined as $\log_2(2A/W)$ for one unit, where A = amplitude of the target, and W = width of the target (Fitts, 1954). Fitts' law applies to older adults as well as young, except that adding the components of age and gender to the equation does slightly improve the prediction of MT for older people (Vercruyssen, 1991). The slope of the Fitts' law equation increases with aging, implying that as individuals age they take a disproportionately longer amount of time on difficult rapid hand-movement tasks (Brogmus, 1991).

Functional Significance of Behavioral Speed

Age-related changes in behavioral speed have great significance for the elderly, both in the slowing of reactions and mental functions and in the execution of movements. The effect that slow reactions and movements have on activities of daily living, such as grooming, eating, and home management chores, were mentioned at the beginning of this chapter, as were the detrimental effects of

the slowing of behavioral speed on automobile driving. These effects, in combination with the age-related changes in coordination that occur, are so important that they are discussed in much greater detail in chapter 8 (see "Automobile Driving" on page 228). But behavioral speed is also significant to researchers who study cognitive processing in the elderly, because behavioral speed contributes to the scores of many neuropsychological time-limited tests. If tests require copying letters or numbers or the completion of scantron answer sheets, handwriting speed can affect the results. This is particularly true if unusual symbols are to be drawn, as in the Digit-Symbol Substitution test, or if lines are to be drawn between targets, as in the trailmaking test. Thus, if an individual generally moves slowly and the movement is not isolated from the general information-processing speed, the specific component of intelligence that is being assessed by the cognitive test may be underestimated.

Intellectual Functioning

Hertzog (1989) argued that age-related slowing of information-processing speed is a primary cause of age-related decline in intelligence. His review of several studies revealed that the relationship between speed of processing and intelligence as measured by these types of tests is substantial for every age group and does not interact with age. He found that a substantial proportion of age differences in so-called primary mental abilities (e.g., verbal comprehension, spatial visualization, and induction) covaries with multiple speed factors, one of which was a composite representing the physical movement necessary to fill in the answer sheets. The deterioration of scores in primary mental abilities, therefore, may not reflect a loss of thinking capacity per se but rather a slowing in the *rate* of intelligent thought (Hertzog, 1989), which also may be slightly affected by the speed and accuracy with which the movements necessary to answer the questions are executed.

Motor behavior contributes even more to the psychomotor tasks frequently used in tests of cognitive decision making. Examples are card sorting, copying letters or numerals, trailmaking, and the Digit-Symbol Substitution test.

One of the earliest attempts to determine how much age-related slowing of movement speed contributed to psychomotor behavior was that by Crossman and Szafran (1956), who measured the time required to deal a deck of cards with 0, 2, 4, or 8 choices to be made while dealing. They were interested in the effects of aging on decision making, and they did indeed find that the differences between young and old grew larger as the number of choices increased. But they also found that small age differences existed even when no choices had to be made.

In the trailmaking psychomotor test, subjects begin with their pencils on the number 1 circle and draw a line connecting each circle in numerical order. The score of the test is the time required by the subject to connect all the circles (Figure 7.17). The primary purpose of this task is to assess visual search time and short-term memory, but clearly the accuracy of short movements and movement speed contribute to the task. The abilities necessary to do this task are highly sensitive to aging, because each older decade takes longer to complete the task.

The Digit-Symbol Substitution (DSS) test, which is a performance subtest of the Wechsler Adult Intelligence Scale (WAIS; Wechsler, 1958), is another neuropsychological task that depends on rate of processing and, to some extent, on movement speed. It is also moderately correlated to the full scale WAIS score ($r \sim$ mid-.60s). Thus, movement speed indirectly influences WAIS scores. In the DSS test, the subject, within a specified time, copies the symbols that match the numerals 1 to 9 into the boxes provided (Figure 7.18). The DSS is extremely age sensitive (Figure 7.19). In the beginning of the task, subjects usually have to look up the matching symbol each time they

copy it. After a few repetitions, however, most subjects begin to remember the appropriate symbol and by the end of the test many do not have to look up any symbols. They just remember which symbol is matched to which number and draw it as quickly as they can. The test assesses the memory and copying speed abilities of different subjects, but it also can be differentially influenced by movement speed and hand control, depending on how dependable the memory is and how much practice has been provided.

To determine how much of the test was assessing memory and processing and how much was measuring copying speed, Storandt (1976) had subjects copy the symbols used in the DSS as quickly as possible without matching them to numbers. Then she subtracted that time from the routine testing time (which included symbol matching). She concluded that the mental coding necessary to complete the task accounted for about 50% of the time, but that the copying speed component of the task also accounted for about 50%. It is easy to see, however, that these percentages could vary, depending on how quickly the subjects memorized the number-symbol pairs. If a subject could completely memorize the symbols after the presentation of 10 or 12 numbers, almost the entire test would be little but a test of movement speed, because no look-up would be required. This could present some problems when comparing greatly disparate age groups, such as 20-year-olds with the oldest-old. If young people memorize these number-symbol matches faster than older people do, an occurrence which is

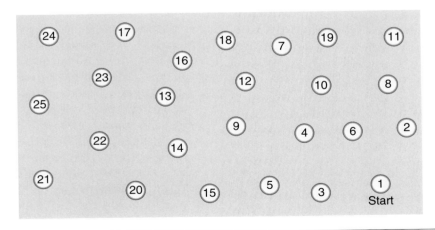

Figure 7.17   The trailmaking test. The subject starts with the pencil on circle number 1, and upon the command "Go" draws a line to the number 2 circle, then to circle 3, and so on until circle 25 is connected. The score for the trial is the number of seconds necessary to move the pencil from circle number 1 to circle number 25.

Digit-Symbol Substitution test

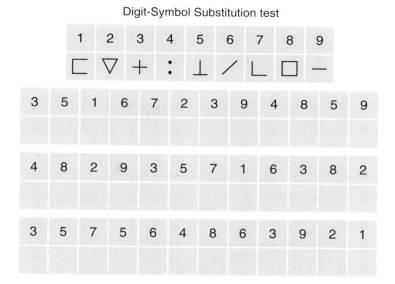

Figure 7.18 A portion of the Digit-Symbol Substitution test. The symbols shown are not the actual symbols used in the test.

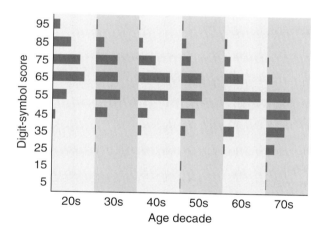

Figure 7.19 Distribution of WAIS-R Digit-Symbol Substitution scores by decade; $n \sim 129$ to 169 adults in each decade. An important observation is that the performance of all subjects, whether in the low, middle, or high parts of the distribution, deteriorated with aging; that is, the means of each older decade were not increasingly worse because a small number of poorly performing subjects "pulled them down." From "What Do Adult Age Differences in the Digit-Symbol Substitution Test Reflect?" by T.A. Salthouse, 1992, *Journal of Gerontology: Psychological Sciences,* **47**, p. P123. Copyright 1992 by The Gerontological Society of America. Reprinted by permission.

highly probable, then the DSS test may be testing visual search and short-term memory in the older people, but movement speed in the young people. Generally, however, although the copying speed

component in the DSS is slower in older adults, it does not account for a high proportion of the overall slowing in this task (Salthouse, 1992). Thus, age deficits appear during both coding and copying in this psychomotor test, but the task is primarily a perceptual-processing task.

Detecting Disease States

Because reaction time serves as a behavioral window through which the integrity of the CNS may be assessed, it also has been employed to identify possible pathological conditions. For example, a slow SRT recorded in an experimental protocol in which the regularity of the preparatory interval is manipulated has long been recognized as being associated with schizophrenic disorders. Schizophrenics not only fail to take advantage of information from regular stimulus intervals, they do worse with it. Unimpaired subjects have faster reaction times with regular preparatory intervals preceding the RT stimulus, but schizophrenics only do better at regular intervals when the preparatory interval is less than 2 seconds. At longer preparatory intervals, they do worse. This characteristic of schizophrenics is known as the crossover phenomenon (Rodnick & Shakow, 1940).

Reaction time also has been used as an indicant of dysfunction to differentiate normal aging from pathological conditions. Discrimination RT, for example, correctly identified 86% of senile patients from controls in one study (Ferris, Crook, Sathananthan, & Gershon, 1976). Also, CRT is sensitive even to relatively mild stages of Alzheimer's disease and deteriorates with the progression of the disease (Gordon & Carson, 1990). Alzheimer's patients can be differentiated into mild, moderate, and severe cases on the basis of oculomotor reaction time, which is strong evidence for a direct relationship between the degree of cortical structural integrity and simple oculomotor RT (Pirozzolo & Hansch, 1981). The Alzheimer's patient is not, however, different in RT characteristics from an unimpaired aged person, only slower. The fact that a reaction time task can be successfully performed even by demented patients has made it a useful tool in the diagnosis of Alzheimer's disease. It is believed that decision making regarding a reaction time stimulus requires analysis by the object perception centers of the temporal lobe, a brain region greatly affected by Alzheimer's. One technique researchers use is to present a large arrow pointing to the left or the right and then require the patients to pull the matching left or right lever as quickly as possible (Ashford, Bice, Vicari, & Feldman, 1989). These authors also suggested that the task was successful enough with Alzheimer's patients to serve as part of the decision process regarding whether to revoke driver's licenses. It has long been known that response speed evidenced by reaction time behaviors is also significantly related to brain damage, cardiovascular disease, and depression. A good review of these relationships is provided in Birren et al. (1979, 1980).

In Summary

Behavioral speed slows with aging. Average correlation coefficients of age with reactive and movement speed task performance are shown in Figure 7.20. Considering that these correlations are averages across several research studies in which the variables were measured differently, the magnitude of the correlations is remarkable.

Slowing is functionally significant to individuals, because it affects the way they perform daily functional tasks, such as automobile driving, and increases the risk of accidents. The functional significance of a slowed behavioral speed for many older citizens is increased accident rates and health insurance rates, age discrimination, job loss

in externally paced environments and in professions such as piloting airplanes, and reduced sports participation. However, as emphasized in chapter 2, a very wide degree of individual variation exists in speeded responses at all ages. Some 50-year-olds are considerably faster than many 20-year-olds, so although chronological age is correlated with speed of response, it is a poor indicator of individual response speed. Generally, the more complex the stimulus display and the decisions to be made, the greater the difference in RT of young and old persons. Similarly, the more complex the movement to be made, the slower the response of older people. The effects of a complicated stimulus display combined with a complex movement are cumulative and reveal the greatest age differences.

All components of the response are slower in aged individuals than in young, but the components that represent central processing (premotor time and information processing) are slowed relatively more than those components that represent peripheral responses (motor time and nerve conduction velocity). Also, gender differences, suggesting that males are faster than females, have been reported for all ages except for those younger than 15 and older than 70. However, because of differential societal expectations, these differences may be spurious.

Theories of age-related slowing in response speed fall into three categories: those that explain slowing via an information-processing model, in which some stages of processing are affected more than others; those that attribute the slowing to characteristics or attributes of aging individuals; and those that explain slowing as biological degradation.

The evidence that aging differentially affects specific stages of information processing, such as encoding, working memory, or response programming, is inconclusive. There is persuasive evidence that manipulations of factors that affect various stages do affect the response time. However, there is no definitive replicated evidence that these manipulations impair the response speed of older people more than younger people.

Speculations that older subjects prepare less efficiently for a task, may use information less efficiently, or may process information differently are largely unconfirmed. The arguments that older individuals develop tendencies, characteristics, or preferences that result in slower responses, though accounting for some of the slowing, do not satisfactorily explain age differences. The speed-accuracy trade-off phenomenon, which has been documented many times, does not explain adequately

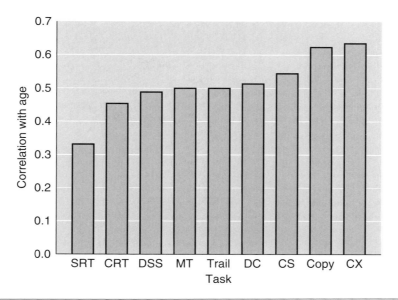

Figure 7.20 Average correlations of psychomotor task performances with age. SRT = simple reaction time; CRT = choice reaction time; DSS = Digit-Symbol Substitution test (from WAIS); MT = movement time; Trail = trail-making performance; DC = digit coding; CS = card sorting; Copy = copy time; CX = crossing out. Data from Salthouse (1985, p. 11).

age differences in response time, and although disuse accounts for some age-decrement and practice can reduce age differences, a rather large proportion of the differences cannot be accounted for by the disuse hypothesis. Also, arguments for a strategy shift in the processing of stimuli and motor control have not been strongly supported by scientific findings.

The most compelling hypotheses to explain age-related slowing are those based on biological deterioration. The bases for these theories include an increase in neural noise, general slowing of CNS function, and disruptions in neural networks. Model parameters such as the connectivity constant or signal loss rate may become powerful predictors of individual differences. At present, the theories that attribute age-related slowing to biological deterioration seem to be the most persuasive explanations, although the results are not conclusive.

References

Ashford, W., Bice, J., Vicari, S., & Feldman, E. (1989). Simple choice reaction vs. Alzheimer severity. *The Gerontologist*, **29**, 140A.

Baron, A., & Journey, J.W. (1989). Age differences in manual versus vocal reaction times: Further evidence. *Journal of Gerontology: Psychological Sciences*, **44**, P157-P159.

Birren, J.E. (1965). Age changes in speed of behavior: Its central nature and physiological correlates. In A.T. Welford & J.E. Birren (Eds.), *Behavior, aging, and the nervous system* (pp. 191-216). Springfield, IL: Charles C Thomas.

Birren, J.E., Wood, A.M., & Williams, M.V. (1979). Speed of behavior as an indicator of age changes and the integrity of the nervous system. In F. Hoffmeister & C. Müller (Eds.), *Brain function in old age* (pp. 10-44). New York: Springer-Verlag.

Birren, J.E., Wood, A.M., & Williams, M.V. (1980). Behavioral slowing with age: Causes, organization, and consequences. In L.W. Poon (Ed.), *Aging in the 1980s: Psychological issues* (pp. 293-308). Washington, DC: American Psychological Association.

Botwinick, J. (1970). Geropsychology. *Annual Review of Psychology*, **21**, 239-272.

Brogmus, G.E. (1991). Effects of age and sex on speed and accuracy of hand movements and the refinements they suggest for Fitts' law. In *Proceedings of the Human Factors Society, 35th Annual Meeting* (pp. 208-212). Santa Monica, CA: Human Factors and Ergonomics Society.

Cerella, J. (1985). Information processing rates in the elderly. *Psychological Bulletin*, **98**, 67-83.

Cerella, J. (1990). Aging and information-processing rate. In J.E. Birren & K.W. Schaie (Eds.), *Handbook of the psychology of aging* (3rd ed., pp. 201-221). New York: Academic Press.

Cerella, J., Poon, L.W., & Williams, D. (1980). Age and the complexity hypothesis. In L.W. Poon (Ed.), *Aging in the 1980s* (pp. 332-340). Washington, DC: American Psychological Association.

Clark, J., Lanphear, A.K., & Riddick, C.C. (1987). The effects of videogame playing on the response selection processing of elderly adults. *Journal of Gerontology*, **42**, 82-85.

Clarkson, P.M. (1978). The effect of age and activity level on simple and choice fractionated response time. *European Journal of Applied Physiology*, **40**, 17-25.

Coles, M.G.H., Gratton, G., Bashore, T.R., Eriksen, C.W., & Donchin, E. (1985). A psychophysiological investigation of the continuous flow model of human information processing. *Journal of Experimental Psychology: Human Perception and Performance*, **11**, 529-553.

Craik, F.I.M. (1977). Age differences in human memory. In J.E. Birren & K.W. Schaie (Eds.), *Handbook of the psychology of aging* (pp. 384-420). New York: Van Nostrand Reinhold.

Crossman, E.R.F.W., & Szafran, J. (1956). Changes with age in the speed of information intake and discrimination. *Experientia Supplementum*, **4**, 128-135.

Ferris, S., Crook, T., Sathananthan, G., & Gershon, S. (1976). Reaction time as a diagnostic measure in senility. *Journal of the American Geriatrics Society*, **24**, 529-533.

Fisk, A.D., Rogers, W.A., & Giambra, L.M. (1990). Consistent and varied memory/visual search: Is there an interaction between age and the response-set effects? *Journal of Gerontology: Psychological Sciences*, **45**, P81-P87.

Fitts, P.M. (1954). The information capacity of the human motor system in controlling the amplitude of movement. *Journal of Experimental Psychology*, **47**, 381-391.

Fitts, P.M. (1964). Perceptual-motor skills learning. In A.W. Melton (Ed.), *Categories of human learning* (pp. 243-285). New York: Academic Press.

Fozard, J.L., Thomas, J.C., & Waugh, N.C. (1976). Effects of age and frequency of stimulus repetitions on two-choice reaction time. *Journal of Gerontology*, **31**, 556-563.

Fozard, J.L., Vercruyssen, M., Reynolds, S.L., & Hancock, P.A. (1990). Longitudinal analysis of age-related slowing: BLSA reaction time data. In *Proceedings of the Human Factors Society, 34th Annual Meeting* (pp. 163-167). Santa Monica, CA: Human Factors Society.

Galton, F. (1899). Exhibition of instruments (1) for testing perception of differences of tint and (2) for determining reaction-time. *Journal of the Anthropological Institute*, **19**, 27-29.

Gordon, B., & Carson, K. (1990). The basis for choice reaction time slowing in Alzheimer's disease. *Brain and Cognition*, **13**, 148-166.

Gottsdanker, R. (1980). Aging and the use of advance probability information. *Journal of Motor Behavior*, **12**, 133-143.

Gottsdanker, R. (1982). Age and simple reaction time. *Journal of Gerontology*, **37**, 342-348.

Greene, V.L. (1983). Age dynamic models of information-processing task latency: A theoretical note. *Journal of Gerontology*, **38**, 46-50.

Griew, S. (1959). Complexity of response and time of initiating responses in relation to age. *American Journal of Psychology*, **72**, 83-88.

Hale, S., Myerson, J., & Wagstaff, D. (1987). General slowing of nonverbal information processing: Evidence for a power law. *Journal of Gerontology*, **42**, 131-136.

Hart, B.A. (1980). *Fractionated reflex and response times in women by activity level and age*. Unpublished doctoral dissertation, University of Massachusetts, Amherst.

Henry, F.M. (1961). Reaction time-movement time correlations. *Perceptual and Motor Skills*, **12**, 63-66.

Hertzog, C.K. (1989). Influences of cognitive slowing on age differences in intelligence. *Developmental Psychology*, **25**, 636-651.

Hertzog, C., Williams, M.V., & Walsh, D.A. (1976). The effect of practice on age differences in central perceptual processing. *Journal of Gerontology*, **31**, 428-433.

Hodgkins, J. (1963). Reaction time and speed of movement in males and females of various ages. *Research Quarterly*, **34**, 335-343.

Inhoff, A.W., & Bisiacchi, P. (1990). Unimanual tapping during concurrent articulation: Examining the role of cortical structures in the execution of programmed movement sequences. *Brain and Cognition*, **13**, 59-76.

Johnson, R.C., McClearn, G.E., Yuen, S., Nagoshi, C.T., Ahern, F.M., & Cole, R.E. (1985). Galton's data a century later. *American Psychologist*, **40**, 875-892.

Jordan, T.C., & Rabbitt, P.M.A. (1977). Response times to stimuli of increasing complexity as a function of ageing. *British Journal of Psychology*, **68**, 189-201.

Klein, H., Dollar, M.L., & Bagdonas, J.E. (1947). Dentist time required to perform dental operations. *Journal of American Dental Association*, **35**, 153-160.

Koga, Y., & Morant, G.M. (1923). On the degree of association between reaction times in the case of different senses. *Biometrika*, **15**, 346-372.

Larsson, L., & Karlsson, J. (1978). Isometric and dynamic endurance as a function of age and skeletal muscle characteristics. *Acta Physiologica Scandinavica, 104,* 129-136.

Laufer, A.C., & Schweitz, B. (1968). Neuromuscular response tests as predictors of sensory-motor performance in aging individuals. *American Journal of Physical Medicine, 47,* 250-263.

Light, K., & Spirduso, W. (1990). Effects of adult aging on the movement complexity factor of response programming. *Journal of Gerontology: Psychological Sciences, 45,* P107-P109.

MacRae, P., Spirduso, W., & Wilcox, R.E. (1988). Reaction time and nigrostriatal dopamine function: The effects of age and practice. *Brain Research, 451,* 139-146.

Marsh, G.R., & Watson, W.E. (1980). Psychophysiological studies of aging effects on cognitive processes. In D.G. Stein (Ed.), *Psychobiology of aging.* New York: Elsevier North-Holland.

McDowd, J.M., & Birren, J.E. (1990). Aging and attentional processes. In J.E. Birren & K.W. Schaie (Eds.), *Handbook of the psychology of aging* (3rd ed., pp. 222-234). New York: Academic Press.

Murrell, F.H. (1970). The effect of extensive practice on age differences in reaction time. *Journal of Gerontology, 25,* 268-274.

Myerson, J. (1987, November). *The search for regularities in cognitive aging.* Paper presented at the annual meeting of the Gerontological Society of America, Washington, DC.

Myerson, J., Hale, S., Hirschman, R., Hansen, C., & Christiansen, B. (1989). Global increase in response latencies by early middle age: Complexity effects in individual performances. *Journal of the Experimental Analysis of Behavior, 52,* 353-362.

Myerson, J., Hale, S., Wagstaff, D., Poon, L.W., & Smith, G.A. (1990). The information-loss model: A mathematical theory of age-related cognitive slowing. *Psychological Review, 97,* 475-487.

Nebes, R.D. (1978). Vocal versus manual response as a determinant of age differences in simple reaction time. *Journal of Gerontology, 33,* 884-889.

Noble, C.E., Baker, B.L., & Jones, T.A. (1964). Age and sex parameters in psychomotor learning. *Perceptual and Motor Skills, 19,* 935-945.

Osborne, L. (1987). The effects of age, modality, and complexity of response and practice on response programming. Unpublished master's thesis. University of Texas, Austin.

Pierson, W.R., & Montoye, H.J. (1958). Movement time, reaction time, and age. *Journal of Gerontology, 13,* 418-421.

Pirozzolo, F.J., & Hansch, E.C. (1981). Oculomotor reaction time in dementia reflects degree of cerebral dysfunction. *Science, 214,* 349-351.

Plude, D.J., Cerella, J., & Raskind, C.L. (1984). *Speed-accuracy tradeoffs in cognitive aging research.* Paper presented at the annual meeting of The Gerontological Society of America, San Antonio, TX.

Plude, D.J., Hoyer, W.J., & Lazar, J. (1982). Age, response complexity, and target consistency in visual search. *Experimental Aging Research, 8,* 99-102.

Rabbitt, P.M. (1965). An age-decrement in the ability to ignore irrelevant information. *Journal of Gerontology, 20,* 233-238.

Rabbitt, P.M.A. (1980). A fresh look at changes in reaction times in old age. In D.G. Stein (Ed.), *The psychobiology of aging: Problems and perspectives* (pp. 425-442). Amsterdam: Elsevier North Holland.

Rabbitt, P.M.A., & Birren, J.E. (1967). Age and responses to sequences of repetitive and interruptive signals. *Journal of Gerontology, 22,* 143-150.

Rich, N. (1987). The effects of age on unresisted and resisted fractionated reaction time. In J. Humphrey & J. Clark (Eds.), *Advances in motor development research* (Vol. 2, pp. 71-82). New York: AMS Press.

Rodnick, E.H., & Shakow, D. (1940). Set in the schizophrenic as measured by a composite reaction time index. *American Journal Psychiatry, 97,* 214-225.

Salthouse, T.A. (1978). The role of memory in the age decline in digit-symbol substitution performance. *Journal of Gerontology, 33,* 232-238.

Salthouse, T.A. (1984). Effects of age and skill in typing. *Journal of Experimental Psychology: General, 113,* 345-371.

Salthouse, T.A. (1985). *A theory of cognitive aging.* Amsterdam: North-Holland.

Salthouse, T.A. (1992). What do adult age differences in the Digit-Symbol Substitution test reflect? *Journal of Gerontology: Psychological Sciences, 47,* P121-P128.

Salthouse, T.A., & Somberg, B.L. (1982a). Isolating the age deficit in speeded performance. *Journal of Gerontology, 37,* 59-63.

Salthouse, T.A., & Somberg, B.L. (1982b). Skilled performance: Effects of adult age and experience on elementary processes. *Journal of Experimental Psychology, 111,* 176-207.

Salthouse, T.A., & Somberg, B.L. (1982c). Time-accuracy relationships in young and old adults. *Journal of Gerontology, 37,* 349-353.

Schmidt, R.A. (1988). *Motor control and learning* (2nd ed.). Champaign, IL: Human Kinetics.

Simon, J.R., & Pouraghabagher, A.R. (1978). The effect of aging on the stages of processing in a choice reaction time task. *Journal of Gerontology*, **33**, 553-561.

Stelmach, G.E., Goggin, N.L., & Amrhein, P.C. (1988). Aging and the restructuring of precued movements. *Psychology and Aging*, **3**, 151-157.

Stelmach, G.E., Goggin, N.L., & Garcia-Colera, G. (1986). Movement specification time with age. *Experimental Aging Research*, **13**, 39-46.

Stern, J.A., Oster, P.J., & Newport, K. (1980). Reaction time measures, hemispheric specialization, and age. In L.W. Poon (Ed.), *Aging in the 1980s: Psychological issues* (pp. 309-326). Washington, DC: American Psychological Association.

Storandt, M. (1976). Speed and coding effects in relation to age and ability level. *Developmental Psychology*, **12**, 177-178.

Strayer, D.L., Wickens, C.D., & Braune, R. (1987). Adult age differences in the speed and capacity of information processing: 2. An electrophysiological approach. *Psychology and Aging*, **2**, 99-110.

Surwillo, W.W. (1964). The relation of decision time to brain wave frequency and to age. *Electroencephalography and Clinical Neurophysiology*, **16**, 510-514.

Talland, G.A. (1965). Initiation of response, and reaction time in aging, and with brain damage. In A.T. Welford & J.E. Birren (Eds.), *Behavior, aging, and the nervous system* (pp. 526-561). Springfield, IL: Charles C Thomas.

Vercruyssen, M. (1991). Age-related slowing of behavior. *Proceedings of the Human Factors Society, 35th Annual Meeting* (pp. 188-192). Santa Monica, CA: Human Factors and Ergonomics Society.

Walsh, D.A. (1976). Age differences in central perceptual processing: A dichoptic backward masking investigation. *Journal of Gerontology*, **31**, 178-185.

Walsh, D.A., & Thompson, L.W. (1978). Age differences in visual sensory memory. *Journal of Gerontology*, **33**, 383-387.

Waugh, N.C., Fozard, J.L., Talland, G.A., & Ervin, D.E. (1973). Effects of age and stimulus repetition on two-choice reaction time. *Journal of Gerontology*, **28**, 466-470.

Waugh, N.C., & Vyas, S. (1980). Expectancy and choice reaction time in early and late adulthood. *Experimental Aging Research*, **6**, 563-567.

Wechsler, D. (1958). *The measurement and appraisal of adult intelligence*. Baltimore: Williams & Wilkins.

Welford, A.T. (1958). *Ageing and human skill* (Oxford University Press, London), for the Nuffield Foundation; reprinted by Greenwood Press, Westport, 1973.

Welford, A.T. (1959). Psychomotor performance. In J.E. Birren (Ed.), *Handbook of aging and the individual*. Chicago: University of Chicago Press.

Welford, A.T. (1965). Performance, biological mechanisms, and age: A theoretical sketch. In A.T. Welford and J. Birren (Eds.), *Behavior, aging, and the nervous system* (pp. 3-20). Springfield, IL: Charles C Thomas.

Welford, A.T. (1977a). Causes of slowing of performance with age. *Interdisciplinary Topics in Gerontology*, **11**, 43-51.

Welford, A.T. (1977b). Motor performance. In J.E. Birren & K.W. Schaie (Eds.), *Handbook of the psychology of aging* (pp. 450-496). Princeton, NJ: Van Nostrand Reinhold.

Welford, A.T. (1981). Signal, noise, performance, and age. *Human Factors*, **23**, 97-109.

Welford, A.T., Norris, A.H., & Shock, N.W. (1969). Speed and accuracy of movement and their changes with age. *Acta Psychologica*, **30**, 3-15.

Wilkinson, R.T., & Allison, S. (1989). Age and simple reaction time: Decade differences for 5,325 subjects. *Journal of Gerontology: Psychological Sciences*, **44**, P29-P35.

Yandell, K.M., & Spirduso, W.W. (1981). Sex and athletic status as factors in reaction latency and movement time. *Research Quarterly for Exercise and Sport*, **52**, 495-504.

Coordination and Skill in Complex Movements

Previous chapters discussed the physical abilities of aerobic capacity, muscular strength and endurance, flexibility, agility, and response speed of older adults. This chapter addresses the effects of age on older peoples' ability to coordinate muscular activity into useful and functional activities. *Neuromuscular coordination* means organizing and activating large and small muscles with the right amount of force in the most efficient sequence.

215

If the particular activation pattern of muscles is complex, this pattern must be practiced many times before it becomes a skill. Even simple forms of locomotion such as walking and running must be practiced and learned. More complex forms of locomotion, such as skipping and galloping, require additional learning and even more complex neuromuscular coordination.

Generally, however, when people describe others as being "coordinated" or "having a lot of coordination," they really mean the ability of the person to coordinate the eyes, hands, and feet so that a particular movement can be made to accomplish a goal. Throwing and catching a ball, hitting a golf ball, and bowling are examples of this type of coordination. When a physical task requires primarily the integration of vision and hands to manipulate objects, the task is said to require *eye-hand coordination*. Eye-hand coordination is defined as the "skillful, integrated use of the eyes, arms, hands, and fingers in fine, precision movement" (Williams, 1983). Sewing, playing video games, slicing a carrot, and turning a knob to change a radio station all have to be learned, and all require eye-hand coordination.

Eye-hand coordination is an incredibly intricate and complex function of the central nervous system. Shown in Figure 8.1, it has been conceptualized as requiring integration of two general schemas: a *perceptual schema* that provides an internal model of the environment and the input parameters, and a *motor schema* that can be programmed to activate the appropriate muscles to complete the physical task. A schema is a set of rules by which decisions are made. Thus, a perceptual schema is a set of rules by which environmental and internal information is identified, organized, and classified. A motor schema is a set of rules that integrates perceptual schema and recalls or initiates motor commands to activate the appropriate muscles in the correct sequence.

A cursory view of Figure 8.1 is sufficient to appreciate the complexity of neuromuscular coordination. To develop a perceptual schema, the shape, size, orientation, and functional significance of objects must be visualized. To develop a motor schema, the nature of the appropriate transitory movement must be determined, and then the processes of finger adjustment, hand rotation, grasping, and manipulation of the fingers must be controlled. Also, as discussed in chapter 6, before and throughout the eye–hand-coordinated movement, the postural reflexes and motor synergies that maintain body balance and locomotion are also being integrated with the action.

When complicated movements, such as throwing balls, shuffling playing cards, tying shoelaces, or typing letters, are first attempted, each specific movement required to accomplish the task is controlled individually. The result is a jerky, poorly timed sequence of individual movements that requires a substantial amount of energy. Gradually, through maturation and thousands of practice trials, perceptual and motor schemas are developed for such movements, and these neuromuscularly coordinated movements can be executed without conscious attention. More complicated physical skills such as typing, which requires an ongoing integration of visual input and motor control, can also become very fluid and reliable as a result of consistent practice.

Even very young children can develop extremely complex eye-hand coordinations. Wolfgang Mozart (possibly the greatest child musical prodigy the world has ever known) was said to have been an accomplished pianist at the age of 5, and the exquisitely sophisticated eye-hand coordination necessary to win a world championship in tennis can be accomplished by 17-year-olds. But what happens to eye-hand coordination as people age? Daily observations of adults' motor skills suggest that these intricate perceptual and motor schemas that have been so painstakingly developed and maintained over many years begin to deteriorate. The 70-year-old golfer does not make the putts he did in his 30s. The 78-year-old embroidery expert's stitches are not as uniform and tiny as they once were. The 85-year-old finds buttoning a blouse, formerly accomplished without conscious thought, to be a challenging task that requires full attention and considerable energy. Age-related changes in performance are obvious, but how does aging affect the *learning* of motor skills? Does practice improve the eye-hand coordination of old adults as quickly as it does that of young adults? Is coordination compromised because of a deterioration of the underlying components of movements, such as strength and steadiness, or because the central nervous system functions of sensory integration and motor programming are impaired?

Because eye-hand coordination and motor skill practice have been studied by relatively few researchers, the information in this chapter is based on a much smaller number of studies than that provided in previous chapters. The number of studies of aging effects on tracking skills or finger

Aging and eye-hand coordination

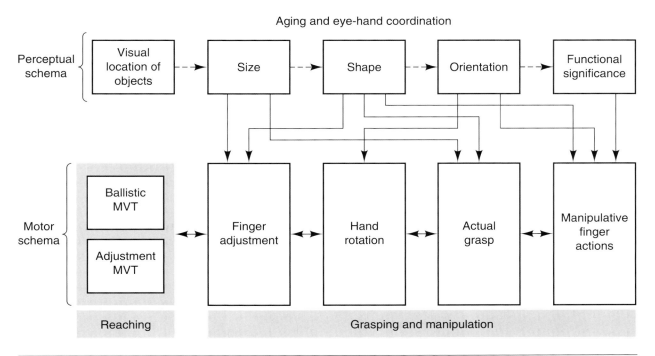

Figure 8.1 Perceptual and motor schema involved in eye-hand coordination: a variation of Arbib's (1981) model. MVT = movement

From "Aging and Eye-Hand Coordination" by H. Williams. In *Eye-Hand Coordination Across the Life Span* (p. 329) by C. Bard, M. Fleury, and L. Hays (Eds.), 1989, Columbia: University of South Carolina Press. Copyright 1989 by University of South Carolina Press. Reprinted by permission.

dexterity is small compared to the abundance of studies on changes in cardiovascular integrity and response speed. The problems of health, fitness, balance, and locomotion have a higher priority than the problems of coordination. Nevertheless, age-related changes in coordination are problems for the elderly. Writing, typing, and sorting papers are important to older adults who wish to continue their employment. The ability to turn the dials of radios and televisions, control a paint brush, or manipulate a camera is essential for some types of entertainment. And in the terminal years, the ability to dial a telephone, remove a jar lid, and grasp, carry, and place objects from pantry shelves into the refrigerator is necessary for independent living. To enlarge the data base available for this chapter, research of somewhat younger "old" subjects has also been included. In these cases, the relative youthfulness of the subjects is noted.

Psychologists, motor control experts, and ergonomists who study eye-hand coordination primarily use laboratory tasks that simulate the day to day physical actions that people use to conduct their business or to enjoy their leisure time. Motor coordination is so complex and difficult to understand that most researchers have used a strategy

of studying either very simple movements or of breaking complex skills into components and studying each component in isolation. Furthermore, to reduce variability, measure more accurately, and place less stress on older subjects, the movements studied have generally been small movements that operate through a small range of motion. One consequence of this research strategy is that many of these studies of coordination are analyses of movements that bear little resemblance to real-life physical tasks. A few researchers have taken a more global approach and studied functional skills. They have developed rating scales or timed tests of the ability to use eating utensils, button buttons, cut with scissors, and to accomplish other manipulative tasks; but generally, research information on coordination is meager and somewhat unsatisfactory from the perspective of really understanding age-related changes in coordination.

Categories of Coordination and Complex Movement

How does aging affect eye-hand coordination and other complex movements? To answer this, it is first necessary to understand the nature and types of coordinated movement and then to consider whether aging affects these movements differently. Although many taxonomies (i.e., classification systems) of movement have been proposed, the simple synthesis of several of them shown in Table 8.1 will serve for discussion in this chapter.

Discrete Movements

Discrete movements or skills appear to have a recognizable beginning and end. Real-life examples are striking a match and zipping a zipper. Discrete movements are unilateral when they are made with one arm or hand, as when raising an arm to vote or attract attention. Bilateral discrete movements are made with both arms simultaneously, as when raising the arms to surrender. One way of analyzing control and accuracy of discrete movements in the laboratory is by having subjects start with one or both hands on a home key and then make a reaching movement forward, sideways, or backward toward another target. Figure 8.2 is an example of a forward-backward paradigm.

The study of aging effects on discrete movements generally follows two lines: One is to measure the speed with which unilateral or bilateral discrete movements are initiated (reaction time)

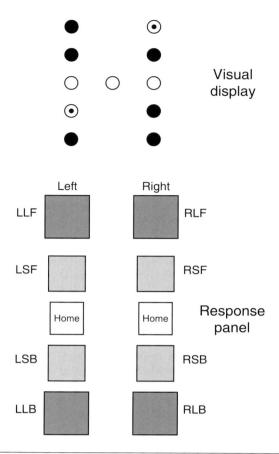

Figure 8.2 Schematic diagram of the visual display and response panel used to study the motor programming of side of body, movement extent, and movement direction in a reaction time paradigm. Dotted circles are the warning lights and open circles the home keys. LLF = left, long, forward; LSF = left, short, forward; LSB = left, short, backward; LLB = left, long, backward; RLF = right, long, forward; etc. This particular display calls for a short backward movement with the left hand while simultaneously making a long forward movement with the right hand.
From "Aging and the Restructuring of Precued Movements" by G.E. Stelmach, N.L. Goggin, and P.C. Amrhein, 1988, *Psychology and Aging,* **3**, p. 152. Copyright 1988 by the American Psychological Association. Reprinted by permission.

Table 8.1
Motor Skill Taxonomy

Discrete movements
 Unilateral
 Bilateral
 Repetitive
 Sequential
 Aiming

Continuous motor skills
 Tracking
 Handwriting

Multilimb skill
 Driving an automobile

Functional skills
 Fine-motor: card sorting, typing, using eating utensils, dialing a telephone, picking up coins, squeezing toothpaste, unwrapping a Band-Aid, zipping a garment

 Gross-motor: shoveling, mopping, sweeping, ironing, throwing

---

and carried out (movement time), and the other is to study the motor programming that precedes and accompanies the movement. When discrete movements are studied in reaction time paradigms, the focus is usually on how aging affects the cognitive stages of information processing that precede the movement. This type of research is discussed in considerable detail in chapter 7.

The second line of aging research on discrete movements is the study of the motor programming involved in the selection of movement parameters needed for the upcoming movement (e.g., side of body, extent, and direction). A reaction time paradigm is used in which a stimulus light panel, like that shown in Figure 8.2, informs the subject as to which movement should be made. To make any discrete movement, the individual must know which side of the body is to be moved (left or right), the extent to which it will move (a short or long movement), and the movement direction (forward, backward, sideways). By analyzing the length of time taken to react to a stimulus light when varying amounts of information about the movement are available before the response, investigators can estimate what movement parameters are being programmed.

When these movement parameters are known in advance, the movement can be preprogrammed before the stimulus. Just like a computer program that is loaded and ready to run at the press of a key, when the stimulus light is activated, the preprogrammed movement can be initiated immediately. If all of the parameters are not known in advance, some movements will have to be programmed *after* the stimulus to move has occurred. If a barrier or external force perturbs the movement so that it cannot be executed as programmed, or if the stimulus calls for a movement that was unexpected, the parameters have to be reprogrammed to execute a new movement.

Research results indicate that older people generally preprogram, program, and reprogram movements the same way that young people do, but they do so more slowly (Larish & Stelmach, 1982). Older adults may differ from young adults in one aspect of reprogramming, however. Amrhein, Stelmach, and Goggin (1991) found that older adults, unlike young adults who restructured all parameters equally well, can restructure their movement plan for a change in direction better than they can for a change in the arm to be used or when both the direction and the arm plans have to be reprogrammed.

Aiming Movements

A host of coordinated movements that are used every day require not only relatively fast movements but also accurate movements. One way to study accuracy is to analyze the ability of a person to make a discrete movement and hit a small target with the hand or with a stylus. In this type of study of aiming, accuracy is determined by the distance the subjects overshoot or undershoot the target.

A well-known law of movement control, Fitts' law specifies that the more difficult the movement to be made, the slower it is made. That is, movements to hit small targets that are far away from each other take longer to execute than movements to hit larger targets close to each other. An aiming movement is made more difficult by making the target smaller or by increasing the length of the movement (Figure 8.3). The reason is that when a task requires both speed and accuracy, the individual must make a choice. Thus the accuracy of speeded performance of older people can be compared to that of younger people by varying the size of the target or the distance between the targets or both.

Another way to study aging effects on discrete aiming movements is to study the nature of the movement itself, the kinematics of the movements made. Even when older adults appear to perform the same motor task at the same speed, they may be using a different movement pattern to accomplish the task. Many of the age-related changes that have been discussed in previous chapters (e.g., loss of strength, balance, and flexibility) may cause the elderly to move in ways that are subtly different from the movement of young people. *Kinematics* is the scientific description of movement, and kinematic methods include filming and

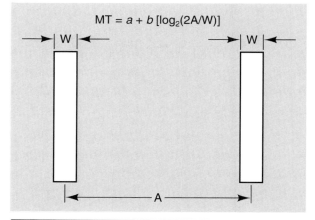

$$MT = a + b\,[\log_2(2A/W)]$$

Figure 8.3 The Fitts paradigm. The performer taps a stylus alternately between two targets of width W separated by a distance A. The formula $MT = a + b[\log_2(2A/W)]$ indicates that if the targets are made smaller (a decrease in W) or the distance is increased between the targets (an increase in A) or both, then the movement becomes slower. The subject must sacrifice speed because the accuracy demands are greater.

From *Motor Control and Learning: A Behavioral Emphasis* (2nd ed.) (p. 268) by R.A. Schmidt, 1988, Champaign, IL: Human Kinetics. Copyright 1988 by Richard A. Schmidt. Reprinted by permission.

videotaping the movement, recording changes in muscle activity (EMG) via electrodes, and measuring the changing angles of the joints through electrogoniometry. Kinematic studies of the elderly are sparse, because kinematic methods are tedious and time consuming. Nevertheless, the few studies that have been reported indicate that there are age differences in the kinematics of movements such as acceleration and velocity.

In an aiming task, in which the individual quickly moves the arm from one target to another, the normal movement pattern is comprised of three phases: an acceleration phase, a steady-state phase, and a deceleration or "homing-in" phase. Young subjects accelerate more rapidly but have a longer deceleration period than older subjects, even though the movement times of the entire task may not be different (Cooke, Brown, & Cunningham, 1989; Darling, Cooke, & Brown, 1989; Murrell & Entwisle, 1960; Warabi, Noda, & Kato, 1986). In another experiment in which subjects made long or short lateral movements on a digitizing tablet, older subjects produced smaller velocities, took longer to reach their peak velocity, and had a prolonged deceleration phase (see Figure 8.4, a and b; also Goggin & Stelmach, 1990). The error correction aspect of aiming may also be different in older adults (Warabi et al., 1986).

Another movement parameter that contributes to the control of aiming movements and in which young and old adults differ is the control of force. Older adults seem to have more difficulty in braking a movement than do younger adults, a difficulty which may be caused by a breakdown in the CNS-controlled reciprocal coordination of agonist and antagonist muscles (Vrtunski, Patterson, & Hill, 1984). For example, if the primary mover of an aiming movement is the biceps (agonist), the triceps (antagonist) may not be activated as quickly as is necessary to stop the movement on the target. The result of a breakdown in control of the force applied by opposing muscles is the jerky, uncoordinated movement sometimes seen in older adults.

The aiming task can be done either fast at the expense of accuracy or accurately at the expense of speed. The relationship of aging to the speed-accuracy trade-off in motor skills is discussed in more detail later in this chapter in "Compensatory Strategies for Losses of Coordination."

Continuous Movements

Continuous movements involve a series of component segments that are interconnected with no discernible break in motion and no obvious beginning or end. One component of the movement blends into the other without interruption. Examples of continuous movements in life activities are controlling the steering wheel of a car, writing, and skeet shooting or bird hunting. In all of these examples, continuous movement adjustments are made to control an implement and guide its path so that its position matches that of a moving target. In the case of driving a car, the wheel must be continuously adjusted so that the car stays in the correct lane between the center and side stripes

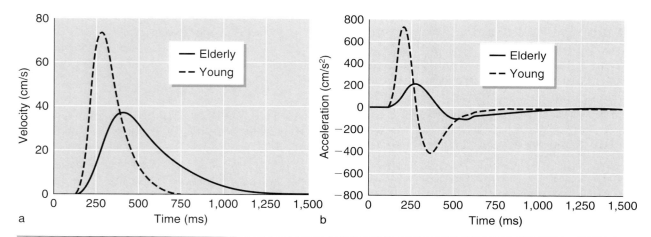

Figure 8.4   (a) Velocity and (b) acceleration profiles of young and older adults.
From "Age-Related Deficits in Cognitive-Motor Skills" by N.L. Goggin and G.E. Stelmach. In *Aging and Cognition: Mental Processes, Self Awareness and Interventions* (p. 146) by E.A. Lovelace (Ed.), 1990, New York: Elsevier Science Publishers. Copyright 1990 by Elsevier Science Publishers. Reprinted by permission.

of the road. In handwriting, a pencil or pen is moved horizontally and continuously adjusted to shape words while staying within the parallel lines on the paper. In hunting, the shooter follows the flight of a clay or real bird until he thinks there is no longer any error between the position of his gun sight and the extended flightpath of the bird. These continuous steering control and hunting types of movement have been studied in the laboratory by a class of tests called tracking tests. The continuous movements of handwriting have been analyzed in terms of direction, velocity, and acceleration.

Tracking

The rotary pursuit task has been a basic instrument of motor behavior and motor learning laboratories for more than 50 years. In first generation versions of this task, the subject, using a stylus, attempted to maintain contact with a small circular target that was revolving on a turntable. This old task can be visualized as trying to keep a pencil (the stylus) in contact with a nickel (the target) glued onto the edge of the turntable of an old phonograph. The faster the turntable goes, the more difficult it is to track the target and maintain contact with it. At low speeds, very little difference exists between the performance of young and old adults. But as the speed of the turntable increases, older persons become more and more inaccurate on this task compared to young persons (Gutman, 1965; Welford, 1958). Potvin, Syndulko, Tourtellotte, Lemmon, and Potvin (1980) reported that the decline in function from 20 to 80 years of age was 15% to 17%.

Rotary pursuit performances of young and old adults over several trials are shown in Figure 8.5 (Wright & Payne, 1985). Several age differences pertaining to overall performance and learning are apparent. First, the young adults were much better than the older adults at keeping the stylus on the target. In the learning paradigm that provided a 40-s rest interval between each trial, the young subjects reached overall levels of tracking ability that were almost twice those of the older adults. Second, when the 40-s rest interval was provided, the young adults made much larger improvements immediately (Trials 1-5) than did the older subjects. Third, when the older adults used the more effective practice schedule (40-s rest), they exceeded the performance of younger subjects who used the less effective practice technique until

Trials 25 to 30, when the younger subjects caught up and no age differences remained.

Wright and Payne (1985) also used a mirror-tracking task in which mirror vision was used to track a small target as it moved clockwise through a narrow star-shaped pathway. The subjects mentally had to reverse the information in order to perform the task. Under these more difficult conditions, the young subjects were 2-1/2 times better than the older adults (Figure 8.6). In this study the young women were better than the young men at the task, but the gender effect was reversed in the older group. These results are typical for both age groups. Young women are generally better than young men at tasks of finger dexterity, but when gender differences in the old are present in physical performance tasks, many times the men are favored. One explanation may be that because fewer men than women survive to very old ages, the men who do survive may be better performers because they represent a select group for their cohort, whereas the larger percentage of surviving women are closer to the average of their cohort. Also, in this particular study, the old women were 4 years older on the average than the old men, so the gender effect was partially confounded by the age effect.

In another version of a tracking task, subjects used a steering wheel to "drive" a pen along a target line on a moving conveyer belt. If the target line emerged from beneath a shield, older (over age 30) persons had a much more difficult time tracking the line than younger subjects, because they had to react to unpredictable changes of the line's direction. But if the older subjects were able to preview the line, that is, to see the line in its entirety as it moved along the conveyer belt, they could almost match the young subjects' performances by looking ahead and predicting the change in line direction (see Figure 8.7; Welford, 1958). The age differences in this study were remarkable because these subjects only had to be over 30 years old to be classified as old; in the example in Figure 8.7, the "old" subject was 40 years old. Today investigators use microcomputers to present a moving target on the computer screen, and the subject tracks the moving target by controlling a cursor with a joystick.

Handwriting

Because handwriting is one of the most important functional continuous movements that all adults

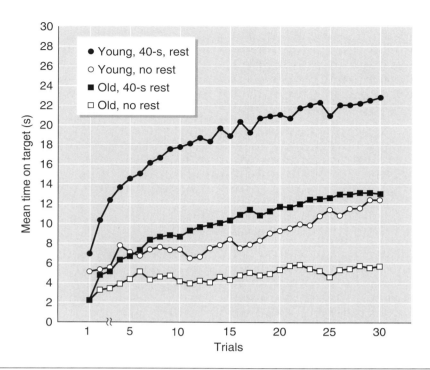

Figure 8.5 Performance in rotary tracking as a function of age, rest interval, and amount of practice.
From "Effects of Aging on Sex Differences in Psychomotor Reminiscence and Tracking Proficiency" by B.M. Wright and R.B. Payne, 1985, *Journal of Gerontology*, **40**, p. 182. Copyright 1985 by The Gerontological Society of America. Reprinted by permission.

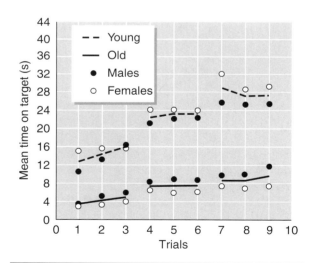

Figure 8.6 Performance in mirror tracking as a function of age and amount of practice.
From "Effects of Aging on Sex Differences in Psychomotor Reminiscence and Tracking Proficiency" by B.M. Wright and R.B. Payne, 1985, *Journal of Gerontology*, **40**, p. 182. Copyright 1985 by The Gerontological Society of America. Reprinted by permission.

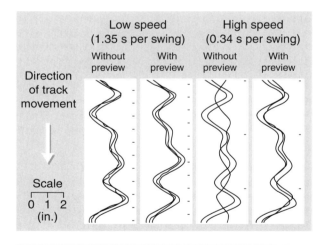

Figure 8.7 Records of the second and third tracking experiments performed by a 40-year-old subject. The track is indicated by the double lines, the course of the subject's pointer by the single line. The small marks on the right-hand margins of the record represent 1-s intervals.
From *Ageing and Human Skill* (p. 87) by A.T. Welford, 1958, Oxford: Oxford University Press. Copyright 1958 by Oxford University Press. Reprinted by permission.

must control, it should be discussed in greater detail. As early as the 1950s it was recognized that handwriting speed of adults, beginning in the middle to late 50s, slows with aging. In Birren and Botwinick's classic study of handwriting (1951), a moderately high curvilinear relationship (eta, where 1.00 = a perfect curvilinear relationship) between age and handwriting was found both for digits and for words, even after education was accounted for. In Figure 8.8, writing speed for both words and digits is relatively stable until the 60s, and then writing speed slows considerably. (These results once again reveal the increased effect of aging on complex tasks.) After age 60, the speed at which words can be written slows more than the speed at which digits can be written. Smith and Greene (1962) duplicated these results a few years later but also noted that the handwriting speed of their subjects who held jobs that required a substantial amount of daily writing was affected less than the speed of their subjects who did little daily writing. Similarly, no age differences were found in the handwriting speed of clerical workers whose jobs required extensive handwriting, compared to skilled laborers or executives who presumably wrote comparatively little (LaRiviere & Simonson, 1965). Also, the need to use visual feedback during writing is no greater in older individuals than in the young. Lovelace and Aikens (1990) found that adults over age 80 could write with their eyes shut as well as younger individuals.

Highly related to studies of handwriting speed are those that measure the time taken to copy numbers, letters, or symbols. Welford (1977) presented a classic case of age effects on number tracing (Figure 8.9). In this figure it is clear that people approximately 20 to 40 years old exhibit little difference in the time required to trace numbers. After age 40, however, the age groups separate. Each increasingly older group traces the numbers more slowly. Adults 70 to 79 years old traced substantially slower than the other groups. Of particular interest was the decreased copying speed, particularly in the older groups, when the numbers were reversed. In the reversed condition, the copying movements had to be made directly opposite to those normally used to make the number. Thus, the copying movements were no longer routine and highly over-practiced; rather, they had to be consciously controlled and reversed. The younger age groups adapted to this change very well, but the oldest groups slowed considerably.

Another measure of copying time independent of scanning time was calculated using the neuropsychological Digit-Symbol Substitution (DSS) test (Storandt, 1976). Explained in chapter 7, the DSS test requires that the subject find the appropriate symbol to be matched with a numeral and then write that symbol in a space below its matching numeral. In a variation of the DSS, Storandt (1976) was able to separate the amount of time taken to copy the symbols from the amount of time needed to search the numbers and symbols. She found that, in addition to a slower search time, older adults were slower in copying the numbers. However, the DSS has been shown recently to be primarily a

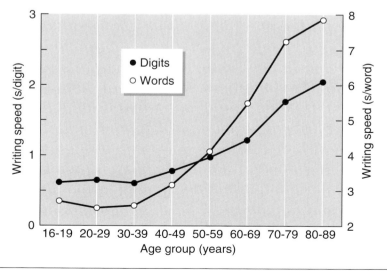

Figure 8.8　Writing speed for different age groups.
Data from Birren and Botwinick (1951, p. 246).

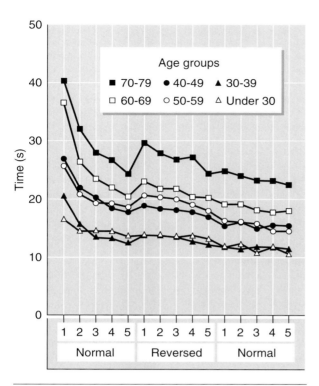

Figure 8.9   Figure-tracing times.
From "Motor Performance" by A.T. Welford. In *Handbook of the Psychology of Aging* (p. 460) by J.E. Birren and K.W. Schaie (Eds.), 1977, New York: Van Nostrand Reinhold. Copyright 1977 by Van Nostrand Reinhold. Reprinted by permission.

measure of perceptual comparison time, and although older adults have a slower copying time than younger adults, it is not the copy time but the perceptual processing that is appreciably slower (Salthouse, 1992; see Figure 7.19, on page 209).

Multilimb Coordination

One of the questions about the effects of aging on the control of movement is whether hand preference may be attenuated in older adults. Children gradually develop a preferred hand use during their early growth and development, so it is reasonable to speculate that as people age they may become somewhat more ambidextrous. To the contrary, however, a few researchers have reported that the prevalence of right-handedness, or dextrality, is greater in older age groups than in young age groups (Annett, 1973; Fleminger, Dalton, & Standage, 1977). One explanation for increased numbers of right-handed older subjects was a shift toward the preferred use of the right hand. Other explanations seem equally plausible,

however. For instance, older people may be more reluctant to admit that they have no hand preference. Also, in the early part of this century, when present septuagenarians and octogenarians were children, neither parents nor school officials were as tolerant of children who demonstrated a preference in writing or using tools with the left hand. Consequently, many subjects over age 60 have a left-hand preference but do not exercise it.

Even though rational social explanations can be made to explain the presence of more right-handed older adults than young adults, a physiological argument can also be made that differential aging of the two cerebral hemispheres causes some left-handed people to become right-handed in their later years. That is, the motor coordination of the two hands may not deteriorate at the same rate. Also, interlimb coordination may decline more quickly than unilateral coordination. The ability to coordinate the two hands may be lost more quickly than the ability to control one hand in an eye-hand coordination test. On visuospatial tests controlled by the right hemisphere, performance declines more rapidly in abilities such as spatial manipulation and arithmetic function than in functions such as speech that are controlled by the left hemisphere (McFie, 1975). Either left-hemisphere controlling mechanisms age more slowly, or they are learned earlier, practiced more, and so are harder to disrupt.

Weller and Latimer-Sayer (1985) found that although both right- and left-hand coordination deteriorate with increasing age, right-hand control is maintained better on first exposure to new manual tasks. Some evidence suggests that there is more neurological redundancy in the left-hemisphere, which controls the right hand, than in the right hemisphere (Lassak, 1954); therefore, the left hemisphere can resist aging effects longer.

Also, older subjects improved more with practice of the left hand than younger subjects, implying that the left-hand skill had deteriorated more and therefore had more room for improvement.

Complex Motor Actions in the Laboratory

Bimanual coordination is the term used to describe the integration of control mechanisms of the two hands during tasks in which the hands work together to complete the task. Bimanual tasks can require discrete movements, as in lifting a box with both hands and placing it on a shelf, or continuous movements such as knitting, dealing cards, or playing the piano. These tasks all share the requirement that the two hands and arms must operate together, coordinating their movements so that the goals of the task are achieved. But life tasks such as knitting or playing the piano are very complex and difficult to analyze, and so more quantifiable and controllable laboratory tasks have been devised to study the effects of aging on bimanual coordination. Examples of such tasks are bimanual tracking, a pinboard task, interfinger grasping and manipulation, and a bimanual reaction and movement time paradigm in which the movements of both hands must be initiated simultaneously and terminated together.

Pacaud and Welford (1989) used a bimanual version of a tracking paradigm to study the two-hand coordination of adults. The subjects (French railroad workers) traced a design by manipulating two controls: One direction of the tracking device was controlled with one hand and the other direction was controlled with the other hand. Bimanual control, measured by the time-on-target in this particular test, was particularly difficult and the older subjects' performances on this task were affected more than their performances on any of the other sensory-motor tasks used in this study (i.e., a paced aiming task and several types of choice reaction time tests). Older subjects were less accurate at keeping within the tolerance limits set for the task, and they tended to maintain their speed of tracking at the expense of accuracy. In tracking, therefore, these older subjects did not trade off speed for accuracy, although as discussed in chapter 7, older adults generally trade off speed for increased accuracy in reaction time and speeded movement tasks. Thus the findings of Pacaud and Welford (1989) with regard to tracking were the reverse of what has been found in speeded movement contexts (Salthouse, 1979; Welford, 1977).

The grooved pegboard test has been used to study eye-hand coordination (Ruff & Parker, 1993). In this task subjects put small pegs with ridges on the side into holes that have matching grooves. The pegboard is a 5- by 5-inch surface with a 5 row by 5 column array of slotted holes, each angled at various directions. Subjects start by working from left to right with the right hand and insert the pegs as quickly as possible, picking up one at a time. The score is the amount of time taken to insert 25 pegs. Figure 8.10 shows the results from 179 men and women using their dominant hand. These results provide evidence for a

clear aging effect on this laboratory test of eye-hand coordination. Note that individual differences (standard deviations) are greater in the oldest two groups and that gender differences are not present in the oldest group.

Older adults (80 years old) have also been shown to be slower (25% to 27% slower) than 20-year-olds in coordinating finger grasping and placing and in interfinger manipulation (14% to 23% slower; Potvin et al., 1980). In other types of laboratory tests, the coordination of older adults is no less effective than younger adults. For example, coordination of lateral reach and tapping were not slowed in the older adults studied by Potvin et al. (1980). Part of the discrepancy among study results may be due to the fact that these types of tasks are difficult for older adults to learn (Welford, 1985), and different results may come from participants who have different levels of learning experience with each task.

Another way to analyze bimanual coordination is to measure the time required to initiate and terminate movements of both hands simultaneously in a discrete movement, bimanual reaction time task. One such task, described previously, is shown in Figure 8.2 (page 218). If subjects place each index finger on a home key and then, with each hand, initiate a response to a target key that is displaced a specified distance from the home keys, a bilateral reaction time is obtained for each hand. If both hands leave the home keys at the same time, then it is assumed that they have been programmed together as one unit of movement. If the two hands land simultaneously on their respective targets, then subjects have controlled the

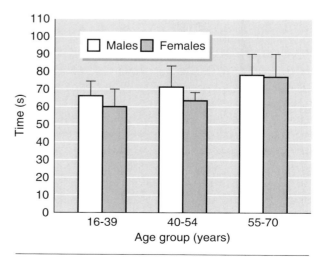

Figure 8.10 Grooved pegboard performance.
Data from Ruff and Parker (1993, p. 1226).

execution of the two arms' movements as one movement. By measuring the reaction and movement time of both hands, the degree of bimanual coordination between the two hands can be determined. When young people are asked to use both hands to leave a home key and contact a target key, they tend to "yoke" the hands together. That is, they program the two hands together into one movement. If the movements are asymmetrical (one hand has to move 6 inches while the other hand moves 18 inches), they still yoke the movements together even though the hand that only has to move 6 inches theoretically could arrive much sooner on its target than the hand that has to travel 18 inches. However, the hands tend to compensate. The hand that has to move a short distance "waits" for the hand that travels the longer distance, so that they arrive on the two targets almost simultaneously, even though the subjects have not been instructed to do so.

What happens with this particular bimanual coordination pattern with increased age? Do older people maintain this coordination, or do the hand movements decouple? Do older people just become slower overall in reaction time and movement time but maintain the same pattern of movement initiation and termination, or do they program their hands independently?

The answer is not yet completely clear. In one study, older subjects (aged 67-75) did not initiate bilateral hand movements as simultaneously as younger subjects (aged 21-25), and they were less able to compensate for this movement asynchrony to terminate the two movements together (Stelmach, Amrhein, & Goggin, 1988). The researchers suggested that as people age, they prepare short movements less well than they prepare long movements, whereas young people prepare long and short movements in the same way. In another study, however, the bimanual coordination of some healthy older adults was not different from that of younger subjects. When groups averaging 19.7, 66.5, and 78.1 years of age were compared in their ability to perform rapid aiming movements of both hands simultaneously to two targets, no age differences were observed (Rothstein, Larish, Petruzzello, Crews, & Naham, 1989). The older groups moved more slowly, but they initiated and terminated the simultaneous movements in the same pattern as the younger group.

Functional Movements

Much of the discussion of neuromuscular coordination to this point has focused on results from laboratory tests. Even though these tests are useful in elucidating mechanisms of control, it is sometimes difficult to see how the findings from such tests could be applied to everyday function. For this reason, many clinical researchers have created tests that utilize functional movements. Though these tests are not as quantifiable as laboratory tests, they have the advantage of being immediately applicable.

Many daily tasks that require coordinating two or more movements at once are so well learned and practiced that they are controlled subconsciously. These tasks include clerical typing, cutting with a knife, using a fork, dialing a telephone, picking up coins, inserting a coin into a vending machine slot, squeezing toothpaste and placing it on a toothbrush, unwrapping a Band-Aid, and zipping a skirt or slacks. Other functions that may be more recreational, such as dealing cards, knitting, crocheting, or playing the piano, also require complex coordination but are carried out at an almost subconscious level. Yet, aging presents some difficulties in the coordination of these tasks for some individuals.

About 13% of a sample of adults older than age 70 had difficulty with several coordination tasks, such as pulling out and inserting a key into a lock, unscrewing and screwing an electric light bulb, and pouring water from a jug to a glass (Aniansson, Rundgren, & Sperling, 1980). Of those who had difficulty, many also had poorer health and inadequate muscular strength (Sperling, 1980).

Potvin et al. (1980) developed some laboratory tests that simulated both functional tasks performed on a daily basis and components of more complex tasks. They measured 61 subjects ranging in age from 20 to 80 years. The top portion of Table 8.2 shows that the decline in the ability to coordinate the two hands in several tasks of daily living increases from a low of 21% in the manipulation of safety pins to a high of 43% in cutting with a knife. In the coordination tests shown in the bottom portion of the table, the decline was least (14%) in the ability to perform interfinger manipulations (rotations/10 s) and greatest (27%) in finger grasping and placing with the right hand. Thus, the findings of the functional and laboratory tests were compatible.

Throwing

The act of throwing an object, such as a ball, rock, or stick, is one category of coordinated movement,

Table 8.2
Reliability and Decline in Function in Coordination and Functional Tasks

Test name[a]	Reliability coefficient (*r*)	Decline in function from age 20 to 80 years (%)
Rising from chair with support	.55	31
Putting on shirt	.63	40
Managing large button	.65	27
Managing small button	.70	22
Manipulating safety pins	.47	21
Zipping garment	.54	34
Tying bow	.66	24
Large peg rotation	.78	27
Speed of handwriting	.84	30
Cutting with knife	.62	43

Coordination tests	Units of measure	*r*	Decline (%)
Finger grasping, placing R[b]	no. pegs/30 s	.88	27
Finger grasping, placing L	no. pegs/30 s	.80	25
Interfinger manipulation R	rotations/10 s	.84	23
Interfinger manipulation L	rotations/10 s	.70	14
Lateral finger reach, tapping R	bits/s	.64	—
Lateral finger reach, tapping L	bits/s	.56	—
Random arm tracking	degrees · s/s	.51	17
Progressive arm tracking R	radians/s	.84	15
Progressive arm tracking L	radians/s	.78	15

[a]For all tests, the measure is tasks completed in 100 s.
[b]R denotes right body side; L denotes left body side.
Note. From "Human Neurologic Function and the Aging Process" by A.R. Potvin et al., 1980, *Journal of the American Geriatrics Society,* **28**, p. 5. Copyright 1980 by Williams & Wilkins. Adapted by permission.

but it is rarely considered when studying the coordination of older adults. In our society, because we no longer use spears or rocks to provide the evening meal, throwing is a movement that occurs almost exclusively in sports. The majority of post-30-year-old adults abandon sports that require throwing, such as baseball, football, and javelin and discus throwing, in favor of golf, fishing, and bowling. A small percentage of older adults do continue playing tennis and badminton, which require a throwing-type motion to serve. Nevertheless, the number of older adults who continue with activities that require throwing is very small indeed. Consequently, studying the effects of aging on throwing has not been an area of great interest. Yet, when the throwing motion of older adults who remain relatively active is studied, age-related changes are seen.

Throwing motion has been carefully studied by film analyses of developing children, and the movement sequences necessary to produce a mechanically efficient throw have been placed into six categories (Roberton, 1977) that have been validated by many other researchers. Children develop and learn the proper movement sequences as they grow and practice throwing, progressing from the least effective category toward the most effective category. The movement sequence categories, therefore, can be used to classify a thrower's level of coordination. Such categorization has been done almost exclusively with children, primarily to determine their developmental progress toward a mature, mechanically efficient throwing pattern. Haywood, Williams, and VanSant (1991), however, wondered whether the throwing patterns of older adults could be categorized using the same movement sequences.

Do older adults throw using the same movement sequences, only with less amplitude and velocity, or do they use different movement sequences? Clearly, they throw with less velocity, and they do not rotate the trunk fully about the vertical axis (Reifsteck, 1982), but many of them include some qualitatively different movement sequences in the throwing pattern. Table 8.3 shows the movement sequences of the backswing used by older adults. Almost half of the older adults studied revealed a qualitatively different sequence of movements in the backswing preparatory to the overarm throw than is usually seen in mechanically efficient young throwers. (These differences are shown as Level 2.5 and Level 3.5 in Table 8.3.) Several factors probably contribute to the qualitatively different movements of the throwing pattern of the older adults. First, loss of flexibility in the shoulder girdle limits lateral rotation of the humerus (upper-arm bone). Second, pain, or fear of pain, probably prevents older adults from pushing their joints to the limit during a ballistic task such as overarm throwing. Third, the desire to protect against injury or postthrowing soreness may be a strong motivator to constrain or change the movement sequences.

These analyses suggest that qualitative changes occur with age in the overarm throw, but two other factors should be kept in mind. The older people analyzed in the Haywood et al. (1991) study were volunteers in a physical activity program, so they were more active than many older people who do not exercise at all. The overarm throw of many very sedentary older adults could not even be tested because of the risk of injury. Conversely, some older adults continue playing sports such as badminton and tennis, in which they execute the overarm throwing motion, several times a week. Although the throwing motion of these athletic individuals has not been cinematographically analyzed, it is highly probable that their movement pattern would reveal quantitative losses in range of motion and velocity but not qualitative differences in the categories of movement sequences. Losses in throwing ability, however, cause very few elderly individuals much concern. The functional movement of throwing is one of the least necessary coordinated motor skills that old adults need to maintain, but driving an automobile is perhaps one of the most important.

Automobile Driving

Driving an automobile is a psychomotor skill that is learned by almost all adults in the United States and executed on a daily basis by a great many people throughout the world, especially in the United States, Canada, and western Europe. It is a skill that most adolescents passionately desire

---

Table 8.3
Modified Preparatory Backswing Sequence for the Overarm Throw for Force

Level 1   *No backswing.* Ball in the hand moves directly forward to release from the arm's original position.

Level 2   *Elbow and humeral flexion.* Ball moves away from the intended line of flight to a position behind or alongside the head by upward flexion of the humerus and elbow.

Level 2.5   *Humeral lateral rotation.* Ball moves away from the intended line of flight by lateral rotation of the humerus in a position of 90° abduction.

Level 3   *Circular, upward backswing.* Ball moves away from the intended line of flight to a position behind the head via a circular overhead movement with elbow extended or an oblique swing back or vertical lift from the hip.

Level 3.5   *Shortcut circular, downward backswing.* Ball moves away from the intended line of flight to a position behind the head via a circular down-and-back motion followed by elbow flexion before the ball comes in line with the shoulders to swing the ball up in a near-frontal plane. The forearm can be pronated, supinated, or in midposition.

Level 4   *Circular, downward backswing.* Ball moves away from the intended line of flight to a position behind the head via a circular down-and-back motion, carrying the hand below the waist and staying in a plane along or nearly along the intended line of flight.

From "Qualitative Assessment of the Backswing in Older Adult Throwing" by K.M. Haywood, K. Williams, and A. VanSant, 1991, *Research Quarterly for Exercise and Sport*, **62**, p. 341. Copyright 1991 by the American Alliance for Health, Physical Education, Recreation and Dance. Reprinted by permission.

to learn and that almost all aging adults dread to lose for the same reason—it affords independence, personal freedom, status, mobility, and self-esteem. Nevertheless, a time eventually arrives when the question has to be raised: Are the perceptual motor skills and judgment of this individual adequate to drive an automobile safely (Persson, 1993; Walser, 1991)? The question of safety is an important one, because it has been estimated that by the year 2020, more than 17% of the population will be over age 65 (Transportation Research Board, 1988).

Age Effects on Physical and Behavioral Attributes Necessary for Driving

Driving an automobile requires acceptable vision and eye-hand-foot coordination to execute the correct sequencing of accelerator, brake, and steering wheel. Vision is extremely important in driving (see Table 8.4). An estimated 90% of the information used in driving a car is visual (Kline et al., 1992). The visual functions important to driving (from the most to the least important) are dynamic acuity, saccadic fixation, acuity, size of the useful visual field, detection of motion in depth, and detection of angular motion (Henderson & Burg, 1974). Older adults do not fare as well as young people in laboratory tests of visual processing speed, dynamic vision, and visual search, and their performance is worse with dim illumination and in near vision (Kline et al., 1992).

Driving a vehicle is a psychomotor skill, because it requires perceptual acuity, vigilance, short- and long-term memory, and motor programming during the information processing that occurs while driving. Automobile driving also presents many situations in which decision making under stress is critical. The requirements for driving have been likened to those necessary for success in complex reaction time and tracking experiments. All of these functions—perceptual acuity, vigilance, memory, and motor programming—are affected by aging. Particularly important in driving is the ability to attend selectively to specific task-relevant stimuli. Selective attention, which is related to driving performance in any vehicle, whether automobile, bus, commercial truck, or airplane, deteriorates with aging. Yet for successful driving, attention must be allocated to different areas of a very complex visual field second by second. Thus, driving requires the ability to divide attention between the perceptual-motor

task of manipulating the controls of the vehicle and the active visual search for information in unpredictable locations. The ability to divide attention (Ponds, Brouwer, & van Wolffelaar, 1988) and visually search (Plude & Hoyer, 1985) is impaired in many adults over age 60.

Panek, Barrett, Sterns, and Alexander (1978) suggested that as people age they become more field dependent, which means they are less likely to detect signs and symbols in the "background" field-of-vision while driving. Old drivers tend to neglect some of the information from road signs, traffic lights, and traffic, particularly if it is overwhelming (McFarland, Tune, & Welford, 1964). It has been fairly well established that it is not a loss of muscular strength or simple reaction time that causes old people to have accidents, but rather the slowness with which they make decisions and their inability to rapidly discriminate relevant information from irrelevant information (Birren, 1974).

Differences in perceptual style, selective attention, and the time it takes to make complex decisions affect aging drivers in particular ways. A driver must scan the environment, retain in memory what was seen at the beginning of the scan, determine relevant information, and make a decision. Older drivers may take a long time to interpret traffic conditions. By the time they look one way and then determine what is happening in the other direction, the information from the first observation will no longer be valid. Because the decisions take longer, corrections also take longer. Older people are more easily distracted by irrelevant information, shifting their attention from one object in the visual field to another, thus making poor decisions. Moreover, their ability to estimate vehicle velocity becomes less efficient (Cremer, Snel, & Brouwer, 1990; Scialfa, Guzy, Leibowitz, Garvey, & Tyrrell, 1991).

Compensatory Changes in Behavior of Older Drivers

Considering all the age-related deficits that have been documented for attributes crucial to the driving process, it seems that older drivers in general must be involved in many more accidents than younger drivers. Exactly the opposite is true, however, for drivers under the age of 70. In terms of traffic fatalities, the driving record of adults between the ages of 40 and 65 is *the safest record*

Table 8.4
Age-Related Declines in Visual Functions That Relate to Driving Problems

Visual difficulties	Driving outcomes

Reading signs in time to turn
    Visual processing speed
    Dynamic vision
    Near vision
    Visual search
	Failing to heed signs

Self-report
    Difficulty judging one's own speed
    Surprised by other vehicles when merging
    Other vehicles appearing unexpectedly in
      peripheral vision
    Believe other vehicles are moving too quickly
Laboratory test results
    Shrinking of visual field
    Estimating velocity
    Visual search for peripheral targets
	Failing to yield right-of-way
	Failing to turn appropriately

Reduction of useful field of vision (UFOV)	Failing to respond to information from many different sources

Decline in
    Retinal illumination
    Acuity in low illumination
    Accommodation reserve
    Resistance to glare
	Difficulty seeing instrument panel at night
	
	Haze and sun-glare on windshield

Binocular field losses	Higher rate of accident

Note. Data from Kline et al. (1992, pp. P27-P34).

of any age. Senior drivers are the least likely citizens to be involved in traffic accidents, whereas teenage drivers are the most likely. Moreover, if the major automobile crash statistics are examined, the evidence is overwhelming that far more 20-year-old males are involved in traffic fatalities than either males or females over 60 years old. Figure 8.11 makes it clear that adults between the ages of 35 and 65 are involved in relatively few traffic fatalities. True, the incidence of traffic fatalities among those over age 80 increases, but it is still the same as or lower than the incidence of such accidents for males between ages 15 and 30. Furthermore, the probability of dying in a traffic accident is at least 10 times higher for 20-year-old men than for either males or females over age 50 (Figure 8.12; Evans, 1988). Conversely, the probability that death will occur from a traffic accident

is almost zero for persons over age 70. Twenty-year-olds are also involved in many more pedestrian fatalities, so older individuals between the ages of 50 and 70 apparently pose no more significant risk to the health and safety of pedestrians than drivers of other ages.

What is the explanation? If so many sensory-motor functions critical to driving are compromised with aging, why is the driving record of older adults so much better than that of young adults? A major reason that older drivers are involved in significantly fewer automobile accidents is that they drive substantially less than younger drivers. For example, male drivers over the age of 70 travel about 5,775 miles a year, compared to 19,251 miles a year for 35- to 39-year-old drivers (Evans, 1988). Thus, younger men drive distances that are more than three times those driven by older drivers every year. The driving fatalities

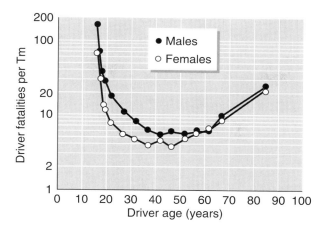

Figure 8.11 Driver fatalities and age. Data are fatalities (all motorized vehicles) per terameter (1 Tm = 621 million miles), 1983 only. Per unit of distance is calculated by dividing driver fatalities by the product of the number of drivers and the average distance traveled. Source: FARS, Federal Highway Administration, and Nationwide Personal Transportation Study. From "Older Driver Involvement in Fatal and Severe Traffic Crashes" by L. Evans, 1988, *Journal of Gerontology: Social Sciences*, **43**, p. S188. Copyright 1988 by The Gerontological Society of America. Reprinted by permission.

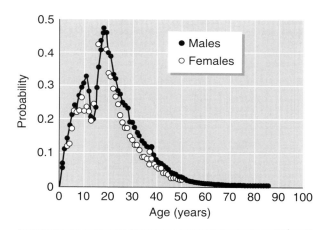

Figure 8.12 The probability of death due to a motor vehicle crash. Source: FARS 1983 through 1985 and National Center for Health Statistics data, 1984. From "Older Driver Involvement in Fatal and Severe Traffic Crashes" by L. Evans, 1988, *Journal of Gerontology: Social Sciences*, **43**, p. S190. Copyright 1988 by The Gerontological Society of America. Reprinted by permission.

shown in Figure 8.11 took into account the distance of travel, and yet younger drivers were involved in a greater number of traffic fatalities than were older adults. If the average distance driven is not taken into account, the number of driver fatalities of 20-year-olds is almost five times higher

than that of 70-year-olds. Another interesting phenomenon that is revealed when distance driven is considered is the comparison of gender and age differences in driving fatalities. Females between the ages of 15 and 18 have as many fatal accidents as males of the same age, but between the ages of 18 and 40, they have substantially fewer fatal accidents than males. At age 50 and older, no gender differences are observed.

Other reasons why older drivers have a better safety record than young males is that they take advantage of their experience and wisdom to take fewer risks when they drive, and they also trade off speed for accuracy to compensate for declining psychomotor abilities. (The speed-accuracy trade-off phenomenon that is exhibited by elderly persons is discussed in chapter 7.) Older individuals drive more slowly to compensate for slower reaction time and visual problems. They avoid driving at night so that their deficit in dark adaptation is not a factor. They avoid driving in bad weather, driving while intoxicated, and generally drive with more caution. (Greater caution is a general behavioral trait commonly associated with increasing age.) These compensatory strategies result in many older persons being safer drivers than many young people. The incorporation of these strategies is also why psychomotor measures, psychological tests, and personality tests alone cannot predict the probability of an individual being in an automobile accident (Barrett, Alexander, & Forbes, 1977).

An Emotional Debate: Should an Age Ceiling Be Established for Driving an Automobile?

Compensatory changes in driving behavior cannot compensate forever for the inevitable effects of aging; shown in Figure 8.11, the driving-related fatalities of adults over age 70 are much higher than all other age groups, except the youngest. At about age 85, older drivers' crash rates are exponentially higher. Also, these older adults are more likely to be involved in more than two vehicle accidents and are four times more likely to be injured or killed (Reuben, Silliman, & Traines, 1988). Medical problems increase and add to the visual and perceptual motor losses that are observed in older adults. In addition to the visual difficulties routinely observed among aging adults, many also experience glaucoma and cataracts. Other diseases, such as Parkinson's and osteoarthritis, restrict head and neck movements. Symptoms of epilepsy and other seizure disorders increase in the elderly. Many also suffer lapses of consciousness from cardiovascular disease or microstrokes; some cardiologists recommend against driving up to 7 months after a heart attack or ventricular arrhythmia. Lapses of consciousness can also occur from uncontrolled diabetes and narcolepsy. Many of the oldest old suffer from fainting spells or dizziness.

Recognizing the danger to the driving public of these medical problems, which are prevalent in the oldest age category, officials in some states have attempted to mandate an age ceiling above which individuals may not drive. Officials in other states have tried to develop and enforce laws requiring frequent physical and mental examinations for older individuals. Legal requirements such as these are extremely difficult to pass, however, because they evoke issues of age discrimination, lessened mobility, social isolation, and possible loss of job and income. Very few states even have laws requiring vision testing on a regular basis after a specific age. Almost none require physical examinations, yet Nelson, Sacks, and Chorba (1992) showed that if visual testing is mandated for renewal of a driver's license, the number of fatal crashes involving older drivers is significantly reduced. Underwood (1992) has recommended that physicians assume some responsibility for screening older citizens to assess their driving ability and for counseling them in terms of safety procedures. His recommendations, some of which could be implemented effectively if state legislative bodies would provide legal support, are shown in Table 8.5. He also suggests that physicians support and work with the families of extremely old adults who refuse to quit driving voluntarily to assist them in making the hard decision to take away the keys.

Some civic leaders, in an effort to avoid age discrimination laws, have recommended innovative changes in the driving environment, the adoption of technological aids for older drivers, and educational programs for those who may have difficulty passing a driving test. For example, the driving environment can be improved for the elderly by using larger highway signs, designing intersections for safer turns, providing better lighting for roads, painting wider stripes on the road shoulders, and using icons rather than text for road signs. Automobiles can be made more functional with pivoting seats, a brightly colored dashboard, clear, untinted windshields, and simplified car interiors. Some impressive technology that will be available in the future includes cars with collision warning devices, lane-keeping systems that tug gently at the wheel when the car drifts out of the lane, signals that advise the driver about upcoming turns or road hazards, and navigation systems that suggest a route to the destination and give the driver turn-by-turn instructions (Sheldrick, 1992). Until such advanced technology is on the market, older adults can be encouraged to drive larger cars, wear seatbelts, take annual night vision tests, and use certain compensatory driving behaviors, such as going around the block to avoid left turns and avoiding rush-hour traffic and freeways.

Learning Physical Skills

Can an old dog learn new tricks? Conventional wisdom has always implied that older adults (and old dogs, cats, and rats) cannot learn new skills as readily as younger adults can, but is this really true? Does the ability to learn physical and verbal skills decrease with aging?

In one of the earliest studies of age and practice effects, Murrell (1970) administered to three secretaries what may be the longest recorded laboratory practice period (over 20,000 trials), spaced over 4 months, to determine if age differences in reaction time could be eliminated. In the early stages of the experiment, the reaction times of the older subject (57 years old) were slower than the two young subjects (17 and 18 years old). It took the older secretary 300 trials before any improvement occurred, but by the end of the experiment the age deficits were completely eliminated. Remember, however, that in Figure 7.12 (page 201), Cerella's (1990) review of 10 more recent studies of the effects of practice on reaction latencies of old and young subjects clearly demonstrated that practice has only a limited effect on actually improving the processing time of older adults. However, the effects of practice on coordination are remarkable, and in cases where information-processing speed is involved, practice can completely negate the losses in processing speed.

Consider, for example, the skill of typing. Many excellent, well-practiced 60-year-old typists can type as fast as 20-year-old typists. They do so by reading farther ahead in the text than younger typists do so that they can anticipate the movements to be made, rather than reading a letter or word at a time and reacting to it as is done in

Table 8.5
Recommendations for Office-Based Assessment
of Risk of Motor Vehicle Injury in Older Drivers

Driving record
  Past crashes or near-crashes, violations, insurability, getting lost while driving, observations of family and friends
  Use of safety belts
  Driving habits
  Importance of continued driving to patient; availability of alternative methods of transportation if driving not advisable

Visual screening
  Evaluation of static visual acuity (near and distant), visual fields (by automated perimetry in selected cases), intraocular pressure measurement, examination for eyelid abnormalities limiting visual field

Auditory screening
  Otoscopic examination and use of audioscope for detection of clinically significant hearing loss

Cognitive screening
  Detailed history from patient and family member
  Systematic, objective testing for cognitive impairment (using instruments of known validity and reliability, such as Mini-Mental State Examination)

Psychological screening
  Assessment for signs and symptoms of depression or behavioral disorders

Assessment of functional status
  Basic activities of daily living: feeding, bathing, dressing, toileting, transferring, mobility, and continence
  Instrumental activities of daily living: use of transportation, shopping, housework, handling finances, using telephone, administering medications

Musculoskeletal screening
  Evaluation for signs of neuromuscular impairment, including testing of cervical mobility, gait, and balance

Screening for sleep disorders
  Inquire about sleep habits, assess for daytime somnolence or other evidence of sleep apnea

Alcohol screening
  History of present or past use and relationship to driving habits

Review of medication list
  Review use of drugs with possible sedative or cognitive effects (including over-the-counter medications)
  Assess for problems due to polypharmacy or drug interactions

Note. From "The Older Driver: Clinical Assessment and Injury Prevention" by M. Underwood 1992, *Archives of Internal Medicine,* **152**, p. 738. Copyright 1992, American Medical Association. Reprinted by permission.

reaction time experiments (Salthouse, 1984). In that study, Salthouse emphasized that researchers are rarely, perhaps never, able to simulate with laboratory practice protocols the vast amounts of practice that people have on daily functional movements or work-day skills such as typing. He calculated that an experienced typist would make as many keystrokes in 17 minutes of 60 words-per-minute typing on the job as he would in 5,000 choice reaction time trials in a research study. The older participants in Salthouse's (1984) study did indeed have slower reaction times than the young typists, but their speed of typing (the whole task) *was no slower* than that of the young typists. Experimental studies of motor learning never provide an amount of practice that remotely approaches the practice that experienced people receive on a daily basis on the job; therefore, investigators should be very cautious in interpreting practice effects data from laboratory learning experiments.

Although very few analyses have been made of age effects on working skills, even complex motor skills can be maintained well into the later years if these skills are practiced many, many times. Older middle-aged men (44-60 years) who had years of work experience on a task with little physical demand were able to perform as well as young experienced men (20-33 years) and better than young men who had little experience with the task (Murrell, Powesland, & Forsaith, 1962). Similarly, men who performed job skills that were similar to copying digits were able to maintain higher speeds of copying performance well into their 60s, whereas men who rarely needed copying skills in their jobs performed more slowly on a speeded copy test (LaRiviere & Simonson, 1965).

Other evidence that huge amounts of practice, or overpractice, can maintain motor coordination into old age comes from studies in which the same type of task is executed with different parts of the body or with movements that are either frequently or infrequently performed. For example, Stones and Kozma (1989) found that in a task that required speeded tapping with the hands or feet, age effects were evident in the hand-tapping task but not in the foot-tapping task. They concluded that because the feet are more active during the daily activities of living, this was an overpracticed movement and therefore was better preserved. Another example comes from a reaction time experiment in which RT was found to be faster when the response movement was arm flexion rather than arm extension (Rich, 1987). This observation is not easily explained. Though Rich hypothesized that arm flexion was faster than arm extension, because arm flexion occurs much more frequently throughout the day for most people, he offered no evidence in support of this.

One of the problems in studying motor skill learning in older adults is that learning is generally studied in laboratory experiments that are customarily, by design, unusual, so that subjects will not have practiced them before. Novelty, however, is more threatening to aged subjects, and thus they are likely to be more timid, cautious, and reserved in their early trials. Additional trials of practice bring older people closer to the performances of the young. Not only does practice on novel psychomotor tasks improve older adults' performance on the tasks themselves, but it also seems to generalize to task-related attributes. In two experiments, older adults who practiced playing video games not only improved their video game scores but also performed much better on a two-choice reaction time laboratory task (Clark, Lanphear, & Riddick, 1987; Dustman, Emmerson, Steinhaus,

Shearer, & Dustman, 1992). They improved in generalized processing ability, specifically, the time needed to select a response.

It is clear that both young and old adults can improve greatly with practice, but do older adults improve *more* than young adults with equivalent or less practice? Some argue that old adults begin a task at a level below that of young adults and thus have more room for improvement. The answers are mixed on this question. Both young and old adults improved with practice on the Digit-Symbol Substitution test, which is one of the performance subtests of the Wechsler Adult Intelligence Scale (Grant, Storandt, & Botwinick, 1978). Similarly, in a study of young and old men who practiced a complex reaction time task for 40 hours spaced over 2 to 4 weeks (Baron & Menich, 1985), and in another study of women who practiced sorting cards every day for 1 week (Falduto & Baron, 1986), both age groups improved substantially and neither group improved more than the other. Because the young subjects in both of these studies also improved, even extensive practice was unable to eliminate the age differences that were apparent at the beginning of the experiment. There was some evidence, however, that practice reduced the adverse effects of increasing the task complexity for the older women (Falduto & Baron, 1986). Conversely, Wright and Payne (1985) found that younger subjects improved more with practice on a pursuit rotor and mirror-tracking task. One of the effects of practice may be to improve within-subject consistency, thereby improving overall performance. Light, Reilly, Behrman, and Spirduso (1989) found that old subjects who practiced for 3 days making movements to short and long targets greatly improved their consistency of performance (Figure 8.13).

The nature of the task may influence the amount of learning that will occur. Older subjects learn simple skills relatively quickly so that, although initially they may not perform nearly as well as young subjects, the gap narrows rapidly with practice (Welford, 1985). Tasks that demand a continuous series of complex and varied movements, however, are more difficult for middle-aged and older people to learn (Welford, 1985). Age effects that differ with respect to the nature of the task can be seen in Figure 8.14, which shows the learning slopes of three different types of tasks. The higher the slope coefficient, the greater the relationship between the number of trials and the task performance (i.e., the greater the improvement seen with

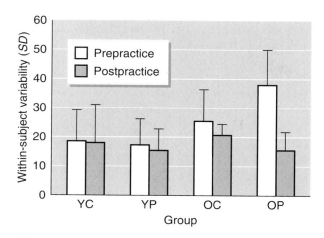

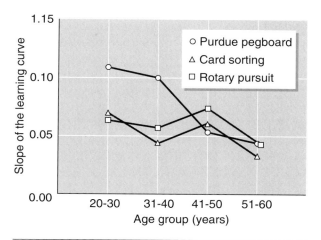

Figure 8.13 Effects of practice on within-subject consistency. Ordinate values are the group averages of each subject's standard deviation about her own mean. YC = young control group; YP = young practice group; OC = old control group; OP = old practice group. The YC and OC groups were tested at the beginning and end of the study, but did not practice. From Light, Reilly, Behrman, and Spirduso (1989).

Figure 8.14 Effects of aging on the performance of the Purdue pegboard, card sorting, and rotary pursuit tasks.
Reproduced with permission of publisher from: Salvendy, G. "Discrimination in performance assessments against the aged." *Perceptual and Motor Skills*, 1974, **39**, 1087-1099. © *Perceptual and Motor Skills*, 1974.

practice). This figure plots the learning slopes of three different tasks—the rotary pursuit, a card-sorting task, and the Purdue pegboard test (Salvendy, 1974). The rotary pursuit test requires the control of a continuous movement of one arm coordinated with finger grasping and manipulation to keep a stylus on a moving target. Sorting playing cards into four piles according to suit requires coordination of fingers, wrists, and arms. The Purdue pegboard task requires fine muscle manipulation to place small pegs into matching holes. Younger subjects learned more than the older subjects on the card sorting and rotary pursuit, but they learned a differentially greater amount than did the older subjects on the pegboard task.

Performance in motor skills can improve after a rest from practice, a phenomenon that has been recognized for many years. *Reminiscence* is defined as a gain in performance that occurs following a rest between Trials n and $n + 1$, in contrast to the gain resulting from practice alone. According to Hull's theory of learning (1943), when people practice a skill on repeated trials, their effort on each trial uses energy and builds up a type of resistance or inhibition to the performance that can be expressed as negative motivation. The more trials performed, the higher the negative motivation and the more the person is inclined to stop practicing. Rest periods, either a few seconds,

hours, or days, dissipate this resistance to practice, and many times performance is better after the rest period.

Reminiscence is demonstrated in Figures 8.5 and 8.6 (see page 222). In Figure 8.5, cumulative performance is much better when 40 s of rest separates each trial. In Figure 8.6, gains in performance occur after each block of three trials. The younger subjects represented in these two figures (from Wright & Payne, 1985) clearly reminisced more than the older subjects, an observation that has been made by several other researchers. Moreover, young women reminisced more in the mirror-tracking task (Figure 8.6) than young men, but older women and men reminisced equally. The explanation provided was based on the hormonal differences between pre- and postmenopausal women (Vogel, Broverman, & Klaiber, 1971).

Neural Plasticity: A Mechanism for Learning

It is clear from the evidence presented thus far that older adults cannot, by extensive practice, eliminate age differences in many coordinated motor performances. They can, nevertheless, improve their performances dramatically. The brain undergoes major morphological and biochemical changes with increased aging, but no matter how old, the brain possesses a remarkable capacity to adapt to new stimuli and new conditions. Both brain morphology and neurochemistry, which are most adaptable in youth and during maturation, maintain a substantial amount of plasticity in aging. Brain plasticity means that the brain has the capacity to make positive changes morphologically and functionally, either in repair or growth processes. For example, significant changes in brain neurotransmitter function have been associated with learned behaviors. The full range of models that have been proposed as explanations for brain plasticity are beyond the scope of this text, but a few examples of morphological changes that occur as a result of aging, practice, and physical activity can illustrate the mechanisms by which learning and improvement occur in the aging brain (see also Cerella, 1990).

Morphological Changes With Age

Morphological changes abound in the aging brain. Many neurons die with advancing age, and of those that survive, changes occur in the axons, dendrites, and cell bodies. Brain weight becomes lighter. One of the most striking changes that occurs is that the dendritic branches, the primary path by which neurons communicate with each other, thin and lose interneuronal contact. It is possible that the losses of dendrites and synaptic contacts are the source of the interruptions in neuronal networks described in chapter 7 as a likely basis for the generalized slowing phenomenon.

Morphological Changes With Practice

Contrary to the losses that occur in aging, morphological changes that represent new contacts and neurochemical changes that facilitate specific pathways are developed by repetitions (practice) of neuronal circuit activity. Many researchers have found that morphological changes in the number, cell structure, and density of neurons accompany physical activity in animals. Large differences in dendritic branching have been seen in young monkeys, rats, and mice that were provided opportunities to experiment and play with toys, compared with animals that were raised in confined cages and allowed few opportunities for physical experimentation and movement (Floeter & Greenough, 1979; Pysh & Weiss, 1979). In the brains of young rats that learned to perform a task with only one paw, the neuronal morphology of the cortical hemisphere that controlled the practiced paw was substantially different from the hemisphere that controlled the nonpracticed paw. Similar physical activity and practice-related morphological changes have also been observed in the brains of very old rats, so that neural mechanisms that support learning in young animals are also present in old animals.

Another example of experience-dependent plasticity in the anatomy of neurons is the plasticity that accompanies enriched physical activity in recovery of brain function. In these studies, unilateral and bilateral sensorimotor lesions were made in the brains of rats, and then the rats were allowed to recover in either a movement-enriched environment (a cage with toys and climbing apparatus) or a movement-impoverished environment (a standard, small holding cage). In these studies, the rats in the movement-enriched environments recovered function to higher levels than the rats in the movement-impoverished environments did (Gentile, Behesti, & Held, 1987; Held, Gordon, & Gentile, 1985).

Taken together, these studies support the hypothesis that the aged brain is capable of morphological and functional change and that chronic physical activity assists in maintaining certain types of brain function.

Attention

To execute a complex motor task, and certainly to learn it, an individual has to pay attention to it. Paying attention means consciously being aware of something. *Attention* is the mechanism by which the central nervous system prepares to process stimuli and determines what to process and to what depth it should be processed. Attention is like a flashlight beam: When the beam is focused on some object, the object becomes visible. The beam of conscious awareness—attention—can be diffused, so that nearby objects are also visible, or it can be intensely focused, so that the viewer is aware of only one object. Attention is limited by the amount of information that can be held in consciousness at a given time, therefore the individual directing the beam of attention has to be selective regarding which objects are illuminated. *Selective attention* is the filtering of information to focus only on information that is interesting or relevant to a goal. Because attention is limited, to "see other objects," the beam has to be moved from object to object. *Attention switching* occurs not only when one's focus moves from object to object, but also when attention is turned from objects in the external environment to objects or operations in memory. The ability to sustain attention in the search for expected short-term stimuli is called *vigilance*. In order to be vigilant, the perceiver must maintain attention on a specific goal. A star gazer watching for the appearance of an anticipated comet has to be vigilant in order not to miss the event.

The importance of attention can be seen in Figure 7.10 (page 197), where attention serves as a gateway between perception and processing operations. Although the ability to switch attention to task-relevant stimuli is critical in order to do the task, attention switching can be very disruptive of performance if attention is inadvertently switched from relevant to irrelevant stimuli. One of the most significant changes that occurs with aging in many people is that it becomes increasingly difficult for them to keep their attention fixed on a task. Events in their environment, intentions, or memories that are irrelevant to the task interject themselves into their thoughts. Controlled and purposeful inhibition of neurophysiological responses to irrelevant information is absolutely essential in controlling movement and learning. Thus, one of the functions of the attention process is the inhibition of unwanted neurological excitation. Infants, small children, and older adults have a difficult time attending only to important stimuli relevant to the task (Philips, Müeller, & Stelmach, 1989; Prinz, Dustman, & Emmerson, 1990). These age differences are depicted graphically in Figure 8.15.

Backman and Molander (1991) provide another good example in their study of golfers' putting capabilities. The older golfers were not able to perform as well when a meaningful noise, such as an informational broadcast, was played as background noise during the putting competition. The older golfers found themselves listening to the broadcast, whereas the younger golfers were more able to block the irrelevant stimuli from their thoughts and concentrate on their putting. The researchers suggested that the background noise increased the cognitive demands of the motor coordination task, placing high demands on memory and on the ability to attend selectively to the task.

In some fine motor skills, the performer must divide attention between the actions of the two hands, because each must perform a different action that is not easily synchronized with the other hand. In these dual tasks, the person must control each hand in a time-shared fashion. Many studies

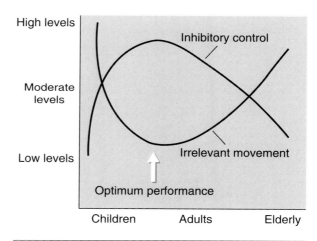

Figure 8.15   Proposed relationship between central nervous system inhibitory control and the initiation of irrelevant movements. Children and older adults exhibit less inhibitory control and make more irrelevant movements than young adults. The ordinate is only a gross scale of the levels of inhibitory control and the number of irrelevant movements made.

have been conducted on age differences in dual task performance, and in general, older adults have more difficulty dividing attention between two tasks than younger adults do (McDowd & Craik, 1988; McDowd, Vercruyssen, & Birren, 1991). A good example of the age effects seen in divided attention is the study by Talland (1962), the results of which are shown in Figure 8.16, a and b. Though this is an old study and many more sophisticated studies have been published since its appearance, it is one of the only studies of divided attention in which both tasks were manual tasks. Most tasks in divided attention studies are computer tasks of memory, visual or auditory vigilance, or perceptual searches.

In Talland's (1962) study, the subjects used tweezers in one hand to transfer small beads from one location to another while operating a manual counter with the other hand. The task required highly developed eye-hand coordination and divided attention. The single task conditions were to transfer red beads to a bowl, to transfer blue beads, which were interspersed among an equal number of yellow beads, to a bowl, and to activate a manual counter with the thumb of one hand as rapidly as possible. The dual task conditions were to transfer the red beads and operate the counter simultaneously (Rc) and to repeat this process for the blue beads (Bc). Thus attention to each task, which was performed by the two hands working independently, had to be divided. The age differences in this type of divided attention task are

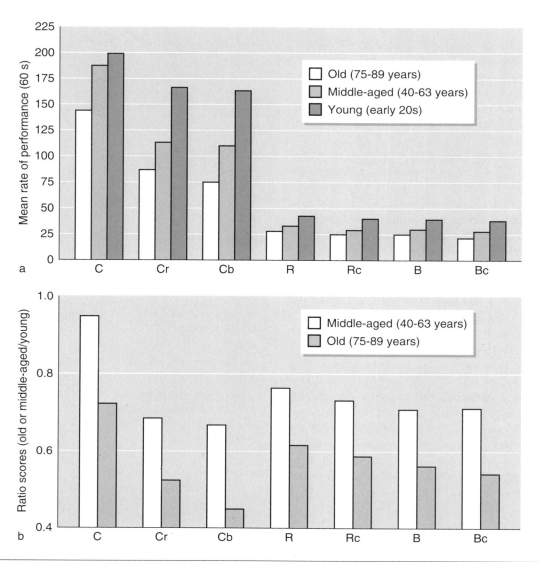

Figure 8.16   The difference between old and young performance on a fine motor skill and the effects of divided attention. The single task conditions: number of red beads transferred (R), number of blue beads transferred (B), and independent activation of a manual counter (C) with the thumb of one hand as rapidly as possible. Dual task conditions: number of red beads while activating counter simultaneously (Rc), number of blue beads while activating counter simultaneously (Bc), number of counts while moving red beads (Cr), number of counts while moving blue beads (Cb). (a) Mean rate of performance: The higher the bars, the better the performance. (b) Old and middle-aged subjects' scores as a ratio of the young subjects' scores: The closer the bars are to 1.0, the closer the performances of the middle-aged and old subjects to those of the young subjects. Data from Talland (1962, p. 72).

shown in Figure 8.16, a and b. In all conditions, the goal was to produce as many "counts" and to move as many beads as possible within 60 s. Figure 8.16a shows the mean rate of performance. The higher the bars, the better the performance. An age effect is clearly apparent for all tasks, whether done singly or in a dual task mode. Figure 8.16b shows the old and middle-aged subjects' scores as a ratio of the young subjects' scores. The closer

the bars are to 1.0, the closer the performances of the middle-aged and old subjects were to those of the young subjects. Both the middle-aged and old subjects were differentially worse at the dual task, more so on the counting task than on the bead transfer task. Because the bead transfer performances did not decline as much as the counting performance did, the subjects probably were attending more to the beads, especially when the blue beads had to be distinguished from among the yellow beads, than they were to the counting task.

Another example is shown in Figure 8.17. In this task, subjects tracked a pursuit rotor target with the right hand while responding in a reaction time paradigm to an intermittent auditory stimulus with the left hand. Doing two independent tasks at once was very distracting to the older subjects, and consequently they were able to stay on the target a much shorter time than the younger subjects were (McDowd, 1986). This finding is consistent with McDowd and Birren's (1990) suggestion that differential aging effects on divided attention are greater when the tasks are more complex.

Nevertheless, two studies did not find older adults to be any worse than younger adults on other types of divided attention tasks. Wickens, Braune, and Stokes (1987) tested young and old subjects (aged 20-65 years) on simultaneously performed pairs of multimodality Sternberg tasks, a mental arithmetic calculation task, and two types of tracking tasks, and found that the divided-attention effect was very detrimental to performance for both age groups, but not differentially problematic for the older group. Somberg and Salthouse (1982), using dual reaction time tasks, found that if they eliminated the age differences existing when each task was executed singly, they also eliminated the age effect on dual task performance.

However, these were the only two studies in which age differences in divided attention were not found. The older subjects of the Wickens et al. (1987) study were relatively young (mean age = 58 years), and the Somberg and Salthouse (1982) study employed a task that may not have taxed the divided attention capacity of either age group. Therefore, McDowd et al. (1991) concluded that aging does take a toll on the divided attention abilities required for dual task performance.

Age differences in dual task performance may be due to deficits in the central mechanisms of rapid decision making and attention switching or to an inability of older adults to combine two motor programs into a single program (Ponds et al., 1988). But age deficits may also be due merely to the fact that requiring divided attention in a task is just another way to make the task more complex, and as discussed in detail in chapter 7, the more complex a task, the greater the age differences. It is also entirely possible that older adults find it increasingly more difficult to deal with complex tasks in a coordinated, holistic manner and that the requirement of parallel processing of information in any task penalizes the older adult (McDowd et al., 1991).

Compensatory Strategies for Losses of Coordination

Although systematic practice can contribute to the maintenance of some types of motor function for a great many years, eventually efficiency and speed of performance decline in the latter part of life. As the passage of time blunts efficiency and reduces the speed of processing, individuals inevitably develop strategies to cope with these losses; thus, for many years the loss of function in a highly practiced, healthy individual is so slight it is unnoticeable. Such compensatory strategies include anticipation, simplification, and the speed-accuracy trade-off, which were discussed in chapter 7.

Anticipation

For some types of tasks, older people develop ways to anticipate movements that they will have to make, so that when the time comes, these movements can be made quickly and efficiently. They

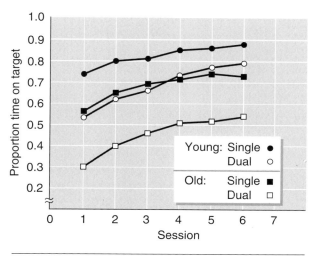

Figure 8.17 Mean time on target during tracking task for old and young adults in single- and dual-task conditions across practice sessions.
From "The Effects of Age and Extended Practice on Divided Attention Performance" by J.M. McDowd, 1986, *Journal of Gerontology*, **41**, p. 766. Copyright 1986 by The Gerontological Society of America. Reprinted by permission.

learn over a lifetime of experience that certain movements will be needed at certain times and knowing this, they can begin their movement planning sooner.

One of the best examples of the use of anticipation to accomplish a task with the same efficiency as young people is the anticipation older typists use to enable them to type as fast as younger typists. Older typists learn to preview letters and words farther ahead, while continuing to type, so that they can type almost as quickly as young typists (Salthouse, 1984). Figure 8.18 shows the correlation of reaction time with age in two studies. On the x axis of the figure are the conditions of preview that were provided for the typists. At the extreme left of the x axis, no preview at all was provided about the words to be typed. Under this condition, the typist had to type words as they were presented; therefore, the task was basically a pure reaction time task with a predictable stimulus. On the extreme right is the condition of normal typing, in which the typist can read far ahead of the words being typed and thus anticipate the words to be typed. The correlation between age

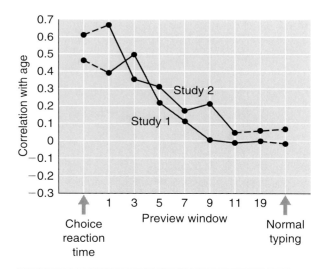

Figure 8.18 Correlation coefficients between interkey interval and typist age across preview window conditions and the choice reaction time and normal typing tasks. When no preview is allowed, the correlation between age and reaction time is moderately high, and the reaction is a straightforward choice reaction time. When typists can preview the material to be typed, the correlation between age and the reaction time drops to zero.

From "Effects of Age and Skill on Typing" by T.A. Salthouse, 1984, *Journal of Experimental Psychology: General*, **113**, p. 357. Copyright 1984 by the American Psychological Association. Reprinted by permission.

and preview condition decreases so that the correlation between age and typing speed is essentially zero under conditions of normal typing. These results are evidence that the opportunity to preview stimuli before needing to react to them is important to older adults. Though some subjects compensated for the ability to preview and others did not, under preview conditions, older adults generally compensated for their slower RT and MT with experience and full use of the preview opportunity. Thus, the correlation between age and typing speed vanished.

Another example of the beneficial effects of anticipation was the superior tracking performance of older subjects under preview conditions discussed previously in the chapter (Welford, 1958; see Figure 8.7 on page 222). In this task, older subjects had a hard time tracking a moving target that appeared very shortly before they were to begin tracking it. But when they could view the moving target before they had to begin tracking it, they performed much better. A real-world example would be retrieving a piece of luggage from a slowly revolving baggage claim at the airport. If a young man is blocked by the crowd from viewing any of the approaching luggage until the moment at which it is immediately in front of him, he can still quickly plan the movements necessary to lean out and retrieve his suitcase. But by the time an older man sees his luggage and begins planning the retrieval movement, the luggage has passed on by and he must wait until it comes around the baggage claim again. However, if the older man can see the luggage coming for several feet, he can plan his movements, be ready when the bag arrives, and successfully retrieve it from the baggage claim.

Simplification

An effective way to compensate for losses in coordination is to make simpler, less complicated movements, so that less complex movements have to be coordinated. When adults find their coordination decreasing, they begin to search for simpler, smaller, or slower movements that accomplish the same goals that were previously met by more complicated coordinated movements. Young adults jump off a low wall instead of bothering to descend by using the steps. Older adults may sit on a small stool to weed the garden, whereas young adults bend over and stand up many times while doing the same chore. A young person may open the refrigerator door with an elbow while holding the newspaper under an arm and a dish in both hands. The older adult places the newspaper and one plate on the table before opening the door. In all cases, the goal is accomplished, but older people find ways to involve fewer muscles and use movements that are less complex. This process is repeated in hundreds of ways during everyday activities, and the simplification process increases with increasing age. George Burns, the nonagenarian comedian who is famous not only for achieving advanced age but for continuing to be humorous about it, said that "you know you are old when, while leaning down to tie your shoelace you think, what else can I do while I'm down here?"

Speed-Accuracy Trade-Off

Discussed in chapter 7, it is well known that older people often trade speed for accuracy, because they generally choose to be more accurate than faster. Older people may use afferent feedback more than young people when monitoring their movements (Rabbitt & Rogers, 1965). By choosing to move slower, old people allow more time for visual and proprioceptive feedback to detect and correct errors, thus they compensate by using additional systems that provide information for the task. They opt for a closed-loop control strategy using feedback, rather than running the program in a rapid open-loop fashion, a strategy in which the entire movement is programmed in advance and executed as one unmodifiable movement (see Schmidt, 1988, for detailed information about closed- and open-loop motor control mechanisms). Thus, older people have a tendency to look at the target longer (Larish & Stelmach, 1982), and they may adopt fundamentally different strategies (Welford, 1958).

A good example of the use of different strategies was provided by Brown (1957). In this study, subjects faced two sheets of graph paper, one of which supported a small steel ball. Using a pointer, the subjects indicated the ball's position on the other sheet of paper. When they thought the plotted position was correct, the subjects pressed a button at the end of the pointer. If the pointer position was correct, the steel ball moved to a new position. Younger subjects adopted clearly different strategies than did older subjects to complete this task. The younger subjects swung the pointer into position very quickly and plotted the ball position almost immediately. If correct, this method was fast and

economical; however, it also produced many errors and required several practice attempts before success was achieved. The older subjects were much more cautious. They plotted along two dimensions, swinging the pointer first one way and then at right angles. When the pointer was in position, they often checked their accuracy by counting the number of grids before plotting the point.

Factors That Influence Coordination and Learning

Motivation

One hypothesis about learning and the aged is that older adults have little incentive to perform well on psychomotor tasks, and so they do not improve as much as young subjects do. Would a special incentive or reward make older subjects learn any faster than young subjects? The answer is probably no (Hertzog, Williams, & Walsh, 1976; Surburg, 1976). Grant et al. (1978) provided two groups of women (aged 19-27 and 64-76) with monetary rewards for fast performance on 20 trials of the Digit-Symbol Substitution test. Neither age group improved substantially more than the other (Figure 8.19), and although it *appears* that the older women improved more with monetary

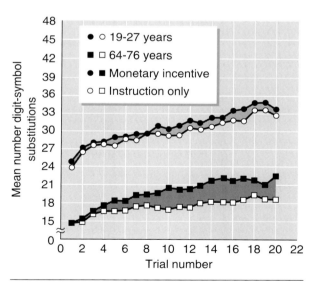

Figure 8.19 Digit-Symbol Substitution performance as a function of age, incentive, and number of practice trials.
From "Incentive and Practice in the Psychomotor Performance of the Elderly" by E. Grant, M. Storandt, and J. Botwinick, 1978, *Journal of Gerontology*, **33**, p. 414. Copyright 1978 by The Gerontological Society of America. Reprinted by permission.

incentive, this improvement was not statistically significant. The monetary incentive did not improve either age group's performance appreciably more than did practice alone. However, high motivation and appropriately provided reinforcement are important for older individuals to reach their optimum performance, and researchers or professional workers may have to attend more to the motivation levels of older adults than they do to those of younger adults in order to ensure that both are functioning at optimum levels.

Anxiety

Anxiety is a state in which high levels of arousal occur from concerns about performance and the outcome of performance. We know almost nothing about how aging affects performance anxiety. The results from the few studies of anxiety effects on cognitive performance are equivocal (Kausler, 1990). However, Lars Backman of Sweden (i.e., Molander & Backman, 1990) conducted an interesting series of studies of the interaction of age and anxiety on aiming and coordinating the hands and arms to sink a golf putt. These studies compared the putting performance of young and old adults (45- to 70-year-olds) under relaxed or highly competitive conditions. The older competitors performed as well as the younger competitors under the relaxed conditions but were not able to coordinate the putting stroke movement as well during competition. Thus, experience might maintain a highly complex skill throughout aging only under conditions that are relatively relaxed, nonthreatening, and low in risk. It was particularly noteworthy that the ability to perform a highly coordinated skill, such as putting, was negatively affected by the stress of competition in "old" subjects as young as 46 to 70 years.

In Summary

Coordination and skill deteriorate with aging. The effects of aging on functions that are more critical for survival—such as cardiovascular efficiency, balance, and locomotion—and the relationship of health to the quality of life rightly have attracted the attention of the National Institute on Aging and other foundations that support research on

aging; consequently, research on basic coordination has not been well supported financially. Although the nature of age deterioration in terms of the extent, rate, and types of skill most affected has not yet been characterized, a few tentative generalizations can be made about coordination in the elderly.

Older people preprogram, program, and reprogram discrete movements in the same way that younger people do, only more slowly. Older people choose accuracy over speed in simple aiming movements of the hands. They may move more slowly in order to sample proprioceptive and external feedback more often during the movement, rather than programming it in an open-loop fashion. In continuous movements, in which the goal is to maintain contact with a target, older people are as accurate as young people if the movement to be made is relatively slow and if they have a preview of the target.

Handwriting, copying of symbols and numbers, and tasks in which both hands must be coordinated are performed more slowly by older adults. Similarly, trying to do one task with one hand and another task with the other hand simultaneously is particularly difficult for older adults, probably because it requires more integration and processing by the central nervous system. Many functional types of movement, such as buttoning buttons, manipulating safety pins, cutting with a knife, and dialing the telephone are impaired in the elderly, and these deficits have particular significance because they affect the ability to live independently.

One eye-hand coordination task that is particularly significant to the elderly (just as it is to teenagers) is driving an automobile. Driving represents freedom, mobility, and autonomy. Older people have deficits in almost all the requirements for driving, but they also develop many compensatory behaviors. Drivers between the ages of 40 and 65 are among the safest on the road in terms of driving fatalities. With people older than 75, accident and injury statistics climb dramatically. Future efforts should ensure that adults who drive well may continue to drive, but those with poorer vision and driving skill should discontinue driving. These efforts should include developing technological aids, more comprehensive and individual performance screening, increased alternatives for transportation, and better counseling of those elderly who may be at risk for traffic accidents.

Even though large decrements are seen in many types of coordination and skills, practice can greatly attenuate these losses. Skilled typists, through almost daily practice, can maintain their abilities well into the 60s, typing as fast and efficiently as much younger colleagues. Because both younger and older adults improve with practice in motor tasks that require speed, it is unlikely that older adults can eliminate the age differences that are seen in the initial trials. The research is not definitive on this issue, but apparently the best that older adults can do is to maintain the same age difference throughout the practice trials. Age differences in learning depend partly on what type of task is to be learned. Age differences are greater in learning some tasks than in others. Some researchers have speculated that the reason older adults may not learn as fast as or faster than young adults is that they are not as motivated as young adults, but this hypothesis has not had much support. The important point is that older adults, no matter what their ages, make substantial improvements in physical skill with practice. Research on animals has shown that the brain remains extremely plastic even into the last third of life, and remarkable morphological changes occur in the structure and function of the brain as a result of practice.

One of the most significant changes that occurs with aging in many people is the increasing difficulty to keep attention focused on a task. Background noise is more difficult for older adults to ignore, and older adults also have difficulty dividing their attention between two tasks that must be carried out simultaneously. The more complex dual tasks become, the greater the age deficit in dividing attention.

Most older individuals maintain for most of their lives the coordinated skills necessary to function socially by practicing and by developing compensatory strategies for age-related losses of coordination. Some of these strategies involve anticipation, in which older adults preview or plan ahead for movements that young adults might successfully achieve by reacting spontaneously to them. Another strategy involves simplification, in which older adults may divide a task into components and execute it one part at a time. A third strategy involves trading off speed for accuracy.

References

Amrhein, P.C., Stelmach, G.E., & Goggin, N.L. (1991). Age differences in the maintenance and restructuring of movement preparation. *Psychology and Aging*, **6**, 451-466.

Aniansson, A., Rundgren, A., & Sperling, L. (1980). Evaluation of functional capacity in activities of daily living in 70-year-old men and women. *Scandinavian Journal of Rehabilitation Medicine*, **12**, 145-154.

Annett, M. (1973). Handedness in families. *Annals of Human Genetics*, **37**, 93-105.

Arbib, M. (1981). Perceptual structures and distributed motor control. In V. Brooks (Ed.), *The nervous system. II. Motor control* (pp. 1448-1480). Bethesda, MD: American Physiological Society.

Backman, L., & Molander, B. (1991). On the generalizability of the age-related decline in coping with high-arousal conditions in a precision sport: Replication and extension. *Journal of Gerontology: Psychological Sciences*, **46**, P79-P81.

Baron, A., & Menich, S.R. (1985). Reaction times of younger and older men: Effects of compound samples and a prechoice signal on delayed matching-to-sample performances. *Journal of the Experimental Analysis of Behavior*, **44**, 1-14.

Barrett, G.V., Alexander, R.A., & Forbes, B.J. (1977). Analysis of performance measurement and training requirements for decision making in emergency situations. *JSAS Catalog of Selected Documents in Psychology*, **7**, 126.

Birren, J.E. (1974). Translations in gerontology—From lab to life. *American Psychologist*, **29**, 808-815.

Birren, J.E., & Botwinick, J. (1951). The relation of writing speed to age and to the senile psychoses. *Journal of Consulting Psychology*, **15**, 243-249.

Brown, R.A. (1957). Age and "paced" work. *Occupational Psychology*, **31**, 11-20.

Cerella, J. (1990). Aging and information-processing rate. In J.E. Birrin & K.W. Schaie (Eds.), *Handbook of the psychology of aging* (3rd ed., pp. 201-221). New York: Academic Press.

Clark, J.E., Lanphear, A.K., & Riddick, C.C. (1987). The effects of videogame playing on the response selection processing of elderly adults. *Journal of Gerontology*, **42**, 82-85.

Cooke, J.D., Brown, S.H., & Cunningham, D.A. (1989). Kinematics of arm movements in elderly humans. *Neurobiology of Aging*, **10**, 159-165.

Cremer, R., Snel, J., & Brouwer, W.H. (1990). Age-related differences in timing position and velocity identification. *Accident Annals Preview*, **22**, 467-474.

Darling, W.G., Cooke, J.D., & Brown, S.H. (1989). Control of simple arm movements in elderly humans. *Neurobiology of Aging*, **10**, 149-157.

Dustman, R.E., Emmerson, R.Y., Steinhaus, L.A., Shearer, D.E., & Dustman, T.J. (1992). The effects of videogame playing on neurophysiological performance of elderly individuals. *Journal of Gerontology: Psychological Sciences*, **47**, P168-P171.

Evans, L. (1988). Older driver involvement in fatal and severe traffic crashes. *Journal of Gerontology: Social Sciences*, **43**, S186-S193.

Falduto, L.L., & Baron, A. (1986). Age-related effects of practice and task complexity on card sorting. *Journal of Gerontology*, **41**, 659-661.

Fleminger, J.J., Dalton, R., & Standage, K.F. (1977). Age as a factor in the handedness of adults. *Neuropsychologia*, **15**, 471-473.

Floeter, M., & Greenough, W.T. (1979). Cerebellar plasticity: Modification of Purkinje cell structure by differential rearing in monkeys. *Science*, **206**, 227-229.

Gentile, A., Behesti, Z., & Held, J.M. (1987). Environment vs. exercise effects on motor impairments following cortisol lesions in rats. *Behavior and Neural Biology*, **47**, 321-332.

Goggin, N.L., & Stelmach, G.E. (1990). Age-related deficits in cognitive-motor skills. In E.A. Lovelace (Ed.), *Aging and cognition: Mental processes, self awareness, and interventions* (pp. 135-155). New York: Elsevier Science.

Grant, E., Storandt, M., & Botwinick, J. (1978). Incentive and practice in the psychomotor performance of the elderly. *Journal of Gerontology*, **33**, 413-415.

Gutman, G.M. (1965). The effects of age and extraversion on pursuit rotor reminiscence. *Journal of Gerontology*, **20**, 346-350.

Haywood, K.M., Williams, K., & VanSant, A. (1991). Qualitative assessment of the backswing in older adult throwing. *Research Quarterly for Exercise and Sport*, **62**, 340-343.

Held, J., Gordon, J., & Gentile, A.M. (1985). Environmental influences on locomotor recovery following cortical lesions in rats. *Journal of Behavioral Neuroscience*, **99**, 678-690.

Henderson, R.L., & Burg, A. (1974). *Vision and audition in driving* (Report No. NTIS PB-238-278). Washington, DC: U.S. Department of Transportation.

Hertzog, C.K., Williams, M.V., & Walsh, D.A. (1976). The effect of practice on age differences in central perceptual processing. *Journal of Gerontology*, **31**, 428-433.

Hull, C.L. (1943). *Principles of behavior*. New York: Appleton-Century-Crofts.

Kausler, D.H. (1990). Motivation, human aging, and cognitive performance. In J.E. Birren & K.W. Schaie (Eds.), *Handbook of the psychology of aging* (3rd ed., pp. 171-182). New York: Academic Press.

Kline, D.W., Kline, T.J.B., Fozard, J.L., Kosnik, W., Schieber, F., & Sekuler, R. (1992). Vision, aging, and driving: The problems of older drivers. *Journal of Gerontology: Psychological Sciences*, **47**, P27-P34.

Larish, D.D., & Stelmach, G.E. (1982). Preprogramming, programming, and reprogramming of aimed hand movements as a function of age. *Journal of Motor Behavior*, **14**, 322-340.

LaRiviere, J.E., & Simonson, E. (1965). The effect of age and occupation on speed of writing. *Journal of Gerontology*, **20**, 415-416.

Lassak, A.M. (1954). *The pyramidal tract*. Springfield, IL: Charles C Thomas.

Light, K., Reilly, M., Behrman, A.L., & Spirduso, W. (1989). *Effects of aging and practice on reaction time and movement time*. Unpublished manuscript.

Lovelace, E.A., & Aikens, J.E. (1990). Vision, kinesthesis, and control of hand movement by young and old adults. *Perceptual and Motor Skills*, **70**, 1131-1137.

McDowd, J.M. (1986). The effects of age and extended practice on divided attention performance. *Journal of Gerontology*, **41**, 766-769.

McDowd, J.M., & Birren, J.E. (1990). Aging and attention processes. In J.E. Birren & K.W. Schaie (Eds.), *Handbook of the psychology of aging* (3rd ed., pp. 222-233). New York: Academic Press.

McDowd, J.M., & Craik, I.M. (1988). Effects of aging and task difficulty on divided attention performance. *Journal of Experimental Psychology: Human Perception and Performance*, **14**, 267-280.

McDowd, J., Vercruyssen, M., & Birren, J.E. (1991). Aging, divided attention, and dual task performance. In D.L. Damos (Ed.), *Multiple-task performance* (pp. 386-414). Washington, DC: Taylor & Francis.

McFarland, R.A., Tune, G.S., & Welford, A.T. (1964). On the driving of automobiles by older people. *Journal of Gerontology*, **19**, 190-197.

McFie, J. (1975). *Assessment of organic intellectual impairment*. London: Academic Press.

Molander, B., & Backman, L. (1990). Age differences in the effects of background noise on motor and memory performance in a precision sport. *Experimental Aging Research*, **16**, 55-60.

Murrell, F.H. (1970). The effect of extensive practice on age differences in reaction time. *Journal of Gerontology*, **25**, 268-274.

Murrell, K.F., & Entwisle, D.G. (1960). Age differences in movement pattern. *Nature*, **185**, 948-949.

Murrell, K.F.H., Powesland, P.F., & Forsaith, B. (1962). A study of pillar-drilling in relation to age. *Occupational Psychology*, **36**, 45-52.

Nelson, D.E., Sacks, J.J., & Chorba, T.L. (1992). Required vision testing for older drivers [Letter to the editor]. *New England Journal of Medicine*, **326**, 1784-1785.

Pacaud, S., & Welford, A.T. (1989). Performance in relation to age and educational level: A monumental research. *Experimental Aging Research*, **15**, 123-136.

Panek, P.E., Barrett, G.V., Sterns, H.L., & Alexander, R.A. (1978). Age differences in perceptual style, selective attention, and perceptual-motor reaction time. *Experimental Aging Research*, **4**, 377-387.

Persson, D. (1993). The elderly driver: Deciding when to stop. *The Gerontologist*, **33**, 88-91.

Philips, J.G., Müeller, F., & Stelmach, G.E. (1989). Movement disorders and the neural basis of motor control. In S.A. Wallace (Ed.), *Perspectives on the coordination of movement* (pp. 367-417). Amsterdam: North-Holland.

Plude, D.J., & Hoyer, W.J. (1985). Attention and performance: Identifying and localizing age deficits. In N. Charness (Ed.), *Aging and human performance* (pp. 47-99). Chichester, England: Wiley.

Ponds, R.W.H.M., Brouwer, W.H., & van Wolffelaar, P.C. (1988). Age differences in divided attention in a simulated driving task. *Journal of Gerontology: Psychological Sciences*, **43**, P151-P156.

Potvin, A.R., Syndulko, K., Tourtellotte, W.W., Lemmon, J.A., & Potvin, J.H. (1980). Human neurologic function and the aging process. *Journal of the American Geriatrics Society*, **28**, 1-9.

Prinz, P.N., Dustman, R.E., & Emmerson, R. (1990). Electro-physiology and aging. In J.E. Birren & K.W. Schaie (Eds.), *Handbook of the psychology of aging* (3rd ed., pp. 135-149). New York: Academic Press.

Pysh, J.J., & Weiss, G.M. (1979). Exercise during development induces an increase in Purkinje cell dendritic tree size. *Science*, **206**, 230-231.

Rabbitt, P.M.A., & Rogers, M. (1965). Age and choice between responses in a self-paced repetitive task. *Ergonomics*, **8**, 435-444.

Reifsteck, J. (1982). *Cinematographical analysis of over-arm throwing patterns of elderly men and women*. Unpublished master's thesis, Washington State University, Pullman, WA.

Reuben, D.B., Silliman, R.A., & Traines, M. (1988). The aging driver: Medicine, policy, and ethics. *Journal of the American Geriatrics Society*, **36**, 1135-1142.

Rich, N. (1987). The effects of age on unresisted and resisted fractionated reaction time. In J. Humphrey & J. Clark (Eds.), *Advances in motor development research* (Vol. 2, pp. 71-82). New York: AMS Press.

Roberton, M.A. (1977). Stability of stage categorizations across trials: Implications for the "stage-theory" of overarm throw development. *Journal of Human Movement Studies*, **3**, 49-59.

Rothstein, D., Larish, D., Petruzzello, S., Crews, D., & Naham, A. (1989). Bimanual coordination in the healthy old. *The Gerontologist*, **29**, 258-259A.

Ruff, R.M., & Parker, S.B. (1993). Gender- and age-specific changes in motor speed and eye-hand coordination in adults: Normative values for the finger tapping and grooved pegboard tests. *Perceptual and Motor Skills*, **76**, 1219-1230.

Salthouse, T.A. (1979). Adult age and the speed-accuracy trade-off. *Ergonomics*, **22**, 811-821.

Salthouse, T.A. (1984). Effects of age and skill on typing. *Journal of Experimental Psychology: General*, **113**, 345-371.

Salthouse, T.A. (1992). What do adult age differences in the digit-symbol substitution test reflect? *Journal of Gerontology: Psychological Sciences*, **47**, P121-P128.

Salvendy, G. (1974). Discrimination in performance assessments against the aged. *Perceptual and Motor Skills*, **39**, 1087-1099.

Schmidt, R.A. (1988). *Motor control and learning*. Champaign, IL: Human Kinetics.

Scialfa, C.T., Guzy, L.T., Leibowitz, H.W., Garvey, P.M., & Tyrrell, R.A. (1991). Age differences in estimating vehicle velocity. *Psychology and Aging*, **6**, 60-66.

Sheldrick, M.G. (1992). Technology for the elderly. *Electronic News*, **38**, 22.

Smith, K., & Greene, D. (1962). Scientific motion study and aging process in performance. *Ergonomics*, **5**, 155-164.

Somberg, L., & Salthouse, T.A. (1982). Divided attention abilities in young and old adults. *Journal of Experimental Psychology: Human Perception and Performance*, **8**, 651-653.

Sperling, L. (1980). Evaluation of upper extremity function in 70-year-old men and women. *Scandinavian Journal of Rehabilitation Medicine*, **12**, 139-144.

Stelmach, G.E., Amrhein, P.C., & Goggin, N.L. (1988). Age differences in bimanual coordination. *Journal of Gerontology: Psychological Sciences*, **43**, P18-P23.

Stelmach, G.E., Goggin, N.L., & Amrhein, P.C. (1988). Aging and the restructuring of precued movements. *Psychology and Aging*, **3**, 151-157.

Stones, M.J., & Kozma, A. (1989). Physical activity, age, and cognitive/motor performance. In M.L. Howe & C.J. Brainerd (Eds.), *Cognitive development in adulthood* (pp. 273-321). New York: Springer-Verlag.

Storandt, M. (1976). Speed and coding effects in relation to age and ability level. *Developmental Psychology*, **12**, 177-178.

Surburg, P.R. (1976). Aging and effect of physical-mental practice upon acquisition and retention of a motor skill. *Journal of Gerontology*, **31**, 64-67.

Talland, G.A. (1962). The effect of age on speed of simple manual skill. *Journal of Genetic Psychology*, **100**, 69-76.

Transportation Research Board. (1988). *Transportation in an aging society: Improving mobility and safety for older people* (Special Rep. 218, No. 1). Washington, DC: National Research Council.

Underwood, M. (1992). The older driver: Clinical assessment and injury prevention. *Archives of Internal Medicine*, **152**, 735-740.

Vogel, W., Broverman, D.M., & Klaiber, E.L. (1971). EEG responses in regularly menstruating women and in amenorrheic women treated with ovarian hormones. *Science*, **172**, 388-391.

Vrtunski, P.B., Patterson, M.B., & Hill, G.O. (1984). Factor analysis of choice reaction time in young and elderly subjects. *Perceptual and Motor Skills*, **59**, 659-676.

Walser, N. (1991). When to hang up the keys. *Harvard Health Letter*, **17**, 1-4.

Warabi, T., Noda, H., & Kato, T. (1986). Effect of aging on sensorimotor functions of eye and hand movements. *Experimental Neurology*, **92**, 686-697.

Welford, A.T. (1958). *Ageing and human skill*. Oxford: Oxford University Press.

Welford, A.T. (1977). Motor performance. In J.E. Birren & K.W. Schaie (Eds.), *Handbook of the psychology of aging* (pp. 450-496). New York: Van Nostrand Reinhold.

Welford, A.T. (1985). Practice effects in relation to age: A review and a theory. *Developmental Neuropsychology*, **1**, 173-190.

Weller, M.P.I., & Latimer-Sayer, D.T. (1985). Increasing right hand dominance with age on a motor skill task. *Psychological Medicine*, **15**, 867-872.

Wickens, C.D., Braune, R., & Stokes, A. (1987). Age differences in the speed and capacity of information processing: 1. A dual-task approach. *Psychology and Aging*, **2**, 70-78.

Williams, H. (1983). *Perceptual and motor development*. Englewood Cliffs, NJ: Prentice-Hall.

Williams, H. (1989). Aging and eye-hand coordination. In C. Bard, M. Fleury, & L. Hays (Eds.), *Eye-hand coordination across the life span* (pp. 327-357). Columbia: University of South Carolina Press.

Wright, B.M., & Payne, R.B. (1985). Effects of aging on sex differences in psychomotor reminiscence and tracking proficiency. *Journal of Gerontology*, **40**, 179-184.

PART IV

Physical-Psychosocial Relationships

Thinking clearly, staying in control of emotion, and feeling good about one's self are considerably easier when health is good and physical capabilities are seemingly unlimited.

*P*ersonal testimonies abound from people who have completed physical rehabilitation or aerobic exercise programs and who believe that their increased physical endurance and abilities have changed their mental outlook and capabilities. Yet what is the hard, scientific evidence? Can people really process information faster and better, keep their anxieties low, ward off depression and other emotional problems, and have an enhanced sense of well-being and life satisfaction if they are healthy and physically fit? This section addresses these questions.

CHAPTER 9

Health, Exercise, and Cognitive Function

A question of major importance to society as well as to individuals concerns the extent to which cognitive efficiency and speed of processing are associated with physical health throughout life. Everyone has experienced the difficulty of thinking clearly and focusing on cognitive problems when in poor health or in pain. Episodes of sickness, disease, and poor health become more frequent with increasing age, and occurrences of chronic disease and physical disability increase in the population as a whole. Indeed,

Fries and Crapo (1981) pointed out that one of the outcomes of aging is that increasingly smaller perturbations of the homeostatic condition of health increase the likelihood of dysfunction or even death.

Throughout history most people have assumed that a decrease in cognitive abilities is an inevitable consequence of growing old, especially in the very aged. In the last 20 or 30 years, however, many researchers in the field of aging have attempted to disassociate the aging process itself (primary aging) from the declines caused by pathological conditions (secondary aging). Diseases have in turn been linked to declines in cognitive function. How much of the age-related cognitive decline that is seen in older populations is due, not to primary aging of the brain, but to secondary aging that accompanies cerebrovascular disease or diabetes? To what extent is cognitive dysfunction related to asymptomatic yet low levels of physical fitness? If age-related cognitive decline could be prevented by improving individual health and physical fitness, health care costs, health insurance, and human suffering might be substantially reduced. Thus, understanding the types of cognitive decline that can be attributed to primary aging and those that can be ameliorated through prevention or postponement of secondary aging could lead to behavioral interventions that would enhance the quality of life for many elderly.

This chapter explores the concepts of health, fitness, and cognitive function and the barriers to understanding their interrelationships in the aging adult. Evidence will be provided that health and fitness are related to cognition, but the counterarguments to this thesis will also be presented. There have been some attempts to differentiate health and fitness relationships with specific aspects of cognition, such as memory and information-processing speed; but the study of these relationships is relatively new, and evidence relating health and fitness to *every* component of cognition (shown in Figure 9.1) is not available. Still, some researchers have proposed biological and psychosocial mechanisms by which health and fitness might influence cognition, both in terms of primary and secondary aging. The chapter concludes with a discussion of how health and fitness may affect cognitive function and the implications of this relationship for society.

The Concepts of Health, Fitness, and Cognitive Function

Because *health*, *fitness*, and *cognition* mean different things to different people, it is necessary to define them before discussing their interrelationships. These concepts, as they are used in this text, are shown in Figure 9.1.

Health

Health professionals define health as physical, psychological, and social well-being, but in gerontological studies of health and cognitive function, health is often defined as the absence of symptoms of disease, particularly those that are age-related, such as cardiovascular disease, adult onset diabetes, and arthritis. In some studies the definitions are further specified as *subjective health*, which is the perception of individuals of their own health (self-reports), and *objective health*, which is the physical examination medical report provided by a physician.

Fitness

Physical fitness includes two types of fitness, aerobic and anaerobic. Aerobic fitness, which is discussed in greater detail in chapter 4, is the maximum level of physical work of which an individual is capable. When directly assessed, the measure of physical work capacity used is $\dot{V}O_2max$, a measure of aerobic capacity reported in milliliters (ml) of oxygen consumption per kilogram (kg) of body mass per minute $(ml \cdot kg^{-1} \cdot min^{-1})$. It is this unit of measure, $\dot{V}O_2max$, that has been analyzed or estimated along with behavioral response speed measures. Because body composition changes with age (discussed in chapter 3), a more appropriate index would be $ml \cdot kg$ lean body $mass^{-1} \cdot min^{-1}$; however, few investigators have reported body density or percent body fat, so only conventional measures will be discussed in this chapter. Individuals who are physically fit have high $\dot{V}O_2max$ levels for their age group, and they can sustain physical work (walking, running, cycling, swimming) for 30 min or longer. In many of the studies discussed in this chapter, researchers estimated the aerobic capacity of their subjects from self-reports of the amount of aerobic-type physical activities in which they participated

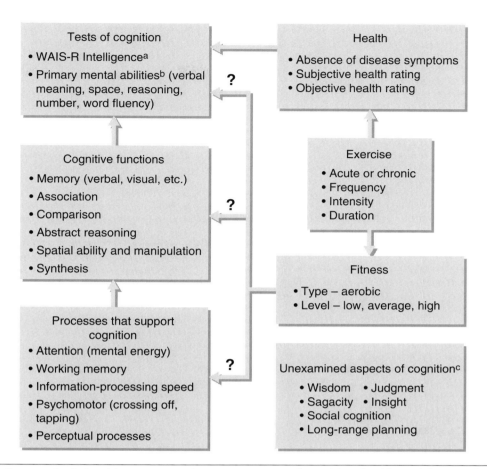

Figure 9.1   Proposed relationships among various components of cognition, health, and fitness. The following references refer only to the development of intelligence scales or proposed cognitive constructs, not to the putative relationship among components in the figure: [a]Wechsler (1981), [b]Thurstone and Thurstone (1949), [c]Salthouse (1991).

each week. Researchers have measured aerobic fitness directly in only a few studies. Anaerobic fitness, which was also discussed in chapter 4, is not a factor in the issue of fitness and cognition.

Cognition

Shown in Figure 9.1; cognition can be thought of in terms of functions of the brain, such as memory, association, comparison, abstract reasoning (verbal and quantitative), spatial ability and manipulation, and synthesis. The processes of cognition—attention (mental energy), working memory, information-processing speed, psychomotor ability, and perception—support the cognitive functions. Together, cognitive functions and processes interact to enable individuals to make decisions and behave intelligently. Intelligence tests have been developed with the hope of assessing the application of brain

functions to psychological and social function. Besides testing cognitive functions, intelligence tests also test verbal abilities, word fluency, arithmetic reasoning, and general information. However, as Salthouse (1991) points out, the tests used to assess cognition of adults rarely include functions such as wisdom, sagacity, judgment, insight, social cognition, and long-range planning.

Barriers to Understanding the Relationships Among Aging, Health, Fitness, and Cognition

Even though the number of studies of the relationship between health, fitness, and cognitive function has increased dramatically over the past 10 years, the relationship, especially in normal adults, remains unclear. All of these factors probably interrelate in some way, and genetic and environmental influences are powerful but poorly understood. It is strongly suspected that some diseases and poor physical health compromise cognition and that improvements in the health of sick individuals also improve cognitive functions. But the role that exceptional health and physical fitness plays in maintaining optimum cognition throughout the aging process is controversial. The relationship of fitness to cognition is difficult to isolate because of the many other variables to which it is related (Spirduso, 1980).

At least five major problems confound the conclusions that might be drawn from existing research. One barrier is that different types of research designs—cross-sectional comparison, pre- and posttest intervention (quasiexperimental) designs, and correlational designs—produce different results. A second barrier is that physical fitness has not been measured adequately in most studies and the physical fitness criterion used by many investigators is questionable. Third, stable measures of cognitive function have often not been obtained. Fourth, cognitive measures are substantially correlated with socioeconomic and education factors, variables not controlled or even reported in most studies. Finally, the age categories chosen for study often exaggerate individual differences in older groups.

Different Research Designs Have Produced Different Results

Three major types of research design have been used in research on older adult fitness. *Cross-sectional comparison group designs* compare young and old groups that differ in levels of physical fitness. *Pre- and posttest intervention designs* compare the physical fitness and cognitive function of a group of sedentary older individuals before and after an aerobic exercise training program. *Correlational studies* compare several health and fitness variables in large groups ranging in age from very young to very old.

Cross-sectional comparison group designs, such as those in which young and old sedentary groups are compared to young and old exercising groups, have generally shown that presumably fit young and old subjects are superior to sedentary control subjects on several cognitive functions

(Clarkson, 1978; Sherwood & Selder, 1979; Spirduso, 1975; Spirduso & Clifford, 1978). In fact, almost all of the investigators who use this type of design have found physically fit subjects to be significantly better at many types of cognitive tasks, particularly reaction time tasks. In contrast, fewer investigators who used a pre- and posttest intervention design reported similar findings, even when significant improvements in fitness were shown. These investigators argue that cross-sectional designs, which compare different age groups, suffer from cohort and genetic effects. Most of these cross-sectional studies used subjects who were self-selected and who probably varied in many other lifestyle activities besides their exercise habits. Another weakness of the cross-sectional group comparison designs is that subjects are not randomly assigned to groups, so the characteristics of the groups can bias the results. Thus, sampling error may be considered one of the primary reasons why fitness effects are found in cross-sectional studies but not in intervention experiments.

Pre- and postintervention designs, in which sedentary older individuals are pretested, assigned to an exercise program for a few weeks or months, and then posttested to determine whether cognitive improvements parallel improvements in physical fitness, have had only negligible results (e.g., Blumenthal et al., 1989, 1991). A major difficulty in comparing results of this research design to cross-sectional group comparisons is that the level of fitness that can be developed over a 4-, 8-, or even 12-month training program is still well below the level present in groups who have a lifestyle pattern of exercise over many years. This was shown in chapter 4, Figure 4.6 (page 107), where $\dot{V}O_2$max averages that have been reported in the literature for each of four subject categories are greatly different.

The problem is that those who have been comparing cohort groups selected for their exercise habits cross-sectionally have been comparing the values of sedentary subjects with those of active or masters subjects, whereas those who have been studying the benefits of intervention exercise programs have been comparing the change in sedentary subjects from before the exercise program to afterward. Consequently, although the confound of cohort groups is not a factor in this research design, the issue of time and the result of the exercise program is. Many of these training studies have either produced no training effect at all or developed only inadequate levels of fitness. Most obtained an improvement of about 15% to 20% in $\dot{V}O_2max$, but some argue that changes of at least 20% to 30% are needed for improvements in central nervous system function.

Physical Fitness Is Hard to Define and Measure

Many researchers, especially those who use cross-sectional designs, have relied on the self-report of subjects as a basis for categorizing them physically. The accuracy of self-reports is always questionable, and it is known that people tend to overestimate their physical activity. For example, in one study it was found that the reliability of one measure of leisure activity, in which subjects were asked "how frequently do you get sweaty," was only moderate ($r = 0.64$) after 2 weeks. The measure also correlated only moderately ($r = 0.38$ to 0.54) with measures of aerobic power and muscular endurance (Godin, Jobin, & Bouillon, 1986).

A more direct measure of physical fitness would be far more reliable, and the gold standard for direct measurement of aerobic capacity is $\dot{V}O_2max$. Although $\dot{V}O_2max$ is generally accepted as the best single measure of physical fitness and is the only measure that is consistent across studies, it nevertheless has some inadequacies that cloud our understanding of the relationship between fitness and cognition and make it very difficult to determine if improvements in cognitive function accompany training-induced increases in $\dot{V}O_2max$. For example, $\dot{V}O_2max$ has a high genetic component (Åstrand & Rodahl, 1977). Some people can train physically for a long time and still not achieve the $\dot{V}O_2max$ that others attain with little or no training. Therefore, individuals who have a natural disposition for high $\dot{V}O_2max$ scores may also have high cognitive processing. Another problem with $\dot{V}O_2max$ is that it levels off after a certain amount of training and cannot be increased even though additional training makes dramatic changes in physical performance and other physiological measures, such as blood lactates, that are generally thought to be associated with fitness levels.

Another indication that $\dot{V}O_2max$ as a sole measure of fitness is an inadequate criterion with which to determine the effects of fitness on cognition is that when composite scores of fitness are used, the relationship between fitness and cognition seems to be higher. Generally, a compound measure of almost any construct is a better indicator of that construct than a single measure, and this has been shown by Chodzko-Zajko and Ringel (1987), Stones and Kozma (1988), and Dustman et al. (1984). In the first study, the strength of the relationship of $\dot{V}O_2max$ with simple reaction time was only $r = -0.20$, and with complex reaction time even less, $r = -0.13$. Conversely, the correlation between a battery of physiological parameters and simple reaction time was $r = -0.36$, and with complex reaction time, $r = -0.40$. Nevertheless, $\dot{V}O_2max$, with all of its problems, continues to be the accepted measure of aerobic fitness.

Measures of Cognition Are Complex and Sometimes Confused With Learning

If the relation between physical fitness and cognition is to be understood, it is important not only to obtain reliable and valid measures of fitness but also to have valid measures of cognition. Many of the comparisons that have been made focus on the levels of fitness and measures of speed of information processing. Processing speed has been estimated from simple and choice reaction times and various timed neuropsychological tests. However, the maximum speed with which an individual can process information is not easy to assess. It is influenced substantially by the nature of the task, the testing environment, the subject-researcher relationship, the motivation of the subject, and many other variables. It takes considerable practice on the task before most subjects learn the requirements of the task, overcome the newness of the laboratory environment, and begin to feel comfortable with the testing situation so that they can concentrate on performing at their absolute fastest capacities. Multiple trials are even more effective if practiced over different days so that consolidation of learning can occur. However, multiple trials over several days take more time to administer, and few researchers have invested the time needed to acquire stable, well-learned performances from their subjects. Consequently, almost all studies of the relationship of fitness to cognition are limited by the fact that the subjects have been analyzed at various points along an acquisition curve.

Furthermore, the variable number of trials provided in different studies places the subjects of these studies at differing points along the learning curve. Subjects of the same age whose reaction time is represented by a mean of their first 15 trials are at quite a different point in their reactive capacity than subjects whose reaction time is represented by the mean of the last 25 of 100 trials. The fewer the number of trials and the more complex the cognitive speeded task, the higher the variance or "noise" of the performance. The higher the variability, the less likely it is that the researcher will find an effect of exercise, especially if exercise has a relatively weak effect on cognition.

These differences are exaggerated when subjects of different age groups are compared. Previously discussed in chapter 7, a small number of trials produces substantial variance in young subjects but an even greater variance and a poorer performance in older subjects. Older subjects deal with novelty less well than young subjects and take somewhat longer to learn tasks. Thus, a small number of trials places older subjects at a disadvantage and probably underestimates their reactive capacity (Hoyer, Labouvie, & Baltes, 1973).

Just as a criterion of physical fitness is better represented by a composite score, so a composite score provides a better estimate of information-processing speed. When composite scores that include both simple and choice reaction time (and several other neuropsychological timed tests) are included in a regression prediction equation, the correlation of these combined scores to health and fitness is higher than the correlation of single estimates of cognition to health and fitness (Era, 1988).

Subjects of Different Ages Are Distributed Unequally Among Age Categories

A final factor that has made it difficult to understand the relationship of fitness to cognitive function is that the ages used in the relevant studies are defined differently and are unequally represented. In most studies, "young" is roughly defined as 18 to 25 years, but in some studies, "young" is between 30 and 40 years. "Old" might be 50 to 60, older than 65, or 70 to 90. Perhaps the greatest violation of research design is the practice of having an increasingly larger and larger variation of age and gender as the chronological age of the groups increases. Gender differences in RT are pronounced and robust (e.g., Fozard, Vercruyssen, Reynolds, & Hancock, 1990), yet because it is sometimes difficult for researchers to

obtain older subjects, it is not at all unusual to see a young group aged 18 to 26 and equally represented in gender, a middle-aged group aged 40 to 55 with slightly more women than men, an old group aged 60 to 79 with more women than men, and a group aged 80 and over composed primarily of women. Furthermore, gender differences in RT are also dependent on the amount of practice and motivation provided (Yandell & Spirduso, 1981). The fact that the variance within age cohorts increases within subjects with age on many variables compounds this problem. The entire phenomenon of group inequality has provided a serious barrier to the understanding of the relationship between fitness and cognitive function (e.g., Hancock, Arthur, Chrysler, & Lee, 1994).

Health and Cognitive Function

Even though there are many formidable barriers in the research designs used to investigate the relationships among aging, health, fitness, and cognition, the results from the growing literature provide a substantial amount of information to be considered. Yet it seems intuitive that disease would take a toll on cognitive capability and judgment. Many years ago Botwinick and Birren (1963) pointed out that the factors of health and sickness play a large role in determining the extent of age differences. Other researchers noted that as cognitive tasks grew increasingly more difficult, the rate of response slowing with increased difficulty was related to a measure of health and fitness—cardiac output (Szafran, 1966).

A study by Milligan, Powell, Harley, and Furchtgott (1984) is an example in which better cognitive performance was associated with both a composite objective health rating score, made by a medical professional, and the subjective perception of an individual's own health. Using the Older Americans Resources and Services Instrument (OARS; Duke University Center for the Study of Aging and Human Development, 1978), individuals answered questions about their physical and mental health, their activities of daily living, and the economic and social supports available to them. Reaction time (RT) measures correlated higher with objective health than any other dependent variable. In fact, the only consistent predictors of reaction time and serial learning were both the subjective and objective measures of health. The subjective rating of health was related to serial learning, and the investigators proposed that because verbal learning is a cognitive task, it is more likely to be influenced by one's subjective perception of his or her disabilities. Thus the relationship of the objective assessment of health to reaction time was a reflection of the relationship of reaction time to inherent motor and perceptual abilities.

Evidence from several studies has supported the hypothesis that in aging populations, coronary heart disease, cerebrovascular disease, and atherosclerosis impair neuropsychological function (see Birren, Woods, & Williams, 1980). Behavioral response speed and verbal learning (Birrin et al., 1980), memory (Wilkie, Eisdorfer, & Nowlin, 1976), and many other aspects of intelligence (Hertzog, Schaie, & Gribbin, 1978) reveal age-related impairments that are partially related to cardiovascular health status. Many other diseases, such as diabetes and depression, also have serious consequences for cognitive function.

Hypertension is a good example of the disease-cognition relationship. Most investigators have found that elevated diastolic blood pressure is associated with poor performance on several types of cognitive tests. For example, hypertension was significantly correlated and was a significant predictor of scores on several neuropsychological tests in the Halstead-Reitan battery: the Category test, Trail-making, Tactile Performance test—Localization, and Tactile Performance test—Memory (Elias, Robbins, Schultz, & Pierce, 1990). In fact, these authors proposed that blood pressure values predict neuropsychological test performance over a wide range of hypertensive and normotensive blood pressure values, not just those values above the clinical definition of hypertension (>140/90 mmHg). They also suggested that, within the age and education range they investigated, the negative blood pressure effects on performance were greater for younger than older subjects.

Speith (1964) found that unmedicated hypertensive subjects were almost as slow on the WAIS Digit-Symbol and Block Design subtests as a group of subjects with cardiovascular disease. The relationship of blood pressure to performance on the Digit-Symbol test was among the highest and most significant of all the neuropsychological items assessed (Wilkie, Eisdorfer, & Nowlin, 1976). The strong relationship between hypertension and cognitive performance has also been supported by longitudinal evidence (Sands & Meredith, 1992). Even in a study of animal discrimination learning,

mice selected for high blood pressure performed worse than mice selected for low blood pressure (Elias & Schlager, 1974).

Waldstein, Manuck, Ryan, and Muldoon (1991) critically reviewed the findings and methodologies of 26 studies of the relationship between hypertension and cognitive function. Their review, summarized in Table 9.1, showed that hypertension is related to some cognitive functions but not to others. Salthouse (1991) also came to this conclusion after reviewing 12 studies in which health was assessed and related to subject performance on one or more tests of memory, spatial abilities, verbal fluency, comparison and association functions, abstract reasoning, and tests of global intelligence in older adults. The intelligence tests included the Cattell Culture Fair Intelligence test (Powell & Pohndorf, 1971), the Wechsler Verbal and Performance Scales (Field, Schaie, & Leino, 1988), and the Primary Mental Abilities test (Clark, 1960). He concluded that on the basis of that evidence, even though a relationship between health and intelligence seems intuitive and is popularly believed, the evidence supporting the relationship is not persuasive. He found that in a number of instances, subjects who reported that their health was excellent did not perform better on tests of intelligence and spatial abilities than average subjects. In some studies, the performances of subjects with cardiovascular disease and hypertension were not significantly worse than the performances of control subjects. Among the studies he reviewed were two longitudinal studies of health changes (self-report) and primary abilities (verbal fluency, abstraction, reasoning, and performance scales) or global tests of intelligence changes over a longer period of time. Neither of these studies produced any support for a relationship between health and intelligence measured by standard tests.

In one of his own studies (Salthouse, Kausler, and Saults, 1990), Salthouse noted that the perceived health status of a large sample of individuals was not related to performance on several memory tasks, so, he reasoned, health status may not be related to this type of cognitive function. However, 77% of his sample said they were "above average" on health, so they may have been an unusually healthy group of subjects. Then too, Salthouse pointed out, many older adults tend to rate their health as better than it is when objectively assessed, so health-rating scales are relatively inaccurate measures of health status. Also, it is possible that poor self-perceptions

Table 9.1
Relationship of Hypertension to Cognitive Function

Cognitive test	Number measures[a]	Number measures related to hypertension	Conclusion
Abstract reasoning	8	6	Related
Memory	39	22	Related
Attention	7	4	Related
Perception	8	4	Mixed results
Psychomotor speed	22	13	Mixed results
Constructional ability	6	3	Mixed results
Mental flexibility			Mixed results
General intelligence			Not related
Verbal skills			Not related

[a]Measures are the number of effect sizes from the experimental analyses. Most studies resulted in several measures, because several different neuropsychological tests were administered.
Note. Summarized from tables in Waldstein, Manuck, Ryan, and Muldoon (1991, pp. 452-454).

of health, particularly of cognitive health, may be the result rather than the cause of poorer intellectual functioning (Perlmutter & Nyquist, 1990). Other investigators have also failed to find a relationship between health, fitness, and memory (Barry, Steinmetz, Page, & Rodahl, 1966; Emery & Gatz, 1990; Gitlin, 1985; Hughes, Casal, & Leon, 1986).

Although the relationships between health and different types of cognition are not yet clearly understood, several conclusions can be drawn from information about health and cognition. First, the barriers to understanding this relationship are indeed formidable, because the question of health and cognition is so complex and difficult to answer. Researchers do not ask the same questions, use the same measurements and instruments, or even review the same literature. For example, Salthouse's review (1991) focused on memory, spatial abilities, and global tests of intelligence and thus omitted all of the studies in which health is related to processes that support cognition, such as information-processing speed and attention. Second, the effect of health appears to be relatively modest compared to the overall cognitive decline that is seen with aging; thus, investigators and reviewers can interpret these small effects in different ways. Salthouse (1991), for example, suggests that when health is statistically controlled, the correlations between age and verbal skills and intelligence are only slightly reduced. They were, however, reduced, which may mean that health effects, though

small, are present. Furthermore, because these relationships are determined by analyzing group performances and group averages, it is probable that for some members of the sample there is a substantial relationship between health and cognition. Finally, almost all studies, including the meta-analysis of Thomas, Landers, Salazar, and Etnier (1994), reveal some evidence that suggests a relationship between health and cognition. It is these positive findings and trends of relationship, not just intuition or wishful thinking, that drives the continued interest and federal funding in this area of study.

Physical Fitness and Cognitive Function

Substantial evidence suggests that behavioral response speed and several other measures of age-associated cognitive function are impaired by cardiovascular disease. What about individuals who are asymptomatic of disease but who are physically unfit? Are their response speed and neuropsychological function significantly better than diseased individuals but worse than individuals who are in excellent cardiovascular health and fitness? When physical training improves physical fitness, does it also enhance cognitive function? If so, does it optimize cognitive function at all ages, or are benefits more likely to occur at older ages when cognitive function may be declining?

Much of the age-related decline in many functions, even when symptoms of disease may be absent, can be attributed to disuse (Bortz, 1982), and unfortunately the majority of North Americans have moderate to low fitness levels (Shephard, 1978). The proportion of 70-year-old individuals who are vigorously active is dramatically smaller than the proportion of active 20-year-olds (Ostrow, 1984). Similarly, the proportion of healthy and physically fit individuals within each age decade is smaller in each older decade (Speith, 1964). Because disuse takes a greater toll as individuals age, individuals selected randomly from different age categories in the population also have different health and fitness levels. A higher proportion of 20-year-olds than 70-year-olds will be healthy and physically fit. Consequently, when the cognitive function of older adults is compared to young adults, unless the physical health and fitness of the subjects is equated, the comparison is really between the healthy young and the less healthy old. Because physical fitness is probably related to cognitive function, the effect of aging on cognition has likely been overestimated in the literature.

The decreasing proportion of fit elderly with increasing age is the basis for questioning whether the decline seen in cognitive function is really a result of primary aging or whether it is the result of secondary aging. Intuitively, regular physical exercise should contribute to cognition by improving general health and retaining physical integrity, thus improving functional age (the age level at which people *function*, not their chronological age). But research findings are equivocal, and the relationships of fitness to specific types of cognitive function have not been clearly established.

Processes That Support Cognition

Shown in Figure 9.1 (page 251), several processes support cognitive function: information-processing speed, working memory, and psychomotor and perceptual processes. Of these, several researchers have examined information-processing speed, attention, working memory, and psychomotor function.

Information-Processing Speed

The speed with which people can react to an environmental stimulus (reaction time), has long been

used as a behavioral assessment of the integrity of the central nervous system (see chapter 7), and it has also long been known that reaction time slows with aging. Reaction time, particularly because it assesses an individual's capacity to respond quickly to environmental events and is extremely sensitive to the effects of aging, has been commonly employed to study the relationship of aging, aerobic fitness, and cognitive function.

Botwinick and Thompson (1966) were among the first to observe that the physical fitness of some of their subjects might have influenced their reaction time results. They noted that several of their younger subjects were athletes and assumed that athletic status and aerobic fitness were associated. This association is true only if athletes participate in a sport in which aerobic capacity is an important component, so these athletes may or may not have been aerobically fit. Nevertheless, the researchers recognized that fitness and reaction time may be related, and since their study many investigations have used reaction time as a measure of response speed.

Simple Reaction Time, Discrimination Reaction Time and Choice Reaction Time

Variations of at least three types of reaction time have been used to study the relationship of aerobic fitness to response speed. Simple reaction time (SRT) provides a behavioral measure of basic central nervous system reactivity. Discrimination or disjunctive reaction time (DRT) adds a go/no-go decision to the preparation of the response; that is, the subject reacts only if a particular color light is activated but not another. In a choice reaction time (CRT) paradigm, subjects react with a specific response that is matched to each of two or more stimuli. Both DRT and CRT paradigms require additional processing time to make the decisions, so that these three reaction paradigms provide an opportunity to determine whether aerobic fitness is associated with basic reactivity speed, simple go/no-go decisions, or the processing of more complex information. Reaction time paradigms are discussed in more detail in chapter 7.

Reaction Time in Exercisers and Nonexercisers in Cross-Sectional Comparison Group Research Studies

Do older people who are highly physically fit have faster response speeds than their cohorts who are not fit but asymptomatic of cardiovascular disease? Spirduso (1975) was the first to use an age-by-physical activity cross-sectional design to compare the reaction times of young and old exercisers and nonexercisers. In this design, people both young (approximately 20 years old) and old (at least 60 years of age) who reported that they participated in vigorous physical exercise at least three times a week for at least 3 years were compared to young and old sedentary individuals. Care was taken to select individuals who were not athletes with the hope that the physical conditioning factor could be disassociated from the talent factor. She concluded that the old exercisers were significantly faster at both simple and choice reaction tasks than the old nonexercisers but not significantly different from subjects 40 years younger.

This general design was repeated several times with similar results (Hart, 1981; Sherwood & Selder, 1979; Spirduso & Clifford, 1978), except in some cases the interaction term was not significant for all types of reaction time. That is, in some studies, for some types of reaction time, the relationship between fitness and cognitive function was strong for all ages, not just for the old adults. When the mean latencies of old subjects were calculated as a function of the young for SRT and CRT in the Clarkson (1978) and Hart (1981) studies, then averaged and graphed (shown in Figure 9.2), the trained old adults' SRTs and CRTs were almost twice as close to the 20-year-olds' times.

Era (1988), unlike many previous researchers, measured directly several physiological and cognitive functions of men in three different age groups, 31 to 35, 51 to 55, and 71 to 75 years of age, and found that $\dot{V}O_2max$ was low to moderate but positively correlated with many of the behavioral speed measures. He also found that *perceived* health was related to speeded functions, but only in the youngest group.

The conclusion to be drawn from these cross-sectional group comparisons is that the relationship of participation in exercise to information- processing speed is compelling. Only Botwinick and Storandt (1974) failed to find a positive relationship between chronic exercise participation and response speed. Whether the relationship is causal is much less clear. Also, whether fitness enhances or maintains response speed more in older subjects than in young subjects is debatable. One of the weaknesses in all of the studies of this type is that the research design does not provide a way to determine whether exercise caused faster reaction

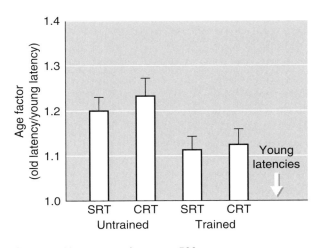

Example: Young mean latency = 500 ms $500_O/500_Y = 1.0$
Old mean latency = 500 ms

Young mean latency = 250 ms $500_O/250_Y = 2.0$
Old mean latency = 500 ms

Figure 9.2   Average age factor score for simple reaction time (SRT) and choice reaction time (CRT) in aerobically trained and untrained groups.

time or whether reaction time caused subjects to be more active. Also, the physical fitness of the subjects was inferred from self-reports of their weekly exercise patterns. Those who claimed to have exercised consistently at a criterion-level intensity were assumed to be more fit than those who said they never exercised.

Reaction Time of Exercisers in Quasiexperimental Intervention Research Programs

A more convincing way to reveal a relationship between physical fitness and cognition, if it exists, would be to show that sedentary persons who participate in an exercise program are better on cognitive tasks after the exercise program than they were before they began. In intervention studies of this type, sedentary persons are tested on cognitive performance, are aerobically exercised, and then are retested on their cognitive function and compared to sedentary persons who did not exercise. However, results from intervention studies have been mixed. Some of these studies support a relationship between fitness and response speed. Three early studies reported that an exercise program had increased the fitness levels and decreased the reaction times of young subjects (Gibson et al., 1961; Tweit, Gollnick, & Hearn,

1963). Tredway (1978) reported a low but significant correlation between $\dot{V}O_2$max and reaction
time. But in an extensive review of the literature
relating to the effects of exercise on various cognitive functions, Folkins and Sime (1981) concluded
that few of these studies had acceptable methodological controls and that the relationship in normal populations was not compelling. They did
concede that in the few studies in which physical
activity programs were initiated for institutionalized geriatric patients, the results were positive
(Powell, 1974; Stamford, Hambacher, & Fallica,
1974; Vanfraechem & Vanfraechem, 1977).

More recently, the index of physiological status
(or IPS, a score combining resting pulmonary, hemodynamic, and blood chemistry variables) was
found to be correlated to two types of CRT
(Chodzko-Zajko & Ringel, 1987): the easy CRT task
($r = -0.36$) and the difficult CRT task ($r = -0.40$).
However, CRT was not significantly correlated with
any single measure of aerobic capacity (e.g.,
$\dot{V}O_2$max). In a correlational study in which the measures of vital capacity, resting heart rate, and systolic
and diastolic blood pressure complemented an
elaborate self-report technique, older groups defined as high exercisers were significantly faster than
low exercisers on simple, two-choice, and four-
choice reaction time (Clarkson-Smith & Hartley,
1989), even when age, education, and vocabulary
were statistically controlled.

Dustman and his group (1984), matched older
men and women between the ages of 55 and 70 on
socioeconomic status and intelligence and placed
them in one of three groups: a sedentary control
group, a strength-and-flexibility control group,
and an exercise group. The exercise group improved their simple reaction time after 4 months
of physical training. The strength-and-flexibility
control group did not improve in aerobic fitness
or simple reaction time. None of the groups improved in CRT. This study has been cited many
times in support of a relationship between fitness
and at least the simplest components of reaction
time (SRT), because appropriate control groups
were used and substantial aerobic capacity improvements resulted from the exercise program.
The subjects' initial level of aerobic capacity was
unusually low, however. In another recent study,
both SRT and CRT improved after a 1-year exercise
program and then remained stable through 2
more years of the exercise program (Rikli & Edwards, 1991). Subjects ranged from 59 to 81 years,
and the RTs of the nonexercising subjects were

significantly slower at the end of 3 years than
they were at the beginning of the research project.
Thus, the apparent contribution of the exercise
program in this study was to postpone age-related
deterioration of RT.

In the only animal study of physical fitness and
reaction time, a group of old rats that exercised
aerobically for 6 months at high levels of intensity
were able to maintain their fastest reaction times,
whereas the reaction times of the old, sedentary
rat group deteriorated over the 6 months (equivalent to about 18 human years). In this study, the
exercised rats increased their oxidative capacity
100%, which is a much higher increase in fitness
than has been recorded in studies of humans
(Spirduso & Farrar, 1981).

Other investigators using the pre- and posttest
designs have found no changes in reaction time
accompanying improvements in aerobic capacity
(Barry et al., 1966; Boarman, 1977; Buccola, 1972).
Blumenthal and Madden (1988) found a relationship between initial levels of fitness and the baseline speed of reacting in a type of reaction time
task, but they found no significant correlations
between the improvement of their subjects' aerobic capacity and their postexercise time. In this
aspect, their results are similar to those of Dustman
et al. (1984), who found that SRT and not CRT
seems to be associated with fitness. The Blumenthal and Madden (1988) finding that initial levels
of physical fitness are correlated with reaction time
also agreed with Spirduso's (1975) conclusions
that high fitness levels are related to faster reaction times.

Fractionated Reaction Time

If reaction times of exercised subjects are faster
than those of nonexercise controls, it might be
argued that speed increases because of stronger,
quicker reacting, highly conditioned muscles and
not because any changes have occurred in the
central nervous system. This skepticism regarding
exercise effects on central versus peripheral components has led to several exercise studies in
which reaction time was fractionated or parti-
tioned into subcomponents (see chapter 7 for a
description of fractionated RT). Fractionating reaction time makes it possible to differentiate premotor time (i.e., central processing time) from
motor time (i.e., peripheral, muscle contractile
events). That is, by subtracting the amount of time
taken for the muscle to contract from the total

reaction time, a more precise measure of information-processing speed can be obtained.

The same experimental paradigm used by Spirduso (1975)—groups of young and old exercised and nonexercised subjects—was used in four studies in which the responses were fractionated. Three of these studies (Clarkson, 1978; Hart, 1981; MacRae, Crum, Giessman, & Green, 1987) confirmed earlier findings that the simple and choice reaction times of old exercisers were faster than those of sedentary individuals, but the fractionation technique also revealed that the major contributor to the significant differences was an exercise difference in the largest component of RT, the premotor time. This can be seen in Figure 9.3 where the PMT, which accounts for 70% of the SRT, is substantially shorter in the exercisers. The contractile time is also shorter, but it contributes only 30% to the SRT.

Only one group of investigators (Panton, Graves, Pollock, Hagberg, & Chen, 1990) failed to find a robust relationship between premotor time and physical fitness, but they analyzed only six reaction time trials before and after the exercise program. Given the great variability in reaction time data of inexperienced subjects, both within and between individuals, it is doubtful that they obtained a true estimate of individual reactive capacity from so few trials.

Event-Related Potentials

The question of the relationship between cognitive events and aerobic fitness can be pursued even further: Can brain function, represented by brain waves, be related to fitness? Event-related potentials (ERPs) (measured by electroencephalography, EEG) are electrophysiological responses in the brain to external stimuli such as a flash of light (visual), a sound (auditory), skin contact (tactile), or movement of a body part (kinesthetic). Explained in chapter 7, ERPs are generally obtained by repeating the stimulus many times and monitoring these responses through EEG surface electrodes placed over the appropriate area of the brain (see Figure 7.7, page 193). For example, electrodes are placed over the occipital lobe when the stimulus is visual, the temporal lobe when it is auditory, and over the parietal lobe when it is a somatosensory stimulus. By computer-averaging the EEG signal response to the onset of each stimulus, an ERP is obtained, which is thought to represent a basic measure of the speed and amplitude with which specific types of central nervous system functions occur. In some research paradigms the subject merely views a flashing light or a changing visual target pattern, thus eliminating factors characteristic of a motor response, such as motivation or speed-accuracy trade-offs. In studies where ERPs are obtained in a reaction time paradigm, the ERPs may provide a measure of information-processing time that is the least contaminated with the motor aspects of the task. Various wave forms of the ERP have been associated with different types of information processing. One of the most pronounced of these wave forms occurs at approximately 300 ms and is called a P300 or P3

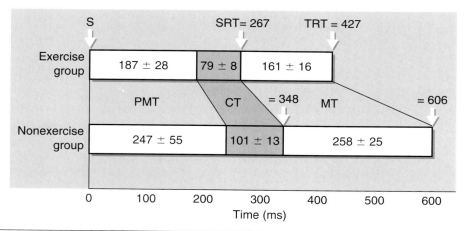

Figure 9.3 Differences between exercised and sedentary subjects' fractionated reaction time components. When a stimulus (S) is presented, the subject reacts by removing the foot from an accelerator pedal and placing it as quickly as possible on a brake pedal. The total response time (TRT) can be fractionated into the simple reaction time (SRT), which in turn is composed of premotor time (PMT) and contractile time (CT). The movement time (MT) is the time (in ms) from the release of the accelerator pedal to the contact of the brake pedal. Exercisers were significantly faster than nonexercisers on all components (Baylor & Spirduso, 1988).

wave. It is measured from the onset of the stimulus to the peak of the wave form and is thought to be associated with decision making in reaction time tasks.

Carlow, Appenzeller, and Rodriguez (1978) found that visual evoked potentials (VEPs) were indeed shorter for physically trained than for untrained men. They also found that VEPs for all subjects of all ages were shorter immediately after a 10- to 18-mile run at training pace. More recently, Dustman et al. (1990) selected two groups of young and old subjects on a rigorous criterion of their exercise habits. They advertised widely for subjects and continued to interview applicants until they obtained a young and an old group who were very high in fitness and a young and an old group who were low in fitness. First they ensured, by analyzing their subjects' scores on vocabulary tests of the Wechsler Adult Intelligence Scale, that the groups did not differ in intelligence. Then they analyzed the P3 latencies obtained from VEPs. Both the P3s and VEP late waves were significantly faster in the young and old highly fit groups than in the low-fit groups, and their results also clearly indicated that the relationship between fitness and the EEG variables was much stronger in the old subjects than in the young subjects. The P3 latencies of the old unfit men were much slower than those of the old fit men or either of the two younger groups (Figure 9.4, a-b).

Emmerson, Dustman, and Shearer (1989) found little correlation between P3 and age in the young; but on the basis of their analysis of 172 subjects ranging in age from 20 to 79 years, they suggested that a major slowing with age occurs between the ages of 45 to 55. They also proposed that an active lifestyle with its resulting fitness seems to attenuate age-related increases in P3 latency. Increases in P3 latency were on the order of 1.68 ms a year for sedentary persons and 0.84 ms a year for active individuals, leading them to conclude that the ERP-P3 latency provides a sensitive measure of age- and health-related processes that affect CNS function and cognitive performance. Because their study was cross-sectional in design, it could not answer questions about the nature and rate of slowing that takes place from early middle age to later life.

Motor Command Processing Speed

Speeded stationary tapping (described in chapter 7) provides a measure of the integrity of central nervous system motor outflow, or the information processing of simple repetitive motor commands. It is highly sensitive to aging, because the CNS of older individuals cannot initiate, control the termination, then reinitiate a simple motor command as quickly as can young individuals. Era (1988) provided evidence that stationary tapping is a potent behavioral marker of longevity. By testing older men and then monitoring death occurrences for 8 years, he found that tapping speed, measured over a 5-s period, was a strong predictor of survival. Borkin and Norris (1980) also found that stationary tapping speed was a useful addition to a biological age test battery and also significantly discriminated between survivors and nonsurvivors in a longitudinally measured sample.

Because stationary tapping speed seemed to deteriorate significantly less in survivors, and because individuals who exercise, even moderately, have a slightly longer longevity (Paffenbarger, Wing, & Hyde, 1978), it seems reasonable that stationary tapping speed would be faster in habitual exercisers than in nonexercisers. However, stationary tapping has not been used in many studies of fit elderly, and when it has been investigated, no differences between exercisers and nonexercisers have been reported. Older individuals are generally slower than younger ones on stationary tapping, but exercise has not been a factor (Spirduso, MacRae, MacRae, Prewitt, & Osborne, 1988).

In summary, the results of many behavioral and neurophysiological analyses of the speed of information processing strongly suggest that physical fitness is related to faster processing, and although the results from intervention studies are mixed, more researchers than not have found positive relationships. Thomas et al. (1994) concluded on the basis of a meta-analysis of 200 effect sizes that the benefits of chronic exercise on RT are small but probably reliable.

Perceptual Processes, Attention, and Working Memory

Though information-processing speed is but one of several processes that support cognition (see Figure 9.1, page 251), other processes have not received as much attention from researchers. Dustman et al. (1984) found that performance on some neuropsychological tests that emphasized perceptual processes (Stroop test, Critical Flicker Fusion

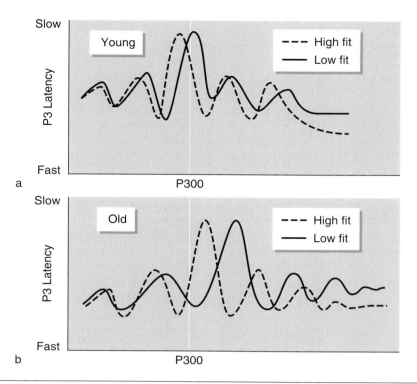

Figure 9.4 Hypothetical event-related potentials (ERPs) showing P3 latencies for (a) young and (b) old men with low and high aerobic fitness levels. The P3 latencies of the old subjects occurred significantly later compared to those of the young men, primarily because the older low-fit men had very long P3 latencies.
Data from Dustman et al. (1990).

Frequency [CFFF], Digit Span, Dots Estimation) improved after an exercise program, but no one has compared physically fit and sedentary older adults on these measures.

Arito and Oguri (1990), however, found that attention, measured by the EEG contingent negative variation (CNV), was greater in young, physically-trained college students than in young, nontrained students. The CNV is a relatively long negative drop in EEG amplitude that precedes, by a few seconds, a reaction or movement; thus, it is interpreted as indicating a capacity to focus attention on a stimulus and prepare for a response. These results imply that physically fit individuals perform better on vigilance tasks than non–physically fit individuals. However, because more than half of the physically trained group were athletes, their results are confounded by the factor of physical talent. Nevertheless, the results support the hypothesis that characteristics of brain activity, as indicated by EEG recordings, are different in at least some individuals who participate in chronic physical activity.

Two tests that have been used extensively in older populations to assess perceptual- and motor-processing speed, coding functions, and working memory are the Digit Span (DS) test and the Digit-Symbol Substitution (DSS) test. In the DS test, subjects are required to remember a sequence of numbers after a short period of time. In the DSS test, subjects must match symbols to the numbers 1 through 9 arranged in sequential order in the key, and the better the symbol-number pairs are remembered, the more symbols the subjects can code and match within the testing time period (see chapter 7 for a description of this test). Several investigators found an improvement in one or both of these tests following an exercise intervention program (Diesfeldt & Diesfeldt-Groenendijk, 1977; Dustman et al., 1984; Stacey, Kozma, & Stones, 1985). In fact, Perlmutter and Nyquist (1990) found that self-reported health was a greater contributor than age to memory measured by the DS test. Improvements in this type of performance have also been found in geriatric institutionalized samples (Powell, 1974; Stamford et al., 1974).

The Symbol Digit Modalities test (SDMT), which is basically the DSS test modified to provide some contextual interference and fewer spatial localization cues, is a rigorous test of short-term memory and visual information processing. Highly fit individuals performed this test (but not the DSS test) better than subjects in poor physical condition (Stones & Kozma, 1989), and the results of these tests also were related to the P3 latencies obtained from EEG recordings of the same subjects (Emmerson et al., 1989).

In their study of fitness and cognitive function, Stones and Kozma (1989), using a coding task (symbol digit) that was similar to the DSS, also found a large age-by-activity interaction that was primarily due to the slowness of the old nonexercisers compared to the performance of the old exercisers and the two younger groups. Exercise apparently compensated for performance on the symbol digit, but not the DSS. This study did not support the hypothesis that enhanced fitness reduces susceptibility to distraction, but it did provide some evidence that exercisers transferred information better from one task to another.

Cognitive Functions

Whether physical fitness enhances or optimizes cognition, particularly neuropsychological performance, continues to be debated. Several cross-sectional comparison studies have been completed. Clarkson-Smith and Hartley (1989) tested 62 older men and women who exercised vigorously and 62 sedentary men and women on several attributes that are generally thought to contribute to intelligence. They found that the exercisers were better on reasoning, working memory (letter sets, digit span, and reading span), reasoning (30 common-word analogies, scaled for difficulty), 20 graded items selected from *Advanced Progressive Matrices, Sets I and II,* and 15 letter-series completion items. These differences remained significant after age, education, and vocabulary were held constant by analysis of covariance. The tests were also untimed, so speed of processing was not a factor.

Clarkson-Smith and Hartley (1990) followed up their 1989 study with an even more interesting one in which they used a statistical technique called LISREL (Jöreskog & Sörbom, 1984) to assess the possibility that amount of exercise is causally related to several aspects of cognition: RT, working memory, and reasoning. Using this technique the investigators proposed three models in which

exercise and fitness are causally related to cognitive function in the elderly: (1) a weak model, in which exercise has a significant but perhaps relatively small effect on cognitive performance, (2) a stronger version, in which some negative cognitive changes associated with aging are primarily due to low levels of physical activity, and (3) the strongest version, in which all or almost all cognitive decline with age is due to declining health. Results of the Clarkson-Smith and Hartley (1990) analysis supported the weakest model. Age, education, and exercise (measured in terms of kilocalories per week; strenuous exercise in hours per week, and previous exercise in hours per week over past 10 years) each had a significant and direct effect on cognitive performance. Health status and morale of the subjects indirectly affected cognitive performance by increasing the likelihood of their participation in exercise. Thus, age, morale, health, and education all affected the subjects' tendency to exercise, which in turn had a beneficial effect on cognition. Exercise also had a direct effect on cognition that was independent of health. The two stronger models, that age-related cognitive changes were either primarily or totally due to disuse and poor health, were not supported.

In a series of exercise intervention studies of middle-aged and older men, Blumenthal and his colleagues failed to find beneficial effects of relatively short-term exercise program interventions on memory search tasks (Blumenthal & Madden, 1988; Blumenthal et al., 1989; Madden, Blumenthal, Allen, & Emery, 1989). In the Blumenthal et al. (1989) study of 101 men and women ages 60 to 83 years, initial levels of fitness were higher than is usually seen in studies of aging, and aerobic capacity gains were low to moderate (11.6%). Although exercise training did not affect memory, some aspects of memory-search were related significantly to the subjects' initial level of fitness. Most subjects continued exercising for an additional 10 months, but there were few improvements in their psychological assessments even after this extended exercise period (Blumenthal et al., 1991). The authors pointed out that their subjects were functioning physically at a higher level than is usually seen in the population and that these subjects were highly motivated. They also emphasized that these subjects did not decline in cognitive function over the 14-month research project, which may also be an important observation. It is also possible that health status accounts for a greater portion of individual differences in older than in younger adults' intelligence performance (Perlmutter & Nyquist, 1990).

In another study, the length of time spent in an exercise program significantly predicted levels of performance on recall and recognition tasks (Myers & Hamilton, 1985, cited in Stones & Kozma, 1988). They suggested that the flexibility and low-intensity aerobic exercises that the subjects participated in may have facilitated memory performance, although it is difficult to imagine how flexibility exercises might contribute to memory.

A few investigators have suggested that the relationship between physical fitness and memory in aged individuals is stronger in cognitive performances that require "effortful processings" (Chodzko-Zajko, 1991; Stones & Kozma, 1988). Free recall and geometric shape rotation are examples of tasks that require more cognitive effort than tasks such as location memory and recognition memory. Tasks that require effortful processing may decline at a faster rate than noneffortful tasks and may also be more affected by the beneficial effects of a regular exercise program (Chodzko-Zajko, Schuler, Solomon, Heinl, & Ellis, 1990; Stones & Kozma, 1988).

Global Tests and Composite Scores of Intelligence and Fitness

Studies of the relationship between health, fitness, and intelligence have analyzed scores from the Wechsler Adult Intelligence Scale (WAIS) or subtests of that scale cross-sectionally either from groups identified as exercisers or nonexercisers, or from groups measured before and after an exercise intervention program. The WAIS test provides scores of abilities that are thought to contribute to intelligence. The processing ability of the system (the hardware) is measured by *fluid intelligence* (problem solving). The ability to perform well on learned material, the database of intelligence, is called *crystallized intelligence.*

Evidence that fluid intelligence is related to health and fitness is unimpressive (Blumenthal et al., 1989; Emery & Gatz, 1990; Perlmutter & Nyquist, 1990). Powell and Pohndorf (1971) found weak correlations between fluid intelligence and measures of fitness but *no* differences between a highly exercised and a sedentary group of relatively young (~50 years) individuals. Only Elsayed,

Ismail, and Young (1980) reported an improvement in fluid intelligence following an exercise program.

The evidence that health and fitness are related to crystallized intelligence is even weaker. Perlmutter and Nyquist (1990) concluded that self-reported health has little effect on crystallized intelligence, and Elsayed et al. (1980) found no difference in crystallized intelligence of physically fit and unfit individuals. The only positive findings regarding the relationship between fitness and intelligence were reported by Dustman et al. (1984), who found that their subjects who participated in an exercise program also improved their scores on the Culture-Fair Intelligence test.

Composite Score of Cognitive Function and Fitness

A composite score, which is created by combining scores from several tests designed to measure a construct, should better represent the construct than does the score of only one test. For example, a composite score combining simple reaction time, stimulus choice reaction time, response choice reaction time, and vocal reaction time should be a better measure of "reactive capacity" than any one of those tests alone, because each requires a unique combination of reactive systems. Therefore, a composite score of cognitive function can be expected to correlate higher to an aggregate score of physical fitness than any single estimate of either construct, physical fitness or cognition.

When Dustman et al. (1984) aggregated their neuropsychological scores into a combined average standard score, the strongest effect of their exercise program, which produced a 27% increase in aerobic capacity, was seen for this composite score. Their cognitive standard score measure was derived from scores on the CFFF test, the Culture-Fair Intelligence test, the DS and DSS tests from the WAIS, the Stroop test, Dots Estimation, and simple reaction time. In another study, Dustman et al. (1990) also found a standard score composite to be more highly related to fitness than to individual tests (Figure 9.5).

Stones and Kozma (1988) found that a composite score, composed of several neuropsychological tests, was related to levels of fitness that differed across five groups: a control group, a group planning to enter an exercise program, exercisers,

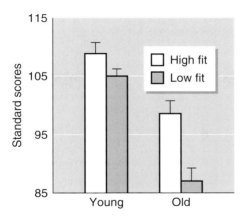

Figure 9.5 Cognitive performance of young and older men with low and high aerobic fitness levels. The cognitive factor measure was derived from scores on the following tests: Sternberg reaction time, Stroop color interference, symbol-digit modalities, and Trails B. Cognitive performance was better for young than older men and better for high-fit than low-fit men. Each mean was based on data for 15 subjects. The error bars are standard errors of the mean.

Reprinted from "Age and Fitness Effects on EEG, ERPs, Visual Sensitivity, and Cognition" by R.E. Dustman et al., 1990, *Neurobiology of Aging,* **11,** p. 198. Copyright 1990, with kind permission from Elsevier Science Ltd., The Boulevard, Langford Lane, Kidlington OX5 1GB, UK.

masters athletes, and Elderhostelers (Figure 9.6). Elderhostelers are older adults who participate in continuing education classes sometimes offered in foreign countries. Stones and Kozma (1988) consider them physically elite, successfully aging adults. The results of this study were particularly compelling because the groups were equated for socioeconomic status. Still, the groups with higher physical activity levels also tested higher in functional neuropsychological capabilities.

Stones and Kozma (1989) retested 200 subjects in an exercise intervention study 1 year after initial testing and classified them into four groups: stay-ins, 76 exercise participants who stayed in an exercise program and had a long history of activity; controls, 80 adults who never exercised; dropouts, 29 participants who dropped out of the exercise program; and 15 enrollees, who had joined the program after the initial measurements but several months before the final fitness assessments. (The groups were matched for socioeconomic status and intelligence.) The results indicated that only the stay-ins differed significantly from the other three groups on the aggregate functional fitness score, which was composed

of tests of balance, vital capacity, flexibility, and the DSS test. The stay-ins' aggregate functional fitness score, which included measures of reaction time, sensory function, DSS (WAIS), and anxiety, among others, improved after 1 year of the exercise program.

Summary of the Fitness-Cognition Relationship

There is a relationship between fitness levels and some types of cognition for those persons who participate in chronic aerobic exercise. Whether this relationship is causal must be determined by future research. In any case, the relationship seems to be more compelling for those CNS functions listed in Figure 9.1 (page 251) that support cognition rather than for cognitive functions or more global tests of intelligence.

Proposed Mechanisms of the Fitness–Cognitive Function Relationship

Several mechanisms have been proposed as rationales for hypothesizing and studying the relationships between health, fitness, and cognitive function, but none have been confirmed in a scientifically satisfying way. So many variables are involved and the research design problems are so great that most of the mechanisms by which fitness might be related to cognitive function remain merely hypotheses.

Mechanisms Acting on Primary Aging

Exercise has been proposed to *directly* affect four major areas of brain function: cerebrovascular function, cerebral neurotransmitter balance and function, neuroendocrine and autonomic tone, and brain morphology. These areas are illustrated in Figure 9.7 (page 267) as overlapping, interacting functions. Primary aging, which is aging that occurs in the absence of disease or environmental accident, is at the core of the four areas. The proposed impact of exercise is shown by the arrow from exercise to the core of aging. Any modulations in cerebrovascular integrity caused by increased physical fitness, because of

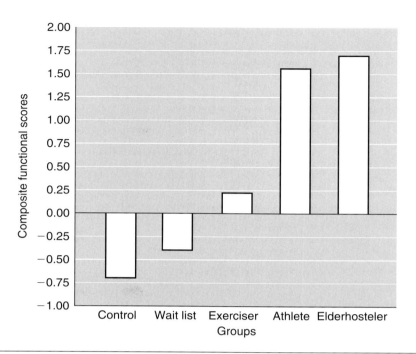

Figure 9.6   Composite functional scores of men varying in habitual exercise. Functional score was developed by combining scores of balance, flexibility, digit-symbol, and vital capacity. Control and wait list groups were men who did not habitually exercise. Exercisers were men who belonged to an exercise program for persons over the age of 50.
Data from Stones and Kozma (1988, p. 321).

the overlap among the areas, also would affect the other three.

Cerebrovascular Integrity and Cognitive Function

An early theory of how increased physical fitness might be related to optimal cognitive function hypothesized that chronic exercise maintains cerebrovascular integrity by increasing oxygen transport, which in turn reduces brain hypoxia (lack of oxygen) in active brain regions. Several types of evidence are suggested to support this theory. First, cerebral hypoxia is common among older people in poor health, and cognitive performance in geriatric patients with chronic, obstructive, and pulmonary disease seems to improve after oxygen administration. Second, cognitive performance is decreased in a high-altitude, oxygen-diminished environment. Third, oxygen is essential for the metabolism of glucose, the brain's fuel, and it also is a critical ingredient in the metabolism of such neurotransmitters as acetylcholine, dopamine, norepinephrine, and serotonin. The weakness in the oxygen

transport-glucose metabolism hypothesis, however, is that brain energy levels can be maintained even under moderate hypoxia (Gibson, Karpovich, & Gollnick, 1961).

The synthesis of acetylcholine and the biogenic amines, however, is susceptible to mild hypoxia. Also, synthesis of some neurotransmitters increases under conditions in which the oxygen level is higher than normal. Even though animal research has shown that the routine supply of oxygen to the brain is 2.5 times greater than the metabolic needs of brain tissue, this research was conducted in animals under anesthesia. The metabolic needs and transport system of oxygen in the healthy, active, and challenged brain are not yet clearly understood and certainly differ radically from the anesthetized animal model. Even with these criticisms, Dustman et al. (1990) maintain that exercise-related increases in oxygen transport and use could affect critical neurotransmitter systems.

Dramatic regional cerebrovascular bloodflow shifts are associated not only with a specific movement but also with the ideation associated with that movement. Sophisticated advances in brain scanning have shown that regional bloodflow asymmetries parallel hand preference asymme-

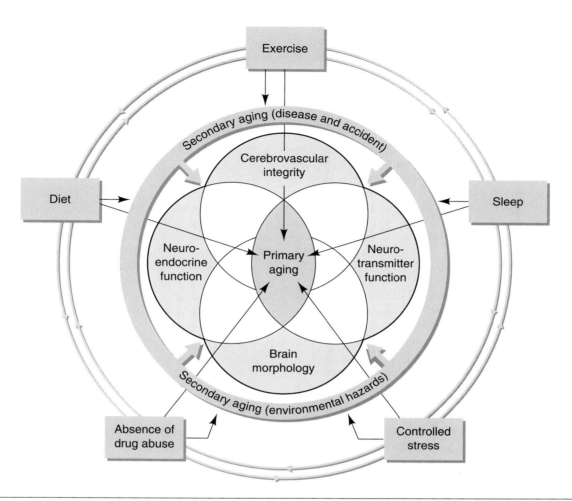

Figure 9.7 Hypothetical model of effects of health habits on primary and secondary aging. The center reflects primary aging of the systems that affect cognitive function: cerebrovascular changes, neurotransmitter depletion or malfunction, brain morphological changes, and neuroendocrine function deterioration. The shaded ring circling the primary aging core depicts factors of secondary aging that can accelerate primary aging: disease, accident, or environmental hazards. The outer ring indicates five health behaviors that may retard the development of both primary and secondary aging (depicted by arrows pointing toward primary and secondary aging). The arrows in the outer ring point in both directions and show that the five health behaviors are interrelated.

tries. That is, when the hands are activated simultaneously to perform the same task, such as touching fingers to the thumb on both hands (Halsey, Blauenstein, Wilson, & Wills, 1979), bloodflow shifts mirror the hand preference even though both hands are doing the same task. It seems likely that the responsiveness of the regional bloodflow shift mechanism to active brain tissue plays a role in the maintenance of functions related to those regions, and exercise-produced changes in blood chemistry remain a viable area of exploration for mechanisms to explain fitness–cognitive function relationships.

Another example of the way that exercise might postpone cognitive aging is by its influence on total cerebral bloodflow (CBF) and regional CBF. Rogers, Meyer, and Mortel (1990) reported that the CBF of inactive retirees 62 to 70 years old significantly declined after 4 years of retirement, whereas the CBF of retirees who continued to work or who remained physically active during the 4 years was unchanged. They proposed several mechanisms (see Table 9.2) by which regular physical activity may be beneficial to the brain, most of them related to the maintenance of CBF and the prevention of stroke, which

Table 9.2
Influence of Regular Physical Activity on Factors That May Retard Age-Related Cerebral Atherogenesis and Sustain Cognitive Functions

Regular physical activity	Beneficial result to brain
Decreases blood pressure	Reduces risk for stroke Assists in maintaining cerebral profusion
Reduces plasma levels of LDL	Reduces risk for atherogenesis Assists in maintaining CBF Reduced risk for stroke
Lowers excessive triglyceride levels	Improves CBF
Inhibits platelet aggregability	Maintains CBF Reduced risk for stroke
Activates the brain	Enhances cerebral metabolic demands, thereby increasing CBF
Improves brain vasculature	More efficient distribution of CBF[a]

Note. LDL = low-density lipoproteins; CBF = cerebral bloodflow.
[a]From Black, Greenough, Anderson, and Isaacs (1987).
Developed from Rogers, Meyer, and Morel (1990, pp. 123-128).

can destroy brain tissue and greatly impair cognition. Thus, exercise can reduce disease-related secondary aging effects on cognitive function.

Neurotransmitter Depletion and Imbalance

Neurotransmitters are the biochemical messengers used by neurons to send neural impulses and to communicate with each other. Each neuron synthesizes one of several types of transmitters, which, by the action of enzymes, is synthesized when neural activity is needed and degraded after the neural activity is completed. Some of the major neurotransmitters are acetylcholine, dopamine, epinephrine, norepinephrine, serotonin, and gamma-aminobutyric acid (GABA). Dopamine, epinephrine, and norepinephrine are collectively

known as *catecholamines*, or *biogenic amines*. Neurons that use acetylcholine are called *cholinergic neurons*.

Normal aging impairs the brain's ability to synthesize and degrade neurotransmitters, some more than others. With aging, a gradual linear decline occurs in some neurotransmitters, two of the most notable being dopamine and norepinephrine. Pathological losses of specific neurotransmitters in late middle age and the resultant imbalances that occur in neurotransmitter function cause neurotransmitter-related diseases. For example, drastic losses of dopaminergic neurons and the concurrent imbalance between dopamine and acetylcholine causes Parkinson's disease, which is characterized by the inability to control movements. However, because dopamine synthesis gradually decreases with each year of normal aging, if everyone lived to be over 100 years old, eventually everyone would display Parkinson-like symptoms. Other neurotransmitter-related diseases include Huntington's disease, which involves, among other losses, an insufficiency of GABA, and Alzheimer's disease, which involves a loss of cholinergic neurotransmitters. Other catecholamines also have been associated with various types of brain function; thus, it is clear that optimal catecholamine function is essential for the performance of psychomotor tasks and many other types of cognitive function.

Catecholamine function, however, can be affected by systematic regular exercise. Several investigators have found that after exercise training, either whole-brain resting catecholamines (Brown et al., 1979) or other characteristics of the catecholamine neurotransmitters in rats were changed in a direction counter to the age-associated changes normally seen (Gilliam et al., 1984; MacRae, Spirduso, Walters, Farrar, & Wilcox, 1987). Also, catecholamine activity is higher in hyperactive rats than in hypoactive rats, suggesting that catecholamine levels may respond not only to acute bouts of exercise but actually may influence activity levels within a species. Almost no work has been completed in which behavioral and brain neurotransmitter changes subsequent to exercise training have been examined in the same animals, but Fordyce and Farrar (1991b) observed enhancement of brain cholinergic functioning and spatial learning in the same rats after 14 weeks of running training. They also found exercised-induced cholinergic changes only in the brain hippocampus (an area associated with spatial learning) and not in two other areas, the parietal and frontal cortices, which are responsible for somatosensory and motor functions, respectively (Fordyce & Farrar, 1991a). Thus, results from animal research support the premise that exercise-mediated changes at the cellular level enhance neural transmission, either by structural or chemical modifications, and may explain the effects of exercise on cognition and learning. Future research may show that habitual exercise, because of either acute effects on a daily basis or long-term changes, can modulate one or more rate-limiting steps (i.e., steps that are critical to the completion of the function) in one or more of the neurotransmitter systems required for efficient, rapid information processing.

Neuroendocrine System and Autonomic Tone

Acute exercise bouts increase arousal of the central nervous system and facilitate some types of information processing (for a review, see Tomporowski & Ellis, 1986). Neural activation and stimulation of the ascending reticular activating system (ARAS) influence attention processes, and physical activity activates the ARAS. For example, there is evidence that the CNS of the elderly is underaroused compared to the young and that neuromuscular stimulation of the ARAS via postural changes (lying to sitting to standing) and exercise (to 40% of maximum heart rate) decreases age differences in CNS processing speed (Woods, 1981). Through this mechanism, chronic activity may enhance the ability of individuals to control attention (Woodruff, 1985).

Chronic exercise also may produce a tuning of neuroendocrine adaptations. The neuroendocrine theory of aging suggests that the neuroendocrine system accelerates aging through hormonal actions on target brain cells (Landfield & Lynch, 1977). For example, aging impairs glucose tolerance and reduces the production of growth hormones and adrenocorticosteroids. Conversely, physical conditioning improves the response to glucose and stimulates growth hormone, thus enhancing the transport of amino acids across cell membranes for protein synthesis. Therefore, staying physically fit may maintain general hormonal regulation such that key enzymatic responses to many different tasks also are maintained.

Exercise-Induced Morphological Changes

As the brain ages, many morphological changes occur. Neurons swell, axons (nerve cables) shrink,

and dendrites (the projections along which neurons communicate with each other) are lost. The dendritic shape also changes, which affects the neurons' ability to communicate with each other. Old brain tissue, when examined under a microscope, has a very different structure than young brain tissue. Furthermore, the rate of these detrimental age-related morphological changes is different not only for different areas of the brain but for different layers of the brain within an area (Diamond & Connor, 1982).

Animal research provides considerable evidence, however, suggesting that morphological brain changes, such as changes in neuronal cell structure, number, and density, are affected by experience, including motor activity. Primates living in movement-enriched environments (i.e., large, room-size cages in which there were toys, ample space to move, and other primates with which to interact) had enhanced morphological changes above and beyond those of primates that were caged alone and also above those of animals that could interact and communicate with other primates but had no opportunity to be physically active (Floeter & Greenough, 1979). Young rats that were forced to use one limb more than the other revealed large morphological changes in the brain areas that controlled the overused limb but not in the brain areas of the underused limb. Also, whole-brain weight is lower in inactive animals compared to active ones (Pysh & Weiss, 1979), although no one has suggested any interesting interpretations of this observation.

Long ago, Vogt and Vogt (1946) proposed that frequent use of neurons served to postpone nerve cell aging. Nerve cells that are active also have a better chance of retaining their maintenance operations. The brain is very plastic, and several researchers have shown that enhanced movement can produce structural changes. Vigorous exercise also induces capillary growth in some brain regions of middle-aged rats (Black, Isaacs, Anderson, Alcontara, & Greenough, 1990) so that the enhanced metabolic activity of the brain can be supported. An enriched environment that promotes manipulation of objects and encourages physical activity also has been associated with the recovery of brain function in animals that have been brain damaged. For example, rats recovering from sensorimotor lesions of the brain in a movement-enriched environment recovered to greater levels of function than did rats living alone in standard housing (i.e., wire mesh cages; Held,

Gordon, & Gentile, 1985; Gentile, Behesti, & Held, 1987). The rats that lived in standard housing were movement-impoverished animals, a condition that appears to impair both the rate and extent of brain function recovery.

Although the old brain is still somewhat plastic, so that morphological changes take place in even very old animals (Diamond, Johnson, Protti, Ott, & Kajisa, 1985), the process is not as efficient as in young animals. The plasticity of the brain, as well as activity-induced development of vascular support, begins to decline in middle age (Black, Polinsky, & Greenough, 1989). Thus, Black, Isaacs, and Greenough (1991) suggested that the major contributions that enriched, complex environments can make to successful aging occur in early youth, when the development of morphological enhancement and vascular support for brain tissue provides a "neural reserve" that can be drawn on in senescence, much as a healthful diet and exercise lifestyle during youth can develop optimal bone mineral density that later in life can postpone the development of osteoporosis.

If reduced nervous activity diminishes dendritic growth and spine formation in aging, confined animals, then enhanced exercise-induced neural activity in aging animals might maintain neuronal cell structure and postpone the age-related morphological changes normally seen. It is possible, therefore, that the continual neural activation caused by physical movement throughout life optimizes the very neurological structures and functions necessary to execute those actions, not only in daily activities, but in communication and psychomotor tasks as well.

Mechanisms Involving Secondary Aging

Exercise may also indirectly affect brain function by preventing secondary aging. One of several good health habits (which include nutrition, adequate sleep, stress control, and absence of drug use), exercise may help prevent premature aging. The *indirect* effect of exercise on aging may operate through the prevention of accidents or disease that may produce secondary aging effects. This is illustrated in Figure 9.7 (page 267) by the wide-band arrows directed toward the circle depicting secondary aging. Finally, exercise also may act indirectly by enhancing and

supplementing other health habits, such as sleep, diet, and freedom from drug use, to postpone premature aging. This influence is also shown in Figure 9.7 by the outer circle of lines that connect all five health habits.

Prevention of Disease

Primary aging is normal aging. Secondary aging occurs in the presence of disease and environmental accidents or insults. The development of cardiovascular disease, adult-onset diabetes, hypokinetic disease, and some types of hypertension accelerate the primary aging process. As discussed previously, these diseases are thought to impair cognitive function. A regular aerobic exercise and diet program can minimize secondary aging in most people, thus preventing these diseases and reducing their deleterious effects on cognitive function.

Complementary Health Habits

One relationship that is repeatedly seen in the exercise literature is that people who exercise also tend to have better complementary health habits than nonexercisers. Usually, exercisers do not smoke or drink excessively, they try to maintain a relatively healthy diet, and they are also at least conscious of the need to control stress. For many, stress control was a motivating factor in beginning an exercise program. As people continue in an exercise program, they may become more and more motivated to improve health habits that counter secondary aging.

Physical fitness may be associated with better cognitive function, because people who are physically fit exercise on an almost daily basis and bouts of acute exercise enhance sleep quality. If individuals are physically fit, exercise vigorously, and do so at a time not too near bedtime, the exercise may enhance the first sleep cycle of the night (Anch, Browman, & Mitler, 1988). Sleep provides an energy conservation function, and to the extent that exercise improves the quality of sleep for older individuals, exercise also may contribute to conserving energy necessary for some types of cognitive function.

Psychosocial Explanations

The possibility that complementary health habits may counter secondary aging and thus influence cognition in older adults leads some critics to doubt a physiological explanation of the role of exercise in maintaining cognitive function. Critics maintain it is not the physiological changes produced by exercise that influence cognition. Rather, it is the constellation of health and personality behaviors that exercisers have that produces superior scores on tests of cognitive function. This has led to a psychosocial explanation of the exercise–cognitive function relationship.

Psychosocial explanations suggest that none of the proposed biological or neurophysiological are mechanisms valid, because what appears to be a relationship between physical fitness and cognitive function is really an indirect result of a relationship between physical fitness and other factors that are also related to cognitive function. Chronic exercisers differ from nonexercisers in many ways other than just exercise habits. They differ genetically in at least some traits. For example, people self-selected for endurance activity differ from inactive people on the basis of inherited traits relevant to muscle fiber composition (Suominen, Heikkinen, Parkatti, Forsberg, & Kiiskinen, 1980). Presumably, the same is true of sprinters, where having a high proportion of fast-twitch muscle fiber is an advantage. Just as exercisers have genetic differences in physical attributes such as fiber types, they also differ genetically in psychosocial factors. Superior performance in several types of psychosocial behaviors has been associated with people who are in better physical health (Milligan et al., 1984).

People who exercise regularly have less physical impairment, higher life satisfaction, income, educational level, and cognitive ability (Stones & Kozma, 1989), and a more positive attitude (Clarkson-Smith & Hartley, 1989). It is also probable that people who are more mentally capable are more likely to exercise, because of their increased awareness of the health benefits of exercise. Cohort differences in combinations of all of these factors make it extremely difficult to tease out a relationship between fitness and cognitive function. Furthermore, lack of education and a low socioeconomic status are correlated with slow psychomotor speed (Era, 1988), a relationship that is more pronounced when studied longitudinally (Lehr & Thomae, 1973). Variables such as socioeconomic status, intelligence, state of anxiety, motivation, and instructional set all interact with the measurement of response speed and have not been well controlled in research studies.

The Process by Which Fitness May Affect Cognitive Function

If regular aerobic exercise indeed enhances cognitive function, does it do so at all ages or are the effects more beneficial and more apparent in older individuals whose cognitive processing speed is declining? Stones and Kozma (1988) articulated two possible models: the tonic and overpractice effect model and the moderator effects model (see Figure 9.8, a-b).

In the tonic and overpractice effect model (TOPE), the effect of exercise is similar for all ages: Vigor and vitality are maintained or restored in a wide range of functions. This model proposes that chronological age and lifestyle factors contribute independently to functional age at all ages. Exercise has a generalized (i.e., tonic) effect across physical and psychological domains. It does not postpone or change the rate of aging on respective functions, but it does compensate somewhat for age-related deterioration in functional capability. Possible mechanisms by which this model operates include exercise-induced regional bloodflow changes, trophic influences of neuromuscular activity, biochemical modulations, and morphological changes that are seen in both young and old and in both cross-sectional and longitudinal studies (Spirduso, 1975; Spirduso et al., 1988). In the TOPE model, exercise also provides an overpractice effect, like that seen in the skillful execution of familiar movement patterns that are relatively unimpaired in older people who practice systematically. Stones and Kozma (1988) suggested that if the TOPE model is correct, investigators should find that exercisers at all ages are superior to sedentary individuals on tests of various types of cognitive function, especially those that require information-processing speed. The results of several studies support this model (Dustman et al., 1984; Stacey et al., 1985; Stones & Kozma, 1988; Vanfraechem & Vanfraechem, 1977).

The moderator effects model suggests that the more people age (up to a point), the more exercise moderates the natural decline in cognitive function that accompanies aging. This model implies a change in the *rate* of aging, or at least a change in the rate of functional aging, and exercise benefits that are greater for the old than for the young. Research supporting this model would have to find differential effects of exercise favoring the elderly, that is, the exercise factor must benefit the older subjects more than the young. Although the

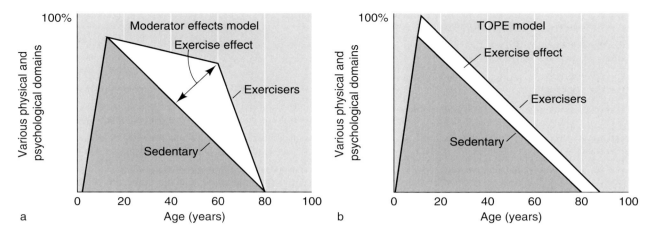

Figure 9.8 Regular exercise may postpone premature mental aging. In the (a) moderator effects model, high physical fitness plays an increasingly important role with each increasing age decade in postponing aging symptoms. The (b) TOPE, or tonic and overpractice effect, model proposes that exercise produces a tonic physiological effect for all ages and optimizes cognitive function at every age, thus postponing premature cognitive aging. Models created from discussion in Stones and Kozma (1988, pp. 273-321).

research results are mixed, the requisite significant interaction that would support the model must be weak, because it is not present in all studies. A complicating factor is that inactive subjects within the older age groups are less active than the inactive 20-year-olds. Thus, old inactive males who are less active than young inactive males produce a weak interaction between physical activity patterns and age.

Implications of the Relationship Between Physical Fitness and Cognitive Function

Based on the amount of highly suggestive evidence, it seems almost compelling that physical fitness optimizes cognitive function. Yet, when these positive results are balanced against the contradictory results from some studies and then weighed against the possibility that exercise habits are just one of a constellation of inherited behavioral differences that covary with cognitive function, the proposed relationship can be accepted only cautiously.

Nevertheless, the potential beneficial impact of physical fitness on enhancing the quality of life of the elderly, through improved cognition and consequently improved psychosocial functioning, is so great that it is unlikely that this topic will lose

momentum any time in the near future. Exercise programs, especially for the elderly who are not yet frail, are so inexpensive and feasible that even the small cognitive advantages to be gained by a small percentage of adults would be cost effective. Studies are currently underway to assist policy makers in determining the administrative costs of implementing exercise programs in long-term care institutions and whether these health care procedures might prevent or postpone patient incapacitation. For long-term benefits, exercise programs in public schools and adult educational curricula cost relatively little but have the potential to improve behavioral health habits, which can substantially decrease individuals' health costs as they age.

In Summary

Cognitive function, particularly as expressed by processing speed, is not as efficient in chronically diseased individuals, such as those who have hypertension and cardiovascular disease, and is impaired somewhat during times of episodic illness. Disuse, or physical inactivity throughout a lifetime, leads eventually to a state of poor health that can compromise cognitive function. Conversely, when some types of cognitive function of highly aerobically fit adults are compared cross-sectionally to those of sedentary low-fit people, these cognitive functions are almost always found to be higher in the physically active individuals. Processes that support cognition, such as information-processing time, working memory, attention, perceptual processes, and psychomotor control may be more related to health and fitness status than other cognitive functions, such as reasoning, spatial abilities, synthesis, and global tests of intelligence.

The faster behavioral speeds seen in physically fit people can be attributed more to a shortening of the central information-processing time than to a shortening of the peripheral neuromuscular aspects of the response. The identification of this major site of slowing has been determined by fractionating reaction times through the use of electroencephalographic and electromyographic recordings.

Although cross-sectional studies generally support a relationship between physical fitness and some types of cognitive function, some exercise intervention programs, in which sedentary older people have been physically trained for 4 to 8 months, have failed to improve cognitive scores. The subjects of these intervention studies, however, never approach the fitness levels of those attained by individuals who exercise regularly throughout their lives.

Several hypotheses have been developed to explain the proposed beneficial effects of exercise on cognitive function. These hypotheses can be categorized as those that act on primary aging— (a) enhanced cerebrovascular integrity and function, (b) improved efficiency of cerebral neurotransmitter function and balance, (c) enhanced tone of the neuroendocrine system, and (d) morphological changes in the brain—or those that act on secondary aging—(e) improved restorative sleep patterns and (f) prevention of disease. Although these hypotheses seem compelling, several valid arguments can be made against a *causal* beneficial effect of exercise on cognitive function. Briefly, these arguments state that the psychosocial characteristics of regular exercisers that drive them to exercise are also highly correlated with other factors that optimize cognitive function—high motivation and instructional set, intelligence, educational level, and socioeconomic status. These characteristics also are probably present at birth, so that people who optimize their cognitive function throughout life do so in many ways, one of which may be maintaining their health and fitness.

Many factors have made it difficult to confirm scientifically whether exercise is causally related to cognitive function, especially in the older population. Findings from cross-sectional and intervention research designs have been contradictory.

Studies have not yielded stable measures of cognitive function, and the variance within and between subjects of different ages is different. Finally, determining physical fitness in older people is very difficult, and older subjects are frequently more difficult to recruit and work with than college students.

Although a fitness-cognitive function relationship is not conclusive, the evidence supporting a strong relationship is compelling enough to continue research on the subject and to make professional and policy decisions that include exercise as an important lifestyle component of older adults.

References

Anch, A.M., Browman, C.P., & Mitler, J.K. (1988). *Sleep: A scientific perspective.* Englewood Cliffs, NJ: Prentice Hall.

Arito, H., & Oguri, M. (1990). Contingent negative variation and reaction time of physically-trained subjects in simple and discriminative tasks. *Industrial Health,* **28**, 97-106.

Åstrand, P.O., & Rodahl, K. (1977). *Textbook of work physiology.* New York: McGraw-Hill.

Barry, A.J., Steinmetz, J.R., Page, H.F., & Rodahl, K. (1966). The effects of physical conditioning on older individuals. II. Motor performance and cognitive function. *Journal of Gerontology,* **21**, 182-191.

Baylor, A.M., & Spirduso, W.W. (1988). Systematic aerobic exercise and components of reaction time in older women. *Journal of Gerontology: Psychological Sciences,* **43**, P121-P126.

Birren, J.E., Woods, A.M., & Williams, M.V. (1980). Behavioral slowing with age: Causes, organization, and consequences. In L.W. Poon (Ed.), *Aging in the 1980s: Psychological issues* (pp. 293-308). Washington, DC: American Psychological Association.

Black, J.E., Greenough, W.T., Anderson, B.J., & Isaacs, K.R. (1987). Environment and the aging brain. *Canadian Journal of Psychology,* **41**, 111-130.

Black, J.E., Isaacs, K.R., Anderson, B.J., Alcontara, A.A., & Greenough, W.T. (1990). Learning causes synaptogenesis, while motor activity causes angiogenesis, in cerebellar cortex of adult rats. *Proceedings of the National Academy of Science USA,* **87**, 5568-5572.

Black, J.E., Isaacs, K.R., & Greenough, W.T. (1991). Usual vs. successful aging: Some notes on experiential factors. *Neurobiology of Aging*, **12**, 325-328.

Black, J.E., Polinsky, M., & Greenough, W.T. (1989). Progressive failure of cerebral angiogenesis supporting neural plasticity in aging rats. *Neurobiology of Aging*, **10**, 353-358.

Blumenthal, J.A., Emery, C.F., Madden, D.J., George, L.K., Coleman, E., Riddle, M.W., McKee, D.C. Reasoner, J., & Williams, R.S. (1989). Cardiovascular and behavioral effects of aerobic exercise training in healthy older men and women. *Journal of Gerontology: Medical Sciences*, **44**, M147-M157.

Blumenthal, J.A., Emery, C.F., Madden, D.J., Schniebolk, S., Walsh-Riddle, M., George, L.K., McKee, D.C., Higginbotham, M.B., Cobb, F.R., & Coleman, R.E. (1991). Long-term effects of exercise on psychological functioning in older men and women. *Journal of Gerontology: Psychological Sciences*, **46**, P352-P361.

Blumenthal, J.A., & Madden, D.J. (1988). Effects of aerobic exercise training, age, and physical fitness on memory search performance. *Psychology and Aging*, **3**, 280-285.

Boarman, A.M. (1977). The effect of folk dancing upon reaction time and movement time of senior citizens. *Dissertation Abstracts International*, **38**, 5329A-5330A. (University Microfilms No. 7732544)

Borkin, G.A., & Norris, A.H. (1980). Assessment of biological age using a profile of physical parameters. *Journal of Gerontology*, **35**, 177-184.

Bortz, W.M. (1982). Disuse and aging. *Journal of the American Medical Association*, **248**, 1203-1208.

Botwinick, J., & Birren, J.E. (1963). Cognitive processes: Mental abilities and psychomotor responses in aged men. In J.E. Birren, R.N. Butler, S.W. Greenhouse, L. Sokoloff, & M.R. Yarrow (Eds.), *Human aging: A biological and behavioral study* (pp. 143-156). Washington, DC: U.S. Government Printing Office.

Botwinick, J.E., & Storandt, M. (1974). Cardiovascular status, depressive effect, and other factors in reaction time. *Journal of Gerontology*, **29**, 543-548.

Botwinick, J.E., & Thompson, L.W. (1966). Components of reaction time in relation to age and sex. *Journal of General Psychology*, **108**, 175-183.

Brown, B.S., Payne, T., Kim, C., Moore, G., Krebs, P., & Martin, W. (1979). Chronic response of rat brain norepinephrine and serotonin levels to endurance training. *Journal of Applied Physiology*, **46**, 12-23.

Buccola, V.A. (1972). *Physiological and psychological changes in the aged following a fourteen-week physical training program.* Doctoral dissertation, Arizona State University, Phoenix.

Carlow, T.J., & Appenzeller, O., & Rodriguez, M. (1978). Neurology of training: VEPs before and after a run. *Neurology*, **2**, 390.

Chodzko-Zajko, W.J. (1991). Physical fitness, cognitive performance, and aging. *Medicine and Science in Sports and Exercise*, **23**, 868-872.

Chodzko-Zajko, W.J., & Ringel, R.L. (1987). Physiological fitness measures and sensory and motor performance in aging. *Experimental Gerontology*, **22**, 317-328.

Chodzko-Zajko, W.J., Schuler, P.B., Solomon, J.S., Heinl, B., & Ellis, N. (1990). *Physical fitness levels and cognitive performance in aging.* Paper presented at the 1990 Gatlinburg Conference on Mental Retardation, Brainerd, MN, April, 1990.

Clark, J.W. (1960). The aging dimension: A factorial analysis of individual differences with age on psychological and physiological measurements. *Journal of Gerontology*, **15**, 183-187.

Clarkson, P.M. (1978). The effect of age and activity level in simple and choice fractionated response time. *European Journal of Applied Physiology*, **40**, 17-25.

Clarkson-Smith, L., & Hartley, A.A. (1989). Relationships between physical exercise and cognitive abilities in older adults. *Psychology and Aging*, **4**, 183-189.

Clarkson-Smith, L., & Hartley, A.A. (1990). Structural equation models of relationships between exercise and cognitive abilities. *Psychology and Aging*, **5**, 437-446.

Diamond, M.C., & Connor, J.R., Jr. (1982). Plasticity of the aging cerebral cortex. In S. Hoyer (Ed.), *Experimental brain research* (Suppl. 5) (pp. 36-44). Berlin: Springer-Verlag.

Diamond, M.C., Johnson, R.E., Protti, A.M., Ott, C., & Kajisa, L. (1985). Plasticity in the 904-day-old male cerebral cortex. *Experimental Neurology*, **87**, 309-317.

Diesfeldt, H.F.A., & Diesfeldt-Groenendijk, H. (1977). Improving cognitive performance in psychogeriatric patients: The influence of physical exercise. *Age and Aging*, **6**, 58-64.

Duke University Center for the Study of Aging and Human Development. (1978). *Multidimensional functional assessment: The OARS methodology,* Durham, NC: Duke University.

Dustman, R.E., Ruhling, R.O., Russell, E.M., Shearer, D.E., Bonekat, H.W., Shigeoka, J.W., Wood, J.S., & Bradford, D.C. (1984). Aerobic exercise training and improved neuropsychological function of older individuals. *Neurobiology of Aging*, **5**, 35-42.

Dustman, R.E., Emmerson, R.Y., Ruhling, R.O., Shearer, D.E., Steinhaus, L.A., Johnson, S.C., Bonekat, H.W., & Shigeoka, J.W. (1990). Age and fitness effects on EEG, ERPs, visual sensitivity, and cognition. *Neurobiology of Aging*, **11**, 193-200.

Elias, M.F., & Schlager, G. (1974). Discrimination learning in mice genetically selected for high and low blood pressure: Initial findings and methodological implications. *Physiology and Behavior*, **13**, 261-267.

Elias, M.F., Robbins, M.A., Schultz, N.R., Jr., & Pierce, T.W. (1990). Is blood pressure an important variable in research on aging and neuropsychological test performance? *Journal of Gerontology: Psychological Sciences*, **45**, P128-P135.

Elsayed, M., Ismail, A.H., & Young, R.J. (1980). Intellectual differences of adult men related to age and physical fitness before and after an exercise program. *Journal of Gerontology*, **35**, 383-387.

Emery, C.F., & Gatz, M. (1990). Psychological and cognitive effects of an exercise program for community-residing older adults. *The Gerontologist*, **30**, 184-188.

Emmerson, R.Y., Dustman, R.E., & Shearer, D.E. (1989). P3 latency and symbol digit performance correlations in aging. *Experimental Aging Research*, **15**, 151-159.

Era, P. (1988). Sensory, psychomotor, and motor functions in men of different ages. *Scandinavian Journal of Social Medicine* (Suppl. 39), 9-77.

Field, D., Schaie, K.W., & Leino, E.V. (1988). Continuity in intellectual functioning: The role of self-reported health. *Psychology and Aging*, **3**, 385-392.

Floeter, M.K., & Greenough, W.T. (1979). Cerebellar plasticity: Modification of Purkinje cell structure by differential rearing in monkeys. *Science*, **206**, 227-229.

Folkins, C.H., & Sime, W.E. (1981). Physical fitness training and mental health. *American Psychologist*, **36**, 373-389.

Fordyce, D.E., & Farrar, R.P. (1991a). Enhancement of spatial learning in F344 rats by physical activity and related learning-associated alterations in hippocampal and cortical cholinergic functioning. *Behavioural Brain Research*, **46**, 123-133.

Fordyce, D.E., & Farrar, R.P. (1991b). Physical activity effects on hippocampal and parietal cortical cholinergic function and spatial learning in F344 rats. *Behavioural Brain Research*, **43**, 115-125.

Fozard, J.L., Vercruyssen, M., Reynolds, S.L., & Hancock, P.A. (1990). Longitudinal analysis of age-related slowing: BLSA Reaction Time Data. *Proceedings of the Human Factors Society 34th Annual Meeting*, **1**, 163-167.

Fries, J.F., & Crapo, L.M. (1981). *Vitality and aging*. San Francisco: Freeman.

Gentile, A., Behesti, Z., & Held, J.M. (1987). Environment vs. exercise effects on motor impairments following cortical lesions in rats. *Behavior and Neural Biology*, **47**, 321-332.

Gibson, D., Karpovich, P.V., & Gollnick, P.D. (1961). *Effect of training upon reflex and reaction time* (Research Report DA-49-007-MD-889). Washington, DC: Office of the Surgeon General.

Gilliam, P.E., Spirduso, W.W., Martin, T.P., Walters, T.J., Wilcox, R.E., & Farrar, R.P. (1984). The effects of exercise training on (3H)-spiperone binding in rat striatum. *Pharmacology, Biochemistry, and Behavior*, **20**, 863-867.

Gitlin, L.N. (1985, March). *Psychological effects of physical conditioning in the well elderly*. Paper presented at the 2nd National Forum on Research in Aging, University of Nebraska, Lincoln.

Godin, G., Jobin, J., & Bouillon, J. (1986). Assessment of leisure time exercise behavior by self-report: A concurrent validity study. *Canadian Journal of Public Health*, **77**, 359-362.

Halsey, J.H., Blauenstein, V.W., Wilson, E.M., & Wills, E.H. (1979). Regional cerebral blood flow comparison of right and left hand movement. *Neurology*, **29**, 21-28.

Hancock, P.A., Arthur, E.J., Chrysler, S.T., & Lee, J. (1994). The effects of sex, target duration, and illumination on the production of time intervals. *Acta Psychologica*, **86**, 57-67.

Hart, B. (1981). The effect of age and habitual activity on the fractionated components of resisted and unresisted response time. *Medicine and Science in Sports and Exercise*, **13**, 78.

Held, J., Gordon, J., & Gentile, A.M. (1985). Environmental influences on locomotor recovery following cortical lesions in rats. *Journal of Behavioral Neuroscience*, **99**(4), 678-690.

Hertzog, C., Schaie, K.W., & Gribbin, K. (1978). Cardiovascular disease and changes in intellectual functioning from middle to old age. *Journal of Gerontology*, **33**, 872-883.

Hoyer, W.J., Labouvie, G.V., & Baltes, P.B. (1973). Modification of response speed deficits and intellectual performance in the elderly. *Human Development*, **16**, 233-242.

Hughes, J.R., Casal, D.C., & Leon, A.S. (1986). Psychological effects of exercise: A randomized cross-over trial. *Journal of Psychosomatic Research*, **30**, 355-360.

Jöreskog, K.G., & Sörbom, D. (1984). *LISERAL VI: Analysis of linear structural relationships by the method of maximum likelihood*. Moonesville, IN: Scientific Software.

Landfield, P.W., & Lynch, G. (1977). Brain aging and plasma steroids: Quantitative correlations. *Society for Neuroscience Abstracts*, November.

Lehr, U., & Thomae, H. (1973). Determinants of "aging": Findings from a longitudinal study. *Zeitschrift fur Alternsforschung*, **27**, 369-372.

MacRae, P.G., Crum, K., Giessman, D., & Green, J. (1987, June). *The effects of age and fitness level on components of reaction time in women.* Paper presented at the meeting of the North American Society for Sport and Physical Activity, Vancouver, British Columbia.

MacRae, P.G., Spirduso, W.W., Walters, T.J., Farrar, R.P., & Wilcox, R.E. (1987). Endurance training effects on striatal D2 dopamine receptor binding and striatal dopamine metabolites in presenescent older rats. *Psychopharmacology*, **92**, 236-240.

Madden, D.J., Blumenthal, J.A., Allen, P.A., & Emery, C.F. (1989). Improving aerobic capacity in healthy older adults does not necessarily lead to improved cognitive performance. *Psychology and Aging*, **4**, 307-320.

Milligan, W.L., Powell, D.A., Harley, C., & Furchtgott, E. (1984). A comparison of physical health and psychosocial variables as predictors of reaction time and serial learning performance in elderly men. *Journal of Gerontology*, **39**, 704-710.

Myers, A.M., & Hamilton, N. (1985). Evaluation of the Canadian Red Cross Society's Fun and Fitness Program for Seniors. *Canadian Journal on Aging*, **4**, 201-212.

Ostrow, A.C. (1984). *Physical activity and the older adult.* Princeton, NJ: Princeton Book.

Paffenbarger, R.S., Wing, A.L., & Hyde, R. (1978). Physical activity as an index of heart attack risk in college alumni. *American Journal of Epidemiology*, **108**, 161-175.

Panton, L.B., Graves, J.E., Pollock, M.L., Hagberg, J.M., & Chen, W. (1990). Effect of aerobic and resistance training on fractionated reaction time and speed of movement. *Journal of Gerontology: Medical Sciences*, **45**, M26-M31.

Perlmutter, M., & Nyquist, L. (1990). Relationships between self-reported physical and mental health and intelligence performance across adulthood. *Journal of Gerontology: Psychological Sciences*, **45**, P145-P155.

Powell, D.A., & Pohndorf, R.H. (1971). Comparison of adult exercisers and nonexercisers on fluid intelligence and selected psychological variables. *Research Quarterly for Exercise and Sport*, **42**, 70-77.

Powell, R.R. (1974). Psychological effects of exercise therapy upon institutionalized geriatric patients. *Journal of Gerontology*, **29**, 157-161.

Pysh, J.J., & Weiss, G.M. (1979). Exercise during development induces an increase in Purkinje cell dendritic tree size. *Science*, **206**, 230-231.

Rikli, R., & Busch, S. (1986). Motor performance of women as a function of age and physical activity level. *Journal of Gerontology*, **41**, 645-649.

Rikli, R.E., & Edwards, D.J. (1991). Effects of a three-year exercise program on motor function and cognitive processing speed in older women. *Research Quarterly for Exercise and Sport*, **62**, 61-67.

Rogers, R.L., Meyer, J.S., & Mortel, K.F. (1990). After reaching retirement age physical activity sustains cerebral perfusion and cognition. *Journal of the American Geriatrics Society*, **38**, 123-128.

Salthouse, T.A. (1991). *Theoretical perspectives on cognitive aging.* Hillsdale, NJ: Erlbaum.

Salthouse, T.A., Kausler, D.H., & Saults, J.S. (1990). Age, self-assessed health status, and cognition. *Journal of Gerontology: Psychological Sciences*, **45**, P156-P160.

Sands, L.P., & Meredith, W. (1992). Blood pressure and intellectual functioning in late midlife. *Journal of Gerontology: Psychological Sciences*, **47**, P81-P84.

Shephard, R.J. (1978). *Physical activity and aging.* London: Croom Helm.

Sherwood, D.E., & Selder, D.J. (1979). Cardiorespiratory health, reaction time, and aging. *Medicine and Science in Sports*, **11**, 186-189.

Speith, W. (1964). Cardiovascular health status, age, and physiological performance. *Journal of Gerontology*, **19**, 277-284.

Spirduso, W.W. (1975). Reaction and movement time as a function of age and physical activity level. *Journal of Gerontology*, **30**, 435-440.

Spirduso, W.W. (1980). Physical fitness, aging, and psychomotor speed: A review. *Journal of Gerontology*, **35**, 850-865.

Spirduso, W.W., & Clifford, P. (1978). Neuromuscular speed and consistency of performance as a function of age, physical activity level, and type of activity. *Journal of Gerontology*, **33**, 26-30.

Spirduso, W.W., & Farrar, R.P. (1981). Effects of aerobic training on reactive capacity: An animal model. *Journal of Gerontology*, **36**, 654-662.

Spirduso, W.W., MacRae, H.H., MacRae, P.G., Prewitt, J., & Osborne, L. (1988). Exercise effects on aged motor function. In J.A. Joseph (Ed.), *Central determinants of age-related declines in motor function* (pp. 363-375). New York: New York Academy of Sciences.

Stacey, C., Kozma, A., & Stones, M.J. (1985). Simple cognitive and behavioral changes resulting from improved physical fitness in persons over 50 years of age. *Canadian Journal on Aging*, **4**, 67-73.

Stamford, B.A., Hambacher, W., & Fallica, A. (1974). Effects of daily physical exercise on the psychiatric state of institutionalized geriatric mental patients. *Research Quarterly*, **45**, 34-41.

Stones, M.J., & Kozma, A. (1988). Physical activity, age, and cognitive/motor performance. In M.L. Howe & C.J. Brainerd (Eds.), *Cognitive development in adulthood: Progress in cognitive development research* (pp. 273-321). New York: Springer-Verlag.

Stones, M.J., & Kozma, A. (1989). Age, exercise, and coding performance. *Psychology and Aging*, **4**, 190-194.

Suominen, H., Heikkinen, E., Parkatti, T., Forsberg, S., & Kiiskinen, A. (1980). Effects of "lifelong" physical training on functional aging in men. *Scandinavian Journal of Social Medicine*, **55**, 225-240.

Szafran, J. (1966). Age, cardiac output, and choice reaction time. *Nature*, **209**, 836-837.

Thomas, J.R., Landers, D.M., Salazar, W., & Etnier, J. (1994). Exercise and cognitive function. In C. Bouchard, R.J. Shephard, & T. Stephens (Eds.), *Physical activity, fitness, and health* (pp. 521-529). Champaign, IL: Human Kinetics.

Thurstone, L.L., & Thurstone, T.G. (1949). *Examiner manual for the primary abilities test* (Form 11-17). Chicago: Science Research Associates.

Tomporowski, P.D., & Ellis, N.R. (1986). Effects of exercise on cognitive processes: A review. *Psychological Bulletin*, **99**, 338-346.

Tredway, V. (1978). *Mood effects of exercise programs for older adults.* Doctoral dissertation, University of Southern California, Los Angeles.

Tweit, A.H., Gollnick, P.D., & Hearn, G.R. (1963). Effects of a training program on total body reaction time of individuals of low fitness. *Research Quarterly*, **34**, 508-513.

Vanfraechem, A., & Vanfraechem, R. (1977). Studies of the effect of a short training period on aged subjects. *Journal of Sports Medicine and Physical Fitness*, **17**, 373-380.

Vogt, C. & Vogt, O. (1946). Aging of nerve cells. *Nature*, **58**, 304.

Waldstein, S.R., Manuck, S.B., Ryan, C.M., & Muldoon, M.F. (1991). Neuropsychological correlates of hypertension: Review and methodologic considerations. *Psychological Bulletin*, **110**, 451-468.

Wechsler, D. (1981). *Manual for the Weschler Adult Intelligence Scale-Revised.* New York: The Psychological Corporation.

Wilkie, F.L., Eisdorfer, C., & Nowlin, J.B. (1976). Memory and blood pressure in the aged. *Experimental Aging Research*, **2**, 3-16.

Woodruff, D. (1985). Arousal, sleep, and aging. In J.E. Birren & K.W. Schaie (Eds.), *Handbook of the psychology of aging* (2nd ed., pp. 261-295). New York: Van Nostrand Reinhold.

Woods, A.M. (1981). *Age differences in the effect of physical activity and postural changes on information processing speed.* Doctoral dissertation, University of Southern California, Los Angeles.

Yandell, M.Y., & Spirduso, W.W. (1981). Sex and athletic status as factors in reaction latency and movement time. *Research Quarterly for Exercise and Sport*, **52**, 495-504.

CHAPTER 10

Health, Exercise, and Emotional Function

Waneen W. Spirduso and Kathleen S. Mackie

Anyone who has watched the gamut of emotions that people exhibit when participating in a competitive sporting event surely recognizes the powerful intertwining of physical exertion and affective responses. The competitor (it makes little difference whether it is a national championship match or a Sunday afternoon game) may be exhilarated one moment and devastated a few moments later. Similar though perhaps more muted emotional responses occur during all types of exercise experiences such as jogging, swimming, and social dance. The underlying theme of most physical activities is that it is almost impossible to perform them without total involvement and commitment—physical, mental, and emotional involvement. This relationship between physical activity and emotional response should come as a revelation to no one, because the relationship is commonplace.

This chapter examines the issue of whether good physical health and regular physical activity are related to the emotional health of older adults. Several questions are important: Do older people who maintain their health and physical fitness reap beneficial effects in terms of their emotional function? Does a high level of health and fitness help older people adjust to the many age-related challenges to emotional balance, such as loss of a spouse, that they often face? Can an improvement in health status and participation in an exercise program remediate emotional dysfunction?

Important though these questions are, the answers have been very difficult to obtain. The measurement of psychological constructs, such as anxiety, depression, and mood, is much more difficult and unreliable than the measurement of physiological functions, like heart rate, balance, and reaction time. However, even though research in the area of physical activity and emotional function may be inconclusive, results from a growing body of literature suggest that the relationship is real. This area of study is called *exercise psychology*, and researchers in the area, often called *exercise psychologists*, have differentiated the *product*, health and fitness, from the *process*, the human behavior of exercising. Health and fitness benefits are derived not only from the physiological changes that occur as a result of exercise behavior, but also from the behavioral process of exercising (Biddle & Fox, 1989; Dishman, 1985, 1986; Morgan & Goldston, 1987).

In this chapter, we discuss health and fitness with regard to various parameters of emotional function, such as moods, coping, anxiety, depression, and personality. (The relationship of health and fitness to self-image, self-esteem, self-efficacy, feelings of well-being, and life satisfaction, which are also aspects of emotional function, will be considered in the next chapter.) This chapter begins by recognizing that some challenges to emotional control are specifically related to the process of aging. It then introduces the basic emotional constructs and briefly summarizes the implications of failed emotional control for the elderly. Next, it discusses some of the difficulties associated with research on this topic, so that the findings presented later can be considered with an appropriate amount of conservatism. The chapter culminates in a discussion of the hypothesized physiological, psychological, and social mechanisms by which health and fitness may influence emotional function and concludes with a brief discussion of the potential negative influences of exercise.

Age-Related Challenges to Emotional Control

The physical, mental, and social changes that accompany aging bring with them challenges to emotional control that are above and beyond those routinely experienced by most younger individuals. As people age, they must adjust continuously to decreasing strength, endurance, physical ability, and health; the deaths of spouses and friends; retirement and reduced income; new social roles; and in advanced age, relocation of physical living arrangements (Schaie & Geiwitz, 1982).

Accumulative Losses

In old age, losses are inevitable and cumulative. Obvious and visible losses are those of muscle mass, strength, physical endurance, flexibility, and coordination. Health status becomes more tenuous in old age, characterized by more frequent and more serious illnesses that require longer periods of recuperation. Biochemical and electrolyte balances change with age, gastrointestinal and metabolic processes become less efficient, hormonal production decreases, and all of these combine to influence the subtle biochemistry of brain function. Coping with emotional challenges when their physical health is compromised is difficult for individuals of any age, but it is even more difficult for older adults who have additional problems and who may have to cope on a daily basis with problems such as arthritis, glaucoma, cataracts, congestive heart failure, or osteoporosis.

Even though some individuals may be relatively free of symptomatic disease, the loss of physical ability and skills may be emotionally traumatic, especially for those who have devoted a lifetime to the development of physical abilities. Physical ability and strength are an integral part of the self for athletes, workers in physical occupations, and individuals who have hobbies that require strength and endurance (mountain climbing, rock hunting, hang gliding, sailing, etc.). As that physical part of the self begins to erode noticeably, it takes substantial readjustment and psychological coping to maintain self-esteem and emotional control. Some individuals deal with the challenge by modifying their self-expectations. Others may have more difficulty dealing with the decline, abandon their physical hobbies or sports, and either substitute less physically demanding activities in their lives or find other compensations for the loss. Dealing with physical changes in appearance or function represents a psychological stressor that all aging people must confront, and for some, the challenge to emotional control is substantial.

Other losses that occur more frequently among aged populations are the deaths of loved ones and friends. In advanced age these deaths begin to occur more often, so that the elderly may find themselves in a state of unresolved and continual mourning (Billig, 1987). They also find themselves with fewer and fewer relatives and friends their own age who can support them psychologically and socially. Their opportunities for nurturing and being nurtured, for expressing feelings, and even for loving decrease with increasing age.

Retirement may often be associated with other types of losses: the self-identity that comes with having a job, financial status, and feelings of independence and worth and of contributing to society. The financial loss itself may be so significant that it imposes a different, often lower standard of living on the retiree. Older individuals also find themselves in new, externally imposed social roles. In advanced age, the elderly may spend hours of anxiety and dread worrying about a potential change in their physical living arrangements. A combination of frequent losses, unresolved mourning, and feelings of increased isolation associated with retirement and changing social roles contributes to a sense of loss of control and helplessness that makes the elderly vulnerable to depression. Also, many elders live in a state of chronic anxiety, sharing the set of fears that are shown in Table 10.1. Given all these losses, it is understandable that one of the greatest challenges that all individuals face is coping with age-related events and demands and managing the emotional responses evoked by them.

Suicide

An added complication of these age-related challenges is the growing and disturbing problem of suicide. Aging brings inevitable losses, bereavement, and possibly depression. Osterweis, Solomon, and Green (1984) emphasize that 10% to 20% of bereaved persons may display symptoms of clinical depression for 1 year or more following their loss, and, as many studies demonstrate, the bereaved are at greater risk of suicide (Bock & Webber, 1972; Carter & Glick, 1976; Gove, 1973; MacMahon & Pugh, 1965). Almost twice as many people over age 65 commit suicide, compared to those younger than 65 (Crandall, 1991). Physical illness and disability can be extremely painful and can result in dependency, social isolation, loneliness, and huge financial debts. The suicide rate for older men is higher than it is for women, presumably because men find the loss of physical independence more intolerable than women do and also because very old men become more socially isolated (Crandall, 1991). This trend is clear in Figure 10.1, a and b (Holden, 1992).

Suicide can be viewed in two ways (Crandall, 1991). *Overt suicide* is a specific act that terminates life, such as the use of poison, a weapon, or the inhalation of carbon monoxide. The second, *covert suicide*, is the adoption of destructive health habits that slowly erode health and eventually cause death. Examples of destructive habits are

---

**Table 10.1
Fears of the Elderly**

- The fear of being old and ill
- The fear of being poor and a burden
- The fear of change and uncertainty
- The fear of insanity
- The fear of losing liberty, identity, and human dignity
- The fear of death
- The fear of poor care and abuse

Note. Compiled from Moss and Halamandaris (1977).

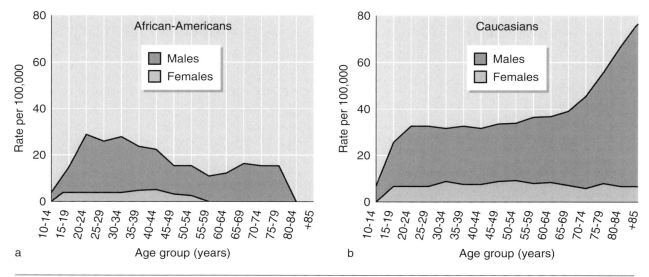

Figure 10.1 Suicide rates by age group, 1989, for (a) African-Americans and (b) Caucasians.
Adapted with permission from "A New Discipline Probes Suicide's Multiple Causes" by C. Holden, 1992, *Science*, **256**, p. 1761. Copyright 1992 by the American Association for the Advancement of Science.

abuse of alcohol and other drugs, refusal to take medications, smoking, neglect of diet, ignoring disease symptoms or weight abnormalities, failure to have regular medical examinations, and failure to plan for emergencies. However, it must be noted that although most people who participate in destructive health habits do not consider them to be suicidal, covert suicide has become a recognized problem. Many times, suicide is tragic evidence that emotional control has been exhausted.

Parameters of Emotional Function

Emotional function is an extremely broad and complex topic. Because of its complexity, we will discuss only those aspects that have been considered by researchers and scholars who are interested in the relationships among health, physical fitness, and emotional function—emotional states versus moods, coping, anxiety, depression, and personality.

Emotional States Versus Moods (Anger Versus Irritability)

In psychology, *emotional states* are those relatively brief but strong feelings that individuals have in response either to thoughts about things that are important to them or in response to environmental events. *Moods* represent temporary and general predispositions toward certain feelings and are weaker than emotions. For example, under the stimulus of a specific event, an individual in a particular mood might react strongly, whereas one who was not experiencing such a mood might ignore it. Emotional states and moods are typically viewed as temporary states, unlike more stable and lasting traits such as personality traits. One instrument used in health, exercise, and mood research is the Profile of Mood States (POMS; McNair, Lorr, & Droppleman, 1971), which includes scales for tension-anxiety, depression-dejection, anger-hostility, vigor-activity, fatigue-inertia, and confusion-bewilderment.

Coping With Psychosocial Stress

Psychosocial stress arises when an individual perceives an event as potentially threatening to his or her personal safety or well-being (Wolfolk & Richardson, 1978). This implies that the event pertains to something that is personally important and that the individual has at least some doubt as to his or her ability to manage or control the event. It evokes the flight-or-fight response, which prepares the body to flee danger or stand and fight. Unfortunately, with few exceptions, the response is no longer adaptive for survival in today's society. Instead, the physiological mechanisms that were once evoked only in times of extreme danger are now evoked in response to job dissatisfaction, traffic jams, unpaid bills, and normal interpersonal conflict. Consequently, the body is flooded with stress-inducing hormones that elevate heart rate and blood pressure, inhibit the immune and digestive systems, and increase muscular tension.

Wolfolk and Richardson (1978) suggested three ways to cope with stress. One is to alter the environment. This can involve moving to another city, finding a quieter place to work, or simply eliminating stress-drivers from one's environment. A second is to change one's beliefs. To use this cognitive approach, an individual analyzes how he or she is interpreting events and identifies the underlying beliefs that may be irrational, or at least, not useful. Changing one's view of an event so that it is no longer threatening can reduce the stress level. The third method is to weaken the connection between stress-producing thoughts and physical arousal, using methods like meditation, progressive relaxation, or physical exercise.

Anxiety

Anxiety can be defined as a vague, uneasy fearfulness (Carlson, 1990). Sime (1984) cautions that anxiety should be viewed in two different ways. First, state and trait anxiety must be considered as independent entities. *State anxiety* is a temporary condition that varies in intensity and fluctuates over time. *Trait anxiety* is more like a personality characteristic, more stable and resistant to change than state anxiety. Sime (1984) also distinguishes between *cognitive anxiety*, which relates to worry, lack of concentration, and insomnia, and *somatic anxiety*, the physiological stress-like symptoms such as nervousness, tension, nausea, headache, sweating palms, and a rapid resting heart rate. These stress-like symptoms of somatic anxiety can also be described as physiological overarousal.

In exercise research, one instrument commonly used to measure anxiety is the Spielberger State-Trait Anxiety Inventory (STAI; Spielberger, Gorsuch, & Lushene, 1970). Another is the Cognitive and Somatic Anxiety Questionnaire (CSAQ; Schwartz, Davidson, & Goleman, 1978).

Depression

Depression is a state of extreme sadness that is generally accompanied by lethargy and slow thinking, but sometimes may be characterized by restless agitation (Carlson, 1990). Other symptoms include a loss of appetite, a lack of interest in living, a sad and confused appearance, and memory loss. These symptoms of slow movements and thinking can also be viewed as physiological underarousal. Depression can be bipolar or unipolar, primary or secondary. Bipolar depression is characterized by extreme mood swings, for example, manic-depression. A unipolar condition is depression alone, be it mild, moderate, or major. Primary depression may or may not be traced to specific cognitive stressors. Secondary depression is related to somatic illness or adverse medication. Instruments commonly used to measure depression in exercise research include the Minnesota Multiphasic Personality Inventory (MMPI; Hathaway & McKinley, 1972) and the Neuroticism-Emotional Stability scale of the Eysenck Personality Inventory (EPI; Eysenck & Eysenck, 1963). Others include the Profile of Mood States (POMS; McNair, Lorr, & Droppleman, 1971), the Beck Depression Inventory (Beck & Beamesderfer, 1974), and the Zung Self-Rating Depression Scale (Zung, 1965).

Personality

Though indicators of emotional function, such as anxiety, depression and coping ability, are influenced by environmental factors like loss of physical capability, retirement and loss of loved ones, they also vary in different individuals. A major factor guiding an individual's reaction to a stressful event is personality. For example, a person who is more extraverted may find it easier to go out, meet new people, and make new friends after the loss of a loved one. Discussions of personality, with regard to aging, health, and fitness, typically focus on personality traits or characteristics. According to trait theory, a person's personality is composed of a number of different, identifiable traits that are stable or fairly resistant to change.

Two trait theorists whose instruments are often used in research with exercise are R.B. Cattell and H.J. Eysenck. The 16 Personality Factor Inventory (16PF; Cattell, 1946) is composed of 16 pairs of traits, each on a 10-step continuum (see Table 10.2). After answering a series of questions, a person's responses can be classified along a continuum in each of 16 categories. In the Eysenck Personality Inventory (EPI; Eysenck & Eysenck, 1963), personality is described on three bipolar dimensions: extraversion-introversion, neuroticism-emotional stability, and psychoticism–self-control (see Table 10.2). Extraversion refers to a high activity level and outgoing nature, whereas introversion characterizes those who avoid crowds and prefer solitary activities. Neuroticism refers to anxiety, worry, and guilt, whereas emotional stability represents a more relaxed outlook and sense of peace with oneself. Psychoticism refers to an aggressive, egocentric, and antisocial character, whereas self-control refers to kindness, consideration, and obedience to rules and regulations.

A third instrument used in some health and exercise research studies is the Minnesota Multiphasic Personality Inventory (MMPI; Hathaway & McKinly, 1972). This personality test was originally developed for pathological populations but is now used with normal populations as well. The scales of this test most often used in exercise research are shown in Table 10.2.

Table 10.2
Personality Scales Frequently Used in Health and Exercise Research

---

Cattell's 16 Personality Factor Inventory items
   Cool-Warm
   Concrete thinking-Abstract thinking
   Affected by feelings-Emotionally stable
   Submissive-Dominant
   Sober-Enthusiastic
   Expedient-Conscientious
   Shy-Bold
   Tough-minded–Tender-minded
   Trusting-Suspicious
   Practical-Imaginative
   Forthright-Shrewd
   Self-assured–Apprehensive
   Conservative-Experimenting
   Group-oriented–Self-sufficient
   Undisciplined-Controlled
   Relaxed-Tense

Eysenck Personality Inventory
   Extraversion-Introversion
   Neuroticism-Emotional stability
   Psychoticism-Self-control

Minnesota Multiphasic Personality Inventory (MMPI)
   Paranoia or vigilance (Pa)
   Depression (D)
   Psychasthenia, or a tendency toward worry, rumination, and agitation (Pt)
   Social introversion (Si)

Issues That Complicate the Understanding of the Health and Fitness–Emotional Function Relationship

Two major issues complicate our understanding of the relationships among emotional function, health, and fitness. The first involves disentangling the high level of interaction between health, fitness, health practices, and emotional function. The second issue refers to specific difficulties associated with research in this area.

Interactions of Health, Fitness, Health Practices, and Emotional Function

One of the difficulties of studying specific relationships between health, fitness, health practices, and emotional function is that they are so highly interrelated. For example, it is possible to be in relatively good health (defined as freedom from overt symptoms of disease) and yet have relatively low physical fitness. Also, poor health can compromise emotional function and mitigate against physical activity, which in turn exacerbates poor health. It is difficult to separate the relationship between emotional health, physical health, physical fitness, and the behavioral process of exercising. For example, depression could be directly related to physical health and only indirectly to physical fitness through the relationship between physical health and physical fitness. Clearly the relationship among health, physical fitness, and emotional function is very complicated.

A second difficulty in studying these relationships is the great diversity of individual health practices, which are affected by such things as health, emotional functioning, and socioeconomic status. Individuals in poor health; those with high levels of stress, anxiety, and depression; and those from low socioeconomic levels are less likely to participate in beneficial health practices.

A third difficulty concerns the accurate measurement of physiological changes related to health and fitness and emotional function. Physiological changes may be affected not only by exercise but also by health practices, stress, and socioeconomic status. For example, behaviors such as smoking and alcohol consumption involve the ingestion of nicotine and ethanol and produce physiological changes that complicate the interpretation of some physiologically based tests of emotional function. Stressful life events, such as the death of a spouse and family members or the loss of a job may have a profound effect on the individual, causing changes in hormone levels that also complicate the interpretation of test results. Problems such as these dramatic life events may occur during an investigative study of emotional function, unknown to the investigator who is testing the affected individual, thus tainting the research project results. Finally, socioeconomic status can affect physiological measurements. For example, low socioeconomic status is associated with lower levels of nutrition, higher levels of stress, and less use of positive health-related behaviors, all of which cause physiological changes.

Research Process Problems

In much of the literature, various methodological and design problems compromise the findings and conclusions drawn about the relationship between exercise and various emotional changes. These problems may be categorized as the limited information on older adults, the subjectivity of subjects' responses, and the wide divergence in research methodologies.

Scarcity of Studies of Older Adults

In comparison to the massive literature on health, physical fitness, and emotional function in the general population, the research on these topics in which older adults are the subjects is very small. Most of the research has been conducted on psychiatric or other hospital patients and on volunteers, resulting in very small sample sizes.

Subjective Data

Information about emotional function from studies of exercise psychology is primarily from self-report data. That is, individuals themselves report how they feel about questions or issues. Emotions can be relatively volatile, changing with one's interpretation of events and with changing mood states in very short periods of time. A person might feel exhilarated one moment to have been chosen to participate in an experiment, but in another few minutes develop anxieties about the implications of a "bad score." In fact, elderly adults who have not been the subject of much attention until a

researcher includes them in a study may experience a roller coaster of emotions within a relatively short time. These short-term changes present researchers with serious problems in terms of the reliability and validity of their data.

Also, in many studies of exercise program intervention, the researchers and exercise leaders have a very positive attitude about the value of exercise, an attitude that is likely to influence positively the responses of the subjects. Older adults, particularly those who volunteer to be subjects, are eager to please, because they believe the investigators are acting in their best interests. In studies of patients or other institutionalized groups, the initiation of an experimental exercise program is a major event in an otherwise grindingly dull routine of daily living in the institution. The new and personal attention from research personnel may also bias the responses of the subjects.

Wide Divergence in Research Methodologies Used

Studies of health, fitness, and exercise vary in terms of the types of exercise studied, the length and intensity of exercise, the types of participants (normal or atypical), and the physical and psychological measurements used. For example, some studies focus on the relationship between emotional function and aerobic exercise, whereas others focus on emotional function and anaerobic exercise. (These types of exercise are discussed in chapter 4.) Investigators who have studied aerobic exercise and its effects on emotional function are usually interested in the chronic effects of fitness on emotional control. Those who study anaerobic activities may be more interested in acute effects of physical activity on emotional factors. Many different types of exercise have been investigated, and it is not clear whether different types have different effects on emotional function. The use of continuous and aerobic exercise, instead of intermittent or anaerobic exercise, is often required to test the hypotheses by which exercise might influence emotional function.

Another methodological issue raised by Folkins and Sime (1981) and more recently by Plante and Rodin (1990) refers to the lack of studies using experimental designs that permit causal inferences. Plante and Rodin point out that threats to internal and external validity abound through failure to use random assignment and control groups and the tendency to use nonstandard instruments.

Investigators also use different psychological measures of emotional function. This may be due to the practice of using intact groups from hospitals, residence centers, or day care centers, in which case the investigators use whichever psychological test has been used by the institution. The residents or patients who make up these intact subject groups are, in some sense, a "captive" audience, in that they may fear that failure to volunteer would result in some type of reprisal from the administrators. Even if no fears of this type exist, volunteer samples are unlikely to represent a random sample of subjects even from the institution, much less from the total population of cohorts. Consequently, the relationship between health and fitness, and even a broad construct such as anxiety, is not well understood; even less well understood is the relationship between the narrower subscales of anxiety such as cognitive versus somatic anxiety, or state versus trait anxiety.

Yet another difficulty is that psychological instruments are generally devised either for clinical or for unimpaired populations. Just as pathological traits cannot be measured satisfactorily using tests designed for the general public, so clinical tests designed for patients are insensitive to emotional differences in unimpaired subjects. Thus, it is often difficult to compare the results of studies in which the samples are taken from these different populations. Further, it is difficult to study the relationship of fitness to emotional function in a sample that includes people who represent a continuum of emotional stability.

Long- and Short-Term Effects of Exercise

Another complicating factor in understanding the relationship between exercise and emotional function is whether the proposed mechanisms underlying this relationship lead to short- or long-term effects. Table 10.3 shows several exercise-induced physiological changes that have been associated with the reduction of emotional stress. These changes might occur in at least three ways. Exercise may affect psychological function on a short-term basis by producing physiological changes that operate for only a few hours after exercise. Or exercise could affect psychological

Table 10.3
Physiological Effects of Exercise Associated With Reduced Emotional Tension[a]

Short-term effects
  Increased cortical bloodflow
  Changes in biogenic amines
  Release of endogenous opiates
  A temporary increase in body temperature
  Improvements in response to stress
    Glucocorticoids
    Increased neurotransmission of catecholamines
    Decreased muscular tension
    Lactate
  Modified brainwave activity (EEG)
Long-term effects
  Changes in levels and characteristics of brain catecholamines
  Changes in aminergic synaptic transmission
  Release of endogenous opiates

[a]All of these have been associated in at least one research study to one or more assessments of emotional function, but all are also controversial.

function by producing structural and functional changes in systems, such as by increasing the effectiveness of catecholamine responses to stress. For example, the release of opiates occurs after a treadmill exercise bout but a long-term exercise program did not affect either the pattern of release or amount of opiates released (Howlett et al., 1984). However, exercise may have both short- and long-term effects on some psychological functions. Of course, the short-term effects of exercise would be tantamount to long-term effects if the exercise was performed on a daily basis.

In summary, numerous factors hinder the understanding of whether and how health and physical fitness relate to emotional function. First, interactions between health, fitness, health practices, and emotional function represent a major source of confusion. Second, issues related to the research process itself, such as the scarcity of studies of older adults, the use of subjective data, the wide divergence of research methodologies used, and the long- versus short-term effects of exercise, lead to difficulties in the interpretation and comparison of results. Nevertheless, some relevant information pertaining to this subject is discussed in the following section.

Physical Activity and Emotional Function

Biddle and Fox (1989) delineated three major topics of interest to exercise psychologists (see Table 10.4). Their findings on exercise and mood, abilityto cope with psychosocial stress, anxiety, depression, and personality are of particular interest. Unfortunately, from the perspective of gerontologists, most researchers have focused on these psychological constructs in athletes, young adults, and institutionalized patients. The number of investigators who have studied psychological contributions of physical activity and physical fitness in older adults is very small. We will emphasize studies of aged individuals, but in areas where such studies on older adults are not available, we will extrapolate the relationship between physical activity and the emotional construct from studies of young adults.

Table 10.4
Research Areas in the Study of Exercise and Mental Health

Acute

1. Psychophysiology
   Anxiety reduction and relaxation through release of muscular tension (EMG)

   Anxiety reduction and relaxation through modified brainwave activity (EEG)

2. Psychobiochemistry
   Heightened mood through the release of endogenous opiates (endorphins) or specific hormones (e.g., catecholamines) during exercise

Chronic

3. Psychology
   Improved self-perceptions, such as self-esteem, through a sense of body, image, mastery, and self-control

   Enhanced ability to resist stress

   Exercise addiction or dependence

Note. From "Exercise and Health Psychology: Emerging Relationships" by S.J.H. Biddle and K.R. Fox, 1989, *British Journal of Medical Psychology*, **62**, p. 208. Reprinted by permission.

Mood

The psychological benefit of exercising most often mentioned by those who undertake aerobic exercise programs, or who have been participating in an exercise program for many years, is that it improves mood. Testimonial evidence is abundant from runners and joggers that their mood improves after running a few miles. Most distance runners are familiar with the phenomenon of "runners' high," a feeling of incredible well-being that floods over the runner an hour or two after a run. Many runners say that they experience dramatic mood shifts. However, scientific documentation of mood shifts, as well as the long-term benefits of aerobic exercise on mood has been less forthcoming.

A few researchers, using a cross-sectional research design, reported that people who are chronic exercisers score higher on psychological tests of mood than people who are sedentary. However, because these were cross-sectional studies, they could not discount the possibility that the relationship was due to a poor mood that prompted physical inactivity, rather than a good mood enhanced by exercise (Brown & Lawton, 1986; Frederick, Frerichs, & Clark, 1988; Lobstein, Mosbacher, & Ismail, 1983; Ross & Hayes, 1988).

Several investigators reported that their subjects experienced an improved mood or morale following extended exercise programs (Brown & Lawton, 1986; Emery & Blumenthal, 1990; Folkins, Lynch, & Gardener, 1972; Gillett, 1989; Prosser et al., 1981; Tredway, 1978). Other investigators found no improvement in mood or morale following exercise programs (Castell & Blumenthal, 1985; Hughes, Casal, & Leon, 1986; Morgan et al., 1970; Stern & Cleary, 1982). In fact, Morgan and O'Connor (1988) flatly state that no published evidence supports the contention that exercise actually *causes* an improvement in mood state. However, in an extensive literature review, Plante and Rodin (1990) conclude that exercise does improve mood.

One exceptionally well-controlled intervention study provided strong evidence that adults between the ages of 50 and 65 who began a systematic exercise program rated their mood states as having been significantly improved after 1 year of exercise (King, Taylor, & Haskell, 1993). This study was unique in that careful statistical controls were employed to account for the possibility of contaminating factors, such as subjects' initial expectations for their exercise program, and for nonindependence of several items on the test battery. It also was unique in having a large sample of subjects who were randomly assigned to different types of exercise programs.

It is possible that exercise may be more effective in improving mood in individuals who are most mood-disturbed. Simons and Birkimer (1988) found that significant improvement occurred on the POMS mood inventory, specifically, on the anxiety, anger, and confusion scales, after 8 weeks of an aerobic exercise program among those who began the study with the lowest moods. The key finding in this study is that mood improvement was not predicted by cardiovascular improvement or by initial fitness, but by initial mood state.

On the basis of current knowledge, it may be premature to state that chronic exercise *causes* mood states in the elderly. The results from the studies previously mentioned, except those of Tredway (1978), Emery and Blumenthal (1990), and King et al. (1993), come from subject samples that are primarily young to middle-aged, atypical (e.g., overweight), or diseased. Research on elderly subjects' mood states and exercise remains sparse, yet it seems entirely plausible that age may interact with exercise in an exercise-mood relationship. Thus, the hypothesis that exercise can enhance mood, although intuitive, appealing, and promising, is yet to be confirmed conclusively.

Coping With Psychosocial Stress

To determine how people react to psychosocial stressors, researchers capitalize on easily measured physiological responses, the "fight-or-flight" reactions. These responses, which are sympathetic nervous system arousal responses, include increased heart rate, blood pressure, galvanic skin response (GSR), and capillary constriction. Thus, emotionally aroused individuals' hearts beat faster, their blood pressure increases, and their hands become clammy and moist (see Table 10.5). These reactions are caused by increased activation of the sympathetic nervous system and the hormonal system, so that adrenaline (epinephrine) and noradrenaline (norepinephrine) are greatly increased in the system. In fact, these psychophysiological responses are called *adrenergic responses*, and people sometimes describe them as an "adrenaline rush." Researchers, therefore, by measuring heart rate, blood pressure, GSR, hand temperature, or levels of adrenaline in the blood before and after a psychosocial stressor can determine how much response an individual had to the stressor.

From an evolutionary perspective, these physiological responses to stress were adaptive, permitting the rapid energy increases required to escape wild animals or other impending environmental disasters. These responses are not very useful, however, for adaptation to stress from psychosocial stressors. Although they may be beneficial for quick reactions to stress, they cannot be easily terminated. Consequently, in modern society, such physiological responses to psychosocial stress, shown on the right side of Table 10.5, can be detrimental in the long term. Sapolzsky, Krey, and McEwen (1986) showed that when old rats are stressed, they can initiate a stress response as well as young rats, but they cannot "turn it off" as rapidly, probably because aging impairs the negative feedback system that suppresses the stress reaction. Consequently, circulating levels of cortiocosterone, which rise dramatically in a stress response but are detrimental on a long-term basis, remain high for a much longer time in old animals.

Table 10.5
Physiological Responses to Psychosocial Stress

Acute response	Chronic response
Increased blood glucose	Muscle atrophy and fatigue
Increased cardiovascular tone	Hypertension
Supression of	
digestion	Ulceration
reproduction	Impotence, amenorrhea
growth	Decreased growth and repair
immune response	Decreased immune response

Some experts believe that people who regularly participate in aerobic exercise have lower levels of chronic stress and can adapt to stress better than sedentary individuals. Both resting and submaximal exercise-induced epinephrine and norepinephrine levels are lower in physically trained individuals (Winder, Hagberg, Hickson, Ehsani, & McLane, 1978). Crews and Landers (1987) conducted a meta-analysis of 34 studies in which physically fit individuals were compared to sedentary persons in terms of their physiological responses to a stressor (e.g., timed arithmetic problems, viewing films of accidents, or keeping a limb immersed in ice water). A meta-analysis is an objective, systematic way to analyze a large number of studies to determine the average difference between, in this case, all exercisers and nonexercisers. They concluded that regardless of the physiological measures used in the various studies, the physically fit groups reacted less to psychosocial stressors than did the sedentary groups. Several other investigators also have concluded that individuals who are physically fit can cope with psychosocial stress better than physically unfit individuals (Brooke & Long, 1987; Sinyor, Schwartz, Peronnet, Brisson, & Seraganian, 1983). Dienstbier, LaGuardia, Barnes, Tharp, and Schmidt (1987) indicated that aerobic exercise may not reduce overall resting levels of adrenaline, but it may depress adrenaline as well as other neurohormonal responses to a psychosocial stressor.

Other experts say it is premature to claim that exercise and its concomitant fitness effects have long-term benefits for the ability to cope with stress. For example, Plante and Karpowitz (1987) suggest that claims that aerobic exercise influences physiological responsivity to psychosocial stressors have not yet been wholly confirmed. They cite, for example, the work of Sinyor, Golden, Steinert, and Seraganian (1986), who found only modest support for the hypothesis that aerobic training reduces responses to psychosocial stress. Their review of 10 other studies found only 4 that reported that aerobically fit individuals recovered more efficiently from a stressor.

Since these criticisms were voiced, however, the exceptionally well-controlled intervention study of King et al. (1993), discussed previously under the topic of mood states, has been published. The scores of their subjects on the Perceived Stress Scale (PSS; Cohen, Kamarck, & Mermelstein, 1983) were significantly higher after 1 year of consistent exercise. Their groups were (a) a higher intensity,

group-based, 1-hr exercise training program conducted in a class situation three times a week; (b) a higher intensity, home-based, 1-hr exercise training program, supervised via telephone; (c) a lower intensity, home-based, 30-min exercise training program, five times a week; and (d) an assessment-only control group. Particularly interesting was their finding that groups who exercised five times a week for 30 min each session, either by themselves or in very small groups, benefited more than the group that met in a regularly scheduled, 1-hr exercise class three times a week (see Figure 10.2).

The strength of the King et al. (1993) study was that they used a randomized controlled design, initially sedentary adults (ages 50-65 years), a moderately long exercise program (1 year), techniques to validate the self-reports of participation, control mechanisms to protect against initial expectations,

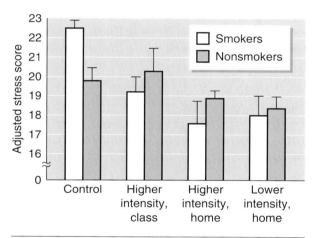

Figure 10.2 Twelve-month perceived-stress score, adjusted for baseline, by condition assignment and smoking status with standard error of the mean. Higher intensity group, class format: 60-min exercise session, three times a week at 73%-88% of peak exercise heart rate. Higher intensity, home-based group: 60-min exercise session, three times a week at 73%-88% of peak exercise heart rate, with telephone and physical activity log supervision. Lower intensity, home-based group: 30-min exercise session, five times a week at 60%-73% of peak exercise heart rate, with telephone and physical activity log supervision. Control group: no participation in a regular exercise program, assessment only, supervision by physical activity log. Groups were also stratified by smoking habits. From "Effects of Differing Intensities and Formats of 12 Months of Exercise Training on Psychological Outcomes in Older Adults" by A.C. King, C.B. Taylor, and W.L. Haskell, 1993, *Health Psychology*, **12**, p. 296. Copyright 1993 by the American Psychological Association. Reprinted by permission.

and actual rather than estimated measures of functional capacity. The only weakness in their study was that, because their primary focus was on cardiovascular rather than psychological changes accompanying the exercise program, they did not control for the Hawthorne effect (when an experimental group knows that it is being studied and performs differently because of this knowledge). However, their study is by far the most comprehensive to date that addresses the issue of exercise effects on older adults' responses to psychosocial stress.

Because of the positive findings of earlier research, and the more recent report of King et al. (1993), the *relationship* between exercise and emotional response to psychosocial stressors is intuitively compelling. It seems reasonable, with an appropriate level of conservatism and skepticism, that adherence to a consistent exercise program is related to an enhanced ability to cope with psychosocial stressors. Several plausible mechanisms for such a relationship have been proposed, and they are discussed later.

Anxiety

Experts also have conflicting opinions about the impact of exercise on anxiety levels and whether exercise differentially affects state-trait anxiety or cognitive-somatic anxiety. Reviews of studies in this area have been particularly critical with regard to the methodologies and experimental designs that have been used (Biddle & Fox, 1989; Plante & Rodin, 1990; Simes, 1984). Anxiety is an extremely elusive construct to measure and to understand, particularly as it relates to health and fitness. State anxiety, by definition, changes over time, and so it is difficult to identify specific causes of anxiety changes. Nevertheless, several researchers have demonstrated relationships between physical fitness or exercise activity and some type of anxiety measure (Biddle & Fox, 1989; Dienstbier, LaGuardia, & Wilcox, 1987; Reiter, 1981; Simons & Birkimer, 1988; Sinyor et al., 1983). Both young and middle-aged subjects (43-62 years; Young, 1979) and older adults (older than 65; Holm & Kirchoff, 1984) reported a decrease in anxiety following an exercise program. Furthermore, the King et al. (1993) study that found exercise effects on both mood and stress response also provided strong evidence that a 1-year exercise program, either in a class format or at home, reduced anxiety. The reduction in subjects' scores on the Taylor Manifest

Anxiety Scale (Bendig, 1956) occurred even though the intensity of the subjects' exercise programs was only moderate. The investigators concluded that exercise does not have to be vigorous, uncomfortable, or painful to realize a reduction in anxiety.

Although the findings of these studies appear to support a general correlation between fitness, exercise activity, and anxiety, the relationship is far from clear. For example, the type of anxiety that may be affected, and the type, intensity, and length of an exercise program necessary to affect anxiety are not known. It may require a longer exercise program to influence trait anxiety than it does to affect state anxiety. For example, McGlynn, Franklin, Lauro, and McGlynn (1983) found that a 14-week program reduced both state and trait anxiety, but Kowal, Patton, and Vogel (1978) reported a decrease *only* in state anxiety after a 6-week exercise program.

Exercise programs may affect cognitive and somatic anxiety differently. In two studies, aerobic exercise reduced somatic anxiety but not cognitive anxiety, whereas a program that emphasized mental training and focused on relaxation reduced cognitive anxiety but not somatic anxiety (Davidson & Schwartz, 1976; Schwartz et al., 1978). Also, exercise in addition to mental imagery (positive thinking) was more successful in reducing anxiety than mental imagery alone (Driscoll, 1976). Sime (1977) also found that an exercise and mental imagery group had lower anxiety levels than a group that practiced mental imagery alone, but only when anxiety was measured by muscular tension instead of by a state anxiety scale.

Depression

Exercise has long been proposed as therapy for depression, although like other psychological constructs involving emotion, causality has been difficult to establish. Chodzko-Zajko and Ismail (1986) found that depression, measured by the Minnesota Multiphasic Personality Inventory (MMPI), was a powerful discriminator between men ages 27 to 64 who were low in physical fitness and those who were high in physical fitness. Of 11 physiological variables and the scores from the MMPI, the depression subscale score was second only to blood pressure in the ability to discriminate between these two groups differing in fitness. An exercise program also reduced depression in college students following negative life events, shown in Figure 10.3 (Roth & Holmes, 1987).

Also in older adults (60-80 years), 70% of those in an exercise program that met twice a week for 9 months reported less depression than they had before they started the program (Uson & Larrosa, 1982). In the King et al. (1993) study, the Beck Depression Inventory scores improved after 1 year of exercise, whether the exercise was of moderate intensity (63%-70% of peak exercise heart rate) or of higher intensity (73%-88% of peak exercise heart rate), or whether the exercise was done three times a week for 1 hour, or five times a week for 30 min. However, the depression scores of the older adults who experienced a much shorter, 4-month exercise program did not change after the program (Dustman et al., 1984).

In another study of moderately depressed older adults (mean age, 72.5 years), McNeil, LeBlanc, and Joyner (1991) found that exercise and social contact groups, compared to a wait-listed control group, experienced significant reductions in depression, measured by the Beck Depression Inventory (Beck & Beamesderfer, 1974). Furthermore, though the social contact group showed equal reductions in total and psychological depression, only the exercise group

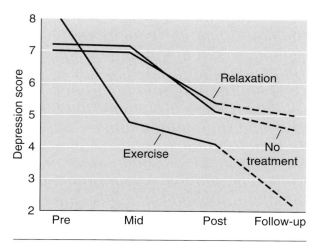

Figure 10.3 Beck Depression Inventory scores from subjects in the aerobic exercise training, progressive relaxation training, and no-treatment control conditions at the preintervention, midintervention, postintervention, and follow-up points.
From "Influence of Aerobic Exercise Training and Relaxation Training on Physical and Psychologic Health Following Stressful Life Events" by D.L. Roth and D.S. Holmes, 1987, *Psychosomatic Medicine,* **49**, p. 362. Copyright 1987 by Williams & Wilkins. Reprinted by permission.

experienced decreased somatic symptoms of depression such as poor appetite, increased fatigue, and disturbed sleep.

Camacho, Roberts, Lazarus, Kaplan, and Cohen (1991) analyzed the data from a very large (they began with 8,023 noninstitutionalized men and women) longitudinal study of adults, about half of whom were over the age of 40. (This is one of few such studies in which older adults were included.) They collected measures of the extent of physical activity and depression for a base line in 1965, and then collected test results two more times, in 1974 and 1983. The critical questions asked in this study were whether people who participated in physical activity had a lower or higher risk of developing depression with aging, and whether a change in physical activity patterns over time could predict the presence of depression. They found that men and women who reported low physical activity at the beginning of the study were at a much higher risk of developing depression 10 or 20 years later than were those adults who reported high physical activity when the study began. This relationship persisted even though the investigators statistically controlled such confounding factors as physical health, socioeconomic status, social supports, life events, and other health habits.

An even stronger relationship existed between physical activity pattern and risk of depression. Those individuals who began the study in 1965 as inactive participants but changed their physical activity habits by 1974 to become active revealed no greater risk for depression in 1983 than those who had been physically active throughout the study. Conversely, those who began the study being active but reported they were inactive in 1974 had a 1-1/2 times greater risk of being depressed in the 1983 analysis.

An important exception in the Camacho et al. (1991) study was the group of adults who were inactive at all three measurement periods. This group was at a higher risk of developing depression than the active groups, both the chronically active and those who changed from inactive to active, but when the factor of physical health was removed statistically, their risk of developing depression was almost eliminated. In other words, the relationship between depression and physical activity pattern was only an indirect relationship, a result of the *direct* relationship between depression and their physical health.

Results of therapeutic exercise programs for clinically depressed individuals have generally been beneficial (Bennett, Carmack, & Gardner, 1982; Greist et al., 1979; Klein et al., 1985; McCann & Holmes, 1984). An important conclusion drawn by Martinsen (1990) is that exercise programs have an antidepressive effect on patients with mild to moderate forms of depression, but the exercise program does not necessarily have to result in an increase in physical fitness in order to reduce depression. Other aspects of exercise programs, such as the social support that generally accompanies therapy programs and the distraction functions of exercise, may also contribute substantially to the therapeutic outcomes for some individuals, although King et al. (1993) showed that social support is not an essential factor for improvements in depression, at least in nonpathologically depressed adults.

Personality

Because of their stable nature, personality traits are the most difficult variables to change by adding a physical exercise program to the daily routine. Most of the research in this area, therefore, focuses on the relationship of various personality traits to physical fitness. However, no causal connections between fitness and personality can be made from these correlational studies because whether specific personality traits, such as calmness, happiness, or emotional stability, are caused by being physically fit or whether people with these personality traits are more inclined to *be* physically fit is indeterminable.

Nonetheless, a number of researchers have demonstrated relationships between fitness (or exercise) and personality. Men characterized as having low fitness also had higher depression scores on the MMPI than men who were categorized as having high fitness (Chodzko-Zajko & Ismail, 1986). In fact, the depression scale was second only to blood pressure in discriminating between the low- and high-fitness males in that study. Schnurr, Vaillant, and Vaillant (1990) studied data from the Grant Study of Adult Development (Vaillant, 1977), a longitudinal study begun at Harvard University in 1938 to determine if young adult personality characteristics could predict levels of exercise at late midlife. After controlling for prior exercise behavior, body build, and fitness in young adulthood, they found that including personality variables improved their prediction of current frequent exercisers. Walker and Hailey

(1987) also found differing personality traits between male and female joggers and their respective cohorts. High-fit men were described as being very calm and relaxed with a sense of well-being approaching elation, whereas highly fit women were described as optimistic, conscientious, organized, and persevering.

However, there is much debate concerning the effects of exercise on personality. Some researchers believe that a causal relationship may exist between exercise and at least some personality variables. After a 10-week running or weight-training program, college women indicated on the 16PF and the Zung Self-Rating Depression Scale (Zung, 1965) that the physical improvements led them to greater happiness and security and made them more inclined to socialize. They also felt a greater sense of control (Jasnoski, Holmes, & Banks, 1988). The men in that study appeared to develop a more extraverted outlook after the 10-week exercise program. Notably, these personality changes were greater after the aerobic training program than they were after the weight training program.

Dienstbier (1984) conducted a meticulous literature review of exercise and personality factors, and on the basis of his analysis of the most well-designed studies, he concluded that the cumulative evidence strongly suggests that aerobic exercise programs can change temperamental dispositions and reduce anxiety and emotionality. On the other hand, in another exhaustive review of the literature, Plante and Rodin (1990) concluded that the effects of exercise on various personality dimensions were contradictory. Further, they found the research regarding personality differences between exercisers and nonexercisers to be both contradictory and inconclusive.

Hypotheses Relating Physical Activity to Emotional Function

Although the research evidence for a relationship between physical activity and emotional function is descriptive, correlational, and not causal, the relationship is provocative and strong enough to have generated several hypotheses to explain it. Remember, however, that these are hypotheses, not scientific explanations, about how exercise might benefit emotional function. The hypotheses can be categorized as physiological or psychosocial.

Physiological Hypotheses

Physiological hypotheses are based on exercise-induced changes in cerebral bloodflow, neural hormones, endorphins, and body temperature.

Cerebral Blood Circulation

One mechanism by which exercise may be linked to emotional change is that it alters regional bloodflow in the brain. The circulating blood of the brain is directed to tissue that is metabolically active. Therefore, when individuals exercise, making decisions about what to do and what directions to move, greater quantities of blood are sent to brain areas that are involved in making these decisions and controlling the exercise. Increased bloodflow generally means an increased amount of oxygen to the area, and increased oxygen may influence the central nervous system and initiate mood changes (Oleson, 1971).

The Monoamine Hypothesis

A more accepted hypothesis is that monoamine neurotransmitters in the brain, which have been linked to anxiety, mood shifts, and depression, are changed by both short-term and long-term exercise. Morgan and O'Connor (1988), citing the catecholamine hypothesis discussed by Schildkraut, Orsulak, Schatzberg, and Rosenbaum (1984), call this the monoamine hypothesis. Monoamines, particularly dopamine, serotonin, and norepinephrine, have been known for many years to be associated with emotion. When people become angry, their adrenaline levels rise, and people who have higher trait anxiety (measured by trait anxiety scales) also have higher levels of adrenaline both at rest and during exercise bouts. Patients with emotional dysfunction have abnormal levels of norepinephrine (noradrenaline). For example, those with paranoia have chronically higher levels of norepinephrine, but norepinephrine is low in clinically depressed persons. This led Kicey (1974) to hypothesize that an inadequate norepinephrine supply at neural receptor sites produces depression, whereas an excess supply produces mania.

Other evidence that points to the relationship between catecholamines and emotional function comes from drug research. Antidepressants function by increasing the amount of norepinephrine

or seratonin in the central nervous system (Forrester, 1987; Laraia, 1987). Reserpine, which is a drug that induces depression, also depletes brain catecholamines (Ransford, 1982). Electroconvulsive shock therapy (ECT), which is used to reduce depression, acts through enhancing aminergic synaptic transmission.

Evidence has been accumulating for several years that these monoamines are influenced by exercise. In animal studies, brain norepinephrine increases after 15 to 30 min of treadmill running or swimming (e.g., Barchas & Freedman, 1963), and animals that were physically trained for several weeks also had higher levels of brain epinephrine (adrenaline) (Brown & Van Huss, 1973; Brown et al., 1979; DeCastro & Duncan, 1985). Whether the animals' norepinephrine levels were raised because of the exercise or because they were psychologically stressed at having to run on a treadmill or swim in cold water is still unanswered. Nevertheless, over long periods of training, the stresses of the laboratory protocol generally dissipate, and the cumulative evidence from these studies is persuasive. In humans, also, changes have been seen in circulating levels of norepinephrine following short exercise sessions (Dulac et al., 1982; Ransford, 1982) and longer bouts, such as from marathon running (Appenzeller & Schade, 1979). A recent modification of the monoamine hypothesis, proposed by Siever and Davis (1985), shifts from the notion of circulating *levels* of monoamines to the idea of monoamine *regulation*. That is, exercise may assist in regulating monoamines, rather than simply increasing or decreasing their circulation levels.

The Release of Endorphins

One theory that has received wide publicity is based on the well-documented observations that the brain produces high levels of endogenous opiates in response to acute physical and psychological stress. These high levels of circulating beta-endorphins might explain the improvements in mood state, sometimes described as euphoria, that people commonly experience following an exercise bout. Many investigators have described increases in beta-endorphins following vigorous aerobic exercise (e.g., Carr et al., 1981; Hollmann et al., 1986; Lobstein, Rasmussen, Dunphy, & Dunphy, 1989; Rahkila, Hakala, Salminen, & Laatkainen, 1987; Risch, 1982), and it is thought that the exercise level must be close to maximum or at least extended for a considerable period of time before any mood change is experienced (Kirkcaldy & Shephard, 1990; Thoren, Floras, Hoffman, & Seals, 1990). These studies share a common theme with studies of the relationship between exercise and catecholamines discussed previously: Resting levels in high-fit individuals are lower than those in low-fit individuals, but in response to a physical or psychological stressor, high-fit individuals both increase their levels of endorphins (or catecholamines) and clear them faster than low-fit people do. The endorphin theory, however, has some serious challengers.

Morgan (1985) researched the topic extensively, evaluated all the research on the subject of exercise-produced endogenous opiates and mood states, and concluded that the researchers' arguments that exercise-produced endorphins contribute to changes in mood state were not compelling. He cited one study in particular, Farrell et al. (1986), in which a drug that blocks the effects of endorphins was injected into subjects before they rode a bicycle at 70% $\dot{V}O_2$max for 30 min. If exercise-induced high levels of circulating endorphins are the reason why people feel more relaxed at the end of an exercise period, then these subjects should not have felt any beneficial change in their mood state, because the injected drug blocked the endorphins before they could act. Yet, these subjects also felt significantly more relaxed after their exercise bout. As Morgan emphasized, these results are a serious challenge to the endorphin hypothesis. At best, exercise-produced endorphins may contribute to the feelings of psychological well-being and relaxation that follow an exercise bout, but they certainly cannot be considered the primary explanation for the tranquilizer effect of exercise.

Thermogenic Hypothesis

Increasing body temperature to produce a variety of therapeutic effects has been known for centuries, dating back to at least A.D. 800 in Finland (Morgan & O'Connor, 1988). Hot baths and saunas represent one way to achieve this therapeutic effect. For example, Raglin and Morgan (1987) found that a 5-min shower at 38.5° Centigrade was associated with a significant decrease in state anxiety.

Body temperature changes during and following exercise may also have the effect of reducing muscular tension (deVries, 1987). Muscle relaxation following exposure to exercise-induced temperature increases may be the result of changes in the brain stem, leading to decreased muscle feedback and synchronized electrical activity in the cerebral cortex (Von Euler & Soderberg, 1956, 1957). This muscle relaxation, in turn, is associated with reduced anxiety. Indeed, the difficulty of maintaining psychological anxiety in the presence of complete muscular relaxation was the basis for a type of aversion therapy (Wolpe, Salter, & Reyna, 1964). In this therapy, the patient concentrated on voluntary control of muscular tension while in the presence of a very mild or abstracted version of a stressor (e.g., a line drawing of a snake). Gradually, the stressor was increased in terms of proximity and reality until the patient could remain physically, and presumably psychologically, relaxed in the presence of a live snake. Wolpe's hypothesis was that by controlling muscular tension, the patient could reduce psychological tension, that is, anxiety. This therapy never gained general acceptance, but it was an interesting hypothesis, because it emphasized the strong link between muscular tension and psychological anxiety. The reduction of electrical activity in the muscles and the parallel reduction in anxiety following an exercise bout have been called the tranquilizer effect of exercise (deVries, Wiswell, Bulbulian, & Moritani, 1981; Hatfield & Landers, 1987). Moreover, some of the exercise-induced changes in physiological systems last for several hours and therefore may be more effective in reducing psychological anxiety than other psychological techniques (Raglin & Morgan, 1987).

The decreased muscular tension that follows an exercise bout may reduce psychological tension, because muscle tone and the central nervous system are greatly affected by body warming. A rise in body temperature may also influence the functions of some of the brain monoamines and may cause a protein that mediates the rise in body temperature to be released into the blood during body heating. (The internal body temperature of rats was increased just by injecting them with plasma from humans who had been exercising; Cannon & Kluger, 1983.) Thus, the relaxed feeling that people experience following a vigorous, prolonged workout may be partly caused by the increase in body temperature that arises from the workout and may last for several hours.

Psychosocial Hypotheses

Though biological theories certainly make a strong contribution to the explanation of the relationships between exercise and emotional function, in and of themselves they are probably inadequate for complete understanding of the relationships (Plante & Rodin, 1990). For example, a study by King, Taylor, Haskell, & DeBusk (1989) found greater psychological improvement based on perceived fitness than on actual fitness. Further, Doyne et al. (1987) found that both aerobic and anaerobic exercise produced similar improvements in psychological health. Therefore, psychological effects must also be factored into the equation. Several psychological and social hypotheses have been proposed, including distraction, mastery, changes in self-concept, and social interaction.

The Distraction Hypothesis

The distraction hypothesis emerged from the observation that time is a contributing factor to changes of emotional state. Exercise takes time, and whether individuals are exercising or not, time passes. Several authors have suggested that exercise may be considered a diversion from the stresses of daily life, a period in which the individual can legitimately take a "time-out" from occupation and family responsibilities (Bahrke & Morgan, 1978; Greist et al., 1979). Thus, an exercise period is a societally condoned activity in which people can "get away from it all," a potentially powerful contributor to exercise-related short-term relief from tension. A study by Bahrke and Morgan (1978) supported this hypothesis by demonstrating that 20 min of meditation or rest in a sound-filtered room was as effective in reducing tension as 20 min of vigorous exercise (see Figure 10.4). However, the reductions in blood pressure and anxiety following exercise may last longer than those produced by quiet sitting. Raglin and Morgan (1987) suggested that, because exercise-related physiological changes, such as reduced blood pressure, last several hours, exercise may have a longer-term effect than planned, quiet sitting.

The Mastery Hypothesis

Another psychological hypothesis of exercise effects on emotional states is based on an assumption that individuals have a psychological drive (i.e., a need) to seek out and master their environment (White, 1959). When people feel that they lack mastery over their environment, this significant need is not being met and emotional health

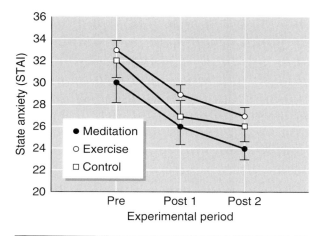

Figure 10.4 State anxiety reductions before and following exercise, meditation, and control treatments. From "Anxiety Reduction Following Exercise and Meditation" by M.S. Bahrke and W.P. Morgan, 1978, *Cognitive Therapy and Research*, **2**, p. 326. Copyright 1978 by Plenum Publishing. Reprinted by permission.

may be compromised. Increases in physical strength, endurance, and ability provide individuals with a feeling that they have more control over their environment, and thus, they are less vulnerable (Greist et al., 1979; Sime, 1984). Therefore, participation in programs that increase these attributes should also enhance emotional health on a long-term basis. However, though mastery experience may be a contributing factor to emotional health, other, less strenuous activities such as softball, bowling, and golf, although offering opportunities for improvement and accomplishment, have not shown antidepressant effects comparable to those that occur after aerobic exercise (Ransford, 1982).

Changes in Self-Concept

Another psychological hypothesis to explain the relationship between exercise and emotional health is that changes occur in self-concept (i.e., the conscious perception and awareness of self). A positive self-concept is required for psychological health, and many studies have demonstrated that some self-variables can be improved through exercise. This explanation of the exercise–emotional health relationship is so important that it is discussed more fully in terms of its contribution to psychological well-being in chapter 11.

Social Interaction and Approval

Many adults who participate in exercise do so in some type of social setting, either with a few friends or in a formal exercise program. Professionals who plan and conduct exercise programs have recognized for many years that the social aspect of the program may be almost as attractive to their older patrons as the health benefits. Because the social interaction that occurs in these settings may contribute substantially to improvements in mood, anxiety, or depression (Hughes, Casal, & Leon, 1986), social interaction is another possible mechanism mediating the relationship between exercise and emotional health. However, the need for social interaction is highly individual, and coercing individuals who do not desire so much social interaction would be more detrimental than beneficial to their mental health. But for those who perceive a social deficit in their lives, participation in an exercise or sports program with other individuals will certainly improve their emotional well-being. Although the social interaction that occurs in exercise classes contributes significantly to older adults' emotional health, it cannot exclusively account for the psychological benefits observed after exercise programs. In two studies of young subjects, jogging alone produced greater improvements from depression than did participation in group activities of softball, archery, and golf (Brown, Ramirez, & Taub, 1978; Folkins & Sime, 1981). Of course these latter studies were of young college students, and social interaction needs change with increasing age.

Another factor that may contribute to the psychological benefits of exercise classes or programs is the social reinforcement that occurs both during and outside of the class. Class participants encourage each other and praise each other for the accomplishment of different activities within the class. Also, class participants' families and friends outside of the class may praise and congratulate them for their participation. Social approval is a strong form of social reinforcement and can elevate mood states (Ross & Hayes, 1988). This type of social approval also has the potential to enhance emotional health on a long-term basis.

and are obsessive about their exercise programs, either continuing each session far beyond its scheduled period or repeating a session several times a day. Exercise, like any other addiction, becomes the central focus of their life and they neglect their personal and social obligations, to the detriment of their family and other responsibilities (Dishman, 1985; Veale, 1987). Kirkcaldy and Shephard (1990) reviewed several studies of exercise addiction and concluded that for some individuals, abstinence from exercising leads to feelings of hostility, headache, frustration, and tension (Glasser, 1976), restlessness, irritability, and guilt (Robbins & Joseph, 1985). It is not unusual to find older adults who, after retirement from work that has been largely sedentary, "discover" running as a pastime and become emotionally dependent on it. Although the effect of age has not been studied in these individuals, older addicted runners probably experience the same negative effects that younger addicted runners do.

A Positive Consensus on Health, Exercise, and Emotional Function

Even though the difficulties in understanding this area seem extraordinary, and it is certainly possible to overstate the contribution of exercise to emotional function, a panel of experts for the National Institute of Mental Health, after reviewing the available evidence, was able to release eight consensus statements, which are shown in Table 10.6. From these statements, we can conclude that a significant relationship does exist between health, fitness, and emotional function, and that this relationship may be even stronger in those who are in emotional distress. There may be substantial gender differences among these relationships, but the small number of studies of aging adults makes conclusions difficult.

Negative Aspects of Exercise

For most individuals and under most circumstances, the behavior of exercise yields benefits in many dimensions. However, for a few individuals, exercise can become a compulsive behavior. These individuals become addicted to exercise

In Summary

Physical health and activity are inextricably interwoven with emotional function. People respond both physiologically and physically to psychological stressors, and in turn, physical health and activity can both produce and mediate psychological

Table 10.6
1984 Consensus Statements From the National Institute of Mental Health

1. Physical fitness is positively associated with mental health and well-being.
2. Exercise is associated with the reduction of stress emotions, such as state anxiety.
3. Anxiety and depression are common symptoms of failure to cope with mental stress, and exercise has been associated with a decreased level of mild to moderate depression and anxiety.
4. Long-term exercise is usually associated with reductions in traits such as neuroticism and anxiety.
5. Severe depression usually requires professional treatment, which may include medication, electroconvulsive therapy, or psychotherapy with exercise as an adjunct.
6. Appropriate exercise results in reductions in various stress indexes such as neuromuscular tension, resting heart rate, and some stress hormones.
7. Current clinical opinion holds that exercise has beneficial emotional effects across all ages and in both sexes.
8. Physically healthy people who require psychotropic medication may safely exercise when exercise and medications are titrated under close medical supervision.

Note. From Morgan (1984, pp. 11-14).

stress. The aspects of emotional function that have been most studied with regard to physical activity are certain factors of mood states, ability to cope with psychosocial stress, anxiety, depression, and personality. The questions of interest are how people cope with losses of physical ability and health and how chronic exercise and other healthful habits may assist individuals in coping with psychological stressors.

Aging presents challenges to emotional control that are beyond those normally seen in younger adults. With aging, all adults must cope with some or all of the cumulative losses that occur as a natural consequence of living longer: decreasing physical ability, deaths of a spouse, family, and friends, retirement and changes in social role, and eventually, in many cases, changes in physical living arrangements. That these significant losses present severe challenges to the emotional control of the elderly is supported by statistics indicating that the suicide rate

of adults over 65 years of age is more than twice as high as it is in younger adults.

The relationship between physical activity and emotional function is very complex, and it is extremely difficult to study because of so many complicating factors. Health status interacts with all aspects of life, so health practices such as dietary choices, smoking, and drinking make it difficult to determine the specific role that physical activity may play in emotional control. Socioeconomic factors and the occurrence of stressful life events (such as divorce or death) also complicate an understanding of interrelationships. One of the biggest problems in understanding the role of physical activity in the emotional function of the elderly is that so few researchers have studied these parameters in the elderly. Exercise psychology is a very large field of study, but most of the emphasis in this area has been on athletes, the health and well-being of young adults, and institutionalized patients. Indeed, because of the scarcity of studies on older adults, most of the conclusions in this chapter are based on research on young adults. In addition to the limited number of aging studies, those available used a wide variety of methods, and the data are largely subjective.

Both physiological and psychosocial hypotheses have been proposed to explain the relationship between physical fitness and emotional function. Physiological hypotheses include changes in cerebral blood circulation, brain catecholamine function, endorphins, and body temperature. Psychosocial mechanisms include exercise serving as distraction, fulfilling the need for mastery of one's environment, enhancing self-concept, and providing opportunities for social interaction that in turn provides social approval.

References

Appenzeller, O., & Schade, D.R. (1979). Neurology of endurance training III: Sympathetic activity during a marathon run. *Neurology, 29,* 542.

Bahrke, M.S., & Morgan, W.P. (1978). Anxiety reduction following exercise and meditation. *Cognitive Therapy and Research, 2,* 323-333.

Barchas, J.D., & Freedman, D.X. (1963). Brain amines: Response to physiological stress. *Biochemistry and Pharmacology, 12,* 1232-1235.

Beck, A.T., & Beamesderfer, A. (1974). Assessment of depression: The Depression Inventory. In P.

Pichot (Ed.), *Psychological measurements in psychopharmacology* (pp. 1-10). Basel: Karger.

Bendig, A.W. (1956). The development of a short form of the Manifest Anxiety Scale. *Journal of Consulting Psychology, 20,* 384.

Bennett, J., Carmack, M.A., & Gardner, V.J. (1982). The effect of a program of physical exercise on depression in older adults. *Physical Educator, 39,* 21-24.

Biddle, S.J.H., & Fox, K.R. (1989). Exercise and health psychology: Emerging relationships. *British Journal of Medical Psychology, 62,* 205-216.

Billig, N. (1987). *To be old and sad.* New York: Lexington Books.

Bock, E.W., & Webber, I.L. (1972). Suicide among the elderly: Isolating widowhood and mitigating alternatives. *Journal of Marriage and the Family, 34,* 24-31.

Brooke, S.T., & Long, B.C. (1987). Efficiency of coping with a real-life stressor: A multimodal comparison of aerobic fitness. *Psychophysiology, 24,* 173-180.

Brown, B.S., Payne, T., Kim, C., Moore, G., Krebs, P., & Martin, W. (1979). Chronic response of rat brain norepinephrine and serotonin levels to endurance training. *Journal of Applied Physiology, 46,* 19-23.

Brown, B.S., & Van Huss, W. (1973). Exercise and rat brain catecholamines. *Journal of Applied Physiology, 34,* 664-669.

Brown, J.D., & Lawton, M. (1986). Stress and well-being in adolescence: The moderating role of physical exercise. *Journal of Human Stress, 12,* 125-131.

Brown, R.S., Ramirez, D.E., & Taub, J.M. (1978). The prescription of exercise for depression. *Physician and Sportsmedicine, 6,* 34-45.

Camacho, T.C., Roberts, R.E., Lazarus, N.B., Kaplan, G.A., & Cohen, R.D. (1991). Physical activity and depression: Evidence from the Alameda County study. *American Journal of Epidemiology, 134,* 220-231.

Cannon, J.G., & Kluger, M.J. (1983). Endogenous pyrogen activity in human plasma after exercise. *Science, 220,* 617-619.

Carlson, N.R. (1990). *Psychology: The science of behavior* (3rd ed.) Boston: Allyn & Bacon.

Carr, D., Bullen, B.A., Skrinar, G.S., Arnold, M.A., Rosenblatt, M., Beitins, I.Z., Martin, J.B., & McArthur, J.W. (1981). Physical conditioning facilities for the exercise-induced secretion of beta-endorphins and beta-lipoprotein in women. *New England Journal of Medicine, 305,* 560-563.

Carter, H., & Glick, P. (1976). *Marriage and divorce: A social and economic study.* Cambridge, MA: Harvard University Press.

Castell, P.J., & Blumenthal, J.A. (1985). The effects of aerobic exercise on mood. In B.D. Kirkcaldy (Ed.), *Individual differences in movement.* Lancaster & Boston: MTP.

Cattell, R.B. (1946). *Description and measurement of personality.* New York: World Books.

Chodzko-Zajko, W.J., & Ismail, A.H. (1986). The discrimination power of the MMPI and selected physiological and biochemical variables to differentiate between high- and low-fit adult males. In J.H. Humphrey & C.O. Dotson (Eds.), *Exercise physiology* (Vol. 2, pp. 99-107). New York: AMS Press.

Cohen, S., Kamarck, T., & Mermelstein, R. (1983). A global measure of perceived stress. *Journal of Health and Social Behavior, 24,* 385-396.

Crandall, R.C. (1991). *Gerontology: A behavioral science approach.* New York: McGraw-Hill.

Crews, D.J., & Landers, D.M. (1987). A meta-analytic review of aerobic fitness and reactivity to psychosocial stressors. *Medicine and Science in Sports and Exercise, 19*(5, Suppl.), S114-S120.

Davidson, F.J., & Schwartz, G.E. (1976). The psychobiology of relaxation and related states: A multiprocess theory. In D.I. Mostofsky (Ed.), *Behavior control and modification of physiological activity.* Englewood Cliffs, NJ: Prentice Hall.

DeCastro, J.M., & Duncan, G. (1985). Operantly conditioned running: Effects on brain catecholamine concentrations and receptor densities in the rat. *Pharmacology, Biochemistry & Behavior, 23,* 495-500.

deVries, H.A. (1987). Tension reduction with exercise. In W.P. Morgan & S.E. Goldston (Eds.), *Exercise and mental health* (pp. 99-104). Washington, DC: Hemisphere.

deVries, H.A., Wiswell, R.A., Bulbulian, R., & Moritani, T. (1981). Tranquilizer effect of exercise. *American Journal of Physical Medicine, 60,* 57-66.

Dienstbier, R.A. (1984). The effect of exercise on personality. In M.L. Sachs & G.B. Buffone (Eds.), *Running as therapy: An integrated approach.* Lincoln: University of Nebraska Press.

Dienstbier, R.A., LaGuardia, R.L., & Wilcox, N.S. (1987). The relationship of temperament to tolerance of cold and heat: Beyond "cold hands-warm heart." *Motivation and Emotion, 11,* 269-295.

Dienstbier, R.A., LaGuardia, R.L., Barnes, M., Tharp, G., & Schmidt, R. (1987). Catecholamine training effects from exercise programs: A bridge to exercise-temperament relationships. *Motivation and Emotion, 11,* 297-318.

Dishman, R.K. (1985). Medical psychology in exercise and sport. *Medical Clinics of North America, 69,* 123-143.

Dishman, R.K. (1986). Mental health. In V. Seefeldt (Ed.), *Physical activity and well-being* (pp. 304-341). Reston, VA: American Alliance of Health, Physical Education, Recreation and Dance.

Doyne, E.J., Ossip-Klein, D.J., Bowman, E.D., Osborn, K.M., McDougall-Wilson, I.B., & Neimeyer, R.A. (1987). Running versus weight lifting in the treatment of depression. *Journal of Consulting and Clinical Psychology*, **55**, 748-754.

Driscoll, R. (1976). Anxiety reduction using physical exertion and positive images. *Psychological Record*, **26**, 89-94.

Dulac, S., Brisson, G.R., Proteau, L., Peronnet, F., Ledoux, M., & DeCarufel, D. (1982). Selected hormonal response to repeated short bouts of anaerobic exercise. *Medicine and Science in Sports and Exercise*, **14**, 173-174.

Dustman, R.E., Ruhling, R.O., Russell, E.M., Shearer, D.E., Bonekat, H.W., Shigeoka, J.W., Wood, J.S., & Bradford, D.C. (1984). Aerobic exercise training and improved neuropsychological function of older individuals. *Neurobiology of Aging*, **5**, 35-42.

Emery, C.F., & Blumenthal, J.A. (1990). Perceived change among participants in an exercise program for older adults. *The Gerontologist*, **30**, 516-521.

Eysenck, J.J., & Eysenck, S.B.G. (1963). *Manual for the Eysenck Personality Inventory*. San Diego: Educational and Industrial Testing Service.

Farrell, P.A., Gustafson, A.B., Garthwaite, T.L., Kalkhoff, R.K., Cowley, A.W., Jr., & Morgan, W.P. (1986). Influence of endogenous opioids on the response of selected hormones to exercise in humans. *Journal of Applied Physiology*, **61**, 1051-1057.

Folkins, C.H., Lynch, S., & Gardener, M.M. (1972). Psychological fitness as a function of physical fitness. *Archives of Physical Medicine and Rehabilitation*, **53**, 503-508.

Folkins, C.H., & Sime, W.E. (1981). Physical fitness training and mental health. *American Psychologist*, **36**, 373-389.

Forrester, D.A. (1987). Affective disorders and suicide. In J. Norris, M. Kunes-Connell, S. Stockard, P. Mayer-Ehrhart, & G.R. Renschler-Newton (Eds.), *Mental health psychiatric nursing—A continuum of care* (pp. 761-767). New York: Wiley.

Frederick, T., Frerichs, R.R., & Clark, V.A. (1988). Personal health habits and symptoms of depression at the community level. *Preventive Medicine*, **17**, 173-182.

Gillett, P. (1989). Aerobic and muscle fitness in high-risk and overweight senior women. *The Gerontologist*, **29**, 258A.

Glasser, W. (1976). *Positive addiction*. New York: Harper & Row.

Gove, W.R. (1973). Sex, marital status, and suicide. *Journal of Health and Social Behavior*, **13**, 204-213.

Greist, J.H., Klein, M.H., Eischens, R.R., Faris, J., Gurman, A.S., & Morgan, W.P. (1979). Running as treatment for depression. *Comprehensive Psychiatry*, **20**, 41-54.

Hatfield, B.D., & Landers, D.M. (1987). Psychophysiology in exercise and sport research: An overview. *Exercise and Sport Sciences Reviews*, **15**, 351-387.

Hathaway, S.R., & McKinley, J.C. (1972). *MMPI manual*. New York: Psychological Corporation.

Holden, C. (1992). A new discipline probes suicide's multiple causes. *Science*, **256**, 1761-1762.

Hollmann, W., Rost, R., DeMeirleir, K., Liesen, H., Heck, H., & Mader, A. (1986). Cardiovascular effects of extreme physical training. *Acta Medica Scandinavia*, **Suppl. 711**, 193-203.

Holm, K., & Kirchoff, K.T. (1984). Perspectives on exercise and aging. *Heart and Lung*, **13**, 519-524.

Howlett, T.A., Tomling, S., Ngahfoong, L., Rees, L.H., Bullen, B.A., Skrinar, G.S., & MacArthur, J.W. (1984). Release of beta-endorphin and met-enkephalin during exercise in normal women: Response to training. *British Medical Journal*, **288**, 1950-1952.

Hughes, J.R., Casal, D.C., & Leon, A.S. (1986). Psychological effects of exercise: A randomized cross-over trial. *Journal of Psychosomatic Research*, **10**, 355-360.

Jasnoski, M.L., Holmes, D.S., & Banks, D.L. (1988). Changes in personality associated with changes in aerobic and anaerobic fitness in women and men. *Journal of Psychosomatic Research*, **32**, 273-276.

Kicey, C. (1974). Catecholamines and depression. A physiological theory of depression. *American Journal of Nursing*, **74**, 2018-2020.

King, A.C., Taylor, C.B., & Haskell, W.L. (1993). Effects of differing intensities and formats of 12 months of exercise training on psychological outcomes in older adults. *Health Psychology*, **12**, 292-300.

King, A.C., Taylor, C.B., Haskell, W.L., & DeBusk, R.F. (1989). Influence of regular aerobic exercise on psychological health: A randomized, controlled trial of healthy middle-aged adults. *Health Psychology*, **8**, 305-324.

Kirkcaldy, B.D., & Shephard, R.J. (1990). Therapeutic implications of exercise. *International Journal of Sport Psychology*, **21**, 165-184.

Klein, M.H., Greist, J.H., Gurman, A.S., Neimeyer, R.A., Lesser, D.P. Bushnell, N.J., & Smith, R.E. (1985). A comparative outcome study of group psychotherapy vs. exercise treatments for depression. *International Journal of Mental Health*, **13**, 148-177.

Kowal, D.M., Patton, J.F., & Vogel, J.A. (1978). Psychological states and aerobic fitness of male and female recruits before and after basic training. *Aviation Space and Environmental Medicine*, **49**, 603-606.

Laraia, M.T. (1987). Psychopharmacology. In G.W. Stuart & S.J. Sundeen (Eds.), *Principles and practice of psychiatric nursing* (pp. 699-738). St. Louis: Mosby.

Lobstein, D.D., Mosbacher, B.J., & Ismail, A.H. (1983). Depression as a powerful discriminator between physically active and sedentary middle-aged men. *Journal of Psychosomatic Research*, **27**, 69-76.

Lobstein, D.D., Rasmussen, C.L., Dunphy, G.E., & Dunphy, M.J. (1989). Beta-endorphin and components of depression as powerful discriminators between joggers and sedentary middle-aged men. *Journal of Psychosomatic Research*, **33**, 293-305.

MacMahon, B., & Pugh, J. (1965). Suicide in the widowed. *American Journal of Epidemiology*, **81**, 23-31.

Martinsen, E.W. (1990). Benefits of exercise for the treatment of depression. *Sports Medicine*, **9**, 380-389.

McCann, I.L., & Holmes, D. (1984). The influence of aerobic exercise on depression. *Journal of Personality and Social Psychology*, **46**, 1142-1147.

McGlynn, G.H., Franklin, B., Lauro, G., & McGlynn, I.K. (1983). The effect of aerobic conditioning and induced stress on state-trait anxiety, blood pressure, and muscle tension. *Journal of Sports Medicine and Physical Fitness*, **23**, 341-351.

McNair, D.M., Lorr, M., & Droppleman, L.F. (1971). *EITS manual for the profile of mood states*. San Diego: Educational and Industrial Testing Service.

McNeil, J.K., LeBlanc, E.M., & Joyner, M. (1991). The effect of exercise on depressive symptoms in the moderately depressed elderly. *Psychology and Aging*, **6**(2), 487-488.

Morgan, W.P. (1984). *Coping with mental stress: The potential and limits of exercise intervention* (Final report). Bethesda, MD: NIMH.

Morgan, W.P., & Goldston, S.E. (Eds.) (1987). *Exercise and mental health*. Washington, DC: Hemisphere.

Morgan, W.P., & O'Connor, P.J. (1988). Exercise and mental health. In R.K. Dishman (Ed.), *Exercise adherence: Its impact on public health* (pp. 91-121). Champaign, IL: Human Kinetics.

Morgan, W.P., Roberts, J.A., Brand, F.R., & Feinerman, A.D. (1970). Psychological effect of chronic physical activity. *Medicine and Science in Sports and Exercise*, **2**, 213-217.

Moss, F.E., & Halamandaris, V.J. (1977). *Too old, too sick, too bad: Nursing homes in America*. Germantown, MD: Aspen Systems.

Oleson, J. (1971). Contralateral focal increase of cerebral blood flow in man during arm work. *Brain*, **94**, 635-646.

Osterweis, M., Solomon, F., & Green, M. (Eds.) (1984). *Bereavement: Reactions, consequences, and care*. Washington, DC: National Academy Press.

Plante, T.G., & Karpowitz, D. (1987). The influence of aerobic exercise on physiological stress responsivity. *Psychophysiology*, **24**, 670-677.

Plante, T.G., & Rodin, J. (1990). Physical fitness and enhanced psychological health. *Current Psychology: Research and Reviews*, **9**, 3-24.

Prosser, G., Carson, P., Philips, R., Gelson, A., Buch, N., Tucker, H., Neophytore, M., Lloyd, M., & Simpson, T. (1981). Morale in coronary patients following an exercise program. *Journal of Psychosomatic Research*, **25**, 587-593.

Raglin, J.S., & Morgan, W.P. (1987). Influence of exercise and quiet rest on state anxiety and blood pressure. *Medicine and Science in Sports and Exercise*, **19**, 456-463.

Rahkila, P., Hakala, E., Salminen, K., & Laatkainen, T. (1987). Response of plasma endorphins to running exercises in male and female endurance athletes. *Medicine and Science in Sports and Exercise*, **19**, 451-455.

Ransford, C.P. (1982). A role for amines in the antidepressant effect of exercise: A review. *Medicine and Science in Sports and Exercise*, **14**, 1-10.

Reiter, M.A. (1981). Effects of a physical exercise program on selected mood states in a group of women over age 65. *Dissertation Abstracts International*, **42**, 1974-A.

Risch, S.C. (1982). B-endorphin hypersecretion in depression: Possible cholinergic mechanisms. *Biological Psychiatry*, **17**, 1071-1079.

Robbins, J.M., & Joseph, P. (1985). Experiencing exercise withdrawal: Possible consequences of therapeutic and mastery running. *Journal of Sport Psychology*, **7**, 23-29.

Ross, C.E., & Hayes, D. (1988). Exercise and psychologic well-being in the community. *American Journal of Epidemiology*, **127**, 762-771.

Roth, D.L., & Holmes, D.S. (1987). Influence of aerobic exercise training and relaxation training on physical and psychologic health following stressful life events. *Psychosomatic Medicine,* **49,** 355-365.

Sapolzsky, R.M., Krey, L.C., & McEwen, B.S. (1986). The neuroendocrinology of stress and aging: The glucocorticoid cascade hypothesis. *Endocrine Reviews,* **7,** 284-301.

Schaie, K.W., & Geiwitz, J. (1982). *Adult development and aging.* Boston: Little, Brown.

Schildkraut, J.J., Orsulak, P.J., Schatzberg, A.F., & Rosenbaum, A.H. (1984). Relationship between psychiatric diagnostic groups of depressive disorders and MHPG. In J.W. Maas (Ed.), *MHPG: Basic mechanisms and psychopathology.* New York: Academic.

Schnurr, P.P., Vaillant, C.O., & Vaillant, G.E. (1990). Predicting exercise in late midlife from young personality characteristics. *International Journal of Aging and Human Development,* **30,** 153-160.

Schwartz, G.E., Davidson, R.J., & Goleman, D.J. (1978). Patterning of cognitive and somatic processes in the self-regulation of anxiety: Effects of medication versus exercise. *Psychosomatic Medicine,* **40,** 320-328.

Siever, L.J., & Davis, K.L. (1985). Overview: Toward a dysregulation hypothesis of depression. *American Journal of Psychiatry,* **142,** 1017-1031.

Sime, W.E. (1977). A comparison of exercise and meditation in reducing physiological response to stress. *Medicine and Science of Sport,* **9,** 55.

Sime, W.E. (1984). Psychological benefits of exercise training in the healthy individual. In J.D. Matarazzo, S.M. Weiss, J.A. Herd, N.A. Miller, & S.M. Weiss. (Eds.) Behavioral health: *A handbook of health enhancement and disease prevention* (pp. 488-508). New York: Wiley.

Simons, C.W., & Birkimer, J.C. (1988). An exploration of factors predicting the effects of aerobic conditioning on mood state. *Journal of Psychosomatic Research,* **32,** 63-75.

Sinyor, D., Golden, M., Steinert, Y., & Seraganian, P. (1986). Experimental manipulation of aerobic fitness and the response to psychosocial stress: Heart rate and self-report measures. *Psychosomatic Medicine,* **48,** 324-337.

Sinyor, D., Schwartz, S.G., Peronnet, F., Brisson, G., & Seraganian, P. (1983). Aerobic fitness level and reactivity to psychosocial stress: Physiological, biochemical, and subjective measures. *Psychosomatic Medicine,* **45,** 205-217.

Spielberger, C.D., Gorsuch, R.L., & Lushene, R. (1970). *State-Trait Anxiety Inventory manual.* Palo Alto: Consulting Psychologists Press.

Stern, M.J., & Cleary, P. (1982). The national exercise and heart disease project: Long-term psychosocial outcome. *Archives of Internal Medicine,* **142,** 1093-1097.

Thoren, P., Floras, J.S., Hoffman, P., & Seals, D.R. (1990). Endorphins and exercise: Physiological mechanisms and clinical implications. *Medicine and Science in Sports and Exercise,* **22,** 417-428.

Tredway, V.A. (1978). Mood and experience in older adults. *Dissertation Abstracts International,* **39,** 2531-2533.

Uson, P.P., & Larrosa, V.R. (1982). Physical activities in retirement age. In J. Partington, T. Orlick, & J. Samela (Eds.), *Sport in perspective* (pp. 149-151). Ottawa, ON: Coaching Association of Canada.

Vaillant, G.E. (1977). *Adaptation to life.* Boston: Little, Brown.

Veale, D.M.W. (1987). Exercise dependence. *British Journal of Addiction,* **82,** 735-740.

Von Euler, C., & Soderberg, U. (1956). The relation between gamma motor activity and electroencephalogram. *Experimentia,* **12,** 278-279.

Von Euler, C., & Soderberg, U. (1957). The influence of hypothalamic thermoceptive structures on the electroencephalogram and gamma motor activity. *EEG and Clinical Neurophysiology,* **9,** 391-408.

Walker, M., & Hailey, B.J. (1987). Physical fitness levels and psychological states versus traits. *Perceptual and Motor Skills,* **64,** 15-25.

White, R.W. (1959). Motivation reconsidered: The concept of competence. *Psychological Review,* **66,** 297-333.

Winder, W.W., Hagberg, J.M., Hickson, R.C., Ehsani, A.A., & McLane, J.A. (1978). Time course of sympathoadrenal adaptations to endurance exercise training in man. *Journal of Applied Physiology,* **45,** 370-374.

Wolfolk, R., & Richardson, F. (1978). *Stress, sanity, and survival.* New York: Signet.

Wolpe, J., Salter, A., & Reyna, L.J. (1964). *The conditioning therapies.* New York: Holt, Rinehart, & Winston.

Young, R.J. (1979). The effect of regular exercise on cognitive functioning and personality. *British Journal of Sports Medicine,* **13,** 110-117.

Zung, W.W. (1965). Self-rating depression scale. *Archives of General Psychiatry,* **12,** 63-70.

CHAPTER 11

Health, Fitness, and Well-Being

Quality of life in dictionary terms means the goodness, excellence, or fineness of life. But whether life is good or excellent really depends not on an absolute dictionary definition but on how each person defines goodness. In fairy tales, the goal of happiness is achieved by being healthy, wealthy, wise, and loved. In real life it is a much more complicated matter. Several components of the quality of life for the elderly were introduced in chapter 1 (see Figure 1.14, page 27). These components were organized into three major clusters: health and physical function, cognitive-emotional function, and social function. Whether individuals feel they are living a high-quality life depends on their feeling of well-being, which includes whether they feel satisfied with their life. Quality of life also depends to a large extent on peoples' health and the way they feel about their health. This chapter explores the relationship of health and physical fitness to feelings of well-being and life-satisfaction. First, the constructs of health and fitness are addressed, followed by a discussion of well-being and life satisfaction and how these are measured. The last half of the chapter presents current information about the role of health and exercise in shaping older adults' perceptions of their well-being.

Health

Physical health has three facets that relate to quality of life: physical condition, functional status, and subjective health status. *Physical condition* is the number of health problems experienced by an individual. A small percentage of older persons are free of chronic diseases, but most individuals over age 70 experience multiple physical conditions, such as hypertension, cardiovascular disease, arthritis, and osteoporosis. Figure 1.8 (page 16) shows the average number of physical conditions for males and females (Guralnik, LaCroix, Everett, & Kovar, 1989); 86% of women and 78% of men over the age of 70 have one or more chronic diseases, so actual health conditions are a concern for most elderly adults.

The second facet of physical health is *functional status*, or the degree to which these physical conditions prevent persons from being able to execute activities of daily living (ADLs, i.e., self-care activities), instrumental activities of daily living (IADLs, i.e., preparing meals, doing housework, and having the mobility to go outside the house), and discretionary activities (hobbies, recreation, and social contacts). *Subjective health status*, the personal evaluation that individuals make about their own health, is the third facet of physical health. Subjective health varies greatly among people. For example, a woman who has two serious physical conditions that substantially constrain her activities may believe that her health is average, or even above average, for her age, whereas another woman with only one, minimally constraining physical condition may consider her health to be poor or unacceptable. Much of the way people view their health depends on their life experiences, their goals, and the coping mechanisms that they use to deal with failure and disappointments.

Because health is a multifaceted dimension and is interpreted differently by different people, it is very difficult to measure and to relate to other dimensions of life. Some investigators focus on the number and type of physical conditions that people have to assess their health. Others emphasize the functional capacities of the elderly, using the ADL and IADL instruments to measure the degree to which the subjects can perform the basic, instrumental activities of daily living. Others measure subjective health by administering single-item subjective health assessments or by using ordinal scales, such as having subjects rate their own health on the basis of the steps of a ladder. Placing themselves on the bottom step (a score of 1) indicates that subjects believe they have a serious illness, whereas placing themselves on the top step (a score of 9) would indicate their belief that they are in perfect health. These types of tests have relatively low reliability and validity. Nevertheless, despite the type of health or the method of measurement, these indexes of health have generally been found to be significantly related to feelings of well-being and life satisfaction.

Fitness

Good health is freedom from disease, and although it is a foundation of physical fitness, it is not synonymous with fitness. Some older individuals are relatively free of chronic diseases, or they may be presymptomatic and not yet experiencing the negative functional consequences of their diseases, but they are not physically fit in terms of having acceptable flexibility (chapter 3), aerobic capacity (chapter 4), and strength and endurance (chapter 5) for their age. Almost all of what is known about the role of health and quality of life in the elderly is related to the notion of health in the most minimal of definitions, that is, the degree to which the presence of chronic diseases influences the ability of individuals to execute minimum survival activities. Little attention has been given to the effect that the loss of participation in a hobby, social experiences, or religious activities might have on a person's perceived quality of life.

Well-Being

The feeling of well-being is a construct that almost everyone understands but, paradoxically, almost no one can define. It is similar to the concept of creativity; most people know what creativity is and can even identify creative individuals whom they know. But defining and measuring creativity has proven to be an almost impossible task. Defining the concept of well-being is very similar. It is a theoretical concept that includes the ideas of contentment, morale, and happiness. Psychologists also suggest that for the elderly, adjustment, emotional balance, and continued development should be included. But even this definition is not complete, because it leaves open the question, what is contentment, happiness, and morale? Contentment can be defined as being satisfied with one's situation. More formal definitions have been provided for happiness and morale (Stock, Okun, & Benin, 1986). Happiness may be thought of as the ratio of positive to negative affects an individual is currently experiencing, and morale is the degree of optimism that an individual has about what his or her life will be like in the future.

The sections that follow examine how well-being is measured and its relationship to health and fitness. Next follow sections on aspects of self-concept—self-esteem, self-efficacy, and sense of control—as they affect well-being. Each of these components is discussed from the perspective of their interacting with health, fitness, and exercise and their interrelationships in the aging adult.

Measuring Well-Being

One's sense of well-being is intensely personal. Therefore, the feelings of well-being that individuals have must be discovered through self-report. The only way to determine how people feel is to ask them. Thus, when well-being is researched, it is generally referred to as "expressed well-being," or "subjective well-being." Because well-being is an emotional feeling, it is personal, relatively transitory, and can be influenced by temporary environmental occurrences. Tests of well-being are difficult to validate and have lower reliabilities than most tests of physical attributes.

Several representative tests of well-being are shown in Table 11.1. The first four happiness scales offer various methods to help people rank their general feelings about their overall life happiness. In these tests people are asked to place themselves on the rung of a ladder or a point on a mountain side to indicate their degree of happiness. Or, they are asked to choose a face that represents the way they usually feel from among

a row of faces ranging from one completely scowling to one completely smiling, or to choose a similar representative position along a dimension ranging from delighted to terrible. The remainder of the global well-being scales use several questions to assess people's feelings of well-being about different aspects of their life (job, family, self, etc.) or include questions that will tap different qualities of subjective well-being (optimism, self-esteem, self-efficacy, cheerfulness, etc.). In these tests, questions are asked to determine the sense of satisfaction that subjects have with themselves, their family, friends, work, recreation, religion, social organizations, health, and economic state. Some of the questions are asked to determine whether individuals believe that there is a place in the world for themselves. Other questions relate to people's levels of zest versus apathy, resolution versus fortitude, and a calculated ratio of their positive and negative states of mind.

Although tests differ in how well-being is described and in the psychological test theory underlying their development, all of them tap a basic conceptual construct. These tests intercorrelate highly, and they also similarly correlate to other constructs. Larson (1978) emphasized, however, that although the estimates of well-being assessed by tests such as these are useful, several caveats must be kept in mind. These tests cannot measure well-being equivalently across ethnic, cohort, and social classes, because people in these groupings have different goals. Also, generalizations from well-being scores cannot be applied to individuals, because individuals, for example, might uniquely interpret key words. All of the responses made by subjects in any study of well-being are quick assessments that are made in a social situation. They represent expressed affective experience and thus should not be used to assess complex psychological factors or mental health.

Subjective well-being is highly related to individuals' feelings of satisfaction about themselves, their families, and their jobs. In fact, it is so highly related that it is difficult to separate the concepts of well-being and life satisfaction. Life satisfaction is really the extent to which an individual is contented with how his or her life has developed. It is measured by asking individuals to compare the overall conditions of their lives (i.e., the actual achievements) to the aspirations they had for their lives (Campbell, Converse, & Rodgers, 1976; George, 1979). Generally when life satisfaction is

Table 11.1
Representative Measures of Subjective Well-Being

Happiness scales

Ladder Scale	Rating of one's current life in relation to the best and worst imaginable life	Cantril, 1967
Mountain Scale		Gallop, 1976
Faces Scale		Andrews & Whithey, 1976
Delighted-Terrible Scale		Andrews & Whithey, 1976

Global well-being scales

Life Satisfaction Scales	"Taking things all together, how would you say things are these days?"	Neurgarten, Havighurst, & Tobin, 1961
Affect Scales	Affective states "during the past few weeks," positive states to negative states ratio	Bradburn, 1969
PGC Morale Scale	Sense of satisfaction with self Feeling there is a place in the world for self Acceptance of what cannot be changed	Lawton, 1975
Kutner Morale Scale	Zest vs. apathy Resolution and fortitude Congruence with desired and achieved goals Self-concept Mood tone	Kutner et al., 1956
Indexes of General Affect and Well-Being		Campbell et al., 1976
Life 3 Scale		Andrews & Whithey, 1976
General Well-Being Schedule		Fazio, 1977
MUNSH-Happiness Scale		Kozma & Stones, 1980
Affectometer 2		Kammann & Flett, 1983

Note. Data from Andrews and Robinson (1991, pp. 61-114).

measured, it encompasses all of the domains of persons' lives: their feeling about the community in which they live, their job or responsibilities, their satisfaction with their marriage or living arrangements, and their health. Researchers generally believe that life satisfaction tends to be stable in the elderly. Persons who have been satisfied with their lives before old age will most likely continue to be satisfied, and those who have been dissatisfied will probably continue to be dissatisfied. The stability of life satisfaction in the elderly is problematic, however, partly because most of the studies are cross-sectional designs and partly because a large percentage of such studies were conducted in institutions. It is expected that institutionalized people have lower life satisfaction and feelings of well-being than community-dwelling people, and so some of the life satisfaction results may represent more negativity than actually exists in the community-dwelling elderly.

Yet, when subjects consider their lives to be very satisfying, they also have a strong sense of well-being. Thus, life satisfaction scales are used as measures of subjective well-being. Both are influenced to some extent by income, race, and employment and to a minor extent by education, marriage, and family (Diener, 1984). Other factors that seem to be related to well-being are friends, a loving relationship with someone, social activity (Okun & Stock, 1987), and the nature of the coping skills people use to deal with negative life events (Matheny, Aycock, Pugh, Curlette, & Cannella, 1986). Aging itself does not decrease well-being independently but only indirectly because aging relates to other factors. For example, the decreased health that sometimes accompanies aging has the potential to negatively affect subjective well-being. The question of how health affects well-being and feelings of life satisfaction is an important one that has substantial ramifications for quality of life.

Health and Well-Being

Health and physical capacity are important components of a feeling of well-being. Ryff (1989) asked middle-aged (52.5 ± 8.7 years) and old people (73.5 ± 6.1 years) what they believed was most important in their lives (the results are shown in Figure 11.1, a-b). Out of 12 items, the middle-aged people listed health as the fifth most important, and the old people listed health as second in importance. When asked what they would change if they could, middle-aged people listed their health fourth in importance and old people listed health second (Figure 11.2, a-b). It is clear that health status is of deep concern to both middle-aged and old-aged people. When they were asked how they had changed from 20 years ago, both groups listed physical changes in the top four (Figure 11.3, a-b, page 309). The older group indicated that their physical being changed more than any other aspect of their lives, whereas the middle-aged group listed physical changes fourth out of 13 or more life dimensions. Both age groups indicated that their personality attributes, concern for others, interests and activities, morals and values, and outlook on life had remained relatively stable. Among the biggest changes over the past 20 years, in addition to the physical changes, was the adjustment to role changes, their ability to relax, and their ability to accept themselves. An important point is that both middle-aged and older groups listed physical changes and health events as the most negative of the changes and events that they had experienced over the past 20 years. These findings match those from other studies, revealing more concern in older groups for health, whereas job and career issues are more important to middle-aged people. A subset of older individuals for whom much of their self-identity has been defined by their career can suffer doubly by a loss of health. Their loss of health also leads to the loss of their job. In these cases, the loss of health is a major contributor to a decline in their sense of well-being.

That personal health is related to well-being, even when other factors such as socioeconomic status, educational level, and gender are controlled, is a very common finding. Larson (1978) concluded, after a comprehensive review of 30 years of research on the topic, "Among all the elements of an older person's life situation, health is the most strongly related to subjective well-being. People who are sick or physically disabled are much less likely to express contentment about their lives" (p. 112). The correlates identified by Larson are shown in Figure 11.4 (page 309). Several investigators since 1978 have corroborated these conclusions. For example, self-rated health was found to be the best indicator of life satisfaction in 40 noninstitutionalized adults aged 80 to 96 years (Gfellner, 1989). In that study, the old-old adults' life-satisfaction, perceived health, and functional ability decreased over a 5-year period, but the deterioration in life satisfaction was less than that of perceived health and functional ability. These elderly were able to maintain a tolerable degree of life satisfaction despite their disabilities and their perception of decreased health and functional ability.

The relationship of health to expressed well-being seems to hold true for all the domains of well-being (community, job, marital satisfaction) and for middle-aged adults as well as older ones regardless of gender, education, marital status, income, number of relatives in the area, number of friends nearby, or frequency of leisure involvement (Willits & Crider, 1988).

The relationship between health and well-being is also bidirectional. Not only does health status influence perceptions of well-being, but people's feelings of well-being also influence their health-related behaviors, illustrated by Figure 11.5 (page 310; Pender, 1982). Although many factors are modifiers of health, people's views of the importance of health, their ability to control their lives, and their self-awareness, self-esteem, and perceived health status have a direct bearing on the likelihood that they will take action to maintain health and prevent disease.

Exercise, Fitness, Well-Being, and Life Satisfaction

Absence of or, at least, a minimum of disease symptoms is positively related to well-being and life satisfaction, but does enhanced health and increased fitness confer a higher level of quality of life? Older adults who consider exercise and physical competition to be a high priority in their lives, that is, masters athletes or age-group sports competitors, report that they experience a high quality of life (Hawkins, Duncan, & McDermott, 1988; Morris & Husman, 1978; Morris, Lussier, Vaccaro, & Clark, 1982). Similarly, nationally ranked women masters competitors (over 40 years of age)

What is most important?

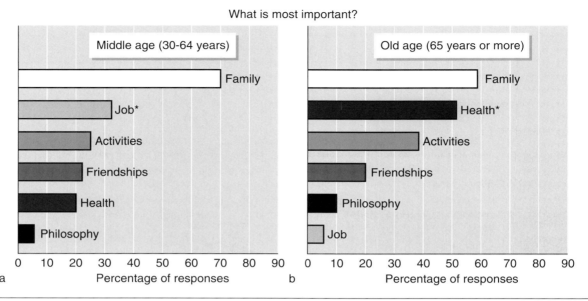

Figure 11.1 The percentage of respondents for each answer to the question, What is most important to you in your life at the present time? An asterisk indicates a significant difference (*p* <0.001) between what is important to (a) middle-aged and (b) older adults.

From "In the Eye of the Beholder: Views of Psychological Well-Being Among Middle-Aged and Older Adults" by C.D. Ryff, 1989, *Psychology and Aging*, **4**, p. 198. Copyright 1989 by the American Psychological Association. Reprinted by permission.

What would you change?

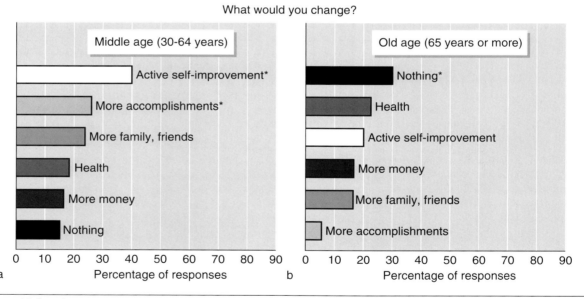

Figure 11.2 The percentage of respondents for each answer to the question, What would you change? An asterisk indicates a significant difference (*p* <0.001) between what is important to (a) middle-aged and (b) older adults.

From "In the Eye of the Beholder: Views of Psychological Well-Being Among Middle-Aged and Older Adults" by C.D. Ryff, 1989, *Psychology and Aging*, **4**, p. 198. Copyright 1989 by the American Psychological Association. Reprinted by permission.

reported a higher quality of life than a group of adults who were similar in many ways except that they did not train and compete in running. But what of older adults who have led sedentary lifestyles and who begin an exercise program? Do

their feelings of well-being and life satisfaction improve after exercise? This question has been approached from two directions: whether a single exercise bout can cause a surge of feelings of physical well-being during or immediately after

How have you changed from 20 years ago?

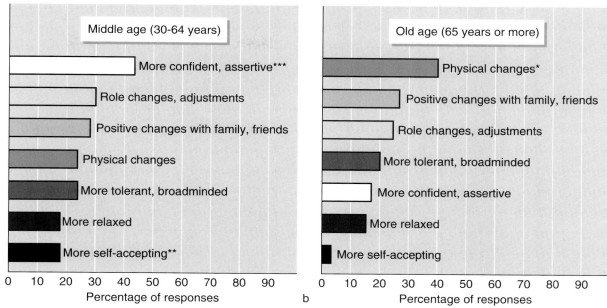

Figure 11.3 The percentage of respondents for each answer to the question, How have you changed from 20 years ago? *p <0.05, **p <0.01, and ***p <0.001 indicate a significant difference between what is important to (a) middle-aged and (b) older adults.

From "In the Eye of the Beholder: Views of Psychological Well-Being Among Middle-Aged and Older Adults" by C.D. Ryff, *Psychology and Aging*, **4**, p. 206. Copyright 1989 by the American Psychological Association. Reprinted by permission.

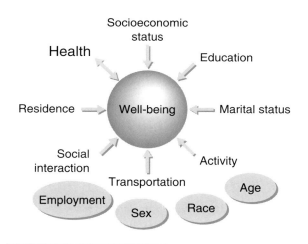

Figure 11.4 Correlates of subjective well-being. The relationships of factors to well-being are shown by arrows, whereas unrelated factors are shown as unconnected to well-being. Health is a somewhat larger correlate, because it was the most strongly related to well-being.

the bout, and whether an exercise program conducted over several weeks can be associated with a longer lasting enhancement in the subjects' feelings of well-being.

Short-Term Effects

Immediately after moderate to prolonged exercise, most people report that they feel good or feel better (Morgan, 1985), and, as discussed in chapter 10, part of this feeling of well-being may be attributed to perceived reductions in anxiety and depression. Some researchers claim that a type of euphoria is achieved by running. Morgan (1985), in his exceptional review of the affective beneficence of vigorous physical activity, rightly called the statements in Mandell (1979) an elegant description of the runner's high:

> Thirty minutes out, and something lifts. Legs and arms become light and rhythmic. My snake brain is making the best of it. The fatigue goes away and feelings of power begin. I think I'll run twenty-five miles today. I'll double the size of the research grant request. I'll have that talk with the dean . . .
>
> Then, sometime into the second hour comes the spooky time. Colors are bright and beautiful, water sparkles, clouds breathe, and my body, swimming, detaches from the earth. A loving contentment

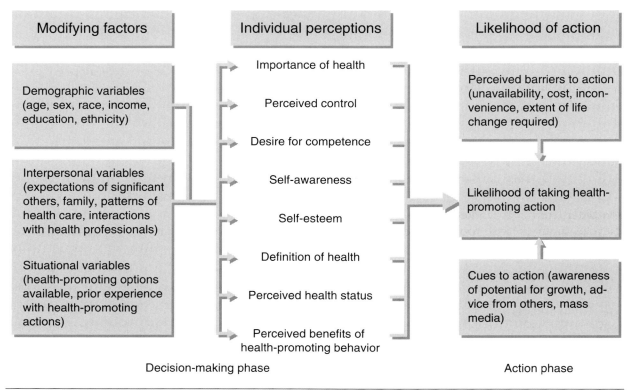

| Modifying factors | Individual perceptions | Likelihood of action |

Importance of health

Perceived control

Desire for competence

Self-awareness

Self-esteem

Definition of health

Perceived health status

Perceived benefits of
health-promoting behavior

Demographic variables
(age, sex, race, income,
education, ethnicity)

Interpersonal variables
(expectations of significant
others, family, patterns of
health care, interactions
with health professionals)

Situational variables
(health-promoting options
available, prior experience
with health-promoting
actions)

Perceived barriers to action
(unavailability, cost, incon-
venience, extent of life
change required)

Likelihood of taking health-
promoting action

Cues to action (awareness
of potential for growth, ad-
vice from others, mass
media)

Decision-making phase   Action phase

Figure 11.5   The Pender health-promotion model.
From *Health Promotion in Nursing Practice* (p. 58) by N.J. Pender, 1982. Norwalk, CT: Appleton & Lange. Copyright 1982 by
Appleton & Lange. Reprinted by permission.

invades the basement of my mind, and thoughts bubble up without trails. I find the place I need to live if I'm going to live. The running literature says that if you run six miles a day for two months, you are addicted forever. I understand. A cosmic view and peace are located between six and ten miles of running. I've found it so everywhere. . . .

After the run I can't use my mind. It's empty. Then a filling begins. By afternoon I'm back into life with long and smooth energy, a quiet feeling of strength, the kind wisdom afforded those without fear, those detached yet full. The most delicious part is the night's sleep. Long an illusive, fickle dealer with me, Father Sandman now stands ready whenever I want. Maybe the greatest power of the second cycle is the capacity to decide when to fall asleep.

This type of testimonial about the feelings of running and the aftereffects abounds in popular literature, but the phenomenon has been extremely difficult to document scientifically. Berger and Owen (1987) reviewed several studies and

concluded that jogging enhances mood and decreases anxiety. In their own research, they reported short-term reductions in anxiety of both beginning and intermediate college swimmers following the swimming period. All of these studies, however, have been of young populations.

Very few analyses have been made of the feelings of well-being that older adults have following acute bouts of exercise. One exception is a study of the transitory effects of a single bout of exercise on young, middle-aged, and older subjects over 60 years old. Subjects in all three groups decreased in negative feelings immediately after exercise (Windsor, Lawton, Sands, Gitlin, & Posner, 1989). But only the young and middle-aged subjects also experienced improvements in positive feelings and feelings of well-being. That is, neither the subjects over age 60 who exercised nor the age-group controls who participated in a 45-min lecture or group discussion improved in positive affect.

Upon further analysis, the investigators hypothesized that improvements in positive affect and perceived physical well-being were positively related to whether subjects enjoyed the exercise and exertion. They suggested three reasons why the older exercisers may not have experienced an increase in positive affect and feelings of well-being: The type of exercise was different, the music was different, and the motivations for exercise may have been different for different age groups. The young and middle-aged subjects were recruited from a local health club, exercised at a different time, and their exercise consisted of fast moves, bending, twisting, and stretching. The exercise leaders encouraged them to endure difficult and tiring floor exercises; consequently, the members of the exercise class developed a type of camaraderie, a sense of "shared pain." In sharp contrast, the older exercisers worked out on treadmills or bicycles in an exercise room at a senior citizens' center. Although others were always in the room, the physical activity for the older subjects was primarily a solitary experience. Thus, the intensity and other aspects of exercise were not equated across the different age groups. Another factor that differed among the age groups was that the music played in the two different exercise locations was also different. The music that accompanied the exercise of the young and middle-aged subjects from the health club was fast and had a pulsing, invigorating beat. The music that accompanied the exercise in the senior center was characterized as easy-listening. The researchers speculated that another significant difference among the age groups may have been that the young and middle-aged participants had elected to exercise to improve their appearance and maintain their health, whereas the older subjects may have been exercising because their physicians prescribed it or because they felt that their health was becoming compromised. In these two extremes, the young and middle-aged subjects were motivated by joy and optimism, whereas the older subjects were driven by fear and necessity (Windsor et al., 1989).

Long-Term Effects of Exercise

Research on the long-term effects of exercise on life satisfaction is mixed. A study of 381 men 45 to 59 years old, who were randomly assigned to either an exercise or control group, found positive changes. The group that exercised three times a week for 18 months reported greater changes in enhanced personal health, increased work performance, and a more positive attitude toward work than the control group (Heinzelmann & Bagley, 1970). Other studies have found that even in the absence of significant effects of exercise on psychological factors such as quality of life, mental

health, or general activity participation, the subjects believed that their sense of well-being improved (e.g., Blumenthal et al., 1989; Gitlin et al., 1986).

However, not all researchers find exercise benefits for well-being and life satisfaction. Sidney and Shephard (1976) found no changes in the life satisfaction scores of older subjects on the LSI-A index after an exercise program that met 4 days a week and lasted 14 weeks. Nor did researchers detect any improvements in psychological well-being at a 3-month follow-up assessment after a 10-week exercise program (Moses, Steptoe, Matthews, & Edwards, 1989).

There are several plausible explanations of why contradictory results have been obtained from studies of exercise effects on well-being and life satisfaction. One may be that exercise interventions may have only short-term effects. A meta-analysis of 31 studies revealed that in most intervention studies, the beneficial effect dissipates within 1 month (Okun, Olding, & Cohn, 1990). Another hypothesis is that exercise contributes to perceptions of enhanced functioning only as long as the individual continues exercising (Emery & Blumenthal, 1990). This supports the proposition that in order to produce long-lasting change, exercise must become a lifestyle rather than an intervention. Another hypothesis is that the questions that have been asked of subjects relating to well-being or life satisfaction may have been too general. Finally, a measurable enhancement of well-being may require improvements in more than one component, such as health, so that it may be unreasonable to expect to see a change in well-being by the intervention of only one factor such as exercise. The results from studies of effects of exercise programs on more specific constructs, such as body consciousness or physical self-efficacy, have been more promising.

Exercise as a Vehicle for Social Interaction

Another way that exercise participation might enhance well-being is through the social interactions that occur during formalized exercise programs. Recall that in Figure 11.1b (page 308), friendships are ranked by older adults as the fourth most important factor in their lives. They also indicated that having more family and friends is the fifth most important aspect of their lives that they would change if they could (Figure 11.2b, page

308). Many researchers have found a significant positive correlation between the number of memberships that older adults have in voluntary community associations and their happiness. Sports clubs and exercise programs provide a group association that is very meaningful to elderly participants, hence these programs contribute to happiness by providing a structured environment for social interaction.

At least part of the reason why the results of research on exercise effects on well-being are mixed may be that global well-being is such a difficult concept for subjects to understand. Instead, it may be more productive to try analyzing the relationship between health and fitness and specific components of well-being, such as self-concept and self-esteem.

Self-Concept

Self-concept is the conscious awareness and perception of self. It is not a unitary construct; rather, it is multidimensional. Shown in Figure 11.6, the awareness that people have of themselves includes perceptions about their intellectual (or scholastic), social, emotional, and physical functioning (Shavelson, Hubner, & Stanton, 1976). Perception of self in the intellectual or scholastic dimension involves recognition of abilities in literature, mathematics, or science comprehension, or of an aptitude for solving problems (e.g., crossword puzzles). The concept of the self as a social identity includes social status, membership in professional or social groups (bridge clubs, teaching), or social labels (e.g., leader, social butterfly, troublemaker). People's perceptions of their personal dispositions include their personality traits, preferences, and predispositions (e.g., anxious, moody, optimistic). Self-concept is developmental in that it changes throughout childhood, throughout adulthood, and with the slow changes that are related to increased aging. In the physical dimension, self-concept includes perceptions about physical appearance and physical skill.

Body concept, an important component of self-concept, is the awareness that people have of their body. It includes their understanding of their physical attributes, for example, their height, weight, and other physical characteristics. Some individuals have a much greater concept of their body and

its functions than others do. For example, some individuals take every opportunity to assess their physical dimension. They know their resting and maximum heart rates, blood pressures (systolic and diastolic), and their grip strength. Other individuals have little interest in understanding their physical attributes and capabilities.

Self-concept is formulated by perception and evaluation, serves as the basis for individuals' beliefs in their competence and capabilities, and is tempered by self-acceptance. That is, it is very difficult to be aware of self in specific circumstances without evaluating and comparing self with a standard, with others, or with one's own performances at different times. Thus, evaluation of self is ongoing. The results of these evaluations and the feelings about them provide the basis for an individual's self-esteem. Self-esteem is composed of feelings of competence, self-approval, power, and self-worthiness. Some people use the terms self-concept and self-esteem interchangeably, but self-esteem is more appropriately used for the evaluative and affective portion of the more general construct of self-concept (Sonstroem & Morgan, 1989).

Self-Esteem

Self-esteem is the respect and appreciation that individuals have for themselves, or the extent to which they feel positive about themselves (Gergen, 1971). Self-esteem, also depicted in Figure 11.6, includes the concepts of general competence, power, normal self-approval, and love-worthiness (Epstein, 1973). Self-esteem is clearly a multidimensional construct (Gergen, 1981), because it includes the regard with which people view themselves in all dimensions of their lives— the psychological, social, and philosophical dimensions as well as the physical. A woman may have one feeling of self-esteem regarding her role as mother, another for her job, and yet another as a church member. With regard to physical movement and exercise, self-esteem is based on self-awareness of physical competence, body consciousness and self-acceptance, and self-efficacy. The next section focuses on the effects of exercise and health on global self-esteem; later sections consider the contribution of individuals' views of their physical body and its functioning to self-esteem.

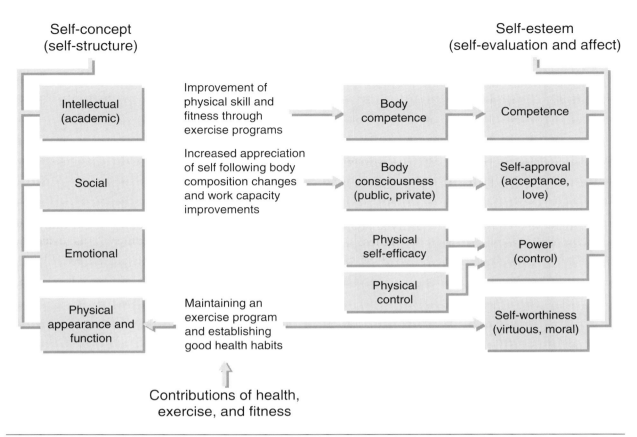

Figure 11.6   The components of self-concept and self-esteem and their potential interaction with exercise.

Physical Skill, Exercise, and Self-Esteem

Very few experiences that people have in life are quite as visible as their physical movements. People may try to understand a book or a movie, to write a poem, or make an effort to learn a language. If they succeed, their success is noted, but if they fail, there are many ways to hide the failure or deemphasize their efforts—even to themselves. Physical efforts, however, are a different matter. When people attempt a physical act, such as running 3 miles or learning to type or play golf, their efforts are usually readily visible. It is hard to tell exactly how much better one person is than another at understanding a difficult social issue, but it is not difficult to see who is still moving at the end of an exercise workout or to determine winners and losers in physical games. It is perhaps because of the stark visibility of accomplishment, success, and failure that accompany physical exercise and skill that these behaviors play so large a role in the development and maintenance of self-esteem. When people physically move, they experience physical self-awareness, and the display of

their physical competence (or incompetence) is excruciatingly visible.

Very little is known about the effects of increases in physical skill or fitness on the self-esteem of older individuals. There have been many studies of the relationship between physical competence and global self-esteem in children, and Harter (1983) concluded from a review of these studies that the relationship between physical competence and global self-esteem is moderately high. This type of relationship may be why Gruber's (1986) meta-analysis of 65 studies showed that physical education programs positively influence self-esteem in children. Similarly, Tucker (1982) found that adult males improved their global self-esteem after a semester of weight training, and Collingwood (1972) and Hilyer and Mitchell (1979) found that relatively short anaerobic exercise programs (4 weeks and 10 weeks, respectively) improved self-esteem. In the case of the latter study, self-esteem was only enhanced when the exercise program was accompanied by instructional information about the effects of exercise, goal-setting, and projections about expected exercise effects. Sonstroem

(1984) found similar results in a review of 16 studies, but most of the samples in his review represented children, adolescents, college students, or psychologically abnormal populations. Only three of the studies included middle-aged adults, and none included large numbers of elderly subjects.

The results from the few studies available of older adults show that maintaining muscle tone, strength, endurance, and physique through daily physical exercise enhances self-esteem. Participation in exercise programs enables people to observe what others their age can accomplish, to explore their own abilities, and to become realistic about their own physical abilities. Understanding their abilities and watching them improve through training gives them self-confidence and facilitates positive lifestyle changes (Ray, Gissal, & Smith, 1983). Participants who exercise in organized programs generally report an enhanced feeling of well-being at the conclusion of these programs (Gillett, 1989; Perri & Templer, 1985; Reynolds & Garrett, 1989). These participants also tend to eat better, sleep better (Reiter, 1981), and take better care of themselves. The pride that they take in maintaining good health habits and the effects of these positive habits tend to interact to further increase their self-esteem.

From his review of the exercise and self-esteem literature, Sonstroem (1984) concluded that participation in exercise programs is related to subjects' increases in the scores of self-esteem tests. He proposed several possible reasons why exercise participation might enhance self-esteem, the first and most likely being the visible increase in physical fitness. Other reasons are that when program participants see a tangible achievement of their goals, they feel better physically, and they develop a sense of competence, which in turn provides them with feelings of mastery and control. In addition, most exercise participants who stay with an exercise program for an extended period also develop other health habits, such as better nutrition and sleep habits, which in turn make them feel better about themselves. Finally, program participants gain new social experiences with their colleagues in the program and with their exercise leaders, they may receive more attention than they have had for awhile from their exercise leader, and they may be praised for continuing the program by their significant others and friends. All of these factors may contribute to enhanced self-esteem.

Sonstroem and Morgan (1989) developed a model to use when studying the role of an exercise program intervention in the development or maintenance of self-esteem (see Figure 11.7). Their model includes the three aspects of self-esteem that have been linked to exercise, starting with lower level elements and proceeding to higher order components: physical self-efficacy, physical competence, physical acceptance, and self-esteem. The intervention shown in this model is an exercise program, and the self-concept components following the exercise intervention are shown as change scores (Δ scores). The authors also suggest that if the model is to be tested, the exercise intervention should follow the American College of Sports Medicine guidelines and be at least 15 weeks in duration.

Body Consciousness

The way individuals perceive their body is called *body consciousness*, and it is an important component of self-esteem. Body consciousness has at least three aspects (Miller, Murphy, & Buss, 1981). The first is public body consciousness, which includes the subjective feelings that people have about their physical appearance, for example, wrinkled skin, hair loss, a sagging stomach, and the way that their clothing fits their body. These and other aspects of external appearance are of concern to many older people, because physical appearance is a large part of the general aesthetic impression that people develop of each other.

A second aspect of body consciousness is the private perception of body function, that is, the awareness that people have of internal body sensations that are not visible to others. People may have very strong perceptions and concerns about cardiovascular, hypertensive, or genitourinary symptoms and problems that only they know. Whereas they may be perceived by their friends as a person of perfect health who has a body to be envied, these individuals may in private be highly anxious and see themselves as having a weak body that has failed them.

The third aspect of body consciousness is body competence. It is the subjective evaluation of the body's ability to accomplish the physical goals that individuals create for themselves. It is also described as self-efficacy. Body consciousness contributes to self-esteem throughout life, but at probably no time in life does it play a larger role

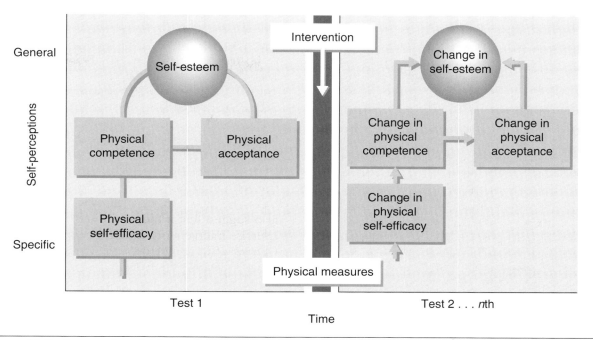

Figure 11.7 Proposed model for examining exercise and self-esteem interactions.
From "Exercise and Self-Esteem: Rationale and Model" by R.J. Sonstroem and W.P. Morgan, 1989, *Medicine and Science in Sports and Exercise*, **21**, p. 333. Copyright 1989 by Williams & Wilkins. Reprinted by permission.

than during the later years when accommodations must be made for an aging body. As listed in Figure 11.3b (page 309), older people consider the physical changes of their body to be negative and the greatest source of change in their lives over the past 20 years (Ryff, 1989).

People of all ages have a negative view of the physical changes that accompany aging. Young and old alike consider the physical appearance of older people less attractive (Perry & Slemp, 1980; Wernick & Manaster, 1984). Older women may have a more negative self-concept than older men do (Kreitler & Kreitler, 1970; Sidney & Shephard, 1976). For both genders, however, perhaps it is the conscious awareness of others' perceptions that made the older subjects of Miller et al. (1981) more negative than the young subjects in their body consciousness, even though the two age groups were similar in health, education, and psychological depression scores. Ross et al. (1989), however, found that although their older subjects had a more negative body image, they viewed their body competence as being higher than the young subjects viewed theirs. The researchers proposed that the older subjects, perhaps because they were volunteers, were above average in health, and thus, when they compared themselves to others of their same chronological age, they thought others to be "older."

Exercise and Body Image

Although it seems intuitive that improving physical function would also improve individuals' perceptions about all aspects of their body consciousness, very little research has been conducted on the effects of exercise on body image. Sidney and Shephard (1976) used a two-part test that was developed by McPherson et al. (1967), and also used by Kenyon (1968), in which young subjects answered questions related to an ideal, "My Body as I Would Like to See It," and an actual, "My Body as It Really Is." In this test, the greater the discrepancy of the actual score from the ideal score, the more negative the body image. Sidney and Shephard (1976) administered this test to older adults (median age = 66 years) before and after a 14-week exercise program. They found that the average discrepancy scores did not change after the exercise program. But, when they analyzed the scores on the basis of the intensity and frequency of exercise during the 14-week program, they found that body image did change for those who exercised the most. Retrospectively, they classified the subjects as high frequency, high intensity (HFHI), high frequency, low intensity (HFLI), low frequency, high intensity (LFHI), and low frequency, low intensity (LFLI). Those subjects who trained the hardest (HFHI) significantly improved their actual body image after the exercise program, bringing it closer to their desired body image. Those who trained at middle levels of exercise (HFLI or LFHI) significantly improved their actual body image, but the improvements were smaller than those of the HFHI group. The persons who exercised the least (LFLI) did not decrease the discrepancy between actual and ideal body image, and thus their body image remained unchanged.

In one other study of body image, nursing home residents participated in rhythmic breathing, slow stretching, and upright exercises twice a week for 8 weeks. Their body image scores improved (Olson, 1975). Research generally has supported the notion that organized exercise programs improve the body image of older adults, thus enhancing their self-esteem (Shephard, 1987).

Self-Efficacy

Physical self-efficacy is another important component of well-being. *Self-efficacy* is an individual's belief that he or she can perform specific tasks. Self-efficacy does not denote the skills that an individual has but rather the individual's perceived confidence to perform specific tasks. An individual must have confidence to have feelings of competency and power. Whereas feelings of body competence contribute to body consciousness, physical task-related self-efficacy refers to the degree of conviction that individuals have that they can perform a physical task. To measure physical self-efficacy, researchers ask individuals what they think they can accomplish and how strongly they believe in their assessment of their ability. For example, an individual may be asked, "How far do you think you can walk (1 block, 6 blocks, 1/2 mile, etc.)?" "How confident are you of your answer?"

Self-efficacy is affected by individuals' interpretations of performance accomplishments, vicarious experiences, verbal persuasion (social expectations), and physiological arousal (Bandura, 1977). In terms of physical self-efficacy, performance is one of the strongest sources of efficacy information. Older adults who have not had much experience with exercise, sport, or physical work have little idea about their physical capabilities. When asked whether they can walk

a mile, they may have no idea, or they may greatly overestimate their ability. This is especially true in many very old women, because their generation had so little experience with physical exercise and sports. These women may instead be influenced by the ageism rampant in America and substantially underestimate their physical abilities (Hogan & Santomier, 1984). They may avoid exercise programs because they have very low self-efficacy concerning their ability to execute the physical movements and may fear embarrassment.

Nonetheless, all people have depended all their lives on their physical abilities to do many things, such as lifting their children (or grandchildren), carrying heavy picnic baskets, or climbing the stairs of a museum while on a vacation tour. One of the adjustments all people must make as they age is how to deal with losses of physical competence that threaten to end or curtail their activities. This may be particularly difficult for athletes and musicians, for whom physical achievement played a large if not dominating role in life. For these individuals, the problem is *not* having an ambiguous idea about their physical capabilities, but rather, having inordinately high internal standards. Even small losses associated with aging can lower their self-efficacy. In many cases, an important part of adjustment is learning to translate objective achievements, such as winning a race, into personal achievements, such as winning the 70-to-79-year-old age-group race. Having a sense of accomplishment was the number one factor in achieving personal fulfillment, according to Ryff's (1989) subjects. For those individuals who have been physically active all their lives, finding a way to continue to be physically competent and to achieve may be extremely important for their sense of well-being.

Physical activity is a precise, quantifiable activity that provides immediate feedback in terms of physical accomplishment and change. After only a few training sessions, individuals can see the increased weight they can lift or the increase in distance that they can walk or run. Participation in exercise programs also can provide experiences that enhance older adults' perceived physical abilities and thereby enhance self-efficacy. When new participants enter a formal exercise program for senior citizens, many of them may change their beliefs regarding their capabilities after just observing other elderly persons who have been performing exercises for several weeks.

Exercise or sports programs for older adults generally improve their self-efficacy for those activities. For example, adults 60 years and older who participated in a swimming program had large changes in their swimming self-efficacy, whereas the comparative control group did not (Hogan & Santomier, 1984). Also, healthy older adults who exercised several times a week on a stationary bicycle reported a higher sense of accomplishment than did the controls with whom they were compared (Windsor, Lawton, Sands, Gitlin, & Posner, 1989). Consistent exercisers may also view themselves as more capable of continuing exercise even in the face of perceived obstacles, such as slow improvement, loss of an exercising partner, or unexpected conflicts, than do individuals who do not exercise on a regular basis (McAuley & Jacobson, 1991). The improvements in psychological well-being that follow exercise programs have been credited to a realization of improved mastery, that is, increased self-efficacy (deCoverley-Veale, 1987).

Exercise has also been associated with increases in self-efficacy in groups that are below average in health. For example, self-efficacy and expectations for exercise and related physical activities improved after an exercise program involving older adults with chronic obstructive pulmonary disease (Kaplan, Atkins, & Reinsch, 1984). In another study, 20 overweight women (ages 59-72) participated in low-impact aerobics and muscle fitness exercises 3 days a week for 11 weeks, and measures of their self-esteem improved slightly (Gillett, 1989). In the comparison group of overweight individuals who did not exercise, there was no improvement.

More importantly, improvements in mastery and in physical self-efficacy have been shown to generalize to other performance-related situations. Hogan and Santomier (1984) found that 78% of older swimmers generalized their feelings of increased self-efficacy to other tasks unrelated to swimming. Other generalizations of self-efficacy also have been reported (Ray, Gissal, & Smith, 1983); thus, improvements in physical self-efficacy may be expected to generalize to physical performances such as completing chores, learning a new skill, or going on a travel tour.

Generally, formerly sedentary older adults who see themselves performing previously impossible physical tasks, whether the task is walking 50 yards instead of 10, or lifting 5 pounds instead of 1, feel a sense of satisfaction and accomplishment.

Physical achievement is always relative to the individual's ability, so however small the physical gains may be, they represent a positive change rather than a negative decline. Positive changes in physical ability as a result of a systematic exercise program mean more than just physical changes. They mean that a goal has been reached, self-efficacy has been increased, self-discipline has been confirmed, and a reversal (albeit, perhaps temporary) in the aging process has occurred. All of these outcomes enhance an individual's self-efficacy and personal feelings of well-being.

Sense of Control

Most people want to feel that they have control over their own destiny, that they have control over their environment, and that they can control what they do in that environment. Acquiring a sense of control is what so strongly impels teenagers to obtain a driver's license and young adults to have their own apartment or home. A sense of control over their lives is essential to individuals' well-being (Kozma & Stones, 1978). As people grow older, they experience losses, many of which are direct threats to their sense of control. Losing the ability to drive an automobile or to travel on a bus instills as much fear and dread of a loss of control as obtaining the license brought the exhilaration of gaining control. Some older adults are described as home-bound, meaning that their ability to move outside of the home is dependent on others. Individuals who enter nursing homes or long-term care centers are even more dependent and suffer a great many losses, some of which are shown in Table 11.2. These losses have profound effects on an individual's sense of control, on self-dignity, and on individual identification.

The sense of being in control is of particular concern to older adults. In addition to losing their mobility outside the home, they lose many other things that contribute to their feelings of control. They lose family members and friends who may have assisted them in ways that enabled them to maintain control over various parts of their lives. They retire and thus lose regular feedback about their competence as contributing members of society. They may have to relocate to a smaller house or apartment, which means a loss of space. Ageism also plays a role in undermining the elderly's sense of control. People around them expect them to

---

**Table 11.2
Losses of People
in Long-Term Care Centers**

---

1. Loss of decision-making power
    Financial matters
    Daily activities
2. Loss of mobility
    Driver's license
3. Loss of control over environment
    Room temperature
    TV channel
    Meal schedule
4. Loss of privacy
    Unlocked doors
    Shared room
    Inability to retreat from meddlers
5. Reduction in human contacts
    Physical contact
    Social interaction
    Lost variety of contact
6. Aesthetic and cultural deprivation
7. Decreased individual identity

---

be unable to do certain tasks and may continually assist them unnecessarily. Such constant assistance, although well intentioned, erodes the sense of control in those being helped.

The fact that older people seek more medical care also makes them more vulnerable to a loss of control, thus increasing the relationship between health and a sense of control in the elder years. Medical care restricts opportunities for control at any age, and it is commonly observed that professional long-term care workers prefer clients and patients who are conforming, obedient, deferential, and treatable. That is, they reward people who willingly relinquish control to them and who seem to be highly receptive to the staff's efforts to help them. Thus, in some centers, dependency and lack of control are encouraged, even though it has been shown that patients who have some responsibilities for their own care attain greater health improvements and postponement of mortality.

Health and Sense of Control

Having a sense of purpose and control over one's life is important to the health of the elderly (AMA-ANA Task Force, 1983). Adults who have a strong

sense of control may feel that they can control, at least to some extent, their own health. They are more likely to take health-enhancing actions, such as gathering health information, engaging in good health habits, interacting with medical providers, and adhering to medical, health, and fitness regimens. If adults see physical decline as inevitable, they may gradually cease these health habits, increasing the probability that they will need even more medical treatment, which in turn reinforces their sense that their health is "out of their hands."

A loss of health and physical ability can quickly erode a previously strong sense of control. In two studies of older adults, those who perceived their health as poor also tended to believe that the locus of control was external, whereas those who rated their health as acceptable to good had a stronger sense that they had control over their destiny (Bonds, 1980; Brothen & Detzner, 1983). Few events are as threatening to feelings of personal control as hospitalization.

Conversely, higher self-esteem and internal health locus of control were significantly related to a history of exercising or being active throughout life and current engagement in physical activity (Hawkins et al., 1988), although habitual exercise is strongly related to social class. People with more education and greater financial resources also tend to take better care of themselves, have somewhat more control over their medical services, and are in the best position to solve problems of ill health. Nevertheless, the contribution of a sense of control to health is much more than just psychological perception. Sense of control, aging, and health strongly interact, such that the older people become, the more strongly sense of control and health interact.

Two physiological mechanisms can serve as examples of how a sense of control is related to health: psychoendocrine responses and changes in the immune system. When people are aroused psychologically, as in anxiety or fear responses, the endocrine system is activated. High levels of epinephrine (adrenaline) are released, blood pressure and heart rate increase, blood lipids increase, and sometimes an increase in ventricular arrhythmia occurs. This is the well-known fight-or-flight syndrome. It occurs when people are threatened or frightened, as might be the case when an 83-year-old woman is suddenly informed that she will be moved from her home into a nursing facility. The perceived loss of control and the unpredictability of the situation can produce classic physiological symptoms of stress, such as gastric lesions and weight loss. Conversely, increasing control over an otherwise anxiety-producing event decreases the neuroendocrine responses in both animals and humans; so does increasing predictability, though to a lesser degree. The high circulating levels of epinephrine and norepinephrine that are produced during introduction to a new and challenging task dissipate with practice, which leads to increased competence and control over the task.

A second physiological mechanism that explains why the relationship of health to sense of control increases with age is that *the association between control and some indicators of health status is actually altered by aging* (Rodin, 1986). When people experience a deterioration in health, it changes their confidence in their ability to maintain control. They experience a new awareness of vulnerability that, in turn, produces feelings of increased vulnerability and anxiety. These feelings can negatively influence resistance to disease. For example, as the immune system ages, it becomes less efficient. The response of the immune system to exogenous antigens (e.g., external viruses or bacteria) decreases with age, but the reverse occurs with respect to endogenous antigens (metabolic by-products that are created by the body). These changes lead to a lessened ability to ward off communicable disease but an increase in circulating autoantibodies, which in essence results in the immune system attacking its own body. But psychological feelings of a loss of control also suppress the immune system, and older people undergo physiological changes that make them more vulnerable to the effects of uncontrollable stress. For example, they experience a decline in metabolism of adrenocortical hormones and an increase in chronic illness. Figure 11.8 depicts the simultaneous effects of immunological aging and psychological feelings of loss of control, showing how both interact to impair the body's defenses against disease. In this diagram, the effectiveness of the immune system is represented by the height of the line. Changes in the rate of immune effectiveness are shown by the steepness of the change over the years. Thus, in youth the immune system is effective, and the changes from youth to middle age are slight. As more and more illness is encountered, however, a feeling of loss of control emerges. This feeling also negatively affects the immune system, adds to the negative effect of aging, and increases the rate of decline in the immune system's effectiveness.

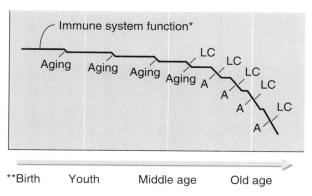

** Birth   Youth   Middle age   Old age

* Symbolic reaction of only one of many immunologic responses to many exogenous antigens.

** Age is not drawn to scale.

Figure 11.8 Diagrammatic relationship of loss of control, immune responses, and aging. LC = feelings of loss of control; A = aging.

Interventions to Increase Control

Because a sense of control is so closely related to health and well-being, many experimental interventions have been implemented to determine whether increasing the opportunities for control also benefit psychological and physical health. Examples include allowing the patients of a long-term care center to plan daily agendas, give input into meals, decide when certain maintenance activities of the center should be done, and assist in making the rules and regulations by which they live. In most cases, increased control is beneficial, with certain qualifications. For an increased control intervention to provide long-term benefits, the opportunities for control must be perceived by the patients or clients to be a permanent opportunity. The effects of increased control can be more negative than positive if control is enhanced during an experiment and then removed. Also, increased opportunities for control only have positive effects when the patients believe that the newly gained control is attributed to their personal abilities and actions or to stable sources. Within this context, they must have opportunities to exhibit competence.

How might enhanced health and fitness improve an individual's sense of control? When elderly individuals live in an institution because they are unable to function independently, their sense of control is very difficult to maintain. Some immediate gains in physical competence can be garnered by many elderly residents through participation in a mild, low-impact fitness program. Increasing strength and lower-body endurance can transform some individuals from nonambulatory to ambulatory status. The capacity to walk and to do minimal or mild exercise contributes substantially to feelings of control.

The ability to walk also provides more options for activity—leaving the room if the program is uninteresting or walking outside to gain privacy. An opportunity to exercise can enable institutionalized individuals to be alone if they choose to be, even if for only a short time, and these additional opportunities can provide some relief from the crushing regimentation of institutional schedules. The simple ability to remove oneself from an unpleasant environment or just change the environment contributes significantly to feelings of self-control. Thus, the increased health and fitness of individuals that accrue from a fitness program also contribute to their confidence regarding their physical competence, a confidence which in turn enhances their feelings of self-control. In fact, it has been shown that physical activity and its accompanying arousal levels can play a role in preventing premature resignation and apathy on the part of those who live in institutions (Lindsley, 1964).

People's preferences for control become increasingly more variable with age, however, and professionals who seek to implement an increased control intervention should consider that some adults are satisfied with less control over the maintenance and daily routine of their lives. They do not want the responsibility, perhaps because of a fear of failure, or perhaps because they think increased control requires more time and energy resources than they wish to expend. Although all older adults want the choice, individuals vary in the amount of control that makes them comfortable. Providing opportunities for more control than an individual wants may lead to anxiety, burdensome responsibility, and feelings of guilt. For these individuals, increasing their opportunities for control may have more negative than positive effects. Astute professionals provide but do not impose opportunities for control, because the need for self-determination also calls for the opportunity to choose not to exercise control.

Health, Fitness, Well-Being, and Life Satisfaction

The relationships among the objective physical condition of individuals, their subjective health, and life satisfaction or well-being are extremely complex. First, physical disease or disability's influence on well-being is partly dependent on the individual's subjective view of the disability and the amount of functional impairment that the disability or disease causes. Second, the psychological mechanisms that the individual uses to cope with the disability can change the degree of functional impairment caused by the disease or disability, the subjective view that an individual has of his or her health, and the amount of life satisfaction that the person experiences. Moreover, the way people cope with health and physical problems influences the relationships between all aspects of physical health and life satisfaction. These relationships are shown in Figure 11.9 (Lohr, Essex, & Klein, 1988), in which all three aspects of physical health (physical conditions, subjective health, and functional impairment) influence life satisfaction, but coping responses influence not only life satisfaction but subjective health and the degree of functional impairment of individual experiences. According to this model, coping mechanisms change people's views of their functional impairment and influence their life satisfaction but have less effect on the relationship of physical condition and functional impairment to life satisfaction.

Coping responses can be categorized into two types: problem-focused and emotion-focused. In *problem-focused coping*, the purpose is to change the stressor, for example, by taking direct action to improve health and avoiding behaviors that are bad for health. This is called *direct-action coping* (see Figure 11.9). In *emotion-focused coping*, the purpose is to neutralize the negative feelings caused by the stressor by modifying the meaning of these feelings and controlling arousal. This type of coping is used more with health stressors. Emotion-focused coping can occur in two ways; with *positive-cognitive coping*, individuals remind themselves of all the good things they have for which to be thankful. Or, they may form the belief that their health is better than most women their age. Those individuals who believe that their health is in the hands of destiny or fate are using a type of emotion-focused coping called *passive-cognitive coping*. Passive copers believe that they cannot do anything about their fate, so they might as well accept it. Their coping mechanism is to attempt to distract themselves by doing other things (Folkman & Lazarus, 1980). However, the women in the Lohr et al. (1988) study who used

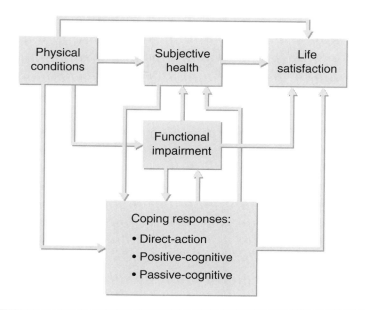

Figure 11.9 Analytic model of physical health status, coping responses, and life satisfaction.
From "The Relationships of Coping Responses to Physical Health Status and Life Satisfaction Among Older Women" by M.J. Lohr, M.J. Essex, and M.H. Klein, 1988, *Journal of Gerontology: Psychological Sciences,* **43**, p. P56. Copyright 1988 by The Gerontological Society of America. Reprinted by permission.

this method of coping were more likely to perceive themselves as impaired and to assess their health as being subjectively more negative.

Women with many physical conditions but few functional impairments can use positive-cognitive coping effectively. Women with many physical conditions in addition to functional impairments cannot use this technique as well and tend to use passive-cognitive coping (Lohr et al., 1988). Older subjects who believed that they had control, that they were not in the hands of "powerful other people" who controlled their health, and who had a high perceived current health status were functionally healthier in all areas. Current status, self-esteem, and exercise were clustered together, supporting other researcher's findings that exercise and self-esteem, in addition to good nutrition, are related to health (Duffy & McDonald, 1990).

Health is a major factor in older adults' feelings of well-being and life satisfaction, critical factors for successful aging. Summarized in Figure 11.10, poor health, low income, and lack of social interaction lead to lower morale, lower contentment, and lower expressed satisfaction, which in turn make individuals more vulnerable to other negative life situations, such as disease. The cumulative evidence, however, supports the proposition that preventive measures and control interventions can improve and maintain health, thus increasing the probability that as individuals age they will maintain a high quality of life. Aging successfully has

huge implications for national health care costs. Table 11.3 (page 323) compares the total health care expenditures from 1970 to 1983 for those who aged well, those who were dependent, and those who died during the study (Roos & Havens, 1991). Those who aged optimally drew on the health care system for $736 each year lived, whereas those who were dependent required $3,850, and those who died during the study required $5,955 a year, an eightfold increase. Clearly, substantial savings can be achieved in the health care system if attention is focused on the health and fitness status of adults in their preelderly years.

Finally, health and fitness contribute to well-being in more ways than just maintaining independence and controlling health care costs. Health and fitness play a crucial role in the involvement and interdependency of individuals in society. Health and fitness enable engagement and interaction with other people. Physical activity not only maintains health, it provides feelings of affect and emotion that are a large part of what it means to be human. Movements have significant meanings to people and enable them to communicate with themselves and with each other. Physical activity, in addition to promoting health, allows older adults to socialize through activities such as folk and social dance groups, golf games, and physical fitness classes. These groups provide not only a social support system,

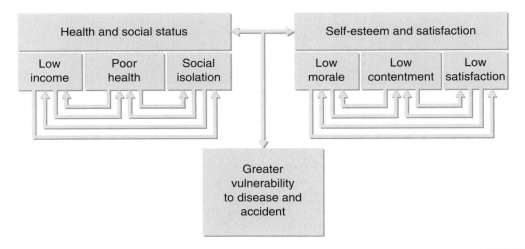

Figure 11.10　Relationships of poor health, low income, and lack of social interaction to low morale, low contentment, and low expressed satisfaction.

but opportunities for older people to interact with younger people. In summary, physical activity promotes well-being by enhancing health and fitness, increasing the opportunities for involvement in the family and community, and enabling individuals to interact with each other in meaningful ways.

In Summary

Physical health is comprised of three components: physical condition, functional status, and subjective health status. Although more than 75% of men and women over the age of 70 have one or more chronic physical conditions, they vary greatly in the ways these health conditions affect their functioning and in how they view their health. Health and physical fitness are not synonymous. Health relates to the presence or absence of disease processes, whereas fitness relates to aerobic capacity, muscular strength and endurance, and flexibility. Most researchers who have studied the relationship of health to well-being and life satisfaction have defined health in the most minimal terms—the extent to which physical function enables activities of daily living and instrumental activities of daily living.

Health is only one of seven major correlates of well-being; the others are socioeconomic status, education, marital status, transportation, residence, and activity and social interaction. Older people rate health and physical status second only to their families in importance for their well-being. Perhaps because older adults often indicate that their physical status has changed more than any other aspect of themselves over the past 20 years, they report that if they could change anything about their lives, health would be their first choice.

The relationship of health and well-being is bidirectional. Not only does health status influence perceptions of well-being, people's feelings of well-being also influence other health-related behaviors. Those who have feelings of well-being and life satisfaction are more likely to take action to maintain their health and prevent disease.

The effectiveness of exercise programs to enhance feelings of well-being is generally positive, but the results of studies are not unanimous. Short-term effects may include enhanced feelings of well-being immediately after exercising. Some investigators found long-term effects in the form of enhanced feelings of well-being among older persons who completed exercise programs of several months' duration. Others, however, have not reported improvements. The effects of exercise on well-being may be essentially short-term, so for individuals to experience an improved sense of well-being, they must exercise on a daily basis. It also may be that exercise programs must be continued for an extended time for physical, morphological, and physiological changes (e.g., weight loss and body composition changes) to occur before long-term feelings of well-being will be enhanced. It is also possible, however, that well-being involves so many dimensions of life and is such a global perception that it is hard to detect any change that can be attributed to an improvement in just one component.

Table 11.3
Total Health Care Expenditures From 1970-1983
by Individuals' Differing 1983 Health Status

	Characteristics of individuals in 1983			
	Aged successfully	Alive but dependent	Deceased	All
Total health resource use[a] 1970-1983 or to time of death (%)				
$0-10,000	67.7	30.5	23.5	33.9
$10,000-25,000	20.7	18.4	22.1	21.0
$25,000-50,000	9.5	19.6	21.8	18.8
$50,000-100,000	2.0	14.0	17.0	13.3
$100,000 or more	0.1	17.5	15.7	13.0
Mean resource use per individual (in $ from 1970-1983 or to time of death)				
Total use ($)	10,304	53,906	50,643	43,354
Use per year lived ($)	736	3,850	5,955	4,441
Number of users	583	666	1,694	2,943

[a]Resource use is estimated in 1984-85 Canadian dollars as follows: $1,610 a day in intensive care, $322 a hospital day, $49 a nursing home day, $17 a physician visit, $4 a day on home care, and actual dollar amount for surgical procedures.

Note. From "Predictors of Successful Aging: A Twelve-Year Study of Manitoba Elderly" by N.P. Roos and B. Havens, 1991, *American Journal of Public Health*, **81**, p. 65. Copyright 1991 by the American Public Health Association. Reprinted by permission.

The physical dimension of well-being includes the role of the body and its functioning in self-esteem, self-efficacy, and sense of control. Body consciousness, public and private, includes the subjective feelings that individuals have about their body. Society in general has a very negative view of age-related physical changes, and it is difficult for aging adults to maintain a healthy body consciousness. Body competence, or self-efficacy, is the confidence that people have about their physical abilities in specific situations. One of the greatest adjustments that all people must make with aging is the adjustment to the loss of physical ability. Exercise programs have been shown to improve self-efficacy and body consciousness in the exercise-related physical activities, and these improvements may generalize to other similar activities.

Physical ability contributes to older adults' sense of control, which is a central component of well-being. The maintenance of health and physical mobility enables older adults to maintain independent living, which is an important contributor to well-being. Even in those older adults who live in long-term care centers, physical health and mobility contributes to enhanced well-being by providing them more opportunities to control their own activities and environment and by increasing the variety of activities in their lives.

Optimizing the health and physical fitness of older adults has three major positive outcomes, two of which benefit the individual and one that benefits society. First, and perhaps most important, enhanced health and fitness have a good probability of enhancing feelings of well-being and life satisfaction, which in turn contribute to high-quality aging. Second, a significant increase in the number of persons who age optimally can have a tremendous impact on reducing the total health care expenditures of this country. The cost of health care for those who experience their terminal years in a state of physical dependency is eight times higher than those who have aged successfully. Third, the healthy and fit older adult is much more capable of being involved with family, friends, and the community and of interacting in emotionally meaningful ways with people who are important to them and to their well-being.

References

American Medical Association–American Nursing Association. (1983). *Report of the Joint AMA–ANA Task Force on the improvement of health care of the aged chronically ill.* Kansas City, MO: Author.

Andrews, F.M., & Robinson, J.P. (1991). Measures of subjective well-being. In J.P. Robinson, P.R. Shaver, & L.S. Wrightsman (Eds.), *Measures of personality and social-psychological attitudes* (pp. 61-114). New York: Academic Press.

Bandura, A. (1977). Self-efficacy: Toward a unifying theory of behavioral change. *Psychological Review,* **84,** 191-215.

Berger, B.G., & Owen, D.R. (1987). Anxiety reduction with swimming: Relationships between exercise and state, trait, and somatic anxiety. *International Journal of Sport Psychology,* **18,** 286-302.

Blumenthal, J.A., Emery, C.F., Madden, D.J., George, L.K., Coleman, R.E., Roddle, M.W., McKee, D.C., Reasoner, J., & Williams, R.S. (1989). Cardiovascular and behavioral effects of aerobic exercise training in healthy older men and women. *Journal of Gerontology: Medical Sciences,* **44,** M147-M157.

Bonds, A.G. (1980). The relationship between self-concept and locus of control and patterns of eating, exercise, and social participation in older adults. *Dissertation Abstracts International,* **41**(04)A, p. 1397. (University Microfilms No. DDJ80-21947)

Brothen, T., & Detzner, D. (1983). Perceived health and locus of control in the aged. *Perceptual and Motor Skills,* **56,** 946.

Campbell, A., Converse, P.E., & Rodgers, W.L. (1976). *The quality of American life.* New York: Russell Sage Foundation.

Collingwood, T.R. (1972). The effects of physical training upon behavior and self-attitudes. *Journal of Clinical Psychology,* **28,** 583-585.

deCoverley-Veale, D.M.W. (1987). Exercise and mental health. *Acta Psychiatrica Scandinavica,* **76,** 113-120.

Diener, E. (1984). Subjective well-being. *Psychological Bulletin,* **95,** 542-575.

Duffy, M.E., & McDonald, E. (1990). Determinants of functional health of older persons. *The Gerontologist,* **30,** 503-509.

Emery, C.F., & Blumenthal, J.A. (1990). Perceived change among participants in an exercise program for older adults. *The Gerontologist,* **30,** 517-521.

Epstein, S. (1973). The self-concept revisited, or a theory of a theory. *American Psychologist,* **28,** 405-416.

Folkman, S., & Lazarus, R.S. (1980). An analysis of coping in a middle-aged community sample. *Journal of Health and Social Behavior,* **21,** 219-239.

George, L.K. (1979). The happiness syndrome: Methodological and substantive issues in the study of social-psychological well-being in adulthood. *The Gerontologist,* **19,** 210-216.

Gergen, K.J. (1971). *The concept of self.* New York: Holt, Rinehart, & Winston.

Gergen, K.J. (1981). The functions and foibles of negotiating self-conceptions. In M.D. Lynch, A.A. Norem-Hebeisen, & K.J. Gergen (Eds.), *Self-concept: Advances in theory and research* (pp. 59-73). Cambridge, MA: Ballingurt.

Gfellner, B.M. (1989). Perceptions of health, abilities, and life satisfaction among very old adults. *Perceptual and Motor Skills,* **68,** 203-209.

Gillett, P. (1989). Aerobic and muscle fitness in high-risk and overweight senior women. *The Gerontologist,* **29,** 258A.

Gitlin, L.N., Lawton, M.P., Windsor, L.A., Kleban, M.H., Sands, L.P., & Posner, J. (1986). *In search of psychological benefits: Exercise in healthy older adults.* Unpublished manuscript, Philadelphia Geriatric Center, Philadelphia.

Gruber, J. (1986). Physical activity and self-esteem development in children: A meta-analysis. *American Academy of Physical Education Papers,* **19,** 30-48.

Guralnik, J.M., LaCroix, A.Z., Everett, D.F., & Kovar, M.G. (1989). Aging in the eighties: The prevalence of comorbidity and its association with disability. *Advance Data* (Vital & Health Statistics of the National Center for Health Statistics), **170,** 1-8.

Harter, S. (1983). Developmental perspectives on the self-system. In E.M. Heterington (Ed.), *Handbook of child psychology* (Vol. 4, pp. 275-385). New York: Wiley.

Hawkins, W.E., Duncan, D.F., & McDermott, R.J. (1988). A health assessment of older Americans: Some multidimensional measures. *Preventive Medicine,* **17,** 344-356.

Heinzelmann, F., & Bagley, R.W. (1970). Response to physical activity programs and their effects on health behavior. *Public Health Reports,* **85,** 905-911.

Hilyer, J.C., & Mitchell, W. (1979). Effect of physical fitness training combined with counseling in the self-concept of college students. *Journal of Counseling Psychology,* **26,** 427-436.

Hogan, P.I., & Santomier, J.P. (1984). Effect of mastering swimming skills on older adults' self-efficacy. *Research Quarterly for Exercise and Sport,* **55,** 294-296.

Kaplan, R.M., Atkins, C.J., & Reinsch, S. (1984). Specific efficacy expectations mediate exercise compliance in patients with COPD. *Health Psychology,* **3,** 223-242.

Kenyon, G.S. (1968). *Values held for physical activity by selected urban secondary school students in Canada, Australia, England, and the United States* (U.S. Office of Education Contract S-376). Madison: University of Wisconsin.

Kozma, A., & Stones, M.J. (1978). Some research issues and findings in the study of psychological well-being in the aged. *Canadian Psychological Review,* **19,** 241-249.

Kreitler, H., & Kreitler, S. (1970). Movement and aging: A psychological approach. In D. Brunner & E. Jokl (Eds.), *Medicine and sport, Vol. 4: Physical activity and aging* (pp. 302-306). Basel: Karger.

Larson, R. (1978). Thirty years of research on the subjective well-being of older Americans. *Journal of Gerontology,* **33,** 109-125.

Lindsley, O.R. (1964). Geriatric behavioral prosthetics. In R. Kastenbaum (Ed.), *New thoughts on old age* (pp. 41-60). New York: Springer.

Lohr, M.J., Essex, M.J., & Klein, M.H. (1988). The relationships of coping responses to physical health status and life satisfaction among older women. *Journal of Gerontology: Psychological Sciences*, **43**, P54-P60.

Mandell, A.J. (1979). The second second wind. *Psychiatric Annals*, **9**, 57-68.

Matheny, K.B., Aycock, D.W., Pugh, J.L., Curlette, W.L., & Cannella, K.A.S. (1986). Stress coping: A qualitative and quantitative synthesis with implications for treatment. *Counseling Psychologist*, **14**, 499-549.

McAuley, E., & Jacobson, L. (1991). Self-efficacy and exercise participation in sedentary adult females. *American Journal of Health Promotion*, **5**, 185-207.

McPherson, B.D., Paivio, A., Yuhasz, M.S., Rechnitzer, P.A., Pickard, H.A., & Lefcoe, N.M. (1967). Psychological effects of an exercise program for post-infarct and normal adult males. *Journal of Sports Medicine*, **7**, 95-101.

Miller, L.C., Murphy, R., & Buss, A.H. (1981). Consciousness of body: Private and public. *Journal of Personality and Social Psychology*, **41**, 397-406.

Morgan, W.P. (1985). Affective beneficence of vigorous physical activity. *Medicine and Science in Sports and Exercise*, **17**, 94-100.

Morris, A.F., & Husman, B.F. (1978). Life quality changes following an endurance conditioning program. *American Corrective Therapy Journal*, **32**, 3-6.

Morris, A.F., Lussier, L., Vaccaro, P., & Clark, D.H. (1982). Life quality characteristics of national class women masters long distance runners. *Annals of Sports Medicine*, **1**, 23-26.

Moses, J., Steptoe, A., Matthews, A., & Edwards, S. (1989). The effects of exercise on mental well-being in the normal population: A controlled trial. *Journal of Psychonomic Research*, **33**, 47-61.

Okun, M.A., Olding, R.W., & Cohn, C.M. (1990). A meta-analysis of subjective well-being interventions among elders. *Psychological Bulletin*, **108**, 257-266.

Okun, M.A., & Stock, W.A. (1987). Correlates and components of subjective well-being among the elderly. *Journal of Applied Gerontology*, **6**, 95-112.

Olson, M.I. (1975). *The effects of physical activity on the body image of nursing home residents*. Unpublished master's thesis, Springfield College, Springfield, MA.

Pender, N.J. (1982). *Health promotion in nursing practice*. Norwalk, CT: Appleton-Century-Crofts.

Perri, S., & Templer, D.E. (1985). The effects of an aerobic exercise program on psychological variables in older adults. *International Journal of Aging and Human Development*, **20**, 167-172.

Perry, J.S., & Slemp, S.R. (1980). Differences among three adult age groups in their attitudes toward self and others. *Journal of Genetic Psychology*, **136**, 275-279.

Ray, R.O., Gissal, M.L., & Smith, E.L. (1983). The effect of exercise on morale of older adults. *Physical and Occupational Therapy in Geriatrics*, **2**, 53-63.

Reiter, M.A. (1981). Effects of a physical exercise program on selected mood states in a group of women over age 65. *Dissertation Abstracts International*, **42**, 1974-A.

Reynolds, B., & Garrett, C. (1989). Effects of exercise on elderly ambulatory functions. *The Gerontologist*, **28**, 258A.

Rodin, J. (1986). Aging and health: Effects of the sense of control. *Science*, **233**, 1271-1276.

Roos, N.P., & Havens, B. (1991). Predictors of successful aging: A twelve-year study of Manitoba elderly. *American Journal of Public Health*, **81**, 63-68.

Ross, M.J., Tait, R.C., Grossberg, G.T., Handal, P.J., Brandeberry, L., & Nakra, R. (1989). Age differences in body consciousness. *Journal of Gerontology: Psychological Sciences*, **44**, P23-P24.

Ryff, C.D. (1989). In the eye of the beholder: Views of psychological well-being among middle-aged and older adults. *Psychology and Aging*, **4**, 195-210.

Shavelson, R.J., Hubner, J.J., & Stanton, J.C. (1976). Self-concept: Validation of construct interpretations. *Review of Educational Research*, **46**, 407-441.

Shephard, R.J. (1987). *Physical activity and aging* (2nd ed.). Rockville, MD: Aspen Publishers.

Sidney, K.H., & Shephard, R.J. (1976). Attitudes toward health and physical activity in the elderly: Effects of a physical training program. *Medicine and Science in Sport*, **8**, 246-252.

Sonstroem, R.J. (1984). Exercise and self-esteem. *Exercise and Sport Sciences Reviews*, **12**, 123-155.

Sonstroem, R.J., & Morgan, W.P. (1989). Exercise and self-esteem: Rationale and model. *Medicine and Science in Sports and Exercise*, **21**, 329-337.

Stock, W.A., Okun, M.A., & Benin, M. (1986). The structure of subjective well-being among the elderly. *Psychology and Aging*, **1**, 91-102.

Tucker, L.A. (1982). Effect of a weight-training program on the self-concepts of college males. *Perceptual and Motor Skills*, **54**, 1055-1061.

Wernick, M., & Manaster, G.J. (1984). Age and the perception of age and attractiveness. *The Gerontologist*, **24**, 408-414.

Willits, F.K., & Crider, D.M. (1988). Health rating and life satisfaction in the later middle years. *Journal of Gerontology: Social Sciences*, **43**, S172-S176.

Windsor, L.A., Lawton, M.P., Sands, L.P., Gitlin, L.N., & Posner, J.D. (1989). *Transitory changes in affect and perceived physical well-being in young, middle-aged, and older exercisers*. Unpublished manuscript, Philadelphia Geriatric Center, Medical College of Pennsylvania.

PART V

Physical Performance and Achievement

At a time in their lives when so many people are telling the elderly that they can't, someone, the professionals, should be telling them that they can.

 verything that has been said to this point about individual differences, the cardiovascular, neuromuscular, and biomechanical systems, and the way they interact with psychological and social factors to influence the physical capacities of the elderly culminates in this final section: What can the elderly actually do?

Physical capacity affects the ability of the oldest-old to maintain an independent lifestyle, the old to maintain a job if they choose to, and many elderly to maintain a high quality of life. In these last three chapters, the vast individual differences that exist in the elderly population are recognized by focusing on those for whom physical independence becomes a challenge (chapter 12), those who struggle to maintain their jobs in the face of physical limitations and ageism in the workplace (chapter 13), and those who find the challenge of maintaining physical ability, the masters athletes, to be one of the most rewarding experiences of their lives (chapter 14).

Physical Functioning of the Old and Oldest-Old

The individual differences of older adults are nowhere more starkly apparent than in the physical functioning of the old (75-84 years) and the oldest-old (85-99 years). In these two age groups, individuals range from those who are extremely mobile, function independently, and who can complete a 26.2-mile marathon race (see chapter 14) to those who have multiple chronic diseases, are physically disabled, and live in a physically morbid condition. Unfortunately the number of elderly who are so physically impaired that they cannot live independently is far greater than the small percentage of those who are described later in this chapter as the physically fit or physically elite. Approximately 7 million elderly are presently in long-term care, and the cost of frailty in this country is roughly $54 billion a year. By 2030, unless some major improvements are made in disability rates of the elderly, 14 million adults will not be able to conduct their daily activities independently (Zedlewski, Barnes, Burt, McBride, & Meyer, 1990).

This chapter explores the full range of capabilities of the old and oldest-old and how these capabilities are assessed. First, it discusses the purpose of testing the physical capabilities of people of advanced age. Next, the chapter presents the general methodological issues and corollary problems of testing this group. Finally, it describes the hierarchy of function of these age groups, ranging from the physically dependent to the physically elite, and several tests appropriate for each level of function. For some levels of hierarchy, tests of physical function have not been well developed, and reasons for this will also be discussed. The last part of the chapter includes a short section on the expectations that health professionals and society in general should have for the physical functioning of the old and oldest-old.

Why Test Physical Function of the Old and Oldest-Old?

Although physical functioning of the elderly is of vital concern to individuals and has substantial implications for national health care costs, people in these age groups receive little attention until they become dysfunctional and require care. Then, clinicians test their capabilities, for the most part ascertaining what they cannot do rather than what they can do. Otherwise, the physical function assessments of these age groups are used to predict the elderly who are at risk of becoming functionally dependent, to determine the appropriate type of institutional care (should it be needed), to predict morbidity and mortality, to determine future health and long-term care needs, and to determine the distribution and type of services required by the elderly.

Although these age groups' health statuses, in terms of presence of disease, have been extensively surveyed, their physical abilities have not received much attention. Why? First, because society more or less accepts the assumption that a sedentary existence is normal and appropriate for

this age group. The primary focus of attention is on the existence and extent of disease and the extent to which disease becomes debilitating in terms of daily functioning. Second, many of the old and oldest-old are physically frail and difficult to measure. For example, surface skin electrodes that are routinely used to measure muscle or nerve activity in younger people are problematic with this group because of their extremely thin, sensitive, fragile skin and the high amount of adiposity (which affects signal conduction) just below the skin. Furthermore, the sensitivity of many instruments is compromised at the very low ends of their scales. Third, the people in these age groups are so individually different that they are difficult to group for statistical purposes. Fourth, this age group is a physically frail group to test, therefore even if individuals exercise systematically and are physically fit, many investigators understandably will opt to use tests that are less valid but safer in terms of health. For example, most investigators will use a submaximal test that estimates oxygen consumption, such as a walking test, rather than determine whether any individuals in the oldest age groups are capable of performing a $\dot{V}O_2max$ test. The consequence of these difficulties of measurement of the oldest groups is that most of what is known about these oldest individuals is known about those with the highest and lowest capacities, because they have been measured more frequently. Those with the highest capacities are assessed by standard tests (e.g., $\dot{V}O_2max$), and those with the lowest capacities are assessed by self-report, observer rankings, or simple observations. The capabilities of the physically fit and the physically independent groups are less well understood.

Tests of physical function should provide norms by which the effectiveness of prevention or treatment programs can be assessed. They should form a basis for the development of preventive physical activity and learning programs for retaining or returning functional ability in the oldest-old as well as information about physical function. Extending the active life expectancy of the oldest-old should be a high priority for health care professionals.

Extension of Active Life Expectancy

Chapter 1 made the point that although most individuals hope that they have a quantitatively long life span, they may not want a long life if the quality of that life is poor. Being physically independent and having the capacity to be active plays a large role in defining quality of life for all older individuals. In fact, the fear of becoming dependent because of physical disabilities is one of the greatest fears of the old. These fears, in addition to the high social costs of dependency, have led gerontologists and public health policy researchers to distinguish between life expectancy and *active* life expectancy (ALE) for older cohorts. Understanding, through health and physical function assessments, the physical capacities that might reasonably be expected at various advanced ages will enable health professionals and gerontologists to develop preventive and intervention programs that will extend the ALE for thousands of adults.

Active life expectancy, defined by Katz et al. (1983), is that period of life that is free of disability in activities of daily living (ADLs). It is an important indicator of the quality of life. Table 12.1 shows the ALE that Branch et al. (1991) calculated for 10,000 Caucasian men and women in three communities. The ALE is always less than the life expectancy, for all ages and both sexes. Figure 12.1, a through c (page 333), shows the percent of remaining life during which 65- to 90-year-old individuals were independent in the Branch et al. study. Several important observations can be made about this figure. First, the ALE declined steadily in all three geographical areas, except that the ALEs of men ages 75 to 85 years in New Haven were a notable exception. Second, the ALE is different for men and women, with the differences increasing in those old subjects over age 85. The percent of remaining independent life is higher in men than in women who live to these older ages. Third, there are geographical differences; the men in New Haven have a much higher percent of ALE than do men in the other two geographical locations.

The concept of ALE is an extension of the concept of an index of health expectancy (the life expectancy of an individual in several different states of health) proposed earlier by Wilkins and Adams (1983). By calculating the number of years that Canadians spent in different conditions (short-term disabilities, restricted or impossible instrumental or daily activities, or long-term institutionalization), they described the age-specific rates of various forms of activity restriction in the total population (Figure 12.2, page 334). They then calculated the health expectancy at birth for a given cohort (Figure 12.3, page 335). The quality-adjusted life expectancy was 3.2 years greater for

Canadians living in cities than for those in rural areas and small towns and 7.7 years greater for persons from high-income families than for persons from low-income families. On the basis of Figure 12.3, noninstitutionalized individuals could expect to have some restrictions on their activities—10.8 years for men and 14.0 years for women. Furthermore, men could expect 3 years and women 1.3 years in the most restricted category, that of inability to do work for employment or housework.

Branch et al. (1991) and Wilkins and Adams (1983) found similar results. For example, Branch et al. pointed out that because the total life expectancy of women is longer than that of men, women will have more years of dependency than men but the ratio of dependent to independent years will be the same. Their added years of life will be a mixture of independent and dependent living, and this can be seen in Wilkins and Adams' data (Figure 12.3). That women's additional years of life are not necessarily just added years of dependency contradicts those who have been warning that interventions to extend life will only extend the years of morbidity (see the discussion on this topic in chapter 1).

Physical disabilities do not always lead to dependent living, because some individuals have transitions in and out of dependency during their later years (Branch et al., 1991). In fact, a significant number of disabled old persons regain independence; thus the occurrence of disability should not be assumed to lead inevitably to a decline in health and functional status. The story of Eula Weaver in chapter 4 is a good example of a person who, after changing her health and exercise habits, moved from dependent to independent status. One way that ALE might be extended is by making periodic assessments of the physical function of older individuals and using the results to prescribe and monitor physical exercise programs and dietary adjustments.

The Need for Periodic Functional Assessment

Functional or screening assessments usually are conducted when there is evidence that instrumental or basic activities may be compromised. But physical health and function are so important in the elderly that several gerontologists have recommended that a baseline of physical capacity of all individuals

Table 12.1
Life Expectancy and Active Life Expectancy Based on Increment-Decrement Life Tables, by Age and Sex for Total Community Population

Age (years)	Total life expectancy								Active life expectancy					
	Men				Women				Men			Women		
	1982 U.S. Caucasians	East Boston	Iowa	New Haven	1982 U.S. Caucasians	East Boston	Iowa	New Haven	East Boston	Iowa	New Haven	East Boston	Iowa	New Haven
65	14.5	11.9	15.3	12.6	18.9	16.3	20.5	19.1	10.6	12.3	10.4	14.4	16.7	15.8
66	13.9	12.2	15.1	12.7	18.1	15.5	19.5	18.6	10.8	11.9	10.4	13.6	15.7	15.3
67	13.3	11.5	14.2	11.8	17.4	14.8	18.5	18.1	10.0	11.1	9.5	12.9	14.8	14.8
68	12.7	11.4	13.5	11.3	16.7	14.1	17.7	17.1	9.9	10.4	8.9	12.3	13.9	13.9
69	12.2	10.8	13.1	10.7	16.0	13.5	17.0	16.1	9.3	9.9	8.3	11.6	13.2	12.9
70	11.6	10.3	12.4	10.0	15.3	12.8	16.4	15.3	8.8	9.2	7.6	11.0	12.5	12.1
71	11.1	10.0	12.3	9.5	14.6	12.0	15.8	14.3	8.4	8.9	7.1	10.2	11.9	11.1
72	10.6	9.8	11.6	8.8	13.9	11.1	15.1	13.8	8.1	8.2	6.4	9.3	11.2	10.6
73	10.0	8.9	11.6	7.9	13.2	10.7	14.1	12.9	7.3	8.0	5.7	8.9	10.2	9.7
74	9.6	8.8	10.6	6.9	12.6	9.9	13.6	11.9	7.0	7.2	5.0	8.2	9.6	8.8
75	9.1	8.3	10.1	6.6	12.0	9.2	13.0	11.4	6.4	6.6	4.8	7.5	8.9	8.2
76	8.6	7.7	9.7	6.7	11.3	8.7	12.3	10.8	5.8	6.3	5.0	6.9	8.2	7.6
77	8.2	7.0	9.4	6.7	10.7	8.3	11.5	9.9	5.0	6.0	5.1	6.4	7.5	6.7
78	7.8	6.4	8.6	6.3	10.2	7.7	10.5	9.0	4.5	5.4	5.1	5.8	6.6	6.0
79	7.4	6.3	8.5	5.7	9.6	7.0	9.8	8.7	4.2	5.3	4.8	5.2	5.9	5.8
80	7.0	5.5	8.1	5.2	9.0	6.7	8.9	8.2	3.6	5.0	4.4	4.8	5.1	5.3
81	6.6	4.9	7.4	5.1	8.5	6.3	8.2	8.3	3.1	4.5	4.3	4.3	4.4	5.4
82	6.3	4.9	6.8	4.2	8.0	5.9	7.5	7.4	3.0	4.0	3.5	3.7	3.9	4.7
83	5.9	4.6	6.4	4.0	7.6	5.6	6.9	6.5	2.6	3.7	3.4	3.3	3.5	4.3
84	5.6	4.1	5.6	3.3	7.1	5.3	6.0	5.7	2.2	3.1	2.7	2.8	3.1	3.7
85	5.3	4.2	4.9	3.8	6.7	4.6	5.3	5.5	2.2	2.6	2.8	2.3	2.6	3.3
86		3.9	4.4	3.7		3.7	4.6	4.7	2.0	2.3	2.5	1.8	2.1	2.7
87		3.3	3.4	2.8		3.5	3.8	4.3	1.8	1.8	1.9	1.6	1.6	2.4
88		2.8	2.9	2.5		2.7	2.9	3.3	1.5	1.7	1.6	1.3	1.1	1.7
89		1.9	2.1	2.0		1.9	2.4	2.3	1.1	1.3	1.3	0.9	0.8	1.0
90+		1.3	1.2	1.5		1.3	1.4	1.4	0.8	0.7	1.0	0.6	0.4	0.5

Note. Source of data: EPESE. 1982-1983. U.S. data: National Center for Health Statistics: *Vital Statistics of the United States.* 1982. Vol. II. Mortality, Part A. DHHS Pub. No. (PHS) 86-1122. Public Health Service. Washington, DC: U.S. Government Printing Office, 1986. From "Active Life Expectancy for 10,000 Caucasian Men and Women in Three Communities" by L.G. Branch et al., 1991, *Journal of Gerontology: Medical Sciences,* **46,** p. M148. Copyright 1991 by The Gerontological Society of America. Reprinted by permission.

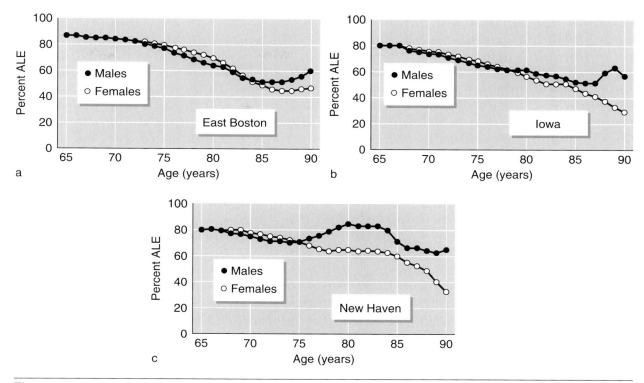

Figure 12.1 Percent of active life expectancy (ALE) in (a) East Boston, (b) Iowa, and (c) New Haven.
From "Active Life Expectancy for 10,000 Caucasian Men and Women in Three Communities" by L.G. Branch et al., 1991, *Journal of Gerontology: Medical Sciences*, **46**, p. M148. Copyright 1991 by The Gerontological Society of America. Reprinted by permission.

over age 65 be established (Besdine, Wakefield, & Williams, 1988; Rubenstein et al., 1989). Only by establishing a baseline of performance can the degree and rate of change of physical function in these individuals be assessed accurately. Baseline assessments are valuable for determining whether deterioration in function is age-related or potentially treatable. The findings can be applied to questions about driving automobiles, housing accommodations, travel, and participation in specific types of activities, such as exercise programs. Systematic assessments can provide longitudinally based norms of function within the population, so that the effectiveness of prevention or treatment programs can be assessed. Periodic assessments also provide norms of age-related changes in function.

For some old and oldest-old adults, a comprehensive geriatric assessment (CGA), which includes much more than just health and physical function, can help determine their capabilities for independent living. Like health and physical function, domains such as cognitive function, affective function, social support, economic status, environmental stressors, and well-being are also important determinants of independent living. The National

Institutes of Health (1988) have recommended one CGA that includes all dimensions of life, as shown in Table 12.2 (page 336). Note that a substantial portion of this CGA involves physical health and functioning. The CGA is primarily a diagnostic process that must be linked to the ongoing care of the clients, and it is more appropriate for the midranges of functional capacity, that is, those who are neither "too well nor too irreversibly disabled" (Reuben & Solomon, 1989, p. 570).

Methods of Physical Function Assessment in the Old and Oldest-Old

It goes without saying that careful consideration of the available tests and the adults to be evaluated is necessary in order to choose the most appropriate test for each situation. Test selection must be guided by the target population, the purpose of the evaluation, and the ease with which the test can be administered (Gromak & Waskel, 1989).

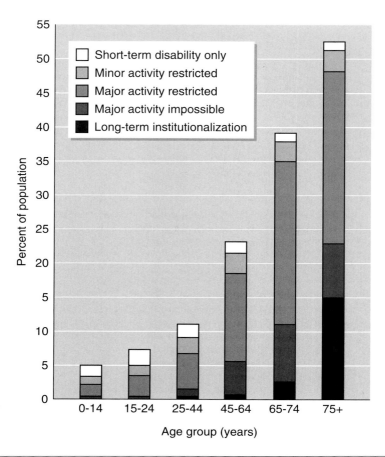

Figure 12.2   Activity restriction by age and severity of restriction, Canada, 1978.
From "Health Expectancy in Canada, Late 1970s: Demographic, Regional, and Social Dimensions" by R. Wilkins and O.B. Adams, 1983, *American Journal of Public Health*, **73**, p. 1075. Copyright 1983 by the American Public Health Association. Reprinted by permission.

There are four basic methods to test physical function in the old and oldest-old: self-report techniques, interviews, observation and functional skill testing, and physical performance and capacity tests.

Self-Report and Interview Techniques

The method routinely used to determine the capabilities of very old adults is simply to ask them (self-report) or their spouses, relatives, or caretakers (interview or questionnaire) about their abilities and to note the tasks they can accomplish. Another technique is to provide an ordered scale on which the older person, or someone else, can indicate his or her level of ability. The example shown in Figure 12.4 (page 337) offered three report sources: the patient (self-report), a member of the patient's family who was providing home care, and the patient's private physician.

The advantage of self-report and interview techniques is that they are easy to administer and score. A self-report survey can be administered by mail. Thus, more people can be tested, and the administrators of the survey do not need extensive training to be effective in obtaining the information. Both self-report and interview techniques present no dangers or risks to the subjects and are much less stressful because the results are known only to the respondent and the administrator. Both the self-report and interview techniques are reliable enough to be useful in clinical settings and in the prediction of morbidity and mortality (Falconer et al., 1991; Reuben, Siu, & Kimpau, 1992). Rakowski and Mor (1992), for example, found that self-reported physical activity and exercise in the 70-and-older age group was predictive of mortality in a 1984 to 1988 longitudinal study of aging (Fitti & Kovar, 1988). They suggested that self-report of physical activity and exercise offered an important contribution to planning patient care and predicting mortality.

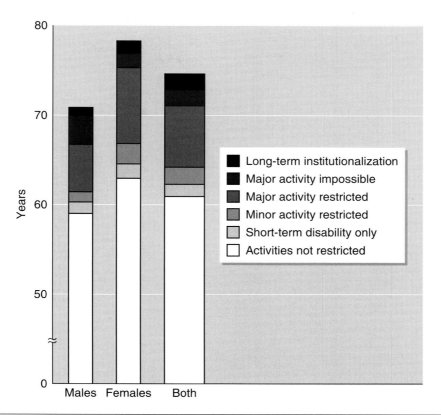

Figure 12.3 Health expectancy (i.e., expected years in each state of health) at birth, Canada, 1978.
From "Health Expectancy in Canada, Late 1970s: Demographic, Regional, and Social Dimensions" by R. Wilkins and O.B. Adams, 1983, *American Journal of Public Health*, **73**, p. 1076. Copyright 1983 by the American Public Health Association. Reprinted by permission.

However, answers from the self-report method are always subject to several criticisms. The validity of self-report instruments must rely on the veracity of the adult or caretaker of the adult being questioned, and as was discussed in chapter 11, it is well known that people are not always accurate in their assessments, either of their own abilities or of their friends'. It is not that people are dishonest; their self-efficacy, or in the case of relatives and friends' reports, their biases, influence their answers. The elderly also are sometimes affected by contextual influences such as the personality or stature of the person asking the questions, by a poor memory, or by a strong desire to avoid being institutionalized. Many times the definitions of terms provided by the test administrators may be unclear. For example, if an administrator asks if a person *can* perform a task without supportive equipment, the answer may be "yes" even though the individual hardly ever *chooses* to do the task without the equipment. Even more confusing is the situation where reports from relatives, friends, or a family physician contradict the

report of the patient or each other. Nevertheless, Elam et al. (1991) found that self-report data on five activities of daily living correlated moderately high with performance data. The reports from family members significantly correlated on four of the five activities, but the family physician's ratings correlated significantly on only one. According to this study, an individual's perception of what he or she can do is probably more accurate than a report from anyone else.

Observation and Functional Skill Testing

Many professionals prefer direct observation of physical performance or objective measurements of physical performance to self-report instruments, because in performance measurement, individuals actually perform the task. Their performance is evaluated in a systematic way using predetermined criteria, with usually much more reliable results. There are three types of performance tests:

Table 12.2
Comprehensive Geriatric Assessment

Physical health
  Traditional problem list
  Disease severity indicators
  Self-ratings of health and disability
  Quantifications of need for, and use of, medical
    services
  Disease-specific rating scales

Overall functional ability
  Activities of daily living scales (bathing,
    dressing, eating, toileting, transferring, and
    walking)
  Instrumental activities of daily living scales
    (household and money management, use of
    telephone, etc.)

Psychological health
  Cognitive function
  Affective function

Socioeconomic variables
  Social interactions network
  Social support needs and resources
  Quality of life assessment
  Economic resources and access

Environmental characteristics
  Environmental adequacy and safety
  Access to services (shopping, pharmacy,
    transportation, and recreation)

Note. From "New Issues in Geriatric Care" by D.H. Solomon et al., 1988, *Annals of Internal Medicine*, **108**, p. 725. Copyright 1988 by the American College of Physicians. Adapted by permission.

tests that incorporate actual physical skills that are performed on a daily basis (e.g., tying shoelaces or buttoning buttons), tasks that simulate daily functional skills (e.g., placing wooden pins in round holes), or tasks designed to test basic attributes or abilities thought to underlie daily tasks (e.g., measures of force control in a pinching task). Performance tests are not affected as much by cultural, racial, educational, or environmental factors as are self-report inventories or interview results. It is much more reliable (and reproducible) to observe an individual walking or measure how far an individual can walk in a specified period (usually 6 or 12 min) than it is to ask the individual or a friend how well he or she can walk.

The disadvantages of performance testing are obvious. This type of testing requires more time, more training on the part of the administrators,

the procurement and maintenance of equipment, and the allocation of specialized space. Also, some physical risk is involved when testing the old and oldest-old; they may fall, have a coronary incident, or experience some other injury during the testing. Some psychological risks are involved as well. As mentioned previously, adults in this age group generally have not had the same educational experiences, with the ubiquitous testing programs, that young and middle-aged adults have experienced. Also, the old and oldest-old may fear that the consequences of a poor score on a performance test will mean even less independence. Consequently, many very old adults see performance testing as very threatening, stressful, and frightening, and high anxiety levels can depress performance.

Physical Performance Testing

A small percentage of the old and oldest-old who are physically fit can be tested using routine physical function tests, such as treadmill and bicycle ergometer tests, and routine strength, flexibility, and agility tests. However, their age does present several problems, particularly if their scores are to be compared to those of younger people to determine how much function has been lost. Most tests of physical function were first developed on younger subjects, and performance norms were based primarily on those subjects. Consequently the interpretation of the test scores of older subjects is problematic. For example, norms in the younger age categories may be very effective using 20-year intervals, but because of the wide range of abilities among those 65 and older, a 20-year interval is useless. The physical performance of a 40-year-old may not be that much different from a 20-year-old's, but the difference between a 90-year-old and a 70-year-old is usually very large. Five-year norm intervals make much more sense for adults over age 70.

Another problem similar to the norming problem is that some parameters are important to test in older individuals but are not discriminatory in young groups. For example, neuromuscular control measured by hand steadiness and static balance measured by a one-leg standing test are important variables to assess in the oldest age groups, but these two tests would not discriminate among 20-year-olds. Virtually all 20-year-olds would have little difficulty with these two tests.

Still other concerns about the testing of physical capacities of the oldest groups are problems

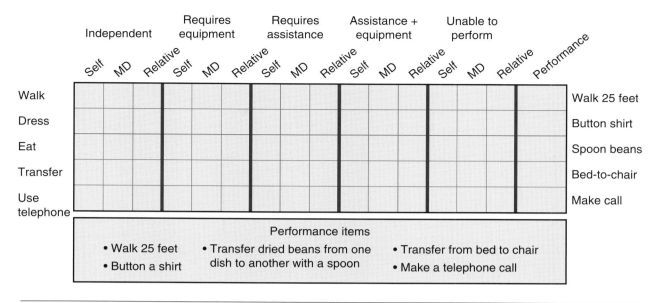

Figure 12.4   Sample self-report and performance test form.

related to other aspects of aging. Cardiovascular disease is more prevalent in these age groups and must be more seriously considered. The tendency of older adults to dissipate heat less efficiently presents problems in endurance testing. Interpretations of aerobic capacity are complicated by age-related differences in body composition, which were discussed in chapter 3. Orthopedic complications in these groups also affect physical performance testing. It is sometimes difficult for the test administrator to determine whether performance is being terminated because the subject can no longer tolerate pain in the joints or because the subject has reached endurance or strength limitations. Most adults in these age groups are on some type of medication, another complicating factor that must be considered. Finally, just as is true in any testing situation, when determining the physical ability of the very old, an important variable to consider is test anxiety and motivation. How nervous and anxious are the subjects about being tested, and how much do they really care about giving their very best effort for the test? When determining physical capacities of this age group, it is important to know whether the performance that is observed during testing is representative of performance on a daily basis. As discussed previously in chapter 10, older individuals are more likely to be excessively and deleteriously anxious about being tested on their physical abilities if they believe that the test outcomes will have

implications for their living independently or participating in other activities that they enjoy. Conversely, if they think the test outcomes have little implication, they may have less motivation to provide their best performance. In either case, the test administrator does not obtain a true picture of the individual's physical abilities.

Comparison of Self-Report and Performance Tests in Predicting Function

The special problems of testing elders have led many professionals to choose self-report of functional assessment over performance measures. This is not true of those who wish to assess the capacities of physically independent and fit individuals, but it is especially true for medical and health care professionals who need to assess physically frail individuals. For these professionals, an important criterion in determining which type of test to use is the test's effectiveness in predicting the need for institutionalization and mortality. If self-report tests are just as predictive as performance tests, then self-report tests would probably be preferred. Reuben et al. (1992) used seven commonly administered self-report measures and three physical performance tests to compare the performance of elderly persons (ages 64-94) whose living conditions differed in level of independence: community-based living, a senior citizens housing unit, and a board-and-care facility. Twenty-two months later, their follow-up showed that most of the self-report inventories and all of the physical performance tests had significantly predicted death and institutionalization. Thus, their study supported the use of both self-report and performance tests for clinical and research purposes.

Falconer et al. (1991) made another direct comparison of predictability by comparing a self-report scale of hand function to several performance tests. The variable to be predicted was whether persons were living independently, whether they were homebound, or whether they needed intermediate care. The researchers found that, in addition to several demographic variables that they studied, one of the hand function performance tests was a strong predictor of living status. Seventy-four percent of the subjects were correctly classified as to their living condition. When the self-report inventory was added to the prediction, however, the prediction increased to 80%. This study is discussed in more detail later in this chapter.

Predictive Capabilities of Physical Function Tests

Whether physical function is assessed by self-report or performance, these tests have some limitations in terms of predicting physical independence. Older adults may discontinue doing some types of activities for many reasons, physical disability being just one of them. An individual may quit climbing stairs, for example, due to lower body paralysis or weakness, pain, poor balance, or inadequate endurance. External physical factors, such as the condition of the stairway, step size, lighting, and the availability of a hand rail, may also influence the behavior. Psychological factors, such as depression, anxiety, and motivation, are also contributing factors. The environment in which a person lives and the social support available make a big difference. One attempt to take these latter factors into consideration was the development of the Assessment of Living Skills and Resources (ALSAR; Williams et al., 1991). This index of IADLs considers available resources in addition to the patient's skills. Consider the example of two individuals unable to drive an automobile but both able to use public transportation.

One of these persons lives one block from the bus stop whereas the other lives 1 mile from the bus stop. The individual who lives closer to public transportation will probably remain more mobile and consequently will reduce the deleterious outcomes of social isolation and physical disuse.

Taking all these factors into consideration, however, performance tests and some self-report inventories are effective in predicting institutionalization and mortality. Impairment on measures of basic activities of daily living (BADLs), instrumental activities of daily living (IADLs), the Tinetti gait test, and the Physical Performance test (Reuben et al., 1992), all discussed in depth later, have successfully predicted mortality.

The next section discusses a hierarchical approach to understanding and testing physical function in the old and oldest-old using both self-report and performance test batteries for different levels of physical function. Test batteries designed for specific subgroups of patients, such as those who have experienced incapacitating illness or severe trauma, the cognitively impaired, those with multiple sclerosis, and those with neurological impairment, are beyond the scope of this text and are not included.

A Hierarchical Approach to Understanding and Testing Physical Function in the Old and Oldest-Old

The physical functioning of the old and oldest-old can be categorized roughly into five levels: the *physically dependent*, the *physically frail*, the *physically independent*, the *physically fit*, and the *physically elite*. Although each level provides a description of individual capabilities, these categories were created to bring some organization to the understanding of physical function in a very old group of adults whose capacities differ widely and who as a group have not been studied very comprehensively by gerontologists. Individual differences are profound, and although most people in any one category will be more alike than they are to those in another category, there certainly are many individuals who will be difficult to categorize—for example, those who seem to fit well in a specific category except for one ability.

A graphic description of a hierarchy of the physical function of old and oldest-old age groups is shown in Figure 12.5, and Table 12.3 lists representative tests of physical function appropriate for persons at each level. Together, Figure 12.5 and Table 12.3 provide a summary of the abilities and the tests available for these abilities at each level of physical functioning, though the table is not a comprehensive list of all available tests, only a representative list. The first column of Table 12.3 shows the category of physical function; the second column provides several examples of tests appropriate for that category; and the third column lists the research resources for these tests. Each of the categories of physical function is discussed in the following sections, beginning with the most dependent and ending with the most capable.

Physically Dependent

The lowest level of the hierarchy of physical function includes the physically dependent,

shown at the right bottom of Figure 12.5. Physically dependent individuals cannot execute some or all of the BADLs and are dependent on others for food and other basic functions of living. The extent of physical disability suffered by these older adults is measured by the degree of their inability to perform activities of daily living, such as dressing, getting into and out of bed, rising from a chair, washing their face and hands, eating and drinking, washing themselves completely, using the toilet, moving around inside the house, going up and down stairs, moving around outdoors on flat ground, and taking care of their feet, fingernails, and toenails. Difficulty with bathing is the most commonly reported problem. Individuals overrepresented in this category are older, female, black, and poor.

Self-report instruments and performance tests have been used to test individuals in this category of physical function. Tests of hand function also have been used to predict an individual's ability to maintain the basic activities of daily living.

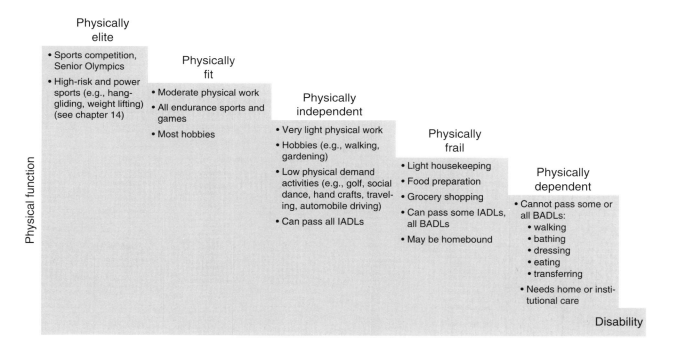

Figure 12.5 Hierarchy of physical function of the old (75-85 years) and oldest-old (86-120 years).

Table 12.3
Performance Tests of Physical Function in Old and Oldest-Old Adults

Category	Example tests	Sources
Physically elite	$\dot{V}O_2$max; modified Balke treadmill	ACSM, 1991
	Bruce treadmill protocol	Bruce, Cooper, et al., 1973
	Resistance strength tests; dynamometry	McArdle, Katch, & Katch, 1991
	Routine flexibility and agility tests	
Physically fit	$\dot{V}O_2$max, as above	ACSM, 1991
	Resistance strength tests; dynamometry	McArdle, Katch, & Katch, 1991
	Fitness tests:	
	jumping, hand strength, flexion	Kimura et al. 1990
	balance, agility, power, flexibility	Kuo, 1990
	jumping, side-step, flexion, reaction time	Tahara et al., 1990
Physically independent	Tests of low-level physical function	
	AAHPERD Field test	Osness, 1987
	Advanced activities of daily living (AADL)	Reuben et al., 1990
Physically frail	Instrumental activities of daily living (IADL)	Lawton & Brody, 1969
	Hierarchical ADL-IADL	Kempen & Suurmeijer, 1990
	GERI-AIMS	Hughes et al., 1991
	Tinetti's mobility assessment	Tinetti, 1986
	Gait assessment	Wolfson, Whipple, Amerman, & Tobin, 1990
	Physical Performance test (PPT)	Reuben & Siu, 1990
	Physical impairment scale	Jette, Branch, & Berlin, 1990
Physically dependent	Basic activities of daily living (BADL)	Katz et al., 1963
	Physical Disability Index (PDI)	Gerety et al., 1993
	Mobility Functioning in Nursing Home Residents	Schnelle et al., in press
	Physical Performance and Mobility Exam	Lemsky et al., 1991
	Barthel Index	Mahoney & Barthel, 1965
	Tests of hand function	Jebsen et al., 1969
	Williams board test	Williams & Hornberger, 1984
	Get-Up-and-Go test	Mathias, Nayak, & Isaacs, 1986
	Timed Up-and-Go screening test	Podsiadlo & Richardson, 1989

Self-Report Inventories

These inventories are widely used and are sometimes specifically developed for local use. Feinstein, Josephy, and Wells (1986) reported that 43 different indexes of BADLs were published before 1985, and a few of these indexes, compiled and described by Kane and Kane (1981), are shown in Table 12.4. However, the original and most widely used is the Activities of Daily Living index (ADL; Katz, Ford, Moskowitz, Jackson, & Jaffe, 1963). Originally designed to assess seriously disabled persons, it is widely used to determine whether older people have the ability to perform self-care activities independently. It is based on six primary tasks that are learned in early life—(in order) feeding, continence, transferring (e.g., from bed to chair), toileting, dressing, and bathing. These same tasks are lost in the latter years of life in roughly the reverse order. These six functions also have a sociobiological function, even in primitive societies.

Using this instrument, an interviewer asks the patient, friend, or caretaker whether the patient can execute the ADLs. A hierarchical structure exists among the items even within this basic scale (Katz et al., 1963; Varekamp et al., 1989). This test is widely used because it is effective in predicting in-hospital mortality and in determining which patients can be transferred to nursing homes. It can also be used to monitor changes

Table 12.4
Tests of Basic Activities of Daily Living

Tests using self-report or reports by others through interviews

Name and items of test	Source
Index of ADL[a] Bathing, dressing, going to toilet, transferring, continence, feeding. Order of items reflects natural progression in loss and regaining of function.	Katz et al., 1963
Barthel self-care ratings[a] Drink from cup, feed from dish, dress, put on brace or prosthesis, groom self, wash or bathe, continence, care of perineum/clothing at toilet, transfer to chair, transfer to toilet, transfer to tub or shower, walk 50 yards, climb stairs, wheelchair, walk outside.	Kane & Kane, 1981
Older American Resources and Services (OARS): Physical ADL[a] Eating, dressing, grooming, walking, getting in and out of bed, bathing or showering, getting to bathroom on time, continence.	Duke University Center for the Study of Aging & Human Development, 1978

Performance tests of basic activities of daily living

Name and items of test	Source
Barthel Index[a] Feeding, moving to bed, grooming, toileting, bathing, walking (propelling wheelchair), climbing stairs, bladder control, bowel control.	Mahoney & Barthel, 1965
Kenny self-care evaluation[a] 17 activities in six categories: bed activities, transfers, locomotion, personal hygiene, dressing, and feeding.	Schoening et al., 1965
PACE II: Physical function[a] ADL section includes going outside, walking, climbing stairs, transferring, wheeling, bathing/showering, toileting, dressing, grooming, eating, range of motion on several joints, strength, balance, and coordination.	USDHEW, 1978
Finger and hand control	(see Appendix, pp. 358-360; Williams & Greene, 1990)
Balance and mobility Balance: sitting, rising from chair, immediate standing, prolonged standing, withstanding nudge on chest, standing with eyes closed, turning, sitting down.	(see chapter 6, p. 174)
Gait: initiation, step length, height, continuity, symmetry, walking stance, trunk sway, path deviation.	(see chapter 6, p. 174)
Get-Up-and-Go Rising from an armchair, walking 3 m, turning, walking back, and sitting in the chair (timed test).	Mathias, Nayak, & Isaacs, 1986

Note. [a]Data from Kane and Kane (1981, pp. 40-42).

in mobility during recovery from conditions such as hip fracture.

The publication of the ADL test gave form to the concept of activities of daily living, and professionals began to use the term ADL to refer not only to Katz's test but to the notion of activities of daily living basic to survival. Later, when the concept of *instrumental* activities of daily living (IADLs) was introduced, people referred to ADLs as basic activities of daily living (BADLs) to distinguish them from IADLs.

Performance Tests

Several performance tests have been developed to measure objectively the performance of individuals on the basic activities of daily living. One widely used gross motor test is the Get-Up-and-Go test (Mathias, Nayak, & Isaacs, 1986). The subject is timed as he or she rises from an arm chair, walks 3 m, turns, returns to the chair, and sits down again. A recent modification of the original Mathias et al. test was developed by Podsiadlo and Richardson (1989). Their modified test was reliable and correlated well with other parameters of function, such as the Berg Balance Scale ($r = -0.81$), gait speed ($r = -0.61$), and the Barthel Index of ADL ($r = -0.77$; Mahoney & Barthel, 1965). It also was useful in predicting a patient's ability to go outside alone safely.

For patients of even more limited physical and cognitive functioning, Schnelle et al. (in press) have developed a mobility test for incontinent nursing home residents. The mobility test provides categorical data on standing, walking, transferring, and wheelchair propulsion (see Table 12.5) and continuous data on endurance and speed that, when combined, provide an assessment of mobility independence. The endurance and speed measures are not susceptible to floor and ceiling effects; thus, they are useful to test various intervention strategies in this severely limited population. Scores are developed by ranking each subject by the level of assistance needed to perform each item. Speed scores are recorded in seconds, endurance scores by the number of times some tests can be completed within 30 s. The strengths of this test are that it provides scores in time and some other variable, and the assessor also ranks the performance according to quality of movement.

The Physical Disability Index (PDI) was developed by Gerety et al. (1993) to measure the physical impairment and disability of frail elderly residents of nursing homes. An observer administers the PDI by quantitatively assessing strength, range of motion, balance, and mobility. The PDI is comprehensive; that is, it provides test items for residents whose abilities range from ambulatory and functional to those who are wheelchair-bound. For residents who are mobile and have some arm and leg strength, level of strength is measured using a Nicholas manual muscle tester, a Cybex EDI 320 strength-testing machine, and a lightweight hand dynamometer. Joint range of motion is measured by a goniometer and the Cybex EDI 320. For those of a lower functional level, the PDI test items include observation and timing of bed mobility (such as rolling to the right side, rolling to the left side, bridging, moving up in bed, and moving from a supine position to sitting up in bed), transferring to a chair from the edge of a bed, sitting unassisted, moving from a sitting to a standing position, standing balanced with feet apart and then together, standing with feet in tandem (one forward and one backward) with or without the assistance of a chair, ambulation through a 180° turn, and ambulation for 50 ft. Finally, the PDI also provides items for wheelchair-bound residents: wheelchair turn through 180° and wheelchair propulsion for 50 ft.

The Physical Performance and Mobility Examination (PPME) was designed by Lemsky, Miller, Nevitt, and Winograd (1991) to be a brief performance test appropriate for measuring the physical function of frail, hospitalized elderly adults. In this test, the patient performs the following items: sit up in bed, transfer to a chair, stand up from a chair once and then five times in succession, stand in a tandem and semitandem position, walk 6 m, and step up and down a 9.5-in. step. The test was validated on a sample of 169 patients (average age, 71.5 years) and on another of 98 patients whose average age was 79.63. Three trained raters assessed the patients' abilities on each item. The PPME's reliability was acceptably high, and it correlated moderately with self-reported activities of daily living ($r = 0.47-0.66$).

Tests of Hand Function

Performance testing of hand function is also predictive of an individual's ability to execute basic activities of living, thus tests of hand ability have been developed to determine whether individuals

Table 12.5
Instructions Given and Measures Collected During Each
of the Four Daily Assessment Trials (Over 2 Days)

Trials	Instructions	Measures		
		Level of assistance	Speed	Endurance
Trial 1	1. Stand once. 2. Transfer chair to chair. 3. Walk or wheel as far as possible.	1. Standing 2. Transfer 3. Walk or wheel	1. Standing 2. Transfer 3. Walk or wheel	1. Walk or wheel
Trial 2	1. Stand as much as possible in 30 s. 2. Walk or wheel as far as possible.	1. Standing 2. Walk or wheel	1. Speed over total distance walk or wheel	1. Number of stands in 30 s 2. Walk or wheel
Trial 3	1. Stand up to four times in 30 s. 2. Walk or wheel as far as possible.	1. Standing 2. Walk or wheel	1. Speed over total distance walk or wheel	1. Number of stands in 30 s (maximum of 4) 2. Walk or wheel
Trial 4	Same as Trial 3	Same as Trial 3	Same as Trial 3	Same as Trial 3

Note. From "Assessing Mobility Functioning in Nursing Home Residents With Severe Cognitive Impairment" by J.F. Schnelle et al., in press, *Archives of Physical Medicine.* Reprinted by permission of J.F. Schnelle.

can live independently. Jette, Branch, and Berlin (1990) studied a group of elderly adults for 5 years to determine what types of disability were most likely to lead to dependency or institutional living. They found that whereas progression of lower-extremity impairments and loss of lower-limb strength led to the deterioration of IADL, decrements in hand function were significant contributors to limitations in basic activities of daily living. That is, the emergence of specific joint and muscle impairment negatively affects the ability to execute the fine motor skills necessary to bathe, dress, and eat. They concluded that musculoskeletal decrement is an important cause of physical disability among the elderly. Those elderly who were 80 or more years old were more likely to experience a decline in hands and upper and lower extremities. Those who were less than 80 years old were more likely to have decreased wrist motion.

In fact, the researchers proposed that musculoskeletal deterioration has a more detrimental influence on BADLs and IADLs than does progressive impairment of sight or hearing. There are technological compensators for hearing and vision losses

that can assist older people in IADLs, but compensations for loss of manual function are not so readily available. Jette et al. (1990) also suggested that the relationship between hand function and disability may be stronger than their study results indicated, because the most disabled of the subject group were unable to complete the tests and thus their scores were not included.

Two of many tests that have been devised to measure hand function in the physically frail or dependent elderly are the Williams Test of Hand Function (Williams, Hadler, & Earp, 1982) and the Jebsen Test of Hand Function (Jebsen, Taylor, Trieschmann, Trotter, & Howard, 1969). The Williams Test of Hand Function correlates most highly with functional dependency (Falconer et al., 1991). This test incorporates a 2-×3-ft plywood board with nine small doors arranged in three rows and three columns. Each door has a different fastener (bolt latch, cupboard latch, screen door latch, doorknob, round knob, padlock, night latch, drawer lock, and turnbuckle). The score is the time taken to open (nine fasteners) and close (eight fasteners, excluding round knob) the doors. The subjects are seated and work with their dominant hand. These tasks require the integration of musculoskeletal and cognitive functions, are nonrepetitive, and test a large number of hand functions. This particular test explained more of the variance in level of dependency than did other variables such as age, mental status score, number of medical problems, number of medications, and morale (Williams & Hornberger, 1984). Furthermore, a summary index from this test (mental status testing, grip strength, and timed walk) highly predicted the need to transfer some individuals to facilities that could provide more care. Grip strength, included in some test batteries of hand function, contributed very little compared to tests of hand dexterity to the prediction of dependency (Falconer et al., 1991).

The Jebsen Test of Hand Function uses seven standardized, timed, and common tasks performed with each hand: writing, turning over 3-×5-in. cards, picking up small common objects, simulated feeding, stacking checkers, and moving large (#303) empty and weighted (1 lb) cans. The Jebsen test can discriminate hand function between 60-, 70-, and 80-year-olds (Hackel, Wolfe, Bang, & Canfield, 1992). Correlations between age (60-89 years) and dominant hand function in men were particularly moderately high, ranging from $r = 0.44$ to 0.62.

Hand function also has been assessed by self-report. Some questions in the IADL relate to hand function, and one of the eight scales of functional status in the comprehensive GERI-AIMS (Hughes, Edelman, Chang, Singer, & Schuette, 1991) is the hand dexterity scale. The interviewer uses this scale to determine, through questioning, the ease with which the subject can write, turn a key, button clothing, tie shoes, and open a jar. This test also provides scales for a generic score and an arthritis-specific score, but these have not been available long enough to be widely used.

Physically Frail

The physically frail elderly can perform the BADLs but have a debilitating disease or condition that physically challenges them on a daily basis. Defined by the American Medical Association, this group comprises those over age 65 who have multiple disease processes that limit normal functional activity (AMA, 1990). They may be unable to execute a few of the IADLs, such as shopping, laundering, and mopping, but with some assistance, either human or technological, they can live independently. Many are largely homebound; that is, meals are brought to them by volunteers or city services groups, and home cleanings may be done periodically for them by others. Elderly persons in the physically frail category walk a fine line between independent and dependent living, and in many cases their level of physical function is the ultimate determiner of their lifestyle.

Physical disability can result from a history of chronic or acute diseases, accidents, or certain lifestyle habits, but common observation indicates that not all people who have chronic diseases or who live certain lifestyles become physically disabled. Potential predictors of physical disability are shown in Table 12.6. Two of these, hypertension and arthritis, are consistent predictors of disability, whereas the other diseases and lifestyle habits are sometimes considered significant predictors. The potential for many elderly people to become physically frail is very high, because the incidence of chronic disease among the elderly is also very high (see Figure 1.8, page 16).

Because this group borders on dependency and suffers many chronic diseases and conditions that eventually lead to physical disability, several different assessment batteries have been developed to determine the extent of their physical function. These test batteries are used with

Table 12.6
Potential Predictors of Physical Disability

A history of . . .	Literature
Hypertension	Consistently reported
Arthritis	
Angina pectoris	Sometimes reported
Coronary heart disease with angina	
Stroke	
Congestive heart failure	
Cancer	
Bone injury	
Obesity	
Diabetes	
Lifestyle behaviors	
Smoking	Sometimes reported
Alcohol use	
High-fat mass	

a variety of populations: hospitalized patients, nursing home residents, those undergoing rehabilitation, and independent members of the community.

Self-Report Surveys

The classic self-report assessment of physical function in the frail elderly is based on the ability to perform physical tasks that are necessary on a daily basis for independent living (Lawton & Brody, 1969). This instrument is called the Instrumental Activities of Daily Living (IADL) survey, in which subjects are asked which of a number of tasks they can or cannot perform. It is an expanded version of the ADL scale previously developed by Katz et al. (1963). Whereas the ADL scale is used to determine the extent to which individuals can carry out activities of daily living that are basic to surviving independently, such as feeding and bathing, the questions of the IADL relate more to complex physical abilities, such as preparing meals, "light" house-cleaning activities, "heavy" house-cleaning activities, washing and ironing clothes, making beds, and shopping. This survey has been very useful in determining whether individuals can live independently.

Kempen and Suurmeijer (1990) developed a hierarchical scale of 18 items in which the tasks of IADL and BADL are combined and ranked according to the percent of elderly adults who cannot execute them. The scores of 78 females and 23 males (average age, 74.5 years) were analyzed to determine the extent to which people with the same total score had problems with the same activities, or the extent to which the scale was hierarchical and cumulative. The scale, shown in Table 12.7, is based on a three-answer possibility for each item: 1, performs activities independently and easily; 2, performs independently but with some difficulty; and 3, depends on others or performs under supervision. Only 2% of their sample were dependent on others for eating and drinking (which are BADLs), whereas 95% had difficulty or were dependent on others for heavy house-cleaning activities.

Kempen and Suurmeijer (1990) proposed that a hierarchical scale such as this has several advantages over other tests of IADLs. It widens the range of measurement of function in the independent-living population and provides information on the distribution of functional problems within populations. It also provides information that can be used

Table 12.7
Eighteen ADL-IADL Items in Ascending Order of Difficulty

1. Eating and drinking (ADL)
2. Washing face and hands (ADL)
3. Using the toilet (ADL)
4. Rising from chair (ADL)
5. Getting in and out of bed (ADL)
6. Moving inside the house (ADL)
7. Dressing (ADL)
8. Light house-cleaning activities (IADL)
9. Washing oneself completely (ADL)
10. Moving outdoors on flat ground (ADL)
11. Preparing dinner (IADL)
12. Preparing breakfast and lunch (IADL)
13. Going up and down stairs (ADL)
14. Bed making (IADL)
15. Care of feet and nails (ADL)
16. Washing and ironing clothes (IADL)
17. Shopping (IADL)
18. Heavy house-cleaning activities (IADL)

Note. Adapted from Kempen and Suurmeijer (1990, p. 499).

to make decisions regarding the delivery of services, determine the amount of care an individual living at home needs, and track changes in ability to function independently.

Two other hierarchical scales, developed by Siu, Reuben, and Hays (1990), incorporate overall levels of function by combining items from other established, frequently used tests: Katz, Downs, Cash, and Grotz (1970); Spector, Katz, Murphy, and Fulton (1987); Older American Resources and Services (OARS) five-item tests (Duke University Center for the Study of Aging and Human Development, 1978); and Rosow-Breslau scales (Rosow & Breslau, 1966). The five-item scale and the six-item scale, shown in Table 12.8, incorporate not only items from ADL and IADL scales, but more complex physical tasks that would be considered advanced activities of daily living.

Other self-report instruments developed before 1981 are described in more detail by Kane and Kane (1981). Examples of some of these tests and others that have been developed since 1981 are shown in Table 12.9 (pages 347-348).

Several performance tests that measure primarily gross or large-muscle physical performance of the frail elderly are also shown in Table 12.9, but tests of this type vary in the kind of assessment made, the setting in which they are appropriate,

---

Table 12.8
Hierarchical Measures
of Physical Function

Six-item scale

Are you able to . . .

Do strenuous physical activities, like hiking, tennis, bicycling, jogging, and swimming?

Do heavy work around the house, like washing windows, walls, or floors?

Go shopping for groceries or clothes?

Get to places out of walking distance?

Bathe, either a sponge bath, tub bath, or shower?

Dress, like putting on a shirt, buttoning and zipping, or putting on shoes?

Five-item scale

Are you able to . . .

Do strenuous physical activities, like hiking, tennis, bicycling, jogging, and swimming?

Do heavy work around the house, like washing windows, walls, or floors?

Get to places out of walking distance?

Bathe, either a sponge bath, tub bath, or shower?

Dress, like putting on a shirt, buttoning and zipping, or putting on shoes?

Note. From "Hierarchical Measures of Physical Function in Ambulatory Geriatrics" by A.L. Siu, D.B. Reuben, and R.D. Hays, 1990, *Journal of the American Geriatrics Society*, **38**, p. 1119. Copyright 1990 by Williams & Wilkins. Reprinted by permission.

and the experience that is necessary to administer the tests (see Table 12.10, page 348). Other performance tests that will be discussed later include tests of refined hand control.

Large Muscle and Mobility Tests

The Physical Performance test (Reuben & Siu, 1990) is a good example of a timed performance test designed to measure physical activities common to daily living. The items were selected either from existing performance tests or created anew to be functionally oriented, simulate activities of daily living, vary in difficulty, and take as little time as possible to complete. Other considerations were that the test items assess upper-body fine

motor function, upper-body gross motor function, balance, mobility, coordination, and muscular endurance. An additional feature is that the test can be administered by untrained assistants. The reliability among different raters is high.

There are two test batteries, a nine-item and a seven-item battery (the seven-item battery is shown in Table 12.11, page 349), that include writing a sentence, simulated eating, putting a book on a shelf, putting on and removing a jacket, picking up a penny, walking 50 ft, and climbing a flight of stairs. Table 12.11 shows the results from 183 adults who were members of several clinical practices, a hospital primary-care unit, a board-and-care home, and a senior citizens apartment. The seven-item performance test meets the standards usually expected of performance tests; that is, the range of scores is very great when administered to groups of different ability levels.

Another excellent example of a physical performance test for this level of functioning is Tinetti's (1986) mobility assessment. This test assesses the individual's ability to get around in the environment. The responses of the individual are rated *normal, adaptive,* or *abnormal* for a wide variety of movements—from maintaining balance during sitting and while rising from a chair to the much more complex control task of turning while walking. Also included are movements such as bending over from a standing position and picking up a small item, and placing a light object on a high shelf. This test may be administered by physicians, nurses, and other trained personnel, and the reliability of ratings made by different raters is high. In one test of reliability, the testers agreed on 85% of the individual items, the total scores never differing by more than 10%.

Hand Control and Function

Hand function is not generally used to test the function of the physically frail, because it is not usually a problem in independent living for this group. This does not mean that hand function problems do not exist, nor that they do not affect quality of life. Many older adults, with great disappointment, may have to give up hobbies or jobs that require fine, meticulous, or tedious hand control. In these cases, the loss of hand function negatively affects their well-being, but it does not threaten their independence. However, there are two types of hand function tests currently being used in laboratory research that have potential for

Table 12.9
Tests of Instrumental Activities of Daily Living

Tests using self-report or reports by others through interviews

Name and items of test	Source
Functional health status Doing heavy work (such as snow shoveling); no physical illness or condition now; not limited in any activities; able to walk half a mile, climb stairs, go out to a movie or meeting.	Rosow & Breslau, 1966
Instrumental Role Maintenance Scale Frequency of meal preparation other than breakfast; frequency of shopping; distance of shopping from residence; manner of doing laundry.	Lawton, 1972
PACE II: IADLs Using telephone; handling money; securing personal items; tidying up; preparing meals.	USDHEW, 1978
OARS: Instrumental ADL Using telephone; shopping for groceries or clothes; transporting self to places out of walking distance; preparing meals; doing housework; taking medicine; handling own money.	Duke University Center for the Study of Aging and Human Development, 1978
Functioning for independent living Vision; hearing and speech; mobility; bowel and bladder control; confused behavior; knowledge of identity; ability to make self understood; wandering; extent of nonconventional behavior.	Gross-Andrew & Zimmer, 1978

Pilot Geriatric Arthritis Project Functional Status Measure (PGAP)
Mobility:
  driving, shopping, walking inside, walking outside, climbing stairs into home, other stairs, curbs; transfer to bed, transfer to chair; transfer to car; transfer to toilet, transfer to bath.
Personal care items:
  telephoning, writing, cutting food, drinking, washing self, turning faucets, teeth care, shaving, combing hair, setting hair; putting on shoes, clothes; buttoning and zipping clothes.
Work items:
  employment; operating stove, oven, refrigerator, sink, faucets; opening cupboards, lifting pots, peeling and cutting; reading; opening containers; laundry, sweeping, mopping; making beds; washing dishes, cleaning bathroom; washing windows, doing home repair, yard work.
Unlocking a padlock
Opening a door
	Deniston & Jette, 1980

Performance tests of instrumental activities of daily living

PGC Instrumental Activities of Daily Living Using telephone; shopping; food preparation; housekeeping; laundry; using public transportation; taking medication; handling finances.	Lawton, 1972

(continued)

Table 12.9
(continued)

Name and items of test	Source
Performance activities of daily living (PADLs) Drinking from a cup; using tissue to wipe nose; combing hair; filing nails; shaving; lifting food onto spoon and to mouth; turning faucet on and off; turning light switch on and off; putting on and removing a jacket with buttons; putting on and removing slippers; brushing teeth; making a phone call; signing name; turning key in lock; standing up, walking a few steps, and sitting back down.	Kuriansky & Gurland, 1976
Physical Performance test (PPT) Writing a sentence; simulated eating; lifting a book and putting it on a shelf; putting on and removing a jacket; picking up a penny; walking 50 ft; climbing a flight of stairs (may be omitted).	Reuben & Siu, 1990

Note. A more detailed summary of these tests prior to 1981 is provided in Kane and Kane (1981). The descriptions of these early tests are primarily from this source.

Table 12.10
Settings for Performance-Based Tests of Function

Setting	Test	Type of assessment	Assessor
Office (for ambulatory clients)	Tinetti gait and balance	Specific	Professional
	Timed manual dexterity	Specific	Lay
	Physical Performance test (PPT)	Global	Lay
	Timed Up-and-Go test	Specific	Lay
	Time to 10 stands	Specific	Lay
Hospital	Physical Performance and Mobility Exam (PPME)	Specific	Lay
Nursing home	Physical Disability Index (PDI)	Global	Professional

Note. Table prepared by D.B. Reuben (1992, personal communication).

clinical diagnosis of hand function loss significant enough to threaten the independence of the frail elderly—precision pinching and grasp control.

The precision pinch, which is the apposition (closing together) of the index finger (and sometimes one or two other fingers) and the thumb, is one of the most important hand movements for daily function. It is with the precision grip that small objects, such as pennies, are picked up from a table. In the precision pinch, grip force has to be matched to object weight, friction, and skin surfaces. Inadequate force results in the object slipping from the fingers, but too much force can result in damage or breakage to the object. Cole and Abbs (1986) developed instrumentation to measure several parameters of pinch control during manipulation of a small object, and Hart and Abbs (1990, 1992), using this instrument, found that older adults use excessive force that is applied too late and is poorly scaled to the object's load.

Sollerman and Sperling (1978) developed a hand-grip classification system that identifies eight prehension patterns common to several activities of daily tasks: four finger-grips (the pulp pinch, lateral pinch, tripod pinch, and five-finger pinch) and four volar grips (diagonal volar grip, transverse volar grip, spherical volar grip,

Table 12.11
Performance on Individual Timed PPT Items

Timed PPT items	% Able to complete	Average time to complete (s)	Range (s)	*SD* (s)
Writing a sentence	94	16.7	7.0-49.0	6.5
Simulated eating	100	15.4	7.5-56.5	6.8
Lifting a book and putting it on a shelf	94	4.0	1.5-40.0	4.0
Putting on and removing a jacket	97	15.6	2.0-71.5	8.4
Picking up a penny	98	3.5	1.5-20.5	2.1
Walking 50 ft	98	25.0	10.5-315.5	31.0
Climbing a flight of stairs[a]	91	10.6	4.0-76.0	11.4

Note. Based on six patient populations:
1) Patients in the UCLA Department of Medicine Practice Group's Geriatric Practice
2) Patients of the Rhode Island Hospital's Medical Primary Care Unit
3) Residents of a senior housing unit in Providence, RI, attending a health screening fair in the unit
4) Patients of a community-based geriatrics practice in Los Angeles
5) Patients entering a board-and-care home in Los Angeles
6) Patients with Parkinson's Disease, Brown University
[a]Excluding subjects at Sites 4 and 5.
From "An Objective Measure of Physical Function of Elderly Outpatients: The Physical Performance Test" by D.B. Reuben and A.L. Siu, 1990, *Journal of the American Geriatrics Society*, **38**, p. 1108. Copyright 1990 by Williams & Wilkins. Reprinted by permission.

and extension grip). Shiffman (1992) provided means and individual difference scores (standard deviations) for frequency of use, performance time, and hand strength of men and women aged 24 to 87. Hand function remained stable until age 65 and then began deteriorating slowly; age differences increased after age 75. This classification system has promise for functional task analysis, if it can be standardized and adapted for clinical use.

Physically Independent

The physically independent elderly are those who do not exercise or pay particular attention to health habits but who nevertheless have not been stricken with one or more diseases so debilitating that they lose the ability to function independently. Some of these individuals have no particularly bad health habits and are relatively free of symptomatic disease. Others may be alcoholics or smokers and have several chronic diseases, but they retain the capacity to function. These people are in delicate health and have meager reserves, yet they have few functional limitations. They remain mobile

and independent. They have enough physical function to participate in some advanced activities of daily living (AADL), so they can participate in social activities such as vacation travel, golf, or gardening. They can complete successfully most or all of the IADLs and all of the BADLs, but they are vulnerable to unexpected physical stress or challenge.

More members of the old and oldest-old age group are in this physical function category than in any of the other four. According to the Established Populations for Epidemiological Studies of the Elderly (EPESE) project, only 5% to 12% of community-dwelling elderly need assistance with bathing and 1.3% to 2.6% need assistance with feeding (National Institute on Aging, 1986). Approximately 25% of elderly are dependent in at least one IADL (Fitti & Kovar, 1988). Considering that probably less than 5% could be considered physically fit or physically elite, roughly 70% of the oldest-old would be correctly classified as physically independent.

It is important to assess the physical capacities of physically independent elderly, because existing tests of function (basic and instrumental activities of daily living) are insensitive to declines of physical function in this group. Also, many members of this group, although still independent, are hovering very near the lower limit. A very small setback in health—the incidence of a minor disease, a small accident, or simply the passage of a little time—could change them from being physically independent to being frail and partially dependent. Physical assessments should be made to determine their "distance from physical frailty" as well as their suitability for exercise interventions.

It is particularly ironic, in light of the large number of old adults who are physically independent, that this group falls between the cracks in terms of understanding their physical capabilities. These individuals continue to live in their homes and are somewhat active, yet they do not have enough aerobic capacity or lower-leg strength to complete even the least demanding protocol on a treadmill test. Most, however, would make a perfect score on any of the tests that are appropriate for the next lower level of physical function. Their scores on traditional resistance strength tests would be so low that they would challenge the reliability of some of the tests. Nevertheless, lower-limb strength is exceedingly important to measure, because a decrement in the lower extremity leads to decrements in IADL (Jette et al., 1990). Leg strength and endurance are necessary for shopping, housekeeping, driving, and food preparation.

Self-reported inventories have been used successfully to identify the limits of physical function of individuals at the lower extreme of the physical function continuum, but the better the subjects' physical function, the less reliable self-reports are. Therefore, several efforts have been made to develop performance tests, such as fitness test batteries, to measure adults in this category. One example of a fitness test battery is the Tokyo Metropolitan University Fitness test, which includes measures of balance (one-leg standing with eyes closed), leg strength (stepping in the sitting position), trunk flexion (sit-and-reach), power (vertical jump), muscular strength (hand grip), and respiratory integrity (breath holding). These can be measured in clinics and in community agencies or institutions. Another example is a test battery developed by the Council on Aging and Adult Development of the American Alliance for Health, Physical Education, Recreation and Dance (AAHPERD).

The AAHPERD Field Test

The AAHPERD Field test, reported by Osness (1987), includes measures of muscular strength and

endurance, coordination, trunk and leg flexibility, and aerobic endurance and was designed specifically for adults over age 60. It was also designed so that it could be administered by professionals and clinicians in the field who lack measurement equipment or resources; what equipment is necessary for the test can be made from materials that are readily available in any institution. The purpose of the test is to provide, through the use of nationally standardized test items appropriate for sedentary, independently living elderly, an estimate of the physical function of those who are not physically fit but also not yet physically frail. This test, in conjunction with a medical examination and medical history assessment, should be administered before any type of exercise intervention program for this group. Because the AAHPERD test was developed and endorsed by a national association of professionals whose primary interest is health and physical function, it bears more complete review.

Cardiorespiratory endurance is assessed by a 1/2-mile walk test in which the subject continuously walks 880 yards (1/2 mile) as fast as possible without running, and the score is the time recorded to the nearest second. Both the temporal reliability (stability) and validity, which is based on correlations of the walking performance score with $\dot{V}O_2max$, are acceptable.

Muscular strength and endurance are measured by a sit-and-stand test. In this test, each subject stands upright from a seated position as many times as possible within 30 s. The score is the number of times the individual reaches a standing position. The internal consistency, reliability, and the test validity, based on correlations with a one-repetition maximum leg extension measurement on Cybex strength-testing equipment, are high. Another measure of strength and endurance that can be used is an elbow flexor test, which is measured by the number of times a plastic milk bottle filled with sand can be raised from an extended elbow position to a flexed elbow position in 30 s. Women use a 2-quart plastic milk bottle (4 lb), which also provides a convenient handle, and men, a 1-gallon plastic bottle (8 lb).

Agility and dynamic balance are measured by the chair agility test. Each subject starts from a seated position and on the command "ready, go," walks around a cone placed 6 ft to the side and 5 ft behind to the right of the chair, then returns to a full seated position in the chair. Without hesitating, the subject repeats the movement, this time walking around a second cone placed at the same distance to the left of the chair. One trial consists of two complete circuits of the agility course. The test reliability is acceptable.

Neuromuscular coordination is measured by the "soda pop" test (Osness, 1987). Six circles with a radius 1 cm wider than a standard 12-ounce can of soda pop are placed in a straight line on a board. The center of each circle is spaced 5 in. from the center of the adjacent circle. Three standard 12-ounce cans of soda pop are placed in every other circle. The subjects must, with their dominant hand, turn all three cans upside down onto the adjacent circle and then return the cans to their original position. The score is the average time of three trials recorded to the nearest 1/10 of a second.

Balance is measured by a one-legged stand with arms extended laterally and eyes open. (A more detailed description of this test is provided in chapter 6.) The score is the time recorded from the moment subjects raise their nonpreferred foot from the floor to the time that they replace it.

Flexibility is measured by a trunk-leg (sit and reach) flexibility test. A yardstick or equivalent is placed on the floor, with a mark at zero (where the heels of the feet are to be placed). The subject, without shoes, sits on the floor, legs extended straight in front of the body, with the yardstick between the extended legs. Keeping the hands together, the subject leans forward as far as possible, and the technician records the number of inches reached to the nearest 1/2 in.

Williams-Greene Classification Schema for Upper-Extremity Function and Mobility

Williams and Greene's (1990) battery of physical function tests, shown in the appendix (pp. 358-362), is particularly attractive because it is based on theory: a movement classification schema. In this classification schema, which is specifically designed to organize and understand movements that are important to the physical functioning of the elderly, movements are classified as either upper-extremity function or mobility movements. Upper-extremity function is dependent on strength and steadiness and is composed of simple arm and hand movements and distal-extremity control, such as occurs in object manipulation and self-help actions. The movements that enable mobility are strength and flexibility, transferring maneuvers from one posture to another (sitting to standing, lying to sitting, etc.), and balance. Gait and mobility functions include

simple gait control, precision gait control, maximum gait control, and body agility. For each of these upper-extremity functions and mobility movements, tests have been developed by these researchers or drawn from the research literature.

Advanced Activities of Daily Living

Advanced activities of daily living (AADLs), a term coined by Reuben and Solomon (1989), are the many luxury functions that people carry out during their daily experiences in social, religious, or physical activities. AADLs are those activities that require abilities well beyond the IADLs. Social AADLs include employment, traveling, hobbies, and participation in social and religious groups. Physical AADLs include recreational exercise and crafting, such as woodworking and gardening. Because these activities are voluntary and social, the range of activities will vary considerably. Thus Reuben, Laliberte, Hiris, and Mor (1990) suggest that a universal measure of AADL probably cannot be developed, but an AADL assessment could be tailored to an individual's particular AADLs so that the individual could be monitored over time. For example, these researchers developed a scale for physical exercise as an AADL, in which subjects are categorized on the basis of frequency and intensity of exercise: frequent vigorous exercisers, frequent long walkers, frequent short walkers, or nonexercisers (Reuben et al., 1990). Using this scale, professionals can plot subtle changes in the physical AADL that might signal a larger than expected decline in physical function.

The development of AADL tests in many different activities, in conjunction with more rigorous tests of hand function, may be an important link to understanding age-related changes in function among the elderly. Those changes that occur in the physically independent are the least well known. AADLs that are sports activities, such as tennis or golf, have built-in performance measures. Also, standardized skill tests exist for sports skills. But for an AADL such as driving an automobile, there are no refined tests for the elderly.

Physically Fit

The physically fit elderly are individuals who exercise two or three times a week, or on a daily basis, but they exercise primarily for their health, enjoyment, and well-being. They do not compete, and they do not exercise as long or as intensely as those who do. Nevertheless, they are consistent in maintaining their good health habits and their exercise protocol. Because of this consistency, their health status is well above that of individuals who do not attend to their health habits (in terms of nutrition, sleep, alcohol, drug usage, smoking habits, and exercise). They are generally estimated by their peers to be much younger than their chronological age. Their physiological characteristics are more robust than those of individuals in lower physical function categories. For example, their $\dot{V}O_2$max is much higher than that of sedentary adults, although their aerobic capacity does not match that of the physically elite (see Figure 4.7, page 108). They may still be working in their chosen occupation or career and may be participating in many activities with people much younger than themselves. Also, because of the relationship of physical health to emotional control (chapter 10) and to feelings of well-being and life satisfaction (chapter 11), they tend to be very active and fully engaged in life.

Most of the physically fit elderly could complete a routine $\dot{V}O_2$max treadmill or bicycle ergometer test, and all could complete regular muscle strength and endurance, flexibility, and agility tests. The Bruce Multistage Treadmill test (Bruce, 1977), which uses the least demanding treadmill protocol, has been used more than any other treadmill test to determine $\dot{V}O_2$max in the elderly. In this protocol, the speed and gradient of walking is increased every 3 min. Four 3-min stages of two MET increments are followed by 2-min stages of one MET increments until the subject declares that he or she is fatigued and ready to quit. During the first four stages, the aerobic requirements are adjusted to the kilograms of body weight. Because of the advanced age of the subjects, they are always evaluated clinically by history, physical examination, and a 12-lead resting ECG *before* attempting any treadmill test of aerobic capacity. A physician specialized in cardiovascular function determines whether heart disease is present, and if so, its extent. If the cardiovascular examination warrants, the treadmill test is initiated, generally supervised by a physician and managed by an exercise physiologist or exercise technician. Blood pressure is monitored throughout the test and both the physician and exercise physiologist stay alert for symptoms of cardiovascular abnormalities. If any occur, the test is discontinued.

However popular the Bruce protocol has been, the American College of Sports Medicine (ACSM) recommends against its use with the elderly, because the increases in speed and grade occur too rapidly. Also, the fact that many very old adults or cardiac patients have to use handrails while taking the test contaminates the $\dot{V}O_2$max values (ACSM, 1991).

The ACSM recommends that the modified Balke treadmill protocol be used with the elderly, because it uses slow but constant walking speeds and very gradual increases in grade increments every 2 or 3 min. The modified Balke protocol also has no awkward speed or grade stages where it is difficult for the subject to determine whether to walk or run (Pollock & Wilmore, 1990). A comparison of the Bruce and modified Balke protocols is shown in Figure 12.6, a and b. The Balke protocol is longer in duration, which is one drawback to its use with elderly individuals. Pollock and Wilmore (1990) suggest that a treadmill test should last at least 6 min but no longer than 15 min.

It is highly probable that physically fit elderly adults could complete either the Bruce or the Balke protocols, which would enable their physicians to obtain the best available measure of their aerobic capacity. Although $\dot{V}O_2$max is not a perfect measure of physical fitness, it is the only reliable single measure of aerobic capacity available. It is the standard by which physical fitness is assessed. Many investigators have tried to substitute other types of tests, such as measuring the length of time subjects can stay on the treadmill and their heart rate during each minute, but these measures are not truly reliable measures of fitness (Tonino & Driscoll, 1988). Because the physically elite and the physically fit elderly can complete either a routine modified Balke $\dot{V}O_2$max or a Bruce $\dot{V}O_2$max test, their aerobic fitness can be assessed reliably. But individuals in the hierarchical categories previously described cannot complete these tests, and consequently the extent of their aerobic fitness can only be estimated.

Individuals in the physically fit category could probably do well on Kuo's (1990) physical function test battery. This battery does not measure aerobic capacity, but it enables the test administrator to assess other components of physical fitness: static balance, agility, lower-limb power, and flexibility. The test was administered (first in 1984 and again in 1985) to 3,562 Japanese subjects, the majority of whom were males (64%) between the

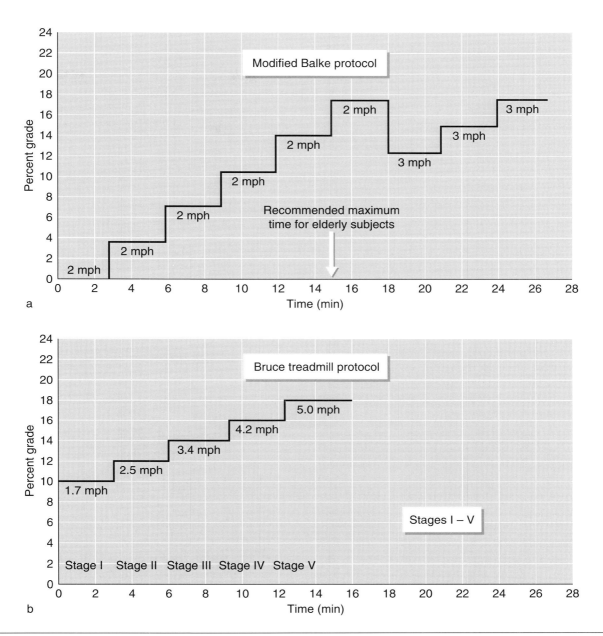

Figure 12.6   (a) Modified Balke protocol vs. the (b) Bruce treadmill protocol. The oxygen consumption at each stage and the length of time the individual can continue to test are used to estimate maximum oxygen consumption.

Adapted from Bruce, Cooper, et al. (1973, p. 693).

ages of 45 and 70. Several subjects were over age 75. Their performances on three of the test items are shown in Figure 12.7.

Several observations of physical function can be made from these graphs. First, it is clear that as the subjects age, their physical capacities decline. Second, the lower scores among older subjects are exaggerated for women. This was a cross-sectional study, so it is incorrect to say that women's physical function deteriorates faster than men's, though

it appears that the physical capacity of older women is much lower than that of older men, except possibly when balancing on one foot with the eyes closed. The greatest difference between men and women is on the test item that measures power, the standing broad jump, where men's scores substantially exceed the scores of women. Not shown in the figure are the scores of trunk flexibility, in which the women were superior to the men. Women older than 55 were only 12%

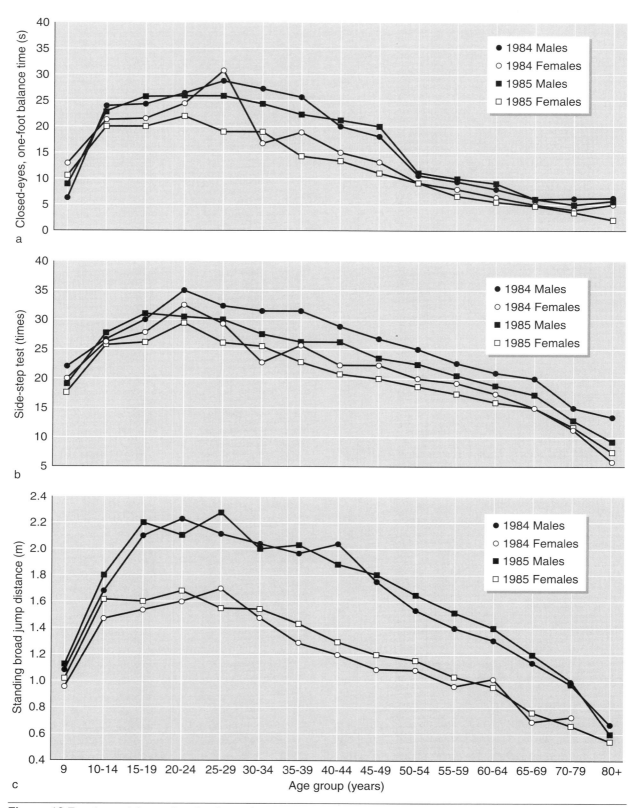

Figure 12.7 Physical fitness levels of people in Taipei in relation to age and sex: (a) balance, (b) agility, and (c) power tests.

From "Physical Fitness of the People in Taipei Including the Aged" by G.H. Kuo. In *Fitness for the Aged, Disabled, and Industrial Worker* (p. 22) by M. Kaneko (Ed.), 1990, Champaign, IL: Human Kinetics. Copyright 1990 by Human Kinetics Publishers, Inc. Reprinted by permission.

less flexible than the 19- to 25-year-old women, but men over 55 were 39% less flexible than the 25- to 30-year-old men. Third, there were very few scores from persons more than 80 years old, and these were all included in one 80-plus category, a practice typical of many studies. Data from the oldest-old on fitness items such as these are almost nonexistent.

The physically fit elderly provide 50% to 75% of the upper scores on laboratory resistive-strength and muscular endurance tests that are administered to persons in this age group, particularly if their exercise protocol includes some activities that require strength. Because of their habitual physical activity, their performances are also better than those of many much younger but sedentary people.

Physically Elite

The physically elite elderly are a very unusual group of people in our society. They train physically on a daily basis and compete in tournaments available to individuals their age. Many participate in the Senior Olympics, in masters tournaments, and in special age-group classifications within a general tournament, such as a 10K running race sponsored by a commercial interest, a city, or a foundation. Another segment of adults in this age group are those who have continued training physically or working in a physically demanding occupation, for example, skiing, scuba-diving, hiking, and mountain-climbing instructors, or forest rangers, fire fighters, and police. Not many can continue working in these occupations to very old ages, but a few do. Their performances are rarely compared publicly to performances of the young, however, so very little is known about them. The physical capacity of the adults in this category, at least in the abilities required by their sport or activity, is generally superior to that of untrained adults decades younger. Because these individuals are so unusual—they represent the maximum physical performance capabilities of these oldest age groups and a high physical standard to which many of the oldest-old should aspire—a separate chapter (chapter 14) is devoted to their performance capabilities.

The physically elite are very active, and they can be assessed safely by tests that are routinely used for young adults. Their maximum aerobic capacities can be obtained using a $\dot{V}O_2$max treadmill or bicycle ergometer test, their strength can

be assessed with cable tensiometers or electromechanical instrumentation, their muscular endurance by multiple trials of submaximum strength production, and so forth. These individuals would score in the top 5% of all physical capacity tests of adults in the four hierarchic categories below them.

Expectations for Physical Performance of the Old and Oldest-Old

On the basis of the information presented in the preceding chapters, it is clear that physical exercise can make significant improvements in the physical functioning of individuals at any age. Even among the oldest participants, aerobic capacity, muscular strength, muscular endurance, flexibility, speed of responses, and coordination all improve following an exercise program. Improvements in some or all of these factors lead to significant improvements in physical functioning. Why, then, do not all of the oldest-old remain more physically active?

Many reasons have been suggested throughout this text, but the most senseless contributor to physical inactivity is the *expectation* for decreased physical performance, both on the part of the individual and her or his support group. Too many people are content to believe that when people grow older than 75 years, their physically active life is almost over. Ageism pressures the oldest-old to become inactive.

A vicious cycle develops. As people age, they become less active. The less active they are, the less physical ability and endurance they have. The less physical ability they have, the less inclined they are to be physically active. And the less active they are, the more physical capacity they *lose*. The less they move, the less they can move. They begin to feel old and act old, which includes not being physically active. When a child or a teenager takes a bad fall and breaks an arm, people tell them to "get back on the horse" as quickly as possible. When an old person has an accident and breaks an arm, people say "better slow down" and "don't be so rambunctious"! The result of this vicious cycle is a steady deterioration of function, depicted by the straight line running from left to right through the circle in Figure 12.8. This line represents the classic average decline that occurs in many functions and abilities. Another interpretation of this line may be seen in the familiar logo meaning "do not" or "not allowed." So why not this line: DO NOT fall into this vicious cycle, or sedentary lifestyle NOT allowed!

Colleagues, friends, health professionals, and finally, old people themselves begin to expect very little in the way of physical function, and these lowered expectations become a self-fulfilling prophecy. Yet, the amount of physical activity that individuals can accomplish and the contribution that it can make to their own quality of life are as different for each individual as is every other aspect of the aging process. The goals for physical functioning among the oldest-old should be *maximum* goals, set as high as possible for each individual. Health care professionals and family members should be aware of the entire hierarchy of physical function and that many individuals in the lower levels of the hierarchy are not there because of fate, but because of inactivity, inadequate information, and low expectations. When everyone around an old individual views disablement and dependency as

the inevitable outcomes of advanced age, then it is easier to give up and become dependent. The two highest levels of the hierarchy of physical function in the old and oldest-old bear testimony to the wide range of function possible in these age groups. The individuals in these groups should provide the basis for much optimism among professionals who, when working with their clients, should share with them expectations for their physical function that are as high as possible.

In Summary

The old and oldest-old probably have a wider range of individual differences in physical function than any other age group. Individuals range from those who are physically incapable of taking care of themselves, and thus are dependent on others, to individuals who are in their 80s and still running marathons. The number of oldest-old who remain very physically active, however, is very small. Rather, the vast majority in this age group are

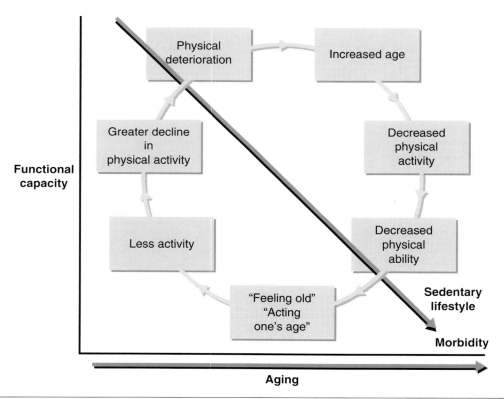

Figure 12.8   The vicious cycle of physical inactivity.
Adapted from Berger and Hecht (1989, pp. 117-157).

sedentary and require substantial health care. A major thrust of professional interest in these age groups has been on assessing physical function for a variety of reasons: to predict which elderly are at risk of becoming functionally dependent and what type of institutional care they should have, if any; to predict future health and long-term care needs, including the distribution and type of services that must be provided to the elderly; to extend the active life expectancy for as many individuals as possible; and to provide a baseline of function by which the effectiveness of prevention or rehabilitation programs can be evaluated.

Four methods have been used to assess physical function in these two age groups: self-report, interviews, observation, and physical performance testing. The self-report technique involves asking the older individuals (or their spouses, friends, relatives, or physicians) about their physical function capabilities. This technique has the advantage of being easy to administer and score, presents practically no risks in the administration of the questions, can be administered by a relatively untrained technician, and is less stressful to the older person. Self-reports provide relatively predictive information. Self-reports also have disadvantages: They depend on the veracity, knowledge, and memory of the responder, and they may be influenced by the administrator of the report. Performance tests, which are thought to be more reliable, are of three types: tests that incorporate the actual physical skills performed on a daily basis, tasks that simulate daily functional skills, and tasks designed to test basic attributes or abilities that underlie daily tasks. Performance tests require more time, more training for administrators, and (usually) specialized equipment and space. Both self-report and performance tests are useful in predicting physical function of the dependent and frail oldest-old.

The physical functioning of the old and oldest-old can be categorized as a hierarchy of five levels of function: the physically dependent, the physically frail, the physically independent, the physically fit, and the physically elite. The physically dependent are those individuals who cannot execute some or all of the basic activities of daily living and are dependent on others for food and other basic functions of living. One of the most commonly used tests of function at this level is

the basic activities of daily living (BADL) self-report scale. Other tests include the Get-Up-and-Go test, the Physical Disability Index (PDI), and the Physical Performance and Mobility Examination (PPME), which are performance tests. Several tests of hand function (i.e., dexterity and strength) also are used.

The next level of the hierarchy includes the physically frail, who can perform the basic activities of daily living but who cannot perform some or all of the activities that are necessary to live independently (e.g., shopping, laundering, and home cleaning). Physical function at this level is tested by self-report of the instrumental activities of daily living (IADLs) and some performance tests, for example, the Physical Performance test and Tinett's mobility assessment.

Physically independent individuals live independently, usually without debilitating symptoms of major chronic diseases, but have relatively low health and fitness reserves. They are vulnerable to unexpected health challenges. More members of the old and oldest-old age group are in this physical function category than in any of the other four categories. Perhaps because this group is in the middle of the hierarchy—neither dependent nor frail, physically fit nor physically elite—their physical function status has not attracted much attention. There are few tests that can discriminate within this group or detect the risk of members of this group moving from physical independence to physical frailty. One type of self-report for this group is the Advanced Activities of Daily Living (AADL) inventory. Another is the American Alliance for Health, Physical Education, Recreation and Dance (AAHPERD) Field Test for older adults.

The physically fit category includes individuals who exercise at least two or three times a week for their health, enjoyment, and well-being. Physically elite individuals train on an almost daily basis and either compete in seniors' sports tournaments or Senior Olympics, work in some type of physically demanding job, such as fire fighting, or maintain a physically rigorous hobby, such as mountain-climbing. The physical function of members in these two groups can be measured with tests that are used with young adults. The physically fit and elite elderly are an inspiration to all people, young or old, because they set high standards of physical function and continue to test the limits of human physical capacity.

Appendix

Williams-Greene Test of Physical and Motor Function*

Harriet G. Williams, PhD
Department of Exercise Science
University of South Carolina
Columbia, SC 29208
803-777-7932

Laurence S. Greene, MS
Department of Kinesiology
University of Colorado
Boulder, CO 80309
303-492-8021

General Classification Schema: Upper-Extremity Function

A. Underlying Components of Upper-Extremity Function
  1. Strength
    a. Hand-grip strength
    Task: Subject squeezes hand dynamometer to produce maximal force. Score is the mean of 3 trials (Potvin et al., 1980).
    b. Elbow flexion
    Task: Using free weights, subject is tested for one-repetition maximum (RM). Weight is added in small increments with 30-s intervals between trials. One RM occurs when subject attempts a weight and cannot fully flex the elbow (Fiatarone et al., 1990).
  2. Steadiness
    a. Aiming control
    Task: Using Lafayette Steadiness Tester, subject holds a stylus in a series of six holes which decrease in diameter from .5 to .125 in. Score for each hole is the number of times the stylus touches the side of the hole in 15 s (counted by an impulse counter). Total score is cumulative counts for six holes (Potvin et al., 1980).
    b. Force control
    Task: Using hand dynamometer, subject watches the indicator dial and squeezes to produce 50% of the maximal force obtained in hand-grip task. Immediately following, subject attempts to reproduce the 50% level without vision. Score is mean absolute deviation from criterion.
B. Simple Arm and Hand Movements
  1. Rapid discrete movements
    a. Moving the arm and hand forward quickly
    Task: With appearance of green light, subject moves the arm and hand from Target A to Target B as quickly as possible. Movement is made forward away from the body. Reaction (nearest ms) and movement time (nearest ms) are recorded. Score is mean of seven trials. Right and left hands are evaluated separately (Pierson & Montoye, 1958).

Note. From *Williams-Greene Test of Physical/Motor Function* by H.G. Williams and L.S. Greene, 1990, Laboratory Report from the Motor Development/Motor Control Laboratory, Department of Exercise Science, University of South Carolina, Columbia. Reprinted by permission.

      b. Moving the arm and hand sideways quickly

         Task: Same as in moving the arm and hand forward quickly *except* that the movement is made in a sideways direction across the body. Score as above.

  2. Repetitive arm and hand movements

      a. Hand tapping

         Task: Subject holds a stylus and taps a metal plate as quickly as possible for 10 s. Score is the mean number of taps in three trials (Greene et al., 1993; Potvin et al., 1980).

      b. Moving the arm and hand forward and backward continuously

         Task: Same as in moving the arm and hand forward quickly *except* that the subject moves the arm and hand back and forth between two target points 10 times. The total time required to perform the series of movements is recorded to the nearest 0.1 s. Score is average of three trials. Both right and left hands are evaluated (Welford, 1977).

      c. Moving arm and hand back and forth sideways continuously

         Task: Same as in moving the arm and hand forward and backward continuously *except* that the movement is back and forth in the horizontal plane across the body (Greene et al., 1993).

  3. Sequential arm and hand movements

      Moving the arm and hand in a changing pattern of movement

      Task: On signal "go," the subject lifts the finger from a telegraph key and performs a sequence of actions that involve two lateral movements, two forward movements, and two backward movements (ordered randomly). Reaction time (nearest ms) and movement time (nearest ms) are recorded. Score is mean of seven trials.

C. Distal Extremity Control: Object Manipulation

  1. Simple unilateral manual dexterity

      Manipulating small objects with the preferred hand

      Task: Frey Pegs-In (Frey, 1979)—Using preferred hand, subject picks up 12 pegs, one at a time from a container, and places them in a pegboard. Score is mean time to place 12 pegs across three trials (Frey, 1979; Greene et al., 1993).

  2. Simple bilateral manual dexterity

      a. Using two hands simultaneously to manipulate small objects

         Task: Purdue pegboard (Agnew et al., 1984)—Subject places pairs of metal pins into columns of pegboard holes using both hands simultaneously. Score is mean time for three trials.

      b. Using two hands in lead-assist to manipulate small objects

         Task: Frey Pegs-Over (Frey, 1979)—Using both hands in a lead-assist manner, subject picks up a peg with one hand and uses the other hand to turn and place peg in slot of pegboard. Score is mean time to place 12 pegs across three trials (Frey, 1979; Greene et al., 1993).

  3. Fine unilateral manual dexterity

      Using preferred hand to complete a sequence of minimal precision movements

      Task: Using a modified version of the Williams's Hand Skills Board, subject uses one hand to open and close a series of fasteners (e.g., screen-door latches, key locks) mounted on a wooden board. Score is mean time for three trials (Williams et al., 1982).

  4. Fine bilateral manual dexterity

      Using both hands to complete sequence of precision movements

      Task: As in 3 above, *except* subject uses both hands to manipulate fasteners.

  5. Finger dexterity

      Using fingers in fine, precision movements

      Task: O'Connor Finger Dexterity—Subject picks up three small pegs at a time and places them into one hole in the pegboard. Score is the mean time to place 12 sets of pegs across three trials (Carter et al., 1993).

D. Distal Extremity Control: Self-Help Actions and Simulated ADLs

  1. Self-help object and implement usage

      a. Using upper extremities to perform selected personal acts

         Tasks: Put on a sweater; button, unbutton, remove; remove and replace lid from small then large jars. Score is time to complete actions (Potvin et al., 1980).

b. Using upper extremities to perform selected self-help acts involving implements
   Tasks: Use a spoon to scoop and transfer five kidney beans from desktop to container; use scissors to cut a circle 8 in. in diameter. Score is time to complete actions (Jebsen et al., 1969).

c. Using upper extremities to perform simple pencil and paper tasks
   Tasks: Subject is asked (a) to draw a series of straight lines in vertical, horizontal, and diagonal directions within specified boundaries, (b) to draw a series of simple geometric figures, and (c) to copy a series of complex designs. Time to complete each task is recorded to nearest 0.1 s. Accuracy of performance is also evaluated (Smith & Green, 1962; Welford, 1977).

d. Using upper extremities to perform complex pencil and paper tasks
   Tasks: Subject is asked (a) to write a series of 10 digits, (b) to copy a series of 10 letters randomly selected from the alphabet, and (c) to copy a sentence made up of 10 words. Time to complete each task is recorded to nearest 0.1 s. Accuracy of performance is also evaluated.

General Classification Schema: Mobility

A. Underlying Components of Mobility
   1. Strength and flexibility
      a. Leg and back strength
         Task: Using Lafayette Leg and Back Dynamometer, subject is tested for maximal strength in a single repetition.
      b. Knee extension strength
         Task: Using a weight-and-pulley system, subject is tested for one-repetition maximum (RM). Weight is added in small increments with 30-s intervals between trials. One RM occurs when subject attempts a weight and cannot fully extend knee (Fiatarone et al., 1990).
      c. Lower back and leg flexibility
         Task: Using standard sit-and-reach test, subject sits on the floor with legs fully extended and reaches forward as far as possible. Score is distance reached at finger tips on measuring device.
      d. Neck flexibility
         Task: Neck turning—Subject stands with feet together and turns head from side to side continuously for 10 s while looking up. Performance is scored on a 3 point scale: 1 = individual begins to fall or needs help; 2 = individual has to move feet to maintain balance or cannot maintain continuous movement; 3 = individual performs continuous movement with no help. Score is total points in two trials (Fiatarone et al., 1990).
   2. General mobility maneuvers
      a. Movement from supine to kneel
         Task: Task is demonstrated; subject lies in supine position; on signal "go," subject moves to a kneeling position. Time to nearest 0.1 s is recorded. Score is average of three trials.
      b. Movement from supine to upright stance
         Task: Subject lies in supine position; on signal "go," subject moves to a standing position. Time to nearest 0.1 s is recorded. Score is average of three trials.
      c. Movement from sitting to standing position
         Task: Subject sits in chair; on signal "go," subject rises from chair and assumes an upright standing position with hands on hips. Time to nearest 0.1 s is recorded; score is average of three trials. Use of hands and process characteristics of the movement are also recorded (Fiatarone et al., 1990; Tinetti, 1986).
      d. Movement from standing to sitting position
         Task: Subject stands with feet together, hands on hips; on signal "go," subject lowers the body onto a standard-sized chair. Task is complete when hands are placed in lap. Time to the nearest 0.1 s is recorded. Score is average of three trials. Process characteristics of movement are also recorded (Jefferys et al., 1969).

     e. Stepping onto and off of objects

      Task: Stable objects of three different heights are placed side by side. Subject stands in front of object, places both feet together, then steps down from the object and places both feet together. Subject immediately continues to next two objects in turn and repeats the task. Time to step onto and off of the three objects is recorded to the nearest 0.1 s. Score is the average of three trials. Process characteristics of the movement are also recorded (Jefferys et al., 1969).

  3. Balance

     a. Static balance with visual control

      (1) Stationary balance on two feet, wide base of support

      Task: Rhomberg stance test is used (Bohannon et al., 1984); score is mean time in balance for three trials.

      (2) Stationary balance on two feet, narrow base of support

      Task: Sharpened Rhomberg stance is used (Heitman et al., 1989); score is mean time in balance for three trials.

      (3) Stationary balance on preferred foot

      Task: Subject stands with hands at sides on rigid surface; eyes are fixated on target 6 ft away. Loss of balance occurs when nonsupport foot is touched to the ground. Score is mean time in balance for three trials (Briggs et al., 1989).

     b. Static balance without visual control

      (1) Stationary balance on two feet, wide base of support

      Task: Rhomberg stance with eyes closed is used. Score is mean time in balance for three trials (Bohannon et al., 1984).

      (2) Stationary balance on two feet, narrow base of support

      Task: Sharpened Rhomberg with eyes closed is used. Score is mean time in balance for three trials (Briggs et al., 1989).

      (3) Stationary balance on preferred foot

      Task: Same as for eyes open. Score is mean time in balance for three trials (Briggs et al., 1989).

     c. Static balance with perturbation of body weight

      (1) Stationary balance on two feet with perturbation on wide base of support

      Task: The Postural Stress test is used (Chandler et al., 1990).

      (2) Stationary balance on two feet with perturbation on narrow base of support

      Task: A modification of the Postural Stress test (Chandler et al., 1990) in which the subject stands with the feet in a tandem position.

B. Gait and Mobility Functions

  1. Simple gait control

     a. Walking a straight, wide path

      Task: On signal "go," subject walks, using a natural gait, through a pathway 10 ft long and 1 ft wide. Time to the nearest 0.1 s is recorded; score is the average time for three trials. Cadence, number of steps, and number of errors are also recorded. An error occurs if the subject steps on or outside the boundaries of the pathway (Carter et al., 1993; Williams & Hornberger, 1984).

     b. Walking a straight, moderately wide path

      Task: Same as for walking a straight, wide path; pathway is 10 ft long and 6 in. wide.

     c. Walking a straight, narrow path

      Task: Same as for walking a straight, wide path; pathway is 10 ft long and 2 in. wide.

  2. Precision gait control

     a. Walking a straight, wide path with precision

      Task: Same as for walking a straight, wide path *except* the subject is required to walk using a heel-to-toe pattern with hands on hips. The path is 10 ft long and 1 ft wide.

     b. Walking a straight, moderately wide path with precision

      Task: Same as for walking a straight, wide path *except* the subject is required to walk using a heel-to-toe pattern with hands on hips. The path is 10 ft long and 6 in. wide.

     c. Walking a straight, narrow path with precision

      Task: Same as for walking a straight, wide path *except* the subject is required to walk using a heel-to-toe pattern with hands on hips. The path is 10 ft long and 2 in. wide.

3. Maximum gait speed
   a. Maximum speed of walking, wide path
      Task: Same as walking a straight, wide path *except* the subject is asked to walk as fast as possible. The pathway is 10 ft long and 1 ft wide.
   b. Maximum speed of walking, narrow path
      Task: Same as walking a straight, wide path *except* the subject is asked to walk as fast as possible. The pathway is 10 ft long and 2 in. wide.
4. Body Agility
   a. Walking a wide, curved or circular path at maximum speed
      Task: On signal "go," subject walks through a curved pathway 10 ft long and 1 ft wide as fast as possible. There is one curve to the right and one curve to the left. Scoring is the same as for simple gait control tasks. Process characteristics of the movement are also observed.
   b. Walking a straight, wide path with two changes of direction at maximal speed
      Task: On signal "go," subject walks through a straight pathway 10 ft long and 1 ft wide. There is one sharp (right angle) turn to the right and one right angle turn to the left. Scoring is the same as in walking a wide, curved or circular path at maximum speed.
   c. Walking a narrow, curved or circular path at maximum speed
      Task: Same as for walking a wide, curved or circular path at maximum speed. The pathway is 10 ft long and 6 in. wide.
   d. Walking a narrow, straight path with two changes of direction at maximum speed
      Task: Same as for walking a straight, wide path with two changes of direction at maximum speed. The pathway is 10 ft long and 6 in. wide.
   e. Moving around obstacles at maximum speed
      Task: Three 2-ft-high rubber cones are placed at equal distances throughout a 10-ft-long pathway that is 1 ft wide. On signal "go," subject walks as fast as possible through the pathway around the cones and returns to the starting point, again moving around the cones as fast as possible. Time to the nearest .1 s is recorded; score is the average of three trials.

References

Agnew, J., Bolla-Wilson, K., Kawas, C.H., & Bleecker, M.L. (1988). Purdue pegboard: Age and sex norms for people 40 years and older. *Developmental Neuropsychology*, **4**, 29-35.

American College of Sports Medicine. (1991). *Guidelines for exercise testing and prescription* (4th ed.). Philadelphia: Lea & Febiger.

American Medical Association. (1990). White paper on elderly health: Report of the Council on Scientific Affairs. *Archives of Internal Medicine*, **150**, 2459-2472.

Berger, B.G., & Hecht, L. (1989). Exercise, aging, and psychological well-being: The mind–body question. In A.C. Ostrow (Ed.), *Aging and motor behavior* (pp. 117-157). Indianapolis, IN: Benchmark Press.

Besdine, R.W., Wakefield, K.M., & Williams, T.F. (1988). Assessing function in the elderly. *Patient Care*, **22**, 69-79.

Bohannon, R.W., Larkin, P.A., Cook, A.C., Gear, J., & Singer, J. (1984). Decrease in timed balance test scores with aging. *Physical Therapy*, **64**, 1067-1070.

Branch, L.G., Guralnik, J.M., Foley, D.J., Kohout, F.J., Wetle, T.T., Ostfeld, A., & Katz, S. (1991). Active life expectancy for 10,000 Caucasian men and women in three communities. *Journal of Gerontology: Medical Sciences*, **46**, M145-M150.

Briggs, R.C., Gossman, M.R., Drews, J.E., & Shaddeau, S.A. (1989). Balance performance among noninstitutionalized elderly women. *Physical Therapy*, **69**, 748-756.

Bruce, R.A. (1977). Exercise testing for ventricular function. *New England Journal of Medicine*, **296**, 671-675.

Bruce, R.A., Cooper, M.N., Gey, G.O., Fisher, L.D., & Peterson, D.R. (1973). Variations in responses to maximal exercise in health and cardiovascular disease. *Angiology*, **24**, 691-702.

Bruce, R.A., Kusumi, F., & Hosmer, D. (1973). Maximal oxygen intake and nomographic assessment of functional aerobic impairment in cardiovascular disease. *American Heart Journal*, **85**, 545-562.

Carter, J.S., Williams, H.G., & Macera, C.A. (1993). Relationships between physical activity habits and functional neuromuscular capacities in healthy older adults. *Journal of Applied Gerontology*, **12**, 283-293.

Chandler, J.M., Duncan, P.W., & Studenski, S.A. (1990). Balance performance on the postural stress test: Comparison of young adults, healthy elderly, and fallers. *Physical Therapy*, **70**, 410-415.

Cole, K.J., & Abbs, J.H. (1986). Coordination of three-joint digit movements for rapid finger-thumb grasp. *Journal of Neurophysiology*, **55**, 1407-1423.

Deniston, O.L., & Jette, A. (1980). A functional status assessment instrument: Validation in an elderly population. *Health Services Research*, **15**, 21-34.

Duke University Center for the Study of Aging and Human Development. (1978). *Multidimensional functional assessment: The OARS methodology*. Durham, DC: Duke University.

Elam, J.T., Graney, M.J., Beaver, T., Derwi, D.E., Applegate, W.B., & Miller, S.T. (1991). Comparison of subjective ratings of function with observed functional ability of frail older persons. *American Journal of Public Health*, **81**, 1127-1130.

Falconer, J., Hughes, S.L., Naughton, B.J., Singer, B., Chang, R.W., & Sinacore, J.M. (1991). Self-report and performance-based hand function tests as correlates of dependency in the elderly. *Journal of the American Geriatrics Society*, **39**, 695-699.

Feinstein, A.R., Josephy, B.R., & Wells, C.K. (1986). Scientific and clinical problems in indexes of functional disability. *Annals of Internal Medicine*, **105**, 413-420.

Fiatarone, M.S., Marks, D.C., Ryan, N.D., Meredith, C.N., Lipsitz, L.A., & Evans, J.W. (1990). High-intensity strength training in nonagenarians. *Journal of the American Medical Association*, **263**, 3029-3034.

Fitti, J.E., & Kovar, M.G. (1988, September). *The supplement on aging to the 1984 National Health Interview Survey. Vital and health statistics*. Series 1, Number 21 (DHHS Publ. No. (PHS) 89-3447). Washington, DC: National Center for Health Statistics.

Frey, C.J. (1979). *Development of alternative fine motor manipulatory tasks*. Unpublished master's thesis, University of Toledo, Toledo, OH.

Gerety, M.B., Mulrow, M.R., Tuley, M.R., Huzuda, H., Lichtenstein, J.M., O'Neil, M., Gorton, A., & Bohannon, R. (1993). Development and validation of a physical performance instrument for the functionly impaired elderly: The Physical Disability Index (PDI). *Journal of Gerontology: Medical Sciences*, **48**, M33-M38.

Greene, L.S., Williams, H.G., Macera, C.A., & Carter, J.S. (1993). Identifying dimensions of physical (motor) functional capacity in healthy older adults. *Journal of Aging and Health*, **5**, 163-178.

Gromak, P.A., & Waskel, S.A. (1989). Functional assessment in the elderly: A literature review. *Physical and Occupational Therapy in Geriatrics*, **7**, 1-12.

Gross-Andrew, S., & Zimmer, A. (1978). Incentives to families caring for disabled elderly: Research and demonstration project to strengthen the natural support system. *Journal of Gerontological Social Work*, **1**, 119-135.

Hackel, M.E., Wolfe, G.A., Bang, S.M., & Canfield, J.S. (1992). Changes in hand function in the aging adult as determined by the Jebsen Test of Hand Function. *Physical Therapy*, **72**, 373-377.

Hart, B.A., & Abbs, J.H. (1990). Load sensitive regulation of precision grip: Differences in young and old subjects. *Neuroscience Abstracts*, **16**, 892.

Hart, B.A., & Abbs, J.H. (1992). Voluntary and automatic components of precision grip force regulation in aging. *North American Society for the Psychology of Sport and Physical Activity Abstracts*, p. 93.

Heitman, D.K., Gossmann, M.R., Shaddeau, S.A., & Jackson, J.R. (1989). Balance performance and step width in non-institutionalized elderly female fallers and nonfallers. *Physical Therapy*, **69**, 923-931.

Hughes, S.L., Edelman, P., Chang, R.W., Singer, R.H., & Schuette, P. (1991). The GERI-AIMS. Reliability and validity of the arthritis impact measurement scales adapted for elderly respondents. *Arthritis and Rheumatism*, **34**, 856-865.

Jebsen, R.H., Taylor, N., Trieschmann, R.B., Trotter, M.J., & Howard, L.A. (1969). An objective and standardized test of hand function. *Archives of Physical Medicine and Rehabilitation*, **50**, 311-319.

Jefferys, M., Millard, J.B., Hyman, M., & Warren, M.D. (1969). A set of tests for measuring motor impairment in prevalence studies. *Journal of Chronic Diseases*, **22**, 303-319.

Jette, A.M., Branch, L.G., & Berlin, J. (1990). Musculoskeletal impairments and physical disablement among the aged. *Journal of Gerontology: Medical Sciences*, **45**, M203-M208.

Kane, R.A., & Kane, R.L. (1981). *Assessing the elderly: A practical guide to measurement*. Lexington, MA: Lexington Books.

Katz, S., Branch, L.G., Branson, M.H., Papsidero, J.A., Beck, J.C., & Greer, D.S. (1983). Active life expectancy. *New England Journal of Medicine*, **309**, 1218-1224.

Katz, S.K., Downs, T.D., Cash, H.R., & Grotz, R.C. (1970). Progress in development of the index of ADL. *The Gerontologist*, **10**, 20-30.

Katz, S.C., Ford, A.B., Moskowitz, R.W., Jackson, B.A., & Jaffe, M.W. (1963). Studies of illness in the aged. The index of ADL: A standardized measure of biological and psychosocial function. *Journal of the American Medical Association*, **185**, 914-919.

Kempen, G.I.J.M., & Suurmeijer, T.P.B.M. (1990). The development of a hierarchical polychotomous ADL-IADL scale for noninstitutionalized elders. *The Gerontologist*, **30**, 497-502.

Kimura, M., Hirakawa, K., & Morimoto, T. (1990). Physical performance survey in 900 aged individuals. In M. Kaneko (Ed.), *Fitness for the aged, disabled, and industrial worker* (pp. 55-60). Champaign, IL: Human Kinetics.

Kuo, G.H. (1990). Physical fitness of the people in Taipei including the aged. In M. Kaneko (Ed.), *Fitness for the aged, disabled, and industrial worker* (pp. 21-24). Champaign, IL: Human Kinetics.

Kuriansky, J.B., & Gurland, B. (1976). Performance test of activities of daily living. *International Journal of Aging and Human Development*, **7**, 343-352.

Lawton, M.P. (1972). Assessing the competence of older people. In D. Kent, R. Kastenbaum, & S. Sherwood (Eds.), *Research planning and action for the elderly* (pp. 122-143). New York: Behavioral Publications.

Lawton, M.P., & Brody, E.M. (1969). Assessment of older people: Self-maintaining and instrumental activities of daily living. *The Gerontologist*, **9**, 179-186.

Lemsky, C., Miller, C.J., Nevitt, M., & Winograd, C. (1991). Reliability and validity of a physical performance and mobility examination for hospitalized elderly. *Society of Gerontology (Abstracts)*, **31**, 221.

Mahoney, F.I., & Barthel, D.W. (1965). Functional evaluation: The Barthel Index. *Maryland State Medical Journal*, **14**, 61-65.

Mathias, S., Nayak, U.S., & Isaacs, B. (1986). Balance in elderly patients: The "Get-Up-and-Go" test. *Archives of Physical Medicine and Rehabilitation*, **67**, 387-389.

McArdle, W.D., Katch, F.I., & Katch, V.L. (1991). *Exercise physiology*. Philadelphia: Lea & Febiger.

National Institute on Aging. (1986). *Established populations for epidemiologic studies of the elderly: Resource data book* (NIH Publication No. 86-2443). Washington, DC: Author.

National Institutes of Health Consensus Development Conference Statement. (1988). Geriatric assessment methods for clinical decision-making.

Journal of the American Geriatrics Society, **36**, 342-347.

Osness, W.H. (1987). Assessment of physical function among older adults. In D. Leslie (Ed.), *Mature stuff*. Reston, VA: American Association for Health, Physical Education, Recreation and Dance.

Pierson, W.R., & Montoye, H.J. (1958). Movement time, reaction time, and age. *Journal of Gerontology*, **13**, 418-420.

Podsiadlo, D., & Richardson, S. (1989). Timed "Up-and-Go"—A useful screen of functional mobility. *The Gerontologist*, **29**, 257A.

Pollock, M.L., & Wilmore, J.H. (1990). *Exercise in health and disease* (2nd ed.). Philadelphia: W.B. Saunders.

Potvin, A., Syndulko, K., Tourtellotte, W.W., Lemmon, J.A., & Potvin, J.H. (1980). Human neurologic function and the aging process. *Journal of the American Geriatrics Society*, **38**, 1-9.

Rakowski, W., & Mor, V. (1992). The association of physical activity with mortality among older adults in the longitudinal study of aging (1984-1988). *Journal of Gerontology: Medical Sciences*, **47**, M122-M129.

Reuben, D.B., Laliberte, L., Hiris, J., & Mor, V. (1990). A hierarchical exercise scale to measure function at the advanced activities of daily living (AADL) level. *Journal of the American Geriatrics Society*, **38**, 855-861.

Reuben, D.B., & Siu, A.L. (1990). An objective measure of physical function of elderly outpatients: The physical performance test. *Journal of the American Geriatrics Society*, **38**, 1105-1112.

Reuben, D.B., Siu, A.L., & Kimpau, S. (1992). The predictive validity of self-report and performance-based measures of function and health. *Journal of Gerontology: Medical Sciences*, **47**, M106-M110.

Reuben, D.B., & Solomon, D.H. (1989). Assessment in geriatrics: Of caveats and names. *Journal of the American Geriatrics Society*, **37**, 570-572.

Rosow, I., & Breslau, N. (1966). A Guttman health scale for the aged. *Journal of Gerontology*, **21**, 556-559.

Rubenstein, L.V., Calkins, D.R., Greenfield, S., Jette, A.M., Meenan, R.F., Nevins, M.A., Rubenstein, L.Z., Wasson, J.H., & Williams, M.E. (1989). Health status assessment for elderly patients: Report of the Society of General Internal Medicine Task Force on Health Assessment. *Journal of the American Geriatrics Society*, **37**, 562-569.

Schnelle, J.F., MacRae, P.G., Simmons, S.F., Uman, G., Nigam, J., Nitta, M., Ouslander, J.G., & Bates-Jensen, B. (in press). Assessing mobility functioning in nursing home residents with severe cognitive impairment. *Archives of Physical Medicine.*

Schoening, H.A., Anderegg, L., Bergstrom, D., Fonda, M., Steinke, N., & Ulrich, T. (1965). Numerical scoring of self-care status of patients. *Archives of Physical Medicine and Rehabilitation,* **46**, 689-697.

Shiffman, L.M. (1992). Effects of aging on adult hand function. *American Journal of Occupational Therapy,* **46**, 785-792.

Siu, A.L., Reuben, D.B., & Hays, R.D. (1990). Hierarchical measures of physical function in ambulatory geriatrics. *Journal of the American Geriatrics Society,* **38**, 1113-1119.

Smith, K., & Green, D. (1962). Scientific motion study and aging process in performance. *Ergonomics,* **5**, 155-164.

Sollerman, C., & Sperling, L. (1978). Evaluation of activities of daily living function—Especially hand function. *Scandinavian Journal of Rehabilitation Medicine,* **10**, 139-143.

Solomon, D.H., Jodd, H.J., Sier, H.C., Rubenstein, L.Z., & Morley, J.E. (1988). Geriatric assessment: Methods for clinical decision-making. *Annals of Internal Medicine,* **108**, 718-732.

Spector, W.D., Katz, S., Murphy, J.B., & Fulton, J.P. (1987). The hierarchical relationship between activities of daily living and instrumental activities of daily living. *Journal of Chronic Diseases,* **40**, 481-489.

Tahara, J., Sakimoto, S., Uchino, K., & Matsumoto, F. (1990). Longitudinal study on motor fitness tests for the aged. In M. Kaneko (Ed.), *Fitness for the aged, disabled, and industrial worker* (pp. 15-17). Champaign, IL: Human Kinetics.

Tinetti, M.E. (1986). Performance-oriented assessment of mobility problems in elderly patients. *Journal of the American Geriatrics Society,* **34**, 119-126.

Tonino, R.P., & Driscoll, P.A. (1988). Reliability of maximal and submaximal parameters of treadmill testing for the measurement of physical training in older persons. *Journal of Gerontology: Medical Sciences,* **43**, M101-M104.

U.S. Department of Health, Education, and Welfare (DHEW). (1978). *Working document on patient care management.* Washington, DC: U.S. Government Printing Office.

Varekamp, I., Smit, C., Rosendaal, F.R., Bröcker-Vriends, A., Briët, E., Van Dijck, H., & Suurmeijer, T.P.B.M. (1989). Employment of individuals with haemophilia in the Netherlands. *Social Science and Medicine,* **28**, 261-270.

Welford, A.T. (1977). Motor performance. In G. Birren and K. Schaie (Eds.), *Handbook of the psychology of aging.* New York: Van Nostrand Reinhold.

Wilkins, R., & Adams, O.B. (1983). Health expectancy in Canada, late 1970s: Demographic, regional, and social dimensions. *American Journal of Public Health,* **73**, 1073-1080.

Williams, H.G., & Greene, L.S. (1990). *Williams-Greene Test of Physical/Motor Function.* Laboratory report from the Motor Development/Motor Control laboratory, Department of Exercise Science, University of South Carolina, Columbia.

Williams, J.H., Drinka, T.J.K., Greenberg, J.R., Farrell-Holtan, J., Euhardy, R., & Schram, M. (1991). Development and testing of the Assessment of Living Skills and Resources (ALSAR) in elderly community-dwelling veterans. *The Gerontologist,* **31**, 84-91.

Williams, M.E., Hadler, N., & Earp, J.A.L. (1982). Manual ability as a marker of dependency in geriatric women. *Journal of Chronic Diseases,* **35**, 115-122.

Williams, M.E., & Hornberger, J.C. (1984). A quantitative method of identifying older persons at risk for increasing long-term care services. *Journal of Chronic Diseases,* **37**, 705-711.

Wolfson, L., Whipple, R., Amerman, P., & Tobin, J.N. (1990). Gait assessment in the elderly: A gait abnormality rating scale and its relation to falls. *Journal of Gerontology,* **45**, 12-19.

Zedlewski, S.R., Barnes, R.O., Burt, M.R., McBride, T.D., & Meyer, J.A. (1990). *The needs of the elderly in the 21st century.* Washington, DC: Urban Institute Press.

CHAPTER 13

Job Performance of the Older Worker

The 1935 Social Security Act established the age of 65 years as the minimum age at which full benefits could be received. Since that time, the age of 65 years has become synonymous with retirement. However, within the past 10 years a concerted effort has been made by many older people to extend the years of their employment. Many older adults want to extend their work life because they are not ready to lose the satisfaction, self-identification, and financial resources that they derive from their employment.

Cultural ideas of oldness have been changing radically, as more and more vigorously active and robust people in their 60s and 70s are continuing their work, hobbies, and social activities. In 1900, people were considered old in their 40s. In the 1960s, people were old in their 60s. Today, many people feel that they are not old unless they are in their 80s. Charles Longino, director of the Center for Social Research in Aging at the University of Miami, calls this "youth creep." He points out that Jane Fonda at age 47, whom most people view as a vital and robust model of energy, was 17 years older than the woman standing next to the pitchfork-holding farmer in Grant Wood's classic painting, *American Gothic*. These robust elderly, whose activities challenge the dogma of aging, are serving as role models for those in their late 50s and early 60s. (Some of these role models are described in chapter 14.) It is understandable that many individuals in their 60s, who expect to live another 20 years and who enjoy their job or need the salary, are outraged when they are arbitrarily forced into retirement. Many older adults feel that being forcibly retired from a job is tantamount to being officially relieved of adult responsibilities and economic contributions to society—in short, being dismissed as a vital and important member of the community. Retirement is especially difficult to deal with when the individual does not feel old psychologically. It also generally means learning to live on a smaller and fixed income.

Employers, especially large corporations, have a long history of embracing the stereotypes of aging. Until recently, many employers reacted to depressed economic circumstances by resorting to early retirement in an attempt to cut costs (Winn, 1991). In some cases, forced early retirement of older workers has a double benefit for employers; not only is the total number of employees reduced, but in most cases the salaries of older workers are higher than those of younger workers. The tension between employers and older workers who want to remain on the job or want to be considered viable applicants for a job resulted in several successful litigations in the late 1970s and 1980s, and in the passage of legislation that has made it somewhat more difficult to discriminate against older adults in the workplace. Nevertheless, many job-related situations exist in which age is a major criterion by which personnel decisions are made.

The Aging Worker

Negative attitudes and discriminatory actions by employers toward older workers may be driven by employers' perceptions that older adults are less mentally and physically competent, that their productivity level is lower, and that their accident potential is higher than that of young workers. These negative beliefs close off job opportunities for older adults by passing them over for promotions and mandating retirement at a specified chronological age. But older adults also have accrued substantial experience, either life experience or job-related experience, that enhances their capabilities and even provides advantages that would enable them to succeed in many types of work. Older adults also have personal and social characteristics that enhance their usefulness to an employer. Each of these issues is important and will be discussed, but our primary focus is on the role that physical competence plays in limiting work opportunities for older adults.

Mental Competence

So many research studies in the psychological literature have produced results that support an age-related decline in cognitive function that this notion is probably the basis for many of the attitudes of employers toward older adults. Results from such studies also have served to support the stereotypes that many young adults believe describe all older adults.

On psychological tests that require rapid information processing, scanning of information, and short- and long-term memory, the "average" older person does not perform as well as younger adults. (These differences were discussed at length in chapter 7.) Older people as a group have been reported to have difficulty mentally manipulating data and monitoring responses (Welford, 1958). Although controversy abounds, many researchers have found older adults to be less successful in laboratory tasks in which they must divide their attention between two or more tasks, sustain their attention in tasks of vigilance, or be selective in their attention to specific goals (McDowd, Vercruyssen, & Birren, 1991). That older adults as a group seem to be more easily distracted from the task at hand has been a robust observation for many years. They tend to allow irrelevant ideas, opinions, experiences, and daydreams to intrude into their thoughts as they perform these tasks. They also as a group tend to approach and execute tasks with considerably more caution, which slows their performance and may limit the number of spontaneous solutions. This same trait, however, may also result in more accurate job performance. Finally, persons of advanced age in key positions may be of concern to employers whose business depends on innovation, product development, and novel ideas, because both informal observation and psychometric measurement have led to the conclusion that creativity seems to peak in early or middle adulthood (Simonton, 1990).

However, when age-related declines in cognitive function are related to job performance, several factors should be considered. Many of the age differences seen in cognitive function in older adults may be attributed more to the generally lower levels of health in these older age groups than to their age per se. Also, most of the age-related deficits that have been discussed have been determined from laboratory tests, which tend to be largely irrelevant to work situations. Such tests have little real-world meaningfulness that would create high motivation for the subjects to perform as well as they can. Also discussed in chapter 7, these laboratory tasks usually require the subjects to work at their utmost capacity, whereas almost no job tasks in the work force require this degree of speed or maximum capacity.

On the positive side of the ledger are the reports that older workers exhibit better judgment and intelligence (Comfort, 1977) and are thought to be less impulsive in their work (Jarvik, 1973). A valid and reliable measure of wisdom has not been developed, but experts in the field generally think that older adults exhibit more wisdom than do younger subjects (Simonton, 1990). Also, as will be discussed in more detail later, on-the-job experience in most occupations can compensate for losses in cognitive function.

Physical Competence

Previous chapters have presented ample evidence that cardiovascular endurance, strength, speed of response, coordination, and skill do in fact decline with age in the average adult. Consequently, on the surface the evidence seems to support the proposition that older adults have inadequate reserves to cope with the production requirements of industry that demand physical endurance (Eisdorfer & Wilkie, 1977). Kovar and LaCroix (1987) surveyed the ability of 38.3 million individuals to perform work-related activities. Individuals included in the study ranged in age from 55 to 74 years and had worked at some time since they were age 45. The five work-related activities analyzed in this study were

- mobility (walking 1/4 mile and walking up 10 stairs without resting),
- endurance for confined activities (standing and sitting for 2 hr),
- lower- and upper-body strength (stooping, crouching, or kneeling and lifting or carrying 10 or 25 lb),
- freedom of movement (reaching up overhead and reaching out to shake hands), and
- fine motor skills (grasping with fingers).

Fifty-eight percent of this population executed the work-related activities successfully. For the remaining 42%, the activities requiring lower-body strength were the most difficult. This was particularly true for women, who found the task of lifting or carrying 25 lb particularly difficult (see Table 13.1). In fact, more women than men had difficulty performing these work-associated activities, though this apparent gender difference is partly a function of the larger body size and weight of the men. That is, the 25-lb weight represented a larger proportion of body weight for women than for men. As age increased from 55 to 74 years, the percentage of the population that had difficulty performing mobility, endurance, and lower-body strength activities doubled. Those activities dependent on freedom of movement and fine motor skills were much less affected by age. Kovar and LaCroix (1987) concluded that when the physical demands of most jobs are considered, many of the people who had retired for reasons other than health could have remained in the work force had they chosen to do so.

For the overwhelming majority of jobs, physical strength and endurance need not be a prohibitive factor for several reasons. First, a relatively small percentage of jobs have large strength and endurance demands, and it has already been shown that many people can resist aging well into their 70s by choosing to lead a lifestyle that maintains cardiovascular endurance (chapter 4) and strength (chapter 5). Second, individual differences are so great that many physically trained older adults can outperform workers half their age (see chapter 14). Third, older workers learn to replace uneconomical responses with less demanding and more economical ones (Bartley, 1977), or to use different strategies to compensate for a loss of psychomotor speed. Fourth, people who stay active and

Table 13.1
Percentage of People 55-74 Years of Age Who Have Worked Since Age 45 With Difficulty or Are Unable to Perform Specified Activities: United States, 1984

Activity	Both sexes				
	Total	55-59 years	60-64 years	65-69 years	70-74 years
	Number				
Sample	9,805	2,000	1,968	3,285	2,552
	Number in thousands				
Estimated population	32,305	9,645	9,235	7,561	5,864
Walking 1/4 mile	Percent of population				
Difficulty	17.6	12.4	16.5	20.0	25.0
Unable	7.6	5.4	8.0	8.7	9.5
Walking up 10 steps					
Difficulty	15.2	10.9	14.5	16.9	21.4
Unable	6.9	5.2	6.9	7.4	9.5
Standing on feet for 2 hr					
Difficulty	22.0	15.1	20.7	26.1	30.1
Unable	9.0	6.5	8.3	10.9	11.6
Sitting for 2 hr					
Difficulty	9.7	8.3	10.6	10.4	9.7
Unable	5.9	5.3	6.5	6.4	5.5
Stooping, crouching, or kneeling					
Difficulty	27.8	20.1	27.0	30.9	37.8
Unable	12.6	9.4	12.5	13.7	16.5
Reaching up overhead					
Difficulty	11.5	9.0	11.2	13.1	14.2
Unable	6.4	4.6	6.7	7.3	7.7
Reaching out to shake hands					
Difficulty	1.8	1.8	1.6	1.8	2.0
Unable	1.0	1.0	1.1	1.0	1.2
Grasping with fingers					
Difficulty	7.8	6.4	7.4	8.7	9.5
Unable	5.0	4.2	5.0	5.2	5.9
Lifting or carrying 25 lb					
Difficulty	23.1	17.0	22.5	24.8	32.0
Unable	6.9	6.2	6.0	7.3	9.1
Lifting or carrying 10 lb					
Difficulty	7.3	5.0	6.9	8.2	10.5
Unable	2.6	2.2	2.5	2.7	3.0

Note. From Kovar and LaCroix (1987, p. 5).

	Men					Women			
Total	55-59 years	60-64 years	65-69 years	70-74 years	Total	55-59 years	60-64 years	65-69 years	70-74 years
				Number					
5,100	1,036	1,067	1,731	1,266	4,705	964	901	1,554	1,286
				Number in thousands					
16,936	5,023	5,037	3,969	2,907	15,368	4,622	4,197	3,592	2,957
				Percent of population					
17.4	12.3	17.0	20.1	23.3	17.9	12.6	15.8	19.9	26.6
7.6	5.0	7.9	9.4	8.7	7.7	5.8	8.0	7.9	10.2
12.8	9.5	12.1	14.2	17.9	17.9	12.4	17.4	19.7	24.8
5.6	3.8	5.3	6.0	8.7	8.4	6.7	8.8	8.8	10.2
20.6	13.5	18.9	25.5	28.9	23.5	16.8	22.8	26.7	31.2
8.1	5.2	7.2	10.6	11.5	9.9	7.8	9.7	11.3	11.6
8.4	7.0	8.9	9.9	7.9	11.2	9.8	12.7	10.9	11.6
4.9	4.2	5.4	5.7	4.1	7.1	6.4	7.9	7.2	6.9
24.6	18.0	23.4	27.7	33.7	31.4	22.4	31.3	34.3	41.7
11.4	8.3	11.1	12.5	15.9	13.9	10.7	14.2	15.0	17.2
10.5	9.0	9.9	12.4	11.6	12.7	9.1	12.8	13.8	16.6
5.7	3.9	6.3	6.9	6.0	7.2	5.4	7.1	7.7	9.5
1.6	1.5	1.3	1.8	2.0	2.0	2.2	1.9	1.8	2.0
1.0	0.8	0.9	1.1	1.0	1.1	1.2	1.2	0.8	1.4
6.3	4.5	6.0	7.1	8.8	9.4	8.5	9.0	10.5	10.2
4.0	2.6	4.0	4.5	5.4	6.1	5.8	6.2	6.1	6.3
15.9	11.6	15.4	16.8	23.1	31.1	22.9	31.0	33.8	40.8
4.8	3.5	3.8	5.6	7.5	9.3	9.1	8.7	9.3	10.7
5.3	3.7	5.4	6.6	6.3	9.4	6.4	8.7	9.9	14.6
1.9	1.6	1.9	2.2	1.7	3.3	2.8	3.3	3.3	4.3

continue their jobs maintain their physical skills and can outperform younger, less experienced workers. Martha Graham, one of the most extraordinary performers in the history of modern dance, did not stop performing until she was well into her nineties. She maintained impressive lower-leg strength, balance, agility, and flexibility to the end of her dancing career.

Productivity

One of the concerns that employers voice about older workers is whether older workers can maintain their productivity and contribute as much as younger workers. It is typical for individuals to suspect that older workers cannot maintain the pace that younger workers set. However, when productivity is systematically studied in the workplace, the results show that this perception is wrong. In several early studies, the difference between young and old worker output was not significant, because the older workers were as accurate as young ones (Kelleher & Quirk, 1973; Kutscher & Walker, 1960; Meier & Kerr, 1976). Furthermore, although workers within each age group varied considerably with regard to their productivity, the older cohorts exhibited less variation than did the young cohorts. In another study, older workers were more accurate than young ones, again demonstrating the classic speed-accuracy trade-off often seen in aging studies (Bartley, 1977).

In a more recent study, the factors of productivity, employee turnover, accidents, and absenteeism were analyzed in two types of jobs in a garment industry; one job placed a premium on speed of performance and the other on skill (Giniger, Dispenzieri, & Eisenberg, 1983). Specifically, they tested the theory that productivity would be lower and employee turnover, accidents, and absenteeism higher among those workers whose job required speed and that the opposite would be true among workers whose jobs required primarily skill, not speed. An example of a speed-intensive job was the clipper, who separates articles by clipping the connecting threads. One of the skill jobs was the marker, who outlined patterns on cloth to facilitate cutting and sewing operations. The researchers based their assessment of productivity on the workers' hourly piece-rate wages and on indexes of turnover, accidents, and absenteeism obtained from company records. But when they reviewed the records of 667 workers, 212 in speed jobs and 455 in skill jobs, their findings did *not* support the age decrement theory (see Table 13.2). The older workers generally earned higher hourly piece-rate wages, were absent less, had fewer accidents, and changed jobs less often than did younger workers.

The results of this study are a good example of the discrepancy between results from laboratory studies of perceptual motor performance, in which older individuals are slower in these types of tasks, and analyses of real-world jobs. Even though many tasks in industry require speed, they do not require that people perform to the utmost capacity of their central nervous system, whereas laboratory tests do. After all, workers of any age must sustain the physical performance of their job for 8 hr every day. The work standards established in these jobs are compromises between speed and maintenance of function, and the older workers in this study were capable of meeting the speed requirements of these tasks. This phenomenon was tested directly by Salvendy (1974), who found that the same older workers who were inferior to young workers on laboratory "work-predictor" tests (the Purdue pegboard, the one-hole test, and the NHP 70/23 nonverbal intelligence tests) were superior to the young workers on actual production performance.

In Giniger et al.'s (1983) study of productivity, experience was the most significant predictor of worker success. However, because the design of the study was cross-sectional, it is likely that the performance of the older groups was inflated due to selective sample attrition. That is, older workers who could not maintain the speed or who were not as skilled quit their jobs, leaving only the highly talented and experienced workers in the older cohorts. The younger cohorts probably had both skilled and unskilled in each age group. Nevertheless, the results of this study provided evidence that, at least in this industry, those older workers who chose to continue working were quite successful in their jobs.

How do older workers, who generally have lower levels of physical capacity, stay as productive as younger workers? They compensate for productivity declines by taking advantage of improved skills and knowledge gained through experience (Schwab & Heneman, 1977). Many studies have shown that the greater the worker's skill, competence, and experience, the smaller the decrease in productivity with advancing age. Older workers learn to use compensatory strategies, such as pacing, anticipation, and planning and organization.

Table 13.2
Comparison of Work Productivity, Absenteeism, Accidents, and Turnover Within Age Categories for Workers in Speed (Top) and Skill (Bottom) Jobs

Age category	n	First quarter				Full year	
		Hourly rate	SD	Hours absent	SD	Accidents	Turnover
Under 25	22	4.06	.89	144	99	1	5
25-34	22	3.75	.82	101	101	3	6
35-44	24	5.01	1.25	75	56	0	2
45-54	44	5.30	1.41	69	60	0	1
55-64	92	5.30	1.33	58	60	1	3[a]
65 and over	8	4.29	2.04	113	112	0	1
Total	212	4.94	1.40	78	74	5	18

Note. For age and hourly rate, $r = 0.33$, $p < 0.001$; for age and hours absent, $r = -0.24$, $p < 0.001$.
[a]Does not include seven workers who retired.

Age category	n	First quarter				Full year	
		Hourly rate	SD	Hours absent	SD	Accidents	Turnover
Under 25	82	4.78	1.48	109	96	13	51
25-34	59	5.26	1.79	107	96	5	19
35-44	40	6.18	3.05	85	79	2	7
45-54	116	6.57	3.20	65	66	7	5
55-64	131	6.43	2.95	78	83	13	5[a]
65 and over	27	7.10	3.52	76	66	0	0[b]
Total	455	6.03	2.82	84	83	40	87

Note. For age and hourly rate, $r = 0.26$, $p < 0.001$; for age and hours absent, $r = -0.14$, $p < 0.01$.
[a]Does not include 10 workers who retired.
[b]Does not include 10 workers who retired.
From "Age, Experience, and Performance on Speed and Skill Jobs in an Applied Setting" by S. Giniger, A. Dispenzieri, and J. Eisenberg, 1983, *Journal of Applied Psychology*, **68**, pp. 471-472. Copyright 1983 by the American Psychological Association. Reprinted by permission.

Accidents

Another fear of some employers with regard to older workers is that in jobs that have a potential for injury, older workers will have a higher accident rate than younger employees. Arthur, Fuentes, and Doverspike (1990) postulated that errors on the part of transport drivers were frequently due to distractions or interruptions while doing the job and used a test of selective or divided attention, the Auditory Selective Attention Test (ASAT; Doverspike, Cellar, & Barrett, 1986) to predict accidents. This test had previously been shown to reveal age differences, with older-adult groups producing lower scores on this test. The test had also been an effective predictor of flying and driving performance. Not surprisingly, when Arthur, Fuentes, and Doverspike (1990) statistically removed the age factor, the ASAT did predict job performance. However, the prediction was due primarily to the older drivers' scores. When these older drivers' (late 50s) scores were removed, age alone was not a significant predictor. They concluded that a very large number of the driving accidents result from factors other than age.

Again, individual differences in selective attention among older adults are more important to consider when making personnel decisions than is chronological age. Accidents that are preventable by using good judgment and common sense decrease with age, whereas accidents that are preventable by rapid response to sudden perturbations in the environment increase with age (Bromley, 1974). That is, younger employees are likely to have a larger number of accidents because they tend to be less cautious, take chances, and have less experience (Tiffin & McCormick, 1968; Van Zelst, 1954).

Experience

Experience is more important than age in terms of the levels of average performance required by many types of jobs (Kutscher & Walker, 1960; Schwab & Heneman, 1977). In fact, a review of several studies showed that the more skill, competence, and experience a worker has, the smaller the loss of productivity with increased age (Giniger et al., 1983). Experience also can offset changes in biological capacity, for the older worker can use expectations, built on a long association with the nature of the task, to compensate for age-related physical decline (Bartley, 1977). However, the predictive power of experience to explain differences in worker effectiveness decreases as the number of years of experience increases and as the tasks get more complex (McDaniel, Schmidt, & Hunter, 1988).

Personal and Social Characteristics

Several personal and social characteristics of older workers as a group also tend to counterbalance age-related physical and mental declines. Older workers exhibit a more serious attitude toward work and use mature judgment in decision making (Bartley, 1977). They are more loyal and conscientious (Giniger et al., 1983), more punctual and attentive to quality (Knight, 1991), and have a lower incidence of absenteeism (Bartley, 1977). Older workers are generally more stable, and they do not change jobs unless forced to do so. They tend to remain on the job until retirement (Porter & Steers, 1973; Riley & Foner, 1968; Speakman, 1956). Employee turnover decreases about 10% a decade from age 20 to 60. This pattern has been shown to be consistent for every industry, for different occupational groups, and varied occupational levels (O'Boyle, 1970).

Age Discrimination in Employment

Ageism is a prejudice against individuals who are old in chronological age. Comfort (1976) states that ageism is "the notion that people cease to be people, cease to be the same people, or become people of a distinct and inferior kind by virtue of having lived a specified number of years" (p. 35). The insidious aspect of ageism is that it is the only type of prejudice that affects *all* people. It is very difficult to combat because people are taught ageism from childhood and eventually come to believe it. "White racists don't turn black, black racists don't become white, male chauvinists don't become women, anti-Semites don't wake up and find themselves Jewish—but we have a lifetime of indoctrination with the idea of the difference and inferiority of the old, and on reaching old age we may be prejudiced against ourselves" (Comfort, 1977, p. 11).

Ageism is expecting certain behaviors and abilities based solely on chronological age. It is using chronological age to define capabilities and certain types of societal roles. With respect to job performance and employment, employers practice ageism when they use chronological age as a criterion in decisions regarding employee selection, promotion, or retirement. Today, legislation prohibits age discrimination except in certain occupations in which it is thought by many that age-related physical performance and psychomotor performance deficits impair job performance.

Age Discrimination in Employment Act

In 1967, the Age Discrimination in Employment Act (ADEA), which forbids discrimination against adults over the age of 40, was passed in order to reduce ageism. Enforced by the Equal Opportunity Employment Commission, the purpose of the act is to "promote employment of older persons based on their ability rather than age, to prohibit arbitrary age discrimination in employment, and to help employers and workers to find ways in meeting problems arising from the impact of age upon employment" (Lake, 1982, p. 4). Canada also adopted, in 1981, the Ontario Human Rights Code, which provides that every person has a right to freedom from discrimination in employment on the basis of gender, age, or disability (Ontario Human Rights Code, 1981).

The ADEA prohibits the use of a chronological age maximum, such as 65, for mandatory retirement. When the ADEA was passed, two occupational groups were excluded. One group was faculty members in higher education. Faculty members were not included in the act and the age of 70 years continued to be a mandatory retirement age, unless a university wished to waive the requirement on a case-by-case basis. In 1992, however, the exclusion of faculty members in higher education was removed from ADEA, and now universities also cannot force faculty members over 70 to retire. Other exceptions were made in the area of high-risk jobs that are protective occupations.

Exceptions to the ADEA

Some types of employment are such high-risk jobs and depend so heavily on some of the variables most affected by age that the courts have allowed these occupations to maintain chronological age criteria in hiring and enforcing mandatory retirement ages *when the public safety is at risk.* Examples are law enforcement, fire fighting, the military, and piloting aircraft for commercial purposes. In these occupations, workers may be required to exert, at a moment's notice, maximum physical strength, power, speed, and endurance. They may have to carry heavy loads of equipment or people and execute split-second psychomotor behaviors under extreme duress. Dealing with physical combat, torrential floods, or emergencies brought on by other types of climatic disasters is part of the job description. The inability of a worker to perform physically and cognitively in these situations could result in serious injury or death for co-workers or other individuals involved in these emergencies.

In the case of pilots, the highly complex instrumentation that requires complicated sequences performed within specified time limitations, especially under emergency conditions, can challenge even the most efficient cognitive abilities. Also, the public worries that a pilot who is in the high-risk age category for heart attack may have a cardiovascular emergency during flight that would imperil the passengers. However, in the history of aviation, from 1930 to present, no airplane accident on a scheduled flight has ever been attributed to pilot incapacitation due to cardiovascular infarct, cerebrovascular insult, or stroke.

Almost all agencies or businesses in which these high-risk, highly physical activities occur have attempted to maintain a maximum entry age for aspiring applicants. Examples of maximum hiring ages for law enforcement agencies in large cities, for example, range from 28 to 40 years (Wolitz, 1974). Several federal agencies have adopted 35

years as a maximum entry age. Many of these agencies also enforce mandatory retirement ages of 65 or 70 years, or offer benefits and encourage their workers to retire after 20 years of service.

However, older adults vary in physical and cognitive capacities so greatly that many of those who are older than the maximum entry age are more capable physically than younger workers who are already employed. It was inevitable that these chronological age criteria would be legally challenged in the courts on the basis of the ADEA. The applicants who challenged the criteria demanded to be employed or tested to determine whether they were capable of performing the job. The employers in these high-risk occupations answered that it was not possible to create a test that adequately simulates the job requirements. They insisted that the best estimate of an individual's physical ability for the job, in the absence of a valid performance test, was chronological age.

The courts held that in the absence of clear standards for evaluation of the abilities of older workers, chronological age may be used as a best estimate of individual capacity as demonstrated in *businesses that involve public safety.* These court decisions were made in cases dealing with airline pilots (Murnane v. American Airlines, Inc., 1981) and bus drivers (Hodgson v. Greyhound Lines, Inc., 1974; Usery v. Tamiami Trail Tours, Inc., 1976). These exceptions are known as a *bona fide occupational qualification* (BFOQ), indicating that age represents the only valid *and practical* criteria by which inference of the ability to perform the job can be made.

Some employers have argued that even in the event that some performance test might be developed that would validly ascertain which applicants and workers can function efficiently in the job, the cost of administering the test to hundreds of applicants would be prohibitive. For example, the story is told of the New York City management's interest in developing a job performance test that would select the best garbage pickup workers for about 150 jobs to be advertised. The city spent several thousand dollars only to find that the test battery predictors were very similar to the actual tasks of the workers and that the performance test would be relatively costly to administer. But far more detrimental to the testing program was the fact that the economy was so depressed when the job openings were published that several thousand people applied for the jobs. Clearly the city could not afford to test thousands of people to select 150 candidates, so to avoid controversy, the city resorted to selecting the first 150 people who applied, with the idea that it would be less expensive to try them on the job and terminate them if they were unsuccessful than to use the newly designed performance test as the criterion. This is an extreme example of the way feasibility plays a role in the performance test process.

Sometimes entry-level maximum age barriers are based on a legitimate belief that physical limitations will preclude efficient, safe performance in the job. But often employers have hidden agendas that are disguised as a concern for the safety of the older worker. Several of the protective occupations have developed a promotion hierarchy within the system in which rookies enter the agency as a "foot-soldier," work "in the trenches," and gradually work their way up the hierarchy to more supervisory and administrative positions. There is a strong tradition in these agencies that in order to make intelligent, wise supervisory and administrative decisions, it is necessary to have worked at all levels of the organization, particularly in the hard, entry-level positions. So even though all high-risk occupations have administrative positions that do not require physical strength and endurance or split-second decision making under stressful conditions, employers do not approve of appointing older rookies to these positions. They argue that, first, if older rookies do not work in the entry positions, they will lack the necessary experience and empathy to understand the problems of the people they are supervising. Second, older rookies would fill an administrative position that traditionally has been viewed as a promotion for a worker who has been coming up through the ranks. Third, for the same investment in training time, older rookies would contribute far fewer years to the agency before retirement. These factors are rarely stated explicitly, but they are frequently considered by upper-management administrators.

Because management of the high-risk occupations have justified the use of chronological age by the BFOQ argument, advocates against ageism have expressed great interest in the concept of functional age versus chronological age and in the development of valid physical performance tests that can test job capability. Several attempts have been made to develop performance tests that can be used as substitutes for chronological age as a criterion for employment, promotion, or retention.

Job Performance Testing: An Alternative to Chronological Age Requirements

Job performance testing is an alternative to chronological age as a basis for hiring, promoting, or enforcing mandatory retirement (Davis & Dotson, 1987; Sothmann et al., 1990). The process of developing such a test involves a job analysis to determine the tasks required by the job, the identification of the tasks that will be simulated by the performance test, the determination of the physical, mental, and physiological characteristics necessary to perform the simulated tasks, and finally the development and validation of the test. The job analysis requires interviewing the work force, making observations of on-the-job behaviors, and obtaining from the workers completed surveys or questionnaires about their responsibilities and behaviors. Several criteria can be used to determine which job-related tasks will be simulated by the test: whether the task is (a) frequently performed, (b) critical to the job, (c) non–skill dependent, and whether it (d) lends itself to objective measurement (Davis & Dotson, 1987). Tasks are selected and the job performance test is field-tested on employees in the occupation. If the superior workers score highly on the test and the less capable workers score poorly on the test, then it is a valid performance test, capable of determining those applicants who could succeed in the occupation. The final version of the test must comply with the *Uniform Guidelines on Employee Selection Procedures*, which are published in the *Federal Register* (1978).

Fire Fighting

Fire fighting is an occupation that requires, during active fire fighting, physical strength, power, endurance, and the ability to tolerate high levels of heat. In addition, many of the fire suppression tasks must be completed with great speed in order to save lives and to keep the fire from spreading rapidly. All of these attributes decline with aging in the general population. The tasks in fire fighting are also unpredictable and unique to each situation, a condition that makes it very difficult to develop performance measures that accurately simulate real-world fire fighting. Davis, Dotson, and Santa Maria (1982) selected several tasks that fire fighters engage in during their work and administered these tasks to incumbent fire fighters while monitoring their heart rates. They found that laboratory measures of $\dot{V}O_2$max, body composition, and muscular fitness correlated well with these field tests and that there was a causal relationship between levels of fitness and improved performance on the job.

Although this and several similar studies provided evidence that a minimum level of $\dot{V}O_2$max (see chapter 4 for a discussion of $\dot{V}O_2$max) might be used as a cut-off point below which a fire fighter could not function effectively, three of the federal guidelines had not been met to allow selection of a $\dot{V}O_2$max cut-off score that could be defended legally. First, the range of aerobic fitness for fire fighters 20 to 65 years old had not been sufficiently documented. Second, indirect indicators had been used to predict $\dot{V}O_2$ of fire fighters during fire suppression activities. Third, the evidence justifying a minimum cut-off score was not adequate. Sothmann et al. (1990) addressed these inadequacies with an elegant study in which they used appropriate measurement validation techniques (see Figure 13.1). They observed actual fire suppression techniques, developed a simulation protocol, and asked fire fighters via a questionnaire to evaluate the simulations. They measured normative groups of fire fighters' fitness levels during simulated fire suppression protocols in order to validate the protocol. They then compared successful to unsuccessful performances on the protocols and set cut-off levels below which individuals might not be successful in fire fighting. Their conclusion was to recommend that a minimum $\dot{V}O_2$max of 33.5 ml $\cdot$ kg^{-1} $\cdot$ min^{-1} be used as a physiological cut-off for hiring and for determining fitness to continue working in an active firefighter role.

The performance times of all the fire fighters who were above the cut-off were compared, and although all of the fire fighters completed the test in an acceptable time and all were matched for similar $\dot{V}O_2$max levels, the older fire fighters took 3-1/2 min more to complete the test than the young fire fighters. In the determination of this cut-off value, they cautioned that a $\dot{V}O_2$max value of 33.5 ml $\cdot$ kg^{-1} $\cdot$ min^{-1} is probably too low to predict accurately those fire fighters who could successfully work in a raging fire that required heavy lifting for prolonged time periods. In addition to the performance criteria they used, they also planned to

select as low a $\dot{V}O_2$max cut-off score as could be tolerated in order to displace as few current fire fighters as possible. They also pointed out that although a large number of the currently employed fire fighters older than 40 years would have failed to reach the cut-off fitness level, this could be attributed more to their lifestyle than to their age. They suggested that fire-fighting departments that incorporate a performance level as a criterion for entry and retention should also actively provide programs of weight control, exercise, and smoking cessation. They also cautioned that a minimum cut-off $\dot{V}O_2$max addresses only the physical performance capabilities, whereas personnel decisions usually are also based on other aspects of the job that are important, such as learning how to use equipment, operating equipment, and interacting with other fire-fighting personnel.

Law Enforcement

Police work requires many different types of physical performance, and job performance tests designed to screen applicants have generally relied on tests that included measures of both physical fitness and performance on tasks very similar to those that police officers frequently encounter. For example, the job performance test developed by Davis and Dotson (1985) included several physical fitness items and a battery of job-related tasks. The physical fitness test was composed of a 1.5-mile run, pull-ups, sit-ups, a one-repetition-of-maximum bench press, and a standing long jump. The fitness section of the test also included several measures of body composition. Items in the job-related portion of the test battery were a lug wrench torque test, a body drag and full-size sedan push for several meters, and a foot-pursuit course emulating chasing a fleeing felon. Each item included in the test battery contributed to predicting success as a law enforcement officer. Interestingly, the only two pieces of information analyzed by the investigators that did *not* contribute to predicting success were the age of the officer and the number of years of service with the department. This test battery was later expanded into two parts. The first part is currently being used to screen applicants for jobs as law enforcement officers, and the second part is being used on an annual basis to monitor job-related efficiency.

McCormick, Jeannerette, and Mecham (1977) also developed a job performance test battery based on the position analysis questionnaire

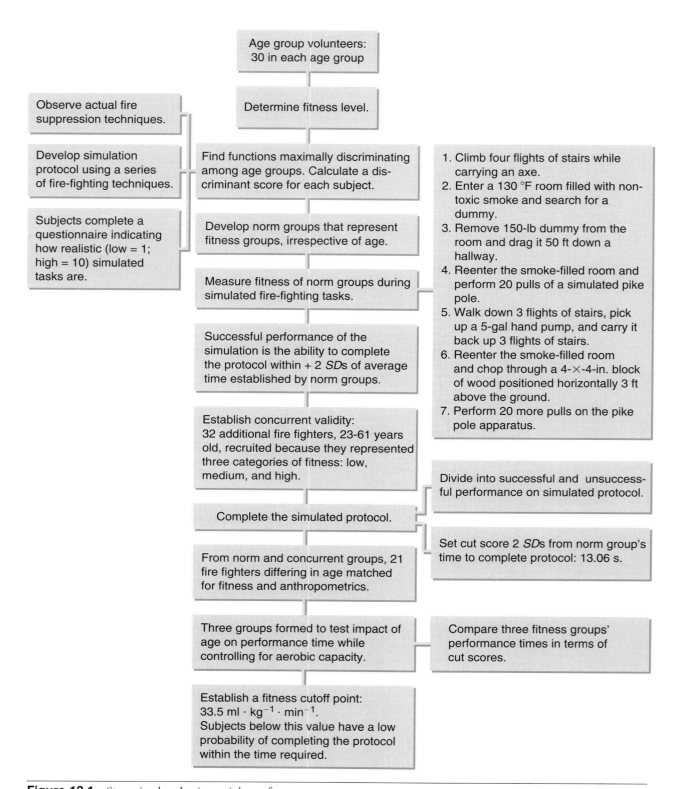

Age group volunteers:
30 in each age group

Determine fitness level.

Observe actual fire
suppression techniques.

Develop simulation
protocol using a series
of fire-fighting techniques.

Subjects complete a
questionnaire indicating
how realistic (low = 1;
high = 10) simulated
tasks are.

Find functions maximally discriminating
among age groups. Calculate a dis-
criminant score for each subject.

Develop norm groups that represent
fitness groups, irrespective of age.

Measure fitness of norm groups during
simulated fire-fighting tasks.

Successful performance of the
simulation is the ability to complete
the protocol within + 2 SDs of average
time established by norm groups.

Establish concurrent validity:
32 additional fire fighters, 23-61 years
old, recruited because they represented
three categories of fitness: low,
medium, and high.

Complete the simulated protocol.

From norm and concurrent groups, 21
fire fighters differing in age matched
for fitness and anthropometrics.

Three groups formed to test impact of
age on performance time while
controlling for aerobic capacity.

Establish a fitness cutoff point:
33.5 ml · kg^{-1} · min^{-1}.
Subjects below this value have a low
probability of completing the protocol
within the time required.

1. Climb four flights of stairs while
   carrying an axe.
2. Enter a 130 °F room filled with non-
   toxic smoke and search for a
   dummy.
3. Remove 150-lb dummy from the
   room and drag it 50 ft down a
   hallway.
4. Reenter the smoke-filled room and
   perform 20 pulls of a simulated pike
   pole.
5. Walk down 3 flights of stairs, pick
   up a 5-gal hand pump, and carry it
   back up 3 flights of stairs.
6. Reenter the smoke-filled room
   and chop through a 4-×-4-in. block
   of wood positioned horizontally 3 ft
   above the ground.
7. Perform 20 more pulls on the pike
   pole apparatus.

Divide into successful and unsuccessful performance on simulated protocol.

Set cut score 2 SDs from norm group's
time to complete protocol: 13.06 s.

Compare three fitness groups'
performance times in terms of
cut scores.

Figure 13.1 Steps in developing a job performance test.
Adapted from Sothmann et al. (1990, pp. 217-236).

(PAQ). They first identified several attributes that were essential for a good law enforcement officer (see Table 13.3; Mecham & McCormick, 1969), then they determined the degree to which these attributes were required under routine versus emergency conditions (see Table 13.4). The higher the percentile, the more the attribute is required during the job in comparison to the attribute requirements for all jobs found throughout the world of work. For example, the attribute of simple reaction time is shown in Table 13.4 to be required in 86% of the emergency situations. Scores on this test battery were then used to screen applicants to the police department.

Large Truck Driving

Driving a large petroleum transport truck and completing the procedures of loading and unloading at specific customer locations is largely a physical occupation that also requires cognitive integration of these physical tasks. In their work, drivers utilize several information-processing functions: memory recall, applying correct rules to the loading and unloading process, adding and subtracting numbers, and map reading. In their study of the comparison of these types of information-processing functions, chronological age, and job performance among truck drivers, Arthur et al. (1990) found that they could better predict job performance, which included a record of job-related accidents, by using a test battery of information-processing tasks than by chronological age. After interviewing 30 drivers, observing them in action, and reviewing the drivers' instruction manual, the authors listed and carefully analyzed each task that was required in the job (Table 13.5, page 381). From this analysis, they determined that distraction from the task was the major cause of accidents for most of the drivers. Therefore, they included in their test

---

Table 13.3
Attribute Definitions

Explosive strength: ability to expend a maximum amount of energy in one or a series of explosive or ballistic acts (as in throwing, pounding, etc.).

Dynamic strength: ability to make repeated, rapid, flexing movements in which the rapid recovery from muscle strain is critical.

Static strength: ability to maintain a high level of muscular exertion for some minimum time.

Speed of limb movement: the speed with which discrete movements of the arms or legs can be made. The ability deals with the speed with which the movement can be carried out after it has been initiated; it is not concerned with the speed of initiation of the movement.

Rate control: ability to make continuous anticipatory motor adjustments relative to changes in speed and direction of continuously moving objects.

Susceptibility to fatigue: diminished ability to do work, either physical or mental, as a consequence of previous and recent work done.

Stamina: the capacity to maintain physical activity over prolonged periods. It is concerned with the resistance of the cardiovascular system to breakdown.

Body orientation: ability to maintain body orientation with respect to balance and motion.

Kinesthesis: ability to sense position and movement of body members.

Spatial orientation: the ability to maintain one's orientation with respect to objects in space or to comprehend the position of objects in space with respect to one's position.

Eye-hand-foot coordination: ability to move the hand and foot coordinately with each other in response to visual stimuli.

Simple reaction time: the time period elapsing between the appearance of any stimulus and the initiation of an appropriate response.

Far visual acuity: ability to perceive detail at distances beyond normal reading distance.

Movement detection: ability to detect physical movement of objects and to judge their direction.

Depth perception: ability to estimate depth of distances or objects (or to judge their physical relationships in space).

Sensory alertness: alertness over expanded time periods.

Note. From McCormick, Jeannerette, and Mecham (1977).

Table 13.4
Physical, Psychomotor, and Sensory Attribute Requirements[a]
for the Entry-Level Police Officer Position

Attributes[b]	Percentile routine conditions[c]	Emergency or physically active conditions
Explosive strength	42	66
Dynamic strength	32	60
Static strength	36	61
Speed of limb movement	35	63
Rate control	50	67
Susceptibility to fatigue	61	83
Stamina	56	81
Body orientation	37	64
Kinesthesis	35	62
Spatial orientation	51	69
Eye-hand-foot coordination	50	67
Simple reaction time	72	86
Far visual acuity	62	72
Movement detection	62	69
Depth perception	54	64
Sensory alertness	65	79

[a]Determined by the Position Analysis Questionnaire (PAQ).
[b]Only attributes of a physical, psychomotor, and sensory nature that are required more than average under emergency conditions (i.e., the 60th percentile or above) are reported.
[c]The level or amount of each attribute required by the entry-level police officer position in comparison to the attribute requirements for all jobs found throughout the world of work.
Note. From *Report to the Houston Police Department*, 1976. P.R. Jeannerette and Associates, 3223 Smith, Suite 212, Houston, TX 77006.

battery several tests related to the attribute of selective attention. Although the purpose of their study was not to develop a test to use as a job performance screening test for applicants for driving jobs, they showed that performance on their test battery was a better predictor of accidents than was chronological age.

Military Work—Infantry

Davis and Dotson (1985) developed a performance test for Marines by observing the physical tasks required of service personnel. The testing included the Marine Corp's three-item physical fitness test, plus chin-ups with a backpack, standing long jump, a 150-m sprint up a 6% incline, and measures of body fat. The tests also included job-related tasks, such as marching with and without snowshoes, weapons, or packs; towing a resupply sled; digging fighting positions; and resupply sprints and firing a rifle. They concluded that improved fitness increased performance on these job-related tasks;

thus, the test was a valid indicator of whether an individual could meet the physical requirements of being a Marine. These tests, then, would be more suitable predictors of successful performance for female and older individuals than chronological age.

Aircraft Piloting

Although unique equipment, such as aircraft simulators and flight performance recorders, has been used to test the performance of Air Force pilots for many years, it has not been used by commercial airlines for entry-level testing. Aircraft simulators and flight performance indicators provide detailed information on an individual's cognitive and perceptual flight skills and overall performance capabilities, including handling emergencies. With regard to mandatory retirement, commercial airlines have access to a complete longitudinal record of performance for

Table 13.5
Unloading Task Sequence for Petroleum Transport Drivers

1. Check all clearances when maneuvering to enter a customer location.
2. Drive transport to unloading position and place transmission in lowest gear.
3. Set parking brake and turn off ignition. Pull battery cut-off switch if lights are not needed.
4. Alight from cab and check transport for hot brakes and deflated hot tires.
5. Open bucket boxes. Remove and place "No Smoking" signs and traffic barricades strategically to protect unloading area.
6. Allow no one to smoke in the vicinity of unloading area. Check for possible sources of ignition.
7. Remove covers from ground fills.
8. Remove caps, both storage and vapor recovery, from tanks.
9. Fetch vapor recovery hose from trailer and connect to trailer.
10. Stick storage tank with gauge pole and record measurements.
11. Refer to map book for storage tank size/type.
12. Refer to the appropriate chart to determine amount of product in the storage tank denoted by the reading on gauge pole. Record amount and decide if storage tank will hold amount of product to be delivered.
13. Connect vapor recovery hose to storage tank.
14. Fetch fitting required for storage tank from trailer and connect it to storage tank.
15. Fetch unloading hose from trailer. Connect hose to fitting and then to the appropriate trailer compartment.
16. Check to ensure that product/compartment indicator dial matches receiving tank.
17. Open internal safety valves to charge system.
18. Open delivery valve to appropriate tank to permit flow.
19. Check hoses and connections for any leaks or drips.
20. Turn product/compartment dial to "Empty" when compartment is emptied.
21. Close delivery valve.
22. Repeat Steps 10 through 21 to unload each compartment.
23. Shut safety valves and replace dust caps.
24. Disconnect unloading hose from compartment. Disconnect hose from fitting and store hose away.
25. Disconnect fitting and store it away.
26. Disconnect vapor recovery hose from storage tank.
27. Gauge tank and record measurement.
28. Repeat Steps 23 through 27 after unloading each compartment.
29. Disconnect vapor recovery hose from trailer and store it away.
30. Replace caps and covers.
31. Return all equipment to storage and check area.
32. Check all tires and wheels.
33. Enter cab and drive to next customer location or company terminal.

Note. From "Relationships Among Personnel Tests, Age, and Job Performance" by W. Arthur, R. Fuentes, and D. Doverspike, 1990, *Experimental Aging Research*, **16**, pp. 15-16. Copyright 1990 by Beech Hill Enterprises, Inc. Reprinted by permission.

each pilot; thus, they can evaluate pilot performance on an individual basis.

Specificity of Job Performance Testing

It is important to remember that different types of jobs require vastly different talents, attributes, and experience, and that these differences interact with the way age affects performance. People in jobs with a heavy emphasis on quick decisions, physical power, or inordinate endurance will be more affected by physical aging than those in jobs requiring low levels of these abilities. Those in clerical, technical, or professional jobs require an entirely different profile of abilities that depend more on information-processing capacity, a function that appears to decrease less with increasing age for skilled than for unskilled workers (Avolio & Waldman, 1987). Performance testing, therefore, must be specific to the job under consideration. It is unlikely that a global test of job performance can be developed for several different occupations. Nevertheless, the examples previously discussed show that performance testing can be developed for specific occupations, and if it is financially feasible, these tests can provide a more valid basis for personnel decisions than the use of chronological age alone.

Factors That Extend the Work Life of Older Adults

It is clear from a statistical analysis of several studies that job performance is not directly related to age but more to performance capabilities, that is, job-related cognitive tests and performance tasks (McEvoy & Cascio, 1989), and to experience. Nevertheless, both aged workers and employers can improve the percentage of older people who continue to work, the physical and psychological cost of their work, and the safety of the work environment. For example, older adults can enhance their employment performance by maintaining their health and fitness. By living a healthy lifestyle, they also can reduce the physical cost of their work.

Worker and Employer Behaviors

Employers, who may adjust job responsibilities within a business to specific attributes and abilities of employees, can make similar adjustments with regard to age. In the left column of Table 13.6 is a list of commonly observed physiological and psychological changes that are known to relate to aging, and in the right column, several employer actions that could compensate for these changes. However, great individual differences exist among adults with regard to the deficits shown in the left column. Indeed, many relatively young adults suffer from some of these deficits more than many old persons do. Employers who wish to maximize the work performance of all their employees should initiate ergonomic and safety analyses of their job descriptions and work sites and fully implement their findings. Implementations of recommendations like those in the right column of Table 13.6 would benefit many older employees more than young workers.

Obviously, not all employers can implement the adjustments in Table 13.6. Specific tasks must be accomplished for some jobs, and adjustments may be impossible. What employers can do, however, is be cognizant of problem areas, make adjustments when possible, and use creative methods to assist when full implementation presents problems. For example, it may be impossible to eliminate all lifting from a particular job description, but employees might be rotated in and out of jobs that require more or less lifting.

National Institute for Occupational Safety and Health Recommendations

Another way that the work life of older adults might be extended is that the United States National Institute for Occupational Safety and Health may recommend a limit to the amount of aerobic power and back loadings a job may require from individuals. The constraints would be in terms of an action limit and a maximum permissible limit for the occupational activity. For example, the action limit would be exceeded if the average work rate is greater than 14.6 kJ $\cdot$ min^{-1}, if the compression force on the lower back exceeds 3.4 kN, or if less than 75% of females and 99% of males can perform the task safely (Shephard, 1987). The *maximum permissible limit* is defined arbitrarily as a work intensity that is three times the action limit. Employers whose occupation requirements exceed these maxima are in violation of occupational safety and health standards.

Automation

One of the great achievements of modern technology is the development of instruments and machines to substitute for or enhance human strength, endurance, and speed. Using Durnin and Passmore's (1967) data, Shephard (1987) compared the energy cost of traditional forms of agriculture to the costs of mechanized farming (Table 13.7, page 384). The energy costs of physical work assisted by technology are much lower than the costs of work completed by manual labor. Similar energy savings probably can be seen in many other industries. Developments in the field of robotics also promise to provide machines that can substitute for the heavy or rapid-repetition components of a job that might unduly tax an older worker. Such rapid developments in technology hold great promise for extending the work life of older adults.

The Future for Older Workers

Within the last few years, signs have been appearing that the future for older adults may be more promising. Mandatory retirement is no longer legal, the eligibility age for Social Security benefits has been raised, gerontechnology is emerging as a field to assist the older consumer

Table 13.6
Adjustments to Enhance the Workplace Environment for Older Workers

Age-related physiological/psychological changes	Workplace/environmental adjustments
Decreased joint mobility Reduced elasticity of tissues	*Avoid* jobs that require or have ■ elevated arm activities ■ prolonged unusual postures ■ twisting of spine ■ large wrist deviations to apply force using tools *Position* objects, controls, displays to minimize prolonged flexing, bending, stooping *Adjust* furniture to individual anthropometry: ■ seats in vehicles ■ office furniture *Design* seats to reduce vibration ■ low frequency vibration (trucks, earth-moving equipment, mining) ■ large wrist deviations to apply force using tools
Loss of strength	*Avoid* ■ controls and tools that require high strength ■ lifting, lowering, pushing, pulling, bearing loads ■ lifting loads >20% maximum of young workers ■ lifting rapidly *Design* tasks so that ■ load is kept close to body ■ task does not require bending, stooping, or twisting ■ adequate rest is provided between loads ■ task assures good foot traction *Teach* workers correct mechanics of lifting and pushing
Reduced work capacity	Jobs requiring energy expenditures should not exceed 0.7 (men) or 0.5 (women) L/min oxygen consumption
Slowed perception and decision making Attention deficits Memory deficits Difficulty with mental transformations	*Provide* ■ longer training sessions ■ practice with written instructions ■ videotapes of desired performance ■ increased signal-to-noise ratio *Assign* older workers to ■ tasks in which work is previewed rather than reacted to ■ tasks that are predictive rather than novel
Visual deficits	*Provide* ■ 50% more illumination for workers 40-55 years ■ 100% more illumination for workers >55 years
Acuity	■ increased task contrast on control panels, writing on labels ■ increased display letters and symbols ■ reduced glare
Color discrimination (blue/green)	*Omit* blue/green discrimination

(continued)

Table 13.6
(continued)

Less tolerance for heat	Reduce heat stress index in workplace
Less tolerance for cold	Maintain optimum worksite temperature
Hearing loss	Increase signal-to-noise ratio in tasks that provide audible cues or instructions
Greater incidence of low back pain (LBP)	*Provide* job training to prevent LBP ■ risks on job ■ basic knowledge of body mechanics ■ specific motions to avoid ■ planning job activities to minimize back stress ■ off-the-job injury prevention
Increased risk of falling	Eliminate slippery walkways Mark steps or ramps Illuminate workplace adequately
Slower rehabilitation from injury or disease	Allow more gradual return to full work load Allow rotation between light and heavy jobs to phase in work requirements Provide information regarding proper rehabilitation and return to work
Higher work stress	Avoid paced work Give worker control over work load Emphasize accuracy rather than speed
Tendency toward inactivity	Provide fitness programs Encourage employees to use fitness programs

Table 13.7
A Comparison of the Energy Cost of Traditional Agriculture to the Costs of Mechanized Farming

Task	Traditional	kJ · min⁻¹	Mechanized	kJ · min⁻¹
Horizontal sawing	Hand	30	Power saw	22.6
Tree planting	Hand	27	Machine	11.7
Mowing	Scythe	23-43	Tractor	7.5-18.8
Grain harvesting	Binding and stooking	21-36	Combined harvester	8.3-13.0
Digging	Pick and shovel	20-42	Mechanical digger	15.5-30.5
Milking	Hand	9.2-21.3	Machine	6.3

Note. From "Human Rights and the Older Worker: Changes in Work Capacity With Age" by R.J. Shephard, 1987, *Medicine and Science in Sports and Exercise,* **19**, p. 169. Copyright 1987 by Williams & Wilkins. Reprinted by permission.

and worker (Bouma & Graafmons, 1992), and several large corporations have experimented with hiring older workers on a large scale basis. For example, in 1986, Days Inns of America began hiring adults over 50 as reservation clerks. They found that these older adults handled the sophisticated telecommunications equipment and the 25,000 daily calls as well as the young adults. In fact, their average training and recruiting costs were only $618 for older workers, compared to

$1,742 for younger workers, and the over-50 workers worked an average of 3 years compared to younger adults' average 1 year on the job. In another example, B&Q, a very large hardware and home appliance store in Britain, experimented with hiring only workers over age 50 in one of its stores. The "over-50" store not only competed successfully with the other five B&Q stores, its profits were 18% higher and the employee turnover was six times lower. Thus, in business arenas where profit is the bottom line, older workers have succeeded.

In addition to increased recent employer interest, more scientific and professional interest has been focused on the older worker (Winn, 1991). Several recent research symposia and monographs have dealt with the topic of the older worker (Czaja, 1990a, 1990b; Leon, 1987; McLaughlin, 1989; Rones & Herz, 1989; Snyder & Barrett, 1988). The American Association for Retired Persons (AARP) has been very active in attempting to change employer (and employee) attitudes about working. *The Working Age*, a bimonthly newsletter published by AARP, covers topics of management, pension plans, attitudes, strategies of foreign countries, and technological assistance relating to older workers. Consequently, as information accumulates regarding the effectiveness of older workers and the increasing number of corporate experiments provide more evidence that older workers are effective, a trend begins to emerge in which the older worker becomes more an experienced and efficient resource than a liability.

In Summary

Many older workers in their 60s and 70s do not consider themselves old and do not want to be forced into retirement. They enjoy the satisfactions of their work, the self-esteem that accompanies the abilities to meet the responsibilities of adulthood, and the feelings that they are accomplishing worthwhile activities that make a contribution to society. They have a very strong motivation to extend their work life.

Employers, however, have several concerns about older workers as a group that sometimes influence the employers' decisions regarding hiring and retaining older adults. These concerns include the workers' mental and physical competence, their productivity, and the possibility of higher accident rates on the job. Older adults do perform less well on many psychological tests of information processing, such as divided and selective attention, short- and long-term memory, and the mental manipulation of data. However, these tests are not always relevant to real-world job tasks, and job descriptions that require employees to work at maximum capacities of speed and information processing, such as required in these laboratory tests, are rare in the workplace.

In most jobs, the work is self-paced and employees use mental capabilities far lower than their maximum capacity. Also, poor health and neurological disease, rather than age, may be responsible for many of the age deficits that are seen. Although physical abilities decline with increased age, more than half of the individuals between ages 55 and 74 can perform work-related activities well enough to continue working if they so choose. Nor must declines in physical strength prohibit older adults from extending their work life, because the activities required in most jobs do not approach the maximum abilities of individuals. Older workers learn to replace uneconomical responses with economical ones and incorporate different strategies to compensate for physical decline. People who continue in their jobs tend to maintain the levels of physical skill necessary to do the job. In industry, older adults generally are more productive, have less absenteeism, have fewer accidents, and change jobs less often than younger workers. The greater the worker's skill, competence, and experience, the smaller the decrease in productivity with advancing age.

Several personal and social characteristics of older workers also enable them to compensate for age-related losses of function. Older workers have been shown to be more serious about their work, more punctual and attentive to quality, more stable, and more loyal to the company.

Ageism is a form of prejudice in which people expect certain behaviors and abilities and define capabilities and role types solely on the basis of chronological age. In order to combat ageism, the Age Discrimination in Employment Act (ADEA), which forbids discrimination against adults over the age of 40, was passed in 1967. However, in occupations where public safety is an issue, such as fire fighting, law enforcement, commercial airline piloting, heavy equipment operation, and the military, age limitations are allowed if clear standards for the evaluation of the physical abilities of the workers cannot be developed. In these exceptions, age may be used as a bona fide occupational qualification (BFOQ).

Job performance tests have been developed in many occupations to provide clear standards of evaluation of performance in high-risk jobs, so that chronological age cannot be claimed to be a BFOQ criterion for hiring, promotion, or mandatory retirement. Because the myriad of occupations require so many different combinations of attributes and skills, performance testing must be specific to the job under consideration. It is unlikely that a global job performance test suitable for all types of physically demanding jobs can ever be developed.

Several factors can extend the work life of adults. First, adults can maintain their health and fitness levels so that they can perform at optimum capacity. Second, employers can adjust job assignments so that older workers can work in self-paced, predictable jobs that put a premium on coordination and dexterity rather than strength and power. Ergonomics researchers have suggested many equipment and workplace design modifications that can be made to adjust for age-related deficits. For example, to minimize problems with attention span, irrelevant details on control panels and switches can be eliminated or masked. To compensate for visual losses, illumination of the task can be increased, the contrast between letters and background can be magnified, and highly contrasting colors can be used on instrument panels. Many other suggestions are summarized in Table 13.6 (pp. 383-384). Third, the U.S. National Institute of Occupational Safety and Health may set a limit on the magnitude of aerobic power and back strength that can be required in occupations. Finally, the exciting new fields of automation and robotics are providing technology that can substitute for or enhance the strength, speed, and endurance of workers employed in the jobs of the future.

References

Arthur, W., Fuentes, R., & Doverspike, D. (1990). Relationships among personnel tests, age, and job performance. *Experimental Aging Research*, **16**, 11-16.

Avolio, B.J., & Waldman, D.A. (1987). Personnel aptitude test scores as a function of age, education, and job type. *Experimental Aging Research*, **13**, 109-113.

Bartley, D.L. (1977). Compulsory retirement: A re-evaluation. *Personnel*, **4**, 62-66.

Bouma, H., & Graafmons, J.A.M. (1992). *Gerontechnology*. Washington, DC: IOS Press.

Bromley, D.B. (1974). *The psychology of human aging*. New York: Penguin Books.

Comfort, A. (1976). *A good age*. New York: Crown.

Comfort, A. (1977). Age prejudice in America. In F. Riessman (Ed.), *Older persons: Unused resources for unmet needs*. Beverly Hills: Sage Publications.

Czaja, S.J. (Ed.) (1990a). Aging [Special issue]. *Human Factors*, **32**.

Czaja, S.J. (Ed.) (1990b). *Human factors research needs for an aging population*. Washington, DC: National Academy Press.

Davis, P.O., & Dotson, C.O. (1985). *Development of a job-related physical performance test for the Jacksonville Sheriff's Department*. Langley Park, MD: Institute of Human Performance.

Davis, P.O., & Dotson, C.O. (1987). Job performance testing: An alternative to age discrimination. *Medicine and Science in Sports and Exercise*, **19**, 179-185.

Davis, P.O., Dotson, C.O., & Santa Maria, D.L. (1982). Relationship between simulated fire fighting tasks and physical performance measures. *Medicine and Science in Sports and Exercise*, **14**, 65-71.

Doverspike, D., Cellar, D., & Barrett, D. (1986). The Auditory Selective Attention Test: A review of field and laboratory studies. *Educational and Psychological Measurement*, **46**, 1095-1103.

Durin, J.V., & Passmore, R. (1967). *Energy, work, & leisure*. London: Heinemann Educational Books.

Eisdorfer, C., & Wilkie, F. (1977). Stress, disease, aging, and behavior. In J.E. Birren & K.W. Schaie (Eds.), *Handbook of the psychology of aging*. New York: Van Nostrand Reinhold.

Federal Register. (1978). *Uniform guidelines on employee selection procedures*, **43**, 38290-38315.

Garg, A. (1991). Ergonomics and the older worker: An overview. *Experimental Aging Research*, **17**, 143-155.

Giniger, S., Dispenzieri, A., & Eisenberg, J. (1983). Age, experience, and performance on speed and skill jobs in an applied setting. *Journal of Applied Psychology*, **68**, 469-475.

Hodgson v. Greyhound Lines, Inc., 499 F.2d 859 (7th Cir. 1974).

Jarvik, L.F. (1973). Intellectual functioning in later years. In L.F. Jarvik, C. Eisdorfer, & J.E. Bluml (Eds.), *Intellectual functioning in adults*. New York: Springer.

Kelleher, C.H., & Quirk, D.A. (1973). Age, functional capacity, and work: An annotated bibliography. *Industrial Gerontology*, **19**, 80-98.

Knight, W. (1991). Taking a new look at the older worker. *Aging Digest*, **8**, p. 9, 15.

Kovar, M.G., & LaCroix, A.Z. (1987). Aging in the eighties, ability to perform work-related activities. *National Center for Health Statistics Advance Data*, **136**, 1-12.

Kutscher, R.E., & Walker, J.F. (1960). Comparative job performance of office workers by age. *Monthly Labor Review*, **83**, 39-44.

Lake, M.B. (Ed.) (1982). *Age discrimination employment act*. Washington, DC: Equal Employment Advisory Council.

Leon, A.S. (1987). Introduction to the symposium: Age as a criterion for work performance—Chronologic vs. physiologic age. *Medicine and Science in Sports and Exercise*, **19**, 157-158.

McCormick, E.J., Jeannerette, P.R., & Mecham, R.C. (1977). *Position analysis questionnaire job analysis manual*. West Lafayette, IN: PAQ Services.

McDaniel, M.A., Schmidt, F.L., & Hunter, J.E. (1988). Job experience correlated to job performance. *Journal of Applied Psychology*, **73**, 327-330.

McDowd, J., Vercruyssen, M., & Birren, J.E. (1991). Age, divided attention, and dual task performance. In Damos (Ed.), *Multiple-task performance* (pp. 386-414). Washington, DC: Taylor & Francis.

McEvoy, G.M., & Cascio, W.F. (1989). Cumulative evidence of the relationship between employee age and job performance. *Journal of Applied Psychology*, **74**, 11-17.

McLaughlin, A. (1989). *Older worker task force: Key policy issues for the future (Report of the Secretary of Labor)* (GPO: 1989 0-227-995: QL 3). Washington, DC: U.S. Government Printing Office.

Mecham, R.C., & McCormick, E.J. (1969). *The rated attribute requirements of job elements in the Position Analysis Questionnaire* (Office of Naval Research, Contract Nonr-1100 (28), Department of the Navy). West Lafayette, IN: Occupational Research Center, Purdue University.

Meier, E.L., & Kerr, L. (1976). Capabilities of middle-aged and old workers: A survey of the literature. *Industrial Gerontology*, **3**, 147-155.

Murnane v. American Airlines, Inc. 667 F.2d 98 (D.C. Cir. 1981).

O'Boyle, E.J. (1970). Job tenure: A special labor force report. *Industrial Gerontology*, **5**, 41-42.

Ontario Human Rights Code. (1981). *Statutes of Ontario (1981). Chapter 53*. Toronto, ON: Queen's Printer.

Porter, L., & Steers, R.M. (1973). Organizational work and personal factors in employee turnover and absenteeism. *Psychological Bulletin*, **80**, 151-176.

Riley, M.W., & Foner, A. (1968). *Aging and society: An inventory of research findings*. New York: Russell Sage Foundation.

Rones, P.L., & Herz, D.E. (1989). *Labor market problems of older workers (Report of the Secretary of Labor)*. Washington, DC: U.S. Government Printing Office.

Salvendy, G. (1974). Discrimination in performance assessments against the aged. *Perceptual and Motor Skills*, **39**, 1087-1099.

Schwab, D.P., & Heneman, H.G. (1977). Effects of age and experience on productivity. *Industrial Gerontology*, **4**, 113-117.

Shephard, R.J. (1987). Human rights and the older worker: Changes in work capacity with age. *Medicine and Science in Sports and Exercise*, **19**, 168-173.

Simonton, D.K. (1990). Creativity and wisdom in aging. In J.E. Birren & K.W. Schaie (Eds.), *Handbook of the psychology of aging* (3rd ed., pp. 320-329). New York: Academic Press.

Snyder, C.J., & Barrett, G.V. (1988). The Age Discrimination in Employment Act: A review of court decisions [Monograph]. *Experimental Aging Research*, **14**(1).

Sothmann, M.S., Saupe, K.W., Jasenof, D., Blaney, J., Fuhrman, S.D., Woulfe, T., Raven, P.B., Pawelczyk, J.P., Dotson, C.O., Landy, F.J., Smith, J.J., & David, P.O. (1990). Advancing age and the cardiorespiratory stress of fire suppression: Determining a minimum standard for aerobic fitness. *Human Performance*, **3**, 217-236.

Speakman, D. (1956). *Bibliography of research on changes in working capacities with age*. London: Ministry of Labour.

Tiffin, J., & McCormick, E. (1968). *Industrial psychology*. Englewood Cliffs, NJ: Prentice Hall.

Usery v. Tamiami Trail Tours Inc., 531 F.2d 224 (5th Cir. 1976).

Van Zelst, R.H. (1954). The effect of age and experience upon accident rate. *Journal of Applied Psychology*, **38**, 313-317.

Welford, A.T. (1958). *Aging and human skills*. Oxford, England: Oxford University Press.

Winn, F.J., Jr. (1991). Preface for special issue on ergonomics and the older worker. *Experimental Aging Research*, **17**, 139-141.

Wolitz, L. (1974). *An analysis of the labor market for policemen*. Doctoral thesis. University of California-Berkeley.

CHAPTER 14

The Physically Elite Elderly

The word *elite* is a strong one, because it literally means *the very best*. Yet, no other word seems potent enough to describe the small percentage of elderly adults who manage to maintain outstanding physical abilities well into their 80s and 90s. Their physical abilities, although not as powerful as those of 20-year-olds, continue to be far superior to the physical abilities of most younger people. When people read the story of Johnny Kelley, who at 83 years of age finished his *60th* Boston Marathon 5 hr 42 min 54 s behind the much younger winner (Kardong, 1991), their first thought may be that aging takes a considerable toll on running performance. On further consideration, however, most people remember that a marathon is approximately 26 miles. How many 20-year-olds can run 26 miles? Kept in perspective, the ability of 80-year-olds to run 26 miles is phenomenal and a testament to the remarkable resilience of the human body when it is properly maintained.

Who are the physically elite elderly? They are older athletes who keep training and competing in tournaments well into their 60s, 70s, and 80s. They physically push themselves on a daily basis, competing in masters tournaments, the Senior Sports Classics, and local tournaments. They are those older individuals who do not quit working in occupations that require strength and endurance and who maintain their abilities through physical training so that they outperform most of their colleagues many years younger. They are front-line, field-working fire fighters, police, military personnel, dock workers, scuba divers, forest rangers, Emergency Medical Services (EMS) workers, and a host of older individuals in occupations that require physical strength and stamina. They are also those individuals like Emil Biener, who has climbed Switzerland's Matterhorn more than 200 times and continues, in his 60s, to guide other climbers (Barnard, 1992). The physical performances of these noncompetitive individuals are not as easy to describe as those of masters athletes, because the types of physical activity they do are not quantifiable. There are no scores for mountain climbing or scuba diving to make it easy to compare their performances with those of younger persons. But every community has them, and people who know them admire them.

Athletic competitions, conversely, provide an easy way for researchers to compare the physical abilities of one age group to another. In athletics, physical ability is rank ordered, and one of the purposes of tournaments and competitions is to identify the best physical performance. Elaborate rules have been implemented to ensure that, inasmuch as possible, the comparisons are fair. Athletics, therefore, is a natural arena to determine how successful humans can be in defying the physical effects of aging.

This chapter focuses on the physical accomplishments of older masters athletes, not because they are the only older adults who perform remarkable physical achievements, but because their achievements are often accurately quantified, recorded, and publicized. First, this chapter describes the groups of athletes and discusses what can be learned from a study of aged athletes. Then, it describes some of the achievements of masters athletes in track and field, swimming, cycling, rowing, weight lifting, baseball hitting, bowling, and golf and discusses several issues related to the analysis of athletic performance records. Finally, there are the nonphysiological factors that limit the

athletic performance of older adults. The chapter closes with some considerations of the question, How do they do it?

Masters Athletes

Masters athletes are competitors who exceed a minimum age specific to each sport and who participate in competitive events designed for masters athletes (e.g., the Senior Sports Classics, the World Veterans Games, or local masters competitions). In track and field, masters athletes are older than 35 years old; in race-walking, they must exceed 40. The minimum age varies according to the extent to which youth is a requisite for success. In swimming, for example, where the world records are held by teenagers, the minimum masters age is 25.

Masters competitions are relatively new in the athletic world. The First World Masters Track-and-Field Championship was held in Toronto in 1975. The National Senior Sports Classics, which began as the Senior Olympics in 1990, are competitions for adults older than age 50 who qualify on the basis of their state Senior Games performance. The events include archery, bowling, cycling, golf, horseshoes, racquetball, road races, softball, swimming, table tennis, track and field, volleyball, 2-mi race-walk, and washer pitching. Each year the Senior Games has many heartwarming stories of successful performances by the participants, such as that of Peter Laurino, who won the 85+ division of the 5,000-m race-walk four times.

The World Veterans Games, which is a biennial track-and-field championship for men over age 40 and women over age 35, was first held in 1975. In 1989, 4,950 athletes from 58 nations competed in the VIIIth World Veterans Championships. Moore (1992) describes an electrifying moment in the 200-m dash:

> Among the men were 94-year-old Wang Chingchang of Taiwan and 90-year-old Herbert Kirk of Bozeman, Montana. Wang bolted to a 5-m lead off the turn. But Kirk charged with 80 meters to go and passed Wang with 40 left, as the crowd stood roaring. Wang, amazingly, dug down and repassed Kirk, winning by a foot, 52.21 to 52.33 sec. But this race wasn't over.

Kirk, who had given up tennis at 86 because he could no longer see the ball, didn't see the finish line either. He kept right on sprinting. Wang, fiercely competitive, went with him, and they dueled for another 70 meters before they were stopped. As they trotted back, it was in front of a delirious, tearful throng. (p. 44)

Masters athletes are also local sports heroes. Every sport and every community has a few legendary elder athletes. Johnny Kelley, at age 83, ran his 60th Boston Marathon in 1991. The race officials set up a special finish line for him and gave him a hat and shirt with the Boston Marathon logo emblazoned on it. Wally Hayward, at 79 years, stunned everyone with his 9 hr, 44 min, 15 s finish in the Charity Challenge 80-km race (48 miles) in South Africa. He finished 5,482nd out of 11,234 starters of all ages. Peter Laurino, a race-walking champion, at 98 years of age won the Charter Hospital's Senior 2-mile Strut. Ruth Rothfarb and Ida Mintz, both over 80 years old, ran the marathon in just a little over 5 hr, and Helen Zechmeister set the world dead-lift record in the female 75-to-79-year age category by lifting 220.5 lb.

Why Study the Elite Physical Performance of Athletes?

The question might very well be raised, Why study and discuss these highly exceptional physically elite older adults? After all, they represent an extremely small number of their cohort. There are several reasons for observing and studying these persons who truly optimize their physical well-being throughout their lives. An obvious reason is that they represent the extreme end of a distribution that ranges from physical disability and dysfunction at one end to elite athletic accomplishments at the other. Because they represent one extreme of this distribution, they should be described and understood. But other reasons are more important. These athletes provide official and controlled physical performance data, they offer a barometer of what is possible in physical aging, and their performances are of scientific value in the understanding of both physical and physiological changes with aging.

Highly Controlled and Motivated Performance

Athletic events have always offered well-documented, quantified evaluations of physical ability. The conditions under which official state, national, and world athletic records are made are highly controlled. Trained officials monitor the performances during events so that no athlete has an unfair advantage. The rules of competition, which take into account weather conditions, facilities, and equipment, are designed to ensure fairness and objectivity of measurement. In fact, considering how highly monitored athletic competitions are, by both officials, observers, and media coverage, the quantification and reliability of physical performance during these events must be considered to be as controlled as field research experiments. Also, the athletes performing in these competitions are doing so willingly and are extremely motivated. Most subjects in laboratory experiments never reach the high level of motivation to produce strength or speed scores that they would reach if they were measured under competition conditions. This is particularly true for high-level athletes. Hagerman (1994) and Foster, Green, Snyder, and Thompson (in press) indicated that the peak $\dot{V}O_2max$ values that they obtained from elite athletes during competition were always higher than the $\dot{V}O_2max$ values they obtained from them during a standard incremental exercise protocol.

A Barometer of the Possible

Those who break records raise the ceiling for everyone. It is well known in athletics that all events have barriers, performances that seem impossible for anyone to surpass. Yet, when someone does break the barrier, then often a flood of people do, and the new record becomes the next barrier. One of the most famous of these barriers was the 4-min mile, a time which everyone thought no human being could accomplish. But after Roger Bannister broke this barrier, the times tumbled. The same metamorphosis is occurring with physical performances of older adults. Previous ideas about the physical limitations of older adults are being reformulated almost monthly with every masters competition.

More and more older adults are competing in local and state tournaments, and more and more events are being modified to include them. Many masters athletes are training in the atmosphere of a sports club, with other athletes of various ages, and under the aegis of a coach who provides them with knowledge about innovative training techniques and new technologies designed to improve performance. In fact, it is not uncommon to find cases where, due to improved training techniques and technological advances in equipment, masters athletes surpass their own collegiate performances.

Describing, recording, analyzing, and publicizing the physical performance of masters athletes can serve as a reminder to all adults and gerontological professionals that physical ability can be maintained at remarkable levels for a very long time. The training and performance of thousands of older adults in these tournaments remind observers that disability is not inevitable. The athletic performances of all the competitors, not just the winners, show what the aging human can do physically in the absence of disease and physical inactivity. Above all, masters athletes' performances reveal what the aging human can accomplish when talent and ability are optimized. Masters athletes raise both physical and psychological ceilings and shatter the barriers of expectations that society has for the aged.

The Scientific Importance of Analyzing Masters Sports

Outstanding achievements in physical performance can partially answer many questions, such as, Are age-related losses greater in aerobic, anaerobic, strength, or power systems? Is the loss of physical ability linear or curvilinear? Do men and women lose physical ability at the same rate? Is there a breakpoint in performance, an age at which the effects of age accelerate? Different energy mobilization and structural systems are necessary for optimum performance in different sports and even across different distances within a sport. *Athletic power* is the production of a large amount of work within a short amount of time, such as occurs in the 100-m sprint race or the clean-and-jerk weightlifting event. These types of performance challenge the peak muscle force generating potential and neuromuscular coordination. In intermediate duration events, ranging from the 400-m dash on the track (or those of about 60 s duration) to the 1,000-m single sculling event on the water (about 4 min), the physiological challenge is to sustain

work outputs far in excess of aerobic capacity in the face of an ever increasing metabolic debt. Longer events, such as a marathon race, challenge the capacity of the aging system to supply continued resources to the muscle (aerobic capacity). High jumping requires exquisite multilimb coordination, whereas running a marathon does not. The marathon, on the other hand, challenges the aerobic system, whereas high jumping does not. By studying the rate of decline of performances that rely exclusively or heavily on specific energy systems and structural integrity, scientists can obtain information about aging effects on these physiological systems. They do this by developing mathematical models, the components of which provide the basis for hypotheses about the mechanisms that control human physical performance. With these models, and other statistical comparisons, athletic competitive performances can supplement laboratory physiological measurements and contribute new hypotheses about how physiological mechanisms interrelate in aging.

Finally, yet another answer to the question, Why study elite masters athletes? is that athletic performance represents the functional significance of physiological theory. If systems such as the aerobic capacity system are found to decrease an average of 1% a year and athletic performance, which depends highly on aerobic capacity, parallels this decline, it provides a functional congruency to theory.

Masters Athletes' Record Performances

Before addressing more theoretical issues of age effects on maximal physical performance, it will be instructive to describe the performance of older athletes in a few sports. Although most sport associations now provide and encourage masters competition, only a few are discussed in detail in this chapter: track and field, swimming, cycling, rowing, and weight lifting. The track-and-field, swimming, and cycling events are included because more older people participate in these competitions than in other sports. Rowing is included because it is a whole-body sport and both field competition and laboratory-rowing ergometer data are available for comparison. Weight lifting is included, not because many older adults participate, but because it is a sport that requires extremes of power and strength. The section concludes with a limited discussion of baseball hitting, bowling, and golf, because baseball hitting represents eye-hand, whole-body neuromuscular coordination and reactive capacity, and bowling and golf are sports in which flexibility, coordination, and accuracy are essential. Together, the task demands of these sports challenge the full range of physical capacities.

Track and Field

The track-and-field events included in this section are the 100-m, 800-m, 10,000-m, 1-mile, and marathon running events and the throwing events: the hammer, discus, javelin throw, and shot put.

Running

The men's and women's world records for the 100-m sprint, the 800-m distance, and an endurance event, the 10,000-m (10K) run, are shown in Figure 14.1, a through c. The decline with age in these trained men and women is very gradual, not slowing at an unusually rapid pace until the age of 80. Past the age of 80, the records are much less consistent, especially the women's records. What is astonishing is that even at the age of 80 some men can run 10K, or roughly 6 miles, in a little over 40 min. A few 80-year-old women can run 6 miles in a little over 1 hr. Compare this to the general public. Most people under the age of 60 cannot even jog 10K without stopping, much less finish the distance in 45 to 60 min. Another enlightening observation about these masters runners is the record for each age group in the mile run, shown in Table 14.1. It is not until the age of 85 that the records for the mile run increase dramatically, becoming much slower. But even at that age, the time of roughly 8 min compares favorably to the time that many sedentary 30- and 40-year-olds need to run a mile.

The masters world records for running events of different distances are shown as a percent of the world records in Figure 14.2 (page 395). Several observations can be made from this graph. The percent of loss is approximately 1% each year, which is about the same as the loss in maximum heart rate over the same period. The first impression is that a striking decline occurs in running speed over the life span. The difference between

the masters runners' records and the world record is larger at each increasing 5-year period. But even though this decline is apparent, a closer inspection reveals that the masters runners maintain *over 50% of their ability* until the 80-84 age category. Even more remarkable, the 85+ masters runners' record in the sprint (100-m) race is 60% of the world record. These figures were based on cross-sectionally derived data, which means that the decline in performance is exaggerated. If longitudinal data of highly trained competitors were analyzed, the proportion of world performance maintained would be even greater (Hartley & Hartley, 1984b; Stones & Kozma, 1982a).

Figure 14.3 (page 395) compares the average running speed (m/s) of male runners over age 40 with that of world-class men and women. On the abscissa of the graph, the distances over which these average speeds were run is shown on a logarithmic scale. One of the most striking features of this analysis is that the decline in speed with increasing distance is almost parallel for men of four increasingly older age groups. Although men over age 70 slow a little more in the extremely long distances, the 40-, 50-, and 60-year-old men have essentially the same declines with distance as the world-class men. Another striking result is the difference in slopes between the world-class men and women and the other runners. The average running speed of world-class men and women, unlike that of men at all ages shown in the figure, declines more precipitously with increasing distances.

Throwing

The world masters records for the discus throw are shown in Figure 14.4a (page 396). In these throwing events, the records decline approximately 2% each year, which is a substantially greater decline than in the running events. Apparently, performance decline is greater in whole-body neuromuscular coordination-limited events that require substantial outlays of power than in cardiovascular-limited events. However, it must be remembered that each point on these graphs is the record of different individuals, not the record of one person from year to year. These year-to-year differences could be due either to a true decline in the performance of a single record holder who nevertheless wins two or more consecutive years or to the individual differences that exist between different people who hold consecutive records. In Figure 14.4a, for example,

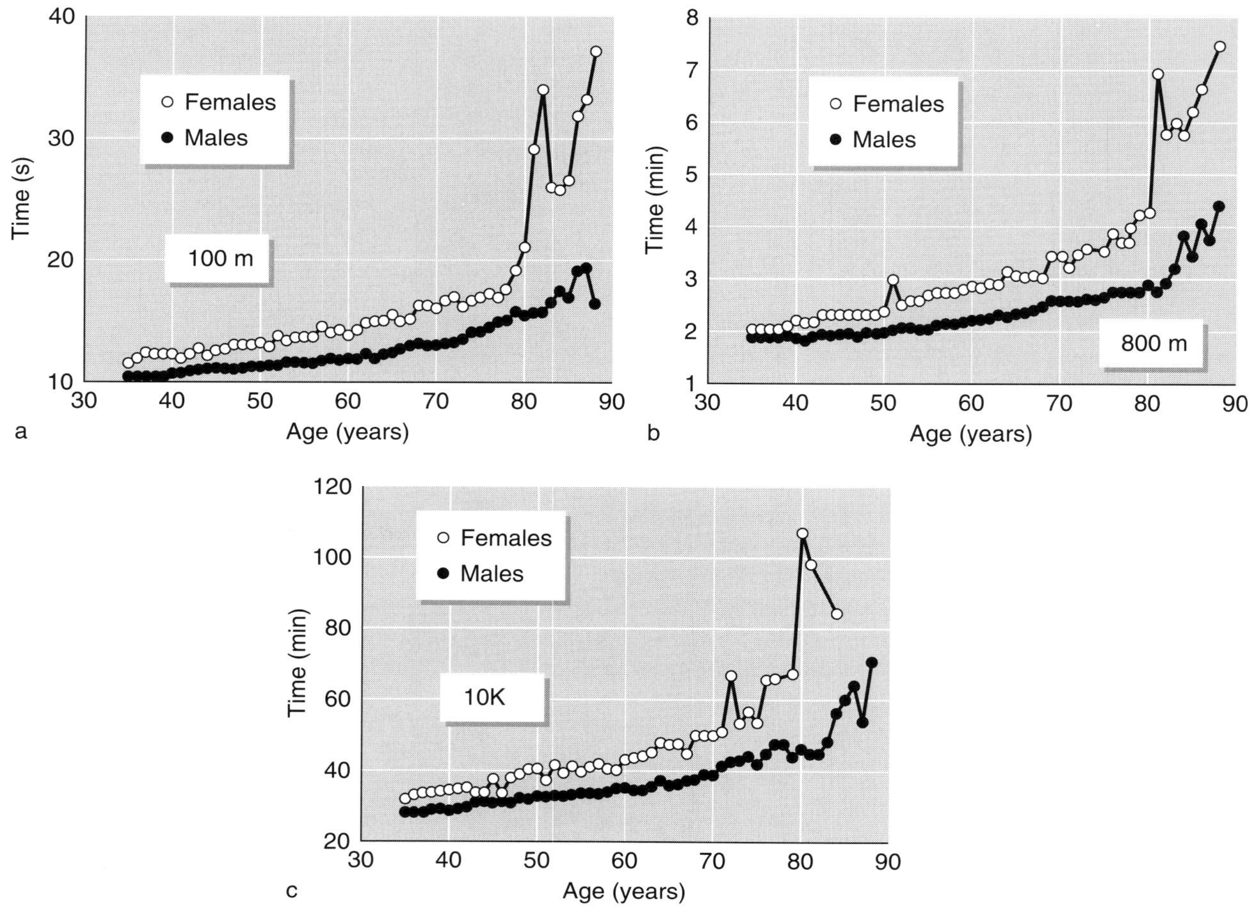

Figure 14.1 Masters world records for males and females in the (a) 100-m, (b) 800-m, and (c) 10K races. Data from *Masters Age Records for 1990* (1991).

Table 14.1
Mile Run Times

Age (years)	Record (min:s)
35	3:55.04
40	4:05.39
45	4:16.75
50	4:32.20
55	4:40.40
60	5:14.20
65	5:05.61
70	5:32.41
75	6:45.00
80	6:43.30
85	8:07.40
90	13:43.60

Note. Data from *Masters Age Records for 1990* (1991).

none of the points on the graph represent the records of Al Orter, one of the finest discus throwers in the history of the event. Rather than competing in masters tournaments, Orter, until the age of 48, competed in the Olympics. His performances from age 35 to 48, if plotted on this graph, would probably reveal no decline at all. These subtleties must be considered when interpreting performance graphs and are discussed in more detail later in the chapter.

Women use a lighter discus than do men. Their overall performance is almost the same as men at age 30 and beyond age 75, and the overall age-related decline is virtually identical to that of men. Women's records are somewhat poorer between ages 45 and 75. It is more difficult to make gender comparisons in the shot-put event because women use a 4-kg shot put from ages 35 to 49 and a lighter, 3-kg shot beginning at age 50 (Figure 14.4b, page 396). Like the discus event, the greatest disparity between men and women is between ages 40 and 50. Once the women change to a

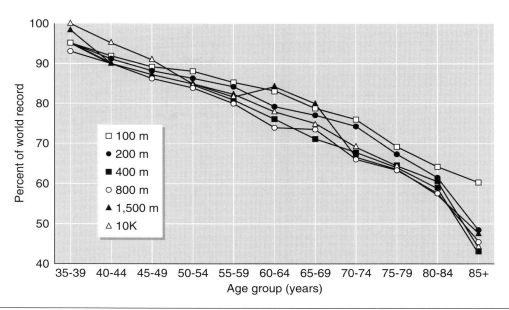

Figure 14.2 Percent of the world record achieved by masters competitors at various ages.
Data from *Masters Age Records for 1990* (1991).

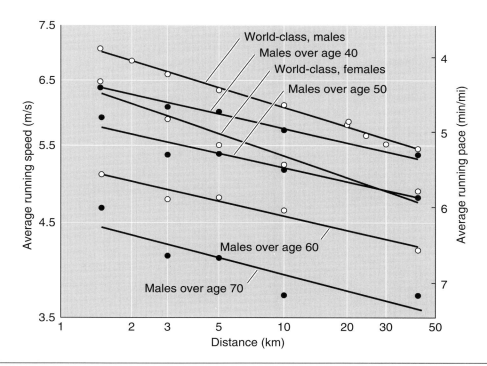

Figure 14.3 Age and gender differences in the average running speed during world record performances.
From "Athletic Records and Human Endurance" by P.S. Riegel, 1981, *American Scientist*, **69**, p. 288. Copyright 1981 by Sigma XI, The Scientific Research Society. Reprinted by permission.

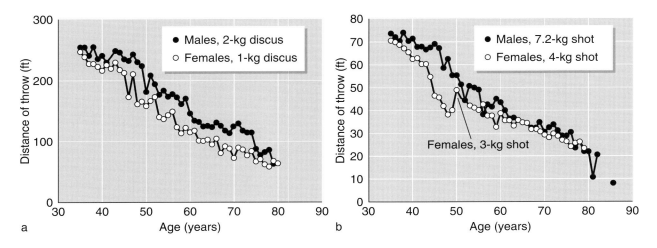

Figure 14.4   Masters world records for males and females in the (a) discus throw and (b) shot put. The arrow in (b) emphasizes that females ages 35 to 49 use a 4-kg shot, and beginning at age 50 they use a 3-kg shot. Data from *Masters Age Records for 1990* (1991).

lighter shot, the performances are virtually identical, although the women are throwing a shot that weighs only half as much as that the men throw.

Jumping

Jumping data for masters men and women are shown in Figure 14.5, a through c. Both men and women decline in jumping distance, but women decline somewhat more. At the oldest ages, women lose 53% compared to mens' 45% loss in the high jump, 69% to 52%, respectively, in the long jump, and 63% to 56%, respectively, in the triple jump. The 50- to 60-year-old men are jumping at about the level of high-school athletes. At all ages, women jump about 22% less than men in the high jump, 28% less in the long jump, and 33% less in the triple jump. Therefore, as the distance to be jumped grows greater (e.g., 7 ft in the high jump, 25 ft in the long jump, 55 ft in the triple jump), the gender differences increase.

Another interesting observation about jumping is how much more it is affected by aging than is running, even sprint running (Figure 14.6, page 398). Performances in events that require complex, whole-body coordination in addition to lower-leg power are more affected by age. The 100-m sprint requires anaerobic energy in what is basically a locomotor activity (running) over a very short time period. It is the simplest motor skill shown in Figure 14.6, and it is affected the least by aging. The triple jump, however, requires even greater anaerobic energy plus coordination, exquisite timing, spatial perception, flexibility, balance, and the

ability to withstand several jarring force contacts with the ground. It is influenced the most by aging.

Swimming

Just as was true of the running records, the swimming speed of masters swimmers slows with age. The swimming speeds of the 10 fastest masters swimmers from the United States Amateur Athletic Union championships were analyzed in 1976, and these same swimmers were also measured in 1981 to provide 5-year longitudinal data that would reflect age changes within individuals (Hartley & Hartley, 1984b). The 1981 data are shown in Figure 14.7, a and b (page 398), and there is a clear decline in performance. Both male and female swimmers were slower at each increasingly older age group; but, as can be seen in Figure 14.8 (page 399), when the 1981 times of the swimmers were compared to their 1976 times (the connected data points in the graph), the swimmers declined little or not at all. Some even improved over the 5-year period, which indicates that age-related declines are substantially less when the performances are measured longitudinally instead of cross-sectionally.

Although the age-related decline in swimming speed appears roughly parallel for these outstanding men and women, according to the statistical analysis, the women declined at a slightly faster rate in the older age groups. Their faster rate of decline is thought to be due to several factors, such as differences in training, in the perceived appropriateness of competitive swimming for

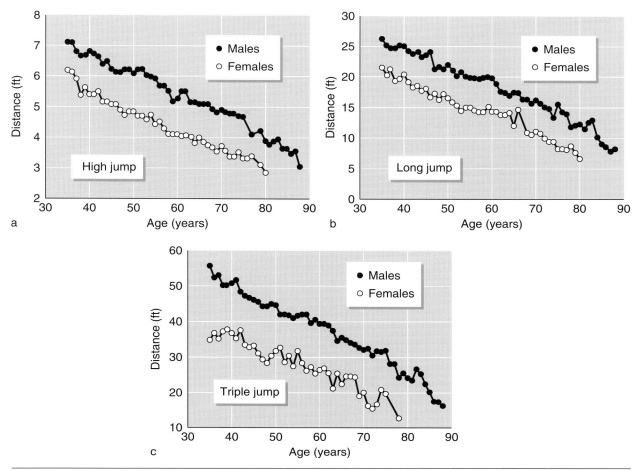

Figure 14.5 Masters world records for male and female jumping: (a) high jump, (b) long jump, and (c) triple jump.

Data from *Masters Age Records for 1990* (1991).

women, and perhaps a faster rate of strength loss. These factors, which influence female performance in all sports, are discussed in more detail at the end of this chapter.

Cycling

At present, older adults maintain their performance capabilities better in cycling than in most other vigorous sports. Shown in Figure 14.9, a and b (page 399), men 60 to 69 years of age only lose 17% of their time in a 40K (24.8 mile) cycling time trial, compared to the loss of about 22% in running a 10K race. It is impressive that highly conditioned men 60 to 69 years old can propel themselves 24.8 miles in less than 1 hr on a bicycle. Women's cycling records are also impressive. The percent losses are almost identical for men and women until ages 60 to 69, at which time the women's record is 29% slower than the national women's

record. However, the percent losses are so similar for men and women up to the 60- to 69-year age group, which is the oldest age group for which U.S. records are kept, that the precipitous loss in the oldest age group is probably due primarily to the fact that few women over the age of 60 compete in cycling races. For example, in the 10K race, an event that attracts many more older women competitors than cycling events do, the women's losses in running are only 21%, which is almost identical to that of men. (This sampling problem is discussed in more detail later in this chapter.) It is surprising that more older women do not compete in cycling, because it seems to be a very popular endurance sport for older men. Competitive cycling, however, also presents a fairly high risk for falling, accidents, and injury, and it may be those characteristics of the event that discourage women.

Cycling records must be considered within the context of the sport as well. As a competitive sport,

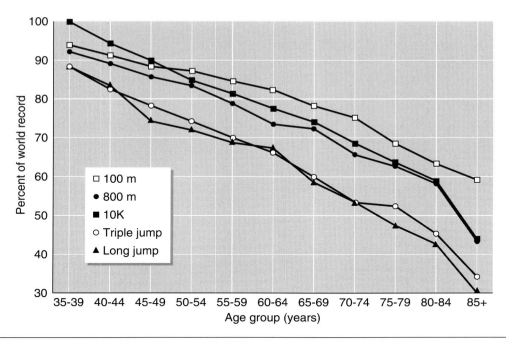

Figure 14.6   Percent of the world record achieved by male record holders of different ages. In the case of the 10K distance, the world-record holder was 35 years old, thus his score was 100% of the world record. The record for the 80- to 84-year-old age category was 60% of the world record.
Data from *Masters Age Records for 1990* (1991).

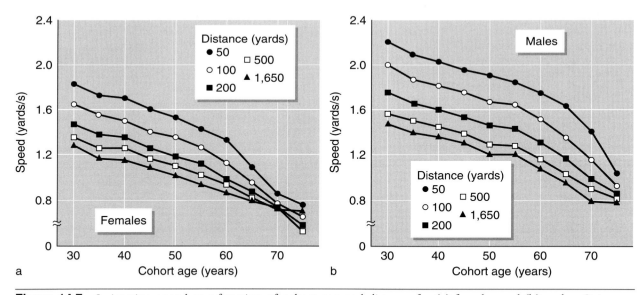

Figure 14.7   Swimming speed as a function of cohort age and distance for (a) females and (b) males. Data are from a repeated cross-sectional study.
From "Performance Changes in Champion Swimmers Aged 30 to 84 years" by A.A. Hartley and J.T. Hartley, 1984, *Experimental Aging Research*, **10**, 146. Copyright 1984 by Beech Hill Enterprises, Inc. Reprinted by permission.

cycling, other than the 40K time-trials event, is somewhat different from other racing sports. In swimming and running races, the competitors more or less swim or run as fast as they can throughout the race, perhaps saving something at the end for a sprinting finish. In cycling, however, wind resistance plays such an important role that the experienced cyclists ride slightly behind one or more of the competitors, making the leaders bear the brunt of the wind and work harder during

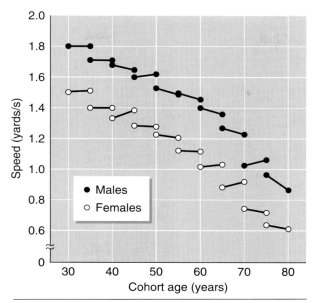

Figure 14.8 Swimming speed as a function of cohort age for males and females. Lines connect performances by the top 10 U.S. performers in a particular cohort in 1976 and in 1981.

From "Performance Changes in Champion Swimmers Aged 30 to 84 Years" by A.A. Hartley and J.T. Hartley, 1984, *Experimental Aging Research*, **10**, p. 146. Copyright 1986 by Beech Hill Enterprises, Inc. Reprinted by permission.

the first part of the race. Those trailing the leaders can then burst out in front at the moment when they think that the combination of more reserve capacity and the element of surprise will leave their competitors unable to catch them. Thus, road-racing times do not reflect the absolute fastest times that the racers could ride but rather the nature of the race strategy. For the sport of cycling, therefore, only time trials in which cyclists race singly against the clock are legitimate races from which to judge the effects of aging on cycling.

Rowing

In this sport one-, two-, four-, or eight-person crews with or without a coxswain propel a shell in as straight a line as possible for speed. Rowing is a sport that requires coordination of almost all of the large muscles of the body (leg, trunk, back, and arms) for relatively long time periods. Most of the events are endurance events and tax the aerobic system. This sport is also somewhat unique in that a rowing ergometer has been developed and performance times on this ergometer have been standardized as world records for the 2,500-m individual race. The results from the ergometer world records

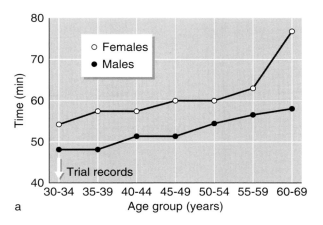

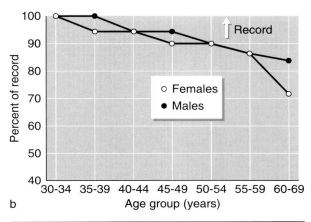

Figure 14.9 Records from the 1990 United States Cycling Federation 40K Road Race Trials: (a) absolute time in minutes; (b) percent of U.S. record for each age group.

Data from the United States Cycling Federation (1990).

provide an interesting comparison to world records in competitive events on the water.

Competitive Events

The results of the 1991 United States Masters Championship in rowing for the light- and heavy-weight men's and women's singles competitions are shown in Figure 14.10. In this particular year, the environmental conditions for all 3 days of the competition were consistent and perfect for rowing, so these competitive times are relatively reliable. As shown in the figure, racing times gradually increase in each older age group (U.S. Rowing Association, 1991). The age of peak performance (i.e., record times) is approximately between ages 28 and 40, although this competition is restricted to masters competitors (over age 27). Some of the fastest rowers who would be in the age 27 to 34

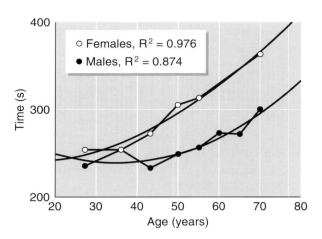

Figure 14.10 Age group records for the men's and women's Single A category, 1991 United States Rowing Championships. The data points for both men and women can be described accurately by a curvilinear (quadratic) equation. Almost all of the womens' data points fall exactly on the curve that describes their performance. The R^2 that is used as an index of the "goodness of fit" of the equation is 0.976, or an R of 0.99. The men's scores do not fall as tightly along the curvilinear line of best fit as the women's do, but they are also predicted quite accurately by a quadratic equation ($R^2 = 0.874$, or $R = 0.93$).
Data from the United States Rowing Association (1991).

category of this tournament, but who consider themselves to be credible contenders in world competitions, rarely enter masters competitions. Rather, these relatively young competitors continue to enter the United States Open Championships. In the masters competitions, both men and women heavyweights row considerably faster than their lightweight counterparts, and men of all ages can move the racing shell much faster than their female cohorts.

Rowing Ergometer Performance

An ergometer is a device that measures physical work output, and as discussed in chapter 4, bicycle ergometers have been used for many years to measure physiological work parameters such as maximum oxygen consumption. The rowing ergometer, however, is calibrated so that the rowing time achieved by an individual on the ergometer is a good estimate of that individual's potential time to row 2,500 m on water. Thus, individuals can test themselves to determine how fast they can row the specified race distance without ever getting in the shell. The technical mastery necessary to balance the body in the shell and keep it

on line with respect to the finish line limits the on-water performance, so that the velocity that can be developed in the rowing ergometer is about 15% higher than the velocity that can be generated on the water. Nevertheless, the ergometer provides a good estimate of rowing potential. Concept II, Inc. developed the ergometer and has established world rankings based on more than 5,000 entrants from 21 countries (Concept II World Rankings, 1991). These data, which are updated each year, are particularly useful for analyzing age differences in rowing performances, because they are free of the influences of the weather (rain, wind, choppy water, etc.) and equipment differences that usually prevail in an outdoor race.

Figure 14.11 compares the effects of age on rowing ergometer performance to the effects of age on competitive on-water rowing. For both events, performance is the percent difference between each age group and (a) the 20-year-old group ergometer scores and (b) the on-water times in the 1991 International Rowing Federation (FISA) championships. The ergometer performances are best represented by a linear decline, and the on-water competitive times are best represented by a curvilinear line. The aging FISA competitors were

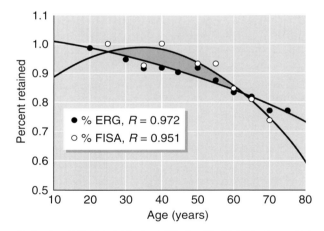

Figure 14.11 The percent of performance retained by different age groups in rowing performance (2,500 m) on the rowing ergometer (ERG) compared to performance in the on-water 1991 championships of the International Rowing Federation (FISA). The ergometer scores were based on performances either recorded during national or world competitions or through club competitions. The regression equations show that the percent of performance retained can be predicted by age with a correlation of $r = 0.972$ for the ergometer and $r = 0.951$ for the on-water rowing performances.
Data from Concept II World Rankings (1991).

able to stay closer to the performances of the young champions for a longer number of years (30-60 years) than to competitors on the ergometer. This difference between the two events appears as a stippled area.

What is the explanation for this difference? In the FISA regatta, everything that a competitor has gained over the years—cumulative training benefits, race, strategy, skill and technique, balance, and ability to cope with the elements—contributes to the outcome of the race. Conversely, the performance times of older competitors in the world rankings on the ergometer primarily represent changes in muscular strength, power, and aerobic capacity. In the ergometer competitions, age-related physiological changes are not counterbalanced by knowledge, technique, strategy, or wisdom. Thus, the performances of the competitors in the two events are statistically represented by two differently shaped regression lines, one curvilinear, indicating the tendency of the on-water competitors to maintain near-peak performances longer, and the other a linear decline, representing the inexorable physiological declines in muscle structure and function.

One additional point about Figure 14.11: Even though the sample size is very large (n = 5,000), the distribution of ages is extremely unequal, as shown in Figure 14.12. In this figure almost one fifth of the entire sample were 20-year-olds, and the samples were very small beginning at about age 55. At this particular age, the performance decrement also becomes noticeably greater.

Therefore, part of the explanation for slower performances by those over age 55 may be due to the smaller number of people that age who compete in the ergometer competitions.

Weight Lifting

Weight lifting is not a very popular sport among older athletes. It is a sport in which the muscular, powerful, and anaerobically talented individual may excel. It requires a tremendous recruitment of energy over a very short period of time and develops extremely high internal pressures during the exertion. In spite of the toll that aging takes on muscle mass, many weight lifters continue to lift weights into their 70s and 80s. Their competitive lift records provide substantial insight into the decline of muscular performance capabilities with aging. It is unlikely that elderly subjects in a strength laboratory ever reach the truly maximum effort that is produced by masters weight lifters in competition. Noncompetitive subjects have rarely experienced the sensation of producing a maximum neuromuscular effort. Not only are competitive weight lifters highly motivated in competition, as a group they also physically train their muscles far more intensively than do any subjects in experimentally designed strength-training programs. From that perspective, the masters weight lifters provide the best data to answer the question, How much strength can be maintained over the years if a person systematically and scientifically weight trains?

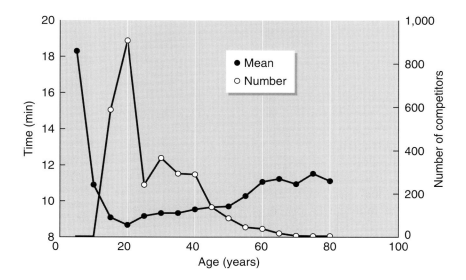

Figure 14.12   Rowing times compared to the number of competitors in each age group.

Olympic weight lifting is a term by which the general public loosely describes all events and activities in which persons lift weight. From the public's perspective, weight lifting can mean resistance strength training, any competition where the athletes lift heavy weights, or even body building. But technically, there are only two types of events in which the participants compete to determine who can lift the most weight. *Weight lifting* officially includes two events, the clean-and-jerk and the snatch. In the clean-and-jerk, the lifter reaches down to the bar (between the two weights) and in one quick motion, lifts the weights to the chest ("the clean"), pauses momentarily, and then explosively drives the bar above the head and holds it with arms extended for at least 3 s. In the snatch event, the lifter must lift the bar all the way from the floor to the fully extended arm position above the head in one motion. Both of these events require not only tremendous power production during the lift but also inordinate agility and flexibility, in order to get under the bar quickly when it reaches its highest point from the first exertion, and exquisite neuromuscular coordination, in order to time the transfer of weight across the different body muscles that absorb and forward the load to its final destination high above the head. Excellent balance throughout the lift is also required to maintain the weight over the center of gravity throughout the lift. Losing one's balance under a 300-lb bar can be disastrous. Both the clean-and-jerk and the snatch are sanctioned by the International Olympic Committee and are Olympic events.

The other major type of weight lifting is *powerlifting*. Powerlifting consists of three events: the dead lift, squat, and bench press. In the dead lift, the lifter reaches down to the bar and must lift the weight only as high as is necessary to get the arms, legs, and back fully extended. The squat requires the lifter to begin with the bar placed on the shoulders, to squat until the crease between the torso and thigh is below the bent knee, and then to return to a full stand. To perform the bench press, the lifter lies on a bench on his or her back, holds the weight at arms-length above the chest, lowers the bar to the chest, and returns it to the original position. Thus, in all three of the power lifts, absolute force production is at a premium. The term *powerlifting* is rather a misnomer for these three events, because speed is not a great factor in the lifts. The clean-and-jerk and the snatch are really power movements, because they require a fast movement to hoist the bar from the floor to a position above the head. Nevertheless, these events acquired their names long before the differences between strength and power were commonly known, and it is not likely that they will change.

Age Effects on Weight Lifting

As shown in Figure 14.13, a and b, aging takes a heavy toll on weight lifting. Only the clean-and-jerk records (United States Weightlifting Federation, 1991) are shown in this figure, because the pattern of change over time is virtually identical for the snatch event. In each successively older decade, lifters in all three weight classes (heavy-, middle-, and lightweight) are able to lift less and less weight (Figure 14.13a). To compare the effects of age on the lifters in different weight classes, the lifts at each age are compared to the lifts that were made at a younger age, when the athletes were at their peak capacity. These comparisons are shown in Figure 14.13b as percentages of the world record for that weight class for each age group. Clearly, the record holders in all three weight classes can only lift about 40% of the world-record weight by ages 70 to 74. All three weight classes experience a highly linear decline from age 40 to age 74. Note that the lightweight lifters in Figure 14.13a lift substantially less absolute weight than the other two weight classes, but when their lifts are expressed as a percentage of the record for lightweights, their decline over age is about the same as that of the other two weight classes.

Age Effects on Powerlifting

The records of the masters in powerlifting are shown in Figure 14.14, a and b. All weight-class records decrease with each increasingly older age group, though the losses are not so great for the middleweight lifters as for the light- and heavyweight lifters (see Figure 14.14a). Middleweight record holders at ages 65 to 69 are lifting more than 60% of their world record, whereas the light- and heavyweight lifters are lifting around 50% of their world record (see Figure 14.14b). Why are middle-class competitors lifting a higher percentage of their record? This apparent superiority may be due almost exclusively to the larger numbers of competitors in that weight class, which makes their weight-lifting meets much more competitive

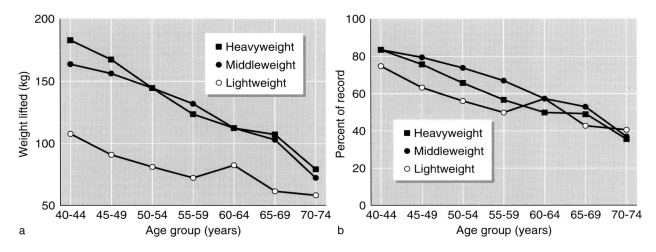

Figure 14.13   Masters national records for the clean-and-jerk. (a) Weight lifted for light- (56- and 60-kg classes), middle- (75-, 82.5-, and 90-kg classes), and heavyweights (100- and 110-kg classes); (b) percent of the world record for each weight class. The decline with age can be described extremely well by a linear equation ($r = 0.988$).
Data from the United States Weightlifting Federation (1991).

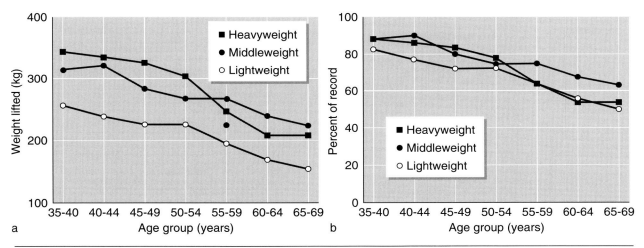

Figure 14.14   Masters national records for the dead lift. (a) Weight lifted; (b) percent of world record for each weight class.
Data from the United States Powerlifting Federation (1991).

and thus more selective. Or, because the anthropometric and biomechanical makeup of middle-class lifters is optimal for weight lifting, their performance may be maintained better over time. Yet another explanation may be that in the older age groups, some of the competitors who were heavyweights lost some weight so they could compete in the middleweight classification and be more competitive.

Comparison of Powerlifting and Weight Lifting

The comparison of powerlifting and weight lifting provides a way to compare the effects of age on pure strength (powerlifting) versus strength in combination with coordination, agility, flexibility, and balance (weight lifting). The brute strength required for powerlifting can be maintained better over the years than the combined attributes of power production, coordination, and balance. This is shown in Figure 14.15, a through c, which compares the U.S. masters records for the dead lift to the masters records for the clean-and-jerk, which requires tremendous power production. In all but one age group for all weight classes, the record holders lift a higher percentage of the world record in the dead lift than in the clean-and-jerk. This difference is greatest in the middle-

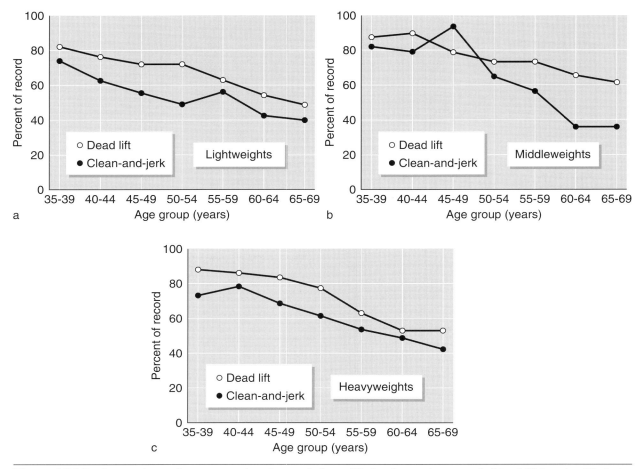

Figure 14.15 Comparison of masters national records for a lift that is purely strength (dead lift) and a lift that requires power, coordination, flexibility, and balance (clean-and-jerk): (a) lightweights, (b) middleweights, and (c) heavyweights.

Data from the United States Weightlifting Federation (1991) and the United States Powerlifting Federation (1991).

and heavyweight classes, where the 65- to 69-year-old powerlifting record is close to 60% of the world record, whereas the record for the clean-and-jerk is less than 40% of the world record. The cumulative effects of aging on strength production, coordination, flexibility, agility, and balance result in older lifters achieving a lower percentage of the world record in weight-lifting events than they achieve in powerlifting events, which require primarily maintenance of strength. In fact, the highest peak movement velocity occurs in the snatch and the clean-and-jerk, the two events in which the difference between old and young competitors is the greatest, and the lowest movement velocity is required in the dead lift and squat, the two events in which the older performers come closest to the world records. Thus it appears that as the peak power requirement increases in these events, the ability to maintain performance decreases.

Implications of Weight-Lifting Performances of Masters Competitors

One of the first things that should be said about the weight-lifting performance of older competitors is that their performances are remarkable. Compared to the physical abilities of the vast majority of older people, it is inspiring to observe that some 70-year-old men can lift more than 400 lb of steel from the floor. The world record in the 70- to 74-year-old category is held by Howard Stupp, who in 1986 dead-lifted 501.5 lb. Just as impressive, an even older Helen Zechmeister set the record for 75-to-79-year-olds in the dead lift by lifting 220.5 lb. If most men and women were to follow good health habits and continue to weight train throughout their lives, it would be reasonable to expect that they could continue to lift more than 100 lb well into their 60s and 70s. In fact, because the data in Figures 14.13 through 14.15 are all based on cross-sectional data, the downward slope seen in these figures is probably an *overestimation* of the age-related decline in muscular strength. Thus, the reason that 16% of older adults over age 55 have difficulty lifting even 25 lb (Kovar & LaCroix, 1987) is largely due to disuse and chronic disease, *not* to massive and inevitable wasting of muscle tissue.

Baseball Hitting

Part of the folklore of baseball is that hitting a fastball is one of the hardest sports skills. Hitting a fastball involves the incredible ability to track a relatively small object (i.e., a baseball) that is moving at a velocity of more than 90 mph and coordinate almost all of the large muscles of the body so that the bat can arrive at the exact point in space at the precise moment in time to contact the ball. Because visual-tracking speed, information processing, coordination, and power are required for this skill, the maximum age of effectiveness in baseball hitting is very young. Figure 14.16, a and b, presents the annual number of home runs and the batting averages of five members of the Baseball Hall of Fame recorded for a 10-year period of their careers. Both hitting power and accuracy peaked at age 27 for these players and then declined. Their careers were essentially over by age 33. Baseball, like football and basketball, requires power and whole-body coordination, a combination that does not fare well during the aging process.

Bowling

Unlike the power, endurance, and reactive sports, bowling is a sport that people can perform successfully for many years. Table 14.2 shows the bowling averages and the number of years in competition for 10 members of the American Bowling Congress Hall of Fame who lived to be at least 60 years old. These older bowlers continued to bowl very high scores into their 70s. This information does not include the age at which the bowlers began their career or whether their careers were shortened by illness, injury, or accidental death, but it does show that high scores can be maintained for a very long time. The next-to-the-oldest

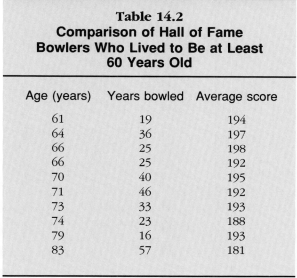

Table 14.2
Comparison of Hall of Fame Bowlers Who Lived to Be at Least 60 Years Old

Age (years)	Years bowled	Average score
61	19	194
64	36	197
66	25	198
66	25	192
70	40	195
71	46	192
73	33	193
74	23	188
79	16	193
83	57	181

Note. Data from Hickok (1971).

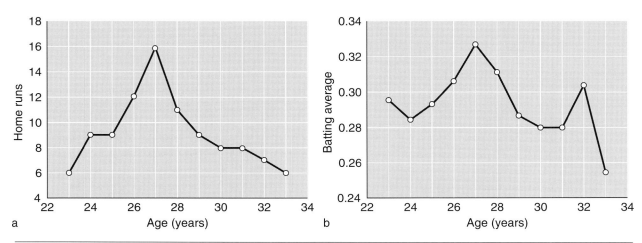

Figure 14.16 (a) Home run and (b) batting average records for five baseball players listed in the Baseball Hall of Fame.
Data from Langford (1987).

person in the table is Ed Easter, who maintained a 193 average during his 16-year career in bowling. He did not begin bowling until he was 60 years old, and he bowled two of his 300 games when he was more than 70 years old (Hickok, 1971). Thus, bowling is a sport that can be started late in life and maintained relatively successfully for a great many years.

Golf

Golf is a very popular sport among older adults, because although the game requires many different abilities, the most important of them are primarily abilities of skill and finesse. Power with the driving and fairway woods helps to make approach shots shorter, but in golf accuracy is much more important than power. More than half of the strokes in an average golfer's score are chipping and putting scores, which require almost no strength at all. Older adults can compensate very effectively for a loss of distance when using the long woods and irons by increased precision in approach shots, chipping, and putting. A good example of this is a comparison of the 1990 Professional Golf Association (PGA) tour players' records with those of the PGA Senior tour players' (Figure 14.17, a-e). Excellent golfers drive the ball far, arrive at the green in "regulation" (1 stroke for par 3s, 2 for par 4s, and 3 for par 5s), get a high percentage of their shots that go in sand bunkers out and in the hole for par (sand saves), have a very low putting average per green (less than 2 strokes per green), and have a low scoring average. The only one of these in which the top senior players are significantly worse than the top younger PGA players is driving distance. The most important statistic in golf is scoring average, and the difference between the two age groups on this statistic is negligible. In professional tournaments, the seniors do not play as long a course as the PGA players, thus the age-related difference in driving distance is negated in these statistics. If the seniors were to play the same length of course as the PGA players, their scoring average would be slightly higher (worse) than that of the PGA players. That is why it is rare for players in their late 40s to win PGA tournaments. Raymond Floyd and Hale Irwin are good examples, however, of the individual differences in older people. Both of them, in their late 40s, won four PGA events. In 1992 Floyd won the Doral Ryder Open tournament at the age of 50.

Among amateurs, the effect of aging is even less apparent, because people differ so much in amount of practice, their skill level, and their psychological approach to the game. It is commonplace to find 60- and 70-year-old amateurs who can soundly trounce 20-year-olds in a round of golf, and in any given round, it is not at all unlikely that even an 80-year-old golfer will chip at least one ball as close to the hole as any professional can or sink a putt as long as that of any 20-year-old. Patience, experience, and wisdom are great compensatory mechanisms for older golfers, and these abilities, in addition to practice, enable people to continue to play golf even into their 90s. One of the goals of many avid amateur golfers is to be able to "shoot their age," but because par is 72 and almost no older amateurs can shoot par, this goal usually is not even possible until a golfer reaches the age of 72. Nevertheless, many people do finally shoot their age, usually in their late 70s and early 80s, and lists of these accomplishments are regularly published in golf magazines throughout the world. The record was made in 1972 when Arthur Thompson, of Victoria, British Columbia, Canada, at 103 years of age, shot 97 on a 6,215-yd golf course (Hains, 1989). Golf is a sport in which dogged determination, constant practice, a positive attitude, and focusing on strengths rather than weaknesses can postpone the negative effects of physical aging on the ultimate goal for a very long time.

Determining Age Effects on Physical Abilities by Comparing Sports Performance

Analyses of aging effects on athletic performance, besides being inherently interesting and serving as a barometer of what is possible at older ages, also supplement scientific knowledge about the effects of aging on the physiological mechanisms that underpin efficient, powerful physical performance. Analysts of sports performance use two strategies. One strategy is to examine the age at which a sport's world record performances occur. If the age at which the world record (for any sport) is 17 years, and the age of the person holding the world record in another sport is 35 years, analysts can derive information about what systems are at a premium in each sport—those that mature early

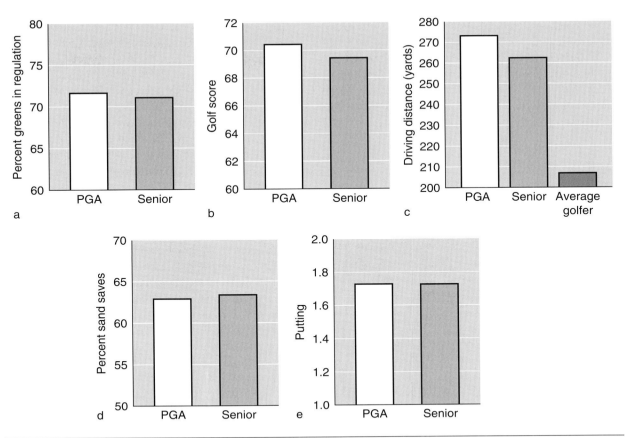

Figure 14.17 Comparison of the 1990 Professional Golf Association (PGA) tour players' golf statistics with those of the Senior PGA players, top 10 players in each tour. (a) Percent greens in regulation; (b) scoring averages (top 3 players in each tour only); (c) driving distance; (d) percent sand saves; (e) putting averages.

and are fully efficient at an early age or those that require experience, patience, and other attributes more commonly seen in older individuals. The second strategy is to study the relative age-related losses that occur at each decade in different sports and then determine which physiological, biomechanical, and structural systems are being taxed. The first strategy can be called the age-at-peak-performance strategy, and the second can be called the statistical modeling strategy.

Age at Peak Performance

The age-at-peak-performance strategy argues that comparing the ages of peak performance across several different sports reveals the physiological demands of each sport (Ericsson, 1990; Schultz & Curnow, 1988). For example, heaving a shot put requires a maximum explosion of anaerobic power, whereas running a marathon requires the production of aerobic energy over a long time period. If the peak age of a shot putter is younger than that

of a marathoner, then it could be concluded that aging exacts a greater toll on the combined systems of anaerobic power production and neuromuscular integration than on aerobic capacity. This procedure seems reasonable, because it makes intuitive sense that if only young adults win championships in a particular sport, aging must affect the basic physiological systems on which great performances in that sport depend. Until relatively recently, the peak ages of those who make records in sports such as running and cycling have remained remarkably stable since records have been kept, enhancing their attractiveness as a potential indicator of age effects on different physiological systems.

However, the validity of this argument hinges on two assumptions. The first is that the time of peak performance corresponds exactly to the time of peak physiological potential. The second is that the athlete begins training at the optimal age and continues to train optimally through the period of peak physiological potential. If these two conditions are met, then consistent differences in the age of peak performance across sports that are limited by different physiological systems (i.e., marathon vs. shot put) may reveal differences in the rate of deterioration of these systems.

On first inspection, age at peak performance seems to be a reasonable means of comparison, and historically this strategy has been used to suggest that the peak performance in sports requiring explosive power over a short period (e.g., sprinting, jumping, throwing) occurs in the early 20s. As the demand for explosive power is replaced by the demand for muscular endurance and tactical experience (middle- to long-distance running, water polo, 1500-m swim), the ages of world-record holders and top performers exceed 25 years. Indeed, *within* some sports the age-power relationship has, until recently, seemed to prevail. For example, the age of the record holders in the running events has supported the notion of a negative relationship between age and power production. For the past 100 years, the order of the race distances (100 m , 200 m, 800 m, 1,500 m, 10,000 m, marathon, and 50K) is roughly the same as the order of the record holders' ages: The shorter the race, the younger the champion.

Extraordinary performances in the early 1990s by athletes at ages previously considered past their prime, however, force a reexamination of the validity of the underlying assumptions regarding age at peak performance. In 1991, the world record in the 100-m dash was shattered by a 30-year-old. In the 1992 Olympics held in Barcelona, the ages of the 100-m-sprint, long-jump, and triple-jump champions were 32, 31, and 30 respectively, whereas previously the peak age for these sports was in the early 20s. The United States 800-m representative (and bronze medalist) in the event was 32 years old; the U.S. decathlon champion was 29. The time when a 17-year-old, like Robert Mathias in 1956, could reign as decathlon champion and "World's Greatest Athlete" has given way to an era in which true peak performance is achieved only after years of training and competing at the highest level. On the basis of these dramatically different competitive results from the 1990s, the concept of age at peak performance merits reevaluation.

The Statistical Modeling Strategy

Another way to use sport performance as an adjunct to understanding differential aging effects on physiological systems is to develop a statistical model that includes age as one predictor and a measure of the type of physiological system primarily used (aerobic or anaerobic) as a second predictor of performance times. Running performances over distances that are finished in less than 1 min depend primarily on the anaerobic system, whereas races over distances long enough to require several minutes (or more) rely heavily on the aerobic system. Therefore, race distance has been used as a proxy for the type of physiological system that is being taxed. If running times (or average velocities) can be predicted accurately by including both age and distance traveled, then an analysis of some of the components of the equation should shed some light on the effects of aging on these physiological systems.

Moore (1975) and Salthouse (1976) developed two early models that included components of strength, endurance, and age. However, the effectiveness of their models was limited by a small database, inadequate sampling, and a limited age range. Moore's (1975) model was an exponential model,

$$Y = A_1[1-e^{A_2^X}] + A_3[1-e^{A_4^X}],$$

where Y = speed in m s^{-1}, X = age in years, and A_1, A_2, A_3, and A_4 are coefficients determined from the age records by least-squares statistical analyses. Moore's (1975) model also was applied separately to each race distance; therefore, it did not include distance as an interactive factor with age and running time.

By far the most comprehensive study of age effects on maximal physical performance, accompanied by proposed performance-limiting physiological mechanisms, has been made by Stones and Kozma (1980, 1981, 1982a, 1982b, 1984a, 1984b, 1985, 1986a, 1986b). Based on their many analyses, they proposed that performance time in running can best be expressed as a product of power function of distance and an exponential function of age (Stones & Kozma, 1980). This exponential function can be simplified, however, to a general linear model in which performance time is related to both age and event distance:

$$Ln(performance) = Ln (0.049 \cdot distance^{1.089}) + b \cdot age,$$

where Ln = log to the base n (natural logarithm), performance = the runner's time, distance = distance of event, and b = coefficient specific to the type of race (i.e., anaerobic or aerobic).

This equation implies that performance, expressed as a natural logarithm, is a linear function of age; the intercept is the log function of distance. From their comparison of the *b* coefficients, which averaged 0.009 for anaerobic events (those shorter than 400 m) and 0.011 for aerobic events (those more than 400 m), they concluded that the age effect is greater for middle- and long-distance events than for sprints (see Figure 14.6, page 398). Furthermore, the rate of decline in the middle- and long-distance events was almost the same as the age-related rate of decline in aerobic power ($\dot{V}O_2$max) when measured by laboratory testing (see chapter 4).

From these results, Stones and Kozma (1985) formulated an energy output-supply ratio hypothesis and later tested its validity against other hypotheses (Stones & Kozma, 1986b). They called their model the power-output-relative-to-power-available model, or the POrPA model. The model is based on two assumptions: that age-related decline is greater on tasks in which the maximal output of power taxes the available power more severely, and that more power is available for short-duration performances than for prolonged ones. How does this work?

In short-distance events, the anaerobic system provides a large supply of energy for a brief time. The classic examples of anaerobic, high maximum energy actions are the high jump, long jump, and short-distance hurdle races, where horizontal force is converted to vertical force by the powerful driving actions of the legs. Physiological evidence shows that the power available from anaerobic sources is three to four times greater than that available from aerobic sources (Bouchard, Thibault, & Jobin, 1981). This principle is also observed in tests of absolute muscle strength, where the greater the mass of muscle tested, the greater the age-related decline. Thus, as was discussed in chapter 5, the decline with age is greater in leg and trunk muscles than in the arm muscles (Åstrand & Rodahl, 1977). In long-distance events, the aerobic system provides lower energy supplies but over a longer time period. Because the energy expenditure over a long period is greater than the energy available, age effects are more pronounced in distance events than in short, power events. In Figure 14.2 (page 395), the event in which athletes over age 70 can best maintain performance is the 100-m sprint—the only running event that is clearly an anaerobic event. The model also predicts age-related decline in the running events rather well (see Figure 14.6, page 398). In running, the decline is greater for the two longer aerobic events (800-m, 10K) than for the anaerobic event (100-m).

These two longer events depend on the maintenance of the oxidative capacity system, which was shown in chapter 4 to decline about 1% a year due to the inevitable decline of maximum heart rate, irrespective of training intensity and duration. The 100-m sprint, however, may be maintained better because the requisite muscle mass can be maintained through training, and biomechanical efficiency and neuromuscular apparatus are less affected by aging. However, the decline is greatest for the two jumping events, which are also anaerobic activities (see Figure 14.6). Although the anaerobic power available for these events may be proportionately greater than the power available for aerobic events, the issue is not this simple. These jumping events also involve multiple systems and factors: complex neurological integration, biomechanical systems, balance, timing, distribution of large impact forces—all of which also are compromised by aging.

Is the Stones and Kozma (1985) model a good predictor of performance *within* a class of events that have similar energy supply categories, that is, either primarily aerobic or primarily anaerobic? Their model states that if the power available is held constant, then the order of deterioration *within a class of anaerobic events*, from the greatest to the least deterioration, should be events that require the greatest power output, followed by events that require less. Their prediction is that within jumping events, advanced age would affect the jump and hurdle events most and the sprint and pole-vault events somewhat less. And that is precisely what they found (Stones & Kozma, 1986b). Their predictions for the category of events that rely on aerobic energy sources were also confirmed. They found that the age-related decline in the performance times of race walks, which require less power output than running events, was less than the age-related decline in any of the running or steeplechase events. In summary, their model predicted, within categories of short- and longer-duration events, that performance deterioration with age is greater in events that require higher peak-power output.

Hartley and Hartley (1984b, 1986) challenged the Stones and Kozma model by showing that, on the basis of their own regression analysis of 5-year longitudinal data on champion masters swimmers, the age-related decline was greatest in the short distances rather than long distances. They also found that the POrPA model failed to predict the outcomes in sprint swimming races that differed only in type of stroke: the butterfly, breaststroke, freestyle, and backstroke. They hypothesized that such age-related declines should be attributed primarily to loss of upper-body muscle strength, not power. However, Stones and Kozma (1984a) maintained that the differences between their research outcomes and Hartley and Hartley's (1984b, 1986) were methodological and analytical, not differences in age effects on performances differing in distance or in type (swimming vs. running). Hartley and Hartley (1984a, 1984b) used age and distance to predict speed (yards/s) of performance, whereas Stones and Kozma routinely used age and distance to predict performance times. Stones and Kozma (1984a) argued that speed is not a good measure to predict, because it is a derivative of distance over time and thus is represented, nonindependently, in two parts of the equation, that is, as one of the predictors (distance) and as the measure to be predicted (speed).

Several interesting observations have emerged from the studies that use the statistical modeling strategy. First, both the aerobic and the anaerobic systems decline with aging, but because of the contradictory results of some of the studies, whether aerobic performance is affected more than anaerobic performance is still unresolved. It is likely that differential aging effects on different systems are much more complex than a simple relationship between power required and power available. The number and interplay of the various systems involved, and the effects of aging and training on these systems, must surely affect the rate of age-related decline in sport. For example, although the 100-m sprint and the triple jump are both anaerobic events that require extraordinary power production, age effects are much greater in the triple jump, because it requires a multisystem effort. Second, physical performances at maximal intensity suffer more from aging effects than do submaximal performances (Stones & Kozma, 1985).

Third, age-related decline in performance is greater and more linear in cross-sectional research designs than in longitudinal designs. This is shown in Figure 14.18, where the cross-sectional studies indicated a larger percent change in performance each year in four out of five distance records. Longitudinal data, because they represent changes within competitors over time, reflect plateaus of performance, a more gradual curvilinear descent in performances, and an accelerated decline in the latter part of life. This curvilinear model is more typical of the growth and decline curves seen in most biological phenomena.

Nonphysiological Factors That Limit the Performances of Masters Athletes

It is clear that aging has a potent negative effect on structural and physiological mechanisms, ensuring that athletic performance must inevitably decline with advancing age. However, several factors other than physical ones also contribute to diminishing performance among most masters athletes. Most masters athletes train less intensely, compete with somewhat less verve and in fewer numbers, and have less psychosocial support for their participation.

Decreases in Training

Although empirical data are scarce, most analysts of older adults' athletic performance believe that with increasing age, masters competitors reduce both the frequency and intensity with which they train. Older people train less strenuously for several reasons. First, many older adults maintain full-time managerial or administrative jobs that carry multiple responsibilities. They simply do not have the time to train that they once did. Second, older adults also have a lifetime of experiences that enable them to place training time and sport competition within a broader perspective than 20-year-olds can. Most can only win so many trophies before additional ones begin to lose their luster. Third, the best that older competitors can achieve is a relative victory, that of their age group, whereas 20- to 30-year-olds are striving for an absolute victory—the winner over all ages. For most people, it is harder to maintain an aggressive training program to gain a relative victory than it is to maintain discipline for a collegiate, state, national, or world record. Fourth, the ravages of time are hard on the body; it is not only difficult psychologically to maintain a heavy training schedule, it is difficult physically. Older competitors are plagued much more by muscular and orthopedic training injuries than are the young, and it takes them longer to rehabilitate from injuries. Consequently, they enter competitions without the

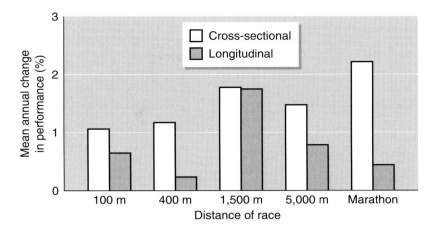

Figure 14.18 Differences in age-related changes for five running distances when data are collected cross-sectionally vs. longitudinally.
Data from Stones and Kozma (1982a, p. 187).

extensive training base that young competitors have.

Because of these training differences, those sports events that require more training to remain in top form reveal greater age declines. It is hard to distinguish whether the greater declines seen in training-dependent events such as distance running, hurdles, and weight lifting are the result of age-related declines in physiological resources, disinclination to train hard, incidence or fear of injury, or a combination of these.

Competitive Fervor Decreases

For some of the same reasons that limit training practices, most masters athletes do not approach competitive events with as much passion as young people do. Besides winning relative rather than absolute victories, and in the life-perspective with which older adults view athletic victories, masters athletes are not likely to view athletics as a potential source of revenue or as a way out of an undesirable lifestyle.

The different ways that young and old powerlifters approach a competition is a good example. Younger men and women in the powerlifting events (not weight-lifting events) wear body suits and use other types of lift-enhancing training equipment and techniques, some of which are relatively painful. These external suits and training apparatus enable the competitors to lift significantly more pounds than they can lift without them. But these external performance aids also substantially raise the blood pressure during the

lift, and they create other physical problems. Older lifters may not use these as enthusiastically; consequently, they do not lift as much as they might be capable of lifting. Also, young competitors do things in competition to evoke the fight-or-flight response just before attempting a lift. Face slapping, ammonia inhalation, and yelling are all part of the game for the younger athlete. For the most part, these types of efforts are absent during masters competitions, suggesting that these age groups also differ psychologically from young competitors.

Another age difference in training techniques is that young athletes are also much more likely to use steroids, growth hormones, or other drugs to enhance their performance, whereas older athletes probably began their careers before drugs were commonly used and are much less likely to begin drug use at an older age. Older athletes, from experience, have discovered that they are neither invincible nor immortal. Young athletes intellectually know that they will not live in good health forever, but they do not believe it. Consequently, young athletes are willing to take more risks with their health.

The Sampling Problem

Perhaps because the motivation to train and to compete decreases with age, many athletes eventually quit competitive sports. Also, many champion athletes do not choose to compete at the masters level when they become less competitive at the national or world level. They would rather not compete at all, than to compete at what they regard as a lower level. A case in point was the great reluctance of Jack Nicklaus, possibly the greatest golfer of all time, to enter the Senior Professional Golf Association Tour on reaching the eligibility age of 50. This is not true of most professional golfers or many champions in other sports, such as certain running events in which some famous runners have continued their competitive careers in age-group events. But in many less visible sports, it is considered unseemly for champions to move from world competition to masters competition. This point cannot be made strongly enough: Masters records do not *always* contain the best performances that adults of each age group can produce.

Because many champions do not compete, and others drop out, the numbers of athletes dwindle with each advancing decade. This is clearly shown in Figure 14.12 (page 401). To acquire performance data that are truly representative of each age cohort, however, it is important to have a large pool of competitors, so that the natural screening process of competition can produce the very highest performances that humans can achieve. Generally speaking, if an event has 500 competitors from 50 countries, the winner of that event will probably have a higher score than the winner of an event with 25 competitors from a single city. In all the states but the one in which the champion resides, state records are not as high as the national records, because the state competitions do not sample as wide an array of human resources. In a marathon event, there may be 750 runners between the ages of 20 and 30, 40 runners between the ages of 50 and 60, but only 3 competitors older than age 80. This contestant-by-age compression phenomenon is even greater in women's events, so performance records and the models that are based on women may be increasingly less representative of actual performance capabilities for the older age groups. Smaller samples mean less likelihood of high-caliber performances.

The sampling issue is more problematic in some events than in others. The number of 80-and-older contestants is much higher in the 10K race than in the shot put, and in the 50-km race-walk than in the high jump. Inequity of sampling is extreme in weight lifting, where the number of weight-lifting records dramatically decreases for both men and women, even as early as middle age. Because the competitions at these older ages have fewer and fewer competitors in them, they serve less effectively as a sample of their age group. In sports that have weight classes, such as weight lifting, boxing, wrestling, and rowing, the sample of competitors is divided into even smaller subunits, so that some weight classes in the older masters categories have only one or two competitors.

Psychosocial Influences

Many psychosocial factors probably influence the participation of older adults in sports, but two obvious factors are societal attitudes toward older participants in sports events (ageism) and societal gender bias with regard to sport. The concept of vigorously active, competitive septuagenarians and octogenarians is a relatively new phenomenon in American society. In the first two thirds of the 20th century, at least, societal expectations were that older adults should rest, take it easy, and be relatively inactive, especially after retirement. Indeed, the dictionary definition of retirement includes such phrases as "to withdraw to a secluded place, to go to bed, to retreat, to give up work because of age, to withdraw from use." Societal expectations are a very powerful influence, so when older adults indicated that they were interested in competing in a tournament, it is likely that they were told, either directly in conversation or indirectly by actions, that they should "act their age," meaning "not compete." Only those few older athletes who were willing to face societal disapproval entered competitions. These societal attitudes still contribute to the sampling problem discussed previously.

Societies also have strong views about what is appropriate behavior for women and men, and although attitudes are changing, gender bias persists in sport. People who harbor these biases believe that tennis and golf are appropriate for women, whereas powerlifting and shot-putting are not. Similarly, pole vaulting is acceptable for men, but ice skating is not. Gender bias therefore influences the size of the pool of competitive athletes. It also limits the opportunities for training and coaching of athletes in those sports that are considered inappropriate for a specific gender.

Consider weight- or powerlifting. Comparatively few young women compete in these events, and even fewer continue to lift into their senior years. Very few U.S. records are available, and in some weight classes, no records are available. A plausible explanation for why almost no women compete in these sports beyond age 50 is that weight lifting places a premium on power production, and social attitudes toward women, especially older women, as power producers are generally negative. Based on the performances of the few women who do compete in their middle-age years, it might be deduced that women cannot maintain strength and power as well as men can. Figure 14.19 compares the percentages of world records achieved by men and women for the dead lift and the bench press. The men 55 to 59 years old lift approximately 70% of the world record, whereas the women lift only about 30% of their world record. It is highly likely, however, that this huge gender difference can be attributed almost exclusively to the difference in the number of women competing and in their training techniques. This is probably also the explanation for the extreme variability of the women's running records in the 80-and-older age groups (see Figure 14.1, page 394).

Fifty years ago it was socially unacceptable for women to participate in even moderately demanding sports. Within this context, weight lifting not only was unacceptable, it was unthinkable. Consequently 70-year-old women today have no youthful experiences of weight lifting on which to build. Those few women who are over fifty who lift weights are usually beginning to lift for the first time in their lives, a pattern of performance that is hardly comparable to that of male masters competitors, many of whom lifted weights in their youth. Even today, when more and more young women are lifting weights, their coaches many times do not require the same demanding training schedules that they demand from their male athletes. These attitude and training differences may also explain in part the findings from laboratory studies, which are generally that the percent loss in women's strength is greater than that of men's strength.

Probably because the baby boomers are aging, and the proportion of the population that is old is increasing, attitudes toward old athletes and women in sport are changing rapidly. The Senior Tour in golf, only 10 years old, is generating a tremendous amount of interest. Both the National Basketball Association and Major League Baseball have initiated shortened Old-Timers All-Star games which precede the All-Star game. Women's professional golf and basketball teams and women's intercollegiate sports are beginning to attract larger followings. The social support system for older athletes, therefore, is improving.

Social Support Systems and the Positive Secular Trend

Previously in this chapter, the point was made that the ages of champion athletes are rising. Similarly, the performances of all masters athletes are improving with each passing decade. This positive secular trend in athletic performance is illustrated in Table 14.3 (Ericsson, 1990). In all categories except the 200-m run, the 1979 records of master athletes from age 50 to 59 were *faster* or almost the same as the best times in the Olympic Games of 1896. It is impressive that not only were the 1979 masters' times faster than the times of those who won Olympic medals in 1896, but the 1990 United States masters records were even faster than those established in 1979. Also in 1979, just 5 years after the first championship, the Canadian masters records were 10% better than the 1974 records (Stones & Kozma, 1980). The secular trend of masters' performance, therefore, is toward better and better performances. Thus, most of the current published records on masters performances may be greatly surpassed, and future sports analysts will interpret present records within the perspective of a transitional period in the history of adult athletics.

Why are athletes performing longer at the highest levels of sport? What conditions may have biased earlier analyses of peak performance ages? Clearly the answer lies not in changing physiology

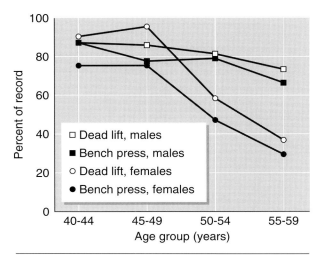

Figure 14.19 Gender differences relative to the world records in the dead lift and bench press.
Data from the United States Powerlifting Federation (1991).

Table 14.3

Peak Performance by Olympic Athletes in 1896 and by Masters Athletes in 1979 and 1990

Event (measurement units)	Best time in Olympic games of 1896[a]	Unofficial world record in 1896[b]	Age category for masters athletes in 1979 and 1990							
			50-54		55-59		60-64		65-69	
			1979[c]	1990[d]	1979	1990	1979	1990	1979	1990
100 m (in s)	12.0	10.8	11.4	11.2	11.6		12.0		13.2	12.5
200 m (in s)	22.2	21.8	23.6	22.9	23.6		24.9		27.9	25.6
400 m (in s)	54.2	48.2	52.9	52.2	54.6	53.8	59.1	55.2	65.1	61.1
800 m (in min:s)	2:11.0	1:53.4	2:01.1	2:00.4	2:11.4	2:05.1	2:19.9	2:12.9	2:27.2	2:20.5
1,500 m (in min:s)	4:33.2	4:10.4	4:14.0	4:05.0	4:20.4	4:14.4	4:53.2	4:30.0	4:59.2	4:41.8
Marathon (in hr:min:s)	2:58.5		2:25:17		2:26:3		2:47:46		2:53:03	

[a]Data from "Olympic games," 1985
[b]Data from zur Megede, 1987.
[c]1979 data from Stones & Kozma, 1981.
[d]1990 data from U.S. Track, 1990.
Note. Adapted from Ericsson (1990, p. 181).

but rather in a changing sports *society*. For example, career longevity in competitive sport seems to be positively correlated with financial incentive. Athletes in professional sports such as baseball, basketball, and football perform at the highest levels of their sport into at least their early 30s (Nolan Ryan at age 44 pitched a no-hitter). Obviously, in these sports high salaries promote career longevity. Conversely, until recently, the track-and-field athlete performed within a very different athletic time frame. Runners generally began running in elementary school, trained and competed in high school and college, and after losing the financial and social support for their passion, retired from competition soon after college and when they were still in their early 20s. It should not be surprising then that the age at peak performance in many track-and-field events was approximately 21 years. Today, with elite track-and-field performers negotiating for lucrative appearance fees and endorsements, the age at peak performance is increasing significantly.

The sport of rowing provides another example. Rowers rarely begin rowing until they are in college, because the equipment and coaching are not available in most public schools. Training and competitive opportunities also are not as readily available after graduation, because the rowing culture is predominantly a collegiate culture. (This was shown very clearly in Figure 14.11, page 400.) But does the age of peak performance really occur within this relatively narrow, culturally defined time span of 18 to 22 years of age? When opportunity for continued training and competition is provided, it appears not. The mean age for all U.S. rowers selected for the 1992 Olympic team was 26 years both for men and women. For men and women competing in one-person or two-person events, the mean age was 30 years.

Athletes over age 50 may be positively influenced by the impressive increase in popularity of masters competitive events and the intensity of media attention that has been focused on masters participants as well as winners in the past two decades. More masters athletes are training harder and more often. More and more older adults are postponing their retirement from competition, and many older adults are beginning to compete in tournaments. Younger cohorts who have grown up in a social environment that promotes good health habits will be increasingly reluctant to give up physical competition. As more athletes continue competing into their older years, these age categories will be sampled better, and their performances will more accurately reflect human capability. Given their different approaches to competition, it may very well be that the athletic performances of young and old competitors in some sports would be more similar if young competitors performed without performance-enhancing drugs and equipment and the old competitors trained as intensely as the young.

Clearly, sport is in a period of transition in which athletes are more likely to continue training throughout the entire age range in which they can achieve their peak physiological potential—their chronological window of opportunity. As this occurs, assumed age limitations for peak performance are being exceeded. It is probably safe to say that 10 years from now, age at peak performance will provide a more accurate measure of the impact of aging on different physiological systems. The qualitative conclusion that aging disproportionately impairs sport performance that requires power or makes multiple system demands probably will be upheld. However, quantitatively, the chronological age of peak performance in different athletic events under optimal training conditions will remain a question—one the current generation of athletes will help to answer as they continue training at older and older ages.

How Do They Do It?

Anyone who studies the physical performances of very old masters athletes or of those who climb mountains, water ski, or hang glide, must be in awe of their successful physical aging. How do they do it? Many factors contribute to the physical accomplishments of these older adults, not the least of which is a superb genetic makeup that has provided them with talent and physical stamina. With all the discussion of special behaviors of these individuals, it should be remembered that they have inherited relevant abilities and resistance to injury, which enable them to optimize their physical performance. They also have been lucky: They have not been in a fatal or debilitating automobile accident or contracted a disabling disease, such as Parkinson's disease, multiple sclerosis, or muscular dystrophy. But given good inheritance and luck, they have maximized their potential by continuing to train physically and by maintaining good health habits, such as good diet, abstinence from smoking and drug use, and low alcohol consumption. They have a psychological makeup in which the body and its functioning is a very important component of their self-awareness and esteem. The combination of these factors produces an individual who physically ages extremely well.

In Summary

One of the best ways to determine human physical potential throughout the life span is to study athletic performances of individuals at different ages. Record performances from events such as the World Masters Track-and-Field Championships, the World Veterans Games, the United States Amateur Union Masters Swimming Championships, and the United States Weightlifting Federation's competition provide measures of maximum human performance throughout aging. These national and world records contribute to an understanding of aging physical abilities, because in masters competitions, the physical efforts are very highly motivated and the performances occur under highly controlled circumstances. These records provide information about the physical abilities of the small percentage of elderly who maintain the maximum amount of strength and fitness possible throughout a lifetime. The records provide a marker of what is physically possible for human beings. In addition, information about the shape of the curve that describes these losses assists scientists in understanding the physiological, psychological, and sociological mechanisms that operate to curtail physical performance.

This chapter described and compared the masters records for selected track-and-field events (running, jumping, and throwing), swimming, cycling, rowing, and weight lifting. The most important conclusion to be drawn from these analyses is that masters athletes produce remarkable physical performances. In a world in which far too many elderly are disabled and physically dysfunctional, the masters athletes stand as a symbol of human strength and resilience. The most striking example is that for men aged 60 to 69 years, the United States record in the 40K (24.8 mile) cycling road race event is only 13% lower than the U.S. record set by young men. This phenomenal maintenance of function occurs in events such as cycling, running, swimming, and rowing, sports in which the systems most resistant to

aging—aerobic endurance and strategy—are predominant. Performances in events that require explosive strength and anaerobic energy reserves, such as jumping, discus throwing, shot-putting, and weight lifting, are less well maintained.

Although national and world records are an important source of information with regard to understanding aged human physical potential, several caveats must be considered when interpreting the records. The older the age group, the fewer the competitors. Also, most researchers believe that even the most zealous of elderly competitors usually do not train as intensely as young athletes do. Both of these caveats are particularly true for women. Thus, individual differences, even in these homogeneous and highly select groups, become greater and greater with increasing age, and because of this sampling problem, it is likely that observed age decrements in the oldest groups, as well as gender differences, are overestimated. Age records have been improving every year as the popularity of masters competitions increases and more and more people compete.

That many adults over age 70 participate in non-competitive, physically demanding activities or occupations bears repeating. This chapter has focused on competitors because their performances are quantified, yet those who remain physically active in other ways are equally admirable. Although those elderly who participate intensely in physical activity, like masters athletes, represent a very small percentage of the old and oldest-old population, they are an important group to study and to emulate. They reveal the limits of human physical potential in all adult age categories. Because they are remarkable and an inspiration, and because they epitomize optimal physical aging, their story is a most appropriate last chapter. They inspire an upward look, provide a standard, and give hope, and that is the note on which any book about the physical dimensions of aging should conclude.

References

Åstrand, P.O., & Rodahl, K. (1977). *Textbook of work physiology.* New York: McGraw-Hill.
Barnard, C. (1992, February-March). Half a mountain . . . the Matterhorn. *Modern Maturity*, pp. 43-49, 66.

Bouchard, C., Thibault, M.C., & Jobin, J. (1981). Advances in selected areas of work physiology. *Yearbook of Physical Anthropology*, **24**, 275-286.

Concept II World Rankings. (1991). *Current world records for 2,500 meters on the Concept II Rowing Ergometer as of April 15, 1991*. Morrisville, VT: Concept II.

Ericsson, K.A. (1990). Peak performance and age: An examination of peak performance in sports. In P.B. Baltes & M.M. Baltes (Eds.), *Successful aging: Perspectives from the behavioral sciences*. Cambridge: Cambridge University Press.

Foster, C., Green, M.A., Snyder, A.C., & Thompson, N.N. (in press). Physiological responses during simulated competition. *Medicine and Science in Sports and Exercise*.

Hagerman, F.C. (1994). Applied physiology of rowing. In D.R. Lamb & H.H. Knuttgen (Eds.), *Perspectives in exercise science and sports medicine: Vol. 7. Physiology and nutrition of competitive sport*. Indianapolis: Brown & Benchmark.

Hains, L. (1989, October). Rarities. *Golf Digest*, p. S-105.

Hartley, A.A., & Hartley, J.T. (1984a). In response to Stones and Kozma: Absolute and relative declines with age in champion swimming performances. *Experimental Aging Research*, **10**, 151-153.

Hartley, A.A., & Hartley, J.T. (1984b). Performance changes in champion swimmers aged 30 to 84 years. *Experimental Aging Research*, **10**, 141-147.

Hartley, A.A., & Hartley, J.T. (1986). Age differences and changes in sprint swimming performances of masters athletes. *Experimental Aging Research*, **12**, 65-70.

Hickok, R. (1971). *Who was who in American sports*. New York: Hawthorn Books.

Kardong, D. (1991). Young at heart. *Runner's World*, **26**, 29, 73.

Kovar, M.G., & LaCroix, A.Z. (1987). Aging in the eighties, ability to perform work-related activities. *National Center for Health Statistics Advance Data*, **136**, 1-12.

Langford, W.M. (1987). *Legends of baseball: An oral history of the game's golden age*. South Bend, IN: Diamond Communications.

Masters Age Records for 1990. (1991). Available from *National Masters News*, P.O. Box 5185, Pasadena, CA 91107.

Moore, D.H. (1975). A study of age group track and field records to relate age and running speed. *Nature*, **253**, 264-265.

Moore, K. (1992). The times of their lives. *Runner's World*, **20**, 44-47.

Olympic games (1985). In *The new encyclopaedia Britannica* (15th ed., Vol. 8, pp. 926-942).

Riegel, P.S. (1981). Athletic records and human endurance. *American Scientist*, **69**, 285-290.

Salthouse, T.A. (1976). Speed and age: Multiple rates of age decline. *Experimental Aging Research*, **2**, 349-359.

Schultz, R., & Curnow, C. (1988). Peak performance and age among superathletes: Track and field, swimming, baseball, tennis, and golf. *Journal of Gerontology: Psychological Sciences*, **43**, P113-P120.

Stones, M.J., & Kozma, A. (1980). Adult age trends in record running performances. *Experimental Aging Research*, **6**, 407-416.

Stones, M.J., & Kozma, A. (1981). Adult trends in athletic performance. *Experimental Aging Research*, **7**, 269-280.

Stones, M.J., & Kozma, A. (1982a). Cross-sectional, longitudinal, and secular age trends in athletic performances. *Experimental Aging Research*, **8**, 185-188.

Stones, M.J., & Kozma, A. (1982b). Sex differences in changes with age in record running performances. *Canadian Journal on Aging*, **1**, 12-16.

Stones, M.J., & Kozma, A. (1984a). In response to Hartley and Hartley: Cross-sectional age trends in swimming records; decline is greater at the longer distances. *Experimental Aging Research*, **10**, 159-150.

Stones, M.J., & Kozma, A. (1984b). Longitudinal trends in track and field performances. *Experimental Aging Research*, **10**, 107-110.

Stones, M.J., & Kozma, A. (1985). Physical performance. In N. Charness (Ed.), *Aging and human performance* (pp. 261-292). London: Wiley.

Stones, M.J., & Kozma, A. (1986a). Age by distance effects in running and swimming records: A note on methodology. *Experimental Aging Research*, **12**, 203-206.

Stones, M.J., & Kozma, A. (1986b). Age trends in maximal physical performance: Comparison and evaluation of models. *Experimental Aging Research*, **12**, 207-215.

United States Cycling Federation. (1990). *Rule book, United States Cycling Federation*. Colorado Springs: Author.

United States Rowing Association. (1991). *The finish line*. Indianapolis: Author.

United States Powerlifting Federation. (1991). Unpublished data. (Available from U.S. Powerlifting Federation, P.O. Box 389, Roy, VT 84064).

United States Weightlifting Federation. (1991). *USA men's and women's records*. Colorado Springs, CO: Author.

zur Megede, E. (1987). *Progression of world best performances and official IAAF world records*. Monaco: International Athletic Foundation.

Index

A

AAHPERD Field test, 350-351
Accidents, job-related, 372, 373-374. *See also* Falling
ACSM (American College of Sports Medicine) recommendations, 109, 138, 352
Active life expectancy (ALE), 27, 331
Activities of daily living (ADLs). *See also* Basic activities of daily living; Instrumental activities of daily living
  Activities of Daily Living Index (ADL), 338, 345
  advanced, 349, 351
Activity. *See* Exercise; General activity level; Training
Adrenergic responses, in emotional function, 288
Advanced activities of daily living (AADLs), 349, 351
Aerobic capacity/fitness. *See* $\dot{V}O_2max$
Age, biological. *See* Biological age
Age at peak performance, 407-408
Age categories, definition of, 7
Age changes, definition of, 42
Age differences, definition of, 42
Age discrimination in employment, 374-376
Ageism. *See also* Age discrimination in employment
  definition of, 374
  masters athletes and, 412
Aging. *See also* Aging processes; Process of aging
  causes of, 16-20
  definition of, 6-7, 45
  theories of, 17-20
Aging attributes models, of response slowing, 199-202

Aging processes (primary aging). *See also* Aging
  cognition-fitness relationship and, 265-270
  definition of, 7
  slowing of, 20
Aiming movements, coordination for, 219-220
Aircraft piloting, 375, 380-381
α-adrenergic function, 98
Aluminum intake, and aging, 19
Alveolar-to-arterial gas exchange, 106
Alzheimer's disease, 210, 268
American Alliance for Health, Physical Education, Recreation and Dance Field test, 350-351
American Association of Retired Persons (AARP), 385
American College of Sports Medicine recommendations, 109, 138, 352
Anaerobic capacity
  exercise and, 110-111
  of masters athletes, 111, 396
  in statistical modeling strategy, 408, 409-410
Androgens, life expectancy and, 15
Android fat patterns, 64
Anemia, 103-104
Anthropometry, 58
Anti-aging strategies, 19, 20-23, 48
Anticipation (compensatory strategy), 239-240
Anticipatory postural adjustments, 165-167
Anxiety
  cognition-fitness relationship and, 271
  cognitive, 283, 290
  coordination/skill and, 242
  definition and types of, 283
  effect on research/testing, 285, 336, 337
  exercise and, 290, 294, 295, 310
  fear of falling, 168
  physiological aspects of, 293, 294

Falling, 173-178. *See also* Balance; Bone fractures
    causes of, 174-177
    characteristics of fallers, 177
    confidence and, 168
    consequences of, 173-174, 177-178
    exercise for prevention of, 178
    muscular strength and, 123-124, 140, 167-168
    postural hypotension and, 99, 102, 112, 176, 178
Fat. *See* Body composition; Body fat
Fat-free mass (FFM), 61-62, 67-68
Fear. *See also* Anxiety
    of death, 17
    of falling, 168
FFM (fat-free mass), 61-62, 67-68
Fine motor skills. *See* Hand function
Finger oscillation (stationary tapping) test, 206, 261
Fire-fighting employment, 375, 376-377
Fitness. *See also* Cognition-fitness relationship
    definition of, 250-251
    emotional function and, 284, 285, 286, 292 (*see also* Emotion-exercise relationship)
    of old/oldest-old, 338-339, 351-355
    quality of life and, 28-29, 204
    reaction time and, 257-261
    self-esteem and, 313
Fit old/oldest-old, 338-339, 351-355
Fitts' law, 219
Flexibility
    coordination for throwing and, 228
    exercise and, 80
    job performance and, 369
    locomotion and, 171
    measurement of, 79-80
    osteoarthritis and, 82
    testing of old/oldest-old for, 351, 353, 355
Fluid intelligence, 264
Food restriction (undernutrition), 20-21, 48
Forced expiratory volume (FEV), 106
Forced vital capacity (FVC), 105-106
Fractionation of response speed, 192-194, 259-260
Frail old/oldest-old, 338-339, 344-349, 350
Frank-Starling mechanism, 101
Free-radicals, definition of, 19
Free radical (damage) theories, 18-19, 20, 37
Functional age. *See* Biological age
Functional movements, coordination for, 226-232

Functional Reach test, 158-159
Functional residual capacity (FRC), 105
Functional status, definition of, 304
Furukawa, T.M., 51-52

Gait. *See* Locomotion
Galen, 17
Gas exchange, 106
Gender factors
    automobile driving and, 231
    in body composition, 68
    in body fat distribution, 64-66
    in bone loss, 70, 78
    in coordination, 221
    in exercise levels, 16
    in flexibility, 353, 355
    in height decline, 58
    individual differences in aging and, 40-41
    in job performance, 369
    in life expectancy, 13-16
    in masters athletes' performance, 396-397, 412-413
    in muscular strength, 369
    in osteoarthritis, 80
    in physical function of old/oldest-old, 353, 355
    in rate of aging, 7
    in reaction time, 187-188
General activity level
    body composition and, 62, 66
    individual differences in aging and, 40
    longevity and, 21
    muscular strength and, 135
    self-reporting by old/oldest-old, 334
General slowing hypothesis, 202-203
Genetic factors
    in body composition, 62
    in individual differences in aging, 35-37
    in life expectancy, 13-15
    masters athletes and, 415
    in training response, 115
    in $\dot{V}O_2$max, 109
Genetic theories of aging, 17-18, 20
Geriatrics, history of, 17
Gerontology, definition of, 5-6
Glucocorticoid function regulation, 48
Glucocorticoids, theories of aging on, 19
Glucose levels, in damage theories of aging, 19
Golfing performance, 393, 406
Gompertz equations, 8

New research, reviews, and articles on older adults

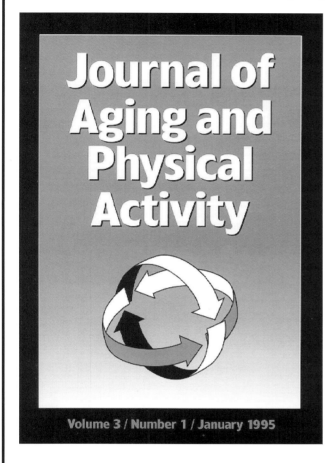

Journal of
Aging and
Physical
Activity

Volume 3 / Number 1 / January 1995

Journal of Aging and Physical Activity

Wojtek Chodzko-Zajko, PhD, Editor

This multidisciplinary journal examines the dynamic relationship between physical activity and the aging process: it focuses on the impact of physical activity on the physiological, psychological, and social well-being of older adults, and it examines the effect of the aging process on physical activity among older adults.

The *Journal of Aging and Physical Activity (JAPA)* is filled with articles that examine the development, implementation, and evaluation of physical activity programs among older adults. These articles are taken from the biological, behavioral, and social sciences as well as from such fields as medicine, clinical psychology, physical and recreational therapy, health, physical education, and recreation.

Frequency: Quarterly (January, April, July, October)

Current Volume: 3(1995)

Subscription Rates (including shipping):

	Individual	Institution	Student
U.S.	$40.00	$90.00	$24.00
Foreign—surface	44.00	94.00	28.00
Foreign—air	60.00	110.00	44.00
Canada—surface	59.00 Cdn	127.00 Cdn	38.00 Cdn
Canada—air	81.00 Cdn	149.00 Cdn	59.00 Cdn

Student rates are available for up to 3 years; along with payment indicate name of institution, year in school, and advisor's name. All journals are shipped from the U.S.A.

Back Issues Available: All

Back Issue Price: *Individuals*—$11/issue ($15 Canadian); *Institutions*—$24/issue ($32 Canadian).

ISSN: 1063-8652 • **Item:** JAGE

Prices subject to change.

Human Kinetics
The Information Leader in Physical Activity

2335